Friends and Enemies

DOROTHY ROWE

HarperCollinsPublishers

HarperCollins*Publishers*
77–85 Fulham Palace Road,
Hammersmith, London w6 8jb

www.**fire**and**water**.com

Published by HarperCollins*Publishers* 2000
1 3 5 7 9 8 6 4 2

Copyright © Dorothy Rowe 2000

The Author asserts the moral right to
be identified as the author of this work

A catalogue record for this book is
available from the British Library

ISBN 0 00 255939 0

Set in PostScript Linotype Minion by
Rowland Phototypesetting Ltd,
Bury St Edmunds, Suffolk

Printed and bound in Great Britain by
Clays Ltd, St Ives plc

To the memory of my dear friend
Hilary Surman

CONTENTS

Preface   1

CHAPTER 1   **Friends and Enemies**   3

CHAPTER 2   **Learning to Become Ourselves**   41
The Meanings in Our Brain   56
Your Meaning Structure   62
Forms of Thought   69
Others – The Necessity and the Threat   103

CHAPTER 3   **Belonging to a Group**   111
Defining Yourself and Your Group   116
Owing Allegiance to Your Group   137
Is Your Group Your Friend or Your
   Enemy?   153

CHAPTER 4   **Belonging to a Family**   177
Becoming Part of the Family   184
What Are Family Values?   229
Family – The Tie That Must Bind Us All?
   251

CHAPTER 5   **Belonging to a Place**   256
Losing Your Place   267
You Can't Go Home Again   285

CHAPTER 6 **Strangers and Enemies**   313

The Necessity of Enemies   320
The Leaders We Deserve   352
The Meaning of Violence   362
The Pleasures of War   374

CHAPTER 7 **The End of Enmity**   387

The Satisfactions and Failures of Revenge   389
Who's Responsible?   399
Becoming Reconciled   419
Is Forgiveness Possible?   441

CHAPTER 8 **The Art of Friendship**   469

Living in a Peaceful World   484
Can Your Lover Be Your Friend?   496
The Art of Friendship   503

Notes   523

Acknowledgements   533

Index   535

PREFACE

Friendship is our greatest invention. No technological construction, no work of art, can compare with the art and skill of friendship which takes us out of the lonely world of our own individual perceptions and puts us close to another person, linked by feelings of love, trust, tolerance, sympathy, generosity, kindness, joy and humour. We can set ourselves the greatest tasks and achieve them, we can become rich, famous and powerful, but all our achievements will be mere dust and ashes if we are friendless. We can have lovers, we can have family, but all these relationships will bring us nothing but misery if they are not imbued with the qualities of friendship.

Friendship has always been of supreme importance in our lives, but today it has taken on a new urgency. Changes in society and in our expectations mean that many people turn to friends to supply what in past years they would have looked for in marriage or family. A businesswoman in South Africa said to me, 'If I had to choose between my husband and my friend I'd choose my friend. She and I talk every day. We tell each other everything. My husband is all right, but we don't talk.'

Moreover, while nations no longer engage in huge wars which mobilize many thousands of troops, across the globe we see conflicts which, though they involve smaller numbers of people, inflict terrible violence and suffering on everyone caught up in them. It is essential to resolve these conflicts if we are to overcome the ecological threats to our planet. Enmity is as old as friendship, yet we seem unable to understand why, when friendship is so glorious and so precious, many people choose to be enemies rather than friends. Of course a friendship has to be reciprocal, two people in tune with one another, while you can hate someone without that person hating you. It is even easier to be hated. You do not have to do anything. You just have to exist. You are sure to have some characteristic which someone hates – the colour of your skin, the place you were born, your sexuality, your religious beliefs.

We seem unable to understand how to turn enmity into friendship. The existence of enmity seems to be taken for granted. We deplore revenge and praise forgiveness but we rarely ask, 'How do we learn the art and skill of friendship?' or 'Why is friendship so hard to achieve?' or 'Why, when we have been wounded by an enemy, does revenge become an imperative?' or 'Can we live without enemies?' or 'How does reconciliation become possible?' or 'Can we choose to forgive, and, if we can, why don't we?'

These and other questions about friendship and enmity I examined in discussions with friends, colleagues and workshop participants, and with people I met on my travels in Serbia, Lebanon, Northern Ireland, South Africa, Vietnam and Australia. Such discussions covered both intimate personal experiences and questions arising from national, racial, political, social and religious issues. As I wrote this book conflicts raged around me. NATO bombed Serbia; the United Nations fumbled their task of protecting the people of East Timor; Russia invaded Chechnya while the West did no more than chide. The Unionists in Northern Ireland continued in their refusal to speak to members of Sinn Fein until Senator George Mitchell demonstrated the skills needed to turn enmity into friendship, but unfortunately he could not reach everyone in Northern Ireland who needed to change. For many people their enemies are more precious than their friends.

Just as I finished writing this book a dear young friend, Hilary Surman, someone I had known for twenty years, died within a few weeks of being diagnosed with cancer. Hilary and I were members of a small group of long-time friends. I find that the pain of losing her is edged around by the sweetness of the closeness of friends.

My thanks to all my friends and to all the people who talked to me about the importance of friendship and the dangers of enmity.

Dorothy Rowe
London, November 1999

1

Friends and Enemies

'You don't make friends. You recognize them.'

This is what people told me, again and again. Somehow, when we meet someone for the first time, we usually know whether that person could become a friend.

For Tima in Beirut it was a matter of trust. She said, 'They have to inspire a feeling of confidence in me, and with me it all has to do with feelings. I can be with one person once and know for sure if this person is trustworthy or not, and in the long run I am usually right about it. It's an instinctive thing, so there's no special criterion where I see shoe size, head size or whatever. It's nothing like that – no measurements or anything, but inspiring a good feeling from within.'

For Jane in London it was a matter of sorting the wheat from the chaff. She said, 'When I meet someone for the first time I know, instinctively almost, whether a person meets my criteria for becoming a friend. If they don't I don't let them through.'

Yet finding a friend is not like finding a diamond which you can put in your pocket and keep. The person you see as having the potential to be a friend has to see you as having the same potential. Only then will the friendship develop. You might like the other person so much that, even though you receive no encouragement, you continue to see the other person as a friend; if, however, the person does not return your feeling, opportunities for you to be together as friends are not created. You might continue to meet at work or in the course of some mutual interest, but invitations to lunch or for you to meet the family do not materialize. You might continue to feel warmly towards the person, but, as time goes by, with no encouragement your warm feelings soon dwindle and fade into what is really the opposite of friendship – a kind of vague interest which shows itself only when an opportunity to gossip about the person arises. You know that the person who did not become a friend feels the same about you because, when you meet, you each go through friend-like rituals, but the spark for friendship is not there.

Enmity is not the exact opposite of friendship. Friendship must be reciprocal, while enmity need not be. There are many mutual enemies, but the objects of enmity often know nothing of the hate they inspire and may even feel warmly towards the unrecognized enemy. The opposite of friendship – vague interest in the other person – tends to remain the same over time. I have a large number of such relationships, some of them going back thirty years. My feelings about these people has not changed in that time, though I do feel sorry when I learn that one of them has met with disaster or death. I am interested to learn about their progress through life from mutual acquaintances and to meet them occasionally, but I do not pine because I have not seen them.

In contrast, none of my friendships has remained the same over the years. Some friendships have followed the vagaries of each of our lives, some have dwindled and vanished, some have strengthened. None can be taken for granted. Indeed, as Samuel Butler once remarked, 'Friendship is like money, easier made than kept.'[1]

Like many people, in conversation I use the word 'friend' loosely and often apply it to people whom I have merely known for some time. For this study of friendship I have been asking people what words they use in making distinctions between the individuals they know. Some distinguish 'real friends' from 'friends', and some distinguish friends from acquaintances, colleagues, chums and team members.

Some people make very careful distinctions. I have been told that:

- 'Friends know me and I know them. We are allies. The next layer are people I like and our paths cross. Then there are the people who cross my path and it's OK and then those where it's not OK.'
- 'I have many acquaintances but few friends. I have people who get close to me – the ones who have the time and interest to

listen and who, in return, feel that they can pour their hearts out to me. I feel that there has to be an exchange – give and take. Some only take, therefore they can never be classed as true friends.'

- 'My categories are: close friends, people with whom I have intimate conversations: professional friends – people I come in contact through work and have special connection with: long-term friends – people I have known for years but don't see very often; friends in Quakers – people I know and trust through the Society of Friends.'
- 'I feel friends vary in degrees. I try to approach people as friends. There are always some who are more easy to relate to and they often become a different grade of friend, and over the years these people become more and more important as trust and shared experiences grow.'

Lesley had written to thank me for the help she had received from my books, and I asked her what discriminations she made about friends. She took great care with her reply.

Friends is the word for a relatively small group of people. It is not necessarily related to the length of time I have known them, as I tend to get a particular feeling upon meeting a potential friend. These people in almost every case have remained in my life, even when geography and circumstances dictate that we may not meet for many years, and contact has dwindled to Christmas-time contact.

Acquaintances is a term I reserve for people I have met once or twice with no special feeling. Then there are *people I know*. I have met them once or twice with no special feelings and know them rather better than acquaintances, I may have known them for years, perhaps coming across them often. There isn't the degree of feeling or liking that would elevate them to friend category.

Finally there is *family*. This is a very diverse category. It encompasses people I like, dislike and occasionally hate. There are people in this category I love more than any others. They are my children who are also my friends. It includes my ex-husband, my ex-mother-in-law and sister-in-law. It includes people with whom I have a blood tie but nothing in common. It is the most complicated category.

Such words, as Lesley and the others quoted have shown, require definitions, so I have been asking people how they define friends and friendship.

Children acquire the concept of 'friend' early in their life. Alice, who was four, told me about Sarah, also four, who was her friend but who was not always friendly. Alice said, 'Sometimes, when Sarah comes to my house, she doesn't let me be the Mummy. We play Mummies and Daddies sometimes.'

I asked, 'And do you think that's not being very friendly?'

'No, I think that's not very nice.'

'How many friends have you got?'

'Loads. I've got so many friends I can't count them. I've got Sarah, one, Chloe, two, James, three, Hayden, four, Elliot, five, Thomas, six, Kate, seven, Marcus, eight, Sam, nine.'

'Do you always play with your friends?'

'Not all the time. Sometimes they get a bit mardy, and they walk off and they say I don't want to play with you.'

Alice's brother Miles, at seven, could define a friend and understand that friendship meant reciprocity. He said, 'A friend is somebody who would be kind to me and wouldn't desert me if I hurt myself or was in trouble. It's somebody who likes you. Sometimes you can like somebody but they don't like you, but that's not a real friend.'

Miles also understood that reciprocity did not mean that two friends had to have identical interests. He told me how pleased he was that his friend Arthur, who had gone to another school, was coming back to Miles's school. I asked him why he was pleased. He said, 'I'm pleased because he was a good friend. Although he wasn't interested in all the things I was interested in he was still a very good friend.'

'So when you were doing something he wasn't interested in, he was still nice about it?'

'Yes, but it was more the other way around. He likes sports and I wasn't really interested.'

When I compared the definitions of friends and friendship which Alice and Miles had given me with the definitions which adults gave me it seemed that as we get older our definitions become more complex, and that many people expect much of their friends.

In a workshop on friends and enemies I asked the participants how they defined a friend. Their answers showed that they saw a friend as someone special.

- 'A friend should be and do. Be: safe, trustworthy, honest, caring, open. Do: share their feelings with me, accept me, believe in me.'
- 'A friend should share my sense of humour.'
- 'A friend will have my welfare at heart and is prepared to accept me as I am and what I want from life, even though he/she may not understand why. A friend needs to be honest with me and open about feelings and opinions even though we differ.'
- 'I need to feel that in dire circumstances that person would be there for me.'
- 'I want a friend to hear what I say.'
- 'A friend – I feel comfortable with and talk, talk, talk and do, do, do, and the time passes without thinking.'
- 'Someone who will be honest with me but care about my feelings at the same time. Importantly, someone I feel comfortable with, easy with, have fun with.'
- 'A friend is able to accept things you do for them.'
- 'They need to tell me, show me, they care for me.'
- 'We share a similar morality.'

I also asked some of my own friends how they defined a friend. Sometimes their answers surprised me.

I had always thought that Elizabeth and Catherine were close friends. They shared considerable work interests and an extensive social life. Yet Elizabeth said of Catherine, 'I speak of her as a friend, we do the things friends do, but she is not *simpatico*.' Elizabeth went on to point out that *simpatico* is an Italian term with no equivalent word in English. She contrasted her relationship with Catherine with her relationship with someone she has known since college. This is what she calls 'eternal friendship', even though she and her friend now see one another rarely.

I have been friends with Judy since 1954, and I regard this as one of my achievements. I love Judy dearly, but in my youth I was always afraid that I would not live up to the high standards Judy set for her friends. Now I am older and wiser I was able to ask her about how she saw friends and enemies. She told me she defined friends as 'People who like me and are faithful to me. They have to be totally faithful.'

I asked her what was involved in being faithful.

'They don't cause trouble amongst other friends. They don't bitch me up too much. They're allowed to say a few things about me because I don't think anybody could go through life not talking about their friends, but they should say positive things about me as well, so that if things come back to me I can say, "That's fair. I can understand why they said that."'

Judy's demand that her friends be totally faithful to her is matched by the love and care she lavishes upon her friends. I have noticed that those people who feel that they have much to offer as a friend and who, like Judy, lavish much time and effort upon their friends are not always greatly surprised when their friends respond in kind, whereas those people whose top priorities include more than friend-ships can be surprised and entranced by what a friend might do for them.

I first met Irene when we were both in our twenties. Each of us had married the same kind of man – selfish, self-centred, someone who demanded that his wife give him her full attention and not fritter away any of her time with friends. In the 1950s this was a typical male attitude. However, Irene understood the importance of friendship better than I did, and she looked after her friends better than I did then. Now, forty years on, Irene has many friends acquired over many years. When I asked her whether she had a talent for friendship she said, 'I do spend a lot of time socializing, but I'm also a disciplined sort of person time-wise, and so I've got my own programme that I follow, and if somebody says, "What about doing such and such?" I'll say, "I can't manage that until later in the day" – because I'm going swimming, or I've got calligraphy, or yoga.'

A few months after this conversation Irene had an accident and injured her hand most severely. She emerged from the casualty ward with her whole arm in plaster and strapped across her chest. This quite ruined her plans for the coming weekend, when her friend Amy was due to arrive for a short holiday. Now Irene knew that it would be a most uncomfortable time for Amy, so she rang her and explained the circumstances. She suggested that Amy should postpone her holiday until she, Irene, was capable of carrying out a hostess's duties. She said, 'Amy, if you come now you'll just be my handmaiden for the whole of the time.'

Amy laughed and said, 'It is better to be a handmaiden in the temple of the Lord than an honoured guest in the tents of the wicked.' Amy arrived soon after and proved to be a most industrious handmaiden, though her attempt to remove some immovable spilt glue from the kitchen floor by scrubbing it with a nail brush was, Irene felt, one task too far. Amy is, Irene told me, 'a dear lady and a very dear friend', but words on paper cannot convey Irene's astonishment and sense of blessedness.

Irene, like me, did not have a childhood where love and a sense of blessedness came as a birthright. I can see what effect such a childhood had on me. I know that there are people who demand much from their friends. I've often had to listen to a torrent of disappointment, anger and sadness from such a person who felt betrayed or let down by a friend. Intellectually I can understand the person's point of view, but, in my heart, I am surprised that anyone can demand so much of a friend, and I get anxious lest to reproach a friend might drive that friend away. I do not expect anything of friends except that they will be nice to me when I am with them, and that behind my back they will speak about me with kindness. If they do not they are not friends. My expecting little of my friends arises not from some great wisdom but from growing up in a family where I found that to ask for anything was to risk refusal and ridicule. When I was a child many shops displayed a sign which read, 'DO NOT ASK FOR CREDIT BECAUSE A REFUSAL MIGHT OFFEND'. That sign always seemed to epitomize all my relationships. 'Don't ask for anything because a refusal always hurts.'

This attitude has meant that I have probably missed out on a great deal, but it also means that anything friends do for me, the smallest gift, the simplest thoughtfulness, comes as a magnificent bonus.

Anthony is one of the warmest, friendliest, kindest people you could meet. When I was in Omagh, Northern Ireland, he took me around, and wherever we went there was someone who greeted him as a friend. Yet, when I asked him how he defined a friend he said, 'I don't think I have any friends. I think in your lifetime you're going to be lucky to meet anyone – two, three at the most, people – whom you could define as friends, in the way that I would perceive

friendship. I think friendship develops over years of trust and acceptance, I suppose. For me, I have no recollection of having friends
who were unconditional. The friends that I have are friends because
it suits them to be my friends, or vice versa. While I think a lot of
them, they're not friends in the sense I think you're asking me about
friendship – except for Anne, my wife, and that friendship took
twenty-five years to come about. I've told Anne this: when we got
married, I didn't know what love was. I walked up the aisle in hope.
She finds it a great source of pain when I say that to her, because
she thinks of her wedding day as a day of such love and hope. She
can't believe that I didn't. I'm totally honest with her. I say, "The
experience I had with you is something very special, but I couldn't
really say I loved you until we had ten years of marriage through
us, through our lives." I realized then that I loved her.'

Anthony was the sixth of eleven children born to a bitterly
unhappy couple. He said, 'Friends weren't encouraged in our family
because there was enough of us in the family not to have friends
around. God, you wouldn't have brought your friend round for tea
as well! There was already eleven children to feed. So I just keep
comfortable distances with people, because of the mask I wear. I
would be a person who has to wear a lot of different faces for
different people, and I find that difficult in the long term. I feel
almost insincere, because the face I would wear for you would be
different from the face from the one at work, or home, or whatever.
These faces sustain me and carry me through life. For a long time
I felt insincere with that, but I've learned to make sense of it. I miss
that relationship that could be there somewhere. I know I'm very
well known and popular, but those people would be at a comfortable
distance. Anne is the only person who really knows me. I think,
too, I've found friendships in books. Certain books, they're close
friends. Books don't betray you.'

Anthony, I guess, is like me in that I can usually detect in others
the wariness that evolves as a defence when a child discovers that
he cannot trust the people who should be caring for him. Adult life
does little to diminish such wariness because once we discover the
treachery of others unconditional trust can never be reborn.

I found this wariness in one of the most delightful people, someone I met in a jazz bar in Beirut, where he worked.

James was magnificently beautiful. Every evening when I was in

Beirut I sat at the bar, where he gave out smiles, drinks, food, and listened to the regulars who, like me, were gathered around him. One evening when the bar was quiet James told me that he came from Freetown, Liberia, but as an adult he had lived in various places in Europe where, I gathered though he did not say, life had been hard. When he was young his parents had been Muslim but his aunt, who brought him up, was a Baptist. He'd helped her to look after the church, and he had learned to believe in God – one God for all of us, even though different people had different names for God. He knew that God saw us as being all the same, all sinners. The idea that the colour of a person's skin or the beliefs that a person held made one person different from another was a human idea, not God's, and very wrong.

When it came to friendship James waited to see how things turned out. He was very friendly. He bestowed his warm, gracious smile on everyone immediately on meeting and in every interaction and seemed so unlike many of the Beirutis, whom the war had left tense and wary. When I asked him about friends he told me that he might meet a person on one occasion and then on another, and each time all would be right no matter how long the time between meetings, and then, perhaps, they would meet and everything would not be right. So, with all his friends, he would just wait and see how things turned out.

He said, 'When people say to me, "I love you, James," or, "I'm your friend," I wonder what it is they want. I wait, I wait and see what happens.'

I did not ask James what he did if 'what happens' was not to his liking. I felt that this would take us into issues of religion and of race, and these were not safe issues to discuss in a bar in Beirut.

However, in South Africa, the enemy is a common topic of conversation. Our guide to the prison where the enemies of the apartheid regime had been incarcerated on Robben Island had been imprisoned there from 1963 to 1978, when prison conditions were at their very worst. He told us, 'The guards and security were my enemies. Robben Island was my first and last enemy.'

His last enemy has now lost power, and life in post-apartheid South Africa is full of ironies. Ex-political prisoners take visitors to a respectful viewing of cell number five, which once housed Nelson Mandela, while in Johannesburg my guide to another holy of holies,

the Voortrekker Monument, was Simbo, a Zulu from Soweto, that
south-western township established to separate the blacks from the
whites.

The Afrikaner apartheid regime had been based on the belief that
God had created blacks inferior to whites in order that they should
work for the whites. Mamphela Ramphele, now Vice-Chancellor of
Cape Town University, mentioned this in her autobiography. She
began her professional education at Bethesda Teacher Training College, which had been started by Dutch Reformed Church missionaries in the 1930s. She described how the white teachers kept their
distance from the black students and how the students were com-
pelled to carry out *huiswerk* (Afrikaans for 'housework'),

> which was a form of forced labour intended to remind students
> that education was not an escape route from the inferior position
> blacks were 'destined' to occupy ... The principal's wife, Mrs
> Grütter, who was our music teacher, was the most unpleasant of
> all [the teachers]. She often reminded those students who seemed
> to her unenthusiastic in their tasks: 'You were born to work for
> us.'[2]

Simbo, like Mamphela, found that his life changed markedly when
apartheid came to an end. He obtained a most sought-after job,
that of a tourist guide. Simbo drove me to the Voortrekker Monument, which looks like a huge, old-fashioned radio set upon a high
hill. It was built to impress on all the implacable power and virtue
of God's own people, the Voortrekkers, who had fought and defeated
the Zulu nation and established their own fair land, only to have it
taken from them by the treacherous English. Inside the monument
Simbo conducted me around the carved frieze on the four walls of
the large interior room. Here the history of the Great Trek was
depicted, and Simbo knew it well. He pointed out the different
characters – the Boer men were all brave and handsome and the
women all beautiful and true – and he showed me how the Boers
had enslaved the blacks.

When we had finished our tour of Pretoria and set off back to
Johannesburg I asked Simbo if he had any enemies. In answer he
spoke of individuals who might know him personally but did not
wish him well.

I asked him how he felt about the Afrikaners. I said, 'When I was here last in 1991 you wouldn't have been allowed anywhere near the Voortrekker Monument.'

He smiled and talked gently about the pass laws which restricted black and coloured people to certain areas. 'See those women?' he said, pointing to two African matrons walking home from work. 'If they'd been there and didn't have their pass book they'd be arrested and put in jail. Now I don't mind the Afrikaners, provided they join with us and make this one country, all of us together.'

The Voortrekker Monument was for him a fine thing. It had given him what he wanted most – a job.

In Lebanon enemies still have power and so it was only in the privacy of a car that I was able to ask Samir, my driver, about friends and enemies as we spent three days together touring Lebanon. He was a large man in his late forties and knew Beirut and the roads in Lebanon and into Syria like the back of his hand.

One day I commented to Samir that wherever he stopped he got into conversation with someone. He seemed to have friends everywhere. He said, 'I want to have friends everywhere and no enemies.'

I asked him if he had any enemies.

He shrugged. 'How can you tell? You don't know who your enemy is. Someone can come smiling, saying, "I am your friend," and then, when you're not looking, he hits you in the back.'

I asked a stupid question: 'Are the Israelis your enemy?'

'They are everyone's enemy.'

Samir had good reason to regard the Israelis as enemies. In the war he had been a driver for foreign journalists, which meant he was often in danger of being killed by the Israelis or their allies. However, Samir's interest in enemies went much wider. On our travels I discovered that he favoured the conspiracy theory of history. He was sure that Princess Diana had died as a result of a conspiracy by the Israelis and the royal family who, on discovering that the Diana–Dodi romance had resulted in her pregnancy, had had her killed. He was equally sure that Monica Lewinsky had been instructed by international Jewry to bring down President Clinton.

Over lunch in a garden in Balbek I gave Samir the benefit of my extensive knowledge of the royal family, garnered over the years that journalists have been asking me to comment on the latest events in the royal soap opera. I am a firm believer in the 'cock-up' theory of history rather than the conspiracy theory. I know that people conspire together, but I also know that stupidity usually triumphs. I assured Samir that Diana's death was an accident, a result of the belief which many drinkers hold – that they drive better when they are drunk. Samir was completely unconvinced. He knew for certain that it was a conspiracy between the royal family and the Israelis to bring down not merely Diana but Dodi and thus strike at Dodi's father, Mohammed al Fayed. I could see from his expression that he thought I was very naïve.

I should have remembered Robert Fisk and The Plot, and held my breath. Anyone who wants to try to understand why Lebanon, once a rich and flourishing country, is now in a state where a long, vicious war has ended but peace has not been made must read Robert Fisk's *Pity the Poor Nation*. Of Lebanon after the war he wrote,

> The events of the 1975–6 civil war have become a fixation for the Lebanese. Even today, the bookshops of Hamra Street and Sassine Square contain shelves of expensive photographic records of the fighting, coffee table books with colour plates in which readers can study at their leisure and in detail the last moments of a young Muslim militiaman before the firing squad, the anguished eyes of a Palestinian mother pleading for her family before a hooded gunman, a Christian family lying massacred inside their home. It is a kind of catharsis for both the Lebanese and the Palestinians who have long understood the way in which these terrible events should be interpreted. Victories were the result of courage, of patriotism or revolutionary conviction. Defeats were always caused by the plot: The Plot, the *mo'amera*, the *complot*, undefinable and ubiquitous, a conspiracy of treachery in which a foreign hand – Syrian, Palestinian, Israeli, American, French, Libyan, Iranian – was always involved. Edward Cody of the AP and I once came to the conclusion that in every interview we conducted in the Lebanon, a special chair should be set aside for The Plot – since The Plot invariably played a leading role in all discussions we ever had with politicians, diplomats or gunmen.[3]

Jean Said Makdisi, in her glossary of terms used in times of crisis, linked The Plot to The Plan and explained that 'The reader should not expect proponents of conspiracy theories to show alarm at their pervasiveness. Rather, a certain perverse comfort is taken from the assurance that someone, at least, knows what is going on and why.'[4]

It is our human nature to create an explanation for everything that happens, even though such an explanation may be entirely speculative and, in many cases, quite far-fetched. We prefer an explanation which enhances our image of ourselves. The thought that someone somewhere is conspiring against us serves to boost our pride. It means that we are so important that other people have to take us into account. The explanation that the suffering of most people in Lebanon was brought about simply because they were in the way when different groups of men, who care nothing for their fellow human beings, were battling for supremacy, is too close to a truth which shows how helpless and insignificant we are in the whole scheme of things. For many people a conspiracy of enemies is preferable because it boosts their sense of personal identity. This is one of the reasons why enemies are necessary.

Asking someone about their enemies is a very intrusive question, and the answers can be surprising. At an Amnesty International party I asked a fellow guest, a strong supporter of Amnesty, whether he had an enemy. He answered immediately, 'My ex-wife.' People can talk about their friendships without revealing much about themselves, but talking about their enemies goes straight to the painful complexities of relationships, as the participants of a workshop showed in their definitions of an enemy. They said,

- 'An enemy is someone who threatens my safety and leaves me feeling helpless.'
- 'An enemy is someone who despises you, doesn't respect you, wishes you were dead.'
- 'Enemies are those who do not allow you to progress, to develop in your own way, but try to impose their own beliefs and opinions.'
- 'An enemy is somebody who doesn't give me respect or trust or openness, who has different values from me and expects me to conform to theirs, who makes life uncomfortable for me by their actions and words.'

- 'I have loads of enemies. There's family, people who have rigid lifestyles and who dictate to everyone. At work there's the people who vie for power with me, and elsewhere, in politics.'
- 'Looking carefully into my life I am aware that I have had, and probably still have, enemies, although I have a fantasy that I haven't. An enemy is someone who wishes bad things for me and who, it seems, no amount of love or understanding will influence otherwise.'
- 'I believe we need enemies to shift rage from family and community to outsiders or causes. Also it gives an illusion of superiority by condemning their beliefs.'
- 'An enemy is a traitor. One who betrayed me. One who had let me down. Rejected me. An unaccepting, narrow-minded person who had not been willing to listen and who sees the truth only from their own view point. Probably envies me and therefore wishes to destroy me.'
- 'As a child I had enemies – other children who bullied me at school and on the way home from school.'
- 'An enemy is someone who is totally without morals. A traitor. Someone who thinks only of self-gain and themselves. Someone who has let me down.'

When I asked four-year-old Alice if she had any enemies she immediately identified the problem of how we can hate the people we love. She said, 'Sometimes Miles is an enemy. With Christopher and Jake. Most of the time when they come to tea he doesn't let me into his bedroom. He just wants to play with his friends.'

I asked her how that made her feel. She said, 'A bit upset. I cry, because sometimes I am trying to get though his door and he slams it shut and I fall down the steps.'

Miles, as I discovered when he told me about his enemies, had encountered the Sex War, though he had not yet recognized it as such. He told me that most of his enemies were girls. There were those who, he said, are 'always telling on you, and telling the teachers, "Miss, Miles did this, Miles did that."' Megan was the chief of his accusers, but she did much more. He said, 'She makes me feel really bad. I say, "Look, Megan, I don't want you playing with me because I can't play with you all the time. I've got other friends." And if I said, "I'm not your friend," she'd go off crying. She'd go all red-faced and make me feel really bad. I just can't leave her alone. And then when I approach her, she runs off.'

Yet at other times Megan would distract him from his work by talking to him. I suggested to Miles that Megan really liked him and did things to annoy him just to get his attention. Miles dismissed this entirely, so I let the subject drop. Time enough for him to discover that sexual attraction is not always mutual and that many miseries arise from that.

Lesley knew these miseries and others only too well. She also knew how important it is to recognize an enemy. She wrote,

An enemy is not only someone who wishes to hurt you personally but has the power, or is perceived as having the power, to do so. In the case of enemies within the family this creates difficulties, because, although a person may to all intents and purposes be your enemy, they in effect have a cloaking device. That is, because they are supposed to love you, you can fail to see them as an enemy and take action to protect yourself. Taking that a step further, you may very well fail to perceive that their words or actions are in fact a result of their malice and projections, and locate the fault in yourself. Unfortunately, this puts you in the usually unrecognized position of being your own enemy. You join the other side and fight against yourself.

If you are brought up to believe that hating or doing harm to others, even wishing it, is wrong you are left very vulnerable to enemies. You bury your own hate, and either cannot see, or feel unable to defend yourself against enemies, people who wish to harm you personally, or who wish to take something that is yours, or you see as vital to your survival.

At a time of great personal stress, a woman moved in on my marriage. I remember being sat on the rug with my two small children when she came to my home to collect my husband for a business meeting and making it as clear as day that she was after my husband by the way she behaved towards him. I didn't feel threatened because I was still locked into the belief that marriage was for ever, but I was appalled by her lack of manners and general demeanour. I can smile in a kind way now at my innocence and naïveté. Things got worse and she was the person my husband

moved on to. She would probably argue that it was nothing personal
and she might refute the idea of being my enemy. But I saw her as
an enemy because she was competition for the resources I needed
for my children, personal as much as financial. Now my children
have grown up the enmity I felt for her is fading. As the threat she
poses diminishes my feelings are moving to the point where she has
no importance.

Lesley's last words echoed those of Irene when I asked her about
enemies. She said, 'I don't think much about enemies at all. I think
an enemy would be someone I disliked or hated, and again that
belongs to youth. It doesn't belong to this age.'

Of course, opportunities for making enemies abound while we
are still involved in competitive work. A university professor, not
English, spoke to me of his colleagues and said, 'They smile at me
and have a drink with me, and then they'll go into committee and
turn down all my applications for research money.'

When I asked Anthony if he had any enemies he said, 'Not that
I know of. There's nobody that I could say that I couldn't see their
point of view. I don't have enemies in the sense that they would
like to hurt me or mine. I could be easily hurt, or offended, but no,
I don't have enemies as such. I don't have friends and I don't have
enemies.'

Yet, as I discovered when he took me to Drumcree, where the
Orange Order supporters manned the country lane, protesting their
right to march down the Garvaghy Road through the Catholic estate
in Portadown, Anthony, in his kindness, had taken me somewhere
where, if it were known that he was a Catholic, he would have been
in considerable physical danger.

Those of us who live in peaceful countries can still have enemies
– friends who betray you. Judy told me about her enemies – a
business partner who had stolen from her and some friends who
had formed a clique and excluded her, and what she had done to
them. She said, 'My way of dealing with people who've been rotten
to me is to pretend they're dead. I feel angry for a long time and
then I get to a stage where, when their names come up, I can say,
"Who?" It takes about two years. We forget about them, people
who've done really rotten things to us. Then they're dead. They've
gone over to the dark side.'

Sometimes Judy's revenge was even greater. She said, 'I have my own revenge. I put curses on them. I beam my energy out.'

I think Judy was so kind she did not beam her energy very far. None of the politicians she hated have dropped dead. But there is a certain satisfaction in hurling a curse, even if it is only at a television screen.

Enemies can certainly play an important part in our life but I had not thought of them as being useful until I met a Serbian Jungian analyst in Belgrade. I asked him whether he had any enemies. 'Internal or external?' he queried.

'Both.'

'I don't think I can talk about my internal enemies where I am an enemy to myself. That's where external enemies are necessary. They see you more clearly than you see yourself. They stop you from having too high an opinion of yourself.'

I would have called such a group of people 'critics' rather than 'enemies' but I did not think this was simply a confusion of terms. He spoke excellent English, so if he said 'enemy' he meant 'enemy'. But only a Jungian analyst would have beneficent enemies.

I asked him if he had any political enemies. 'Of course,' he said. 'Americans.'

I wonder if many Americans realize how big a part they play on the world stage as the universal enemy. But that is one of the dilemmas of friendship. The more powerful you are the fewer friends you are likely to have.

I am sure that many Americans would be greatly hurt to know that millions of people beam great amounts of enmity at them and take no account of how many Americans – though not always the American government – have tried to help impoverished people and, however ineptly, to secure world peace. Fortunately, not all foreigners do this. When I was in Vietnam in 1997 I discovered that the Vietnamese discriminated carefully between the American government that inflicted the most dreadful war on the Vietnamese and the Cambodians, and Americans generally, whom the Vietnamese saw as friends or potential friends. Such subtle discriminations require a subtle mind, which is lacking in those people who want to divide the world into two groups, friends and enemies.

Yet friends and enemies are rarely discrete categories. Friends can easily become enemies. In Northern Ireland I met Martin at a Sinn

Fein Advice Centre in Fermanagh. He had recently been released from Long Kesh jail, where he had been serving an eight-year term. We got on to the subject of education and he told me how, in many places in Northern Ireland, Catholic and Protestant children would attend the same primary school. His best friend at primary school was William, a lad from a Protestant family. He said, 'We played football together, we went fishing together, we did everything boys do together. In our last year in primary school, when I was eleven, I was one of six boys who passed the eleven-plus exam to go to the Christian Brothers School. William went to the local Protestant high school. The next time I saw him it was on a street in Castlederg. He was in an Ulster Defence Regiment uniform. He stopped me and made me get out of my car. He knew who I was but he didn't let on that he knew. He asked me my name, then he searched me and he searched my car.' Not long afterwards Martin became a volunteer in the IRA.

Sometimes friends become enemies because the groups to which individuals belong demand that it be so. Sometimes individuals themselves decide to change from friend to enemy. Sometimes it is hard to know who is your friend and who your enemy. Mark Twain once observed that 'It takes your enemy and your friend, working together, to hurt you to the heart: the one to slander you and the other to get the news to you.'[5]

Irene spoke of the spite which can lurk in the heart of a friend. She said, 'Spite is one of the things I dislike, probably because I have a spiteful reaction inside myself sometimes and I find it horrible. There's that desire to hurt. I think envy's different. You can envy someone for having a terrific relationship you'd like to have, or having freedom from financial worries. I think that's fine because it doesn't mean you want to do them down or make them feel unhappy. Whereas spite has a real sting. To take them down, make them feel unhappy with themselves and what they've got.'

When we act out of spite and enmity we want to hurt other people and know that they are hurt, yet at the same time we do not want to know how the hurt feels to them. We have to refrain from empathizing with them. Empathy can bring us close to other people, but it can cause us much pain and that sense of helplessness when we know what another person is feeling and we can do nothing to ease that person's pain. A mother told me how upset she was by the way her teenage son's friends were also his enemies. They hurt him and they got him into trouble, but he still trailed after them, entranced by what he saw as their style and glamour, and proud to call them his friends. Friends can indeed be enemies.

When I asked my workshop participants to list what they saw as the dangers of friendship they had no difficulty in doing so. Here are some of the dangers they described:

- 'The fear of the loss of the friend through death or separation.' (Someone pointed out that people will commiserate with you when a relative dies but not when a friend dies.)
- 'It means trusting someone with very sensitive parts of myself, so I am vulnerable and can be hurt. If I become dependent on that friendship that person might let me down.'
- 'They can tell you things when they're in difficulty and you want to make it all right and you can't.'
- 'Being taken for granted is an abuse of a friendship.'
- 'There are dangers in becoming too familiar or involved in a situation in their lives, as with their spouse. It's important to remain neutral in aspects of other relationships in their lives.'
- 'You have to trust them and sometimes this trust is broken. They may gossip and not keep a confidence – or you may let them down in some way.'
- 'To be a true friend you have to expose yourself, and this means you always risk being rejected.'

The pain of losing a friend was often mentioned as one of the dangers of friendship, but for Andrew Sullivan the death of a friend meant something more. He wrote, 'It is only, perhaps, when you absorb the notion that someone is truly your equal, truly inter-changeable with you, that the death of another makes mortality real. It is as if only in the death of a friend that a true reckoning with mortality is ever fully made, before it is too late.'[6]

Andrew Sullivan was writing about the death of a friend from Aids and describing how 'homosexuals, by default as much as any-thing else, have managed to sustain a society of friendship that is, for the most part, unequalled by any other part of society.'[7]

This is a major claim to make, though he did acknowledge that heterosexual women could sustain friendships if their familial responsibilities have not overwhelmed them. Heterosexual men have suffered 'great spiritual and emotional impoverishment' because 'the fear of male intimacy, which is intrinsically connected to the fear of homosexuality, has too often denied straight men the bonds they need to sustain themselves through life's difficulties. When they socialize they often demand the chaperone of sports or work to avoid the appearance of being gay.'[8]

Tim Lott's novel *White City Blue* concerns four men who call themselves close friends but whose friendships fail through lack of intimacy. Fear of homosexuality is certainly present in their relationships, but so is intense competition. In an article accompanying the publication of his novel Tim Lott commented on how women, unlike men, will talk to one another at length on the phone and even make conversation in a public washroom:

> This seems to me a fundamentally different approach to male friendship. For men, friendship is far more a performance art. You go out, and you try to entertain each other. You grandstand, you try and get attention, you aim for the loudest laugh. This need for competition – which is another way of saying this need for domination – is an increasingly thin shell, and I believe it is slowly cracking up. Men are showing all the signs of admitting to be humans rather than just men, and, in this case, this means admitting to being more like women.[9]

I have not observed homosexual men being any less competitive than heterosexual men. Most hold the distinctly masculine view that competition is what life is about. I am not sure the homosexuality itself creates a special talent for friendship. Having sex with another person does not constitute a friendship, and, while some homosexual men form loving relationships with a long-term partner, many homosexual men spend an enormous amount of time and energy in promiscuous sex. I do not think that this is because homosexual men have a particular propensity for sex. If women were as interested in sex as men are, heterosexual men would be able to be as promiscuous as homosexual men.

Having sex is an excellent way of avoiding intimacy. You do not have to talk. Or you can talk but it is sex talk, which nowadays goes on in bed, out of bed, in entertainment and in selling things. The journalist Charlotte Raven, a very sharp-eyed observer, wrote,

> This is what the sexual sell does. Far from revealing reality, it ends up concealing the truth. This may strike us as strange. We are used to reading sexual candour as evidence of openness. We tend to believe, as a culture, that the more we talk about sex, the more we are revealing of ourselves.
>
> This may once have been true, but in the current over-stimulated climate sex talk is, perversely, becoming an excuse for not revealing anything important. All the usual rules have been inverted. Sex talk is small talk, a kind of background gibberish that covers up our inability to have real conversations. Therefore, the more we reveal about orgasms and erectile dysfunctions, the less we really know about ourselves.[10]

I agree with Charlotte, though I have to say that I have never known a time when talking about sex revealed the truth. When I discovered sex in the late forties women said nothing publicly about sex and many did not talk about it privately. My mother never mentioned menstruation or conception or childbirth to me, though she did, by implication, give me to understand that marriage entailed something unpleasant for a woman. In my teens I had to keep secret from her the fact that my sister, who was training to be a teacher, had given me a pamphlet to read on menstruation. I was in my thirties before I said the word 'fuck' publicly, and then only in the context of the punchline of a then very daring joke. I had had to learn the word, though not the joke, from my husband in bed.

In the sixties and seventies we thought we were being open and truthful about sex. But actually the same secrecy, misunderstanding and refusal to listen were still there, though the context might have changed. Men still operated on the old principle of propositioning every woman because, as my husband once explained to me, even though you got a lot of knock-backs, you get some acceptances, only now men expected every woman to be on the pill and so to have no reason to refuse their offer. Women were prepared to forgo the security of a marriage ring but they still wanted a relationship along with the sex.

Nothing of importance had changed because sex still posed the danger that it had always posed. Sex renders us vulnerable in the way we fear the most. We have to protect our sense of being a person for in failing to do so we risk being annihilated as a person. In orgasm our sense of self can dissipate in splendour, but we can also be wiped out as a person by the power of our partner, or, in the case of men, by failing to perform. So we lie about sex to one another and, sometimes, foolishly, we lie to ourselves.

During the seventies the Women's Movement enabled many women to reveal that their sexual interest was in other women. After so many centuries in the shadows it was only human for them to claim that they were special. Having been less than nothing they needed to be more than most, as all disadvantaged groups do when they claim their birthright. So the myth was born that lesbians were able to combine the sensitivity, caring and empathy which all women possess with the passion of sex, and lesbian relationships would therefore not be torn apart by the jealousies, angers, hatreds and betrayals that turn heterosexual relationships into nightmares.

This myth completely ignored the fact that some women have all the sensitivity, caring and empathy of a pile of old bricks, and that sex and love, whatever the gender of the couple, are always accompanied by the passions of jealousy, anger, hatred and betrayal. A lot of women were hurt by this myth. I remember a young woman who came to talk to me about a book she was writing but who drifted off the subject to tell me about her partner's faithlessness. What troubled her most was her guilt for failing to live up to the myth. She was jealous.

If you want an untroubled, utterly faithful relationship get a dog. Did you know that a survey by the British Veterinary Association revealed that 93 per cent of pet owners questioned bought their pet a Christmas present, and more than half the pets also received Christmas cards?[11]

Friends as friends and lovers as friends might be difficult but what about family? Can family be friends?

Alice was very clear that people as friends were different from family as friends. When I asked her if Miles was a friend she immediately answered yes, but when I pointed out to her that she hadn't included him in her list of friends she said, 'Well, he's my brother.'

'And what's the difference between being a friend friend and being a brother friend?'

'Well, he's living with you. Friends don't live with you, and brothers do. Eli's my friend too.' Eli was then only a few weeks old but he was fascinated with Alice and no doubt regarded her as a friend.

I asked, 'Is Mummy your friend?'

'Sort of. In the middle, I think.'

'In the middle of what?'

'In the middle means a bit of my friend – half. Half of my friend.'

Her mother Jo looked stricken.

I asked, 'Is Daddy your friend?'

'Yes. Daddy's my friend.'

We went on to talk about enemies and then Jo, who was cooking, asked Alice why she did not think Mummy was a friend. Alice went over to Jo and, smiling broadly, started thumping her. She said, 'Mummy, sometimes you shout at me and say I'm horrible.'

I said, 'You're banging into Mummy now. Does that mean you're not her friend? If you hit Mummy, are you being a friend to her?'

Alice went on smiling and thumping Jo. She said confidently, 'She likes it.'

That's the kind of logic which families use.

When I asked Miles if Alice was his friend he said, 'Some of the time she is but some of the time she isn't.' However, when he went on to consider the matter he decided that Alice was his friend even though she did not always do what he wanted her to do.

I asked Miles if Mummy was a friend. He said most emphatically, 'Yes,' but went on, 'Most of the time, except when she gets cross.'

'Is Daddy a friend?'

Miles's 'Yes' was more hesitant so I said, 'You seemed like you weren't too sure about that.'

'Well, I was going to say that my dad's a bit harsh on my mum because he makes her seem to be the baddie. He's always threatening us with things like 'Quick, get into the bath before your mum comes up.'

'And what do you think of that?'

'I don't think it's nice. I wouldn't like it if I was made the baddie all the time.'

'Do you think your mum and dad are friends with one another?'

'Yes, or they wouldn't have married and I wouldn't probably be alive.'

Miles and Alice illustrate the perils parents face if they take their children's point of view seriously and allow them to express their opinions. Such children do not hesitate to criticize their parents. But Miles and Alice also reveal the security which they take for granted like the air they breathe. They can criticize their parents, and everyone can get cross and shout at one another, but it is never more than a storm in a teacup, and the teacup is rock solid.

Not all families are like that. I asked my workshop participants, 'Can family be friends?' Here are some of their replies:

- 'No. What prevents them being friends is trust. I cannot trust them with my emotions. My parents never respected my feelings and I could no more trust them now than I could as a child. We do not relate our feelings to each other.'
- 'We have totally different value systems.'
- 'I love my son but he is not my friend. The relationship is one-sided. I love my daughter and she is a friend. We have a supporting relationship.'
- 'I can't say that anyone in my family was a friend. My mother was particularly forbidding, full of repressed anger and without humour.'
- 'I would like to think this is so but know that it is not because we come from the same situations with similar knowledge but different feelings.'
- 'Many of my family will only accept me very conditionally and I am not willing to sacrifice myself in order to be accepted by them.'
- 'Blood's thicker than water because you share the same history and are used to familiar relationships. But it is harder to set yourself free.'
- 'I have a sister I haven't spoken to for several years because she hurt me many times. I feel it is safer for me not to have a friendship with her.'
- 'I love my brothers but wouldn't call them friends. There's no one in my family I share myself with deeply.'
- 'Sometimes it's difficult for a relative to be a friend because they can't stand back from the situation. They get too involved and emotional.'
- 'I do not see all members of my family as friends but maybe

members of the same tribe. Some are friends: all are friendly.'
* 'Blood's bloodier than water.'

Andrew Sullivan considered the question of friends and family:

Families and marriages fail too often because they are trying to
answer too many human needs. A spouse is required to be a lover,
a friend, a mother, a father, a soulmate, a co-worker, and so on.
Few people can be all these things for one person. And when the
demands are set too high, disappointment can only follow. If husbands and wives have deeper and stronger friendships outside the
marital unit, the marriage has more space to breathe and fewer
burdens to bear. Likewise, a lack of true family can, I think, impinge
on friendship. If we have many friends and no real family, we tend
to demand things of friends which are equally inappropriate. The
two relationships, then, family and friendship, are surely rivals, but
they are also complements to one another. There is no reason why
most human lives should not have a deep experience of both.[12]

That is a wonderful aspiration, but many of us fail to achieve it.
I used to think that some people have a talent for friendship but
now I am not so sure. I have learned that when people speak of the
wonders of universal love, or of spirituality, or of caring for others,
or of friendship I should look at what these people actually do. I
have worked as a visiting lecturer for far too many charity, psychotherapy and counselling groups where all the talk was of how much
they care about other people but where that 'other people' did not
include me. In their eyes I had no needs like being fed, being
protected from importunate members of the audience, assisted with
transport or simply given a glass of water. The world is full of people
who believe that to say you do something is the same as doing it.
St Paul did say that the thought is the same as the deed, which
probably explains why I have found so many Christians prone to
such oversights.
    Even when someone does show all the behaviours we might
associate with having a talent for friendship I have found it necessary
to ask the person whether that is so.
    My friend Una seemed to me to have a talent for friendship.
She had retired from a long and distinguished academic career in

psychology. I doubt that there would be many of her erstwhile students who did not consider her to be a friend, while in the often bitchy world of professional psychology in Australia she had no enemies and masses of friends.

Una remembered and kept up with the events in her friends' lives. She always kept a photographic record of us, pictures which she kept in albums on the coffee table beside the couch where she read her beloved newspapers. Her passion was current affairs. She told me, 'A lot of my friendship is carried on in my head. I think about you a lot, and I think about Patricia sitting in her London house. I've got pictures of all of you here. There's Polly in Scotland. I think of you all living your lives as I know them now.'

What Una liked about friendship was the conversation, exploring a topic together. She was conversing most of the time, directly with friends and neighbours, and her cat, or indirectly by telephone and letters. Yet, when I said to her that she had a talent for friendship she denied it.

She said, 'I have a talent for friendship like when the plumber came today. I can talk like that very easily. I can get on with working men in pubs in England as very few people can. And there are certain people in shops I can talk to, and my neighbours, but I have been living here for twenty years so that's not surprising. We have over-the-fence chats to each other but we have got absolutely nothing in common except neighbourliness. When I go into groups with my peers I'm one of the less comfortable ones. I think people like me and they look to me for certain things. I do have close friendships but they took a long time to build up and they're often quite ambivalent. At a distance I can be friendly and helpful, but I find it hard to cope with intimacy. That's why I live on my own, I suppose. I find it hard to tell people, "I like you. Can I see you again?" Maintaining a friendship is a problem with me. I am grieving over several lost friendships where we have just drifted apart. And that's hard. My friend Belinda, we shared flats together and so on, and even after she married and had a kid we saw each other quite frequently. Now she no longer rings me. I ring her and keep in contact. But she has got grandchildren and her husband has retired, and it's very rare that she gives me a thought, I think, and I find that hard.'

I asked my workshop group if there was a talent for friendship and, if so, whether it was innate or learned. They answered:

- 'I have learned to respect others through therapy. I learned from appropriate modelling of others who have been through similar processes.'
- 'I haven't a talent for friendship. I think friendship is learnt; by giving friendship to others one receives friendship back and people benefit and grow.'
- 'No talent. I was brought up by a puritanical grandmother who allowed no one into the house. No child was quite good enough for me to play with.'
- 'In the main, we learn how to make friends by observing others, initially our parents and siblings and, as we get older, our peers and work colleagues. To observe the making of a friendship by others teaches us to behave in a fashion to create our own.'
- 'I grew up with no social skills apart from being polite. My best friend grew up with good social skills and she became my role model.'
- 'I think I have a talent for friendship because I am open and honest and I have a great faith in people. Unfortunately this sometimes leads to my downfall because other people then hurt me.'
- 'I value friendships highly. Because I think friendships are important I think I make a good friend.'
- 'I think that I probably choose not to develop any talent I may have for friendship as I do not feel the need for many friends, although I do like other people to accept me in a friendly way as a friendly person.'

Underlying these answers and indeed the words of everyone quoted here is a division which runs like a great fault-line across the world of friendship. It is the line which divides us all into one of two groups, according to how we experience our sense of existence. These groups I have called extraverts and introverts. In my earlier books and especially in *The Successful Self* I have looked at how this division affects our relationships. What I have said has arisen out of extensive research. I now know that whenever I talk or write about this matter some people, usually those I call introverts, will say, 'Yes, I recognize myself in what you say,' and some people, usually those I call extraverts, will not recognize what I say and instead be puzzled or insist that they are a bit of both, no matter how much I explain that it is not a matter of what you do but why you do it. However, it is not surprising that such a difference arises because introverts turn inwards to their internal reality of thoughts and feelings, and thus are likely to be aware of why they do what they do, while extraverts turn outwards to their external reality, where they are more interested in doing than in examining the reasons why.

Other people are of enormous importance to extraverts because extraverts experience their sense of existence in relationship to other people. Lesley, an extravert, explained this. 'If you are an extravert who feels in danger of disappearing, friends are vital landmarks on your map who need to be kept in place at all costs. Without them there is the feeling that you don't exist because you can only get some sense of yourself if it is reflected back at you. It is as though the reflection is real and exists but you do not exist without the mirror of people relating to you. If you feel like that any expenditure of effort on friends is worthwhile.'

The writer Fay Weldon told me, 'I had the art of placating and always had fans, even as quite a small child. I would always have a little group of supporters who would fight my corner for me with teachers. I just like friends. I just like talking to people, I enjoy conversation. I just went to school because I liked my friends.' It has always amazed me that Fay ever gets any writing done because her home is always full of people, but she explained, 'I've rather cunningly always surrounded myself with children, which is another way of creating your own world downwards because there isn't anything particularly solid behind you. So now there are children, and grandchildren, and Nick has three boys – one, fifteen years old, lives with us and the other two visit. I just think I was born sociable and gregarious.'

Extraverts often envy introverts for having – or appearing to have – a deep, still centre, but Lesley clearly does not envy introverts. She wrote,

> Then there are those strange people called introverts. I have the feeling that many of these characters are so bound up with what they are doing or thinking and are so happily and securely independent that they don't realize that extravert partners may feel shut out

and neglected. I misunderstood my introvert ex-husband, because he was much more bound up in his medical practice than in what I and the children were doing or feeling. I reached the perfectly logical conclusion that he didn't care about us. In fact he did and does, but he doesn't want his family to take up much of his valuable time.

What Lesley was describing here was how introverts experience their sense of existence through a sense of achievement, organization and control. They often lack the social skills which extraverts acquire so easily.

Some introverts do learn the art of being sociable. Irene described her progress to me: 'Control is important to me. Wild emotion and a lot of impinging of emotion I can't deal with. Sex drives I could understand, but I could never understand why people were dependent on one another. Even as a child I couldn't. There was all that marvellous, exciting world out there, and so many things to see and do. I resent people who try and restrict me from being myself, from doing what I want to do. It took me a long time to be part of a group. Right up until I was fifty I hated groups, but gradually I've learned to cope. I've done it, I feel, successfully, and it's been a great help in my life. I remember talking to you years ago – I'd just turned thirty-six, I think, and I said to you, I just suddenly felt that everybody else felt the same sort of inadequacies, fear and anxiety as I did. I didn't feel isolated any more. Because that's what I felt before, that I felt this and everybody else was going along having a great time. I think that gradually in the eighties – it was doing those various personal development courses and group activities – I realized more fully that everybody's much the same. It was good to learn to work with a group and accept a role in that group, and usually, if I'm not the leader, I'm close to the leader. I would hate to be without friends. The fact that they exist and are part of the circle that I can relate to is very comforting to me. I haven't got perfect friends, but I'm not a perfect friend either. I can be happily occupied by myself, fiddling around with paints and looking at things, but friendships are part of the pattern of my life.'

Extraverts, as Lesley described, need other people to maintain their sense of existence, and introverts, as Irene mentioned, need other people to reduce their sense of isolation, but for extraverts relationships with other people are their top priority while for introverts the top priority is a sense of achievement. Of course, everyone wants both – good relationships and a sense of achievement – but often life forces us to choose between them. If we are wise we know what our top priority is and we make sure we fulfil it in some way. No matter how vast Fay's work commitments are she always surrounds herself with family and friends. When Irene was diagnosed with lung cancer she chose not to go immediately into treatment. Instead she flew to Paris from Sydney to spend two weeks touring the art galleries. What mattered most to her was exploring 'that marvellous, exciting world out there'.

Opposites, so they say, attract, and where love and sex are concerned a couple is always a pairing of an introvert and an extravert. We see in the other something we do not have. The central character in Tim Lott's *White City Blue* is Frankie, an estate agent and an extravert. He says of himself,

> I've always liked to be liked. Everyone does, I suppose. I'm just prepared to admit it. It's more of a naked need than a desire for me. I hate it if someone doesn't like me. And so a job which seemed to turn so much on making people like you, on making them trust you, appealed to me. And you don't have the effort afterwards of maintaining a friendship. If you sell their flat at a good price, or find them a nice one, they love you. I get kissed, hugged, praised, thanked. It's terrific for self-esteem. Then it's goodbye and on to the next person to woo.[13]

Frankie's affairs are as transient as his customers. Then he meets Veronica. He does not understand her, but he recognizes that she has something he does not have.

> As I chatted to her, I realized with a certain amount of surprise that I actually *did* like her – not only her looks but the way she kept herself apart from herself. There was – how can I put this – a *decent gap* between when she thought and when she spoke, there was *consideration*. It was a mark of self-possession, something I find greatly attractive for that reason. Perhaps because it's the quality I've always lacked. Events sweep me up, clean my clock, leave me gasping.[14]

We might not always be what we appear to be. A couple might appear to be two extraverts, but one of them is a socially skilled introvert; or two introverts, but one of them is a shy extravert. Where friendship is concerned, introverts can be friends with introverts and extraverts with extraverts, but often a lengthy friendship, one that withstands the changes that life brings, is between an extravert and an introvert. One of the reasons that the friendship John McCarthy and Brian Keenan formed when they were hostages together in Beirut was so strong was because John was the extravert and Brian the introvert, and each was prepared to supply what the other lacked.

However, misunderstandings and enmities can arise because one person does not understand or will not accept that the other has a different priority. Only now does Lesley see how she, the extravert, misunderstood her introvert husband. Often such misunderstandings turn into intolerance. To an extravert the introvert's refusal to display emotion can seem to betray a complete lack of feeling, while an introvert can despise the way in which an extravert puts relationships above principle. When I was in Greece I met a designer, a woman in her fifties from New York, who told me how she had lost a friend.

She said, 'I was invited to submit a design for a particular project. I was interested in doing this because it was something I hadn't attempted before and it was a chance to try out some ideas, but I wasn't passionately wedded to the design I developed. I'm too long in the tooth now to get overinvolved in the work I do, but it was interesting and I wanted feedback from the man who'd commissioned it. Well, this person was someone I'd known for years. I knew him socially as well as through work, and I thought of us as being friends, not close friends, but friends. One thing I knew about him was that he really liked to be liked. I never saw this as a problem because he's a really likeable guy. Everybody likes him. I never thought this would take precedence over the work. Yet this is just what happened. He couldn't bring himself to say he didn't like my work because he thought that would mean I wouldn't like him. That was just ridiculous. It never crossed my mind that his opinion about this piece of work would cause me to dislike him. I never think about whether I like or dislike people because on the whole I really like people. I can think of only one person I actually dislike, and that's very personal. A lot of people I judge very harshly but I don't dislike them. It mightn't always be liking but I guess I feel sorry for people. Everyone gets a rotten deal one way or another. Anyway, what happened was that there was a big performance in which he talked to other people but he didn't talk to me. The first I knew of it was when a mutual friend – you know the sort of friend who can't get to you quick enough with bad news – rang me to say he'd spoken to her husband and of course her husband had told her. He should have just given me his opinion straight but he didn't. It really wasn't any big deal but at the time I thought it was important. I came to feel that he'd acted in bad faith. That's a harsh judgement but that's me. I think that worrying about whether people like you is a weakness.'

The lack of understanding and tolerance between an introvert and an extravert can become the basis for enmity.

Perhaps the greatest contrast between friendship and enmity is that friendships are often difficult to establish and always hard to maintain, while enmities are easy to establish and simple to maintain. Friendships always involve trying to understand another person and, in opening yourself to that person, making yourself vulnerable. Enmity always involves turning the enemy into an object which requires no understanding and, in closing yourself off from the other person, making yourself aggressive and strong. Enmity always makes us less of a human being and friendship makes us more. To achieve that more is not easy.

I have been asking people whether they find friendship easy. The consensus of opinion is that friendship is demanding and difficult.

When I asked Miles if he found it easy to make friends he said, 'It is quite hard.' I asked him what he found hard about it and he said, 'Well, if there's someone new the teachers want you to be nice to her and if you really don't like her, or him, at all, it's very difficult and she can't be a real friend to you.'

'When you meet somebody you think you might like, do you find it hard then to be friends?'

'Sometimes, but sometimes it's easy.'

'What makes the difference?'

'Well, if it's someone you like but they're not so keen on you, it's quite hard. Or if you like one thing and the other person didn't, and that person hated it and threw it away, then that would be quite hard because you'd be using it and the other person would be wrecking it.'

Miles has spent seven years of his life negotiating his friendships, first with family and family friends, and then with fellow pupils. He is a warm, outgoing boy, keenly interested in other people and in the world around him, he has the unwavering support of his parents, yet he finds friendship far from easy. How much more difficult is friendship for someone who, no matter how warm and friendly they might be, has no secure background.

Diyana was enjoying her life in Sarajevo when the war came and destroyed much of what she held dear. After enduring months of shelling and sniper fire from the Serbs she made a desperate and dangerous journey with her little daughter from Sarajevo to London, where she found asylum. I asked her, 'How easy are you finding it to meet people here and really make friends?'

She said, 'It's easy to meet people, very easy, but it's very difficult to make a friend and start a real friendship. First of all you don't understand the people – it's not just a matter of language, it's a matter of a different mentality as well. Sometimes you don't understand somebody who is maybe offering you help, maybe really wants to help you and to make a friendship with you, but you just can't understand. It can take years and years to get used to English people. I don't think they're worse than my people, or that they are any worse than any people in the world, you just need time to get to know the English.'

How many times have I heard an Australian or an American say that about the English! I said, 'Everyone who comes here says that.'

Diyana went on, 'I find it very easy to communicate with them because they don't ask you very much – maybe they don't want to know much about you. In this situation it's very good for me not to speak a lot about my past, so if they don't ask me it's good. But you can't start a real relationship with somebody who doesn't know anything about you and you don't know anything about them. It's maybe too idealistic to expect that. You have to ask somebody about their home town, their family, their parents.'

'Do you feel they aren't interested or do they feel they shouldn't ask questions?'

'I think they were brought up not to ask questions, to keep at a distance. I think maybe they could be much better, much closer to foreigners, but they don't know how to approach. Maybe it's better for me to think that. I don't want to think they don't want to approach.'

I talked about my experience as an Australian in England. I said, 'Sometimes people don't know how to frame a question because they don't know enough about your background to frame a sensible question. I've met hundreds of English people – they know I'm Australian as soon as I speak – and the only thing they know about Australia is the weather. They say, "Don't you miss the wonderful weather?" But they don't ask other questions unless they've been to Australia, or they've got a relative there, when they'll say, "Perhaps you've met my relative. She lives in New Zealand." New Zealand is fifteen hundred miles away from Sydney.'

Diyana recognized what I was describing. 'When I'm asked where I'm from – because after the first sentence they discover I'm not from here – and I say, "I'm from Europe." "Which part of Europe?" they'll say. "Is it Poland?" And I say, "Not Poland. It's Bosnia, the former Yugoslavia." And they say, "There was a terrible war down there. Is it still on?" or something like that. And I can't go on with the conversation. It's finished before it's started. I just answer sometimes, "Fortunately not. It's finished now." But that's all they can ask you. Not all of them, of course – I don't want to insult them.'

After a year or so in London Diyana had met a few people who had a good knowledge of what went on in Bosnia, and who knew that in Bosnia, as in Lebanon, the war might be over but the peace has not been made. She had made friends, but friendship is not easy to maintain when one has little money and every day brings more problems to be overcome.

Indeed friendship is not easy for any of us. This is the consensus of opinion of the many people of whom I asked the question, 'Is friendship easy?' Here are some of the answers from the participants of my workshop:

- 'I don't think it possible to maintain the sort of relationship which I call friendship with any more than a small number of people because it requires me putting a lot of myself in. So for me the talent is recognizing someone who has the qualities for friendship with me. If you mean a talent for having lots of

acquaintances – that's not where I choose to invest a lot of my energy. That's not important for me.'
- 'I can easily strike up a conversation with perfect strangers and form a relationship leading to a friendship. I think if you can communicate and make an opening for the other person to interact you have the makings of a friendship. You then have to learn the skill of maintaining that friendship.'
- 'I find it difficult to talk to and "read" people.'
- 'I have a talent for getting along with people and so I think this helps in making friends. But I only have a few close friends.'
- 'Once someone has become my friend I try always to be there for them and enjoy making a fuss of them on their birthdays. I feel I've got a lot of love to give.'

In two other workshops I asked the participants to answer the question: 'How easy or difficult do you find the whole business of being friends with people?' using a scale from 1 to 7, where 1 was 'easy – like breathing – you don't have to think about it – just natural, no problems' and 7 'difficult – where everything in friendships is difficult, a hassle, a burden, painful, something you can't manage, something always goes wrong no matter how much you try'. After they had answered this question I asked them if they would have answered the question differently when they were younger and, if so, why.

The people in both these workshops were not strangers to the experience of reflecting on what one does and why. The participants in one workshop were women, each of whom was, in her own way, pursuing enlightenment, while the other workshop was for an international group of high-flying managers who were well aware of the necessity of self-knowledge for a successful career. In both groups the ratings generally hovered about four. Friendship was both hard and easy. However, their comments were more revealing of how hard they found friendship to be.

The comments from the women included:

- 'I find the initial art of making friends the most difficult. When it's made it's the problem of keeping in contact. I find this is often down to me.'

- 'When I was younger I was much more judgemental of who was right to be a friend. Now I'm more expansive and relaxed.'
- 'Friendship was easier when I was younger. I was more blithe, less enquiring. I felt life was full of opportunity to make friends. Now it seems more complex. Now I'm friendly but I'm more self-conscious, more inhibited.'
- 'I never know if people feel the same about friendship and often get it wrong; thinking that people are closer than they are, or thinking that people don't want to get close to me when they do.'
- 'Friendship was easier when I was younger. I've had hurtful relationships. Now I'm more picky.'
- 'Being friends is much more difficult than making friends. I am easier in friendships which are not too demanding. Then they become like relatives and I tend to draw back. I can give a lot to friends who don't ask too much.'
- 'I found friendships much harder when I was younger and more judgemental. For me the key is acceptance and trying to see the wider picture. If I rejected the people who behaved in a way I didn't like I would be very lonely.'
- 'I find as I get older it is harder to meet people and make friends. As people get older they become more inhibited, myself also.'

Here are some of the answers from the men:

- 'It is difficult to have too many friends but often after the selection process is over I normally go to any length to maintain that friendship even if it means a lot of sacrifice.'
- 'When I was younger I was less concerned with rejection. It did not register as an issue.'
- 'I used to be able to find common interests much more easily as a child because children spend a lot of time with each other. They've pretty much no barriers. They're open to each other to begin with. Whereas as an adult, I didn't have much time or sufficient time to make friends. I must admit I have developed some barriers. Also I have to make commitment and effort to maintain it.'
- 'I am a very social person who needs to feel needed and

accepted. I think that I tried to work hard at developing and maintaining friendships when I was younger.'

- 'As we grow in age experience catches up with us and we tend to be more suspecting, rather cautious of relationships. A friend in need is a friend indeed. The older you get the more relevant this adage gets.'
- 'I would have answered a little differently when I was younger. I have forgotten so much about sharing, having become guarded by my experience and somewhat unable to give and receive trust on fresh ground.'
- 'I grew up in many different places and tended to be careful about not being too friendly with too many people I knew I'd leave behind. The modern marriage makes it difficult for men to maintain friendships. Non-work time must be devoted to the family.'
- 'As I get older I find it easier to make friends. I believe it's the result of greater self-confidence and a reduced fear of rejection.'
- 'When I was younger I was less flexible with family. There has to be certain coordination with my wife. She might not feel the same for a person. Female friends are less likely to happen now. There's too little time for developing friendships. I stick to (prioritize) a few.'

Only one of the women had rated friendship as completely easy, but she had written, 'I seem to offer and receive a very durable and rewarding level of friendship, but I do screen people out if I don't take to them.' Only one man had rated friendship completely easy, but in the two days I was with the workshop group I saw how he worked ceaselessly to make and to maintain friendships. I could see why when he told me of one of the worst experiences of his life when, in his last year at school, all his friends left and he was completely alone facing what he felt was his annihilation as a person. He now put a great deal of highly skilled work into making sure that that never happened again.

Creating and maintaining friendships and overcoming enmities are not easy tasks. Ed Cairns, a psychologist who had studied the effects the Troubles in Northern Ireland had had on the people there and who was an elder of the Presbyterian Church, told me, 'I think that for us to move on, all that we have to do in Northern

Ireland is to learn to *tolerate* each other at some level; we don't actually have to learn to *love* each other; we don't have to learn to *forgive* each other. It would be nice if these things come about, but I think in the first instance we just have to *tolerate* each other, which people are often not prepared to do at the moment.'

My friend Judy told me, 'I'm prepared to put in the work it takes to become friends with people. It takes work, it takes a while, doesn't it? You can't just walk into a party and pick up four people, it takes a whole lot of work. You say, well, come over and have a coffee, and you find out if you've got anything in common or not, and vice versa, and maybe you never see them again. And if you've got something, great, and it goes on from there. It's a sort of commitment.'

With her lifelong devotion to friends and friendship Judy would see much truth in what Andrew Sullivan said of that which is central to the experience of gay men: friendship. He wrote, 'It is a form of union which is truer than love, stabler than sex, deeper than politics and more moral than the family.'[15]

However, friendship is always open to betrayal, and betrayal, real or imaginary, is always at the heart of enmity. Aaron Hass, writing about the betrayals experienced by Jews in the Holocaust, said, 'Betrayal leaves one feeling exceedingly alone. The boundary between I and Other becomes impermeable, perhaps forever.'[16]

Friends and enemies, closeness and isolation. When friendship is so vital to us, why do we betray and are betrayed? Why is it that we find that most precious condition, friendship, so difficult?

2

Learning to Become Ourselves

Why do we long for friends who understand us and why do we find friendship such a difficult task?

It is because we are all such peculiar people.

If we were not such peculiar people the lonely hearts pages would always be successful in matching one person to a soulmate, with disappointments only when the advertisements did not tell the truth. My friend Helena, once an enthusiastic practitioner of the absolute freedom of love, had turned forty and was looking for a lifetime relationship. Somehow there were fewer attractive men around. She knew it had become fashionable to advertise for a partner, and so she did. 'Professional female, into personal growth, classical music, walking and travel.' All of this was true, and so was the advertisement which caught her eye – 'Spiritual man, loving, caring, well-travelled, loves art, music, literature and poetry.' I do not know who contacted whom, but Helena and Ian met. All went gloriously well at first. They each recognized that they had the same need to find a partner, not just for a sexual fling, but someone who would assuage that terrible ache which they would name only in the dark night of the soul – the ache of loneliness. What they wanted was a true friend, but somehow, despite great sex and much impassioned discussion of travel and the arts, despite the skills they had each acquired in getting along with people, a friendship did not grow. Together they each felt lonely. For all their education they did not know why.

They invited me to dinner, and I soon discovered it was not just for the pleasure of my company. They wanted my expert opinion. Helena showed me the advertisements which had brought her and Ian together, and explained that, as much as they enjoyed one another's company, somehow they weren't getting anywhere. I did not waste any time on the subtleties of psychotherapy but went straight to the tough question. I asked Helena, 'Why is personal growth important to you?' and Ian, 'Why is being spiritual important to you?'

Their answers could have revealed that there were some common elements in the importance she gave to 'personal growth' and he to 'being spiritual'. It could have turned out that they were using these terms in very similar ways, perhaps in that they both placed great importance on self-knowledge and being open to change. As it turned out, they were each talking about very different things. Helena saw 'personal growth' as the means to understanding other people, forming good relationships and being better able to care for other people, while Ian saw 'being spiritual' solely as a way of seeking a close, individual relationship with God, a relationship where worldly goods and people were of no importance at all.

I could then have asked each of them, 'Why is travel important to you?' but through what they had told me in other contexts I felt I knew what their answers would be. It would have been nice to discover that each saw travel as one of the ways of making their life rich and exciting, but I knew that Helena gave to 'travel' a meaning which betrayed her restless and desperate need of excitement, while Ian no longer felt that travel to exotic places was important to him. The only travelling he wanted to do was inside his head.

It is these underlying but vital meanings which determine whether a friendship ever takes root. The underlying meanings of two people do not have to be identical. As often as not complementary meanings do very well. Someone who gives prime importance to looking after people can get along very well with someone who gives prime importance to being looked after. But where the underlying meanings are antagonistic the relationship will either never start or, having begun because each person was ignorant of the other's underlying meanings, will fail once these meanings are revealed through the person's actions.

If asked, Helena and Ian would have said they had a good knowledge of how their bodies functioned. They understood about nutrition and exercise, and they always read the self-help best sellers, but, like many educated people, they did not understand the curious physiology of our bodies which makes us, in essence, meaning-creating creatures. We exist by creating meaning. Every moment of our lives we are in the business of making sense of everything we perceive. Indeed, perception and creating meaning are an identical process. Our perceptions are what Richard Gregory[1] called 'Perceptual Hypotheses' – guesses about what is going on. Seeing something and making sense of something are the same, even if the sense we make is: 'I can't make sense of this.' The meanings we create are ours alone, and alone is the operative word, because no two people ever create exactly the same meanings. To see a rainbow we need the sun to be behind us and rain ahead, but the existence of that multi-coloured bow depends on the particular perspective of an individual's eyes. *We each see our own rainbow.* Even when we share an experience with others, the meaning we each give to that experience will be different. One person's rainbow might have the connotations of magic and a pot of gold, while another person's rainbow is no more than a sign that the evening will be dry. Thus each of us is alone in a separate individual world of meaning, and when we try to contact other people our messages are often misunderstood.

Over the last twenty years I have been writing about this because our failure to understand the nature of our existence is the basis of all the suffering and sorrow we inflict on ourselves and on other people. However, over those twenty years what I can say about our curious physiology has changed because scientific knowledge and interests have changed.

Twenty years ago physics, neurophysiology and psychology were entirely separate disciplines with nothing to say to one another. Now physicists have made it very clear why it would not be in the interests of animals like ourselves to be able to directly perceive reality, that is, everything that is actually going on, instead of, as we do, relying on the guesses we make about reality. The physical world is very different from what we perceive it to be, and every advance in fundamental physics distances it even further from what we understand about the world we live in. Psychologists now know a great deal more about how we create meaning and how, when we change the meanings we have created, our behaviour changes. Meanwhile, the study of consciousness has become fashionable. In the past hard-headed psychologists and physiologists eschewed the study of consciousness because it was subjective, and subjective, as they saw it, was bad. Now philosophers, psychologists, physicists, neural systems engineers, neurophysiologists and media commentators have taken consciousness up, and there is a great deal of jolly chat about it.

Much of this chat is no more than that, but some of the conversations across disciplines have proved to be extremely fruitful, although many of the scientists are now so entranced by the notion of consciousness that they overlook the fact that consciousness is just a special case of what we are doing all the time: making meaning. The brain used to be thought of as a kind of computer but it is now clear that brains are very different from computers. However, the marriage of the computer concept of neural learning to the physiological concept of neuronal networks, along with the results of research using non-invasive scanning of the active human brain, appears to be providing some part of the missing link between the functioning of the brain and the functioning of the mind. It seems possible that when we create a meaning we simultaneously create what the neurophysiologist and psychologist Susan Greenfield calls a 'neuronal gestalt'.

Physicists have always been interested in finding the ultimate 'stuff' of reality of which everything is composed. At present they seem to agree that this ultimate stuff is quanta – tiny packets of energy. However, these quanta behave in peculiar ways very different from the kind of matter we humans can experience, and so there are currently two kinds of physics – quantum physics and classical physics, which is the kind of physics which explains why apples fall downwards and planes fly.

The big question for physicists is how to link quantum physics and classical physics. Subatomic particles behave very differently from the way in which we expect objects to behave. An electron will in one situation behave like a particle and in another situation behave like a wave. If you try to measure subatomic particles the actions of taking the measurements affect what you are trying to measure. Then there is the problem of the behaviour of a photon in one place apparently being able to affect instantly the behaviour of another far distant photon. Three solutions have been suggested for this problem of the link between quantum and classical physics, but each solution seems to suggest a reality which we humans could never see. Indeed, it is difficult even to imagine what this ultimate reality might look like.

Einstein argued that quantum particles have definite position and momentum but these are obscured by wave function. It is possible to imagine little quanta darting about at great speed, but then does this mass of tiny dots turn into a seething mass of something else which is itself an illusion? Niels Bohr said that the classical realm and the quantum realm never meet except in measurement, which suggests that we all operate simultaneously in two different realms. Hugh Everett said that there is set of actual states in which a quantum particle is simultaneously a wave and a particle, the implication of which is that there are many parallel universes. Being able to see an infinite number of universes would definitely be an information overload for us. More recently a number of physicists have talked about how time functions in the behaviour of particles, but the time physicists talk about is very different from the time you and I experience.

In short, physicists are showing that we cannot see reality, or, even if we could, we wouldn't be able to deal with it.

If that is the case, what is it that we do see?

In 1994 Terence Picton and Donald Stuss summarized much of what had recently been discovered about the localization of brain functions usually associated with 'being conscious'. They said, 'The human brain forms and maintains a model of the world and itself within that world. This model can be used to explain the past events and predict the future.'[2]

That is, what our brains do is make a guess about what is actually going on and present that guess as a model or picture of ourselves in our world. Curiously, our brains not only construct these pictures, they also persuade us that, instead of the picture being inside our head, we are in the middle of the picture and it is all around us. As I am writing this I have a picture in my head of the gum trees at the bottom of my garden, but what I am experiencing is that I am sitting in my conservatory and looking at the gum trees at the bottom of my garden. Even as I look at the garden my picture is out of date. It takes my brain between a tenth and half a second to form my picture, so what I see my trees doing they have already done. Moreover, because my eyes, like everyone else's, jump about, I have taken a string of snapshots of the garden, but my brain has turned these snapshots into a smooth, flowing film of trees waving in the wind.

Clever though my brain may be, there is much it cannot do. The models that our brains create are limited first by the basic physiological equipment we are born with and second by what our environment has to offer.

The physiological equipment which humans are born with is different from the equipment other animals have – in some cases very different. Take the humble octopus. It does not just sit there waving a tentacle or two. The *New Scientist* pointed out,

> To plumb an octopus's thought will require a huge leap of the imagination. As earthbound humans we are not even very good at imagining the world of other animals that move around in three dimensions. Scuba divers know how easy it is to be lost at the right place but the wrong depth ... Cephalopods [which include octopuses, squid and cuttlefish] have boneless bodies and keen senses. Their complex eyes, as large as car headlamps in some deep water species, can distinguish detail as well as mammalian equivalents. Although cephalopods are thought to be colour blind, they can see polarized light, which we cannot. They also have highly developed senses of touch, taste and smell, and can detect gravity, a sense which is used in the co-ordination of muscles during movement. And in the past few years, researchers have even discovered what can be best described as hearing: fine hairs along the head and arms that, in cuttlefish at least, can detect disturbances made by a metre-long fish up to 30 metres away.[3]

Thus an octopus's picture of the world must be quite different from our own. Even the domestic cat occupies a world very different from its owner's. To claim to know what an animal is thinking is, in fact, to claim the impossible.

It is sad to think that cephalopods are colour-blind when to most of us humans the sea is full of colourful delights. Actually it is not, nor is the world a colourful place. What we see as colour is the response of the cones in the retinas of our eyes to different wavelengths of light. Our eyes respond to light, and so we see a world which is complex and detailed. Yet within that world there is much we cannot see. What we see as light is only a part of the electromagnetic spectrum, which extends from extremely low-frequency radiation with wavelengths of more than 1,000 kilometres to gamma rays with wavelengths measured in billionths of a millimetre. Only a narrow band somewhere near the middle of this spectrum provides us with wavelengths to which our eyes respond.

In contrast, plants 'see' much more of the electromagnetic spectrum than we do. They do not have eyes but they do have proteins latched on to light-sensitive compounds which can then harvest the packets of light energy called photons. They not only 'see' more wavelengths than we can see but they can also identify the intensity, quality, direction and periodicity of light. Most plants can also taste, touch and perhaps even hear. Plants create their own kind of meaning, but their construction of themselves in their world must be very different from our construction of ourselves in our world.[4]

When we see we do not simply record things in the way that a video camera does. When we see, wrote Richard Gregory, we 'receive signals from the physical realm, and then create everything we see. Shape, size – all the properties we assign to the world around us – are largely a result of our visual intelligence.'[5]

Different parts of our brain deal with different aspects of vision. They select and combine, and we see a picture which seems to be reality. It is only when one or two of these specialized cortical areas are damaged that the selecting and synthesizing functions of the brain are revealed. After such damage a person might be aware of colour without form or form without motion. Thus a person might be able to see a red mass but not recognize it as a bunch of roses, or be able to recognize a car but not see it as moving from one place to another. When we are seeing, different parts of our brain are used to put the picture together. What the picture means to us depends on our past experience. The retina of your eye might register a small upright rectangle with a triangle on top of it but what you see on the horizon is the huge bulk of the Canary Wharf Tower.

However, not everything we 'see' is experienced consciously as a picture. It seems that we have two visual modes, 'one that allows us to consciously perceive the world and a second, subconscious mode that helps us move around in it by, say, informing a foot where to place itself.'[6] Letting the conscious visual mode override the unconscious visual mode can make us stumble or drop things, while letting both modes work in harmony can mean typing fast or making a brilliant return in a game of tennis.

We learn to use both these visual modes when we are tiny babies

learning to see. When we are born we do not just open our eyes
and see. We open our eyes and set about learning to see the world.
In the womb in the developing brain neurons divide and then
migrate to their correct locations in the brain. Susan Greenfield
explained,

> As soon as the neurons have proliferated, migrated to the appropri-
> ate brain region, they effectively set down roots, initiate com-
> munications with neighbouring neurons by establishing a synaptic
> circuitry. Much of the increase in brain size after birth is actually
> due to the development of these connections, rather than simply to
> the addition of more neurons ... As our development continues
> after birth, the jostling, restless neurons in our brain are very sensi-
> tive as they form circuits, to whatever changes, or simply signals,
> are imposed from the outside world. Inside the brain, right up to
> sixteen years of age, a bloody battle is being raged between our
> neurons. It is a battle for establishing connections. If a new neuron
> does not make contact with a target neuron, then it dies ...
>
> Another related and very important factor in determining cell
> survival, once contact is established between neurons, is activity, the
> sending and receiving of signals. This point is tragically made by
> the recent example of a six-year-old Italian boy. This boy was blind
> in one eye. Yet the cause of his blindness was a medical mystery.
> As far as the ophthalmologists could tell, his eye was totally normal.
> Eventually the enigma was solved. It finally emerged that when he
> was a baby, the boy's eye had been bandaged for two weeks as part
> of the treatment for a minor infection. Such treatment would have
> made no difference to our older brains with their more established
> connections. But two weeks after birth the connections of the eye
> were at a critical period for the establishment of eye to brain circuits.
>
> Since neurons serving the bandaged eye were not working, their
> normal target became taken over by nerves from the normal, work-
> ing eye. In this case the neurons that were not signalling were treated
> as though they were not there at all: the target for these inactive,
> functionally non-existent neurons was readily invaded by the active
> brain cells. Normally this rule would be beneficial as it would mean
> that neuronal circuits were being established according to the work-
> ing cells which reflected in turn the environmental requirements in
> which the person had to live. Sadly, the bandaging of the eye was

misinterpreted by the brain as a clear indication that the boy would not be using that eye for the rest of his life.[7]

In those weeks following our birth we learn to structure space and distance as we look around us and, if we are not swaddled as many babies still are, we reach out and discover what is near and what is far and how something feels when we put our hand around it or hold it in our mouth. Once we have learned this we can look at something and know how that shape would feel even though it is too far away or too large for us to put it in our mouth or hold it in our hand.

While, through our experiences, we are learning a basic structure for our perception of space we are also having the first of a multitude of experiences which determine how our brain selects and combines to form a picture of the world. No two people ever have the same experiences, so no two people ever have the same picture of the world. If you listen to a group of people discussing an event in which they have all participated you'll see how individual experience shapes individual perceptions.

I went with a group of friends to the Proms, where the Chinese composer Tan Dun was presenting the European première of his symphony 'Heaven Earth Mankind'. An important part of this symphony was the Imperial Bell Ensemble of China, who perform on a set of sixty-five ancient Chinese bells made 2,400 years ago and excavated from the tomb of Marquis Yi of Zeng in 1978. The bells are amazingly wonderful and we were all entranced by them. We were also amazed and intrigued by the soloist Yo-Yo Ma, who used his cello in ways we had never seen before, and by the string section of the Scottish Symphony Orchestra, who treated their instruments as things to be slapped and banged as well as played. Moreover, behind the orchestra was the New London Children's Choir singing as we had never heard a children's choir sing before.

Afterwards we talked about what we had heard and seen. We all agreed that it had been a special occasion for us, but when we talked about certain details in the performance it was clear that we had each seen a different event. Although we had all watched and listened intently we could still inform one another about what we had seen and the other missed. The parents of children in the choir gave precise accounts of their child's behaviour. The musicians in our group commented upon the structure of the symphony and the qualities displayed by the performers. I realized that I had missed the significance of the different shapes and textures of the bells and was glad to have this explained to me, but, inveterate people-watcher that I am, I had seen, and others had not, many of the interactions between the participants which were not part of the actual performance.

Every meaning we create is a selection from a vast array of possible meanings. The meanings we choose to create arise from all the meanings we have created in the past. The old saying, 'If I hadn't seen it I wouldn't have believed it,' might be correct in particular circumstances – for example, when we see an extraordinary sporting achievement or when we see an old friend act out of character, but in general the saying should be, 'If I hadn't believed it I wouldn't have seen it.' Those people who believe in astrology see in a person's life the effect of the movement of the planets, which is something that I cannot see.

When I ask myself, 'Why did that person do that?' I come up with answers that have to do with the person's feelings, desires and fears. I do not create theories that have to do with the influence of the planets or evil spirits or God's mysterious ways, even though I am familiar with the ideas in astrology and in the various religions. However, as I make sense of any situation there are certain meanings which are not in the vast array of possible meanings presented to me because they are meanings which I could not possibly apprehend.

Some of these meanings are beyond my apprehension because I have never had the required experience to form them. I am largely ignorant of mathematics. I speak only one language. I was born at a particular time in the history of the universe and I have lived in particular places and not others. Similar restrictions apply to each of us, but, along with these, there is the restriction which our physiology imposes on us.

Each of our senses responds to some aspect of our environment in a particular way – that is, our senses respond only to change or contrast. The uniform green of a thick bush hides from our eyes a green tennis ball or a green lizard. The tennis ball is visible only when its texture is seen in contrast to the texture of the leaves; the lizard is visible only when it moves.

This necessity for contrast carries over into the meanings we create. Every meaning contains its opposite because, if the opposite did not exist, no meaning could be created.

If, from the moment of your birth, you had been surrounded by loving people who protected you from every pain and disappointment and met your every need, you would have no concept of happiness because you would never have been sad. If you had been born into a world where everyone without exception was kind, caring and tolerant of everyone else you would have no concept of friendship because you would never have encountered enmity.

Sometimes the contrasts we see actually do exist. Sadness is part of the human condition and enmities abound. Sometimes the contrast exists only in our imagination because the actual contrast is for us literally inconceivable.

For instance, we cannot conceive of the actual opposite of meaning. We would say that the opposite is 'meaninglessness', but that itself is a meaning. Usually when we call something meaningless we mean, 'I don't know at the moment what meaning to give this' or 'I don't approve of this', as in the phrase popular with politicians and media commentators, 'meaningless violence'.

When we are reaching into our imaginations to create a contrast we often come up with images from our past experience which seem sensible but are actually quite misleading. When physicists talk about the edge of the universe or before the Big Bang we can picture a cliff-like edge to the universe or a time before the universe existed. Our image presupposes an observer. However, the physicists are talking about a timeless nothingness which is the actual contrast to our timeful somethingness, but a timeless nothingness which, like the opposite of meaningful, lies for ever beyond our comprehension.

When I talk about meaning I can only use words, and this can give the impression that meanings exist only in words. Many of them do, but many, perhaps most, exist in wordless forms. Many exist as visual or auditory or tactile or kinaesthetic images, or mixtures of all four – the kinds of images we create before we acquire language. Many exist in that wordless but vital knowledge we call skills. Ask a champion golfer, a master potter or an experienced cook how to produce a winning drive, a superb pot or the perfect soufflé and their description will fall far short of what they actually do. Each is likely to say, 'I'll show you.'

Even when we construct our meanings in words we do not, and

Friends and Enemies

cannot, report the world as it is. Just as our past experience limits what meanings we can create so does the language we speak limit what we can say.

As they left the forest for the savannah our far distant ancestors weren't chattering away as we do now. They would have communicated with one another, but language as we know it evolved over many thousands of years. As Richard Gregory has pointed out,[8] they would have evolved perceptual classifications of objects and actions, knowing, say, which leaves to eat and which to avoid, and it was from these classifications that language developed. There had to be changes in the brain, changes in the larynx and pharynx to make possible a wide range of vocalizations, and these changes had to be underwritten by changes in the genetic structure. Linguists and anthropologists argue about the rate of these changes. Could the Neanderthal people talk? Did our species, *Homo sapiens*, have, right from its first appearance, language as we know it, or was there some major explosion of language ability coinciding with an explosion, between 60,000 and 30,000 years ago, of artistic creation, implying the ability to think in symbolic forms? The only thing these scientists seem to agree on is that we evolved language in order to talk to one another, to inform, warn, trade, or, as Robin Dunbar said, to gossip.[9]

Different languages developed as different groups of people spread across the continents. The best time to learn more than one language is in early childhood when neuronal connections are being set up. In adulthood learning another language is for most of us quite difficult, and different languages can seem to be extremely diverse, yet what linguists following Noam Chomsky have shown is that every language has within it the same Universal Grammar, and that small children learning to speak exhibit an innate ability to use this grammar.

Language might be universal to our species but different languages developed in different groups of people in different places, dealing with different kinds of environment and having different interests and needs. Steven Pinker in his book *The Language Instinct*[10] scornfully demolishes the belief disseminated by the linguist Benjamin Lee Whorf that the Eskimos had some 400 words for snow. The Eskimos, said Pinker, had about as many words for snow as English speakers have.

This rather schoolboy-like harangue overlooks the fact that

Eskimos had a particular interest in snow quite different from the interest in snow taken by the inhabitants of London, where snow sometimes falls, and from the inhabitants of Cairo, who are little troubled by snow. It is not a matter of individual words. People who live in an environment dominated by snow have to develop a language with the power to make fine discriminations in situations involving snow. Over recent years the inhabitants of the Australian Antarctic research base have developed a large collection of words and phrases which refer to the peculiar conditions under which they live and which must be learnt by any newcomer in order to communicate. There is fast ice and brash ice, ding nights, pissaphones, dongas, slushies, tradies, Larcies, jafas and jafos.[11]

No language, not even English with its huge vocabulary, can describe the world in all its vastness and complexity. Languages differ in what they can hide and reveal. For instance, in languages which add suffixes to indicate gender one cannot say, as one can in English, 'A friend is staying with me,' and keep ambiguous the gender of the friend.

A language can force its speakers to lie even when they think they are telling the truth. The history of psychology and psychiatry is littered with such lies. This is because the English language loves nouns, words that refer to things, far more than it loves verbs, words that refer to people and things in action. Psychologists and psychiatrists study people in action, but when they talk about 'people-doing' they find it hard to resist turning 'people-doing' into abstract nouns, which they then talk about as if the abstract nouns were referring to real entities. Thus 'people-intelligently-doing' became 'intelligence', and 'people-depressedly-doing' became 'depression'. Holding the mistaken idea that if a name exists there must be an object that has that name, psychologists and psychiatrists set about measuring the lumps of intelligence that people were supposed to carry around inside them and searching for different kinds of lumps of depression which might or might not be dissolved by drugs.

Every language uses metaphors to convey meaning. Sometimes these metaphors give an accurate picture of what actually happens and sometimes they do not. 'The rain poured down' uses the metaphor of river water pouring over a cliff or water pouring from a jug, and accurately describes a particular type of rain. The metaphor contained in 'I gave her the news' is not an accurate metaphor. If I give you a cake, the cake which leaves my hands is the same cake which you take, but when I give you my news the story which I tell is not the story which you hear. You do not hear my story. You hear your interpretation of my story, something which is always different from what I say.

When we talk about communication, when we say things like 'That book is full of good ideas', or 'He gave me his opinion', or 'She poured out her feelings', the metaphor we use implies that communication is a thing which can be inside something, or passed from one person to another, or a liquid which passes from source to receptacle. But this is not what actually happens. In communicating, one person creates a meaning and displays this meaning to another person who then interprets the displayed meaning to create his own meaning. Many errors can be made along the way in both the display and the interpretation of the display. All these errors are compounded when we talk about communication without understanding that the metaphors we are using are leading us astray.

Because we do not always remember that what a person says is different from what we hear that person say we often fail to distinguish when a person is using a metaphor as an empty cliché and when a person has chosen a particular metaphor in order to describe a particular truth. Consider the following conversation between John and Mary.

MARY: Hello, John. What's it like out?
JOHN: It's pouring with rain.
MARY: Did you see Betty?
JOHN: We had a long talk. She's very upset. She just poured out all her feelings.
MARY: How did you cope?
JOHN: I felt quite overwhelmed.

'I felt I was drowning' might have been a better description of what John had experienced but John chose 'overwhelmed' because it is a word which reveals a little but not too much. Many people use the word 'stress' in the same way. You let others know you're distressed but you do not reveal how that distress actually feels. John had felt the force of Betty's revelations as a torrent of water that threatened to drown him. Another person might feel being overwhelmed as being buffeted by a tornado, or being engulfed by falling rocks, or being run over by an immense tank, and so on. The words we say can be simple and ordinary, yet hide our actual truth, which we experience as an image. A question I have often used when I was trying to understand the meaning a person has given to a situation is, 'If you could paint a picture of what you're feeling, what sort of picture would you paint?' Answers to this question often reveal a discrepancy between the person's statement about his meaning and the underlying image. The image accompanying the words 'I'm upset' might be 'I feel that everything around me is crumbling and I can't hold it together'.

The meanings we create often exist both as words and as images. Sometimes the words can give the better account of that meaning, and sometimes the image is the best rendition of the meaning. But the meanings we create do not exist in isolation. They are always linked to all the other meanings we have created.

Some of the links are associations formed from past experiences. My meaning that I call 'Australia' I link with 'the wide brown land' from a poem all Australian children learn at school,[12] but for many English people 'Australia' links only with the soap operas *Neighbours* and *Cell Block H*.

Some of the meanings are in hierarchies of value judgements. Asking the question, 'Why is that important to you?' can reveal these hierarchies.

When I asked Helena, 'Why is personal growth important to you?' her answer had to be a more general statement of a principle. She replied, 'Through personal growth I expand myself and become better in my relationships with other people. I blossom as a person, and people can get to know me and I can get to know them.' I then asked, 'Why is it important to you that people get to know you and you get to know them?' Helena looked at me in surprise. It was as if I had asked her why it was important to her to breathe. She said, 'That's what life's about, isn't it? Having friends, caring about other people.' Helena's home was always awash with people and cats in need of comfort.

The word 'spiritual' has become very fashionable, but it seemed to have as many meanings as there were people using it. I asked Ian what he meant by 'spiritual' and he talked about a close relationship with God, but not a God who was a person. It was a blending with everything that exists, but it was not the merging whereby individuality vanishes, as the eastern philosophies teach, but a kind of enlarging and developing of his own individuality. Part of this was becoming a better person and part the gaining of knowledge and power. As Ian talked, Helena looked increasingly stricken. Ian was talking of a striving towards an achievement in individual development which had no place for other people. It was clear that he enjoyed the company of friends whom he found interesting, and what he wanted was someone like Helena to look after him and do the necessary socializing for him so he could continue striving for his goal.

This, of course, was not enough for Helena, and so their friendship faltered and failed. Such is the power of the meanings we create.

The Meanings in Our Brain

The brain, it seems, is the most complex object on this planet and exactly how it works no one knows. There are lots of ways of examining the brain – looking at brain tissue, planting electrodes in an animal's brain, using X-rays and various scanning techniques – and lots of interesting things have been discovered, but the great problem is to construct a suitable model of the brain. Our brains think in a peculiar way. To understand anything we have to decide what it is like. We have to find something from our past experience which is similar to what we are examining. If you have to describe a pizza to someone who's never seen one you might start by saying, 'It's something like a pie but without a top.' The trouble with the brain is that there is not anything like it. It operates with various chemicals, but not in the way our heart and lungs do. It uses electrical impulses, but not like any piece of electrical equipment that has been devised. People who love computers often liken it to a computer and there are Artificial Intelligence experts who believe that if they make a sufficiently large and clever computer it will turn into a conscious brain, but such a view is based on a supreme ignorance of how human beings actually operate. Models of the brain have now become a growth industry in science and philosophy but nothing satisfactory has yet been devised.

However, one way of thinking about the brain seems to be full of possibilities. Back in 1949 the psychologist Donald Hebb suggested a model for understanding the functions of the neurons in the brain. It seemed that the more two neurons communicated with one another the easier communication became. The neurons seemed to set up a relationship which Hebb called a neural net.

This has proved to be a most useful way of thinking about the brain's activity, especially with the development of scanning techniques like positron emission tomography (PET), nuclear magnetic resonance (NMR) and magnetencephalography (MEG). Because human subjects can tell researchers what they are doing – looking at something, daydreaming, silently doing sums or reciting a poem – while they are being scanned many interesting relationships between thinking and brain activity have been observed.

For instance, Petry and Meyer showed how when we are perceiving the world around us and when we are imagining or dreaming we are using much the same regions of our brain.[13] Whether we are lost in imagination, or asleep and dreaming, or looking at the world around us our brain is creating a picture in our heads. We have the task of deciding whether what we are experiencing is the world around us or an image inside us. Most of the time we get it right but sometimes we do not. If something utterly unexpected happens, be it a tragedy or the best of good fortune, the world around us can take on a dreamlike quality, and we turn to others for assurance that what seems to be happening is real. If, on the other hand, we feel totally overwhelmed by events and utterly powerless to make reasonable sense of what is happening to us we can lose the ability to distinguish between the voices of our thoughts in our head and the voices of people around us. Our thoughts seem to be the voices of unseen people around us. These voices might be friendly and comforting, but often they are criticizing us and urging us to commit terrible acts. When this happens to us we need real people around us who will not tell us that we are mad but rather will assure us that our voices are simply our thoughts and help us find ways of keeping our thoughts in order. Singing can quieten the voices, as can telling them loudly and firmly to shut up. If you have to do this in public a mobile phone can be very useful.

In research on the functioning of the brain there is still a big gap between scanning an active person's brain and looking at the firing individual neurons. The images from scanning might not be showing the mental processes themselves, but only emissions from them, somewhat analogous to showing emissions from a car's exhaust rather than the functioning of the internal combustion engine. However, Hebb's neural net has provided the key to finding what might be a suitable model for understanding how the brain creates meaning. Susan Greenfield defined the model of a neuronal gestalt as 'a highly variable aggregation of neurons that is temporarily recruited around a triggering epicentre. Not all neuronal assemblies are gestalts but all gestalts are neuronal assemblies.'[14] A stimulus produces an epicentre of arousal in the brain and a group of neurons firing in a particular pattern form around the epicentre. If the stimulus is repeated the pattern of the epicentre and the neurons is repeated. Further repetitions of the stimulus turn what was a transient pattern into a gestalt, a schema where the whole is more than the sum of its parts. (A common example of a gestalt is that particular positioning of an oval shape, two dots and two straight lines which to our eyes is a picture of a face.)

Neurons communicate with one another by using a chemical transmitter to empty into the synapse – that is, the gap between the axon terminals of one cell and one of the dendrites of another cell, where the transmitter binds to a target molecule. In the transmitting neuron the electrical signal is put into a chemical code and, when it crosses the synapse, it is decoded back into an electrical signal in the neuron which received it.

In the womb a baby's brain begins working long before it is fully formed. Neuronal patterns for pleasure and pain and certain kinds of sounds are laid down before birth (babies are born knowing the sound of their mother's voice) but even so the baby's brain still contains some 100 billion neurons whose connections are yet to stabilize into patterns. Trillions of synapses are available, but, unless the baby's environment calls a synapse into use, it will be eliminated. The brain, said Susan Greenfield, operates on 'a law of the jungle – use it or lose it'. A baby who is wrapped like a parcel and left to lie except when being fed will lose many more synapses than a baby who is little restrained and talked to and shown things. The more synapses you retain the brighter you're likely to be. The more you use your synapses the more you retain them.

Susan Greenfield reported,

Although the brain is particularly impressionable whilst it has been developing, such adaptability does not cease, but merely lessens somewhat in maturity. It is actually possible to manipulate the environment and observe long-term changes in the brain. For example, adult rats were exposed to what is referred to as an 'enriched environment' where they had lots of toys, wheels, ladders and so forth to play with. In contrast, other rats were kept in an ordinary cage, where they received as much food and water as they wanted: it was just that they did not have anything to play with. However, when the brains of these two groups of rats were examined, then it was found that the number of connections in the brain had increased only in the animals in the enriched environment, not in those from the ordinary cages. It appears that sheer numbers of neurons are not so important as the connections between them in the brain, and these connections are not fixed but are highly changeable, not just in development but in adulthood. Specific experiences will enhance the connectivity in highly specific neuronal circuits.[15]

The more synapses you have the more neuronal gestalts your brain can create. If neuronal gestalts, or patterns of neuronal gestalts, are meanings, then the more synapses you have the more meanings you can create.

Being born into a uniformly bland and uneventful environment would limit ability generally. Most of us were born into an environment which was rich in some kinds of experience and limited in others, and so we grew up with differing abilities. Babies born into households where music was constantly being played are more likely to grow up with a liking for, if not an ability in, music. Babies who are taken swimming are more likely to develop a feeling for water and movement in water than babies whose bathing is confined to a wash in a small bath. Babies born into households which ring with the sounds of people's voices are likely to have a very different sensitivity to voices and language than those born into homes where silence reigns supreme.

Included in all these possible configurations will be the issue of whether the baby found the experience determining the configuration pleasant or unpleasant. To the baby who is sung to or talked to gently and sweetly words and music will mean something very different than they will to those babies who are continually surrounded by angry voices, by shouting, screaming and crying. Neuronal configurations can change and dissipate, but there is some evidence that those configurations laid down in experiences where the person is afraid have a greater permanence than those configurations laid down where the person is happy. There is a good reason for this. If we are to keep ourselves safe we need to remember where there could be danger, but this is a burden to carry when the danger is long in the past and not likely to recur. Our ancestors needed to remember where the wild beasts might lurk, but do we need in adulthood to remember the adults who were cruel to us when we were children?

What is clear is that each individual brain develops its own unique set of configurations. No two brains ever have the same set of configurations because no two people ever have the same experience. Your set of particular configurations and your meaning structure are intimately related and are unique.

Models of neuronal gestalts can be generated by certain computer software. Professor Igor Aleksander, head of Neural Systems Engineering at Imperial College, has developed Magnus, which stands for multi-automata-general-neural-units-structure, a piece of learning neural software. When Igor sits at his computer and clicks on the icon called Magnus his computer becomes a large neural network. This network is used 'to see if a bunch of simulated (or artificial) neurons can carry out some of the feats that their living counterparts, the cells of human or animal brains, perform in going about their daily lives. The feats are feats which when performed by humans are described as the result of "conscious thought".'[16]

The problem for computer software like Magnus is that it cannot reach out and explore the world through touch, it does not start as baby software and slowly change and grow through interaction with the world, and it does not interact with and learn from people as human beings do. Igor told me, 'Your point about growing minds has been on my mind for some time. I think that the only way for Magnus-like-things to develop is for their minds to grow. But they do this in the sense of what in my book *Impossible Minds* I have called a growth of state structures (or thinking structures). I distinguish physical growth from "thinking structure growth" as the first puts the machinery in place to do the second. In babies the two are concomitant, and I have no idea what the effect of this is. All I know is that from a scientific point of view it is hard to understand.'[17]

Igor had been engaged in building machines which recognized patterns, but a question from a young girl at one of his public lectures set him thinking about how to model the way in which humans see. Our vision is far more complex than simply seeing patterns. We can see the quality of things – for instance, we perceive the qualities of roundness and redness, and put them together to identify a red ball. We can see when our eyes are closed. We can create images of what is not there and images of things we have not seen. Igor's audiences never have any difficulty in imagining a blue banana with red spots.

Magnus does not have any difficulty in imagining such a banana either. To imagine something we have not seen we have to be aware, and Magnus now contains a set of software which Igor has labelled 'Awareness Area'. It is unlikely that Magnus's awareness resembles ours in any way, except in that it is a model based on the hypothesis put forward by Francis Crick and Christof Koch that 'Everything of which we are aware is fully represented by the firing of some neurons.' Francis Crick called this 'an astonishing hypothesis' but it seems that the only people to be astonished are those who like to think that human beings have certain powers and qualities which are not based on the functioning of our bodies. The only way to prove or disprove such a belief is to establish just what it is that the brain does. We are a long way from this goal, but meanwhile the study of the brain provides much astonishment.

The problem with models is that they can only suggest what something might be like, not what it actually is. Mathematics, like art, describes events, though in very different ways from art. To describe the activity of some object in terms of algorithms might allow for some very accurate predictions, but that does not mean that the object itself is using algorithms. Newton's equations predict the orbit of the moon, but this does not mean that the moon itself is computing. In the same way, even if certain activities of the brain can be described in algorithms, it does not mean that the brain itself computes. Indeed, there are a number of scientists who now argue that the brain can be understood only as a dynamic system, an organ which evolves its pattern of activity rather than computes it.

The argument has been that if the brain operates like a computer then the output of each cell in the brain encodes a message. The trick was to find the 'neural code'. Researchers tried to discover what aspect of a cell's activity revealed the code. If brain waves were measured, could the code be found in the strength of a spike, or the average number of spikes per second, or in some numerical synchronization with the activity of other cells? Many of the results of this research looked promising, but such promises were not fulfilled. Instead, there were results which threw the whole notion of a neural code into doubt.

This research showed that the output of any individual neuron depended not just on a stimulus but on what was happening in the rest of the brain – that is, on what the brain was thinking at the time. According to John Maunsell, one of the neuroscientists carrying out this research, 'We are coming to the end of one generation of effort. The next generation is going to have to look at the whole system [and] understand the effect that plans, decisions and actions can have on what neurons do.'[18]

If the brain did operate like a computer then, when nothing was happening, the brain would be a blank screen. In fact, even in a brain which seems to be doing nothing there is a steady tick-over of cell activity of at least three or four spikes a second. This might be just a leakage of current, but those scientists using a dynamic model of the brain argue this background firing maintains a certain level of tone in the brain and presumably creates some meaning. It is possible that 'the brain stores memories as patterns of connections between cells – new experiences prompt the strengthening of old connections, or the growth of new ones. The tick-over firing echoing around the brain could be a defocused representation of everything you have ever learnt or known.'[19]

'Everything you've ever learnt or known' – that sounds very much like all the meanings you've ever created. These meanings altogether form a pattern or structure – your meaning structure.

Your Meaning Structure

The brain is a dynamic system which operates and evolves. There is no little person sitting in the brain telling it what to do. There is no special part of the brain which organizes and operates the rest of the brain. The brain is a self-generating, self-running system. It learns, it stores memories, it creates meanings. Old meanings create new meanings. Meanings evolve and change, but all are stored and linked together into a structure. You know the structure very well because your meaning structure is you. You are your meaning structure.

You are, in effect, your memories and your hopes and expectations. To paraphrase Picton and Stuss, quoted earlier, 'Your brain forms and maintains a model of the world and yourself within that world. This model uses itself to explain the past events and predict the future.' Like your brain, your meaning structure is a self-generating, self-running system. There is no little self sitting inside it, running it. Your meaning structure is your self.

Your meaning structure operates with two basic rules:

1. Every part interconnects with every other part;
2. The aim of the meaning structure is to maintain its structure.

Some of the interconnections in your meaning structure are easy to recognize when you remember how hard it is to think about one thing only and not be distracted by other thoughts. A simple task like drawing up a shopping list can easily involve, say, a memory of once disliking the tea that you now cannot live without, a feeling of anxiety about the size of next month's credit card bill, irritation at the fuss your family makes about the wrong kind of muesli – which leads you on to irritation with the way in which your children leave wet towels on the bathroom floor, a fantasy about escaping from all of this and living on a South Sea island and a brief meditation on the state of your best friend's love life.

The connections which are not so easy to discern are the meanings which underlie the decisions you make. When you're drawing up your shopping list you accept or reject the idea of buying yourself some treat and might not recognize your underlying meaning of how you feel about yourself. This could be 'I've made a mess of things, therefore I don't deserve a treat', or it could be 'I've done really well so I deserve a treat', and thus this meaning, which you need not make conscious, determines whether or not the treat goes on your list.

Another underlying meaning which is often hard to identify concerns what you regard as your absolute top priority in life. You

might, like Ian, have as your top priority gaining a sense of achievement, organization and control, or you might, like Helena, aim to
establish and maintain good relationships with other people. In
either case, your top priority can lead you to put 'thick bleach' on
your list, in order either to remove disorder and establish organization and control or to make sure that people will not reject you
because your house is dirty.

Our meaning structure must maintain its structure as a unified
whole because it is this wholeness which gives us our sense of
existence. Out of this sense of existence comes our experience of
consciousness and our notion of 'I'. When we talk of 'holding myself
together' it is not just a matter of keeping our emotions and our
behaviour under control. It is a matter of holding our meaning
structure together so that our sense of 'I' does not dissipate and our
sense of existence fall apart.

The aim of our meaning structure to maintain itself as a whole
is so much present in our lives that we are not always aware of its
existence. We are aware that we have to survive physically, as a
physical body. So we take vitamin pills and look both ways when
we are crossing the road. We are not always aware that we have to
survive as a person because we are always using one or other of the
range of well-practised defences we have created to prevent our
meaning structure from falling apart. These defences range from
the practical, like organizing clocks, watches and diaries to keep
time under control, to lifetime strategies, like never making a commitment to anyone and thus preventing anyone from finding out
how awful we really are.

Thus it is that many of us do not discover how essential it is to
survive as a person until one day we discover that we have made a
major error of judgement and we feel ourselves – our meaning
structure – falling apart.

Our meaning structure is always in danger of falling apart because
at any moment life can reveal a huge discrepancy between our
picture of what is going on and what is really happening. It could
be that you have always seen your environment as solid and reliable,
and one day it convulses into an earthquake. It could be that, even
though you know that people die, you didn't think that meant you,
and one day you're in a car accident and barely survive. It could
be that you expect to spend the rest of your life in one loving

relationship, and one day your lover leaves you for ever. It could be that you have always prided yourself on being a good judge of character, and one day the friend and colleague you trusted most betrays your trust.

In these and many other situations you can discover that you have made a major error of judgement. You think, 'If I was wrong in that I could be wrong in every judgement I have ever made.' Such a thought undermines your meaning structure. It starts to shake and fall apart, just as a strong building will shake and shatter as the earth beneath it begins to shake and crumble.

If you understand that you are your meaning structure you will know what is happening and be prepared to ride out the storm until you can get yourself together again, but if you do not understand this you will feel that you yourself are shattering, crumbling, even disappearing. This experience is utterly, utterly terrifying.

A friend once told me what had happened to her when she discovered that she had made a major error of judgement. She was a senior social worker and, as I well knew, prided herself on her feet-on-the ground, common-sense approach and especially on her ability to sum people up and see through the artifice which hides deceit. One day she discovered that one of her clients, a man whom she had seen as a good father and husband battling illness and other harsh circumstances to provide for his family, was in fact a key figure in the local drugs syndicate with a hobby of beating up women.

She said, 'The implications for me were enormous. It wasn't just the official inquiry about what had gone wrong. I wasn't the only person who'd been taken in by him. It was how I felt. For months I was too scared to look in the mirror. I felt I wasn't me any more. I felt I'd become an empty eggshell, and if I looked in the mirror I'd see that I was all cracked and about to fall into tiny pieces. I had to go on leave and spend time on my own to put myself together. I'm different now. I don't know that I'm wiser but I'm different.'

What makes this experience particularly terrifying is that, buried in your memories of the time when you lived in a world of giants who misunderstood you and laughed at your attempts to talk, are memories of falling apart not once but often. How frightening those experiences were, and how hard it was to put yourself together again! Very likely the adults around you called these experiences 'temper tantrums', and they might have scolded or slapped you, making the experience very much worse. They did not understand that, because little children have a limited knowledge of the world, the way they have made sense of the world is often disconfirmed by events. Then the children can feel completely overwhelmed and unable to make sense of what is happening. Their meaning structure falls apart. They scream and cry, and need to be held and talked to gently.

Small children quickly develop defences to keep their meaning structure intact. One such defence is to become very particular about what they eat. They have discovered that food can spring big surprises. As we all know, sticking to the familiar makes us feel safe.

If parents understand and accept this they can put aside their anxiety that their child is not getting an adequate diet and wait patiently for this phase to pass. Children can choose a most peculiar range of foods but still get an adequate diet provided they do not feel threatened by parents who want them to eat properly.

Here 'eating properly' means eating the right kind of food at the right time in the right place and in the right way. It is the parents' 'right', not the child's 'right', and when the parents try to impose their 'right' on the child the child has to resist because, in trying to remove the child's defence and impose their ideas on the child, the parents, in the eyes of the child, are threatening to annihilate him as a person.

This is the issue at the heart of all our relationships, be they loving relationships with friends, family and lovers, or hateful relationships with those who try to do us down, or power relationships with those who want to tell us what to think and do – people like teachers, clerics, politicians, advertisers. Without exception, other people are always a threat to our meaning structure. By trying to impose their ideas on us they can get us to doubt the validity of our own meanings. We might gratefully accept our mother's advice to stay healthy by eating lots of fruit or the bank's advice about a mortgage, but if we find ourselves being streamrollered into doing something we do not want to do, or if constant criticism leads us to lose confidence in our ability to make even the smallest decision, we start to lose that which an intact meaning structure gives us: the sense of being who we are. Even more, we can become frightened that we are going to be annihilated as a person,

Other people live in the world around us, and so, like everything else around us, they cannot be known directly by us. All we can ever know of other people is the picture we create of them, a guess which always carries a degree of error and uncertainty. The only direct knowledge we can ever have of anyone is our knowledge of ourselves, our own thoughts and feelings, our own personal truth. Everything else is a guess.

Unfortunately, many children lose the ability to know exactly what they think and feel. The adults around them tell them that their thoughts and feelings are childish, wrong, irrational, even wicked. Moreover, adults can behave in such a way that the child becomes confused. If a parent beats his children and treats them cruelly while at the same time demanding the children's love the children cannot freely love or hate the parent. Some children deal with this confusion and with being told that their thoughts and feelings are wrong by turning away from what goes on inside them and instead paying attention only to what goes on around them. In adult life they cannot distinguish anger from fear, they cannot recognize what their most important priorities are, and they say of themselves, 'I don't know who I am,' or even, 'I'm a role without an actor'.

As adults we can try to protect ourselves from all kinds of uncomfortable emotions by lying to ourselves, by telling ourselves that we are not angry when indeed we are, or that we really have not hurt other people but have acted only in their best interests. Such lies might bring short-term relief, but their long-term effects are destructive, not least because we have destroyed the only truth about which we might be absolutely sure.

If we want our meaning structure to be as accurate a picture of the world as possible we need to develop ways of checking the accuracy of the meanings we create. The starting point for this is the acceptance that things are not as they seem. My colleague Chris French, reader in psychology at Goldsmiths College, has done a great deal of research into the paranormal and what people are prepared to believe. Chris divides us all into sheep and goats. The sheep, he says, tend to believe in the paranormal while the goats tend to doubt such claims. I have always been a goat, but Chris, so he told me, began with a sheeplike belief in the paranormal but, like all good scientists, when his results did not support his beliefs he changed his beliefs. Nevertheless, like all wise goats, he knows

that there is much going on in the universe which we cannot apprehend, and so he keeps an open mind and is prepared to be surprised.

To check the accuracy of the meanings we create we need to
develop our own scientific method. We need to be aware that the
meanings we create are hypotheses, theories about what is going on.
We have to test out these theories by looking for evidence which
supports or disproves them. We can develop the habit of looking
very closely at a situation before creating our own theory. We can
become skilled in collecting evidence, asking questions, and compar-
ing our observations with those of other people. We can refuse to
become tightly wedded to our theories and, when we are proved
wrong, we can, without too much pain, relinquish our theories and
create new ones.

Alas, a close, honest inspection of the natural world and the people
in it does little to bolster our confidence in our own significance in
the scheme of things. The planet we inhabit and the universe of
which it is part are indifferent to our existence, while most – perhaps
all – of our fellows are far more interested in their own concerns
than they are in us. This state of affairs is very disturbing to many
people and, rather than getting to know the world and their fellows,
they prefer to create fantasies where the universe came into being
in order that they could exist and where their lives have an absolute
significance which time and other people can never destroy.

Such fantasies can give comfort and, when times are hard, courage
and optimism, but events can easily throw doubt on the truth of
such fantasies. It can be a great comfort to believe that you live in
a Just World where, inevitably, the good are rewarded and the bad
punished. You can assure yourself that if you are good nothing bad
can happen to you. But what do you do when something very bad
happens to you? Do you decide that in your case the system of
justice has failed and you have been denied your rewards? Or do
you decide that you had been kidding yourself and that you really
are a bad person deserving of such punishment? Or do you abandon
your belief in a Just World and accept the large amount of evidence that life can be very unfair simply because things happen by
chance?

Meanings which we acquired in childhood can be very hard to
change. I have met many people who are unable to abandon their
belief in a Just World and who spend lives of great misery alternating

between bitter resentment at not getting their deserved rewards and guilt at their wickedness, for which the disasters they have suffered are a punishment they deserve.

Being able to change our meanings is not just a matter of how long and how strongly we have held these meanings. Meanings too can be held in place through the forms of thought in which they are contained.

Forms of Thought

The pattern of genes which each of us inherits is an array of possibilities. How each of these possibilities becomes an actuality depends on the experiences each individual encounters.

The array of possibilities is an array of forms. There is the form of a heart, a brain, a hand and so on. One individual's form of a hand might become a hand which is soft and slender. Another individual's form of a hand might become a hand which is large and muscular, while for another individual the form of a hand might become corrupted by the effects of Agent Orange with which the baby's father was sprayed during the Vietnam War, and the baby is born with two stumps at the end of his arms but no fingers.

Similarly, that array of genetic possibilities which can become the ability to create meaning contains *forms of thought*. These are forms which are found in all human beings. Just as we explore our environment using the form of the hand so we think about our environment using our different forms of thought.

Just how many forms of thought there are I do not know, but it seems to me that there are three forms which are essential for the effective functioning of the meaning system, so that we can each live as an individual in a society where other individuals are essential to our survival, both as a body and as a person, yet where other individuals, while they might cherish our body and indeed our existence, often threaten our survival as a person. In families this happens all the time.

These three forms of thought are:

1. The Face, the means by which a baby bonds with a mothering person;

2. The Story, the means by which an event becomes meaningful to us;
3. The Strategy for Survival – Primitive Pride, the means by which the meaning structure maintains its existence in the face of threat.

The Face

Amongst the artefacts in the National Archaeological Museum in Athens is a statue much older than the beautiful gold jewellery and the charming pottery of Mycenean Greece also in the museum. This statue comes from the Cyclades and was sculpted nearly 3,000 years before the birth of Christ. Despite its age it looks remarkably modern. It is a representation of the human form, about five feet high, in cool, pale marble, elegant and calm and without adornment or accretions of hair or clothes. The head is smooth, the face oval, the eyes no more than dots, nose straight and vertical, mouth no more than two half moons, the ears small circles. All human faces are more complex and irregular than this simple design, yet each of us, whether we lived five thousand years ago or now, sees this simple pattern as a face. To us an upright oval which encloses a vertical line in the middle, topped by two small circles on either side and below its base a horizontal line, is a face.

This interpretation of this design seems not to be a learned but an innate response. Newborn babies prefer to look at a face than at anything else, be they real faces, photographs of faces or cartoon faces. When a baby is offered an array of designs where each design consists of a vertical oval containing two small circles and two straight lines in various positions the baby fixes his eyes on the one particular arrangement of circles and lines which we call a face. The form of thought which enables us to recognize a face allows us not only to identify the basic form of a face but to make fine distinctions which allow us to distinguish one person from another. 'We are our faces. To our fellow human beings, if not to ourselves, they are the key identifiers. Our brains have exquisite machinery for processing and storing a particular arrangement of eyes, nose and mouth and for picking it out from other very similar arrangements.'[20] Computer experts are now turning this ability of ours into algorithms which can identify one particular face in a crowd of faces and give it a name. Big Brother is indeed watching you.

The form of the face is essential to the formation of relationships. With this form of thought the baby has a hook for catching hold of other people. Offered a number of faces and particularly a face which appears frequently the baby elaborates the basic form. If a baby at two or three weeks is offered an array of photographs, one of which is the face of his mother and the others the faces of women who look like his mother, the baby will identify his mother's photograph and gaze at that in preference to all the other photographs. Of course the baby has more information about this face than he has about the others. 'The distance between the eyes of the baby at the breast and the mother's eyes is about ten inches, exactly the distance for the sharpest focus and clearest vision for the young infant.'[21] Now he knows her smell, her touch, and the comfort, satisfaction and pleasure she can provide. He learnt the sound of her voice when he was still in her womb. (Babies are born interested in human voices. At birth babies prefer to listen to human speech than to other sounds, and at four days they can distinguish certain properties of their mother tongue from those of other languages.)

Cartoons and photographs are all very well, but what the baby wants is a face which responds, which moves and talks, and shows those changes which reveal something of what is always hidden: the other person's thoughts and feelings. Just as the stony face of the Cycladian statue is as disturbing as it is intriguing, so we are all disturbed by someone whose face reveals nothing of their thoughts and feelings. The face of authority, emotionless, unrevealing, is adopted by those who want to inspire anxiety in those over whom they wish to have power.

It is impossible to establish a relationship with someone whose face reveals nothing of their thoughts and feelings. A baby who is born to a mother who is depressed soon discovers this.

Studies of depressed mothers and their babies show how, when the mother fails to respond to the baby or when the mother begins an interaction with the baby and then does not complete it, the baby is profoundly affected. Daniel Stern, who has been studying the interactions between mothers and babies for many years, described what happens.

Compared with the infant's expectations and wishes, the mother's face is flat and expressionless. (I am assuming that the mother has become depressed recently enough that the infant has a set of schemas of her normal behaviour with which to compare her present, depressed behaviour.) She breaks eye contact and does not reestablish it. Her contingent responsiveness is less, and her animation and tonicity disappear. Along with these invariants coming from the mother, there are resonant invariants evoked in the infant: the flight of his animation, a deflation of his posture, a fall in positive affect and facial expressivity, a decrease in activation, and so on. In sum, the experience is descriptively one of 'microdepression'.[22]

Those people who claim that, since depression 'runs in families', it must be caused by a gene are ignoring the profound effects a depressed mother has on a child. What neuronal gestalts does a 'microdepression' form and what behaviour do they later produce?

The form of the face which we each inherit carries with it the information not just that the face is significant for the baby but that it is qualitatively different from those other patterns which the baby learns are called 'bottle', 'cot', 'rattle', 'dummy' and so on. Human beings are different from objects because, even though there are objects which move and make sounds as humans do, objects do not have thoughts and feelings.

Babies are born with the potential to acquire this information but they cannot make this potential actual unless they are presented with one consistent, caring, interacting face. This face does not have to belong to the baby's biological mother. Adoptive mothers, fathers, aunts, grandmothers, siblings or one attentive nurse can provide the relationship which becomes a model for all subsequent models in the baby's life. This model states that *all human beings have thoughts and feelings, and that a relationship consists of an engagement of the thoughts and feelings of two people, one with the other.* In acquiring this model the baby becomes a fully paid-up member of the human race.

Babies are tenacious in their search for a face, and thus many babies born in less than favourable circumstances still manage to acquire their model of a relationship. However, for some their search is not successful and, while they might grow up knowing intellectually that human beings are different from objects, experientially, in their bones and in themselves, they do not know the difference between a person and an object. To them human beings other than themselves are no more than a particular kind of object.

I have spent much of my life both professionally and personally in the company of people who treat other people as a particular class of object. For many years I worked in a psychiatric hospital where one of the consultant psychiatrists specialized in the treatment of people diagnosed as psychopaths. I observed no successful treatment. The current view of psychiatrists in the UK is that those people who are deemed 'to suffer from a psychopathic personality disorder' are untreatable. Consequently such people cannot be detained in a psychiatric hospital no matter how great a danger they might be to other people. Some terrible tragedies have followed from this. I think that one of the great tragedies of the twentieth century is that, although the importance of a baby bonding with a mothering figure was recognized in the 1950s, little money and effort have been spent in determining whether a deficit in bonding can be overcome. A remedy for this deficit would have a widespread effect far greater than the cures for various genetic physical disorders which are now being discovered.

A remedy for this deficit in the ability to create human relationships would need to be applied early in a child's life because the lack of this ability has profound and long-term effects. I saw this in the many hours I was able to spend talking with these patients called psychopaths. What I learned explained much of what I had observed.

We all treat objects in the same way. We either manipulate them, or use them for our benefit, or ignore them. On occasions we destroy them. Those people who have never acquired the model of a relationship treat other people in the same way. They manipulate them, they use them for their own benefit, they ignore them, and occasionally they attempt to destroy them. Being on the receiving end of such treatment is difficult and painful because every interaction can become a threat to the integrity of one's meaning structure.

It is out of our model of relationships that we create that model we call 'conscience' or 'superego', a model which causes trouble for us for the rest of our lives, but which enables us to live in groups. Those who lack the model of relationships and, consequently, the model of conscience live lives unimpeded by guilt. Many such people end up in jail, but many more become extremely successful politicians and entrepreneurs. Many, fearing the punishments which breaking the law can bring, lead what are apparently normal lives. They might marry, have children, but because they are adept in making excuses for themselves and inspiring guilt in others, and because they are untroubled by the need to tell the truth, they become the most powerful member of the family, the centre around which all the other family members revolve.

From such little acorns do massive oaks grow, when all that the baby wanted was some regular interaction with another person.

The interaction which the baby seeks always follows a particular pattern. It is a pattern we all know, and thus adults who would say they know nothing about babies can still be drawn into this interaction and know how to play.

Face to face either the baby or the adult can invite the other to play by looking into the other's eyes and making a noise or a movement such as pushing out the bottom lip or wrinkling the nose. If the other responds with sounds and facial movements what follows is a conversation: this begins with an interchange which sets the scene, rises to a crisis, and falls away in a dénouement. The interaction follows the pattern of a play, and a play is always a story.

The Story
Stories so abound in our lives that, like the man who was surprised to discover he talked prose, we can be surprised to find that everything we know comes in the form of a story.

The form of a story is very simple. It has a beginning, a middle and an end. For us to find a story satisfactory it has to be complete. If someone says to us, 'I was on a train the other day with some people and you'll never guess what happened,' we are being given the middle of a story and invited to guess the end. But before we can make a guess we need to be told the beginning of the story. What train was it? Where was it going? Who were the people? Once we know the beginning we might or might not be able to guess the end, but, if we have become intrigued by the story, we cannot feel satisfied until the story is complete – beginning, middle and end.

There are many different ways of telling a story but each way must complete the basic form. Novelists, journalists and essayists often try to draw the reader in by telling the middle, or part of the middle, of the story first. Such a device aims to surprise and intrigue the reader, something which scientists telling the story of their research must not do. Academic journals require that the story be told twice, first in a brief summary and then in the detailed form of introduction, method, results, discussion and conclusions. Cookery recipes have the ingredients as the beginning, the preparation as the middle and the cooking and serving as the end. This cooking and serving we might actually do, or we might simply imagine doing it, and thus complete the story. The story told by instruction manuals for video recorders and the like requires the reader to enact the story. The beginning is to take the recorder out of its box and to name the parts. The middle of the story is to decipher the prose and the diagrams, set up the recorder and work out how to use it, and the end to sit back in successful satisfaction.

The form of the story is the means by which we link one event to another. We cannot survive physically or as a person when all we see is a passing phantasmagoria where events occur with no connection one with the other. We need to see connections between events, and our need often overrides what is actually happening. Thus some people explain an individual's character and life in terms of the movements of the planets, while other people use as the explanation some mythopoeic gene.

The most prosaic way of seeing a link between one event and another is the simple observation that one event is always followed by another particular event. From such an observation we go on to use the occurrence of the first event to predict the second. The observation and the prediction take the form of a story. Thus we can be sitting in our garden on a sunny day (the beginning of the story) and we see black clouds massing on the horizon (the middle of the story). We predict the end of the story: 'It's going to rain.'

This particular prediction/end of story comes out of our past experiences. We have seen lots of black clouds followed by rain. But the way in which we have linked these events together comes from that form of thought which is innate, the story.

Babies while still in the womb, from about twenty-four weeks' gestation, show that they are using the form of the story. Even before the cortex of their brain is complete they are able to observe that one event always follows another event and to use the occurrence of the first event to predict the second.

Perhaps the commonest example of this is in the way that babies in the womb can link the feeling of pleasure with certain sounds, particularly rhythmic, sweet music. No doubt for a baby in the mother's womb the ride can be quite rough and constricted when the mother is busy and active. When she sits down and puts her feet up to rest, the stillness and easing of constriction must create in the baby a feeling of pleasure. Many mothers, just before they sit down to rest, switch on some music. If the mother has sat down to watch or to listen to her favourite soap opera the baby comes to hear the same music every day and, soon after the music begins, the baby feels a sense of ease and pleasure. The baby creates the story 'I'm feeling uncomfortable' (beginning), 'Here's the music' (middle), 'Something nice is going to happen' (prediction/ending). When the baby is born and the music is switched on the baby remembers the story, and looks in the direction of the music with what is called the 'alerting response', the expectation that something nice is about to happen.

Daniel Stern calls this ability of the baby to create a story 'the protonarrative envelope'. This is 'an emergent property', which is

> an organization that is in the process of coming into being or that has just taken form ... an emergent property of the mind ... has coherence and sense in the context in which it emerges. That is to say, the diverse events and feelings are tied together as necessary elements of a single unified happening that, at one of its higher levels, assumes a meaning ... More recent developmental research is beginning to suggest that the infant is intuitively endowed with some kind of representational system which can apprehend the intentional states of agents ... The ability – in fact the necessity – to see the human interactive world in terms of narrative-like events and their motives, goals and so on, is achieved very early.[23]

We use the form of the story not just to link one event to another. We also use it to create meaning. Nothing is fully meaningful to us until we have embedded it in a story.

You might be in your house or office when, quite unexpectedly, something happens. You immediately name this unexpected happening 'an extraordinarily loud noise'. Your naming of this event could be quite accurate, but the meaning of the event cannot be complete until you create a story around it. Immediately you create a theory about what the noise was. You might decide that it was a clap of thunder, or an explosion, or a traffic accident, and so on. Your theory must include the beginning of the story – what led up to the clap of thunder or the explosion or the accident – and the end of the story – what effects the thunder, the explosion, the accident will have. By creating this story you complete the meaning you have given to the event. Then you might decide to check the accuracy of your story by going and looking, or you might decide that you are sure you are right, and get on with what you are doing.

We are busy creating stories and listening to stories all the time. We gossip, we watch television, we daydream and tell ourselves stories. We love stories, but the story which matters most to us is our own life story.

Our meaning structure is a collection of stories, but all these stories are held within one story, our life story. Our sense of identity – that is, the person we experience ourselves as being – and our life story are one and the same. We can think of them as being separate – 'This is me and this is my life story' – but in fact me/my life story is the form which holds the meaning structure together and gives it a certain coherence.

It is our life story which embeds us in time and place. Our actual experience of living is a string of present moments. The form of the story gives us a sense of time (or it might be that our sense of time gives us the form of the story, or that the form of the story and the sense of time are aspects of the one form). We never actually experience the past or the future. They are just ideas, parts of the form of the story. Out of the story form/sense of time comes our life story/identity.

In our life story the middle is where we are now. The beginning is not just about our own past life. It is about our family, our roots. Knowing who our family was and where we came from is tremendously important in creating a complete sense of identity. In 1994 many Sydney suburbs were threatened and some houses engulfed by huge bushfires which, leaping at high speed from the top of one tall tree to another, would bear down on houses where the occupants, believing they were safe, were peacefully going about their business. Many families had to flee with little time to gather up valuable possessions. All Australians considered the question,

'What's the most important thing to take with you if you have to leave your home in such a hurry?' There was universal agreement on what to take: the family photograph albums. There could be no replacement or recompense for such a loss.

One of the cruelties inflicted on children down the centuries has been to deny them the right to know where they came from and who their family was. Orphanages have often been guilty of this crime against the children in their care. Nowadays some child-care agencies have a policy of helping children separated from their families to put together a 'life story book' containing the letters and photographs which enable the children to create the beginning of their story. Children thus helped speak of their life story book as giving them great comfort, but, alas, there are still many adults involved in child care who do not realize the importance of the life story and they fail to provide children with the means of creating and maintaining the beginning of their story.

The ending of our life story has yet to be lived. It is made up of expectations and predictions about what our life will be. This is where the coherence and stability of our meaning structure is at its most vulnerable. If ever we discover that we have got the beginning of our life story wrong, if we discover that our parents were not the people we thought they were, or the circumstances of our birth were markedly different from what we had been told, we can feel quite disturbed, particularly if these discrepancies have implications for how we have chosen to live our lives and how we see our future. However, such discoveries are made by only a few of us. What happens to us all is that at least once in our lives the ending of our life story is disconfirmed. Our life is not going to turn out as we expected. We discover that John Lennon was right: 'Life is what happens while we're making other plans.'

Usually it is other people who disconfirm the ending of our life story. They die, or they betray us, or reject us, or simply turn out to be different from what we thought they were. When they do this, or when other events show us that we have got the ending of our story wrong, we feel our meaning structure tremble and threaten to collapse.

Dangerous though other people may be, we need them to confirm our meaning structure. The ancient Greek philosopher Xenophanes spoke of how all we know is but 'a woven web of guesses'. We need to check and to keep checking whether our guesses have some close relationship to what has happened, what is happening and what will happen. To do this we can see for ourselves and we can ask other people what they see. When people tell us that what we see is what they see we feel strengthened and more confident. But if someone keeps telling us that we have got it wrong we can come to doubt every meaning that we create.

Women who are married to men who constantly denigrate them can lose their self-confidence and come to believe that they are so stupid and incompetent that they cannot manage without the man who is destroying them in order to overcome his own sense of weakness. Such women create life stories, not of escaping or of fighting back, but of being the passive victim of whatever their husband, or life, might do to them.

Children need adults round them who confirm the child's meanings, or, when the child has got it wrong, will gently steer the child to a more accurate representation of the circumstances the child is trying to understand. Alas, many adults do not do this. Instead, they tell children that they are stupid, or they shame them by laughing at them. Even worse, they tell the child that he has lied when he knows that he has not.

This was a favourite ploy of my mother whenever I told her something which did not fit with the way she saw things. When I was twenty-seven and pregnant I was working very hard. In the last few weeks of the pregnancy I developed the early symptoms of toxaemia and was sent to hospital. My doctor told me that I had not been getting enough rest. When I told my mother this she said, 'That's not true, Dorothy. You never work hard.' This for me at twenty-seven was a story I could joke about with my friends, but when I was a child such a rejection of my truth was very disturbing.

At four I developed symptoms which could signal the onset of diphtheria, a disease from which, in those pre-antibiotic days, many children died. I was put into the infectious diseases ward in the local hospital and my parents forbidden to visit. I remember my stay there extremely well. For the first few days I was in a cot but some days later I was shifted to a bed, not my own bed but one which I shared with another girl. She was older than me and was already at the head of the bed where she could use the radio headphones. I was at the foot, and so did not hear the message my parents had arranged to be broadcast over the local radio. Eventually I was sent home (I didn't have diphtheria, just the incurable bronchiectasis which has plagued my life) and my mother asked me if I had heard the radio message. I said I had not and explained why. My mother told me I was lying. 'They wouldn't put you two to a bed,' she said. No doubt she had her reasons to say that. Her own anger and disappointment that I had missed the radio message, and, possibly, her guilt at not being there to look after me, were hard for her to deal with, but she held the view, as most parents did then, that one of the uses of children was to be a scapegoat on which parents could vent their feelings.

My big sister must have observed my mother's success in being able to deny inconvenient facts because she adopted the 'Dorothy's lying' ploy. Such constant assaults on my understanding of what went on around me had devastating effects on my self-confidence. I could not show that I was distressed by what they said because, if I did, they would tell me I was stupid to be so sensitive. Consequently, I grew up doubting my perceptions and in my teens and early twenties there were times when I nearly lost my grip on reality completely. Years later I worked with people diagnosed as schizophrenic and I heard stories of childhoods where the child's truth had been denied by the family, stories which made my heart turn over just as it does whenever I discover I have just had a close brush with death.

What we all want is that others should know our life story and acknowledge the truth of it and that we have lived. This is why graves are marked, memorials are built and histories written. If no one knows your story it is as if you are nothing and, when you die, it will be as if you have never existed. This is why many people are pleased that their name has been in a newspaper or that they have been glimpsed on television by millions. The fear of being a nothing, of never having existed, can feel like utter shame, the utter terror.

It was this utter shame and utter terror which the SS militiamen guarding the German concentration camps visited upon the prisoners. Primo Levi recorded that

the first news of the Nazi annihilation camps began to spread in 1942. They were vague pieces of information, yet in agreement with each other: they delineated a massacre of such vast proportions, of such extreme cruelty and such intricate motivation that the public was inclined to reject them because of their enormity. It is significant that this rejection was foreseen well in advance by the culprits themselves.[24]

He went on to quote Simon Wiesenthal, who described these SS militiamen in the last pages of his book *The Murderers Are Among Us*. They told the prisoners that

'However this war may end, we have won the war against you; none of you will be left to bear witness, but even if someone were to survive, the world would not believe him. There will perhaps be suspicions, discussions, research by historians, but there will be no certainties, because we will destroy the evidence with you. And even if some proof should remain and some of you survive, people will say that the events you describe are too monstrous to be believed: they will say they are exaggerations of Allied propaganda and will believe us, who will deny everything, and not you. We will be the ones to dictate the history of the Lagers.'[25]

Primo Levi described how

Almost all the survivors, verbally or in their written memoirs, remember a dream which frequently recurred during the nights of imprisonment, varied in its detail but uniform in its substance: they had returned home and with passion and relief were describing their past sufferings, addressing themselves to a loved person, and were not believed, indeed, not even listened to. In the most typical (and most cruel) form, the interlocutor turned and left in silence.[26]

This dream became a reality for many of the survivors of the Holocaust. People did not want to hear their story because it threatened their own meaning structure. In a television news report about the fiftieth anniversary of the foundation of the state of Israel, one woman, a survivor of Auschwitz, told how, when she finally arrived in New York, her relatives did not want to hear about her experiences because they had suffered so much during the war. They told her, 'The queues for food were dreadful.'

Perhaps her relatives prided themselves on their ability to suffer and they did not want to acknowledge that someone else's suffering was greater than their own. Perhaps they did not want to examine the question of why God would let good people suffer in this way, or perhaps they could not tolerate a story which showed how a person can be trapped and helpless. Concentration camp survivors who did tell their story were often challenged by their listeners, who asked, 'Why didn't you try to escape?'

Sometimes listeners would offer suggestions based on what they thought they would do in such a situation. Primo Levi recalled such an event. He wrote,

> I remember with a smile the adventure I had several years ago in a fifth grade classroom, where I had been invited to comment on my books and to answer pupils' questions. An alert-looking little boy, apparently at the head of the class, asked me the obligatory question: 'How come you didn't escape?'

Primo explained to him how the Lager was organized. The boy wanted a diagram, which Primo supplied. The boy studied it and presented Primo with a plan:

> At night, cut the throat of the sentinel: then, put on his clothes; immediately after this run over there to the power station and cut off the electricity, so the searchlights would go out and the high-tension fence would be deactivated; after that I could leave without any trouble. He added seriously: 'If it should happen to you again, do as I told you; you'll see that you'll be able to do it.'[27]

The dangers of not being believed were recognized by the South African Truth and Reconciliation Commission. A system for briefing and debriefing those people who testified was set up, and though it did not work perfectly, it went some way to prevent those who had to talk about the traumas they had suffered from feeling that they had not been believed.[28]

Just as we need other people to confirm our story, so we need to confirm our story to ourselves. That is, we need to tell ourselves the truth. Our story is a construction, and if we want to lead a reasonably peaceful life we need to create a life story in which the pieces fall into a pattern where the pieces fit and which does not conflict with our need for a sense of pride and self-worth. But what if the events in our life conflict with this need? One solution is to lie to ourselves. It is an easy thing to do, but the results are always disastrous.

I have met many people who describe their childhood as idyllic and their parents as perfect. Some of these people say that they do not actually remember their childhood but they are sure it was a perfectly happy one. Not all these people were suffering from depression and anxiety. Some led apparently normal lives, though they were often troubled by their inability to maintain good relationships with others.

No childhood is idyllic and no parent is perfect. All children suffer, but some are fortunate enough to suffer less than most. One of the tasks of adult life should be to inspect the beginnings of our story and see it clearly and truthfully. From our adult perspective we can modify the interpretations of events we constructed in childhood.

In a workshop I once ran one of the participants talked about the brutal punishments his father administered. In adult life his great problem was his rage, which had disrupted all his important relationships. Later he and I travelled by train together, and we talked about our fathers: they were both men of considerable ability who had never had the chance to put that ability to good use. Limited by education and opportunity, they had seen it as their duty to work in demanding, unsatisfying jobs in order to support their families. As my companion talked about his father he acknowledged that he could take some pride in him, and with this some of the sadness which lay beneath his rage showed through, the sadness of a child who had offered his father love and been rejected.

In looking at his story from an adult perspective he made the story more complex. It was no longer about a brutal father who terrorized his son. It became a story of a man who was trying to be what he thought a good father should be, and a son who loved, hated and feared his father. A more complex story, but a more truthful one.

Simple stories lay blame simply. 'My father was totally wicked,' or, 'I was wicked and my father was right to punish me.' Complex, more truthful stories apportion not blame but responsibility.

Responsibility properly applied relates to that over which the person has control. Parents have a great deal of control over what happens to their children when they are small, and so have great responsibility for the care of their children. Parents have no control over what happens to their adult children and how their adult children interpret what happens to them, so parents cannot be held responsible for what their adult children do. However, the question of responsibility becomes more tricky when the parents see a link between what they did when the children were young and what their children do when they are adults. Had they acted differently would their children now be acting differently? In those past years could they have chosen to act differently or was their choice constrained by what they knew at the time?

This is the question which plagues many parents when they review their lives, often at the behest of their adult children. As a parent concerned about your children's education you might have surveyed the options for secondary schooling and, after much deliberation, you might have decided to invest your savings in your children's education and send them to a well-regarded boarding school. As an adult one of your children talks of how the boarding school was the best experience ever, while the other child says, 'How could you be so cruel as to send me away from home?'

No doubt the child who disliked being away from home would say, 'You didn't listen to me,' but parents can listen to their children and still get it wrong. The circumstances of their lives did not offer them an infinite range of choices, and they could not foresee how ideas about education and families would change. They could act only with the knowledge they had then. Later perhaps the best they can do for their life story and for their adult children is to say to them, 'Yes, these things did happen. I tried to do my best but I can see now I made mistakes. I'm sorry.'

The question of responsibility is quite different when our choice of action was not constrained by what we knew at the time. If we know that something is wrong and we still choose to do it we are fully responsible for our actions. Every adult who accepted Hitler's plan to exterminate all those people who impeded his plan for a pure Aryan race, and who by action or non-action helped put his plan into operation, is responsible for what each one of them did. It was not only Germans who chose this course of action. Such people came from all the European states. What they had in common was an inheritance of ideas from European civilization and from the Christian tradition. Most would have claimed an allegiance to one of the Christian churches, but even those who did not call themselves Christians would still have been aware of Christ's teaching about the necessity of loving one another and forgiving our enemies. Not one could honestly claim, 'I didn't know it was wrong to humiliate, torture and kill other people.'

Knowing that we have acted wrongly should provoke guilt and shame, but these are very painful emotions. One way of dealing with them is to lie to yourself. You tell yourself a story which is not true.

Most adults who lie to themselves begin by lying to other people. Certain facts are inconvenient for them: they do not want to take responsibility for what they do. They act in bad faith towards other people, and they slip into acting in bad faith towards themselves. They start believing their own lies, and, as I now observe in my contemporaries who have done this for most of their lives, as the years pass their memory becomes confused. They have lost the ability to distinguish between what did happen and what they fantasized had happened, what they themselves did and what other people did. Through their lies they have denied themselves the strength and comfort our life story can give us when we reach an age where the inevitability of death cannot be denied. For this we need a life story which is grounded in the truth that we have made mistakes, we have suffered, we have endured life's blows, but we have come through and it was good. Though we might fear the processes which lead to death, we do not fear death itself for it is the appropriate end to our story.

To arrive at such a story is not easy. Primo Levi acknowledged how hard it is when he wrote about Louis Darquier de Pellepoix, former commissioner in charge of Jewish affairs in the Vichy government around 1942, who was personally responsible for the deportation of 70,000 Jews. After the war, wrote Primo Levi,

> Darquier denies everything: the photographs of the piles of corpses are montages; the statistics of millions of dead were fabricated by the Jews, always greedy for publicity, commiseration and the indemnities . . . I think I can recognize in him the typical case of someone who, accustomed to lying publicly, ends by lying in private too, to

himself, and building for himself a comforting truth which allows
him to live in peace.

To keep good faith and bad faith distinct costs a lot: it requires
a decent sincerity or truthfulness with oneself, it demands a continu-
ous intellectual and moral effort.[29]

Some people are not prepared to make such a moral effort. They
are not prepared to suffer the pain of shame and guilt or the difficulties which can follow the making of a moral choice.

In 1998 the German news weekly *Der Spiegel* carried a story by
Bruno Schirra about his visit to the eighty-seven-year-old Dr Hans
Münch, a Bavarian doctor who could attest to the accuracy of the
film *Schindler's List*. He told Bruno Schirra, ' "The selection process
is portrayed completely authentically. Every detail is right. It was
exactly like that." '

Bruno Schirra wrote,

Hans Münch spent 19 months in Auschwitz. He served in the
Hygiene Institute of the Waffen-SS. He carried out his work as
conscientiously as all the other SS ranks. 'To eradicate the Jews, that
was the job of the SS at the time,' says Münch. 'I could do experiments on people, which otherwise were only possible on rabbits. It
was important work for science.'

Münch wanted to be a scientist and Auschwitz gave him what he
wanted. He said,

'These were ideal working conditions: a laboratory with excellent
equipment and a selection of academics with worldwide repu-
tations.'

His job was to fight epidemics. Typhus, dysentery and typhoid
were always breaking out, and since SS people were dying, there
was a need for action.

But fighting epidemics in Auschwitz meant 'that all the huts were
closed off. Nobody came out and nobody went in. Everybody was
gassed, because it was possible that someone could pass it on. That
was the usual treatment.'

He talks about it casually. There is no doubt and no emotion.

'Did it bother you?'

'No, no, not at all, because it was the only way not to let things get much, much, much worse.'

'Gassing was better?'

'Of course! Of course! If you think it through to its logical conclusion, it was the only way to prevent the whole camp from being destroyed.'

Münch still believes today that this was the only possibility. For him, it was a humane act. 'If they hadn't been gassed, they would have died terrible deaths from epidemics.'

For Münch, the notorious SS doctor Josef Mengele was 'the kindest of colleagues. I can only say the best things about him.' On 29 June 1944 Mengele sent him the head of a twelve-year-old child. Münch examined it and sent the findings back on 8 July. 'It was an everyday event,' he says today. 'Mengele and the others sent us heads, livers, spinal cords, whatever they had, and we analysed them.' Did he ever refuse? Even today the idea is unthinkable. 'That was my duty, and duty was duty, and schnaps was schnaps.'

Dr Münch's wife was with him in Auschwitz. During the interview she became increasingly distressed. She said, ' "My God, I'm so ashamed of being German." Münch looks up. "I'm not." Well, he says, the Jews might have had it bad in Auschwitz. But it wasn't easy for him either.' When asked, ' "What does Auschwitz mean to you?" ' he answered calmly, ' "Nothing." '[30]

What can we say about Dr Münch? To say he is a monster might relieve our feelings but it does not explain what he is actually doing when he eschews shame and guilt and denies the suffering of other people. One way of explaining the process which led him to make such a monstrous choice is to see that when Dr Münch was offered a choice of disobeying orders, or fighting and perhaps dying on the Russian front, or, as he saw it, advancing his career, he chose his career. In doing so he retreated to an unelaborated form of thought which is concerned with the survival of the meaning structure no matter what the cost. This form of thought is the primitive form of pride.

Primitive Pride

On 15 April 1945 the British army entered Bergen-Belsen camp in north-west Germany. The soldiers who liberated the camp and the medical staff who came to assist them were among the first to report through their letters what they saw. Lieutenant-Colonel Mervin Willett Gonin, DSO, TD, wrote,

I can give no adequate description of the Horror Camp in which my men and myself were to spend the next month of our lives. It was a barren wilderness, as bare and devoid of vegetation as a chicken run. Corpses lay everywhere, some in huge piles where they'd been dumped by other inmates, sometimes they lay singly or in pairs where they'd fallen as they'd shuffled along the dirt tracks ... One knew that five hundred a day were dying and that five hundred a day would go on dying for weeks before anything we could do would have the slightest effect ...

Piles of corpses, naked and obscene, with a woman too weak to stand propping herself against them as she cooked the food we had given her over an open fire; men and women crouching down just anywhere in the open relieving themselves of the dysentery which was scouring their bowels, a woman standing stark naked washing herself in water from a tank in which the remains of a child floated ...

It was shortly after the British Red Cross Society teams arrived, though it may have had no connection, that a very large quantity of lipstick also arrived. This was not at all what we men wanted, we were screaming for hundreds and thousands of other things and I don't know who asked for lipstick. I wish I could discover who did it, it was the action of genius, sheer unadulterated brilliance. I believe nothing did more for those internees than the lipstick. Women lay in beds with no sheets and no nightie but with scarlet lips, you saw them wandering around with nothing but a blanket over their shoulders, but with scarlet lips. I saw a woman dead on the post mortem table and clutched in her hand was a piece of lipstick.

Do you see what I mean? At last someone had done something to make them individuals again, they were someone, no longer merely the number tattooed on the arm. At last they could take an interest in their appearance. That lipstick gave them back their humanity.

Perhaps it was the most pathetic thing that happened in Belsen, perhaps the most pathetic thing that's ever happened, I don't know.

But that's why the sight of a piece of lipstick today makes my eyes feel just a little uncomfortable.[31]

And how hugely important is that uncomfortable feeling in our eyes, the tears of sorrow and pity that come when we recognize the humanness of another person, a fellow human being. We recognize them and their story, and we see them in us and us in them. We can guess at what they are feeling and why they did what they did. There is something both pathetic and brave in what these women did. Wearing lipstick was not going to make one iota of difference to the physical condition of these women, but it was a way of defending themselves against the assaults they had suffered on the sense they had of being a person.

Lieutenant-Colonel Gonin knew that the women who wore the lipstick were making a statement about their identity and their pride. He knew that he did the same, not by wearing lipstick but by wearing his army uniform, and that using lipstick, a uniform or whatever to express identity is characteristic of our species *Homo sapiens sapiens* or Modern Humans. Our distant ancestors, the Early Humans, had no beads, pendants or necklaces, no painting on cave walls. In his study of the development of the mind the archaeologist Steven Mithen wrote, 'A characteristic feature of all Modern Humans, whether they are prehistoric hunter gatherers or twentieth century business people is that they use material culture to transmit social information'[32] – that is, to define their identity and to demonstrate to others their definition of their identity.

Babies are not born wearing some identity statement – their mothers press that upon them soon enough – but they are born with the need to be a person and to be treated as a person. Most adults recognize this though they might not articulate it as such. They know that a regular pattern to the day benefits the baby and that a baby needs company. The regular pattern reinforces the baby's meaning structure and the company of other people confirms the baby as a person. If the baby is deprived of company or if the regular pattern of care is badly disrupted the baby becomes distressed. It seems that at birth, when the baby encounters an environment not as supportive and predictable as the womb, the baby is primed to survive both as a body and as a person. Just as a baby whose mouth and nose become covered will scream and wriggle in order to breathe, so a baby who finds his meaning structure under threat will demand the conditions necessary for its survival.

The purpose of life is to live, and just as everything that is alive will strive to survive physically, so every meaning structure strives to maintain its coherence and thus survive. The mechanism for doing so is given by the form of thought which I have called primitive pride.

I first became aware of this way of thinking when, in the early seventies, I was spending much of my working day in conversation with people who were severely depressed. To become depressed you have to turn against yourself and hate yourself. My patients were experts in hating themselves. In utter humility and pain they would describe to me how they had failed in everything, how they were responsible not only for every disaster they had suffered but for every disaster that had befallen their family and friends. Some claimed responsibility for world poverty and the degradation of the planet. If I tried to suggest that they were claiming responsibility for matters clearly not in their control they would correct me by telling me that they must be responsible for all these disasters because, if they had been really good people, these disasters would not have happened. They were inherently inadequate, unacceptable, bad, the wickedest people the world had ever seen. At every encounter they would thank me for listening to them and say, 'You shouldn't waste your time with me. There are many more deserving patients than me.'

In the face of such a massive, relentless attack, how does a meaning structure manage to remain whole? I found that, as I listened to these people, in the welter of self-castigation and humility something else would occasionally show through. It might just be a facial expression, a tone of voice, or a remark made in casual conversation while we were preparing a cup of tea or standing in the queue at the canteen.

What showed through was pride. I was first aware of this pride as I listened to some of my patients talking about their suffering. I was very familiar with this way of talking. It is the voice of the expert sufferer. Expert sufferers take pride in their ability to suffer. My mother was an expert sufferer. The suffering of anyone else paled into insignificance when compared with her suffering, and in the family she brooked no competition. Thus I never acquired the knack of talking about my own suffering. I find it very difficult to say, 'I'm ill,' or 'I'm anxious.' When I'm on my deathbed and you ask me how I am I shall say, 'Fine.' This, I am sure, was one of the reasons my husband found me so attractive. He was an expert sufferer and needed a silent and attentive listener.

Expert sufferers can specialize not just in physical suffering but the mental suffering that goes with guilt. If you say to such an expert sufferer that something has gone wrong and perhaps they could put it right you will find that they do not make a move to do so. Instead they fall to suffering, saying, 'It's all my fault, I'm so guilty, I'm sorry I've done this to you, how can I ever make it up to you, you don't know just how guilty I feel,' and so on and so on. Their aim is to make you feel guilty for having made them feel guilty. Not that your suffering guilt can ever match the agony they suffer. Expert sufferers take great pride in their capacity to suffer and they resist anyone who tries to take their suffering away from them. Martyrdom can be a wonderful source of pride.

Most of my depressed patients revealed a pride in how bad they were. They were not ordinarily bad. They did not want to be ordinary. If they could not be the Most Perfect, Wonderful, Intelligent, Beautiful, Successful, Admired and Loved Person the World Has Ever Seen they had to be the Worst, Most Despised, Confused, Evil Failure and Outcast the World Has Ever Seen.

Over the weeks and months that we talked the life story of each of my patients gradually unfolded, and primitive pride was revealed in the codicils that came with their statements about who they were and what the ending of their story would be. Each life story was unique, but they had some common themes such as:

- 'I am a shameful person and must creep around the edges of society, asking permission to exist and expecting a refusal.' Primitive pride then adds, 'God sees my suffering and will one day comfort and reward me.'
- 'I am wicked, the cause of my disaster, and depression is my deserved punishment.' Primitive pride then adds, 'But I'm a better person than everyone else because I know how wicked I am whereas other people don't recognize how wicked they are. Through my suffering I shall find redemption.'
- 'I shall expunge my shame and guilt by dying.' Primitive pride

then adds, 'I will force those who shamed me to witness my suffering and know that it is their fault.'
- 'I will never forgive those who shamed me.' Primitive pride then adds, 'My revenge will be merciless and eternal.'

In telling their story some of my patients recognized and confronted their primitive pride. They saw that it kept them in the prison of depression, and they decided that the cost was too great. There were other and better ways of creating a life story, and, in realizing that they were free to do so, they freed themselves from their prison. Some of my patients found that the immediate rewards their primitive pride gave them were too delicious to relinquish. They remained depressed.

The meaning structure is a self-regulating system. All self-regulating systems have within their structure some mechanism which maintains the integrity of the system, preventing it from grinding to a halt or shattering to pieces. Our body, a self-regulating system, has a number of such mechanisms. The mechanism which forms blood clots to stem the flow of blood through a wound is one. In the meaning structure primitive pride is the form of thought or mechanism which selects from within the individual meaning structure a collection of meanings; when put together, these meanings serve to give immediate protection to the integrity of the meaning structure. This collection of meanings may have little relationship to what is actually happening or in the long term be an adequate defence. Indeed, it usually creates more problems than it was assembled to solve. Its importance is that it can be assembled immediately, in the blink of an eye.

In psychoanalysis one of the mechanisms of defence is rationalization, which is a concept with a passing similarity to primitive pride. With rationalization, as Otto Fenichel explained,

Emotional attitudes become permissible on condition that they are justified as 'reasonable'. The patient finds one reason or another why he is to behave in this way or that, and thus avoids becoming aware that he is actually driven by an instinctual impulse. Aggressive behaviour is sanctioned on the condition that it is viewed as 'good'; a like situation holds true for sexual attitudes.[33]

In the 1930s the psychoanalyst Karen Horney developed the concept of compensatory 'pride systems' which, as described by the psychotherapist Chris Mace,

> attempt to minimalise internal anxiety by maintaining self images that are inconsistent with social realities. These are identified with characteristic goals and fixed attitudes, providing a source of inconsistent behaviour at any time. If reality threatens to impinge, conflict and anxiety are the inevitable result as the fragile balance between these internal systems is disturbed.[34]

Two American psychologists, Daniel Gilbert and Timothy Wilson, though working quite differently from psychoanalysts and from me, encountered primitive pride, which they called a 'psychological immune system'. They had wanted to discover how quickly people recovered from the shock of some disaster or some unexpected good fortune. They found that when people were asked how long they thought it would take them to recover from, say, being jilted or being elected to a much wanted position, they had predicted that it would take far longer than it actually did.

What happened was that the psychological immune system, which was 'an army of rationalizations, justifications and self-serving logic, soothes our psyche during bad times'. Daniel Gilbert said, 'People are famous for making the best of bad situations and rationalizing away their failures – which allows them to remain relatively pleased with themselves despite all good evidence to the contrary.'[35]

Primitive pride is concerned with choosing from the array of possible interpretations of a situation that interpretation which will best keep the meaning structure intact. It can act swiftly without having to resort to conscious thought. It is not concerned with testing an interpretation against reality nor is it concerned with the long-term implications of a particular interpretation, even if the implication is that the person will suffer.

This action of primitive pride can be seen in the pattern of events which leads to a person becoming depressed. Some disaster occurs which causes the person to see a serious discrepancy between what he thought his life was and what it actually is. The meaning structure cannot adjust to this discrepancy without a major reorganization, and so the person starts to feel himself falling apart. Primitive pride comes into action and provides an interpretation which serves to hold the meaning structure together, namely that the person himself is the cause of the disaster. The holding together operation is successful because the interpretation is simply an enlargement of what the person believes, but what comes hard on its heels is the imprisoning isolation of depression.[36]

Not only is primitive pride not concerned with testing meanings against what is actually happening, it can perform its function of maintaining the integrity of the meaning structure simply by denying that certain things are actually happening. The story which many Serbs have always liked to tell themselves is that, throughout history, Serbs have, without exception, been virtuous victims. In June 1999, as NATO troops uncovered more and more evidence of the massacres by the Serbian army of Albanian Kosovans and the Serbs in Kosova fled their homes for the safety of Serbia, many Serbs preferred to believe what their state media told them, that they were the innocent victims of NATO aggression, while some denied the evidence of their own eyes. Rory Carroll, an English journalist in Belgrade, reported:

> Asked whether Serb refugees should be interviewed about possible atrocities, Belgrade shoppers yesterday gave blank responses. The refugees fled because the Kosovan Liberation Army was a gang of murderous terrorists, not because they had done something to provoke retribution, many said. As for the refugees, they deny any wrongdoing against their Kosovan Albanian neighbours. Questioned about the March 26 massacre at Suva Reka in which men, women and children were shot at close range, Serb refugees from the town claimed that not a hair had been touched on a single head.
>
> Reports of mass executions, grenades tossed at children, trucks ferrying bodies, were a fantasy. 'Not one Albanian has been killed, not one,' said Bravko Petkovic, 32, who worked in Balkan Tyre factory.
>
> A crowd of young men, arms folded, said it was inconceivable that they or any other Serbs could have killed their neighbours. 'Do we look like murderers? Come on, we're family men,' said Vesko Mladevovic. 'We got on very well with the Albanians, even though they were kidnapping and shooting us.'[37]

Primitive pride can also keep us alive when the conditions of our life are at their most dire. Instead of giving up and dying we stay active and, even without conscious thought, we carry out those actions which can ensure our survival. That is how people torn from their homes and robbed of everything they hold dear manage to go on living day by day.

As the many millions of people who live in great poverty show, it is possible to survive on very little. The trick seems to be to keep our expectations in line with what's on offer. 'What's on offer' is not just a matter of physical survival. It is also a matter of what's on offer that will maintain our sense of identity/our life story. It is easier to survive on very little if you live in a community where you have a place and where the other members of the community treat you with respect. Poverty is much harder to bear when you are utterly alone.

Does your environment allow you to be yourself and do other people see you as you see yourself? Whenever your answer to that question is 'No' primitive pride comes to the rescue. It might perform a reconstruing of your life story, perhaps, 'Even though other people spurn me, God loves me and will reward me for my virtue,' or it might say, 'If I cannot live my life as I am I shall die my death as I am.' Where primitive pride is concerned, the meaning structure must survive even if that means letting the body die.

Primitive pride, like all the mechanisms which keep us functioning, will at some time come to an end because no living thing lives for ever. In the face of overwhelming disease, injury or simply old age, the mechanisms which keep us breathing and thinking close down. They come to an end and we die. Sometimes primitive pride closes down first, and with that a reasonably healthy body dies. This is a common phenomenon in hospitals dealing with an ageing population. A patient whose physical condition could have supported many months of life simply, as it is usually described, 'loses the will to live', and dies. As we get old some parts of our meaning structure change and adapt to the inevitability of death. We might not want to die this very minute or even next month or even next year, but the inevitability of death brings some unexpected comforts. Whenever I read about the extreme changes of climate predicted for the middle of the next century I think, 'Well, I don't have to

worry about that.' 'Losing the will to live' might be the meaning
structure becoming one simple idea: 'It's time to go.'

This is not what happens to those people who find that the terrible
disaster they have suffered completely confounds their expectations
of what life was about. If they cannot construct another set of
meanings, if primitive pride cannot overcome such an assault on
their meaning structure, they cannot survive. Nearly fifty years after
the Second World War the psychologist Aaron Hass interviewed
some of the survivors of the concentration camps.

> Jack Diamond was forced to watch as his brother was hanged in
> Auschwitz. He told me what it was like to be a teenager in that
> universe. 'In the camps you became an adult overnight . . . I was
> like a general planning for a war . . . not to be noticed . . . The
> intellectuals were the first to die . . . They thought about it all. How
> could humanity do this? Who wants to live in a world like this? . . .
> I just put my head down and didn't ask the larger questions. I think
> it was easier being an adolescent, because I wasn't mature enough
> to ask the larger questions. My father, he died spiritually before he
> died physically. He kept asking, 'Where is God? How is this possible?'
> I got frightened, I got scared, but I wasn't internally destroyed. So
> many adults lost their *will* to survive . . . Sometimes I created an
> invisible wall shutting out what was happening . . . as if it wasn't
> happening. My father did see everything that was going on around
> and it destroyed him.'[38]

Losing the will to live, that is, primitive pride closing down, results
in death. Suicide is unnecessary. In fact, suicide is primitive pride
asserting itself. Whenever we contemplate, and perhaps carry out
our suicide, it is primitive pride deciding that there is a conflict
between the body's need for survival and the meaning structure's
need for survival. In such a conflict the body has to go. It has to
be killed.

The actress Kathryn Hunter, in an interview with Lyn Gardner,
spoke of this. 'When she was twenty-one and in her final year at
RADA, locked in an unhappy relationship from which she could
see no escape, and in a trough of depression so deep that "I could
hardly be bothered to kill myself", Hunter leapt from a window.'
She didn't die, but her injuries left her with long-term difficulties,

the overcoming of which made her reputation as a fine actress all the greater. She said of her suicide attempt, ' "The fall was just something that happened. A long time ago. A stupidity. The action of a child who discovered that things were not as she wished." '[39]

Primitive pride demands that reality conform to its wishes. Through time and experience we might gain the wisdom to know that reality is indifferent to our wishes and that this is not to be deplored but seen as something that makes life interesting. If we could make everything predictable how dull life would be.

Most of us, as children, develop that set of ideas which is commonly called a conscience, and out of that set of ideas comes a pride of which we are always conscious. This is moral pride which, like primitive pride, endeavours to protect the integrity of the meaning structure, but which, unlike primitive pride, takes some account of what is actually going on. Moral pride is concerned with avoiding shame and guilt which always threaten the meaning structure, and with maintaining the ideas we have about how we ought to live our lives. Whenever we say, 'My conscience will not allow me to do this,' moral pride is operating.

However, despite the fact that moral pride does take some account of what is going on, we can still set ourselves some rules which will lead us into danger. If we insist that our beliefs about the purpose of life and the nature of death – that is, our religious and philosophical beliefs – are absolute truths then our meaning structure is threatened every time we meet someone who holds beliefs different from ours. If we take pride in the way we are unchanging in all our beliefs and opinions, a significant discrepancy between what we thought our life was and what it actually is will sooner or later appear and threaten our meaning structure.

Refusing to change our views is always a sign of weakness. To be able to let our views evolve along with our experience, to be able to reflect upon events and consciously choose a wise interpretation, to be able to say, 'Yes, I was wrong,' or, 'I used to think such and such but now I think so and so,' we need to feel that, even as we modify our views, our sense of identity has a basic strength which is able to withstand the assaults made upon it by unexpected events and by other people. It is a tensile strength which flexes but does not break. This strength comes with overcoming our fear of the world and of other people. If we see the world as a frightening place and most other people as enemies we never feel strong because we see the world and its inhabitants as being stronger than us. We feel that we are in constant danger of being overwhelmed. We can become inflexible, and pretend to ourselves that refusing to change your mind is a sign of strength. Alas, inflexible structures, be they buildings or meaning structures, are always in danger of breaking. Buildings are always assaulted by wind and rain, and meaning structures are always assaulted by other people.

Even when other people are most benignly disposed towards us they are always a threat to our meaning structure because they are a constant reminder of how our way of seeing things is not the only way. Moreover, other people have the ability to deprive us of our greatest protection, our pride.

Primitive pride is a form of thought with which we are born and takes no account of other people or of what is actually happening. It is concerned only with our survival. It can fit comfortably with the form of the story because it is adept at creating a life story where we are justified in everything we do.

The form of the face can be a challenge to primitive pride. The face is the face of others, and all these faces have eyes which look at us. Are these accepting, friendly eyes or do these eyes say something else?

Primitive pride can override the form of the face, especially in those people who, as babies, formed no secure bond with one mothering person. Such people create life stories which absolve them of all responsibility for what they do, but their stories, like the story of Dr Münch, provoke in other people the response, 'Have you no shame!'

Shame precedes a sense of guilt. Guilt requires a sense of time – past actions and future punishment. Small children who have yet to develop notions of yesterday and tomorrow do not have a sense of guilt, but they do have a very profound sense of shame. They can be held in the gaze of another person and feel exposed and vulnerable. Daniel Stern wrote,

> Babies act as if eyes were indeed windows to the soul. After seven weeks of age, they treat the eyes as the geographic centre of the face and the psychological centre of the person. When you play

peek-a-boo with a baby, she quickly shows some anticipatory pleasure as you lower the blanket to reveal your hair and forehead. But
only when the baby sees your eyes does she explode with delight.
Six-year-olds illustrate this psychological centrality of the eyes in a
different way. When a six-year-old covers her eyes with her hands,
and you ask her, 'Can I see you?' she will answer, 'No!' Although
we used to think that the child could not imagine you could see
her if she couldn't see you, that is not the problem. She is perfectly
aware that you can see not only her but even her hands covering
her eyes. What she really means by 'No' is, 'If you can't see my eyes
you don't see *me*.' Seeing her means looking into her eyes.[40]

Shame evolves out of the form of the face, and so becomes part
of the meaning structure at an early stage in its development. Small
children suffer many experiences of shame as they go through the
difficult process of learning to be clean. We do not forget these
experiences of shame, and later our enemies can use them against
us to destroy us.

In Yugoslavia under Tito nationality was no barrier to marriage
and there were many intermarriages between Serbs, Muslims and
Croats. But once they came to power Serbian Nationalists were
affronted by these mixed marriages because they showed that people
of different nationalities could live happily together. Serbian Nationalists developed a policy of getting rid of mixed marriages, that of,
as Diyana said, 'Either kill them or send them out of the country.
It was easy to get a visa for Australia or America because the Nationalists wanted to get rid of you.'

Diyana was a Serb married to a Muslim and lived in Sarajevo.
After eight months of enduring the siege, Diyana and her small
daughter Sarah were able to join a busload of women and children
leaving the city. They suffered many horrors along the way. Eventually the bus arrived in Split in Croatia. Diyana, like many of the
other women refugees, had friends in Split who would have given
her and her child shelter but this was not allowed. She told me,
'One of my husband's relatives came and paid a policeman to let
me out with the child but he couldn't do anything. I think it was
political. If we get out, we will stay in Croatia and they don't want
refugees in Croatia. And that was the first time I was humiliated as
a refugee.'

She went on, 'There were about a thousand women and a lot of children who had travelled days to get there in buses, without water, without food. The authorities locked us in a new swimming pool complex and let us sleep on the floor. And round the swimming pool were tiles.'

A new swimming pool complex would undoubtedly contain showers, toilets and ample water. The Croatian authorities refused to let these Serbian and Muslim women use them. Diyana said, 'They allowed us four toilets, with a small handbasin to wash hands, and by the time I got to the toilets there was no water and the toilets were very dirty. We were locked in. We couldn't get out. We couldn't get to a pharmacy to buy the things we needed. My daughter had already got gastroenteritis. I developed the most terrible thrush. I'd never experienced such an uncomfortable feeling, and I couldn't do anything about it. It was purely stress, caused by stress, and I couldn't do anything. I didn't have water to wash myself and I was ashamed. I was clean in Sarajevo. You hear stories about humiliation, when you are not allowed to wash yourselves, you are not allowed to change yourself. You soon realize that you stink. Your hands are dirty; you don't have anything to wash them. And it's a humiliation for me, and I don't want to remember. I don't want to think about that, because I always remember those terrible two days.'

Shame is very threatening to our meaning structure because we are held in the eyes of other people and are seen. For our meaning structure to stay whole it needs privacy. Pride, both primitive pride and moral pride, erects barriers so that people cannot peer in, and the barriers become the ways we want to present ourselves to the world. But we are always conscious of the danger of being exposed to shame, no matter how excellent our credentials that we present to the world.

I saw an example of this outside Waterloo International Terminal when I had arrived from Paris on the Eurostar. I hurried to join the queue for taxis. Within seconds there were twenty people behind me in the queue. Immediately ahead of me was a tall, well-dressed man who turned round and, over my head, called his two colleagues further back in the queue to join him. They were also tall and well dressed and the three of them immediately fell into conversation. They were Americans of power and influence either in business or government.

I spoke up, distinctly and sternly. I said, 'I trust that you are all going in the same direction and in the same taxi.'

They looked round at me. One nodded, the others said, 'Er, yes,' and they turned away. I had interrupted a busy conversation but now they fell silent. I thought that was because they were surprised at being reprimanded by a little old lady, but this was not so. It was the silence of shame. They had lied, and within minutes their lie would be revealed.

The queue was at right angles to the line of taxis so I had a clear view of what happened. Our queue shuffled forward as taxis arrived, loaded and departed until the two groups of travellers immediately ahead of the Americans claimed the next two taxis to arrive. As these people were loading their bags the three Americans, keeping close together, walked some ten yards away from me to the next empty taxi. The three of them appeared to be conferring with the driver and then getting into the taxi, but then one of them sneaked away and took the next empty taxi.

I watched and made sure they could see me watching. As his taxi moved past me the one whose lie was now manifest kept his head turned away as if he were deeply interested in the wall on the other side of the road.

No doubt the three of them could deal with their shame by assuring themselves they had only slightly inconvenienced me and the other waiting passengers. There was a long line of empty taxis coming to pick us up. I was amused at their behaviour, and relieved. If they had shown no shame I would have been furious at being outwitted. I was pleased they had shown some shame because in their positions of power and influence their ability to feel shame would help keep them honest. I once worked with a consultant psychiatrist who never felt shame. He would lie in front of people who, he knew, knew that he was lying. His lack of shame frightened and confused those who did have the power to challenge and rebuke him, and so, never being called to account, he could continue to improve his own position while bringing havoc into the lives of others.

Shame might be dangerous to our meaning structure, but it is one of the means by which we can establish and maintain good relationships with other people. We have to take other people's interests into account. But shame is not just a matter of being seen by others. It is also a matter of being seen by ourselves. We can become the viewer and stand naked in our own eyes. In this situation the threat to our meaning structure can be immense and so, knowing this, we can deny ourselves much in order not to be shamed in our own eyes. We can do this in extreme conditions, as Primo Levi recalled:

> I entered the Lager as a non-believer, and as a non-believer I was liberated and have lived to this day; actually, the experience of the Lager with its frightful iniquity has confirmed me in my laity. It has prevented me, and still prevents me, from conceiving of any form of providence or transcendent justice. Why were the moribund packed in cattle cars? Why were children sent to the gas? I must nevertheless admit that I experienced (and again only once) the temptation to yield, to seek refuge in prayer. This happened in the October of 1944, in the one moment in which I lucidly perceived the imminence of death. Naked and compressed among my naked companions with my personal index card in my hand, I was waiting to file past the 'commission' that with one glance would decide whether I should go immediately to the gas chamber or was instead strong enough to go on working. For one instant I felt the need to ask for help and asylum; then, despite my anguish, equanimity prevailed: you do not change the rules of the game at the end of the match, nor when you are losing. A prayer under these conditions would have been not only absurd (what rights could I claim? And from whom?) but blasphemous, obscene, laden with the greatest impiety of which a non-believer is capable. I rejected that temptation: I knew that otherwise were I to survive, I would have to be ashamed of it.[41]

When we act as the other and shame ourselves we become a threat to our own meaning structure. We know what matters most to us, and when we want to criticize ourselves we know what to say to throw the whole meaning structure into doubt. I like to pride myself on being intelligent and well organized. When I took the wrong set of keys and locked myself out of my house my immediate reaction was to say to myself, 'How can you be so stupid?' This is the same phrase I often hurl at the television screen or a newspaper as yet another story of the blind stupidity of those in power or who want to be in power unfolds. This is but one small example of how, although our physiology condemns us to the isolation of our own meaning structure, other people are always part of us.

Others – the Necessity and the Threat

Other people are essential to us because they can confirm our exist-ence. They can break through our essential isolation and confirm our meaning structure. But they can harm and even destroy us by withholding this confirmation. Torturers and jailers the world over know this. In May 1998 Graziella Dalleo was interviewed on the BBC.

> While Argentina hosted the World Cup in 1978 and celebrated its success, many of its citizens were being tortured. Graziella Dalleo was one of Argentina's 'disappeared' at that time. She described the extreme situation in Radio 5's 'Watt in the World – a guide to footballing countries'.
>
> She said, 'Those of us being "re-educated" during the World Cup were allowed to watch the games on TV in the "fish tank" [where hard labour was enforced] . . . After watching the World Cup final in the "fish tank", the commandant of the camp whose name still fills me with terror . . . came in and embraced us one by one and said, "We won! We won!" I remember feeling that if *he's* won we've lost – if this is a victory for him, it is a defeat for us. The guards then told five or six of us to get into a car. I remember it to this day – a green Peugeot 504 – and he drove us to the centre of Buenos Aires. It was incredible.
>
> 'There were so many people out on the street celebrating Argen-tina's victory I asked the general if I could stand up and put my head through the car roof. I stood up and looked out – I couldn't believe what I was seeing. Rivers and rivers of people singing, danc-ing, shouting. I began to cry, because I remember thinking if I start shouting "I've disappeared", no-one's going to give a damn. This was the most concrete proof I ever had that I had ceased to exist.'[42]

Such an experience is not uncommon in those countries where torture is the routine way of dealing with prisoners, especially those who are regarded as a threat to society. Most of us have experienced a milder but still distressing form of torture where our companions have a mental picture of us which bears little likeness to the person we know ourselves to be. When this happens we can feel very, very lonely. When my friend Ann Hocking wrote to me after her dog died she said,

The other evening when I was at a musical evening at the church I saw a man from Mosborough whom I used to know. I said, 'You don't remember me, do you?' He said, 'Yes I do. You're Martin's mother, aren't you?' I said, 'No, I'm Ann.' He shouted across to another mutual acquaintance, a woman, 'Look who's here. Do you remember who she is?' 'Oh yes,' the woman said, 'It's Sarah's grandmother.'

I hate that. When I was little my mother would never use my name. She would say, 'This is my daughter, Jim's sister,' as if I didn't exist in my own right. Now I'm Martin's mother, Ray's wife, or Sarah's grandma. It makes me sick. I've got a name. Why don't people use it?

I guess that's why I miss the dog so much. He would never go away from me. He would never take his eyes off me while he was awake. He didn't care what I looked like or how old I was or that I'd got no job and no money. People want you to try to merit their love all the time. The dog never did, even when I shouted at him. He still loved me. I didn't have to give him breakfast in bed to make up for it. He just accepted me for what I am. People have a lot to learn from dogs.[43]

Ann as Martin's mother, Ray's wife and Sarah's grandma slots her neatly into the working-class suburb of Sheffield where she lives. If her family, friends and acquaintances saw her as she really is she would be constantly confounding their expectations, thus troubling their own meaning structures. She is a mother, wife and grandma, but she is also a skilled artist, a philosopher who asks the big questions and a sharp observer of other people with a keen eye for hypocrisy and lies. I doubt if there is any society who could see her as she is and find her easy to fit in, but there would be certain societies, certain artistic societies, where her individuality would be appreciated.

Ann is a threat to her society only in so far as she does not conform exactly to her society's expectation that she be a modest mother, wife and grandma who complains only about domestic matters and who confines her interests to gossip and television. While she does not fit that picture exactly, her existence does not threaten the image other members of that society have of themselves, as did the existence of the survivors of the Holocaust when they emigrated to Israel after the Second World War. Aaron Hass recorded,

Perhaps the fiercest blow to survivors who emigrated to this hazardous territory was the psychological distance imposed by the sabras (those born in Palestine) . . . Jokes deriding the victims circulated. A popular one began with the question 'How many Jews can you fit into an ashtray?' . . . Far from being perceived as heroes, they were considered reminders of all which the glorious modern Jew must shun. Even among their own, in a Jewish state, survivors were kept from speaking out. In 1949, David Ben-Gurion referred to survivors as 'demoralizing material' who needed to be retrained and imbued with 'national discipline'. A few years later Moshe Sharett, the Israeli foreign minister, declared that survivors were 'undesirable human material' . . .

It was not until the 1960s, spurred by the trial of Adolf Eichmann in Jerusalem, that education about the Holocaust was perceived as desirable by Israeli society. (It took until 1979 for the Holocaust to be introduced as a compulsory subject in Israeli school curricula.) During the Eichmann proceedings, the witnesses whose Holocaust experiences had been silenced for the preceding fifteen years were now asked to render precise account and encouraged to disclose the most horrifying details. Suddenly, the country's leaders realized that this newly acquired consciousness of a common destiny was an invaluable asset in consolidating a national identity and promoting Israel's case abroad.

The primary intent of the Eichmann trial was not punishment. If that were the case, he could have simply been liquidated on Garibaldi Street in Buenos Aires, where he was abducted by the Mossad. Instead, Ben-Gurion's objectives were twofold: (1) to remind the world that the Holocaust obligated support of the State of Israel; and (2) to impress the lessons of the Holocaust, particularly

upon the younger generation of Israelis. What was the most fundamental lesson of the Holocaust from Ben-Gurion's perspective? That
Israel was the only country which could guarantee the security of
the Jews . . .

Events six years later accelerated the humbling process as immediately before the Six Days War in 1967, Israelis felt that they were in
the ghetto under siege. They felt alone and isolated and spoke of
the necessity 'to prevent another Holocaust'. An identification with
the Jews who had been annihilated two decades previously was now
possible.[44]

Perhaps, having at last been given the kind of attention they
needed, some of the Holocaust survivors started to experience the
opposite fear, that attention by others may be so intense that it
threatens to take us over. I once overheard a woman talking about
the way her family had tried to press her into an arranged marriage.
Women relatives who had made arranged marriages assured her
that she would have no difficulty with such a marriage. It was, they
said, just a matter of adjusting. She exclaimed, 'Just adjust! That
would be to die!'

This fear of being taken over, robbed of our will, comes from
our childhood, when the adults around us pressed their ideas on
us, often with considerable force. We knew that if we accepted all
their ideas and relinquished our own we would be annihilated. We
would no longer be a person in our own right. We could not explain
why but we knew that it was imperative that we had secrets and
never became totally obedient.

In our fantasies these adults became figures of power whose only
aim was to take us over and force us to do their bidding. We loved
stories where the small hero or heroine, through cleverness, courage
and daring, defeats the powerful enemy. Then we discovered that
the adults around us also feared some inscrutable, powerful enemy.
It might be the devil, or witches, or a force of evil, or spirits which
could turn a man into a zombie. We might be told how Nazism or
Communism took people over and turned them into automatons.
During the Korean War of the fifties the term 'brainwashing' was
created, as if brains could be washed clean of thoughts and new
thoughts implanted. Stories about aliens from outer space abounded.
Television was seen to threaten to take us over, and then computers

and the Internet were expected to pose the same threat. Meanwhile popular series like *Star Trek* and *The X-Files* told stories about people who fall into the hands of some alien power and cease to be themselves. The central factor in all these scenarios is that the person cannot comprehend and relate to the thought processes of some alien power and consequently loses the power to think for himself. Survivors might have been released by the alien power, but more often have to work out the alien power's secret before they can escape.

The fear of being taken over by an alien power is one of the disadvantages of possessing consciousness. Being conscious might allow us to create a much wider range of meanings and to be more flexible in our techniques for maintaining the coherence of our meaning structure, but it also means that we know just how alone we are. Moreover, we have some awareness that our sense of self is not a solid thing but a fragile structure entirely dependent on the accuracy of its representations of reality for its stability and permanence. This awareness of the fragility of our meaning structure reveals itself in the words we use when we feel that our meaning structure or that of someone else is in danger of collapsing. We say, 'Get a grip on yourself,' or, 'Pull yourself together,' or 'I'm falling apart.'

As life evolved on this planet there were many forms and functions of forms which evolved and then disappeared. Evolutionary biologists and psychologists argue that those forms and functions which persist did so because they were useful. The psychologist Nicholas Humphrey suggested that we developed consciousness in order to work out what other people were thinking, and so be able to predict what they were going to do. Consciousness allows us to know what we are thinking, and so we can use our own experiences to guess what is going on in other people's heads. But it is always a guess. We can never be sure. Consciousness is always private.

Susan Greenfield argues that consciousness in a baby comes on slowly like a dimmer switch on a light being turned on. However, the process of consciousness lighting up is also the process of being involved with other people.

Babies are born being interested in faces, human voices and what people do. The psychologist Dr D. Premack argues from his research that a baby is born with what he calls two 'innately specified causal predicates', one which allows the perception of 'non-self-propelled objects' (something has to happens to an object for it to move) and one which allows the perception of 'self-propelled motion of biological beings' (humans and animals choosing to move). Babies find the movements of human beings much more interesting than the movements of objects.[45] They would rather be propped up in their basket watching Mum get dinner than be lying in their cot looking at a mobile.

The ability to distinguish people from objects quickly develops into the ability to project on to objects and on to animals the characteristics of humans. For young children toys become people, and these people can comfort and support the child. They become immensely important when adults around the child fail to do so.

I watched a television programme about dolls in which one woman, Catherine, now sixty-four years old, talked about her doll Sailor Boy. She had been born into a family which did not want her. She was the youngest and her siblings all rejected her. Her mother was a distant figure and her father an authoritarian whom she feared. She was looked after by nannies and servants. The only person she could talk to was Sailor Boy. He understood her feelings. One evening she had Sailor Boy close to her while she was being given supper in the kitchen. The room was hot from the range oven and she wasn't feeling well. Her father came into the room, and in her sudden fear she vomited over Sailor Boy. Her father, a fastidious man, immediately ordered the nanny to put Sailor Boy in the fire. The nanny took the poker, lifted the lid above the fire and thrust Sailor Boy in. He blazed up and was gone. As she told her story Catherine showed that she was still mourning Sailor Boy, but she finished her story by saying that some time later she was able to get another Sailor Boy and she has him with her to this day.

Toys and pets can listen and appear to understand, but, alas, they cannot talk. We can imagine them talking, but, because what they say is what we have imagined, they cannot surprise us as real people do. We can imagine our toys and pets saying things which support, comfort and confirm us, but only other human beings can show that our wish to be supported, comforted and confirmed has been fulfilled in reality and not just in fantasy.

Language is a social activity. Indeed, according to the psychologist Robin Dunbar, we evolved language because we wanted to gossip.[46] When we evolved language we were already communicating in the way animals do by touch and gesture. Robin Dunbar has made a special study of how primates communicate. He wrote,

> A light touch, a gentle caress, can convey all the meanings in the world: one moment it can be a word of consolation, an apology, a request to be groomed, an invitation to play; on another, an assertion of privilege, a demand you move elsewhere; on yet another, a calming influence, a declaration that intentions are friendly. Knowing which meaning to infer is the basis of social being, depending as it does on a close reading of another's mind. In that brief moment of mutual understanding in a fast-moving, frenzied world, all social life is distilled in a single gesture.[47]

This reminded me of an incident that occurred when I was in Hanoi in Vietnam. I had just left a shop when I felt on my right shoulder blade a touch which was as soft as silk yet with the power to draw my immediate attention. I looked round, and there was a little old woman dressed in black, her hand cupped in supplication. A soft touch for someone she hoped was a soft touch.

Primates spend much of their time touching one another in mutual grooming. Being groomed is very pleasant because it stimulates the body's natural endorphins. In a group of primates grooming is one of the chief means whereby alliances are formed and hierarchies within the group established.

However, grooming takes time. Human groups were much bigger than primate groups so required a more efficient means of grooming. Through language we can groom more people and be groomed by more people. Language makes social interaction more efficient. Hence its evolution.

Psychologists have always unwisely divided their subject into individual psychology and social psychology, but now they are coming to understand what sociologists and anthropologists have always understood – that, as my friend and colleague David Canter said, 'the essence of humanity is in interactions between people in groups.' The profession of psychology virtually came into existence with society's need to understand why some people think more quickly, accurately and creatively than most other people. Psychologists invented the notion of intelligence and claimed it was a measurable thing lodged inside each person and genetically inherited. In 1999

Ken Richardson, a psychologist who had studied intelligence for many years, demonstrated in his book *The Making of Intelligence*[48] that human organizations require what he calls 'sensitivity to hyper-structural information' – that is, knowledge of how knowledge is organized, of how knowledge of knowledge organization is organized, and so on. Professor David Canter, reviewing Robinson's book, concluded that 'Intelligence is a sophisticated creation of social inter-actions embedded in particular cultures, not the genetic endowment of any individual.'[49] Knowledge of how knowledge is organized and so on is a matter of interpreting interpretations and so on. The more quickly, accurately and creatively we can interpret other people's interpretations the more intelligent we are.

What are we usually doing when we are interpreting other people's interpretations? We are gossiping. We tell one another stories. Such stories are not just for entertainment or for imparting information. They are for managing reputation, for determining the place each of us occupies in society. What better story than one which besmirches your enemy's reputation and enhances your own? No wonder that the media thrive on gossip. No wonder the activity which combines both gossip and grooming – hairdressing – is so popular.

However, while we use language to communicate with others, our communications are never completely accurate and unambiguous. While we might all speak the language of the society we live in, no two of us use that language in exactly the same way. We use the same language but the meanings we hold for those words are different. Two people might agree that the word 'Christmas' refers to 25 December, but for one person the connotations of Christmas are entirely religious while for the other person Christmas means fun and family. To discover the similarities and differences in our meaning structure we have to talk to one another.

We are indeed peculiar people, with a language which simul-taneously brings us together and pushes us apart. This is but one facet of the peculiarity which is our essence. Our physiology deter-mines that we should live in isolation in our own world of meaning, yet our world of meaning is elicited and maintained by the presence of other people. At the same time other people can always threaten our world of meaning. To survive we have to find ways of main-taining our identity while being a member of a group.

3

Belonging to a Group

Meeting someone for the first time and wondering whether you are going to be friends can be stressful, but how do you manage when you meet a crowd of people and you are all going to be together for some time? I felt extremely anxious when I sat in the domestic air terminal in Athens and wondered which of the people around me were going to be the participants in the group I was to run at the Skyros Centre on the island of Skyros.

Ten days later, when I knew and liked my group very much, I asked one of them, Janna, how she had fared in meeting all the people who would be at the centre. I had travelled to Skyros on a small plane a day early and so had met the staff and some of the participants in twos and threes, but Janna, who was travelling on her own, making the long journey by coach and ferry with those bound for either the Skyros Centre or its twin centre Atsitsa, was presented with what she saw first of all as 'an amorphous mass of people'.

Janna told me, 'It was quite a stressful time because you don't know these people, and you're wondering who's going to be in your group and all that. Then I ended up sharing a room with Inger, and that's been great. But that amorphous mass I experienced mostly at breakfast and the first few meals. People seemed to talk so much. There was a heightened state of chatting. I'm not sure what that was. I think it's because we all wanted to engage with other people. There were gales of hysterical laughter which happened a lot. It was very noisy, which, certainly at the beginning, made it seem as though there was a huge body of people.'

I had experienced this 'heightened state of chatting' when I went on several game drives in the African bush with a group of American tourists. There were nine of us, including the ranger, who drove our vehicle, and the tracker, who rode shotgun. The great silence of the African bush was there to be savoured, but savour it we did not because everyone except the tracker and me talked all the time. The ranger made no idle conversation. He informed us about what we were seeing, and answered every question, no matter how inane or repeated it was, in a courteous and informative way, but around him words were being wasted at a prodigious rate. My fellow tourists bombarded the ranger with questions which might be about matters of detail but were rarely profound. One woman asked, 'Do people ride zebras?' and, on being told that zebras were untameable, commented, 'What a pity. They'd be so colourful at a rodeo.' When the questions were exhausted the tourists engaged one another in earnest chat on a wide variety of impersonal topics. I found it bizarre being driven through this magically alien bush while behind me the conversation was about the relative merits of certain e-mail servers.

But, of course, it was the alien bush that was the problem. *I* might have had faith in my ranger and the game reserve's system of constant radio communication but my companions did not. So they talked to one another to keep their fear at bay. The same thing happened when, one evening after a very hot day, a fierce but very beautiful electrical storm converged on our camp. Dinner for some twenty tourists was being served on the veranda, where the noise of conversation all but drowned out the thunder.

One way of dealing with fear is to turn it into a story, a fantasy about what is feared and how that fear might be overcome. On the third of our game drives my companions did just this. One of them was a literary agent, and he began developing an idea for a novel about a group of people who are on a game drive in this very same park when, for some reason, the ranger and the tracker disappear. How would these people survive?

This was the nub of the fear they were feeling. They were a group of professional people and therefore useless if left to fend for themselves in this bush full of dangerous animals. They needed a fantasy to assure themselves that, if abandoned by the ranger, they could survive.

Their fear was not just about abandonment in this alien place. It also had to do with the hierarchies in the group. In the conversations amongst the tourists not just on the drives but over meals there was constant jockeying for position. Evidence of position, power and wealth was cunningly presented by being implied not just in their statements about their nationality and work but also in the extensiveness of their travels. 'When we were in Botswana' could be topped by 'We much preferred Namibia to Botswana'. Such conversations were not merely to improve one's position in the hierarchy. Along with the conversations about cameras and computers the conversations were aimed at showing that the person speaking was knowledgeable and in control.

The rangers were well aware of this. One of them told me, 'The South Africans are the worst. They always want to make out that they know more than the ranger.' A hierarchy might be established over dinner with, say, a captain of industry or a judge claiming superiority, but such a hierarchy would be thrown into doubt the next morning, when the ranger became the leader on whom the tourists' lives depended. This was a particular problem for some of the people in the group which I had joined. They did not like being dependent on a twenty-two-year-old, no matter how skilled and conscientious he was, and one of them at least made sure that before he departed he had patronized our ranger and reasserted his authority to his satisfaction, even though it meant being offensive to his hosts. This man had built his identity – his meaning structure – on being a powerful leader. No matter what the reality of the situation was, he could not cope with feeling helpless and dependent.

At the game park tourists came and went every two or three days so the groups and the hierarchies existed only briefly. At the Skyros Centre twelve of us had committed ourselves to being together for two weeks, so forming a group and sorting out hierarchies and allegiances was tremendously important. None of us had ever met before so it was very much a matter of stepping into the unknown.

When Janna was a university student she had recognized that she had anxieties in joining a group. Like most extraverts she had feared that, as she saw alliances being made, she would be left out completely. She said, 'Everybody else might come together and I'll be the one on their own.' However, she discovered that 'Things do shake down and you find yourself with the kind of person you want to be with.' Years later, at work or when she went on retreats, she realized that this was always the case. She knew that out of that amorphous crowd of people one or two would emerge with whom she would connect straight away. When she met a number of people for the first time they had for her a certain 'feeling tone' which grouped certain people together, and then out of these groups individuals emerged. At Skyros someone who stood out immediately became a close friend. Janna told me, 'Sandra and I connected up early on. We laughed a lot together, so that's a good start. And she had interesting things to say. So it's a take on the world. That's what I'm looking for, I suppose, an interesting take on the world, which is maybe complementary or different to mine.'

Understanding how we operate in groups is not easy. Robin Dunbar, in his book about language and gossip, commented, 'It's now clear that understanding the social world is a far more difficult task for children to master than understanding the physical world.'[1] Adults have the same problem. It is much easier to understand the physical world than the social world because we can separate ourselves from the physical world and observe its behaviour. In the social world we might like to think that we can separate ourselves from other people and observe their behaviour but there is one crucial difference. When I observe the workings of an internal combustion engine that engine is not observing me and forming ideas about me. When I run a workshop and observe the behaviour of the participants they are busy observing me and one another, forming interpretations and adjusting their behaviour accordingly. We do not just interpret one another's behaviour, we interpret one another's interpretations, and so on.

My workshop which Janna had joined was about how we make sense of the social world, but, of course, while I was trying to give the participants some tools for understanding their social world, their actual social worlds were evolving and changing. Each of us entered that workshop at a certain point in our life story. Initially each of us was drawn to the people whose life story had some features similar to our own, what Janna called 'a take on the world', but this disparate collection of people turned into a group because they listened to each other's stories and saw similarities and contrasts with their own story. With this the group gelled. Once this had happened no one left the group and no outsider was allowed to join. We knew that the group would fragment at the end of the fortnight, but while we were at Skyros we stuck together and enjoyed the security of the group.

We like to think that belonging to a particular group will give us a sense of security, but groups, like everything else in the universe, are changing all the time. A group of friends have life stories which overlap and intertwine, but as time passes the stories change, both in their present circumstances and in their expectations. Then the group might not survive. A television documentary on BBC2 called *Modern Times: Friends*[2] captured some of the tensions in a group of friends who, as thirtysomethings, led a very enjoyable social life. Now the threat and the promise of marriage loomed. One man said, 'It's difficult for men. The pressure is on for men to stay a player for as long as possible. There used to be pressure to marry and settle down. Now the pressure is to stay a player.'

Another man said that his friends are 'a big cushion behind you all the time. If you fail yourself you've got these friends to back you up.'

One woman said of her boyfriend, 'He uses the group of friends as a marker. That's made it difficult for me to move on in our relationship as I would like.'

The men showed a great need to hang on to their youth. They were unable to decide whether this period of their life was over and that they must move on. The women knew it was time to move on. They were strong and wanted children, and they could, and probably would, inveigle the men into getting married and settling down, but if they did this they were likely to be dissatisfied because their man had not made the decision to change himself but had merely drifted, tugged along by her. He had shown himself, in the last analysis, to be weak, indecisive, childish, and in time she might come to despise him.

How easily a man goes from being 'a player' to being 'a married man' depends on how he defines 'a player' and 'a married man'. Does he define 'a player' as 'what a man should always be' or as 'a good experience, but something you have to grow out of'?

How we define our groups determines what we do in them.

Defining Yourself and Your Group

To know something we have to know its opposite. To define something we have to define what is not that something. Thus we define
our groups in terms of those who are excluded from them. The
group 'golfers' is defined by those who do not play golf. If everybody
played golf we would not need a group called 'golfers'. We do not
talk about 'breathers' because everybody who is alive breathes but
we do talk about 'drivers' because not everyone drives a car. When
asked to define Britain the film-maker Terry Jones said, 'We are
set apart as Britons by our lack of French-ness, German-ness or
Italian-ness.'³

No doubt, if asked to list the groups to which we belong, each
of us could produce quite a few. However, some of these groups
would be no more than collections of people with whom we
occasionally spend some time while other groups would be an integral part of our identity. These groups are usually those of gender,
family, race, religion and nationality, but all these categories are not
necessarily applicable to everyone. If someone calls me an atheist I
can only reply that I am an atheist only in the same way as I am
an 'a-fairy-ist' or an 'a-Father-Christmas-ist'. When the broadcaster
Jon Snow was asked if he was British he said, 'I think that Britishness
has died off in my lifetime and nothing has replaced it. When I was
a child it was Winston Churchill, beefeaters and lots of pink on the
globe. Now it's an irrelevant concept. Personally, I'm a Londoner
living in Europe.'⁴

The groups which we join only transiently we can usually define
very simply – 'the crowd I drink with on Friday nights', 'the people
who live in my street', 'the guys with me at college', but the groups
which are part of our identity, while they might have simple labels
like 'Church of England' or 'Australian', have complex definitions
which are difficult to make entirely explicit. 'Australian' might mean
anyone who carried an Australian passport but it also means a wide
range of different attributes. Recently my son sent me two videos
made by the Australian Broadcasting Commission. One was the film
The Castle, a funny, sentimental story about a family whose home
was to be requisitioned for an airport extension, and the other a set
of four episodes of the satirical series *Frontline* about a television

current affairs team in Melbourne. The family whose home was their castle were all loving, kind, tolerant and simple-minded to the point of stupidity. The television team were murderously competitive, hurtful and cynical, with an intelligence used only for self-interest. Yet both the film and the series were an accurate representation of what I would recognize as Australian.

A complex definition of our group allows us to align ourselves with certain aspects of our group and to distance ourselves from other aspects. We can claim to have all the virtues of our group and none of the vices. Primitive pride can make good use of this ploy whenever certain events threaten our meaning structure. Primitive pride is not wedded to truth or logic, and so, as the Truth and Reconciliation Commission in South Africa revealed more and more of the abuses of the apartheid era, those who had benefited from that era did not reject their group but continued to claim its virtues while denying that they ever knew that such atrocities had occurred. When F. W. de Klerk was in the UK to promote his autobiography he told BBC Radio Four listeners that, on the one hand, his government had done much to promote the welfare of blacks and, on the other hand, he had known nothing of what happened at Vlakplaas, a farm near Pretoria which was used as a base for police hit squads. He had to admit that he had known of the existence of Vlakplaas but he thought it was simply a place where ANC activists were 'turned round'. The assassins of Vlakplaas were unruly elements who wanted to keep their activities secret from him.[5]

The chutzpah of primitive pride in action can often leave onlookers flabbergasted. They are unable to point out to the exponent of such pride that every idea we hold, every meaning that we create, has bad implications as well as good. De Klerk might claim ignorance of what was going on in the country of which he was President, but this has the bad implication that he was not doing his job properly. People were acting in his name, and so he was responsible for the matters of which he claimed ignorance.

However, many people feel that it is better to be charged with incompetence than to be charged with wickedness. By saying, 'I'm just a poor, fallible human being trying to do my best,' we can show humility and contrition while taking pride in our humility and contrition. We are all extremely skilled at reinterpreting events in order to hold our meaning structure together.

One area where we frequently redefine is that of responsibility. Like de Klerk, we can deny responsibility for events for which we were clearly responsible, or we can claim responsibility for events over which in fact we had no control. Such a redefinition, the writer and biologist Barbara Ehrenreich surmises, could be at the beginning of our concepts of sacrifice and religion.

When, some 100,000 years ago, our species first emerged it was into a world dominated by large animals. We were small creatures, much smaller than we are today, and we were prey to the beasts. It took us many thousands of years to develop tools to defend ourselves. Artificial fire-making and action-at-a-distance weapons like the bow and arrow were not invented until some 15,000 years ago.

Only then did we turn ourselves from prey to predator. However, the fear of being prey is still very much with us. Barbara Ehrenreich pointed out that grief, depression and helplessness are the experiences of those who are prey. It seems from the research on phobias that people much more readily develop fears of spiders or snakes than they do of cars or guns, even though in a modern world people are much more likely to be killed by cars and guns than they are by spiders or snakes. The psychiatrists Isaac Marks and Randolph Nesse regard panic disorders, phobias and chronic anxiety as evolutionary adaptations to an environment which required human beings to be very readily alarmed at the possibility of danger.[6] Fear serves to keep us alive.

This fear not only drove us to flight or fight but also inspired our ancestors to devise ways of outwitting the powerful beasts. They would have noted that the beast was often satisfied with just one kill. They might have reasoned that if they gave the beast some food, even if the food was one of them, the rest of the group might be spared. Thus the idea of appeasing a great power with a sacrifice could have been born, and then flourished as an integral part of the ritual of religion. The idea of sacrifice allows us to reconstrue a disaster over which we had no control as a sacrifice which we had chosen to make. Barbara Ehrenreich considered the possibility that

Sacrifice, in its most archaic form, was not a ritual at all, but a face-saving euphemism for death by predation. Perhaps no victims were ever thrown to the wolves or lions, but it somehow pleased our hominid ancestors to think of those who died in the jaws of predators as victims voluntarily offered up by the group.[7]

The concepts of prey and predator, sacrifice and appeasement are still today central to the way in which we define the groups with which we identify. We might no longer think of ourselves as prey to the beasts of the African savannah, but in the economic jungle we're either the exploited or the exploiter.[8] Modern religions might not demand blood sacrifices, but the belief in the importance of sacrifice still operates powerfully. In Hinduism, as recounted in the *Rig-Veda,* the entire world is a result of a sacrifice by the gods. All Christian churches remind the faithful that Christ sacrificed himself for them, and, in all religions, the faithful are reminded of the necessity of personal humility and abasement.

The concepts of prey, predator and sacrifice are central to our definition of the group because they are central to our experience of being an individual in a group. In the hierarchy of the group we might have enough power to prey on others and force them to make sacrifices, but each of us started life as small and weak and at the mercy of people around us, so even the most powerful know what it is to be prey. This is one of the reasons why the powerful usually hate to relinquish power.

The concepts of predator, prey and sacrifice have both good and bad implications. To be prey is bad, but if there is a power strong enough to prey on us it might also be strong enough to look after us. The beasts which preyed on our ancient ancestors also provided our ancestors with much of their food. They could scavenge the kills made by the beasts. Thus a sacrifice was both an appeasement and a reward. A savage god might be appeased by a sacrifice and coaxed into generosity. Throw in a few hymns of praise and the prey might be safe.

Being the predator has its disadvantages too. If the prey becomes an enemy the predator can become prey. When our ancestors turned from being prey to being predators, the most successful predators the world has ever seen, they remained mindful of the dangers of being a predator. It was not just a matter of being mindful of the dangers of having an enemy. To become too strong, too powerful as an individual, was to invite retaliation either by the gods or by the group. The Greek gods punished anyone who displayed hubris, while every group developed its own way of punishing those who were not mindful of the necessity of humility. In Australia, as they say, tall poppies get cut down, in Japan the nail that sticks up gets hammered down, while the English quietly damn those who are too clever by half. A popular group pleasure is that of schadenfreude, the joy felt at the spectacle of someone who has flown too high being brought down to earth.

Thus the group constantly presents us with a conflict between pride and humility. We need pride, both moral pride and primitive pride, to maintain our individuality. Too much humility threatens our meaning structure because humility requires us to value other people's ideas more than our own. Most of us deal with this conflict by developing ways of appearing to be humble while privately maintaining our pride. However, this is merely a tactic. The overall strategy is always problematic because this strategy is always about justice.

Every meaning structure, left to itself, would seek to make the entire universe conform to its expectations and demands. In real life other meaning structures get in its way and spoil its plans. Every meaning structure has to compromise, and the compromise always has to do with justice. The idea of justice is essential to the maintenance of the meaning structure. Long before a child can utter the words, 'It's not fair!' the child will demonstrate the anger we all feel when life is not fair to us.

Life is rarely fair. We do not mind that when we are the ones benefiting from its unfairness, but when we feel hard done by we want justice. We want this justice to be applied to all the trades we do with other people. These might be trades in goods or services, or simply in feelings. We can believe that 'If I am patient with you, you must be patient with me,' or 'If I love you, you must love me.' Sacrifice is a trade. 'I give you this offering. Now you must benefit me.'

Every group develops its own rules or laws about justice. Our ancestors lived in small bands which, as the centuries passed, swelled into or came together as a tribe. Tribal law could deal with goods and services trades between people and sort out some of the issues which arise in relationships, but it could not deal with disasters which were beyond the control of the tribe. A brave man who had led a blameless life might die in an avalanche, a good wife and mother might die in childbirth, or the tribe itself might be threatened with starvation by an unforeseen change in the climate. How can such disasters be explained? How can good people be recompensed and rewarded? How can the wicked who go beyond tribal law be punished?

Now the meaning structure's great capacity for fantasy could come into play. What if there was a law of justice greater than the tribe, something that covered the land, sea and sky which the tribe knew and beyond to realms which could only be imagined? What if this justice decreed that ultimately all people get their just deserts. The good are rewarded and the bad are punished. Thus the idea of the Just World was born.

It seems that all tribes at some point in their existence arrived at the idea of a Just World. In their imaginations what that Just World looked like was different for different people, and so a vast number of religions came into being, each with its own story which gave a meaning to death and the purpose of life, and an explanation of why suffering exists.[9] The supreme power which administered universal justice took on the features of those who had conjured it into being, and its abode took on the features of the territory the conjurers inhabited. The practices of tribal law were enlarged and elaborated to become the practices of the universal power, and the rewards and punishments of tribal law were transformed into universal rewards and punishments whose enactment might take an instant or an eternity. However terrible and mysterious the power might be, weak, frail humans could know that they were secure provided they were good.

But what was 'good'? The power might demand absolute belief and constant praise, and the tribe might have rules about good behaviour, but what was good enough? What was an adequate sacrifice – one virgin or twenty? Would a smidgen of doubt about the existence or competence of the Almighty cast you into hellfire for ever? If you coveted your neighbour's wife but did not act on your thought did that make you a good person or a bad person?

You could spend your life trying to be a good person and still be struck by disaster. Did that mean that you had not tried hard enough and this was your punishment? Or had there been some failure in the system of justice and you had been treated most unfairly? Or had the suffering been sent to try you and, if you suffered expertly enough, would you get your reward? The highly talented but severely disabled actor, film-maker and broadcaster Nabil Shaban told how

> Many disabled friends have admitted to me they think they are disabled as a punishment. My own mother told me I was born disabled because I had been very bad in my past life – and that, if I continued to be an atheist, I would be in an even worse position in my next life . . . When I was working in Calcutta on the movie *City of Joy*, an old Hindu hotel porter every time he saw me would bow. Eventually he told me I was a god. What he meant was that my being born disabled was not a curse but a divine blessing as I would end this life a spiritually stronger person than someone who didn't have to suffer as I did, and would come closer to God and end my cycle of lives and achieve Nirvana.[10]

Fertile though our imagination might be in creating scenarios which we hope will give us security, such scenarios always produce as many problems as they were created to solve. The same has happened in the financial world, where 'products' were conjured into being to give us financial security – banks, insurance, pensions, futures and options – only to produce new and worse kinds of insecurity.[11] Where religion is concerned it would seem best to choose the set of beliefs which would give you personally the greatest chance of happiness – provided nothing happened to you to confound your choice. However, not many of us are given the opportunity to exercise such choice. Jean Said Makdisi, who recorded her life in Beirut during the religious and political war there, was brought up as a Christian but, as she said, 'I think of Islam as part – a large part – of my inheritance and revere it as such.' However, as Lebanon was being increasingly segregated according to religion, she wrote,

> I have felt repeatedly that religion has worked like a stamp with which cattle are branded . . .
> And so are we all, like it or not, branded with the hot iron of our religious ancestry. Believers and nonbelievers alike, struggle though we may, we are being corralled into the separate yards of our fellow coreligionists by the historic events of the moment. Belief and political vision have less to do with how one is seen, and

then is forced to see oneself, than with external identification – the brand.[12]

Most of us are born into a religious group and much of our early education is concerned with learning the tenets of that religion. Muslim children have to memorize the Koran while Jewish children study the Torah, and, while they can ask questions in order to increase their understanding of the holy books, they are not allowed to question the veracity of the books themselves. Catholic, Protestant and Orthodox Christian children are taught that God sees everything they do and will reward or punish them accordingly. In those homes where the adults speak of their god or gods in the same way as they speak of a revered but absent grandparent, the idea of a deity can become for the child as firm and fixed as the meanings the child has created about his parents.

The neural connections which underlie these ideas must for some children at least become firm and fixed. I have met a large number of people who have told me that, although they had been given a religious education, in adulthood they had rejected or drifted away from religion only to find that when they became depressed all the shame, guilt and fear which their religious education brought them in their childhood had returned to haunt them. The brand was still on their hide. Some of these people were determined to resolve the conflict between their sense of who they were now and the demands of their childhood religious beliefs. They challenged these beliefs, changed them into beliefs which gave them courage and optimism, and ended their depression. Others dared not challenge their child-hood beliefs and so remained depressed.[13]

Religion might have had its origins in the search for justice, but it was justice for the tribe, not for all human beings. Religious groups, like all groups, define themselves in terms of who is excluded. Matt Ridley in his study *The Origins of Virtue* wrote,

The universalism of the modern Christian message has tended to obscure an obvious fact about religious teaching – that it has almost always emphasized the difference between the in-group and the out-group: us versus them; Israelite and Philistine; Jew and Gentile; saved and damned; believer and heathen; Arian and Athanasian; Catholic and Orthodox; Protestant and Catholic; Hindu and

Muslim; Sunni and Shia. Religion teaches its adherents that they are the chosen race and their nearest rivals are benighted fools or even subhumans.[14]

The wickedness of those excluded from the religious group has to be emphasized by the group's leaders in order to deter any of their flock from straying. During my Presbyterian upbringing I heard much about the wickedness of the Catholics. Nowadays we often hear about ecumenicalism, and in public the clerics of different religions are polite to one another. In private ideas might not have changed that much.

At a refugee centre in London I met Father Rossi, a Catholic priest from Italy, who told me about the wickedness, not of the Protestants, but of the Italians from southern Italy. I asked him about the current situation in the debate on whether the northern states of Italy should secede from the south. He said quietly but very firmly, 'It's not likely but it should happen.' He told me that he was from the north. He spoke of the south with bitterness and hatred. 'They should be left to themselves, cut off from the north completely.' He spoke of the corruption in the bureaucracy, politics and the police. 'Every manager's chair,' he said, 'is filled with someone from the south.' (My parents used to talk about how a Catholic church and presbytery always occupied the best land in any Australian town.) He showed none of the tolerance and forbearance which many Christians like to think are peculiarly their own.

I remembered my conversation with my Italian friends Lorenzo and Magdalena when they, devout Catholics, told me that Italy is no longer a Catholic country.[15] I asked Father Rossi, 'Is Italy a Catholic country?' He replied immediately, 'No, it is not.' In asking him why it had changed I spoke of how the school system was now predominantly a state system where religion was an optional subject. I saw this as part of the explanation why Italy was no longer a Catholic country, but he saw this as the effect of a deeper cause, which was the work of the Devil.

I asked him if he was speaking literally or metaphorically. His answer was quite unambiguous. The Devil is real, and the Italian people had been seduced by him. The Devil, he said, cannot make people do things but he can suggest things, and people can be too weak to resist these suggestions. He hated the Devil and he hated southern Italians. His defence against the Devil was exorcism. 'I am an exorcist,' he said. So the Devil must be exorcized and the southern Italians driven from the north and confined in the south. Italy should be two nations, north and south.

The schools, he explained to me, had ceased to teach history, philosophy and religion, and instead taught frivolous subjects like screen printing. Without a knowledge of history, philosophy and religion people were rendered vulnerable to the blandishments of the Devil. I thought, but politely did not say, that the history, philosophy and religion he wanted taught in the schools would be those versions which are approved of by the Catholic Church. In his view, not believing what the Catholic Church teaches is evidence of being seduced by the Devil.

Implicit in Father Rossi's definition of Catholics and non-Catholics are ideas which clearly relate to national groups. Indeed, our religious and our national groups can overlap markedly in the characteristics we give them and in what we want to get out of them. Chiefly what we want from our groups is support for our meaning structures. According to Jean Said Makdisi, being forcibly labelled as belonging to a certain group is a terrible insult to a person's individuality. Mamphela Ramphele found sustenance from both her political and religious beliefs through her darkest days as a political activist under apartheid, but she saw a similarity between religious and activist communities. She wrote,

As in the case of religious conviction, political activists are moved by something greater than themselves – a belief in a future which might be better than the present, a desire to be engaged in the establishment of a better order, and compassion for the underdog. Secondly, they share a sense of fellowship with others who are similarly committed. The need for renewing such fellowship in ritualized meetings – church services or political gatherings of the faithful – is also a common feature . . .

Then again there is a common desire of individual members of such communities to conform to the group. The more fundamentalist the tendency, and the more insecure the community feels, the more likely conformity will be enforced . . .

The willingness of individuals to sacrifice or subordinate their personal ambitions or goals for the sake of the group is also a notable similarity. This tendency is often closely tied to a willingness to engage in communal sacrificial acts, either symbolic or involving actual physical violence. Such sacrificial violence is sometimes justified as an important and necessary act to contain communal violence by focusing it on a sacrificial victim. Some of the most gruesome necklace murders [killing a victim by setting alight a motor-car tyre filled with petrol which is placed around the person's neck] committed by political activists in the 1980s involved the sacrificial death of fellow activists suspected of disloyalty.[16]

Whenever we identify with a group we immediately put ourselves in jeopardy of being expelled from the group. As children we discovered how painful this could be when other children refused to play with us, or when our parents, in order to discipline us, threatened that we would be expelled from the family. In our teens our peers became very important to us, and our happiness depended on being accepted by them. A pair of shoes or a certain haircut could put our meaning structure under threat because we had failed to conform to our group.

Because the group demands conformity individuals must adapt their meaning structure to what the group sees as the correct set of ideas. For some people this is a serious threat to the integrity of their meaning structure, while for others just about any change is acceptable because they value the security and support which the group gives them above all else. However, the group itself might not be secure because it is under attack from other groups. Then, as Mamphela Ramphele pointed out, conformity is likely to be enforced.

In such a situation the fear of being prey comes to the fore. The group then can create a defensive solidarity, not just against the outside enemy but against a member of the group. Coming together to sacrifice a scapegoat can produce in the group what Barbara Ehrenreich called 'a burst of fear-dissolving strength'.[17]

The choice of a scapegoat is never random though it might be mistaken. The scapegoat is someone who is considered to have betrayed the group; the punishment will serve as a warning to those group members whose loyalty to the group might be less than absolute.

To many whites in South Africa necklace murders were simply utter barbarism, acts of mindless violence which showed that the

blacks were incapable of governing themselves. Such an interpretation maintained the whites' sense of superiority and thus their own
meaning structure, but it failed to take account of how all actions,
whether peaceful or murderous, arise from the way in which the
participants have interpreted the situation.

William Finnegan is an American journalist who, in the eighties,
spent long periods in South Africa, where he worked with black
journalists. He recounted the story of Ruth, a secretary in her forties
who lived in the township of Alexandra. She told him about her
background: her teenage son had been jailed without charges for
three months.

For the first month she had not known where he was, or even
whether he was alive: many mothers were simply informed by the
authorities that their children were dead and already buried; others
never heard. 'When he was released there was something wrong
with his heart,' she told me. 'The police struck him too many times.
The doctor told me he must not get excited. But how can you tell
a seventeen-year-old boy that he must not get excited? Especially
with all that is happening to us now.' Ruth's son was on the run.
She saw him occasionally when he came home for a change of
clothes, and friends of his who were also running sometimes slept
at her house. But the police came regularly, bursting in, hoping to
find her son, and seizing any other comrades they found there. 'I
have not slept properly for a year or more,' Ruth said, and I believed
her.

The conversation then moved on to a recent incident when a
woman who had been informing for the police was caught and
necklaced. William Finnegan wrote,

Ruth turned to me and said, emphasizing every word, 'I think the
necklace is a good thing.' Her eyes were full of strange, sad anger.
She went on, 'It makes people think twice before they will collabor-
ate, even if they have no job and the system offers them money to
inform. We are unarmed. They are armed. We must take and use
what little weapons we have. Informers have been the system's greatest weapon for a very long time. Finally, now, we are stopping
them.'[18]

There is no way of knowing how the woman who was caught informing interpreted the events which followed, but, just as the act of necklacing can be interpreted in at least two different ways, so the act of being scapegoated can be interpreted in at least three different ways, each then having a different effect on the meaning structure of the victim.

Victims might accept the verdict of the group and believe themselves to be wicked and deserving the inevitable punishment. This punishment might be viewed with utter dread because it is ultimate and for ever, a hellfire from which no escape is possible. Or the punishment might be seen as an expiation of sins; out of such hellfires the person will be redeemed. Both primitive pride and moral pride may prefer the second interpretation.

Victims might see themselves as unjustly charged and the punishment totally undeserved. This may well be the case. Groups are not infallible. Or it might be that primitive pride has come to the fore, determined to maintain a sense of feeling good about yourself no matter what the evidence against you. After the people of the Philippines deposed President Marcos, who had enriched himself at the expense of his country, his wife Imelda demonstrated that she was a past mistress of this kind of interpretation. She always insisted that everything she did was for the good of her people and that she was, actually, very poor, despite the fact that she still lived in a most luxurious fashion.

Choosing the 'I am innocent' interpretation can arouse in the person great anger and resentment and even paranoia. Or it can lead to a third interpretation, one which Imelda Marcos has often demonstrated – that of being a martyr.

Groups often need martyrs and martyrs always need groups. Martyrs might feel themselves to be alone and isolated, but they need a group to play the support role in the drama of their lives. The group, or at least some influential members of the group, must first heap scorn and suffering upon the martyr before casting him out. (Men as martyrs usually choose a very public role for their martyrdom while women down the centuries have found a special niche as domestic martyrs. For domestic martyrs, being taken for granted by those for whom you sacrifice yourself is the equivalent of scorn and suffering and being cast out.) In the course of time members of the group must discover the error of their ways, whereupon they repent and forever revere the martyr. A martyr is, by definition, superior and good, therefore any group which has a martyr must itself be superior and good.

To turn yourself from a scapegoat into a martyr you must have the opportunity to say a few last words. The victims of necklacing never did. Some of the most fraught and painful testimony at the Truth and Reconciliation Commission hearings was from the relatives of those who had been necklaced. We need to learn how to live together in groups without resorting to scapegoating in order to maintain group solidarity, but we will not be able to do this until we can deal effectively with our fear of being prey.

The history of religious and national groups is full of scapegoats and martyrs. The nation state was a product of the eighteenth and nineteenth centuries. Nationality is now an idea that has common currency, but not everyone feels the need to claim membership of a national group.

Nationality becomes a vital part of a person's identity when little else is available to sustain that person's pride. If you feel that you have considerable control over your own life, if you have work which bolsters your identity and you have an income which meets your needs, nationality becomes an add-on extra, something you can assume when your national football team looks like winning the World Cup and abandon when you go abroad and wish to demonstrate your international skills. However, when you feel that you are utterly helpless, that your fate is in the hands of other people, even though you might have work which bolsters your identity and an income which meets your needs, and even more so if you do not have such work and income, nationality can become vital to the integrity of your meaning structure. Thus Jon Snow, an acclaimed and successful journalist and broadcaster, could abandon the idea of nationality while my friend Dusan, professor of psychology at Belgrade University, held on to his. When I visited Dusan in the summer of 1998 he told me that he felt helpless in the political and economic upheavals Yugoslavia had suffered. He had always loved his country and especially his city, Belgrade, but the break-up of Yugoslavia and the following war intensified his feeling of being a Serb. I found this intensity most striking in contrast to the nonchalant way psychologists in England and Australia treat their nationality.

Then I remembered how intensely we all felt about nationality during the Second World War. It was vitally important both to one's meaning structure and to one's physical survival to identify with the nation which was winning the war and to avoid being identified as belonging to an enemy nation. The history of nations is a history of war. Every nation has to invent a national story, and that story becomes its official history, where the great milestones are wars. In official histories Britain looked to Crécy, Agincourt and Trafalgar; France looked to Marengo, Austerlitz and Jena; Serbia to Kosova; America to Lexington and Bunker Hill; Australia to Gallipoli and the Somme. Such events defined the nation, but the event which defined the nation did not have to be a victory. The Serbs were defeated at Kosova, the Australians at Gallipoli. Defeats mean sacrifices.

The story goes that on the eve of the fateful Battle of Kosova in 1389 Prince Lazar told his men,

'It is better to die in battle than to live in shame. Better it is for us to accept death from the sword in battle than to offer our shoulders to the enemy. We have lived a long time in the world: in the end we seek to accept the martyr's struggle and to live forever in heaven. We call ourselves Christian soldiers, martyrs for godliness to be recorded in the book of life. We do not spare our bodies in fighting in order that we may accept holy wreaths from that One who judges all accomplishments. Sufferings beget glory and labour leads to peace.'[19]

The Serbs have long memories. Six hundred years later Slobodan Milošovic, President of the Yugoslav Republic, could persuade the Serbs that the sacrifices at Kosova justified many more sacrifices.

In 1922 the *Sydney Morning Herald* declared that 'The Gallipoli campaign has been described as "the most glorious failure in military history"', and went on to ask, 'But was it failure to Australia? It has made us a nation. Was the price worth paying? Are not nations like individuals? If the nation is to be born, if the nation is to live, someone must die for it.'[20] Which is what our ancestors must have thought when they saw a sabre-toothed tiger devouring one of their group.

Belonging to a national group can be a source of comfort and pride, and it can also be the cause of much pain and suffering. Those of us who are free to choose or reject the national group on offer are very fortunate because most people have their nationality branded on them – often in such a way that they are not aware of the process. I am free to change my nationality if I wish and if another nation would accept me. Whenever I arrive at Heathrow from overseas and have to stand in a long queue to go through Immigration I wonder why I do not save myself some time and get a UK passport. But I do not, and I know why. If I gave up my Australian passport I would feel disloyal to Australia. The Australia I mean is not the land mass which is called Australia and its inhabitants, but my idea of Australia, which I created when I was a child. This idea grew out of my happiest experiences playing in the bush or going swimming, out of Australian poetry like *The Wide Brown Land*, out of the way Australian history was taught in schools during the years of intense wartime propaganda, and out of the stories my father told me of the time when he was a soldier in the Australian army. This idea is part of my identity. To change my passport would mean feeling disloyal to myself.

I was reminded of how my idea of Australia took shape when I was in South Africa in 1998 visiting my friend Andy Dawes who, at Cape Town University, is conducting with his colleagues a large study of how teenagers see their country and their future in this post-apartheid era. One of the tasks these schoolchildren were set was to write a brief essay entitled 'My Nation and My People'. This topic assumed that these teenagers could see the country, which contained many different racial and tribal groups, which had eleven official languages and huge discrepancies in wealth and education, as one nation. Andy let me read some of these essays, and I found in them factors similar to those which had formed my idea of Australia. There were the children's own experiences alongside what they had been told by parents and teachers, and both sets of ideas were coalescing into the child's own idea of 'my nationality'.

Two of these essays struck me particularly because they were written by children of very similar backgrounds. They were both white, at the same school and from comfortable middle-class homes. One was a girl of thirteen, the other a boy of fourteen.

The girl wrote,

My nation is affected by the government. The people are scared.
Where I live we hardly ever go anywhere at night because the squatters are on the other side of the hill. If they walk over the hill they
will be by our houses. Most white people have moved away. We
are going to move but everywhere you go it is the same. The African
people are breaking and ruining things. Mandela is the worst president we have ever had. We are affected by the Africans because
there is more of them than us.

The boy wrote,

I am very proud of my Nation because it seems as though we have
come out of a dark place into the light for now we are the rainbow
nation. We have a new president who is very popular throughout
the world. Black people are now being properly educated and are
getting jobs so they can support their families. Even though some
people think this is a bad thing, many are working still together to
save our country. It will still take years though to get our country
to its full potential. And hopefully those people who do still think
this is a bad thing will change their outlook on life.[21]

We could look at these essays in the context of society and ask
whether a nation will be able to contain such divergent views. Or
we could look at these essays in terms of the individual's future.
How can the girl live with such fear and resentment? In the future
will the boy find that his idealism and optimism have been betrayed?
However, in making this division between society and the individual
I am perpetuating a gross error made by my professional group,
psychologists. The study of psychology, which is concerned with
what people do and why they do it, has always been divided into
social psychology and individual psychology. Groups do one thing
and individuals do another: there are group reasons and individual
reasons.
    Thus psychologists have based much of their work on a false
dichotomy. Individuals are never separate from groups, and groups
are never separate from individuals. There is a constant interaction
between the ideas a group holds in common and the ideas an individual holds, and between what a group does and what an individual
does. Of course, each individual has a particular interpretation of

the group's ideas, but the starting point of this interpretation is the group's ideas. I did not create the image of Australia as 'the wide brown land' any more than the girl created the idea of Mandela as the worst president or the boy the idea of a rainbow nation.

An individual meaning structure might seem like a self-enclosed system, but it is not. My interpretation of your interpretation changes my meaning structure, while your interpretation of my interpretation changes your meaning structure. If I believe that you always tell me the truth, then my interpretation of everything you say will be that it is true, and, as it is true, I will take your interpretations into my meaning structure. Small children usually believe that their parents tell them the truth, and so they take into their meaning structure their parents' interpretation of the world. An important part of the parents' meaning structure will be the parents' interpretation of the ideas of the group to which the parents belong.

One study which illustrated this and which is very relevant for an examination of friends and enemies is one carried out by the psychologists Richard Nisbett and Dov Cohen on the functioning of the culture of honour in the southern states of the USA.

When anthropologists talk about a culture of honour they are not talking about probity of character as in 'Brutus is an honourable man', but about power and status. This has to do with a man's reputation for strength and toughness. A culture of honour functions on 'the rule of retaliation. If you cross me, I will punish you.'

Nisbett and Cohen explained,

> To maintain credible power of deterrence, the individual must project a stance of willingness to commit mayhem and to risk wounds or death for himself. Thus, he must constantly be on guard against affronts that could be construed by others as disrespect. When someone allows himself to be insulted, he risks giving the impression that he lacks the strength to protect what is his. Thus the individual must respond with violence or the threat of violence to any affront.[22]

It is perhaps not surprising that the murder rates in a culture of honour tend to be high, but what does require explanation is that, in the USA, while the rates of murders committed by black males show little regional differences, amongst white males there are more homicides, especially those involving arguments, in the southern states than in the north. The highest rates were in rural areas where cattle are herded. The difference, Nisbett and Cohen postulated, might be explained in terms of attitudes, beliefs and behaviours concerning honour, self-protection and violence.

To do this Nisbett and Cohen brought together the different groups of ideas which serve to define the group of southern white American males – ideas coming from economics, history, child-rearing practices – and showed that they meshed together to create a concept dearly prized by the group, that of a man's honour. They then looked at the behaviour of some of the individuals in the group and contrasted this behaviour with that of individuals who were northern white American men. The behaviour studied was how these individual men responded to an insult.

The northern states of the USA were first settled by farmers from England, Germany and Holland, while the south was settled by Scots and Irish herdsmen. Worldwide, an economy based on the herding of animals tends to be associated with concerns about the upholding of honour with violence when necessary. This can be seen in the life of a Greek shepherd, a Masai warrior, a Druze tribesman, a Sioux Indian, a Scottish chieftain. Herdsmen can easily lose their entire wealth through the loss of their herds, so by showing that they will be quick to retaliate to the slightest insult they are more likely to deter thieves. In the sparsely settled southern states of the USA the law of the state was little in evidence. Instead, men followed the advice given by the North Carolina proverb, 'Every man should be sheriff in his own house.'

Toughness had to be demonstrated. The autobiographies of sou-therners of the eighteenth and nineteenth centuries tell of pastimes and games involving great violence. Fighting was no holds barred, which meant that the contestants sought to maim their opponents. Children were disciplined by receiving severe beatings from adults. When they fought amongst themselves, as children who are beaten usually do, their aggression was seen by adults as appropriate. The whole socialization process of boys was aimed at making them physi-cally courageous and ferocious in defending their reputation. 'From an early age small boys were taught to think much of their own honor and be active in its defense. Honor in this society meant a pride of manhood in physical courage, physical strength and warrior virtue. Male children were trained to defend their honor without a moment's hesitation.'[23]

Ideas are handed down from one generation to another, and often each successive generation accepts them without question. Thinking is hard work, and questioning your parents' ideas runs counter to the Fifth Commandment, 'Honour thy father and mother, so that thy days will be long in the land.' That means, criticize your parents and you're dead. So it is not surprising that today in attitude surveys southern men and women show that they hold the beliefs of their ancestors. They say that they favour corporal punishment for children, they oppose gun control and they support the use of violence in response to an affront, whether the person affronted is a man or a boy.

Attitude surveys can be misleading because we often say we believe something and then we do something different. In questionnaires and interviews most of us 'fake good' – depending, of course, on what we think good is. To find out what a person really thinks we have to see what that person does.

This is what Nisbett and Cohen did. They selected two groups of college students, one of men from the south and one of men from the north, and they involved them in a series of experiments where, as they described,

> We examined the sequence of reactions following an insult, in an effort to determine whether southerners become more upset by affronts and are more likely to take aggressive action to compensate for the diminishment they experience. We brought southerners and northerners into the lab, where an associate of the experimenter, who did not appear to be part of the study, rudely insulted them. We observed the subjects' emotional reactions, physiological responses, and actions in response to this insult.[24]

Nisbett and Cohen predicted that they would find differences in the behaviour of the two groups, but the degree of the differences surprised them. They found that insulted southerners believed that the insults damaged their appearance of strength and masculinity in the eyes of another, they were made more upset by the insult, as indicated by their rise in cortisol levels and in the pattern of emotional responses as rated by observers, they became more cognitively primed for future aggression in insult situations, they showed preparedness for dominant and aggressive behaviours, as indicated by their rise in testosterone levels, they behaved in more domineering ways during interpersonal encounters, and they actually behaved in physically aggressive ways in subsequent challenge situations.[25] Nisbett and Cohen concluded that 'An insult simply has a fundamentally different meaning for northerners and southerners. For the southerner, the insult has something to do with himself and his reputation; for the northerner, the insult has something to do only with the person who delivered the insult.'[26]

We are each born into a gender, family, race, religion and nationality group, and these groups together make up the culture in which we live. We each had to learn the definitions and rules of that culture. Very few families teach their children these definitions and rules in the framework of 'Many different definitions and rules can be constructed but in this culture these are the definitions and rules which we prefer.' Most families teach in the framework of 'This is how things are.' When the child subsequently discovers that there are other cultures which do things differently the adults' response is usually: 'Those people are wrong and wicked.'

Even though our wishes sometimes run counter to the rules, as children we found the absoluteness of the definitions and rules a strength and comfort in a changing, confusing world. I remember when I was in my early teens thinking angrily, 'What am I supposed to do?' My mother showed me endlessly what I was not to do, namely anything which ran counter to her wishes, but she gave me no guidance in how I should behave in the new social situations in which I was finding myself. She was quick to point out when I got things wrong but she never praised me when I got things right.

Children who are born into families where the definitions and rules are presented as clear and absolute absorb these definitions and rules into their own meaning structure, along with the fear that if they do not adhere to the rules they will become prey in the eyes of the other members of the group. They will be scapegoated and cast out. They know, even though they might not think about it consciously, that their group has ways of forcing their allegiance.

Owing Allegiance to Your Group

The basic relationship of an individual to a group is that of a trade. 'I'll give you something provided you give me something in return.' The individual gives allegiance to the group provided the group gives the individual the kind of security which helps to maintain the individual's meaning structure.

This kind of security requires that there be considerable similarity between the ideas held by the group and the ideas held by the individual. The history of the group has to form part of the life story of the individual. The way in which the group operates has to be known by the individual members of the group so that they can predict what is going to happen in the group and behave in ways acceptable to the group. These ways of behaving include the way in which stories are told and what they are told about. You can never feel yourself to be a member of a group until you can understand its jokes.

One day when I was in Belgrade I visited the imposing St Mark's Church in the centre of the city. I had been to some of the Byzantine Orthodox churches in Athens earlier that year and I was interested to see how this church compared.

The centre of the church was a large square space supporting a very fine glass dome. The space was bare of furnishings except for three icons on ornate gold stands, a circular sand tray containing candles lit as offerings, and three rickety wooden chairs. I sat on one of these and surveyed the scene.

Worshippers came alone. Each stood in front of one of the icons, made the Orthodox sign of the cross, bent and kissed the icon, stood silent for a moment and then slowly left the church. Only one person in the church moved rapidly. This was a middle-aged woman dressed in black. She bustled around extinguishing those candles which had burnt to a stump and, with her white duster, cleaned and polished the glass which protected each icon. That piece of housework gave me great satisfaction. I had been worried about whether it was hygienic to kiss icons.

That evening Dusan and I had a long talk. I told him what I had been doing during the day, and the conversation turned to religion, and Dusan discovered that I did not understand the proper meaning of icons. They were not at all like those Catholic statues and paintings which Presbyterians are taught to regard as idolatrous. Icons, Dusan told me, were the eyes of God. Through the eyes of the icon God surveyed the world.

I said, 'So that woman in the church was polishing God's spectacles.'

I thought my joke merited a smile if not a laugh, but Dusan's face was stern and still. He was shocked. One does not make jokes about God.

I was uncertain whether Dusan was a very religious person for whom jokes about God were unthinkable or whether this was a typical Serbian attitude. When I met Steve, an Australian theatre director who had been working in Belgrade for four years, I asked him what kind of jokes Serbs made. He said, 'Nationalism. They joke about Montenegrins, they joke about Bosnians. And they joke about sex. Sex is very important in their culture – as a game. But mainly you'll find the whole range of Irish jokes you're familiar with translated here as Bosnian jokes, and more.'

'Do they joke about God, do they joke about religion?'

'Not really. There were a number of jokes along the lines that Milošovic died and went to heaven, but using it as a political joke, not really about religion.'

I told Steve of my conversation with Dusan about icons, but before I had got near the end of my story Steve interrupted me and stole my punchline with 'She was cleaning God's spectacles.' Australians make jokes about everything.

I seized the opportunity to ask my question again when I was talking to the Serbian psychiatrist Johan Maric, who had written a book about the psychology of the Serbs in which each chapter was devoted to a particular Serbian characteristic. One chapter, he told me, was about 'Our joy. Yugoslavian jokes. We are very productive. It's a sense of mental health, I think, when people make so many jokes.'

'Do they make jokes about God?'

'Rarely, very rarely. But about St Peter, when Slobodan Milošovic dies and goes to St Peter, that sort of thing.'

Very likely if I had asked around some more I would have found a Serb or two who ventured a joke about God that fell into the Jewish, Protestant and Catholic traditions of jokes about God. However, what came across to me in a workshop on depression which I ran for post-graduate students at the University of Belgrade was that in the Orthodox Church emphasis is placed on the transcendence of God – that is, God as a power over and above our world, invisible, unknowable but seeing everything. In the Catholic, Protestant and Jewish traditions transcendence is given its due, but much is made of the immanence of God – that is, God here in the world, mingling with people. In our minds an immanent God readily turns into a person, and people make jokes about one another. So we tell stories where we make jokes about God, and God makes jokes about us. Indeed, some people see God as the Ultimate Joker. How else can you explain what goes on in the world?

Very much of what goes on in the world involves suffering, and making jokes is one way of trying to cope with suffering. When the cause of our suffering is beyond our control and there is no end in sight we can feel like helpless prey. One way of maintaining our pride and thus lessening our sense of being prey is to make a joke about the cause of our suffering. A joke made privately, just to yourself, can be helpful, provided it does not arise solely out of bitterness and resentment, but it is much more heartening to share a joke with others. Shared jokes pull a group together, just as shared suffering does.

Shared suffering welds a group together much more effectively than shared happiness. You can have a really good time with a group of people and part promising to keep in touch, but somehow that does not happen, whereas when a group of people, however diverse their backgrounds, have gone through a bad time together they can forge bonds which are unbreakable even though circumstances keep them apart. Andy Dawes told me about scenes outside meetings of the Truth and Reconciliation Commission, where people who had perhaps not seen one another since some terrible events had brought them together fell into each other's arms with tears and rejoicing.

We can be happy together but still be using our pride to hide ourselves from the others. Suffering strips that pride away and we see one another as we are. We cannot use our pride to feel superior to the person who suffers as we do. We become equals, and only as equals can we form bonds where the fear and envy involved in our ideas about hierarchy have no place. Once these bonds are formed the group itself can create an allegiance which allows its own form of pride to emerge.

In the seventy-seven years during which the British government used transportation to deal with the growing number of convicts created by the government's harsh laws, some 45,000 Irish convicts were transported to Australia in conditions of great cruelty and deprivation. Many of them had been convicted of rebelling against the British rule in Ireland. In 1801 the then governor of the colony, Governor King, reported back to London that

> We have been very quiet until the arrival of the *Anne* transport from Cork with 137 of the most desperate and diabolical characters that could be selected through that kingdom, together with a Catholic priest of the most notorious, seditious and rebellious principles – which makes the numbers of those who, avowing a determination never to lose sight of the oath by which they are bound as United Irishmen, amount to 600, are ready, and only waiting an opportunity to put their diabolical plans into execution.

He went on to plead that 'no more men of a violent Republican character, and particularly the priests (of whom we now have three), should be sent.'[27]

A long-time English resident of the colony also remarked upon the character of these Irish convicts.

> The worst trait is the ill-feeling they display to all but their own class. A spirit of free masonry exists among them to a great extent, and the greater the ruffian, the greater the pet he is. The man who endeavours to reform or to give satisfaction to his master is barely tolerated while he who has been subjected to excessive punishment is considered a hero.

The police were very much despised by the convicts, and the convicts who became constables were seen to have betrayed their mates.[28]

Economic prosperity reforms the character of thieves, vagabonds and rebels far more efficiently than do harsh punishments. Many of the convicts remained in the colony and prospered. But some of the ideas developed in the time of suffering still feature in the thinking and language of Australians today. There is the concept of the 'larrikin', the young man of dash and verve who refuses to conform to law and customs. There is also the condemnation of anyone who informs on someone else to the authorities. It is a dangerous and unworthy act to 'dob someone in'.

Australian English is different from English English in more ways than in accent. When I moved to England I had to stop using many words and phrases which were incomprehensible to the English. I much regretted not being able to respond to something said to me with 'raw prawn' or to use the word 'rubbish' as a verb. 'Raw prawn' was an abbreviation of 'Don't come the raw prawn' which meant 'Do not be so foolish as to think that I am believing the lies you are currently telling me.' In my encounters with the English, especially with those psychiatrists who wanted to persuade me that behaviour can be fully explained by biology, I often felt the need for 'raw prawn'. The verb 'to rubbish', meaning to speak about someone or something in a derogatory way, has now entered English English, thus showing how useful it is.

All groups take their language very seriously. Language creates reality, and not reality language. The language a group speaks creates that group's reality. When an outside force tries to change a group's language, either by altering it or by preventing the group from speaking it, the meaning structure of each person in the group is threatened. So groups try to protect their language and maintain its status.

In France the 1994 act, the *Loi Toubon*, named after a previous minister, tried to prevent any advertisement, radio or television broadcast, official document, public notice and so on from containing any foreign term or expression where an 'officially approved' French equivalent existed.[29] When the Cambridge University Press reached its third volume of a six-volume history of the English language and relegated the Scots tongue to the level of a recently derived version of English, linguists in Scotland were outraged. They retaliated with a weighty history of the Scots language.[30] The arguments over whether the UK should join the EC are often reduced to 'Would you give up the pound for the euro?' Yet, as the economist Larry Eliot has pointed out, 'In economies increasingly driven by the service sector, language matters. Indeed, a single language is more important to the smooth working of the single market than a single currency will ever be.'[31] Perhaps the prestige of having

English as the chief language for the EC will outweigh the abandonment of the idea that the pound is an essential part of what it is to
be English.

If you are not French, Scots or English these concerns might seem
laughable, but there is nothing laughable in the tragedies which have
followed attempts by one group to destroy another's language.

In Sri Lanka the Tamils, who are mostly Hindu, and the Sinhalese,
who are mostly Buddhist, have lived together for two millennia with
little hostility. Then, after independence in 1948, Sinhalese politicians
decided to make Sinhalese the only official language.

> Tamils felt deprived of access to government and of their traditional
> route to advancement, jobs in the civil service. There followed a
> series of laws setting up separate schools for Sri Lanka's different
> language-groups and establishing quotas for Sinhala-speakers in uni-
> versities. Many of these measures were later recognized as discrimi-
> natory and overturned. But by then it was too late. Angry young
> Tamils had started their terrorist movements, among them the Tamil
> Tigers, and so the terrible cycle of destruction and retribution
> began.[32]

This quote was from *The Economist* in 1993. The terrible cycle
continued.

In 1652, when the Dutch settled at the Cape of Good Hope, they
brought with them High Dutch, the language which was enshrined
in their Bible, but the language they spoke had been mixed with
French and German. As a port on the route between Europe and
the Far East, the Cape was home to many tongues, while the descendants of the first settlers, like the Hottentots they were displacing,
simplified the declensions and other refinements of High Dutch. A
Cape language developed which the British, when they arrived as
the overlords in 1806, tried to suppress. All education had to be in
English. This was one of the reasons the Boers set out on their Great
Trek and established the republics of the Transvaal and the Free
State. Their language, Afrikaans, at this stage hardly existed in writ-
ten form. In 1875 a group of young Afrikaners held a meeting in
Paarl and set about writing a history of South Africa in their own
language, and in 1876 produced their own newspaper, *Die Afrikaanse
Patriot*, the first publication to appear in Afrikaans.

When the British defeated the Boers in 1902 the Afrikaners were faced with the loss of their republics and their language. The High Commissioner for South Africa, Lord Alfred Milner, was determined to stamp out Afrikaans. 'Had it not been for Milner and his extreme measures,' says Kowie Marais, former judge and later Progressive Federal Party spokesman on education, 'we Afrikaners would probably all quite happily have been speaking English by now. By his opposition to our language, he helped create it.'[33]

Milner swept away the whole educational system of the Transvaal and the Free State. In its place he put a system where all the teachers and inspectors were English. Despite the fact that most of the pupils did not speak English virtually all the teaching was given in English and children were punished for speaking Afrikaans in the playground. The punishment was often the 'Dutch mark': a placard was placed around the offending child's head and the child made to stand on a chair to be ridiculed by the other children. The placard always bore some derogatory remark about the child. In Afrikaans mythology this was always 'I am a Donkey – I speak Dutch'.

In 1966, five years after South Africa became a republic, the Afrikaners held a festival at the Voortrekker Monument to celebrate their language. The huge backdrop to the festival bore the legend 'I am a Donkey – I speak Dutch'. The Afrikaner government could not eradicate the English language but they could demote it by requiring that everyone who dealt with the public in whatever capacity should be able to speak Afrikaans. The languages which they did try to eradicate, or at least banish from South Africa itself, were those spoken by the majority of people in South Africa, among whom relatively few spoke either English or Afrikaans. The requirement to speak Afrikaans was applied in many petty and cruel ways. Visitors to the political prisoners on Robben Island were required to speak only Afrikaans. One word of another language and the visit was over. The law which required that all the teaching in schools in black townships should be in Afrikaans sparked off school boycotts by the students and riots which led to many deaths.

Not learning from experience, the apartheid regime repeated the mistake. By trying to eradicate the tribal languages the regime strengthened them. Now the tribal languages are part of the eleven official languages, and tribal membership has become even more important for many people. When I was in South Africa in 1998 I was impressed by the number of people who introduced themselves to me with a reference to their tribe. The future of South Africa does not just depend on the relationship between the blacks and the whites, which is usually the way the situation is presented to people outside South Africa, but between all the tribes, including the Coloureds, the Indians, the English and the Afrikaners.

Much will depend on education, the way in which a group hands down its ideas to younger generations. For the rainbow nation to become unified it will have to develop some stories which are meaningful to all the people in it. It is the myths and legends of the American dream which hold the diverse groups of Americans together. However, in South Africa, as in many countries, there is a conflict over which of the two models of education should be used. One model is represented by the word 'education' itself. It is from the Latin 'to lead out'. The child is seen as born containing something very valuable – that is, the potential to learn and to become. All the educator has to do is to encourage the child to fulfil that potential. The other model of education sees the child as containing something undesirable and dangerous. The aim of the educator is therefore to control and to mould the child into the shape desired by the group. The Russian word for education is *obrazovanyi*, which has its root in *obraz*, meaning shape, form, mould.[34] These two models of education relate directly to ideas about the desirability of free speech and free thought.

National groups who pride themselves on free speech and thought may have difficulty in getting people to absorb the group's myths and legends without question. Children who are allowed to think for themselves always do. National and religious groups who regard free speech and thought as unnecessary do not have this difficulty. Right from the beginning they teach children that those in authority know what is right and true, and that anyone who doubts this is wicked. Such teaching uses repetitive rituals and prayers and the memorizing of a holy text, which are an efficient means of instilling the required meanings and preventing the individual from thinking. This is an effective way of creating group allegiance but it also severely limits creativity. If you grow up believing that the world actually is the way your group has presented it you will find it difficult, if not impossible, to see the world in any other way no matter how much it might benefit you to do so. Moreover, when the world behaves in ways contrary to your predictions you will become very frightened. On the other hand, if you grow up knowing that the world can be interpreted in many different ways you are likely to question what your group wants you to believe.

To deal with such fear and such questioning and to maintain allegiance groups develop rituals. These are enactments of the group's story.

For a ritual to achieve its aim the participants have to believe in it, or, at least, be able to suspend disbelief. I have always been unable to do this because as a child I saw very little ritual. To my mother weddings, christenings, funerals, Christmas, New Year and birthdays were bothersome events to be got over as quickly as possible. She sent me to Sunday school and church but she did not attend herself. St Andrew's Church, where I reluctantly went, had very little drama in its rituals, and the only part of the rituals I liked was when the organist struck up 'Praise God from Whom All Blessings Flow' and I knew that in a few minutes I could escape.

I gave ritual little thought until I moved to England, where I had a number of encounters, some prolonged, with the Church of England. I have witnessed the Anglican rituals and, more often, the enthusiasm and fascination many of the clergy have with the ritual. If any man – and, more recently, woman – wants to be an actor but does not have the talent for success on the stage, then becoming an Anglican priest is a possible alternative. Indeed, the Church can be seen as the preferable stage. The buildings are more solid and can be much more dramatic than ordinary theatres. The audience is there to praise, not criticize (though they sometimes do). Best of all, while the theatre is an as-if presentation of life, the Church promises believers access to the real thing. One does not even have to be a believer. The theatre asks us only for the suspension of disbelief, and so does the Church. The only difference is that the theatre requires our suspension of disbelief for only an hour or two, while the Church demands it for a lifetime.

As a child I might have been able to keep myself separate from the rituals of religion but I could not separate myself from the rituals of nationalism. At school we had to march and do it well. We spent hours forming fours and marching around the playground. I could not see how children marching would actually help the Allies win the war, but that was how it was presented to us. To refuse to march was unpatriotic as well as disobedient, something my mother would not countenance.

Now I wonder whether the politicians and civil servants in the Department of Education realized that they were copying, in a milder form, what Hitler had imposed on German children. Primo Levi described how

> the insipid violence of the drill had already in 1934 begun to invade the field of education and was turned against the German people themselves. Those newspapers of the period which had preserved a certain freedom in reporting and criticism tell us about exhausting marches imposed on adolescent boys and girls within the framework of premilitary exercises: up to fifty kilometres a day, with knapsacks on their shoulders and no pity for stragglers. Parents and doctors who dared to protest were threatened with political sanctions.[35]

Drill is one of the means by which ordinary young men are turned into obedient soldiers willing to kill and be killed. Medieval wars had been fought by relatively small groups of men, often under little or no central command. Killing was done at close quarters. However, the English archers at Crécy and Agincourt changed that. Killing at a distance could be done by archers, but they needed to operate in great numbers and to be well trained to act in unison.

> There were methods developed at the end of the sixteenth century to ensure that discipline was so thoroughly internalized that no one would think of disobeying an order – that, ideally, no one would think at all. A Dutch prince, Maurice of Nassau, came up with the idea of the drill. Instead of being trained once and trusted to use their skills on the battlefield, troops were to be trained incessantly from the moment of induction to the eve of battle. They were to form ranks, march, and manipulate their weapons, over and over, in any kind of weather, as a full-time occupation.[36]

Thus it was that 'well before notions like "France" or "Italy" or "the fatherland" had the power to stir and uplift people, soldiers in the new mass armies were experiencing directly what it meant to feel like "part of something larger than oneself".'[37]

This 'something larger than oneself' is what many people experience when they all act in unison, not just in drilling but in singing, dancing or doing the 'Mexican wave' at football grounds. In such situations the individual can lose that sense of boundary which surrounds each person and experience a oneness with other people. For this to happen there must be, however temporarily, bonds of mutual trust. When you are swaying to the left you need to be sure without looking that the person beside you is doing that too.

Where there is no trust rituals are no more than gestures. In activity courses which promise self-development much is made of mutual trust. Teams of disparate individuals are given exercises to carry out, such as devising a way for the group to cross a river when no boat is available; the aim is for the individuals in the group to learn to trust one another so that at the end of the course each person will emerge stronger and wiser. Such courses have now become part of the rituals used in business and government organizations. However, we can believe in a ritual only if we believe in the ideas held by the society which created the ritual. Many organizations spend vast sums of money on such courses – to little effect because there is a disparity between the ideas of the managers who purchased the course and those of the employees who were sent on the course. The managers might be thinking in terms of creating a smooth-running organization and of making bigger profits while the employees think in terms of how much they distrust the management. On the other hand, where the participants share the ideas which provide the context for the ritual profound change is possible.

The wars and insurrections in Africa have involved many children and, even if they survive physically, their experiences can make it very difficult for them to settle back into ordinary life. Some communities use special rituals to enable a child to do this, but to understand how these rituals work we need to understand the beliefs held by the community which developed the rituals.

Andy Dawes and Alcinda Honwana described one such ritual used by some tribes in Mozambique.

Nine-year-old Paulo was kidnapped by Renamo soldiers during an attack on his village. He stayed with them for about eight months and managed to escape a few weeks before he was due to start military training. When he arrived home he was taken to the *ndomba* (the house of spirits) to be presented to the ancestral spirits of the family. The child's grandfather addressed the spirits informing them that his grandchild had returned home alive and thanked them for their protection. A few days after his arrival Paulo was submitted to a ritual of purification. His father, *nyanga* (healer) described it as follows:

'We took him to the bush (about 2km away from our house). There we built a small hut covered with dry grass in which we put the child, dressed in the dirty clothes he wore back from the Renamo camp. Inside the hut the child was undressed. Then we set fire to the hut and Paulo was helped out by an adult relative. The hut, the clothes and everything he might have brought from the Renamo camp had to be burned. This symbolizes the rupture with the past. Then, Paulo inhaled smoke from herbal remedies and was bathed with water treated with medicine. This was aimed at cleansing his body internally and externally. Finally he was "vaccinated" (*ku thlav-ela*: small incisions made in certain parts of the body, which are then filled with special remedies) to be strong and protected from evil forces.'

In a society heavily influenced by ideas from psychotherapy this ritual might seem bizarre, frightening for the child, and, at best, useless. The received wisdom nowadays is that the only way to deal with trauma is to talk about it. However, for the people of Mozambique

health is defined by the harmonious relationships between the individual and the natural environment, with the ancestors, and with other community members. Rather than being narrowly defined realms, the social world (which includes the spirits and the living) and the natural world are united within a larger cosmological universe. If this harmonious state fails to come about, it is perceived to be the result of malevolent interventions of the *valoyi* (witches and sorcerers) or due to the intervention of the ancestral spirits who wish to correct inappropriate social behaviour . . . The healing rituals performed for Paulo bring together a series of symbolic meanings aimed at cutting his links with the past and at cleansing and reintegrating him into the community . . . the cleansing process and the practice of closing the way to malevolent spirits are associated with the notion of social pollution. Individuals are believed to be potentially exposed to pollution in their contacts with other social groups and environments . . . Social pollution may also arise from being in contact with death and bloodshed. Thus, individuals who have been involved in a war are believed to be potential contaminators of the social body of the community . . . Thus the cleansing process to which Paulo was submitted was a fundamental condition for his reintegration into society. It was designed to manage his traumatic separation, his reintegration, and the community's anxiety concerning the impact of his return.[38]

The ritual of healing and the ritual of psychotherapy, though arising from two very different sets of ideas, have some important features in common. Both the child soldier and the person considering psychotherapy have lost their capacity to feel at ease with themselves. They feel themselves to be bad, unworthy, valueless, unacceptable, and with that they feel very alone. They expect to be rejected and cast out by other members of the group. For the healing and the psychotherapy to work the healer and the therapist have to persuade their client that this will not happen. They will not reject their client. The healer and the therapist must take their client seriously and believe his story, and they have to be able to persuade their client that they do so. If the client does not believe that the healer or therapist believes him, or if the client believes that he is so wicked that no healer or therapist has the power to cleanse him of his wickedness then the healing or the psychotherapy will not be successful.

The central feature of psychotherapy is that the client tells his story. To tell your story truthfully is to 'come clean'. Every religion has rituals involving washing away pollution, be it the actual washing performed by Muslims and Hindus before praying, or symbolic washing, where Christians speak of being washed in the blood of the Lamb. The pollution which is washed away is the sin which the individual has committed and the shame and guilt which arise when the individual acknowledges that sin.

The group can thus claim to have the power to remove guilt and shame, but it also has the most effective means of causing the individual to feel shame and guilt. Indeed, provoking shame and guilt is a very effective means of maintaining group allegiance.

Politicians often try to inspire patriotism by making people feel guilty. Guilt is the subtext of President Kennedy's 'Do not ask what your country can do for you. Ask what you can do for your country.' Many young Americans who heard him utter these words were so inspired that they planned their lives accordingly. Kennedy strengthened the import of his message by dying soon after, and his death was seen by many as a tragic sacrifice. Had he lived to serve a second term the privacy he enjoyed in his private life might not have continued. Revealed as a very fallible man who was a stranger to marital fidelity, he would no longer have had the power to inspire guilt in impressionable listeners.

One of the most effective guilt-arousing calls to patriotic self-sacrifice was that delivered by President Paul Kruger in 1904 from his exile in Switzerland to his people, the Afrikaners, who were now being forced by the British to become part of the British Empire. In this last message he thanked those 'who have spared a thought for their aged State President during their deliberations about the present and the future: for by doing so they show they have not forgotten the past.' He went on,

> For he who desires to build a future dare not neglect the past. Seek, therefore, all that is good and beautiful in the past, build on it your ideal, and strive to realize that ideal for the future. It is true much of what has been built is now destroyed, despoiled and ruined; but through singleness of purpose and unity of strength what now lies shattered can still be restored.

He warned them, 'Do not forget the grave warning that lies in the words "Divide and rule"; never let these words apply to the South African nation. Then our people and our language will endure and prosper.'

Now he let them know that he was close to death:

> What I myself shall live to see of this, rests with God. Born under a British flag, I do not want to die under it. I have learnt to accept the bitter thought of death as a lone exile in a foreign land, far from my kith and kin whose faces I am not likely to see again; far from the soil of Africa, upon which I am not likely ever to set foot again; far from the country to which I devoted my whole life in an effort to open it up for civilization and where I saw my own nation grow.

But this grief will be softened if I may cherish the belief that the work, once begun, continues; for then the hope and the expectation that the work will end well, will give me strength. So be it.

What son or daughter could live with the guilt of failing to fulfil such a father's wishes? Andy Dawes told me, 'Few people outside South Africa can appreciate how difficult it was for an Afrikaner to oppose apartheid, no matter how much he or she might want to do so.'

At Paul Kruger's house in Pretoria, preserved as a museum to him, I bought a facsimile of his hand-written letter. My guide Simbo did not accompany me into the house and did not say why. Perhaps he just wanted a rest, or perhaps the people who ran the museum would not have welcomed him. While I was studying the historical display about Kruger's last years I heard a man, who seemed to be associated with the museum, give to two foreign visitors an account of the Boer War which differed markedly from what I had been taught when I was at school. The basic facts were the same but in his version the Boers were the heroes and the British the villains. The subtext of his story was 'We were robbed.' Perhaps Simbo did not want to be reminded of what the implications of Kruger's letter were for him.

Most groups use shame and guilt as a means of maintaining group allegiance but groups differ in the amount and kind of punishment they inflict on group members who fail to meet the standards and demands of the group. Severe punishments have severe effects.

Until I went to South Africa in 1991 I had not appreciated the prevalence of physical violence used by adults against children. In this there seemed to be little difference between the whites and the blacks. In the crowded, deprived schools in the black townships teachers used the cane as the first means of keeping order. When I was in Pietermaritzburg I ran a workshop on depression for a group of about thirty people. Some had an Afrikaner background, most an English background. One of the exercises I used in this workshop was aimed at showing how the conclusions we draw from our experiences in childhood can be most salient in adult life. I asked the group 'to recall an incident in childhood which led you to draw the conclusion that you were in some way bad and unacceptable'.

When a group in the UK or Australia does this exercise the stories produced are usually sad but funny. Sad because the child has been hurt, misunderstood and humiliated by an adult, but funny because the child was, as we all were, an innocent fool. The stories related by most of these middle-class, educated South Africans were of a child being beaten for doing something which angered an adult. What shocked me was not just the prevalence of physical violence in these stories but the way in which the narrators treated physical violence as a natural phenomenon. They would say something like, 'I was late and my mother beat me with a strap,' in the same tone as I might say, 'I was caught in the rain and I got wet.'

This seeming indifference to the pain and humiliation of being beaten is an example of the way primitive pride reconstrues an interpretation in order to maintain the integrity of the meaning structure. In his account of his boyhood where he refers to himself as 'he', J. M. Coetzee showed how fear and shame can be turned into pride. He wrote,

> When his father and his father's brothers get together on the farm at Christmas, talk always turns to their schooldays. They reminisce about their schoolmasters and their schoolmasters' canes: they recall cold winter mornings when the cane would raise red weals on their buttocks and the sting would linger for days in the memory of the flesh. In their words there is a note of nostalgia and pleasurable fear.[39]
>
> . . . [At school] every teacher, man or woman, has a cane and is at liberty to use it. Each of these canes has a personality, a character, which is known to the boys and talked about endlessly. In a spirit of knowing connoisseurship the boys weigh up the characters of the canes and the quality of the pain they give, compare the arm and wrist techniques of the teachers who wield them. No one mentions the shame of being called out and made to bend and being beaten on one's backside.[40]

The boy Coetzee is ashamed because he has never been beaten. 'He comes from an unnatural and shameful family in which not only are children not beaten but older people are addressed by their first names and no one goes to church and shoes are worn every day.'[41] His father would have beaten him but his mother does not allow this.

He is caught between two shames, the shame of never being beaten and the shame of being beaten. If he is called to the front of the class to be beaten

> so bad will be the shame, he fears, so daunting, that he will hold tight to his desk and refuse to come out when he is called out. And that will be a greater shame: it will set him apart, and set the boys against him too. If it ever happens that he is called out to be beaten, there will be so humiliating a scene that he will never be able to go back to school; in the end there will be no way out but to kill himself.
>
> So that is what is at stake. That is why he never makes a sound in class. That is why he is always neat, why his homework is always done, why he always knows the answer. He dare not slip. If he slips, he risks being beaten; and whether he is beaten or whether he struggles against being beaten, it is all the same, he will die.[42]

If he resists being beaten, the shame which follows would destroy him/his meaning structure. If he is beaten he/his meaning structure would also be destroyed. He knows that 'if the violation of his body can be achieved quickly, by force, he will be able to come out on the other side a normal boy, able to join easily in discussion of teachers and their canes and the various grades and flavours of the pain they inflict.'[43] But he does not want to be a normal boy because 'his father is normal in every way'.[44] He hates and despises his father. He cannot become like him.

He is engaged in a battle to defend his meaning structure against the group to which he belongs. So are we all. The only difference between each of us lies in how wonderful our group is as our friend and how terrible it is as our enemy.

Is Your Group Your Friend or Your Enemy?

There is only one answer to this question. It is always both.

Your group can give you security and a sense of belonging. It can bolster your pride, both your primitive pride and the pride you take in belonging to a group which you see as good. However, these are not free gifts. In return your group demands your allegiance. If you fail to be loyal in the way your group demands you will be punished. As punishment some groups will criticize you, some freeze you out, and some will kill you.

When a group demands loyalty from its members it is demanding that each person accept a certain set of ideas. If you want to join Newcastle United football supporters' club you need to believe that Newcastle United is a great team, even when it loses. If you want to be a Muslim you have to believe in Allah. If you can accommodate your meaning structure to the ideas of the group then the group is your friend. If you cannot, the group becomes your enemy because it is a threat to your meaning structure.

The meanings which we create do not exist in separate boxes. All meanings have implications which lead to other meanings. Often in our groups we might have no difficulty in accepting the group's ideas but problems can arise for us in the implications of those ideas. You might believe that your nation is the greatest in the world, and then the leader of your country declares war and you find yourself having to leave all those aspects of your life which support your meaning structure – your family, friends, job, home – and face the prospect of your death.

This is where primitive pride can come to the rescue. You can resolve your conflict by reconstruing. The group is not your enemy. Your enemy is another group, and you are going to fight and defeat your group's enemy. Nothing could be nobler than to die for your country. When other members of your group heap praise upon you such praise can, at least temporarily, replace the support for your meaning structure which your family, friends and familiar surroundings once gave you. This is one of the reasons why propaganda is so important in the conduct of a war.

Some people make the patriotic reconstruction of the meaning structure and do sacrifice themselves in a war. Others make a similar reconstruction but then make some adjustments to the implications of this reconstruction so that they are not too discomforted by their patriotism.

When I was in Serbia I was told by several people that the Serbs are spiritual people. Johan Maric said, 'We have a sense of a non-material value of life. We don't like so much gold and things. Our sense of a non-material value of life is a spiritual linking with friends, with the neighbourhood, but not so many *things*. I know that in lots of western cultures Saturday is the day for buying things. Shopping. Saturday shopping. Some of our younger generation like shopping, but the older generation of Serbian people – also all Slav people – don't like this. Because of this I think that all Slav people are not typical of civilizations, like the Italians, Greeks, Egyptians. Serbs have never been the first nation. Why? Some other investigator said this is because they don't like things or money. They are interested in the spirit and in art.'

I flew from Belgrade to London in the week when NATO began warning Slobodan Milošovic that, if he did not prevent the Serbian army and police from attacking the Albanians in Kosova, NATO would bomb military installations in Serbia. My plane was full. Most of the passengers were Serbs and from those generations which Maric described as older and, presumably, spiritual. Yet I witnessed something which I have never seen on a plane before. In my experience, when the duty-free trolley does its rounds only a few passengers purchase something. On this flight it took the steward with the trolley most of the remaining flight time to make a very slow passage up the aisle. Everybody was buying and everybody bought big. Afterwards the steward told me that every duty-free item on the plane had been sold. He said, 'It's always like this coming from Belgrade.'

I had seen how empty the shops were in Belgrade. Human beings love things, and the people on the plane were human beings before they were Serbs. We are all human beings and that is the group to which we all belong. We should remember this, particularly when we are claiming membership of a smaller and more special group. The people on the plane were more fortunate than most Serbs because they had the money to fly and to buy things. Money can be so useful when you want to reconstrue. If I had been able to ask these people why they were buying so many things, some might have said, 'Because I'm greedy. I want things.' But most would have been likely to explain their purchases in altruistic terms. These things were not for themselves but for friends and family. They would keep for themselves only the tiniest smidgen of perfume or whisky. They were spiritual people.

Back in Serbia most Serbs were struggling. They had little money and little prospect of getting money. To be well off a person had to be a crony of Milošovic and his wife or a gangster who drove expensive cars and traded in drugs and guns. Consequently most

Serbs were left only with a choice of how they could interpret their
situation.

They could feel angry with their leader, who cared nothing for
his people, and thus risk the punishment which dissent would
bring. Or they could feel helpless and defeated, the prey of their
predator leader. Or they could see themselves as noble but tragic,
betrayed, not by their leader, but by the enemies of the Serbs.
Their virtuous spirituality stood in splendid contrast to the wicked
materialism of the Americans. They might suffer, but do not all
martyrs suffer?

The first interpretation leads to an uncomfortable way of living,
but it enables people to maintain the standards set by their moral
pride and to see clearly what is actually happening. The people who
choose this interpretation will not compromise their own truth, and
they prefer to know this truth, and the truth of their situation, no
matter how terrible that truth might be.

The second interpretation is dangerous. It is physically exhausting
and debilitating, and so can lead to illness and even death from
disease or the extinction of primitive pride. If the people who choose
this interpretation blame themselves for their situation their misery
turns to depression.

The third interpretation is seductive. The people who choose this
interpretation see themselves not just as virtuous but as significant.
Their sufferings serve only to heighten their sense of virtue and
significance. However, all this is purchased at great cost. To maintain
their interpretation they have to remain oblivious of what is actually
happening. They have to interpret what their nearest and dearest
say and do in ways which fit in with their interpretation, and so
they fail to take proper account of those they love. They have to
create blanket explanations, like 'the Western media never tells the
truth', to prevent events disconfirming their interpretation. They
might find themselves forced into more and more serious actions
in order to protect their own interpretation. Events move on, and
the day comes when events can be denied either by turning the
interpretation into a delusion which has no accord with reality, or
by undertaking a major reconstruction of the meaning structure.

Thus it is that when we belong to a group whose set of ideas
includes pride in its history we can always bolster our pride by
wrapping ourselves in the pride of our group. Sometimes this works.

Sometimes it does not. But what do you do when your group has no history?

In South Africa the conversation is usually about crime, and so Andie Miller, the resources manager at the Johannesburg Centre for the Study of Violence and Reconciliation, and I were talking about crime and the groups of young men who commit so much crime. These men were thieving, but using considerable violence and brutality in their thefts. Violence and brutality is what they had known all their lives. They had been beaten at school. They had been beaten by the police and they had seen people die. Violence was part of their meaning structure.

Andie commented that South Africa was 'an extraordinarily materialistic society' and went on: 'Since the election a black middle class is beginning to emerge. Everyone has the right to do what they want and get what they want, but not everyone has the resources to do that, so once again it's a very small minority that is able to improve their circumstances. I am completely stunned by how rich the rich in this country are, and the poor are just getting poorer. Even I feel the pressure that this consumerism places on one. I think when people's self-esteem has been that eroded they can only define themselves in terms of what they have. And I really do feel that in our society people don't have a sense of who they are, of their worth, beyond what they have.'

During the struggle against apartheid many blacks learned to define themselves in terms of their political group. The Black Consciousness movement of the 1970s was tremendously important. Mamphela Ramphele wrote,

> Mr Mbeki and others of his generation, who grew up as members of a proud peasant class in the Eastern Cape, have never had to doubt their own worth as human beings in spite of the racism around them. But for those young blacks in the townships of the 1960s, it was much more difficult not to have self doubt. A Black Consciousness perspective was essential for these young blacks growing up in a racist country.[45]

Black consciousness was tremendously important for Mamphela Ramphele, especially when she went to work in 'the white stronghold' of Cape Town University: 'One of the enormous benefits of having been steeled in the furnaces of Black Consciousness is that I have been liberated psychologically. I feel I belong in any part of my country, and I treat any major public institution in my society as part of my heritage.'[46]

There was a place for Mamphela Ramphele in the new South Africa, but for many young black activists there was none. For those who could prove their ANC affiliation there was a place in the army, but in the struggle many activists had to keep their ANC affiliation unrecorded. With the breakdown of the school system in the townships most of the young black activists entered their twenties lacking the education to get a job. Their experiences had aged them, so it was hard for them to return to the classroom, even if they had the money to do so.

Andie said, 'When the youth played a major role in the liberation struggle, they tended to identify with their political affiliations, but since that role has been taken over by government, by middle-aged exiles to a large extent, younger people no longer have a place where they belong.'

So what could these young men do to maintain their meaning structure? The only advantage they possessed was that they had each other. They knew one another's story. They had shared great suffering. They knew what attributes were needed in a leader, and one of them became the group leader whom they would follow just as they had followed their activist leader. They formed their group and gave their group a purpose – that of getting their rewards for what they had done to overthrow apartheid. What others would not give they would take. They were highly skilled in the methods of violence.

For many of these young men their group is their only friend. But it is also their enemy because it cannot give them security and a place in society. They cannot leave the group except by dying, either at the hands of the police or a rival group, or through the effects of drugs and alcohol.

The lives of these young men had not brought them into easy contact with a wide range of people. They knew only their kith and kin. Everyone else was a stranger. Their groups were tight-knit. And the more tight-knit a group is the stranger other people appear to be.

Group leaders who want their group to be tight-knit and obedient do what they can to prevent group members from having contact with people outside the group. In a tight-knit group every member holds without question the ideas common to the group. Outsiders must be shunned because they may carry ideas which would challenge the ideas held by the group. The USSR and its Communist satellite states put in place extremely onerous sanctions against any of their citizens who had unauthorized contact with any person or literature from a non-Communist country. When I visited Moscow in 1984 I became very anxious when I discovered that I had inadvertently brought with me some extremely subversive literature, namely three issues of the BBC journal *The Listener*. Fortunately, one of the people I was meeting in Moscow was a publisher who, when I met him, had all the hallmarks of being a senior member of the party. He spoke excellent English, he travelled abroad often and he looked sleek and well-fed. I offered him my copies of *The Listener* and he accepted with great pleasure. He said that *The Listener* was amongst his favourite reading. I had learned in a visit I had made to the Karl Marx Clinic in Leipzig in the seventies that powerful members of the party were in no danger of being contaminated by foreign ideas. They could indulge in the ideas and practices of the decadent West and their Communist beliefs would remain untouched. It seems that power can create a most accommodating meaning structure.

However, for those members of such a group who are denied contact with those outside the group, such a restriction has long-lasting results. John Parry, a journalist who lives in Madrid, described the effects of the Franco regime in Spain. He wrote,

Knowledge of other cultures during the Franco era was sparse, except among a small, well-travelled elite and the intellectual fraternity. Most Spaniards who were more than ten when Franco died in 1975 and are now in their mid-thirties and above, are not naturally tolerant of other cultures because they have not been exposed to them until recently. The groups which come in for the most ostracism are the permanent community of 'gitanos' (gypsies) and the moros (North African migrant workers) . . .

But even fair-skinned strangers from the north of Europe get odd looks. In central Spain, which was particularly isolated from the rest of Europe during the dictatorship, older people are very wary of the unknown. Even in the capital city, Madrid, the prevalent attitude among the older generation is that any foreigner living here is to be regarded as at best eccentric, at worst suspicious, unless proved otherwise.[47]

Such exclusion and fear of the stranger can become embedded in the language and culture. In Belgrade Stephan told me about the Serbian word 'naš'. He said, 'Serbs don't speak of "the rest of the world", they speak of "the world", meaning "not Serbia". Serbian is one of the strongest national identities I've known. They constantly use the word "naš" meaning "ours". Is he ours or is he not? Our man – "naš covek". It means brother. It doesn't matter how long I live here and how much people like me, I can never be naš covek. My friends accept me as a brother-in-law but I'll never be a brother.'

Yorkshire people often use the word 'our' to denote a member of the family. 'Our Bill' is distinctly different from all other Bills in the world. The demarcation of who is family is broader in Yorkshire than in Serbia. When our Bill marries Pat she usually becomes 'our Pat'.

The idea of 'our' can be submerged but still powerful for people who like to think of themselves as being liberal in their views on nationality, race and gender. Outsiders can often see the functioning of 'our' when the person concerned does not. Women can see 'our' in the implicit sexist attitudes of someone who thinks of himself as a New Man. Blacks can see 'our' in the implicit racist attitudes of people who think of themselves as white liberals.

The simplest word can carry different meanings in different contexts. I met a number of white liberals while I was in South Africa, and with some of them I was struck by the way in which their use of the word 'they' came across to me when they were talking about blacks. It sounded different from the way in which Australians might use the word when talking about Americans or the English talking about the French. This particular South African liberal 'they' seemed to carry connotations of separation and difference. When I asked Andy Dawes whether I had just imagined this he laughed and said, 'Have you heard the whites from Zimbabwe and from here who talk about "our blacks" as distinct from "their blacks"?'

I raised this matter with Andie Miller at the Centre for the Study of Violence and Reconciliation in Johannesburg. She was part

American, part South African, and she had given much thought to matters of race and nationality. She said, 'I think of myself as South African (though I sort of balk at saying "I'm proud to be South African"). But in terms of my cultural preferences – what foods I enjoy, what books I enjoy, what music I enjoy – I'm very, very Western, and I feel that as much as we may be different, you and I, there's still a level at which Western culture predominates in the world. My life has not been racially polarized, as I grew up mainly surrounded by coloured people, in Cape Town. But for the most part I have little clue about the experience of black people's lives; it's just really, really foreign.'

She spoke of how 'Americans will walk in and assume that their way of doing things is the only way; their assumptions about the world.' She told me about an American black who had been an intern at the centre; she could not understand, no matter how often it was explained to her, why one black member of staff had not finished high school until he was in his twenties. In the USA everyone matriculates when they are seventeen. Andie went on, 'This was a very narrow way of viewing the world. And I think it's a very Western thing. It tends to develop along racial lines, although it's not always just white people who make these assumptions. It's a Western standard. We've entrenched a Western standard throughout the world, and in subtle ways we insidiously undermine people from other cultures.'

The liberal attitude, Andie said, 'is very much abstract. One very good example for me – this is a stereotype but it does happen – some people are incredibly liberal about their intellectual ideas but they pay their domestic workers badly. There's a level of liberalism that has very little to do with living in the real world, or living in the real South Africa; there's a liberalism of *attitude* but sometimes less tolerance, kindness and caring. Whereas many Afrikaners I've encountered use racist terminology but are more caring about the people around them.'

Many of the white liberals in South Africa were emigrating. Andie commented, 'There's a difference between the reality of change and the academic ideal of that. For me the difference between the English and the Afrikaner is that the Afrikaner has nowhere else to go, so where there may be racism it's *honest*. I think that racism is inherent. We all, to a greater or lesser degree, are prejudiced towards people who are different from us, and in this country it tends to manifest along the lines of skin colour.'

There is a body of psychological research which shows that we are extremely skilled at identifying faces we have seen before. Knowing someone's face but not the person's name seems to be a limitation which comes from our inheritance from our tribal ancestors. In those days our kith and kin might, over our lifetime, never number more than 150, and we might not ever actually meet that number of people. So the bit of our brain which developed to link names to faces did not have to be very large. We now live in a society where the number of faces each of us knows must run into thousands – far too many for that bit of our brain to store. However, we have not lost our ability to recognize a stranger. Researchers have found that when subjects are shown, in rapid succession, a series of photographs of people they have never met, and then are shown a second series of strange faces into which some of the first series have been inserted, the subjects are very adept at identifying the faces they have seen before. Distinguishing an acquaintance from a stranger can be very important. The question is, what meaning do you give to the person who is not a member of your group?

I was sitting at a bar in Beirut when a young man came in wearing a T-shirt with the message 'MORE GUIDE DOGS NEEDED'. Fleetingly I wondered whether, in all my reading of the history of the war in Lebanon, I had failed to note that many people had been blinded during that war, but then I decided that this message had a deeper meaning. So I asked him, and he told me that people in Lebanon were blind because they looked only at a person's skin. 'They judge you on your skin. They don't look at what's beneath the skin.'

This bar was a gathering place for lonely people. Loneliness is part of the human condition, but if we see the people who are outside our group as strange we increase our sense of being alone. Yet this is what many people do. They do not look beneath the skin to see the person. Rather than seeing a person like themselves in the basic human characteristics, they see an object.

Babies, as I have described, are born with the capacity to distinguish people from objects, and to be more interested in people than in objects. We must have evolved this capacity as a way of overcoming the great disadvantage of being for ever trapped in our own individual world. Physically we cannot survive on our own. We must have some way of relating to other people, of being able to imagine what their own individual world is like, even though we can never literally share it. Consciousness gives us the ability to imagine a situation which we cannot physically experience. When we use this ability to imagine what another person's individual world is like we are using that special kind of imagination called empathy. We are all born with the capacity to empathize with other people, no matter what the colour of their skin or what groups they belong to.

However, innate characteristics can always be overridden by later experience. Thus we can decide that strangers are not merely strange, they are not people.

Thus we turn people into objects. Whenever we do this we harm ourselves. We fail to use our capacity for empathy and, as Susan Greenfield reminds us, if you don't use it you lose it. You increasingly treat your kith and kin as objects and, most harmful of all, you increasingly treat yourself as an object. You ignore other people's feelings and you fail to be aware of your own.

When we turn people into objects we mislead ourselves into thinking that these people actually behave like objects. We fail to notice that, while objects do not observe us and judge us, other people always do.

When the First Fleet arrived at Sydney Cove the white settlers decided that the inhabitants of the Australian continent were not people. The land was deemed to be empty. The settlers seemed unaware that their behaviour was being observed and moral judgements made. The Bidegal people of Port Jackson were repulsed by the treatment of certain of the whites, who were flogged and forced to walk around in chains. They were distressed to see the soldiers and convicts cutting down the trees, and they would embrace the stumps and weep over them.[48] The soldiers and convicts were part of a brutal system in which people had to relinquish their capacity for empathy in order to survive in that system, and so they were likely not to see the distress they were causing.

Treating certain groups of people as objects can become part of a culture and be handed down from one generation to another. Just how this treatment is carried out can change over time, but the underlying meaning remains the same. In societies where one group of people are slaves or servants they can be deemed by their masters

to be unaware of everything their masters do and say except when
their masters give them orders. The ancient Romans considered
themselves to be alone when no one was with them but their slaves.
One of the cherished beliefs held by many whites in South Africa
is that the blacks do not study the behaviour of the whites. Stephen
Francis, the American member of the team of three cartoonists
who produce the 'Madam and Eve' cartoon strip for the *Mail and
Guardian*, observed this when he first arrived in South Africa:

> I was amazed how families who employed domestic workers spoke
> so openly in front of them – as if they weren't even there. One
> night, during a family dinner, and a particularly candid conversation
> – I mentioned this and was told, 'Ag, they're not interested in what
> we say and do. They don't even hear us.' At that point – and I'm
> sure it wasn't my imagination – the maid serving dinner winked at
> me.[49]

Julian Sonn, writing about the sensitivity of blacks to white racism,
said, 'Our survival has depended on our ability to assess white people
effectively.'[50]

Blacks far outnumber whites in South Africa, and so the changes
in the expression of racism there are different from those in Australia, where the whites far outnumber the blacks. Over my lifetime
the expression of white racism in Australia has changed markedly.
From the days of the first white settlement Aboriginal people were
ignored and derided by the whites. It became government policy
for Aboriginal children to be taken from their families and sent to
orphanages, where they were taught white ways and deprived of
their own language. Most Aboriginal people lived in poverty, with
little opportunity for education. But in the sixties there were changes.
Aboriginal people were for the first time included in the census. In
1966 some 200 Gurindji people, including eighty station hands,
walked off Wave Hill Station in the Northern Territory in protest
against poor wages and poor conditions, and began a fight to get
title to their tribal territory, thus marking the beginning of the fight
for political rights.

However, while politicians made some efforts to improve health,
housing and education for the Aboriginal people, they refused to
see these people's situation in political terms. According to Mud-

rooroo, the leading writer and activist, 'Political problems are seen as social problems and the social welfare state seeks to coerce us into accepting what they regard as the prevailing norms of the Australian community.' He went on,

> The Master refuses to see the Other, the Native, as being equal, as being capable. It is a colonial discourse, a way of speaking which seeks to disarm, a way of removing a threat. Examples of such a discourse abound, and it is little wonder that in Australia those in control find it easier to accept a Native as an artist, a musician, or a writer, but as a politician, as an equal vying for a sharing of power, never.[51]

Helping someone can be an effective way of making that person feel inferior. Another method of doing this is to make him the object of study. Go into any large Australian bookshop and you will find a sizeable section devoted to the study of 'the Aboriginal'. Mudrooroo was scathing about this.

> There is a whole, almost completely white organisation, the Australian Institute of Aboriginal and Torres Strait Islander Studies, devoted to the study of the Native, and often this study is concerned not with the Native but with the structure of the Master text, which has now been changed to include the Mistress. As ideological shifts have occurred in the Master culture, the text must now be broadened to include the Mistress. Anthropology, that Master text limiting the Other, has thus become bisexual. The European woman has taken her place beside the Master and now produces studies that ape his text, or at least add to the Master text and give it a certain bisexuality. Thus, because the Master subject has bifurcated into male and female, so has the Other, the Native, and the Native female has entered anthropology as a legitimate concern of study, so that we now have books on topics such as 'women's business'.[52]

Whenever we want to exclude a group of people but we want to think well of ourselves and want other people to think well of us we have to create another form of racism. In Australia, the UK and the USA it is not politically correct to use the old racist language, so racist sentiments have to be expressed in another way. One very popular way is that of romanticizing the native. The efforts that indigenous people have made to build up their sense of identity and self-worth by re-establishing their history, art and crafts are used by the white romanticists to develop their own sentimental stories about the natives, who are so at one with their land and who have such great wisdom and spirituality that they do not need political rights and access to good housing, education and health care.

We want to see the people outside our group as strange and inferior because this means that we can preserve our belief that our group is not just good, it is especially good, better than all the rest. In this there is no clash between our individual needs and wishes and those of the group. We know that all the people in our group are good and that, even when we do not feel happy with ourselves, we can cheer ourselves up by remembering that we belong to the best group in the world. Our group has the highest possible standards.

Thus in 1996, after the first Asian–European summit, Malaysia's Prime Minister, Mahathir Mohamad, declared that, 'Asian values are universal values. European values are European values.' Asian values have been defined as attachment to the family, the primacy of personal relationships over legal relationships, consensus over confrontation, respect for authority, and a high value placed on education. However, attachment to family can become nepotism, a stress on personal relationships can lead to cronyism, consensus to corrupt politics, respect for authority to rigidity and an inability to innovate, education rote-learning and a refusal to question. Such Asian values played no small part in the financial crash of the Asian economies in 1998.[53]

Believing that your group is good means believing that your group has the right values and sees the world as it is. This is a very comforting and heartening belief when events admit of being interpreted in that way, but what happens when they do not?

Life in South Africa can be very risky, but the degree of anxiety felt by the older, middle-class whites is often much higher than the situation actually warrants. I found that in 1998 the doomsayers amongst the older generations were predicting that when President Mandela retired the following year and Thabo Mbeki took over all would be doom and disaster. These people lived in the relative security and comfort of wealthy suburbs which reminded me of the wealthy suburbs of Australian cities. Like those suburbs, they ran smoothly. Traffic flowed, gas, water and electricity were delivered, garbage was collected, and the trains ran on time. The change from the Nationalist to the ANC government had not disturbed the tenor of these people's lives in any major way.

Yet this was not what they had predicted. When they were children they had been told – and shown over and over – that they were superior to the blacks because they were white. Blacks were like children and could not be trusted to run their own affairs. It was the duty of the whites to look after the blacks, and so this burden of responsibility justified the riches and power which the whites possessed.

But what if the blacks demonstrated that they could not only run their own affairs but the country? Then the meanings on which the whites had based their identity and justified their power would be shown to be false. This threat of annihilation was too great to be ignored. It had to be overcome. Rather than admit they had been wrong in their judgement they maintained their judgement and prophesied doom. Where was the evidence? Why, in the violence, the murders and the burglaries. Living behind complex security systems, they terrified themselves with stories of violence in the inner cities and in the townships. They did not count their blessings but grew increasingly afraid.

Yet, if what they feared came to pass and they died at an assassin's hands, what pleasurable confirmation they would feel with the assassin's blow, that all along they had been right.

There are many people who would rather be right than happy. If being right means suffering, then suffering is to be welcomed. Indeed, by suffering you can show that you are both right and virtuous. In South Africa I was told that in the current discourse between those who carried on the struggle inside the country and those who were exiles now returned there can be competition to determine who suffered the most.

Suffering is at the heart of the Serbian Nationalist story, and suffering is part of the Serbian culture. Steve told me, 'Here there's an expression "mora da boli", which means "it has to hurt". The Serbs are very much into suffering. There was a funny incident one night. This young friend of mine, who's now eighteen, three or four years ago, his mother and I had decided to take him to a bar. It was the first time I'd ever taken him into an adult place. We were

sitting there with him in between us. In the middle of the conversation, he was sitting like this, bending down with his hands over
his head and his head down, rocking, and he said, "I'm sad. This
place reminds me of somewhere I was once a long time ago, and it
was one of the happiest days of my life and it will never happen
again, and I'm really unhappy because of that." And his mother
turned round to me and said, "Don't take any notice of him. He's
a Serb. He has to practise suffering." And he practised, and now at
the age of eighteen he's very good at it, and has days where he
suffers. To me, it's very exotic.'

I thought of how Australians will tease someone whom they consider to be suffering too dramatically and asked, 'Do other people
take him seriously when he suffers?'

Steve replied, 'I think they just take it for granted. Yes, it's serious
but it's no big deal. Serbs are very kind people if someone's suffering,
or if they think someone is suffering. Sometimes even if they think
someone ought to be suffering, they'll arrive with lots of sympathy,
and they are happy to come and have a bit of vicarious suffering with
you. It's rather nice, actually, and they have litanies of homespun
philosophies for everything. And chief among them always is "it
has to hurt".'

Johan Maric told me about Serbian masochism. 'In our restaurants a Serbian will drink and then break a glass and blood his
arm. In exaltation – he enjoys. His joy of suffering – he's enjoying
the situation. I think that's a specific form of masochism.'

In my work and in my personal life I have encountered a number
of people who felt that they were truly alive only when they were
suffering. They found periods of calm and peace in their life increasingly intolerable, and they would actually create some disaster in
order to suffer, gain attention and, if not exult, feel that things were
the way they expected them to be. I wonder if this way of making
sense of life is, in some small part, an explanation of the tragedy of
Yugoslavia. I toured there in 1972 and found it a most beautiful
country. With the fall of Communism the Yugoslavs could have
realized their country's potential: not least, they could have built up
a great tourist industry, and then sat back and enjoyed the profits.
Was Slobodan Milošovic one of those people for whom suffering is
a necessity, and his people, believing that suffering is a virtue, followed him?

Most people do not enjoy suffering, but when the group's beliefs include that of the Just World suffering can become an inevitability.

The belief in the Just World does not allow for chance. If a disaster occurs, then some person or some spirit or force must have caused it. The people of South Africa's Northern Province, the Venda, Sotho and Shangaan, believe that when a disaster occurs, such as a lightning strike which burns houses and kills cattle, it has been caused by a witch. Someone in the village is then likely to be identified as a witch and, if unable to flee, is burnt to death. The motive for selecting one person rather than another is usually envy. The person might have worked in a city and earned a pension, thus making him or her slightly wealthier than the other villagers, but to them that person's good fortune is not just. They had been good and where was their reward? So justice must be done.

No doubt some of the vulnerable people in these villages try to escape the fate of being deemed a witch by pre-empting the punishment and punishing themselves in some way. An illness can be seen as a suitable punishment, or an accident. Sometimes the tension of waiting for something bad to happen to you can be unbearable, so people will punish themselves and feel that the balance of justice has been restored. In Africa there is a large black bird called the hammerkop, *scopus umbretta*, which builds a huge nest in the branches of a tree and incorporates all manner of things in its nest. It collects bones, sometimes human bones, and this habit has led to its bad reputation. It is considered to be extremely bad luck if the hamerkop flies over your house. Some misfortune will certainly befall you. Consequently the sight of the bird over a house will prompt the inhabitants to perform some ritual self-punishment in order to ward off the misfortune which is coming their way.

Suffering is always a problem to those whose belief in the Just World centres on one all-powerful, all-beneficent God. To state the problem in its simplest form, here are three statements: God is all powerful; God is all good; suffering exists. For two of those statements to be true one must be false. Since suffering undoubtedly exists, we are left with the question, 'Is God all good or all powerful?'

The members of St James Church in Kenilworth, Cape Town, were faced with this question in the starkest way on 25 July 1993. At the church service that evening there was a massacre, leaving eleven people dead and fifty-five injured. A year later the vicar, Frank

Retief, wrote a book, *Tragedy and Triumph: A Christian Response to Trials and Suffering*, as an answer to the question of why bad things happen to good people. 'There is an unspoken feeling among Christians,' he wrote, 'that, if there should be suffering, it should be bearable and that we should not experience the same horror that unbelievers do.' But here the congregation had encountered suffering that was not bearable. Frank Retief wanted to assure believers of God's love and power, but on the question of power he had a problem. On page 51 he wrote, 'Ultimately everything is under God's control – no thing is outside God's plans and purposes – no power can thwart His purpose.' Yet on page 146 he wrote, 'Sin is a principle lodged in our very natures. There is nothing God can do.' In an attempt to reconcile these opposing statements he concluded that 'We have to accept that there are things about which we will always be ignorant ... [We have to] come to terms with the mysteries of life.'[54]

His conclusion is that there is no overarching Grand Design of a Just World whose workings-out we can see, but some ultimate and unknowable mystery. We just have to trust God. Such a way of seeing the world can accept the existence of chance; events no longer have to be related to our relative goodness and badness. Such an understanding takes away the security of the Just World, but it also takes away its inevitable punishments. In admitting uncertainty it allows hope, because hope can exist only in uncertainty. In such uncertainty we might come to feel less certain of the superior virtue of our own group and admit the possibility that groups other than our own might be good.

If we see our own group as superior to all others we will find ourselves in dire straits when our group disappears.

Recent world events have left vast numbers of people bereft of the group to which they had devoted their lives. Major parts of their meaning structures have been disconfirmed, and the construction of new meanings has proved to be extremely difficult. When a person finds a reconstruction impossible suicide can become the solution. Since the fall of Communism the suicide rate in Lithuania, Russia, Estonia and Latvia has soared.[55]

When I was in Cape Town I went with Andy Dawes to visit Justine Evans at the Trauma Clinic which had been set up in the wake of the Truth and Reconciliation Committee's work. I thought we would be discussing the TRC and the process of forgiveness, but what we talked about was the pressing problem of how people cope when their group no longer exists. Towards the end of our discussion I tried to sum up my understanding of what we were saying with, 'Are we saying that what must be happening now to a lot of people is that they come through the door of the clinic with their ticket of entry as "I had this terrible trauma ten years ago", but that's just the presenting problem? The real problem in the here and now is their faith in the struggle, or their faith in the beneficent, all-powerful God, which is now severely under strain. The situations which sustained that faith are no longer there.'

For many long years people had given themselves to the struggle against apartheid. Andy had supported the struggle in many ways, not least as a psychotherapist for political activists. In a paper about this work he wrote about the activists' devotion to their cause, which was such that 'Many of the activists who came into therapy did not regard it as legitimate to take time off to go to the sea with their families once in a while, or go to a cinema. To have done so would have indicated that they did not care while their comrades were suffering.'[56]

In our discussion I talked about the implications of the belief in a Just World. Andy said, 'With the Truth Commission stories, as they came out, yes, A did this to B and B was my child, you still hear people say this: "Why did I let Johnny go into the street? Why did I not do this?" So there's a hell of a lot of self-blame. "If I'd been a really good mother I'd never let him go near the stuff." And that comes out again and again, even though it's quite obvious that they have no responsibility at all. And, listening to these stories, it struck me forcibly – yes, this and that happened, somebody was tortured – but coming back over and over to self-blame. People take on an almost superhuman responsibility for something they could not possibly have responsibility for. That seemed to offlay the sense of "the bastards who did this". Quite often there seemed to me to be a sense of failure to protect one's own from the bastards.'

I said, 'Whenever you blame yourself for doing something, or failing to do something, you're making a claim that you were actually capable of doing that, so when you say, "If I'd really been a good mother I'd have supervised my fifteen-year-old every minute of the day and night," you're making this huge claim to power, and for many people, they'd rather live with that inflated claim than acknowledge their helplessness.'

Andy replied, 'Otherwise it would be in a sense to give up. "There was nothing I could do" diminished your power completely in a situation like that. And to give up power in a situation like that is very difficult, because then *they* have the power, not you.'

I mentioned Frank Retief's book and said, 'If you believe in the Just World, you've got to bring God into the argument. You've either got to blame God – if God's all-powerful He ought to have prevented this – or you see God as dangerous. There are plenty of pictures of a wrathful God in the Old Testament. If you want to preserve this notion that God is all-good and could be powerful if He chose to exercise His power, the only way to hang on to that is to say, "Well, we have to be patient. God knows best. Sooner or later." Which is sort of giving up your power, to say that God's all-powerful.'

Andy said, 'Though in a positive way. If you give up power on your own, you've lost it. You're useless, there's nothing you can do. Whereas if you give up power to God, He's on your side, and He will work through you to see that it's OK. So it's a very powerful situation.'

'Provided,' I said, 'you can go on trusting God.'

'Yes, of course,' said Andy. 'But it's a choice between being utterly alone with your uselessness and being co-opted into the God system, which will work with you. It's a massive existential crisis.'

Justine pointed out that for many people the struggle was God.

Andy agreed. 'All the way through. And you gave up your children, not to God this time but to the struggle. And that was valid and made a lot of sense. When people began to question *that*, then the wheels came off. And the whole dilemma of the mental health workers of that time was how far do you take someone towards saying, "I'm not sure I want to be part of the struggle any more. It's too scary, it's blowing my head off, it's messing up my family." As soon as that starts going, it's like a loss of faith, isn't it? A lot of people involved in these things were very wary of psychological workers for that very reason. Like you don't sit and have a counselling session with a soldier in a trench, and say, "How do you feel about this? Do you want to go back home?" You say, "Bloody well get on with it." So the military metaphors were very much part of the struggle. This child was not your child, he was the child of the nation. So everything was expropriated, and that's maybe why the private sense of grief couldn't be, because the child wasn't yours to grieve over. It was something you'd given to the collective. So in a certain sense you didn't deserve to grieve privately.'

Justine said, 'But there was that sense of belonging all through that time.'

'But not now,' said Andy. 'Then there would have been the comradely support group, to make the tea and so on, but not now. Now you're on your own. Once there were instruments of containment of a kind – the fact that you knew you'd be able to go to a funeral tomorrow and re-engage with people and milk them for their strength. I think we all did that. Sometimes we were running around like headless chickens. But part of that was being close to other people who are in those situations with you. You could feel contained by that, and what do you get contained by now? I don't know.'

Often to maintain that sense of being contained by the group we will hang on to the beliefs of the group even though they are no longer appropriate. One of the unfortunate legacies of the belief in unquestioned loyalty to your comrades in the struggle is that loyalty is now being expressed by some of the comrades now in power in terms of political favours and turning a blind eye to corruption. Economic success can be built only on democracy and a system of just laws which are respected by all. It will be a tragic irony if the loyalty which freed South Africa from apartheid goes on to destroy it.

Even while the struggle continued many people discovered how hard it is to live outside their group with all their connections severed. One of the weapons used by the apartheid regime was a banning order, whereby the banned person could be sent far away and prevented from contacting any friends or family. When Mamphela Ramphele was first banned she was sent, without any of her belongings and with none of her friends and family knowing where she was, to the Naphuno district of Tzaneen in northern Transvaal. Her first thought was to make contact with those she had left behind. With the help of the priest and nuns at the Sacred Heart Mission in Ofcolaco she phoned Steve Biko. Later she wrote,

A sense of calm descended on me after this call. At least the people who mattered to me knew where I was. There is something frightening about being in 'non-space' – unknown and amongst people with whom one has no real contact. I experienced the frightening emptiness of it all during the two days whilst being transported to my place of banishment. Many narratives of ex-detainees and ex-prisoners attest to the same overwhelming sense of not feeling like a complete human being until one has made some contact with those to whom one is connected, those who in a sense define one's humanity. It is not surprising that solitary confinement is used as a mainstay of torture.[57]

We can be in peril of that dangerous isolation when we lack the characteristics that would enable us to be a member of what appears to be our appropriate group. These characteristics are ways of behaving and thinking which we learn in childhood. However, some of us have childhoods where we cannot acquire these characteristics, and we have instead what Fay Weldon called 'a sense of not belonging'.

Fay had a very unusual childhood in New Zealand. When I asked her about friends and enemies she told me, 'I woke up this morning remembering someone once saying that I was a demimondaine. And I was really upset by that because there was a time when I was really trying to be like other people. But you weren't, you see – you couldn't be, and they detected it somewhere. They wouldn't make you a prefect at school because they detected something in you which meant you didn't belong. And you partly wanted to belong and you were partly glad you didn't. And in retrospect you're glad you didn't. And then you end up in advertising, along with everyone else who's a demimondaine – all people who don't quite belong.'

When you know that you do not belong, when you feel yourself to be an outsider, you have to find some way of maintaining your sense of existence. Just what you do depends on how you experience your sense of existence. Extraverts experience their sense of existence in the relationships they have with other people, while introverts experience their sense of existence in terms of a sense of achievement, organization and control. Outsider extraverts like Fay and my friend Judy survived by gathering around them a group of other outsiders.

Judy, who grew up in the same town as I did, Newcastle in Australia, also had an unusual childhood. Her parents saw no reason to send her and her sister Deirdre to school. Just out of her teens she married Alan, and they have a much-loved daughter, Fiona. However, having failed to learn the customs and beliefs of a Novocastrian, Judy found many of her friends among other outsiders, gay men and women. I asked Judy about these friendships and she said, 'My close friendships are with gay men. Even in Newcastle I had gay men I really liked and had these intense friendships with. I feel that they need me. And I like their sense of humour. I like the fact that you can have a friendship with them without giving them anything else, without the clingy bit – putting their hand on your knee and all that nonsense you don't want – and so they're the people I feel most happy with. Gay men, and gay women for that matter. I'm always attracted to gay people, because it seems to me they have so much sense of humour and none of them have children. I've never liked children. Gay people mostly adore animals the way I do, and like getting drunk and being outrageous and partying.'

I am an introvert, and for ever an outsider. My mother kept herself to herself, and she kept me with her. When I was a child she seemed like a wall between me and the rest of the world. As I got into my teens I wanted to escape but lacked the confidence to do so. Yet, on occasions she would insist that my sister take me on some outing, but Myra, six years older than me, had made it clear to me, right from the beginning, that she wanted nothing to do with me except when I could be of use to her. So, pushed out of the house by my mother with an air of being glad to get rid of me, I would hover, anxiously and awkwardly, on the edge of my sister's group of friends. This group sometimes included Robert, whom she later married, and his brothers Colin and Frank. Colin went to sea during the war and then lived abroad, so it was some fifty years before we met again. He told me then that he always remembered me as 'tag-along'.

I was not able to gather a group of friends around me as Fay and Judy had done. My mother disapproved of the neighbours' children. She also disapproved of the primary school nearby, and sent me to a school several miles away. I had a few friends there, but I did not get to know them well since I rarely saw them out of school. So, like many lonely children, I turned to books and found some friends there. My secret ambition was to be a writer.

I also did what Fay and Judy, and all children who find that they do not belong, do. We let primitive pride come to the rescue. We learnt to scorn the group which excluded us, and were proud to be separate and different. Fay told me that as a teenager she was pleased not to be part of ordinary English society. She said, 'I was pleased because you knew it was an advantage, you knew you could see what was going on, and they couldn't. You looked at things differently. They never saw that it was strange, what was going on, but you could see that looking at it from the outside was actually more of an advantage than being part of it.'

Fay sees a connection between being an outsider and becoming a writer. I see a similar connection between being an outsider and becoming a psychologist. Right from birth I had to keep a clear and steady eye on that most wonderful and most dangerous group, the family.

4

Belonging to a Family

'What's special about a family,' said Naomi, 'is that there's no one else in the world who can work you up so much by saying something like, "Press play on the video."'

Naomi is a member of one of the happiest families I have ever known, but she readily identified the one characteristic that distinguishes friends from family. No matter how close you are to your friends, and no matter how important they are to you, they cannot get past your defences and touch your inner core in the way that your family can.

We join this special group, our family, when we are born. We had no choice. They are the reason we exist. We are stuck with them for the rest of our lives. Even if they all die, or we sever every tie and live elsewhere, we take our family with us in our family resemblances. We might think that we look nothing like our parents, and then one day we look in a mirror and there they are.

Just how we feel when our parents gaze back at us from the mirror depends on what love they inspired in us. I saw this in two very different workshops which I ran. The first was part of an extensive international course for high-flying, successful managers in their thirties and forties. Over lunch one man leaned back in his chair and put his hands behind his head with his elbows spread. He said, 'My father always sat like this and when I was young it annoyed me intensely. Now I do it often. I find it comfortable.'

That set the rest of the group talking about how they were discovering that they had developed ways of thinking, talking and moving which were just like the ways their fathers had thought, talked and moved. They were surprised by their discovery and, what surprised them even more, they were actually pleased to find that they were growing to be like their fathers.

Two days later I ran a workshop for a group of women whose ages ranged from early twenties to late sixties. The theme of the workshop was anger, revenge and forgiveness. In the morning I set them the task of examining how the family they had grown up in had dealt with anger, forgiveness and revenge. Then, in turn, each woman described her experience to the group, and we discussed some of the issues arising from this.

What had brought these women to this workshop was the unhappiness in their lives. This was not their first experience of exploring their childhoods. Each of them had for some years been reading books and entering into discussions in order to unravel what had gone wrong in their lives, so each of them could speak frankly and reveal the emotions they felt. They gave lots of support and comfort to one another throughout the day.

All the women told stories of parental neglect and cruelty which took many forms. One of the themes which emerged in many of their stories concerned the woman's mother who was still alive, still making demands on her child and maintaining her child's unhappiness. As they spoke several of the women said, 'I hope I don't get like my mother.'

The ties to family do not end with death. In childhood we take our parents inside us and there they remain, commenting, criticizing, giving us instructions. I have more than once purchased a new outfit to wear for a television engagement because I could hear my mother saying, 'They'll think you've got only one dress.' The likelihood that 'they' will remember what I was wearing in each of my brief television appearances is decidedly slim, but I obey my mother's voice.

I think that this voice is my memory of my mother and not a message from her in some afterlife, but the majority of people do believe that their family has some kind of eternal life separate from them. In many of the conversations I have had with people who were depressed the person would talk about how, in making their decisions, they would take into account the views of the family members who were in heaven. One man, very seriously depressed and longing for death, told me that he would not kill himself because, if he did so and arrived in heaven, his domineering father would not welcome him but instead be very angry.

For Zulus the dead are deemed to live on as spirits in the family home, where they support and advise the living. Should a Zulu die away from home someone in the family has to go to where the person died and bring the spirit home.

This is done by using a twig of *mpafa* tree, which is a very tough thorn bush. The Voortrekkers called it the *blinkblaar wag-'n-bietjie*, the shining leaf wait-a-while tree. It has two kinds of thorns, one hooked and the other straight. If these thorns got hooked into your skin you were forced to wait a while.

Ian Player, renowned for his conservation work in KwaZulu-Natal, wrote about his friendship with Qumbu Magqubu Ntombela, a Zulu game guard who had a profound influence on his life. Magqubu was a brilliant story-teller, and one of the stories he told Ian Player was about how he had brought his father's spirit home from the hospital in Durban where he had died. Magqubu took a piece of the mpafa tree with him to the hospital, laid it on his father's death bed and called out to the spirit, 'Woza, Baba [Come, Father], I am here to take you home.'

Magqubu went on,

'When the mpafa had lain on the place where my father had died, his spirit entered the mpafa and I began the journey home. But there were two of us, my father's spirit and myself . . . I bought two tickets at the stimela [steam train], one for my father, one for me. The train left for Mtubatuba in the night and I bought food for the journey. When I ate, I spoke to my father and said I was eating for him too. I put the mpafa branch on the next bunk. The other Zulus in the compartment respected my father's spirit and did not lie on the bunk. [Once home] I took the mpafa branch and pushed it into the eaves of my father's hut, which was made from the same umuNga [Acacia karoo] poles we had brought from Ongeni when the government removed us in 1945 . . . My father, he beat me when I was a grown man with two wives. When I put the mpafa branch in the eaves, I remembered everything about him, and I said, "Father, you are now home with us and we want you to keep the peace in this muzi of the Ntombelas."'

Magqubu told Ian Player how at the time of the big battles at Isandlwana, Kambula, and Inyezane in the Anglo-Zulu War of 1879, the bodies of many men lay on the veld and were eaten by the animals and the vultures. He said,

> 'The bones were mixed together. No one knew which body they came from. The relatives of the men who died walked from their homes carrying a piece of the tree, and when they came to the battlefield they held up the mpafa and called out the name of their father, brother, son, uncle, cousin, or the man from their area, and they would say, "We have come to collect you, to take you home to your muzi on the hills of Hlabisa, or Hluhluwe, Nongoma, Mahla-batini, Lebombo." The people would turn and walk back, and all the time speak to the spirit in the mpafa. When they drank at streams or ate at homes on the way, they would do so twice, as I did for my father. At home the mpafa twig would be put into the eaves of the huts, a beast killed, and the dead person would then join all the other amadhlozi in the muzi.'[1]

The mpafa provides an economical way for the family dead to be brought back home. In the USA dead soldiers are brought home in body bags, and the number of body bags affects government policy. One of the reasons American sanctions against Vietnam were eventually relaxed was so that American teams of investigators could search for the bones of American soldiers still missing in that war. The American army's disastrous foray into Somalia in 1992 and the sight on American television of so many body bags being brought home led to a change of policy on intervention in foreign conflicts. Rather than sending in the troops missiles were to be used against distant targets. Foreign civilians might die but no American troops would come home in body bags.

The belief that the spirits of your ancestors are safe beneath your roof or that the bones of your loved ones must be decently interred nearby helps to maintain the one quality that the family can provide better than any other group, a sense of permanence and continuity. This is vital in a world of continual change of which all we can ever know is 'a woven web of guesses'. When we are small we need to believe that those who look after us are fixtures in our world. As that part of our meaning structure called consciousness develops we need to believe that we ourselves are fixtures and not something which could disappear. When we discover death, as we usually do when we reach five or six, we have to create a meaning for death with which we can live.[2] To overcome our fear of death we try to imagine some way in which we can continue on after we have died. For many people the most attractive option is reincarnation.

This belief became increasingly popular in the West during the seventies, when the study of Eastern philosophies like Buddhism and yoga was the vogue. Western believers in reincarnation tended to see it in terms of the survival of the individual rather than the group. They identified themselves as the reincarnation of some fascinating and significant person from some important time in history. They did not see reincarnation as an intimate part of the social strata, as it is seen in Hinduism, or of the family, as it is for the Druze.

The Druze community was formed in the eleventh century and went on to play a significant part in the history of Lebanon and Syria. According to Druze belief,

> Human souls were created at once, their number is fixed for all time, it is not subject to diminution or increase. Upon death, the soul is immediately reborn in another body, the body serving to envelop or robe the soul . . . The process of transmigration goes on to the end of time. In the process souls rise through their attachment to the truth to a higher degree of excellence, or deteriorate to become degraded by neglecting the teachings of religion . . . The soul, in its repeated transmigrations, experiences all conditions of life: fortune and misfortune, riches and poverty, health and illness.[3]

'There is no other group who believe in reincarnation in this particular version, that at the point of death the soul is instantly reincarnated in a newly born baby. So as you take the last breath in the old body, you take your next breath in a new body.' This is what Dr Chris French told me when I went to interview him about his research, which involved, amongst other things, making a television film showing some Druze children speaking about their previous life and their previous family. The present family of these children might then set about finding their child's previous family.

Chris French is well known for his work in the study of the paranormal – not in proving or disproving its existence, but in exploring 'just what psychological processes might be involved in making people think that something paranormal happened when in fact it hadn't'.

What he has found is that we will readily believe that something paranormal has happened when that belief serves to maintain our meaning structure. He told me, 'People often think that the reason you're trying to point to possible motives is to indicate that there's some deliberate fraud or hoaxing going on, but it doesn't mean that at all. It just means that there are obvious benefits to that individual from the world being that way – reincarnation being an obvious example where, in the cases that we looked at there were obvious benefits to both the current family of the child and the past life family. There's a very strong tendency for the reincarnated child to have reincarnated in a lower social class than in their past life. In the vast majority of cases the child will say that in their past life they were of a higher social class, that they were more powerful in their past life.'

He went on, 'Apart from the kind of wish-fulfilment angle, there can also be real material benefit. If the past-life family accept the reincarnation, they will of course feel a certain obligation to help that child out in terms of providing opportunities. It may be actual financial benefits, or it may be in terms of providing guidance, advice and so forth. But they will take an interest, and because they're of a higher social class, they will have influence. Which is not to say that the children, or the parents of the child, are therefore deliberately manufacturing the whole thing. On the other side of the equation, you've got the past life family who obviously are helped to come to terms with the grief they have felt, by having this person presenting themselves as being the reincarnation of their dead father, or whatever. So it works on that kind of micro level. On the higher social level there is the increase in social cohesion that this kind of system allows for – especially in a closed community like the Druze, where they've been persecuted for centuries. On the one hand it extends links into the community. So you've not only got your biological family – again there's lots of intermarrying there because a Druze must marry a Druze – but you've also got the past life family to link into, so the whole social cohesion is increased in that way.'

This belief serves to create a cohesive group, but in its working out in real life some creative construing is required to explain the anomalies which arise. For instance, more than one child might claim to be the reincarnation of the dead person, or the dates of the death and the birth do not coincide. In theory, since conversion either in or out of the Druze community is impossible, the population should stay the same size, but in practice fluctuations do occur. However, a family can give so much comfort and security that putting your reason into some kind of abeyance can seem a small price to pay.

Each religion offers a way of denying death, and each religion does this by offering a way of eternal life which is modelled on the family. The gods are the parents, the faithful the children. All the varieties of parents, as they can be seen by the children, are represented by the gods – the Greek gods capricious and sensual, Jehovah stern and punitive, Shiva magical and powerful, Kali the murderous mother, the Holy Spirit distant and unknowable, Jesus the good shepherd and the martyr. The trade which the gods offer us is the same trade which parents offer their children: 'I'll look after you and you'll be an obedient child.'

However, ordinary parents expect their children eventually to become independent adults who take responsibility for themselves. Eternal families demand eternal childhoods, and this is what many people want, to be the eternal child and never have to take responsibility for themselves. When the largest Mormon temple in Europe was opened in Chorley, Lancashire, Sister Luke from California was quoted as saying, 'I was born into the church. I know I can be with my family for ever and that I can be married to someone I love for all eternity.'[4]

Not everyone wants to be an eternal child. Ingrid told me, 'I became involved in the Friends of the Western Buddhist Order (FWBO) at a time when my life scored very high on the stress counter. Like many others who were interested in FWBO, I was looking for a peg to hang my beliefs on during a time of crisis. I had already rejected the dreariness of the Church of England, which had been imposed on me as a child, but was attracted to the exotic and peaceful face of Buddhism. Naïvely, I assumed that all would be peace and harmony with my fellow travellers on the spiritual path. It was a shock to discover that going on retreats was not the answer, and that FWBO was no better than the world I was trying to escape. For those who wanted to make a commitment, and become

ordained members, the FWBO seemed to offer a ready-made family,
complete with lifestyle. I never felt able to make that kind of commitment and become a fully fledged Friend. To me, the FWBO soon
became a kind of benevolent prison, in which dissension was hidden
from public view. For me to have joined such a community would
not have solved anything at all. I would have felt powerless and
childlike all over again. So I opted for uncertainty and stayed
outside.'

Staying outside the family is an option open only to adults. Children need to be in care of adults, so each of us has to spend our
first years of life in some kind of family group.

Becoming Part of the Family

Something that has always seemed to me to be odd about us is that
we readily accept complex ideas when we want to understand objects
but we are reluctant to accept complex ideas when we want to
understand ourselves. If we want to learn how to programme a
computer or send a rocket to Mars we see it as natural that we will
have to absorb some very complex ideas, but if we want to learn
how people form relationships or parent a child we demand that
these complex processes be reduced to one or two simple ideas. No
wonder we have made so little progress in learning how to live
happily together!

However, underlying the complex processes involved in the
behaviour of objects there are some universal laws of physics. Within
complexity there is simplicity. Psychologists always fancied themselves as scientists like physicists, and they have searched for universal laws of human nature. There has been no shortage of ideas which
have been presented as universal laws – Freud's unconscious and
his id, ego and superego, Jung's collective unconscious and arche-
types, for example – but that is what they are, ideas, metaphors
which can be more or less helpful in understanding what we do
and why we do it. The problem is that human beings do not behave
like objects. They function like human beings – that is, they are
constantly in the business of interpretation. They interpret what is
going on around them, they interpret what other people do and
say, they interpret other people's interpretations, and then other

people interpret their interpretations of the others' interpretations
and so on and on and on. We all live in this complex, ceaselessly
active, multidimensional world of interpretations interpreting
interpretations, and most of the time we do this fairly well, but
when we want to understand what is actually going on what we
look for is one simple idea.

When I came into psychology in the late forties the prevailing
simple idea was instinct. There was the maternal instinct, the sex
instinct, the aggression instinct, the avoiding-walking-under-ladders
instinct, the listening-to-the-radio instinct and so on. Whatever anyone did could be explained as the functioning of an instinct.

Times have moved on and we are now much more scientific.
Now we have genes. There is the maternal gene, the sex gene, both
hetero and homo, the avoiding-walking-under-ladders gene, the
watching-television gene and so on. My son Edward rang me from
Australia not long ago to tell me that he was listening to a psychologist on the radio who was talking about the psychotherapist gene
and the psychotherapy-client gene. These must be mutant genes in
existence only for a few decades. Edward does not have either of
these genes but he does have the sending-up-psychologists gene.

The term instinct gradually disappeared from the discourse of
psychologists as more and more of them realized that the so-called
universal law of instincts was no more than a circular argument
which went:

SEEKER AFTER TRUTH: Why is that person aggressive?
PSYCHOLOGIST: Because he has the aggression instinct.
SEEKER AFTER TRUTH: How do you know he has the aggression
    instinct?
PSYCHOLOGIST: Because he is aggressive.

Now genes explain behaviour in the same circular way. Replace
the word 'instinct' in the above by the word 'gene' and you have
the genetic argument about how genes cause complex behaviour.
Advocates of the genetic explanation of complex behaviour claim
to be scientific. They talk of twin studies and the Human Genome
Project, but in such a way that reveals their ignorance of both.

Twin studies have three major flaws. The first is that the earliest
studies were done for political reasons to do with eugenics and

racism, and the results were fabricated to that end. Although this is now well documented, psychiatrists who want to prove that mental illnesses like schizophrenia are genetic still use the data from the early studies to bolster their own data.[5] The second flaw is that in studies using identical twins separated at birth little or no attempt is made to assess just how different the two environments were where each twin lived. Growing up with a granny who lives just around the corner from Mum is a very different experience from growing up in a country and with a language different from your twin. The third flaw is that identical twins do not necessarily have the same genetic traits, they do not necessarily have to be carried in the womb in the same gestational sac, and, in competition in the womb for space and blood supply, one twin can do better than the other, and both have experiences different from those of a single baby in the womb.

As for the argument that the Human Genome Project will discover the gene for homosexuality, for depression and so on, let me quote Susan Greenfield writing in the *Sunday Times* so that we can all understand it.

Some [people] point to recent advances in molecular biology and say that it is only a matter of time before we have the wherewithal to suppress the gene 'for' shyness, or introduce the gene 'for' intelligence. Once we have fully mapped the human genome, once we know what every gene in the human body expresses, then surely it will be scientific child's play to tweak a few strands of DNA to fine-tune our brains.

But what these people who make these claims do not seem to realize is that the brain is not merely a genetic potpourri. The human body contains about 1m genes. This sounds enormous, until you take in the fact that the human brain has 100 million brain cells. And that number is as nothing compared to the number of synapses, or connections. There are 1,000 to 100,000 synapses for every brain cell, bringing us to a total of about 100,000,000,000,000! It is unlikely that genes dictate the formation, distribution and functioning of each of these individual connections, but even if we assume that they dictate 1m of them, we are still left with a billion-fold discrepancy.

So what does determine the configuration of these other circuits?

The answer is: real life; recent studies have shown that synapses are forged, strengthened or suppressed by personal experience.

The biggest problem lies in what we perceive genes to be 'for'. It would be wrong to point to the gene 'for', say, criminality. All a single gene can do is express a tiny chemical. It does not contain a sophisticated behaviour pattern trapped in the structure of DNA. True, the chemical will aid and abet the functioning of certain brain cells in certain circuits, which in turn are nested in ever more complex brain hierarchies, which eventually add up to a complete brain structure. But these brain structures are not independent mini-brains. There are no 'centres for' love of children, or patriotism. Just as a single brain function such as memory is distributed among many different brain regions, so, too, can a single brain region be involved in many different functions.[6]

There might well be some universal law which will describe the functioning of the brain and bring together the individual patterning of synaptic connections and the individual meaning structure, but its discovery is not imminent. What the current stage of knowledge of brain function shows is the importance of individual personal experience. This should make us very wary of claims that any particular form of behaviour is universal, found in every human being irrespective of race and culture.

There are some universal characteristics found in all people, though I doubt that there would ever be universal agreement amongst psychologists, anthropologists and biologists on what should be included in that list. My list of universals is:

1. We are in essence meaning-constructing creatures.
2. We each create our own individual meanings.
3. These individual meanings cohere into a structure which we experience as our sense of self or identity.
4. Each meaning structure has certain intrinsic forms which enable it to function. These include:
   • the form of the face, on which the creation of relationships with other people depend;
   • the form of a story, whereby everything becomes meaningful once it is embedded in a story;

- the form of primitive pride, which has the function of keeping the meaning structure together.
5. Meanings exist as images or as language or as emotion or as combinations of all these.
6. Meanings have some as yet unknown relationship to the individual patterns of synaptic connections in the brain.

This is the basis on which each of us operates. However, as soon as we want to examine what particular meanings we or anyone else has created we must take into account the environment and culture of that particular person. While each of us is born with the capacity to create an infinite array of meanings, the meanings which we do create are limited by what possibilities of meanings our particular environment has to offer. We come into the world capable of forming relationships with an infinite array of faces, but we find the only faces available are those of our family. We come into the world capable of absorbing an infinite number of stories, and the story we are presented with is that of our family.

The last thirty years have seen some tremendous advances in our understanding of how infants develop. The clever use of film and video has allowed some remarkable observations to be made of what infants and toddlers do. However, problems arise when the researchers interpret their observations. An American researcher observing a number of white, middle-class American babies, or an English researcher observing a number of white, middle-class English babies can easily fail to draw the simple conclusion that this is what American or English middle-class babies do and instead generalize their observations to say that this is what *all* babies do. This is Western imperialism in operation, and it is so implicit in much of the information and advice given by Western pundits that you can be led to believe that because a black, working-class baby in Africa does something different there is something wrong with that baby.

Of course some of the information and advice given by Western pundits does apply to all babies. All babies like being in the company of other people and having something interesting to look at. It is when pundits talk about how adults ought to behave and how babies ought to respond that Western imperialism can take over, and what is lost is the understanding that babies have to learn how to fit into their family and their culture. Not all families and not all cultures are the same.

I have certainly given a great deal of advice about how babies should be helped to develop and what that development should be. No doubt a close reading of any of my books would reveal some effects of Western imperialism, but I think that my basic message has some universality. This message is that to live peacefully with ourselves and to have the courage to face life's difficulties we need to value and accept ourselves and to feel that others value us and accept us as we are. In general terms this statement would apply to all people in all cultures, but how 'value' and 'accept' actually operate would be different in different cultures. What is valuable and acceptable in one culture is not necessarily valuable and acceptable in another. Each culture has its own way of teaching children the kind of behaviour which that culture values and accepts.

Studies which compare the child-raising practices of different cultures usually show how these practices arise both from the economic circumstances and from the metaphysical beliefs of that culture – that is, from the practicalities of daily living to the meaning of life. One such study was that carried out by Robert A. LeVine and his colleagues at Harvard University. They compared a group of middle-class mothers and babies in Boston, USA, with a group of Gussii mothers and babies in Kenya.[7]

The Gussii people number about 1 million and live in the fertile highlands of south-western Kenya. They are quite successful farmers – the weather and politicians permitting – and have one of the highest birth rates in the world, with quite a low infant mortality rate for Africa. The average woman bears about nine children and manages to raise most of them, while at the same time providing the children's food through labour-intensive agriculture whether or not their husbands are in employment. In contrast the Boston mothers, if they did work outside the home, did so only part time because the husband could provide an adequate income.

In any community where insurance and pensions do not exist, where workers do not earn enough to build up savings for old age, and where one disaster can reduce a worker to penury, the only way parents can try to ensure an adequate income and make some provision for their old age is to have many children. When a woman has to bear and raise many children, run a household and do a demanding job outside the home she does not have time to give her children much individual attention.

It is hardly surprising that the Harvard research team found that the Boston mothers spent much more time interacting with their babies than did the Gussii mothers. The Gussii babies were held or carried by their mothers or other people all the time, and fed and soothed, but they were not played with and talked to in the way that the American mothers played with and talked to their babies. But this reflected not just the amount of free time each group of mothers had. There was also a great difference in what LeVine called 'the models of virtue that guide mothers in the socialization of their children'. He explained that,

> Middle-class American mothers typically want alert, active, responsive, talkative and independent children, and they look for precursors of these qualities to reinforce during infancy. Gussii mothers, although their primary goals in the first year of life are growth and survival rather than behavioural or psychological development, typically prefer respectful children who are attentive to adult commands without being talkative or attention seeking. In infancy they try to cultivate a quiet, easily soothed baby who will fit easily into the domestic hierarchy of the household under the daytime care of siblings as young as five years of age. Mothers assume that the sibling group will socialize each toddler with only occasional maternal intervention. This model of child development helps explain why, when Gussii mothers were asked why they do not play with or teach their infants more than they do, their typical response was that this was something for the other children, not the mother, to do.

When Western parents of large families are questioned about their child-rearing practices they usually talk about how they try to spend a certain amount of time with each child in order to make sure that the child feels 'special' and able to talk openly to each parent. The principle that a child should be seen and not heard, which dominated Western child-rearing practices until the 1950s, has now faded away, except in those families where the parents have managed to avoid all those agencies which teach parents how to listen to their children. Children who are listened to by their parents grow up expecting to be listened to, and they complain when their expectations are not met. Parents who listen to their children have to adapt to being told what they would often prefer not to hear. My young friend Miles, who was listened to assiduously by his parents Jo and Jeremy from the moment he was born, developed the habit of uttering truths which could be devastating. When he was six he told his hard-working father, 'You've been doing your PhD for as long as I've been alive' (though a year later he was greatly impressed when he saw Jeremy graduate). Miles was never slow to complain when he felt he had not been treated fairly, and he did not hesitate to exaggerate to get his point across. He might tell his mother, 'You're only interested in Alice and Eli, you're not interested in me,' and Jo would take this seriously and consider carefully what she had done, or failed to do. If she felt she had neglected him in the smallest way she would hasten to make amends.

It was not like that in the family I grew up in. I remember an incident when I was about eight and trying to puzzle out how our family operated. I must have been seeking to reassure myself that everything was really all right because I said to my mother in a tone which implied that I thought this was fair, 'It's like a balance, you love Myra and Dad loves me.' In my effort to feel that I was being treated fairly I overlooked the fact that my father loved my sister as well as loving me. Whether my mother saw the implication in my statement about her relationship to me I do not know, because she looked very annoyed but said nothing.

Miles and Alice would certainly correct their parents if they thought they had got something wrong. They could do this without fear of punishment, something I risked if I corrected my mother. At school I could correct my teachers, say, if they got the date or the time wrong, provided I did it respectfully. This was not the case in many African tribes and not merely in the Gussii. Such is the respect which children in these tribes must show to their elders that they must never even hint that an adult has got something wrong, even when this mistake causes much misery.

This was explained to me by Richard, a very pleasant young man from Ghana who works for the cab company I use. He told me how he was his mother's first born and, as she was very young, he had been brought up by his aunt. As an adult he came to England and, once in work, he wrote to his mother and promised to send her some money. His aunt opened and read this letter, and, believing that he had favoured his mother over her, turned against him and subsequently acted in such a way as to harm him. He told me that he had intended to send his aunt much more money, 'five times over', than he would send his mother, because his aunt had raised him and looked after him so well.

'Couldn't you explain to your aunt?' I asked, operating in the Western myth that good communication solves all problems.

Richard did not say, 'No, I can't,' but instead talked around the subject, using illustrations which allowed me to deduce that, no matter how serious an error an adult might make, a younger person could not correct an adult because that would be disrespectful. I put my deduction to him, and he said, 'Yes, that's right.'

For Gussii children all their training from birth onwards is aimed at ensuring that they know their place in the family hierarchy. Part of this training is to show children that they are in no way special. LeVine wrote,

> [Gussii] parents provide little explicit support for the young child's self-assertion and pride in personal achievement. Mothers and fathers eschew praise for a child of any age as fostering conceit ... Gussii mothers believe that keeping infant expectations for adult attention low prevents young children from becoming morally 'spoiled' (*ogosaria*), that is, demanding and cranky, which can lead to conceit and arrogance. From the parents' point of view, Gussii infant care provides the child with expectations that are realistic and morally appropriate.

How could a child growing up in such a family be able to value and accept himself? The Western self-esteem school of child development advocates lots of praise and positive reinforcement. LeVine's answer to that question was that in the traditional Gussii community everyone became competent in all the skills necessary for the survival and maintenance of the tribe. All these skills had to be committed to memory and passed on to younger generations, all of which could be a source of a sense of personal satisfaction. By contrast, the Western advances in technology have been accompanied by increasing ignorance amongst most people about how that technology actually works. We might be able to take pride in our ability to operate that technology, but few of us know what to do when that technology breaks down, except to phone for some expert whose fee will be well in excess of his expertise. Some people try to sidestep this problem with the help of primitive pride. They constantly congratulate themselves on their ignorance of all technology except those items with which they grew up. Over the years I have watched many of my contemporaries refuse to learn how to use answer phones, video machines, computers and mobile phones, but they do use telephones and they drive cars.

Gussii children might acquire all the necessary skills, but how could they know if what they did was good enough if their parents never praised them? If their parents noticed them only to criticize them, would they not grow up feeling crushed and defeated? It is likely that they would, just as any child in any family would. No doubt there were Gussii parents who criticized their children endlessly, and no doubt their children became dispirited and depressed, but in families where the parents were proud of their children's accomplishments the giving of praise would be subtle but significant. Thus a Western child, surrounded daily with a parental chorus of 'Darling, you are wonderful, I love you,' would take parental praise for granted, whereas a Gussii child, receiving a parental nod or a pat on the shoulder, would feel his heart near burst with pride. When Richard read these pages to check whether I had quoted him correctly he suggested that I add here that 'when these children become adult their parents give them respect, particularly if the parents are being well looked after by their children.'

When parents love their children they cannot help but feel that their child is wonderful and special. One of the measures of friendship, I think, is that your friend will listen patiently while you boast about your children. If the Gussii parents do not show their pride in their children there must be some heavy sanctions that force them not to do so.

And there are. The Gussii believe in the Just World. They try to be good and get their just rewards, but when disaster befalls them they are faced with the choice: was the disaster their fault or that of someone else? Do they become depressed or paranoid? Depression could mean the end of the tribe, so they choose paranoia. It becomes their way of life.

LeVine wrote,

Gussii men and women tend to feel extremely vulnerable to the imagined jealousy of others when they contemplate receiving any potentially invidious distinction . . . [They] were extremely anxious about being publicly recognized for special accomplishment or good fortune, exaggerating the destructive power of their neighbours' jealousy and going to great lengths to postpone public awareness of any advantage gained by themselves, their children, their family . . . To the Gussii, a display of pleasure in one's good fortune is an open invitation to the jealousy and destructiveness of others less fortunate, even when they are not present. Children are particular targets for the witchcraft of envious neighbours. Thus a Gussii healer showed me the medicine he had for children who do well in school, to protect them from the dangers their good fortune would inevitably attract. Gussii mothers do not make a display of love and attachment to their babies for the same reason they do not announce that they are pregnant.

LeVine asked whether the Gussii mothers, when alone with their babies, looked at and talked to their babies. He answered that question, firstly, by saying that they were rarely alone and, secondly, that it seems that 'their suppression of behaviour interpretable as a display of personal pride is not dependent on the actual social conditions of the observation; from their point of view the danger is ubiquitous.' In the Gussii woman's Just World evil spirits were always present and she would have to act appropriately to keep herself and her family safe.

The Gussii children learn of the ever-present danger of the malevolence of envy in the same context where they learn to be circumspect in their behaviour and thus earn the very subtle signs of their parents' pride in them. They learn to behave in ways which make them acceptable to their families, and, in doing so, they learn to see the world in terms of enemies. As we shall see, in all cultures enemies play an important part when a child is taught to be an acceptable member of the family.

The ideas which we acquire as small children have a quality quite different from the ideas we acquire later in life. First-time experiences have an immediacy and a vibrancy which repeated experiences never have. Often these experiences occur in situations where a great deal of emotion is being expressed by all the people present. Children might, in their own eyes, be doing nothing that they have not done before, like running to look at something interesting or relieving the pressure in their bowels, and suddenly there is an adult shouting and punishing the child.

With first-time experiences synaptic connections are formed, and, if the experience is repeated several times, groups of these synaptic connections form the neural gestalts which underlie all meanings. Repetition is not necessary for the formation of some neural gestalts. Some experiences so command our attention that we learn something immediately and for ever. Such experiences in adult life can lead us to question all our previous assumptions, whereas for a small child such experiences seem to present the world as totally real, absolute and unquestionable. If no adult notices that this has happened and hastens to explain to the child the relativity of the child's interpretation of the experience, the child is likely to hold that belief through childhood, if not through life.

This is what often develops from those experiences where the child is being taught to be good. When parents are trying to teach their children how to behave in ways which fit in with what family and society want they often include in their instructions information about the child himself. Such information is to the parent entirely relative, and often completely wrong since the parent might be exercising the parental right of taking his bad feelings out on the child.

I was involved in such an event not long ago when I was returning to my home from the local shops. This involves a short walk along a narrow pavement which lines a busy road. I have to pass a bus stop, where at any time there could be ten or more people waiting for a bus. Most commonly these people position themselves without regard for the people like me who want to get past. I refuse to walk on the road to get past because not only is there a great deal of traffic but many of the drivers who have been held up while passing the shops put on a burst of speed once they are clear of shops and the pedestrian crossing.

On this particular day, as I approached the bus stop, I could see that my path through the crowd was blocked by a little boy of about five who was absorbed in playing with the folded pushchair his mother had beside her. She was oblivious of me. As I came up to the little boy I gently put my hands on his shoulders and said,

'Excuse me, please, dear.' He looked up, surprised, but before he could move his mother yanked him to her side and said, 'Get out of the way,' and then, 'That's just like you. You're always in the way.'

I walked on pondering whether I ought to have stopped and asked the mother why she blamed her son for her own failure to anticipate that I would need to get past, and whether she really did want to teach him that in her family he was surplus to requirements.

Had I said this no doubt the mother would have taken offence. She might, amongst other things, have been one of those parents who believe that children are very selective in what they learn from their parents. They will – or they should – learn rules of behaviour like 'Don't get in other people's way', but they will not remember parental remarks like 'You're always in the way.' Such a belief arises from the activities of primitive pride. If we take responsibility for all our actions we run the risk of disconfirming our meaning structure when we realize that we are not as good, tolerant, wise and far-seeing as we like to think we are. The mother at the bus stop could not bear to blame herself for failing to see me approach, and so she blamed her child.

Children are always a threat to their parent's meaning structure. They can prevent the parent from doing the things which maintain the integrity of the parent's meaning structure. The parent might need to reassure himself that he is still a member of his group of friends, or she might need to maintain her career in order to have a sense of achievement, but the requirement to look after a small child cuts across both these needs. The parent, to think well of herself, might need to feel that she is knowledgeable and in control, and the child presents her with situations which she does not understand and where she feel helpless. The parent might need to feel that the way in which he sees the world is the only right way, and the child, not trained to see the world as his father does, constantly presents other perspectives.

Many parents, not wanting to admit how often interactions with their children have left them feeling anxious and helpless, prefer to see the influences on their child's behaviour as something other than the behaviour of the family members. In the family I grew up in I was seen as a distinct, bounded object whose actions had no more significance than 'that's what Dorothy does'. If I was angry, or upset, or dejected, or silent it was because that was what I did. What I did could not be the outcome of what others in the family did. If I told my mother and sister very little about myself it could not be because they were likely to use any confidence I might make against me. It was simply because I did not talk very much. To be fair, my father did see that there was a connection between my behaviour and the behaviour of others, though he sometimes misdiagnosed cause and effect, but in that household his interpretations of reality were not likely to prevail. My mother would get very angry with anyone who dared to suggest that everything she did and said had anything but an entirely happy outcome, and my sister learned to do the same.

This kind of denial of responsibility often leads people to claim that parents in no way influence their children. Yet parents do influence their children, though just how this influence works is difficult to predict. When Nisbett and Cohen began their research into the functioning of the culture of honour they saw this as a study of masculinity, but as their work progressed they saw that this was a false division. They found that

> in many societies females not only prepare their male children for
> the culture of honour and force it on their menfolk, they participate
> in it themselves. In some Mediterranean cultures, it is the women
> who routinely carry out some of the homicides, for example, the
> stoning to death of a woman who has been unfaithful. In others, it
> is understood that if there is no man available to carry out a homi-
> cide, a woman must do it.

In their own studies Nisbett and Cohen found that 'southern women, like southern men, are more likely than their northern counterparts to endorse violence for answering an affront, to oppose gun control, and to support spanking.' A result from one of their studies surprised them. Here they asked

> about the regional background of the subjects' parents. The number
> of cases was small, but it seemed that having a mother from the
> South was important in producing the 'southern' response to our
> insult – and, indeed, having a mother from the South seemed to
> be a better predictor of the 'southern' response than having a father
> from the South.[8]

It is not just parents who influence their children. Other family members do. Richard, a journalist who talked to me about the importance of the family to him, said, 'We had my mother's mother with us for a few years when I was a kid, and she made life pretty miserable at the time. She had quite strong views about who was the wage earner in the family. If you weren't a wage earner, you were nothing. Even though I was only thirteen or fourteen, a schoolboy, I was very low down her pecking order in esteem.' Later, when he was telling me how he regretted that his parents had not encouraged him to go to university, he said, 'From the age of fifteen to eighteen I used to work about twenty-six hours a week, and that's a big slice out of your week – Saturday, Sundays and two nights a week from five to ten, stuck in a supermarket. So studies didn't get done.'

However, when I said that parents influence their children, I glossed over what makes being a parent so very, very hard. If you are a parent, it does not matter how carefully you consider your every word and deed with regard to your children and how hard you try to make your influence on your children entirely beneficial, it is not what you say and do which determines your child's behaviour. It is how your child interprets what you say and do that determines your child's behaviour.

If parents are unaware that the child's interpretations are the determining factor in the child's behaviour they do not spend any time trying to work out what are the implications for the child of what they say and do. Thinking along these lines is really hard work, and there is always the danger that in doing so a parent's meaning structure could be disconfirmed, or, at least, that the parent comes to see the necessity of behaving in ways that are not convenient or pleasurable for the parent. My mother never ran these risks. Like the Gussii parents she did not want a child who was 'spoiled' – that is, demanding – and so she forbore to give praise and signs of affection. I have a memory of something which happened when I was coming up to eleven, an event which then seemed to me to be quite ordinary but now seems to me to be very odd. When you are a child you lack comparisons, and so things seem to happen in the context of 'this is what happens everywhere'.

Like all sixth-class pupils in the Newcastle and Lake Macquarie district I had to sit for the primary final examination, where the pupils competed for places in the various secondary schools. Some weeks after the examination there was an evening event at my primary school where the results of the primary final were to be announced. I went to this event on my own, and travelled home alone in the dark. My journey involved a tram ride and a long walk over a hill on the outskirts of Newcastle. I reached our home, rang the front doorbell, and Dad let me in. Just to the right of the front door was the doorway to my parents' bedroom. Mother was already tucked up in the big double bed at the end of the room. The foot of the large bedstead faced me and blocked Mother from my view. I stood in the doorway and told them that in the examination I had come second in the district and thus secured my place at Newcastle Girls' High School. Dad looked pleased and shook my hand. Mother may have murmured something from the fastness of her bed but nothing encouraged me to approach her. I took myself to bed.

I think that my mother expected that I would love her, irrespective of what she did or said. Daughters loved their mother, and I was her daughter. But did she love me? There was so much about me which disgusted, repelled and angered her that she convinced me that I was unlovable. The logic of that did not escape me. If I was unlovable then certainly my mother could not love me.

Central to our meaning structure is the complex of meanings which concerns how we feel about ourselves. This includes how we value ourselves, how we care for and look after ourselves, what standards we set for ourselves and how harshly we judge ourselves on these standards. Some of these meanings we lay down in early childhood following events which did not suggest to us that any alternative meaning was possible. For instance, some children have mothers who do not love them, and some have mothers who are incapable of showing their children love, but not all these children lay down the absolute and unquestionable meaning 'I am unlovable'. They see that their mother does not love them, but they are also able to see that other members of the family do love them, and so they can understand that lovableness is not an absolute quality which some people possess and others do not but a relative quality which, like beauty, lies in the eye of the beholder.

That form of thought which I have called 'the face' develops in the small child into an acute perception of how the other person perceives the child. Though lacking a language in which to understand and describe this perception, the young child not only knows whether his mother is happy or unhappy but can make subtle distinctions between, say, the unhappiness of anger and the unhappiness of anxiety. The young child can also detect pretence.

Currently there is considerable interest in the psychology of deceit in ourselves and other animals, and some researchers argue that the capacity to deceive and to perceive deceit in others marked a major advance in the development of our species. It is difficult to determine just how early a young child becomes capable of detecting deceit in others since the subtleties of a relationship between one person and another are often hard to put into words, even when we are fully in command of our language. Yet it is possible to observe the small child detecting pretence in the games the child plays with adults. When Daddy says to the child, 'I'm going to throw you up to the sky,' or Mummy disappears in a game of peek-a-boo the child laughs rather than becomes distressed.

The child's response to another kind of deceit might not be so obvious but the child's awareness of deceit is just as acute. Small children need to know whether the love they are being given is real or counterfeit, whether they are going to be looked after or devoured as prey. They seem to be able to assess the quality of the love which they are offered.

The father of Jean-Paul Sartre died shortly after Sartre's birth and his mother returned with him to her parents' home. There his grandparents and his mother lavished love on him, but Sartre as a small child came to feel that he was not worthy of their love. When they told him he was a gift from heaven he felt that he was an impostor. No doubt these three people were genuine in their love for him, but they showed their love in the context of 'poor fatherless child, we must make up for what he has lost'. Never having known his father, Sartre could have no concept of being fatherless until he was much older, so their pity for him meant to him that there was something intrinsically wrong with him. Thus, when they told him he was the delight of their life he knew that either they were lying or they were deceived by him.

When I read Sartre's autobiography *Words*,[9] where he tells this story, I got the shock we all feel when we discover in a book, a play or a poem an account of an experience very similar to an experience which we have had and which we thought was ours alone. My father had always shown his love for me, and my grandparents and my aunts and uncles were always loving and kind, but I never felt I could rest secure in their love for me because right from the beginning their love had this quality of making up for something I had lost. I had no idea what it was that I had lost. No one in the entire family would utter in my hearing anything which might suggest that I had anything but a perfect mother. Everyone in my mother's family were frightened of her because her easily provoked temper could readily turn into a serious attack of asthma. She bullied many more people than me into submission with the threat of her anger and her asthma. No one would tell me that they thought she treated me unfairly. Consequently, I could only assume that her bad moods and harsh punishments were my fault because there was something intrinsically wrong with me.

I can remember being aware of this 'making up for' kind of love when I was about four, and somehow I knew it was not quite right. Something was missing. It was the 'I love you because you exist' kind of love. I think it likely that I had been made more aware of the 'making up for' kind of love because I had already experienced the 'I'm pretending to love you' kind of love. It was my father who confirmed this.

I was home from university and sitting by the living-room fire with my father. Mother had retired to bed in a furious sulk because my sister had told her she was pregnant. Myra was a respectable married woman who had established her career as a teacher before she decided to start a family, so 'what will the neighbours think' was not an issue. [For younger readers: this was in the 1950s, when having a baby out of wedlock made a woman a social outcast.] Dad and I knew what we were in for. Some eleven years before Mother had reacted like this to the news of her youngest and favourite sister's pregnancy which came, like my sister's, some considerable time after her marriage. That furious sulk lasted some six months. When, some years later, I had been married long enough to fall respectably pregnant I had to laugh at my state of cognitive dissonance when Mother took the news of my pregnancy quite calmly. I was glad that there was not going to be any high drama, but I could not help but feel a little aggrieved that my pregnancy troubled her considerably less than those of my sister and of my aunt.

So Dad and I sat beside the fire and we talked. No doubt following Mother's instructions bellowed from the bedroom, 'Don't you talk

about me,' Dad talked about himself. He told me that when I was
born he had been greatly disappointed that I was not a boy. He had
always been a sportsman and he would like to have had a son. He said
that he had felt nothing for this new baby, and to try to overcome this
lack of interest and to generate some affection for me he made a
point of playing with me each evening when he came home from
work. But he was stricken to the heart when he heard six-year-old
Myra say to her mother, 'Doesn't Daddy love me any more?'

Over the last hundred years untold billions of words have been
uttered about the effects parents have on their children, but considerably fewer words have been uttered about the effects siblings
have on one another. Yet such effects are profound and long lasting.

One day, when Eli was about two months old, Jeremy and I were
with the three children in the playroom at their home. Eli was lying
on his back on the floor in a state of huge delight. Alice was kneeling
beside him, talking to him with her face just an inch or two away
from his. Miles was leaping around him and now and then crouching
down to push his head against the top of Alice's head. Eli was seeing
Alice's face and, above that, Miles's face upside down, and he was
hearing their voices. The synapses in his little brain must have
been busy elaborating their Alice neuronal gestalt and their Miles
neuronal gestalt. Jeremy remarked, 'Younger children are imprinted
on their older siblings.'

Imprinting, a very basic form of bonding, is well documented in
the research into animal behaviour. Newly hatched ducklings and
goslings imprint on their mother and follow her wherever she goes.
Babies are born being able to distinguish children from adults, which
suggests that the bond babies form with their mother might be
qualitatively different from that which they form with their older
siblings. Gussii mothers must know that they can rely on a special
kind of bonding to occur when they hand their baby into the care
of an older sibling who might be no more than five years old.

The neuronal gestalts that are laid down as 'my sister' or 'my
brother' are remarkably long-lasting. When I visited my Auntie Doff
in her nursing home in 1997 she was very pleased to see me and
told me I looked young and well. I suppose a sixty-six-year-old does
look young to someone in her nineties. However, once we had
exhausted all we could say about how well I was and how well she
was, my aunt began talking about my mother. She asked, 'Is she

expecting you? She'll be glad to see you,' and went on to tell me how the person she called Mother – that is, my grandmother – was not very well. She spoke of Grandmother as I remember her from the past: an old woman who was often ill. I asked her about Grandmother when Doff was a child and Grandmother was young and strong. 'What was Grandma like?' I asked. She smiled at me and said, 'I don't remember,' and then a moment later she said, 'Mother always favoured Jack.'

Jack was Grandma's fifth child and the youngest boy. He was born in 1900. Doff came along later, an afterthought and not particularly wanted. Now she had forgotten most of her very long life, yet the memory that her beloved mother had preferred her brother Jack had not faded.

Young babies find their older siblings to be wonderful and infinitely interesting. They hope their siblings will feel the same about them. Whether they do or do not depends on how the parents have prepared them for the arrival of a new baby.

My arrival was a shocking surprise for my sister. Since my mother never spoke about anything to do with sex, she had not warned Myra of my impending arrival. After my birth Mother was physically ill and probably depressed. She felt she could not cope, and so sent my sister to stay with an aunt. Myra saw this as an intensely hurtful rejection, so with that and the attention Dad was giving to me, it was unlikely that she looked on me as anything but a resented and unwanted interloper.

It was very different in the Halstead family when Eli was born at home. Miles and Alice had known of his presence in the family ever since Jo's pregnancy had been confirmed. They had listened to his heart beat and felt his movements through his mummy's tummy, and when he kept delaying his arrival they had shouted instructions to him to hurry up.

A few minutes after Eli was born Alice and Miles came into the bedroom and saw and held their baby brother. I have never seen such wonder and astonishment on children's faces. From then on, no matter how much trouble Eli might be to them, he would always be someone very special, and they would always be special to him.

One such younger brother told me how special his big sister was to him. When Richard and I began our conversation about how he saw the importance of the family, I asked him to name the members of his family. He listed his wife, his children, his father, his brother (with his wife and child), and his in-laws. Our conversation went on to be very much a monologue since Richard is very fluent and the subject was central to his life. Suddenly he stopped. I thought he looked upset so I waited.

Then he gathered himself together and said, 'I've made a serious omission, which I'm disturbed about really. I never mentioned my sister, who died when I was eleven, and who obviously is no longer part of the family, but emotionally, historically she is very much part of the family. She was about to be twenty-one and I was eleven. She was quite an influential figure, someone I looked up to enormously and admired. She was the one person in the family who had this amazing talent of painting. She could paint marvellous pictures. She had polio when she was three and she was severely physically handicapped. I've told my children about her but I haven't told them enough. For years and years after she died I couldn't talk about it. But I do think that some of her did go into me. We were born into the same family and were very close. I think we were similar people. I sometimes think that if she couldn't live a life, then I could live it for her. It's difficult to put that sort of feeling into words. It's not about faith, or religion, or superstition either – but I do think that character isn't something that is lost when you die. Character is something that you can enthuse into other people: leave a bit of yourself in other people. I'd like to think that a lot of her was left in me.'

This is one of the great peculiarities of close relationships. We can never literally get inside another person's private world, literally become part of that person's meaning structure, but we can feel that we have taken another person inside us. This process can happen between very close friends, but it always happens in families. One school of psychoanalysis has made 'internal objects' and 'object relations' central to their work. These internal objects are not versions of the actual person, in the way that some Druze children think that they are particular people who have died. They are simply the group of meanings we form about the people close to us, and they are our own individual perceptions. Thus the internal object of Mother which I carry around in me is very different from the internal object of Mother which my sister carries around in her.

Internal objects speak to us. Some of us can hear these voices as clearly as if the person was in the room because the memories we have stored of that person include the sound of his or her voice. Others do not store the sound of the person's voice but we do store the words. Many first-time parents are shocked when they hear themselves using to their children the very words which their mother used to them – often the words which they had vowed they would never say.

When these internal objects are benign and loving they help us to maintain our optimism and courage. But when they are constantly making harsh criticisms of us, or taunting and threatening us, we suffer greatly. Deeply depressed people find themselves in the grip of intense and infinite guilt as they are pursued by implacably critical internal objects. The voices heard by people in a psychotic state are the memories of voices they once heard, but these voices are now so intense and persistent that they are now experienced as if they were real. Our internal objects are not necessarily our friends.

Much of the work done by object relation therapists has been concerned with parental objects, but for some people their sibling internal objects are of considerable importance. Not everyone takes their siblings inside as objects. Their siblings might have played little part in their lives, or they might have had little interest in their siblings. The youngest child in the family might not get to know a sibling some fifteen years older, or the older sibling, locked into the self-regarding teenage state, might barely register the existence of a young child in the family. But when a person does form an internal object of a sibling a bond is formed, though not necessarily a bond of friendship.

It can be difficult for siblings to be friends because they have to contend with that primitive but powerful emotion, jealousy. As much as Miles loves Alice and Eli, he has to share something which he once had all to himself, his parents' love and attention. Sometimes he cannot help but feel that his siblings have taken something which is rightly his.

Often when I have sat with a depressed client, helping him to unravel the layers of meanings which have resulted in his intense distress, somewhere close to the bottom we find primitive pride saying, 'I ought to have had perfect parents and had them all to myself.' This meaning is not peculiar to those who get depressed. We all create this meaning when we are small children and discover that our parents are not perfect. When we are small children we know that we are vulnerable and that only perfect parents who are always available to us can protect us from all dangers. This is not conscious knowledge, of course, but the feeling that we are safe only when we are close to our parents. On discovering our parents' imperfection some of us are able to arrive fairly easily and in a short space of time at 'that's OK', usually because our parents' imperfections do not threaten us in any way. We can see their imperfections as lovable quirks. But when their imperfections do threaten the stability of our meaning structure we cannot deal with our primitive pride's resentment of their deficits until we have developed efficient ways of protecting ourselves from them. Some people do this by being confident in their ability to look after themselves, but others, whose self-confidence has been undermined by their parents, remain resentful that their parents have failed them.

Perfect parents give us their undivided attention. This attention does not necessarily mean that the parent is in constant conversation with the child, just that the parent is close by and available if needed. Thus a Gussii baby, asleep and snug on his mother's back as she hoes her garden, could feel his mother to be perfect, while an American baby, talked to by his mother for eight hours a day but now put to sleep alone in his cot, could feel the stirrings of resentment. The irony of this demand for perfect parents is that if we did have perfect parents, ones who would anticipate our every need and meet it faultlessly, we would have no incentive to grow up. We would remain for ever babies and never become independent adults.

The demand for perfect parents allows no place for siblings. Resentment against siblings is felt as jealousy, not envy. These terms, jealousy and envy, are often used interchangeably, but it is useful to distinguish between the two emotions. Jealousy is what we feel when we see someone enjoying what is rightly ours. Siblings take from us what our primitive pride tells us is rightly ours: our parents' undivided attention. Envy is what we feel when we see someone owning what we would like to have. Thus, when we see our siblings achieving something which we would like to achieve, we can envy them. Jealousy and envy – no wonder sibling relationships can be so terribly fraught.

The way we are constructed as meaning-creating creatures means that we are always seeing the present in terms of the past. This can be a very efficient way of dealing with the present. Once you have learned to recognize a car you do not have to repeat the process every time you encounter a car. Because you have learned to recognize a car you can note the similarities and differences between the car you learned to recognize and the ones you later encounter. The process of understanding objects in terms of past experiences with objects can be so efficient that we are not always aware that this process is not so efficient when it comes to dealing with people.

It seems that we are born with the ability to distinguish people from objects. However, we have to learn how to assess individual people, and here our learning can be faulty. Our first encounters with individual people are usually with our parents, and, just as we come to see other cars as being like the first car we knew, so, when we encounter people other than our parents, we see them as being like our parents. This way of giving meaning to the people we meet can remain with us throughout our life, and, if we are not aware of this and seek to counteract it, we can make some grave errors. It is not just a matter of what meaning we give to another person but how we act on that meaning.

A common example is that of the child with a parent who wishes to be in complete authority over the child. An authoritarian parent is always a threat to his child's meaning structure. If the child accepts his parent's ideas without question, is always obedient and never acts autonomously, the child develops only a tenuous hold on his sense of being a person. He does not know what he does think and feel, only what he ought to think and feel. Some children are browbeaten into this state by an authoritarian parent. Most children sensibly rebel. However, when they go to school and encounter other people in authority over them, they interpret them as being like their father and so rebel. Unless they quickly learn that other people are different from their father, they rebel when there is no need to rebel, and this has grave consequences for the rest of their lives.

The same process often occurs in relationships with siblings. Envy and jealousy can be the dominant emotions in a group of siblings all their lives. Just as some parents can never see their children as being grown adults, so some siblings may continue in adult life to see one another in the ways they saw one another in childhood. Such siblings never become a group of friends who cooperate and enjoy one another's successes. Quarrels over sharing toys become quarrels over sharing in their parents' wills, and the feeling of 'It's not fair' is provoked by every sign of another sibling's success.

Any history of the institution of the family has to dwell at length on the quarrels among siblings about family property and the inheritance. If royal parents had taken more care in the upbringing of their children and dealt with sibling rivalry when their children were small the history of Europe would have unfolded in quite a different way. Property laws, where wealth and possessions were entailed to the eldest son in the family, did not help in the resolution of quarrels among siblings. To assist families in dealing with the problem of inheritance and to maintain a steady supply of priests and nuns, the Church encouraged parents to send at least one or two of their children into the Church.[10]

The first experience of having to survive in a group of siblings can become the unquestioned template for all adult relationships. When a person has grown up in a family where the parents have dealt sensibly with the siblings' rivalry that person can usually deal very effectively and realistically with relationships with colleagues at work and with friends. But when parents have done little to help their children deal with feelings of jealousy and envy, or have added to these feelings by favouring one child over another, the children can carry into adult life a way of seeing relationships with their peers solely in terms of sibling rivalry. Much of the conflict which arises in the workplace stems from this, as do the fallings out among friends. In couples it is not unusual, when one partner is unfaithful, for the deserted partner to direct his or her anger and jealousy, not at the faithless partner, but at the new lover, and so to relive all the anger and jealousy felt when the person's parents appeared to prefer a sibling.

Of course some siblings do become good friends. According to various reports, Cherie Blair, Queen's Counsel and wife of the Prime Minister, Tony Blair, always showed concern and care for her six half-sisters, all daughters of her father, Tony Booth. The writer Nicci Gerrard wrote a loving tribute to her sister Jackie, who lived and worked in Angola.[11] My friend Una lived in Sydney and her sister in a country town some 400 kilometres away. Una told me, 'I remember driving up to Young to see my sister and thinking, if I see my sister six times a year as I do – either I go up there or she comes down here – and we both live to the age when my parents died – which is seventy-three in both cases – I did a little sum and worked out I'd probably see her two hundred times. That's not an awful lot of times in a lifetime for someone who's very close to you.' She added wryly, 'There are divergences. I really cannot understand why she's so wrapped up in croquet, but her whole time is spent with this old buffers' group of men and women.'

When parents do not get along together the children can feel that the only way to survive is to stick together. Anthony, the sixth of eleven children, told me how his childhood was 'like being in a lifeboat. That sense of insecurity – you were afraid to rock the boat, to move in the family. I think because there were so many of us we lost our individuality. We felt unwanted from the very start. Another baby coming along was another passenger in the lifeboat. In our family the person who got up earliest was the best dressed. Clothes were bought not for individuals but for the family. We shared toys and bicycles as well. I felt almost an intruder in my own family. We children, we didn't fight and pull against each other as normal children do. There was enough strife, enough conflict, enough tension going on between our parents.'

However, divergences are to be expected. Siblings, no matter how well they get on together, are different people. They see things differently. This comes out all too clearly when they compare their memories of the past.

Yasmin Kureishi publicly denounced her novelist brother Hanif for the way in which he wrote about their family's life.[12] Jon Snow's brother Tom was furious at Jon's description of their mother in his memoir about mothers and sons. Tom Snow wrote a letter to the *Guardian*, where he said, 'I cannot see how anything in his childhood can now justify the humiliation of our mother, whose memory of those times has been wiped out. It is simply pitiless. Self-indulgence has gained the upper hand over decency.' Two years later Jon Snow again raised his brother's ire by describing in negative terms their family's search for a decent nursing home for their mother.[13]

In contrast, when the writer Linda Grant decided to write about what she had learned about her family and herself through her mother's slow journey into senile dementia she did so with the full consent of her sister Michele. Linda, in commenting on Yasmin Kureishi's reaction to Hanif's work, wrote,

When it came to *Remind Me Who I Am, Again* – both a family memoir and an account of my mother's unsuccessful battles with senile dementia and the decisions my sister and I took in assuming control over her life – I would not have agreed to write it at all without my sister's consent, co-operation and commitment. But in writing it, I discovered that each of us had at times quite different ideas about our family's varied truths, and even when we agreed, we might be flatly contradicted by one of our cousins.

She concluded, 'Unlike Hanif Kureishi, I have been fortunate to have a sister who understands the many dilemmas that writing poses. The last words of my book are hers: "But most of all I gave my permission because my sister is a writer and to suppress the impulse to write about the very core of oneself would be an unendurable waste." '14

Writing about our families can be an excellent way of coming to understand what has happened, and out of that understanding can come a significant degree of peace and acceptance. I know that if I had not been able to set out on a journey of understanding and to write about that – the writing is part of the journey of understanding – I would long since have killed myself or be living out my days on the back ward of a psychiatric hospital, forgotten by my family. However, such journeys of understanding are not always appreciated by other family members. They are likely to fear that they will be blamed, or that, if they fail to protest, they will be punished for breaking the Fifth Commandment: 'Honour thy father and mother, so that thy days will be long in the land' ('Criticize your parents and you're dead'). This is one of the reasons why many people find it impossible to confide in a therapist.

Then there is the question of family secrets. They must be kept. One absolute rule which my mother demanded was that everyone in the family should keep was 'Don't tell strangers about family business.' For Mother everyone who was not a close family member was a stranger. Many families have such a rule, and this is another reason why some people find it impossible to confide in a therapist.

The sanctions against divulging the family secrets can be so great and the family rules against such divulgences so long obeyed that you may be unaware that you are guarding a family secret. I discovered this about myself when I was in my early fifties and went to Canada, where I visited a distant cousin whom I had not met before. Some years earlier this cousin had made several visits to Australia and had stayed with my sister and brother-in-law. We talked about her visits there, and she confided to me that this had not been the happiest time for her as she had become increasingly uncomfortable to observe how my sister and brother-in-law chastised their children.

I knew precisely what she meant, but, even as I acknowledged this, I was overtaken by intense feelings of disloyalty and fear. I had often written and talked about how unwise it is to use corporal punishment in disciplining children, and I had talked about how my mother used to beat me, but of what went on in my sister's family I had never spoken.

Yet Myra and Robert were only doing something which practically every other family in Australia – and indeed the world – was doing in the sixties. They were continuing the centuries-old tradition of corporal punishment for children. 'Spare the rod and spoil the child' was the principal rule for child-rearing. My brother-in-law, one of three boys, grew up in a family where the parents enforced their demand for absolute obedience in this way. My sister once told me she could not remember being slapped by Mother, but she has also told me that she remembers little of her childhood. Mother was not a woman to keep her hands to herself if a child were disobedient. Our beloved father, who never hit us, kept a large leather razor strop in the bathroom and, if Myra and I did not obey his order to stop fighting, he would bring the strop from the bathroom and threaten to use it. That threat brought us to heel immediately, but my sister and I had learned the lesson that all children who are slapped and beaten learn: that it is permissible to hit other people.

So, as children, Myra and I hit one another. By the time I was eleven and very solidly built I could land an effective hit, but when I was younger I was at the mercy of a sister six years older than me and well versed in the tactics of bullying. With that and the attacks my mother made on me it was no wonder that for most of my childhood I felt like prey at the mercy of predators who had no pity for me.

So years passed and I grew up and moved first to Sydney and then to England. Despite time and distance, I continued to find visits to my sister's home very stressful. There were reasons for this which are not relevant here, but not until this cousin spoke to me of her visits there did I recognize the secret I was keeping and the fear that accompanied that secret.

My secret was that I was afraid of my sister and afraid of what I might do. When I saw my nephews being punished I felt for them, a real physical hurt, but overriding that was my fear that my sister might turn on me as she had done when I was a child. She still yelled at me if I annoyed her by, say, not switching an electric hot plate off quickly enough, so my fear was not such a wild exaggeration. I felt like prey, and then I feared that I would retaliate, and become again that eleven-year-old, desperately, blindly hitting out, and everything that I had learned since would disappear. Even after my nephews had become tall, handsome, witty young men well able to defend themselves I still felt frightened.

Whenever we are being fiercely loyal to our family it is likely that there is something about ourselves which we are defending. However we might define that 'something' it is always a feeling which we fear might overwhelm and annihilate us were we to acknowledge it. Sometimes we do not recognize, as I did not, that we are now strong enough to deal with the threat. But sometimes the threat continues because it is seen as a threat to the whole meaning of one's existence. When Betty Scott, mother of the serial killer Dennis Nilsen, was interviewed for a BBC television film about the relatives of murderers she insisted that her son had been a 'kind and caring' child. The responsibility for what he became did not lie with her. 'It was nothing I had done,' she said. 'He was brought up the same as the other children.'[15]

No doubt Betty Scott had tried as best she could to bring up her children to be good. Unfortunately the process whereby a baby gradually learns to form bonds with parents and siblings, and learns how to fit in with the demands of family and society is too complex to be directed successfully merely by a few slaps and the instruction 'Behave yourself'.

Learning how to fit in with the demands of your family and your society is not easy. Babies are born with many skills but self-control is not one of them. Learning self-control is not like learning to walk, or ride a bicycle, or swim, where, once you have learned how to do it, you can go on doing it without difficulty for the rest of your life. Instead, the techniques of self-control are always in a constant tension with the techniques of self-expression. Strong emotions and the importunate demands of the body can override the most skilled and practised techniques of self-control. A failure of self-control can leave us overcome by shame, and with that the threat of annihilation looms.

Newborn babies do what they want to do when they want to do it. Left to themselves they would go on behaving like this for the rest of their lives, but when they first start a conversation with a face, and that face reappears again and again, they gradually discover that unbridled self-expression is not necessarily the best option. Their expectation that the face will reappear strengthens into a bond, and with that bond comes a need to please that face. Babies have no difficulty in distinguishing a happy face from an angry one, and a pleasant voice from an unpleasant one. As the months go by babies work out that some of their actions will produce a happy face and some an angry face. Thus Gussii babies learn to be quiet and easily soothed while American babies learn to be cheerful and chatty in company and to sleep alone.

In some families the process of learning to behave as the family expects is on the whole calm and smooth because the parents do not demand from the child what the child cannot yet produce, and they follow the policy of rewarding the responses they desire and ignoring or only minimally punishing the responses they do not want. However, even children born to the calmest and most enlightened of families will encounter several dramatic situations from which the child draws those kinds of conclusions which create a conscience and lead the child to believe from then on that 'I am bad and have to work hard to be good.'

In these situations the parents might be trying to do nothing but the best for the child – to teach the child to be clean, or to eat nourishing food, or to get adequate sleep. The parent might have brought into the situation some anger and tension from elsewhere, or the child might have seen the parent as demanding a degree of compliance which the child at that moment finds threatening, and so the child finds that what was an otherwise ordinary situation is now imprisoning and dangerous. These are not extraordinary situations. Unfortunately some children find themselves in very dangerous situations where they might be the victim of an adult's physical or sexual abuse.

Whatever the degree of danger, the child finds himself in a situation from which there is no escape. Though he may not have an exact language in which to describe it, he interprets the situation as 'I am being unjustly punished by my bad parent.'

He then realizes that he is in double jeopardy. The bad parent who is punishing him is also the parent on whom he depends. What can he do?

He can do what we all can do when we find ourselves in a difficult or dangerous situation from which there is no escape. We redefine the situation.

As he struggles to cope the child decides that it is he who has got himself into this situation and it is he who is keeping himself there. It is his fault. Now a redefinition is at hand: 'I am bad and am being justly punished by my good parent.' The parent is preserved as good, but at the cost of the child's unselfconscious self-acceptance with which he was born. He has diminished himself. He sees himself as not acceptable, and from now on he must work hard to be good.

For some children these extreme situations are repeated no more than is sufficient for the belief 'I am bad and have to work hard to be good' to be reinforced to the point where it becomes an absolute and unquestionable truth, the standard against which they constantly measures themselves. The dimension ranging from 'I am perfectly good' to 'I am totally bad' becomes the centre of their meaning structure on which all other meanings depend. Every one of us who in babyhood formed a bond with a mothering person has such a dimension at the centre of our meaning structure. When we feel that we are operating successfully we see ourselves as being on the 'good' half of the dimension, but when we make mistakes we feel ourselves sliding to the 'bad' half of the dimension.

We each have our own way of defining 'good', and, indeed, we might never use that word. We might think in terms of working hard, or being unselfish, or never getting angry, or being an accepted team member, or being responsible, or being involved in politics or in saving the planet. No matter what we call it, most of us are experts in being good. We could not function as a society if we were not.

Some of the children who learn to be good in extreme situations learn something else when these situations are constantly repeated.

Each repetition threatens the stability of the reconstruction because the punishing adult persists in behaving in ways which are difficult to define as good. So the suffering child creates another redefinition in order to keep the first redefinition in place. This is, 'I am bad, and am being justly punished by my good parent, and when I grow up I will punish bad people in the way that I was punished.' This is the belief which generates the behaviour of those tough young men who, having received severe physical punishment in their childhood, take their bad feelings out on those whom they see as the enemies of their group. Without this belief the British National Front and similar right-wing and fundamentalist groups would not exist.

This belief enables cruelty to be handed down from one generation to another. Those people who were punished now punish others. Generation after generation of parents down the centuries have justified the cruelty they perpetrate on their children by saying, 'I was beaten as a child and it never did me any harm.' They fail to realize that the damage the beatings did to them was to rob them of much of their humanity, because to endure the pain inflicted on them by the 'good' parent they had to become indifferent to their own pain, and even take pride in their toughness. If you become indifferent to your own pain you become indifferent to the pain that others suffer.

The functions of a conscience are to set standards and to judge whether those standards have been met. These standards always relate to what we see other people expecting in terms of our good behaviour – that is, what we think they see as deserving approval, acceptance, affection and admiration. Adults, when they want to create feelings of shame and guilt in a younger person, will often say to that person, 'You've let yourself down,' but the standards where this letting down occurs still relate to other people – usually the other people whom we experience as internal objects.

A judgemental conscience and a feeling of irredeemable inadequacy, if not downright badness, does not lead to a comfortable life. People who live like this, and vast numbers do, have to find some way of relieving themselves of at least some of the tension which living this way creates. One way is to be unremitting in your efforts to be good. I have among my friends and acquaintances a number of people who never take a minute off trying to be good.

They feel that if they take a minute off they will be overwhelmed by guilt and the punishments that guilt entails. If I say to them, 'Why don't you give up being good? Do something else,' they think I am mad. What I said to them was equivalent to saying to a passenger in a plane some 30,000 feet over the Pacific, 'Why don't you get off the plane now and travel by train?'

Another way of trying to deal with that sense of essential badness is to gather it up and hurl it out of yourself and on to those people who are outside your group, in particular at those people whom your family and group call enemies. Thus you can say to yourself, 'I mightn't be perfect, but I am better than those whites/blacks/Muslims/Christians/Serbs/Albanians/Protestants/Catholics . . .'

When I talk about dealing with a sense of badness by gathering it up and hurling it at another person I am not speaking metaphorically but trying to describe an experience as real as taking off a dirty coat and hurling it at the floor. When we are subject to much abuse and criticism, or when we have been betrayed by those we have trusted, or when our important plans have failed, or when we have suffered great loss we may find that something very unpleasant, something dark and foreboding, gathers around our heart, lungs, stomach and bowels. So palpable and powerful is this 'something' that our ancestors regarded the heart, lungs, stomach and/or bowels as the centre for our intelligence and feelings. The brain was not considered to be important.

Just as we can try to rid our lungs, stomach and bowels of noxious substances, so we can try to rid ourselves of this dark 'something' which is in some way bad by seeing it as not lodged in us but in other people, particularly the people who appear to be a danger to us. Much family strife consists of one family member trying to rid himself of this sense of badness by seeing it as lodged in another family member and then attacking that person. So husbands attack wives, parents attack children, and siblings fight amongst themselves. Peace within a family can be preserved by projecting this feeling of badness not on one another but on to those people who are seen as the family's enemies.

This method of relieving feelings of badness is available to those who have never formed a bond with a mother person and who therefore never went on to develop a conscience. Lacking relationships, these people never receive the great benefits which family and friends can give, the affection and reassurance which can help to balance the feeling of badness. Friendless, conscienceless, frustrated by the fact that the world does not behave as they want it to, they seek relief from the inchoate, disturbing feelings which they lack the ability to understand by putting these feelings on to the people whom they see, not as people, but as worthless objects. They join racist, nationalist and religious groups where they find like-minded people, or they join the military and find the closest they ever come to a family. There their contribution is likely to be greatly valued by their leaders because they will do things which soldiers with a conscience might not be prepared to do.

The process whereby a group identifies and defines its enemies is intimately related to the process whereby a child is educated to become a member of that group.

All families have rules about cleanliness and, right from the beginning, the family imposes these rules on the infant. Even the kindest and most tolerant of parents convey the importance of these rules in the energy and competence with which they enact them. Nappies are changed, hands and faces washed, baths given and clothes changed. Modern fathers, keen to show how active and involved they are as parents, discuss the relative merits of different brands of disposable nappies with the same intensity with which they would discuss the relative merits of different brands of cars. The message the baby receives is clear. Clean is good; dirty is bad.

Not all children are treated with such tolerance and patience by their parents. Most are still punished, shamed and humiliated for being dirty. 'Dirty is bad' becomes deeply embedded in the way children feel about themselves.

Just how embedded, unchangeable and unquestioned this idea becomes is seen in the way groups describe their enemies. The first adjective always used is 'dirty'. Hence the Serbs embarked on 'ethnic cleansing' of the Muslims in Yugoslavia, and the Nazi propaganda about Jews portrayed the Jews as rats.

Such a way of thinking is not confined to the Serbs and Nazis. It is prevalent in all societies.

I was travelling on the London Underground from Highbury to Oxford Circus when the train pulled into King's Cross. Some people got off, some got on. The doors closed and then opened again. The guard's voice came loud and clear over the tannoy: 'That woman with the baby who just got on, get off the train. And the other one further down the train, get off the train.'

None of the people in my carriage spoke or even looked at one another, and no one craned to see who got off the train. Most of us knew who had been ordered off the train. Some of the Romanies who had fled persecution in Slovakia had come to England where, as they always had done, they tried to supplement their income by begging. Women in long dirndl skirts and usually clutching a small child would sit in the Underground walkways or walk through a moving train silently soliciting for money. This could hardly be a profitable enterprise because generally they were ignored.

The train doors closed and the train went on to Euston. As the train left the station the guard came back on the tannoy. He said, 'I'm sorry, ladies and gentlemen, to interrupt your journey but these people have to be stopped. Don't encourage them. Don't give them any money. They are lice and they've got to be got rid of. If you give them money they keep coming back. Just remember, they are lice and we don't want them here.'

No one in my carriage either agreed or complained, though many of the people on the train must have been the victims of racial discrimination. We did what good Germans did in the 1930s. We minded our own business.

Of course we would, because we are good people and therefore never aggressive. It is bad people, enemies, who are aggressive. No nation, no racial or religious group ever chooses to go to war. Even if they are getting their retaliation in first, they have always been driven to it by their wicked, aggressive enemies.

Enemies have to be seen as aggressive because families generally have never found a really satisfactory way of dealing with their offspring's anger and aggression. The problem is that, while learning to be clean is simply learning to organize the external world into categories of clean and dirty, anger and aggression are an essential part of our survival kit. Our species would not have survived if we did not have the capacity to defend ourselves with anger and aggression. Physically we were puny compared with the huge beasts with whom we once had to contend, and, as ever, we have to defend our meaning structure against those who would annihilate us.

Some families, like those in the southern states of the USA, as described by Nisbett and Cohen, define anger and aggression as being, in some situations, necessary and good, but such definitions are often interpreted as applying to situations where defensive aggression turns to offensive violence. In many families no attempt is made to work out a policy about anger and aggression because the parents have never learned to deal with their own anger and aggression, and the children grow up confused about when and where aggression and anger might be appropriate. In other families all anger and aggression is defined as bad, and the children grow up unable to acknowledge and deal with their own anger and aggression and are terrified by that of other people.

Over the years when parents tussle with the problem of dealing with their offspring's anger and aggression they also have to deal with the children's completely self-centred outlook. The parents tell the children, 'You must share with others.' Those parents who want their children to grow up not seeing strangers as the enemy advise their children to share their possessions with everyone they meet, but parents who see the world as full of enemies will tell their children not to share with those the parents deem to be strangers. My friend Lou told me how her parents made sure that she shared everything she had with her sister but, because biscuits were still luxuries in the 1950s, they instructed her that when she was at school she should not share her playtime biscuits with her friends. Since she found sharing with friends to be much more fun than eating on her own she continued to share her biscuits with her friends but worried about the consequences if her parents found out.

Parents teach their children who their enemies are. Sometimes the teaching is explicit. The picture of the great leader is displayed everywhere and children learn how to praise him and how to condemn their enemies. They learn all about the vices of America, or capitalism, or Communism, or the infidel, or the Pope and so on. Sometimes the teaching is implicit. Children hear what their parents say to one another and to friends and family, and they believe it to be true. Their parents have told them many things which have proved to be true. Touch anything hot and you do get burnt. Go out without your coat and you do feel cold. Break a window with your football and you do get a hiding. So it must be true that the council gives the blacks the best housing, that gypsies are dirty and the Pakis are getting all the jobs. Thus enemies get handed down from one generation to another and become an integral part of the family's life story.

Enemies have four main uses. First, they help families to bring up their children to fit into the family and into society. In learning to be good children they do not have to run the risk of being overwhelmed by their sense of badness. Second, the threat of an enemy binds the group together. As soon as NATO began bombing Serbia in April 1999 the disparate groups of Serbs came together as one. Third, anger and aggression can be turned against the enemy and the stability of the group preserved. In wartime football hooligans disappear and re-emerge as military heroes. Fourth, enemies can absolve a person or a group of responsibility and guilt.

Dusan in Belgrade told me that his father 'came from a very monarchic, royalist family. "For king and country" sort of family.' As a young boy before the Second World War he went to court and became a friend of the young prince. Dusan showed me his father's photos from that time and told me that these had to be hidden away during the Communist years because his father could have gone to prison for possessing them.

He went on, 'Yet all those photos talk about what our life would have been like if we were not occupied by the Communists after 1945, after the German occupation. As a child my life was made up of two realities: one I got at home, with my father and mother, which told me that the people who ruled the country were not honest, but one day freedom will come. The internationalists will go away and we won't be suppressed any more. We will be able to say, "We are Serbs," and all the lovely people devoted to the king will crawl out of their holes and they will show what good leadership looks like, and how good life can be. And they are honest – as opposed to Communists, who are bad. And then back at school I was told that all those "honest" people are actually traitors. Horrible people who left their own people and that the best regime in the world is the Communist regime and the self-government regime of Yugoslavia which was introduced by Marshal Tito. So I really know what it means to have two hemispheres in the brain! The problem with the two realities was that I could believe either one or the other, and yet they were both wrong.'

Dusan returned to talking about his father and the photographs. He said, 'The whole life of my father could be put in those pictures.

And the idea with him was that he had something very precious, and I didn't have that. I don't know if it was good or bad but he had this hen laying golden eggs, because he had those enemies he could blame for every problem he had in his life. Every failure he had, he would blame on the Communists. He was not chosen to be a professor at the university just because he was not a Communist – the Communists did not allow non-Communists to be professors. And then he had a failure in his marriage – and that was because he didn't have a big apartment. Big apartments are reserved for party members: he was not a party member, so if he had been his marriage would have stayed intact. He was drinking heavily, and he'd say he wouldn't be doing that if he'd been given all the things he actually deserved.' This story shows how the belief in the Just World fits so neatly with having enemies. If you do not get the rewards you deserve you do not have to blame yourself. You can blame your enemy.

To the question 'Can we live without enemies?' the answer is, 'No.' Thus we commit ourselves to more years of war, conflict and violence. Unless, of course, we can change.

The key to change lies in the way we bring up our children. Needing enemies is not an absolute but a relative relationship between how children are brought up and how much subsequently they need enemies. The more gently and tolerantly children are brought up the less they need enemies: the more harshly they are brought up the more they need enemies.

It is only in the last forty or so years that there has been a major change in the way in which some parents bring up their children. These parents see their children, not as objects which they possess, but as people in their own right to be treated with the same dignity and respect as adults are treated. I stress that only some parents do this because only in a few parts of the world has this change come about, and even in those parts many parents still pay only lip service to the change. There are parents who read all the right child-rearing manuals and they know the right jargon, but they treat their children as designer accessories to enhance their own image. There are still many parents who want their children to be seen as a credit to them, proof that they are good parents. It is the parents who decide just how to define such credit. The definition always has little to do with the child's individuality and everything to do with conformity and obedience, and continues the age-old traditional idea of children being the parents' possessions.

Such an attitude has ruined the lives of many children. In Mamphela Ramphele's autobiography I came across a story which reminded me of families in the UK and in Australia whom I have known where the parent decided the child's fate irrespective of what the child needed and wanted. In writing her book Mamphela usually went to extraordinary lengths to be even-handed but with this story about her father and her brother Sethiba she did not try. She wrote,

> Sethiba was unfortunate in being taken in by my paternal grand-parents at the age of twelve to help the ageing couple look after their livestock. It was a cruel decision by my father, who, like many of his contemporaries, viewed children as part of their possessions with no independent voice. The decision did not enjoy my mother's support, but women at that time were given little choice in such matters – the children belonged to their fathers. My grandparents were not nurturers by any stretch of the imagination. My father's younger brother added insult to injury by the manner in which he and his wife made Sethiba feel unwanted and unloved. His pain must have been immense then, but as a child he was not given a hearing, and my mother's pleadings for him to come back to the family home fell on deaf ears.[16]

According to Mamphela, her brother's hard life as a child and adult led to his early death from a rare form of cancer.

Some parents believe that, as they gave their children life, so they have the right to end their life. In the UK every six or eight weeks a parent, usually a man, kills his children and then kills himself. In Australia murder-suicide occurs twice as often as in the UK, and in the USA, where guns are readily available, the rate is higher still.[17] What is not known is how many parents threaten their children with murder. My mother, when she was upset and angry and alone with me, would tell me that she was going to kill me and then kill herself. My friend Mike told me how his father, who beat his sons regularly, would frequently threaten, 'I'll swing for you.' Mike and I found that this behaviour did not endear our parents to us.

Terrible though these experiences were for Mike and for me, they were not unusual, and, compared to many children, we got off lightly. When I was researching for my book *Time On Our Side* I wanted to investigate why old people are generally treated badly by young adults. The only cultures where this does not occur are those in which the old retain their power. This enquiry took me to the history of childhood, and there I found, down the centuries, a kind of Holocaust of children. Writing about this was difficult. My thesis was that the pattern has always been of the parent generation using children for their own ends; when such children who survive become adults they take their revenge on their parents' generation, who are now old. Unfortunately, few children learn anything from their experience but simply repeat the pattern of using their children for their own ends. Their attitude is, 'If I had to suffer so must you.' I wanted to present enough evidence to support my thesis, but I did not want to present so much evidence as to cause the reader too much pain.

It has been estimated that between 90 and 99 per cent of human history has been spent in small nomadic tribes, and in many ways we still think in tribal terms. Conditions of life for a tribe are always chancy and often hard. In order for the tribe to survive when food is short the active adults must survive. Seen in these terms they are more important than the children because they have the skills and they can have more children. So children become the prey of the predator adults.

When our species became farmers and then manufacturers children were still seen as prey – useful prey. They were put to work as soon as they were old enough to do something useful, or, if born into a powerful family, they were put into arranged marriages in order to secure the family's interests. Moreover, since children were seen as objects in the same way as enemies were seen as objects, they could be treated with the cruelty which an enemy might expect. In the treatment of children around the world generally very little has changed.

The research by the Truth and Reconciliation Commission in South Africa showed that it was the young people, those between fifteen and twenty-five, who bore the brunt of rights violations.

Children and youth were killed, abducted, raped, tortured, poisoned, imprisoned for long periods without trial, denied rights (granted in law) while imprisoned, and harassed mercilessly for actions taken and beliefs held in relation to political conflict or for just being in the firing line ... Terror tactics including threats, misinformation, smear campaigns, harassment of kin, intrusion into domestic space, interference with education, sophisticated techniques to turn people into enemies of their colleagues, intensive interrogation, false executions, isolation and denial of contact or care, were all used to divert the young from their political purposes and destroy cohesion among their peers. The need to control the young was inscribed on their bodies in countless ways as power was expressed through the infliction of pain. Limbs were broken, joints crushed, heads smashed so that brains no longer functioned well, eyes were gouged out, and so on.[18]

It was not just the black youth who suffered. 'Millions of white adolescents were militarized through participation in the school cadet system. During compulsory military service in the townships, they were forced to participate in the oppression of their fellow South Africans.'[19]

Turn from the TRC report involving many thousands of children to a story about one, an eight-year-old boy in Arkansas. Associated Press reported,

An eight-year-old Arkansas boy shot himself as his mother was outside getting a stick to whip him because he had received a bad report from his school, police said yesterday. Christopher Parks later died in hospital, they added.

The boy was believed to have climbed on to a dresser to get a gun hanging from a nail on the wall. He straightened the doily on the dresser he had wrinkled and then shot himself in the head, Detective Rusty Quinn said.

'The mother was apparently unhappy with the report card and was going out to cut a switch to discipline him,' he said.[20]

The detective Rusty Quinn, who examined the scene, must have surmised that Christopher had straightened the doily, but it is a detail that for me rings very true. I have known families where wrinkling a doily was an offence which merited a beating.

In April 1999 Sean Sellars, who had spent thirteen years on Death

Row in Oklahoma, was put to death by lethal injection for three murders which he committed when he was sixteen. The family of those he murdered came to watch his death, and then complained that they thought it was 'too easy'. They were further infuriated by Sean's last words: he told them that his death would make no difference to them because they would go on being angry. It seems that thirteen years on Death Row had taught him something which the family had failed to learn – that wanting revenge is an absolutely certain way of being unhappy.

Even though the twentieth century has been in the West the century for self-understanding – therapists and theories about therapy have flourished – little of the knowledge which came from such activities has seeped into public life. Whenever a child commits a murder, like Sean Sellars, or Mary Bell, or the boys who killed Jamie Bulger, the reaction of the media shows that if we still had public executions there would be no shortage of crowds to watch children die. When someone like Gitta Sereny tries to understand what led the child to this outrageous act and in the course of such a search uncovers a history of crimes committed by adults against the child who later killed, the public reaction is not one of 'Now we can see what happened. How can we prevent this ever happening again?' Instead, the seeker after truth is vilified and the anger against the child criminal increased.

Two things are happening here. The first is that many people become very uneasy when child-rearing practices are discussed. They do not want to consider their own upbringing for fear of breaking the Fifth Commandment, and, if they have children, they do not want to consider what they have already done.

As I know from the discussions which follow my lectures, some people are able to acknowledge their unease with regard to child-rearing practices. What most people – and certainly the leader writers in the tabloids – cannot acknowledge, is the second factor: that of sibling rivalry. They are jealous because this criminal child is being given something which they have always wanted but never got – an adult who takes them seriously and tries to understand them.

This same way of thinking is often present in groups of people who ought to know better – teachers. Children whose families have failed to prepare them to fit into school life are labelled 'uneducable' and expelled from school. Stories about such children are told in staff rooms and conference halls – 'I don't know what the youth of today are coming to,' adults say to express their hatred of children. Meanwhile, children who bully other children are deplored and punished, and what is ignored is that children learn to bully by being bullied. Children learn how to bully from other children, from their siblings, and from their parents. They have a great incentive to learn to bully because bullying is one of the most effective methods of maintaining the integrity of one's meaning structure. Bullies always justify their actions by claiming that they are merely applying much-needed punishment to someone who deserves it. They are good. Their victim is bad.

In families bullying can take many forms. Parents have great power over children. They are bigger than them, they know more about the world, if they have trained their children to be good they know how to make them feel guilty, they control the conditions of their children's lives and can manipulate these in order to punish the children, they can threaten physical punishment and they can inflict it. It is the last power which many parents do not wish to lose.

Over the past ten years a number of countries have passed legislation which protects children against assault in the same way as adults are protected by the law against assault. Such legislation was not passed without difficulty. In South Africa, where horrific violence threatens the very stability of the state and where traditionally teachers have relied on corporal punishment to keep order, the organization Christian Education South Africa, an association of 205 Christian schools across South Africa, applied to the Constitutional Court to have the ban on corporal punishment declared unconstitutional.[21] Fortunately the Constitutional Court rejected on technical grounds the Christian claim that it is right to inflict pain on children. In the UK a group of fundamentalist Christian schools threatened to challenge the ban on corporal punishment in private schools, which was due to come into force on 1 September 1999.[22] In August 1999 the ban on the use of corporal punishment in state schools in the UK was extended to private schools. Immediately forty religious schools mounted a challenge to the law in the European Court of Human Rights. Was beating children what Jesus meant when he said, 'Suffer little children to come unto me'? Who was doing the suffering?

Corporal punishment is the most inefficient way of educating children. Children do learn from it, but never what the adult inflicting the punishment intended them to learn.

For nearly thirty years Murray Straus at the Family Research Laboratory, University of New Hampshire, has been researching the effects of corporal punishment on children and on the adults they subsequently become. The results of a recent large-scale study, along with the results of other studies, showed quite clearly that

The more corporal punishment was used the greater the tendency for antisocial behaviour to *increase* subsequent to the corporal punishment. Of course other things also influence antisocial behaviour. For example, girls have lower rates of antisocial behaviour than boys, and children whose mothers are warm and supportive are less likely to behave in antisocial ways. Although these variables do lessen the effect of corporal punishment, we found that the tendency is for corporal punishment to make things worse over the long run regardless of race, socioeconomic status, gender of child, and regardless of whether the mother provides cognitive stimulation and emotional support.[23]

Murray Straus pointed out that

Studies show that talking to children, including pre-speech children, is associated with an increase in neural connections in the brain and in cognitive performance. Those findings led us to theorize that if parents avoided corporal punishment they are more likely to engage in verbal methods of behaviour control such as explaining to the child, and the increased verbal interaction with the child will in turn enhance the child's cognitive ability.[24]

Other studies reported in Straus's book *Beating the Devil Out of Them*[25] showed that

The benefits of avoiding corporal punishment are not limited to enhanced mental and verbal ability. Ending corporal punishment is likely also to reduce juvenile violence and other crime ... The benefits of ending corporal punishment are likely also to include less adult violence, less masochistic sex, a greater probability of completing higher education, higher income and lower rates of depression and alcohol abuse.[26]

Despite all these unfortunate outcomes, corporal punishment, threats of corporal punishment, threats of banishment from the home and of divine retribution, guilt-arousing techniques, shame and humiliation remain popular with parents because they are sanctioned by the community, they require little thought and allow the parents to rid themselves of their own anger, fear and feelings of inadequacy. The easiest way to bring up children is to terrify them into obedience. Bringing up children by listening to them, trying to understand what they are experiencing and taking their point of view into account in every decision you make is the most difficult way to bring up children.

If the mere presence of a child in the family can be a threat to the parents' meaning structure children who are allowed to question, to express their opinion, to criticize, argue and bargain are a thousand times more threatening. I have a number of friends who, by the time they were twenty-five or so, felt that they had really sussed out what life was about. They were liberal in their views, tolerant, generous, eschewing the slightest smidgen of racism and sexism, and happy to criticize those who did not share their views. Then they had children, and launched upon parenthood secure in the knowledge of how to bring up a child with unfailing positive regard, unfailing love, tolerance, forbearance and encouragement. They found that their children challenged them on every one of their most cherished meanings. The longer they were parents, the less certain they were about anything. Children see things differently from adults, and, if allowed to express themselves without fear of punishment, they will readily demonstrate that their view of life should not be dismissed as silly and childish.

At the same time as these friends were reeling from the challenges to their meaning structure which their children presented they had to endure the criticisms of those who did not approve of their child-rearing methods. There were grandparents who were offended that their children were not using the methods which they had used. There were teachers and doctors who dismissed their concerns about their children's welfare by letting them know that they were time-wasting, anxious parents. There were strangers in the supermarket who would say loudly when a child was upset, 'If that was my child I'd give him a good hiding.'

The years have passed, and I can now witness the products of these parents' labours, now people in their teens and twenties. They are all wonderful people, talented, well-educated and, unlike many young people, at ease with themselves and other people. For me one thing about them is very striking. In their childhood their parents had sometimes been exasperated with them, on occasions they had lost their temper and shouted, but they never used their power to terrorize their children into obedience. The result in these young adults is easy to see. The children like their parents. They enjoy their company. They want to spend time with them. They and their parents are the best of friends.

Some people will say that parents and children being friends is all very well, but families are more important than friends because families have family values. Not a day goes past but some politician or cleric will direct us to remember the importance of family values.

What Are Family Values?

I was once asked to write an article about family values so I made a list of all the values which might be relevant. These were loving, wishing the other person well, treating people as people, not as objects, treating people with generosity, respect and dignity, valuing friendship, accepting the other person's point of view, being flexible, patient, loyal, cooperative, hospitable, kind, and interested in people and events.[27]

These are all wonderful values but they are not specific to families. Indeed, they are the values of friendship. What other values could apply only to families?

Whenever anyone extols the importance of family values we should ask how that person defines 'family'. It is clear that many clerics and people of a conservative bent think of the ideal family as a man and woman tied together for life by indissoluble marriage vows, their children born in wedlock and all living together under one roof. The theory is that in some ideal past all families were like that but the wickedness of our modern age has ruined marriage and families. The only way forward is to get back to the golden age of the family.

Just when this was is hard to determine. Historians of the family have shown that what might be called 'the family' has, down the centuries, changed its form, and always in accordance with economic conditions. In the seventeenth century a man might decide to marry in order to beget children who would work for him in his cottage industry of weaving, while in the later twentieth century a young woman might decide that being a single mother was a better option both economically and personally than spending her lifetime in unemployment. Wally Seccombe in his book *A Millennium of Family Change* remarked, 'What we now term, in retrospect, "the traditional family" is a recent invention, the product of a period of exceptional stability and uniformity in family relations, culminating in the 1950s.'[28]

The number of traditional families might have dwindled since the 1950s, but this is a trend which has been seen at other times in our history.

> By the time of the Napoleonic Wars, it has been estimated that a fifth of the English population lived at one time or other in common-law unions. The rise of casual cohabitation among the swelling ranks of the proletariat has also been noted in France and Germany ... Young people seized the initiative, their actions increasingly governed by the balance of market forces as they sought jobs, unsupervised accommodation and eligible marriage partners.[29]

Young men and women of the early nineteenth century had to contend with the lack of divorce laws and the lack of adequate means of contraception. Now that divorce and contraception are readily available groups of people who call themselves families can come in all shapes and sizes. The traditional family still exists – perhaps as just the husband and wife and their children, perhaps as what is called an 'extended family', which includes grandparents, uncles and aunts and cousins of many degrees. Such extended families can be a complex mixture of family connections when one or both of the parents have been married previously and so 'the family' includes not merely the children of the earlier marriages but the grandparents and the ex-spouse, and even the ex-spouse's chil-

dren from subsequent marriages. Life would be simpler for
researchers into family life like me if families stayed traditional!

Then there are the families composed of a single parent and one
or several children. Such families might function as a small group
or be part of a larger group which include the parent's parents and
siblings. There is an increasing number of lesbian families with
children. Two friends of mine, like quite a few middle-aged women,
gave up trying to find happiness with their respective husbands
and found great happiness with one another. They have their own
household, which has to be well organized because between them
they have seven children. Other lesbian couples have decided that
they should have their own children and used the mechanical services of a man to achieve this. Some homosexual men have decided
that, as their relationship is a marriage, they should adopt a child.

None of these different kinds of family has solved the problem
which ordinary families have always had – that it is the family which
both sustains and threatens the individual's meaning structure. Just
having one parent or two parents of the same sex does not solve
the problems that arise between parents and children. Moreover, all
these families can encompass what I have identified as four values
that apply only to families. The first of these is:

A Special Kind of Loyalty

Good friends are loyal to one another, but such loyalty does not
usually extend to loyalty to the friend's family no matter what these
individuals might be or do. No matter how close two friends are,
their relationship will not be satisfactory if they do not take into
account that each of them has loyalties elsewhere. There are times
when a relative has to be considered ahead of a friend.

However, family loyalty is an absolute. Escapees from families
might be able to limit their loyalty to the family, but for those who
remain and who want the benefits a family can provide, loyalty is
the prime value.

Family is central to Richard's life. I asked him, 'Why is the family
important to you?'

He replied, 'Only your family really know you, really know what
you're like. You don't have to explain, you don't need a preamble.
That's terribly important, that there's somebody there for you, who
won't question if anything happens in your life. I think the worst

thing that can happen in families is "never darken my door again".
I think it would be something pretty heinous for me to do that with
my children. The loss would be mine as much as theirs. I'd like to
think that I would always be there to help them out. I think the
responsibility of being a parent is enormous, and you have to make
sure that your children are going to behave as responsible citizens.
You're preparing your children for life after you, as your parents
prepared you, and that forms huge bonds and duties.'

For Richard such parental loyalty required a similar loyalty from
his children. He said, 'So often you hear in families about parents
saying to their children that as they get old they don't want to be
a burden to their children. It upsets me, that idea. I want to be a
burden to my children. I like the idea that they look after me when
I'm old, and I hope they do. But for that to happen they've got to
be successful. I'm not joking when I say this – I see them as an
investment. It might not be a sensible investment, because I'm aware
it can go all wrong, and they might not do financially well, but I
suppose I want us to be friends really. I'd like to feel we'll always
be friends.'

In a programme about the revival of the Jewish community in
Berlin the BBC television programme *Correspondent* told the story
of Gad Beck who, as a Jew and a homosexual, had been fortunate
to survive the Holocaust. He immigrated to Israel but years later
returned to Berlin. He was still haunted by his failure to save his
first love, his schoolfriend Manfred Levine. Manfred and his family
were rounded up by the Gestapo and imprisoned in the Jewish
school both boys had attended.

Determined to rescue Manfred, Gad had borrowed a Hitler Youth
uniform and had gone to the school. Now, as an elderly man pictured in front of the school door, he said, 'I came here to the school
and said to the guard, "Heil Hitler. You have the Jew Levine here.
I need to take him. He has all the keys to our business." The guard
said, "All right, take him but bring him back." "Of course," I said.
"What would I be wanting with a Jew?" We left together and then
Manfred stood just a few steps away from here and said, "No, Gad,
I will never be free. I have to go back, to go along with my family,
with the sick little ones. I have to go back." He just turned around
and went back through that door. The whole family perished. Not
one of them came back.'[30]

For Dusan in Belgrade loyalty to his family was absolute, even to the point of behaving in the way that his grandfather behaved. He showed me a photograph and said, 'This is my grandfather whom I adored. He was absolutely the best person in the world. He spent a lot of time teaching me when I was a kid and I learnt about Belgrade with him. He was teaching me how to haggle on the market. How never to buy the first thing you see. You first have to go all the way around, and then if they say it's ten dinars, it's probably worth seven. I was only four or five years old, but every time I go to the market I remember my grandfather. It turns my wife crazy, but it's part of the ritual and I still do it.'

Dusan told me how Serbian Orthodox families had their own saint. The family was loyal to the saint and the saint was loyal to the family. He said, 'The custom of having a saint and having a day in the year when you celebrate your saint is peculiar to Serbian Orthodoxy. I think it is a leftover from a pagan religion. And this is something also very important because under the Turkish reign we actually kept our identities because the Turks were very cruel but did not forbid religious gatherings. They knew that this was very important to the people, so they let them gather around. And these were the places where upheavals were planned. During Tito's reign it was not a good idea to celebrate your saint, and if you did you would be seen as an enemy of official policy. Only after Tito died Serbs started to do that more often. On many occasions in my life when I felt low or I was being afraid or I was being anxious, I could hear my mother, or grandmother, or grandfather or father saying, "Well, St Gabriel will help you. St Gabriel will guide your way. St Gabriel won't let anything horrible happen to you." Sometimes, when something nice happens I look up in the sky and say thanks.'

Dusan went on to tell me that he had been in London at a conference during a very difficult time in his life. Several potential disasters were looming, and one afternoon he found the conference unendurable. He said, 'I went out and wandered around in the neighbourhood. I saw this lovely church, built in the eighteenth century. As I came nearer I saw it was St Gabriel's Church and I said, "This is God's sign. This has some hidden meaning." I couldn't go in because it was locked, and I was standing in front of this tall building, communicating with St Gabriel, and I felt this inner calm, and I felt it was going to be all right. I felt this inner strength and confidence that even in London he was protecting me, taking care of me, and I should just carry on with my projects. I returned home and got the post I had applied for, I married my wife and my daughter was born. All those lovely things began to happen.' He laughed and said, 'And I wonder, was it English Gabriel, or Serbian Gabriel on holiday in England? I don't know the answer to that.'

Tima in Beirut was more critical of the loyalty a family might demand. I asked her about families in Lebanon, and she said, 'Families are very important, and usually they are so important that they deprive the different individuals of the right to make their own decisions, because the family always knows best, the family's interests are the first to be taken into consideration. Sometimes it's good, but sometimes it backfires, like somebody is coerced to, say, major in a particular subject at university because it suits the family. And you have an individual who's totally unhappy because he's been forced to do something that doesn't appeal to him. They interfere in your private decisions, and who to marry, where to live. The closeness has put no barriers to what they can say about your life. But for many people they can't live without their family. I doubt that they'd be able to make their own decisions anyway.'

She went on, 'When somebody's sick, or somebody dies, every-body is there. Sometimes I don't know whether it's for the sake of being together or being supportive. Sometimes I feel it becomes more of a social event, but they are there, and there are situations where some people feel that they need to be surrounded by a lot of people; it makes them feel better.'

Tima was very much a strong individual. I asked her how she had achieved this. She said, 'No one gave me the chance. I had to take it, by force. It was painful for my parents, but I knew at sixteen that this was the moment to do it, or I was never going to get out, never doing my own thing, never asserting my existence, and so I had to do it. It wasn't very easy. I left my parents' house and started work and went to college – a college I chose with a major I chose – and I was working very hard and was also a volunteer with the Red Cross so my days were full and I was able very shortly to support myself financially – I was seventeen – which was the time when the break was hard for my parents. They knew that even for the money they couldn't get me back.'

Tima had been in Beirut all through the war there. She survived, even though she had deprived herself of one of the important benefits of family loyalty. Robin Dunbar recorded,

> The absence of kinship networks has a surprisingly bad effect on people's health. This was dramatically highlighted among both Captain Smith's Virginia colonists in 1626 and the famous Donner Party wagon train that set out to cross the American West in 1846. In both these cases, mortality was heaviest on those who had no relatives in the group. Despite often being fit young men at the outset, many of those who travelled alone with the Donner Party were unable to cope with the depredations of the journey. They died earlier and they died in significant numbers. The same effects have been noted in a study of the slum dwellers in north-eastern England during the 1950s: Those families with the smallest kinship network suffered the highest levels of both child morbidity (sickness) and mortality, as well as being generally more susceptible to conditions like depression.[31]

On the television news I saw pictures of an elderly man being helped over the border between Kosova and Albania by a Serbian guard. The man collapsed and staff from an Italian field hospital took him to their unit, where he was diagnosed as having a severe lung infection. There was no accommodation for him at the unit. The doctor said, 'If he hasn't got a family to look after him, he will die.'[32]

Of course it can be easier to be loyal to your family if your family enjoys some distinction. In Vietnam a young man told me how the children of parents who had taken part in the liberation felt superior to children whose parents had not. On the other hand, being a child of a famous family does not always increase the child's self-confidence. One young man, the youngest son of a world-famous sportsman, told me, 'You never see the sun standing in the shadow of the family tree.'

However, famous and/or powerful families can reward their members in ways that few other organizations can because the family is the organization which has been around the longest. Our earliest ancestors lived together in small bands, a collection of people who were united by some blood relationship. Our form of thought, the face, enabled everyone in the band to identify readily those who were family and those who were not. Since the probability was that those identified as family would be more likely to help an individual than a stranger would, there were sound reasons why, if favours were being given out, family members should be the recipients.

As our early ancestors increased their numbers and the bands grew to tribes, and the tribes to groups of tribes under the rule of a chieftain or king, nepotism became a political way of life. It is only quite recently that political systems have emerged which require people to relegate family relationships to the purely personal. However, loyalty to the family dies hard.

Lebanon has an extensive democratic system, but the real power still lies with certain families. Amir, who lived abroad and was making a brief visit to Beirut, told me, 'Success depends on whether you belong to certain families. If you do, you get everything. If you don't life is very hard. That's why I went away.'

People who lived under Communist governments were expected to put the Party above all else. The family was to be as nothing. Yet party members themselves rarely set a good example. When the USSR and its satellite states fell, revealing the bankruptcy of their economies, the Communist Party leaders in Vietnam felt that they had to prevent their country from going the same way. In 1986 they drew up plans for economic development known as *Doi Moi* or 'renovation'. However, as Robert Templer recorded in his book about Vietnam, 'The country had not so much gone from plan to market as from plan to clan; this idea is neatly reflected in an old adage that "once a man becomes a Mandarin, his whole lineage can depend on him".'[33]

In a political system where loyalty to the family comes before all else corruption flourishes. In Vietnam, Templer wrote,

In 1997, the Party did tentatively announce changes that might have cracked open its hard shell of secrecy by forcing all officials to disclose their assets. The measures were half-hearted as it was unclear whether they applied to family members of Party officials. It is often the spouses and children of cadres who run the businesses profiting from their family connections. Party members themselves are supposed to maintain the fiction that they cannot dirty themselves with the exploitative world of capitalism. Plans for officials to declare what they own were quietly dropped as unworkable; nobody was willing to stir up such a hornet's nest of problems.

He concluded, 'The system that creates a warm and nourishing environment for corruption, also nurtures a hubris and arrogance that threatens Vietnam's future by blocking any solid commitment to reforms.'[34]

There is now evidence to show that a country's economy will grow steadily and securely only if there is a truly democratic political system, an efficient and incorruptible system of justice, a population of people who generally obey the law, and, across the society, a very low level of corruption. It was corruption arising from family loyalties and from the Chinese system of *guanxi* or connections which was largely responsible for bringing down the economies of Thailand, Indonesia and Malaysia in 1998.

Meanwhile, in Western democracies family loyalty is still quite strong. When an enquiry revealed that many of the EU commissioners, a group of men and women who, like Caesar's wife, should be above suspicion, had not always acted with the principles of law and democracy in mind, one commissioner, Edith Cresson, was criticized for giving an EU job to her dentist. Turning on her detractors in Brussels she angrily demanded, 'Are we supposed to employ only people we don't know?'[35]

The rewards for loyalty to the family can be great, but the punishment for what is seen as disloyalty can be even greater. Jack Diamond, who survived the Holocaust, grew up in a middle-class, modern Jewish Orthodox home. He told Aaron Hass,

'I was angry with my parents because they wouldn't leave Germany when we could have. My mother couldn't believe that the world would let Hitler do what he promised . . . I implored my mother to get out. After Kristallnacht, we could have left. But we had a good life in Germany and she wouldn't leave it. Perhaps if I'd pushed more . . . My brother left for Palestine and we in the family never forgave him. We decided, we as a family should stay together.'[36]

The Hezbollah in Lebanon, the enemies of Israel, take an even stricter view of family loyalty. It has been estimated that when, in the 1980s, the Hezbollah were following a policy of taking hostages as many as 300 were taken. Terry Anderson, who spent seven years as a hostage, commented,

> '[It was] an amazing number considering no one was ever near finding or locating the hostages – and many did try. The reason for this well-kept secret was due to ideological and religious loyalties and fear. First of all, they are two-thirds family. Most of them are convinced both ideologically and theologically, in other words, they are homogeneous in their beliefs or pretty close to it. And the danger to the family who broke the secret was extreme. If they found out that anybody had leaked information about us, they would kill him, his brother, his sister, his wife, his mother, his father and his dog.'[37]

No doubt there were members of the Hezbollah families who might have liked to opt out of the family, but, like many people, they stayed close to their family, not because of love and friendship, but because they felt guilty and afraid. Many people stay close and loyal to their family because they feel they have nowhere else to go. To them strangers are, at best, unknown, and, at worst, enemies. Their upbringing has not given them a broad perspective on society.

Family loyalty can bring out the best in us, but it can do this only when we are loyal to one another out of real affection and not out of guilt and fear, and when we always remember that, no matter how wonderful our family might be, it is still only a small part of the society to which we belong.

'Anyone Who Isn't Family Doesn't Count'

One very good reason for being a member of a family where everyone is independent and self-reliant is that disasters never happen to such families – or so I have come to understand from the media's description of families which have suffered a disaster. They are always 'close-knit'.

'Close-knit' is presented as a virtue, and so it is when the ties between family members are those of love, kindness and mutual support. However, for many of these families 'close-knit' is not a virtue but the outward manifestation of how the family divides the human race into two groups – family members (who count) and the rest (who do not).

This way of seeing people provides the framework in which priorities are ordered and decisions made. The question which many people find hard to answer – how much help should be given to a person in need? – is for such families easy. If the person is family, endless help; if not family, no help.

Eileen talked to me about what she called the 'family centredness' of her neighbours. She said, 'For a long time until the end of last year, when he was found a place in a residential home, I had been seeing to a disabled man with failing sight and hearing, but was constantly being scolded by other neighbours for this. "Why should you bother about him?" "It's nothing to do with you." "His relations should look after him." "It would be different if he were one of your own family." In other words, an unrelated person is to be ignored – and trying to be a Good Samaritan to a stranger is just plain stupid.'

In such families the definition of who is family can be very restricted. Marrying into the family might not be sufficient qualification. Richard told me,

'There's an expression "blood's thicker than water". On my wife's parents' side, that's quite strong, and no matter how long I live, how long I've been married, how settled our marriage might be, I don't think I'll ever be wholly accepted by my mother-in-law. It comes down to blood being thicker than water. My father-in-law firmly believes in it. I don't think I'll ever be accepted on equal terms. They love me, they like me, for all my faults – and probably because of them – but I'm not family, not their family.'

In close families friends might visit and be welcomed and entertained most hospitably, but friends can never be treated in the way that a family member might be treated. A particular friend might be given the highest compliment the family can bestow – he is 'just like family'. However, 'just like family' never becomes 'family', and it is easy for the family to close ranks and exclude the friend.

I was on a train travelling to Edinburgh when I met Alec who, as it turned out, knew my work. He asked me what book I was working on, and, when I mentioned friends and enemies, he told me his story of a close family. As a shy young man whose family had dwindled to three distant cousins, he had gone to university, where he had met Steve who, like Alec, was a keen amateur footballer. After a match Steve would take him home for tea. There

Peggy, Steve's mother, who kept her children around her, presided over the family like a great earth mother. She felt sorry for Alec and invited him to visit often. She told him, 'You need feeding up,' and when one of Steve's sisters married and moved to a house just two doors away Peggy offered to take Alec in as a boarder.

Alec felt that he had at last found his family. Indeed, the family would introduce him to visitors as 'Alec, he's just like one of the family.' After he had graduated as an engineer his work took him all over the world, but he always stayed with Peggy when he was in England and kept in touch with all the family. He never failed to make sure that they knew where he was on his travels and how they could get in touch with him.

One day, when he was working in the south of France, he saw in a daily English newspaper that Peggy had been killed in an accident. He phoned Steve, but spoke only to Steve's wife, who told him that the funeral was the next day and was 'for family only'.

Alec travelled overnight and next day arrived at the church as the last of the mourners were going in. Steve stood at the church door. He said, 'Hi, Alec. I hope you don't mind, but this is for family only.'

Alec was too surprised to speak. Close families can deal friends some terrible blows.

Children who grow up in families where the parents' prime rule is the importance of staying close, or the importance of seeing other people as the enemy, are robbed of the opportunity to learn that, no matter how diverse our customs and habits are, we are all more alike than different, because we are all members of the one species. We are all meaning-creating creatures, wanting to make our way in the world and to have strong, affectionate relationships. When a child is not helped to understand that, the child sees strangers as being excessively strange. When I was an undergraduate I had a room in a house. My landlady Gladys was a Catholic with a six-year-old daughter who was being educated by nuns at the local Catholic primary school. One day, when my landlady and I were talking, the little girl picked up something that I had said and asked her mother, 'Is Dorothy a public?' 'Public' was someone who went to a public or state school and who therefore was not a Catholic. At that time Catholic parents were not allowed by the Church to send their children to state schools. On being assured by her mother that I was, the little girl drew back from me and gasped, 'Look at the devils jumping around her!'

Close families can give one another love and support, but when there are tensions and disputes within the family the knives can go in deep. Often the best protection from someone who hurts you is simply to put physical distance between you and that person, but children of a close family, even when adult, may be unable to envisage the possibility of living outside the family. Their mental map of the world shows that life is possible only within the family space. Beyond that lie dragons and all the terrors of the deep.

Thus a circular pattern is set up in the family where family members stay close to one another but, in so doing, increase the opportunity for an individual's meaning structure to be constantly under threat. Since the individual believes that the outside world is peopled only by dangerous strangers he or she cannot look there for help, but, in fear, clings closer to the family which has created the fear in the first place.

This threat often arises from the use of the third family value:

'Be What I Want You to Be'

Many babies are born already in debt to their families – some literally so, as in those Third World families which are in the bondage of an irreducible debt to a rich landlord. These babies are condemned to a lifetime of working to pay part of the debt. Some babies, indeed many babies, are born to parents who wish to be recompensed for the trouble and expense the baby has cost them. 'After all I've done for you' is a constant parental refrain in such families. Only the most rebellious of children dare to reply, 'I didn't ask to be born.'

Sometimes the birth of a baby can provoke one member of the family to feel deprived and to look to the baby to provide recompense. My sister felt this way about me, but, no matter how much I did for her, my very existence meant that I could not provide what she regarded as an adequate recompense: a return to the state of an only child. In some families where there is a sick or handicapped child the parents impose a debt on their healthy children: that of special affection and care for the child who has been deprived of good health.

Many babies have a role imposed upon them. There is the role of being the competent one. Tima was obviously a most competent person. I said something to her about how, if you are a competent woman, other people let you be responsible for matters which by rights are their responsibility. She corrected me. 'They don't *let* you take responsibility. They *dump* it on you. They dump it all your way.'

If members of your family see you as competent they usually cannot conceive of the possibility that you might be having difficulties yourself. Anything you might say about feeling anxious, or vulnerable, or doubting your own competence, is either ignored or brushed aside with, 'But of course you can cope.' This is the family's way of controlling 'the competent one'.

In some families the role thrust on the child is that of protecting the parent. Sometimes children have to provide physical care for the parent, but often they are given the task of protecting the parent from the difficulties and unpleasantness of the world. Often these children are presented with the parental demand that they be perfect, because anything less than perfect would expose the parents to realities which they wished to avoid. Sheldon Kopp, the famous American psychotherapist, was one such child. He commented, 'Some of us have learned to believe that we should feel ashamed every time we turn out to be less than the perfect child our parents expected us to be. Making a mistake, doing something foolish, finding ourselves momentarily unable to cope, means we are not worthwhile human beings.'

Kopp told the story of how, when he was eleven, he hurt himself quite badly while roller skating. He then had to go home and face his mother.

It was a summer day and the apartment door was open. I was careful to peer in with only one eye, shielding the battered side of my face from view. I called out loudly, 'Ma, don't get upset. I got hurt a bit but it'll be all right.'

Only after warning her could I feel free to enter. Her response was completely predictable. 'What now? Again you don't stop to think about how much it would hurt a mother to see a boy who gets into so much trouble?'

I spent the next hour apologizing for my thoughtlessness, reassuring her that I would try to be a better boy. I consoled her in *her* grief at having such an inadequate son.[38]

Some families have a strict hierarchy, with the person at the top of the hierarchy wielding great power over the rest. In such families small children, particularly girls, can be given the role of the object to be sacrificed for the sake of the family. These children follow in the footsteps of our ancestors' children who were sacrificed to appease the wild beasts, only now the wild beasts are economic circumstances. In south-east Asia many young girls have been sold into prostitution by their families. 'A line in "The Story of Kieu", Vietnam's national poem that traces the life of a woman eventually forced into prostitution, reflects a common acceptance of prostitution if it provides sustenance for a family or village: "What does it matter if the flower falls if the tree stays green?" '[39]

In other families it is the wild beast of public opinion that demands a sacrifice. I have known two women who have had this role thrust upon them. Jessica was a Southern Baptist and lived in Louisiana, Maria a Catholic who lived in Malta. The head of each family was a grandfather, who was much respected in the community. As children each woman was sexually abused by her grandfather. Jessica told her mother, but her mother would not hear a word said against her father, a minister of the local Presbyterian church. Maria was too frightened to tell her mother, so she told the priest, who then sexually abused her. Both women went on to live fraught and unhappy lives, but the reputation of each family remained intact.

The fact that a child has been given a special role does not necessarily mean that the child will accept it. Some do because the role gives the child power. As the eldest sibling, being the competent one can mean that the child dominates the younger ones and interferes in what they do, and, in adult life, continues to do so. However, roles like 'the stupid one' and 'the fat one' are not pleasant roles to have and give the child feelings of falseness and loneliness which are a constant threat to the individual's meaning structure.

Once family members have given a child a role they are often very reluctant to change their perception of that child, even though the child might have grown to adulthood. I have told the story of how my mother still saw me, at twenty-seven, as 'the lazy one', despite the fact that I led an extremely busy life as wife, mother and teacher. I have had clients who, having arrived at the point where they can see that an unhappy marriage and an unfulfilled life have

led them to be depressed, then embarked on an educational course
or accepted a job which required the competence which they now
saw that they had; members of their family – spouse, parents, siblings
– then did everything they could to scupper the project so that they
did not have to change how they saw my client, 'the stupid one'.

Counsellors who have specialized in counselling people – usually
women – who are extremely fat, have told me how they constantly
come up against the problem of the family who want 'the fat one'
to stay fat. Diets are decried and 'the fat one' is showered with gifts
of food. How could a loving daughter refuse the cream sponge her
mother made especially for her? The mother wants her fat daughter
to remain at home at her beck and call, while her slim sisters want
to look good beside their fat sister.

Looking good beside someone fat is often the reason why young
women will include a fat girl in their group. If she tries to slim,
they criticize and reject her. However, even though friends can be
extremely cruel, they would demonstrate that they were not a friend
at all if they behaved like the families which adhere to the fourth
value.

'Why Should I Be Polite to You? You're Family'
In family photographs my mother looks sweet and gentle, and so
she was – to strangers. If a stranger, and by stranger I mean anyone
who was not family, angered her she would say nothing, and then
contrive never to have to speak to that person ever again. Nor would
she criticize a stranger to that person's face. When a childless couple
who were friends of my sister decided to adopt a baby, Mother,
within the family circle, condemned this decision. Who in their
right mind would bring a child of unknown parentage into their
home? However, she did accept an invitation to see the new baby,
and there she was everything the new mother would want. Mother
was entranced by the baby and asked to hold him. Yet when my
son was born, within my hearing she greeted the news that I had
had a son with, 'Not another boy!' She had wanted a granddaughter,
and Dorothy had failed yet again.

Courtesy to strangers and endless discourtesy and criticism for
family members is a rule which many families follow. It is something
which has always puzzled me. Surely we should be polite to the
people who matter to us the most? My friend Jeannie explained to

me why this was so. She said, 'In families people treat abominably those family members who will not run away.' Many family members feel that they cannot run away because, as my friend Jane said, 'Blood ties have to be obeyed no matter what.'

It is not just a matter of being courteous. It is even more a matter of thoughtfulness. One couple I know, when they have a friend to babysit, make sure that the children's meal has been prepared, and that plenty of food and drink is provided for the friend. Yet when the grandparents babysit, the purchasing and preparation of the food for the children's meals are left to the grandparents while the drinks cabinet is bare.

Then there are those family members who readily identify those in the family who can be used.

Lettie, who was in her late sixties, told me about her cousin Fred and his wife Beryl. After Lettie's husband died Fred and Beryl visited Lettie. Lettie hardly knew them, but they were family and she was pleased they were interested in her. They gave her lots of instructions about what she should do, and they pressed her to spend a holiday with them in their caravan on the coast. Lettie made excuses, but they kept insisting and so, at the end of the summer, she agreed to spend a weekend with them while they packed up the caravan for the winter.

They drove to the caravan late one Friday afternoon and stopped to get fish and chips along the way. Lettie was concerned that such a meal might give her an uncomfortable night so she ate little. Next morning Beryl gave her what Lettie assumed to be a cup of morning tea, but as time passed and no food was forthcoming Lettie realized that this cup of tea must have been breakfast. She could see that the kitchen area of the caravan contained not a scrap of food. The caravan was parked in a field, miles from shops and houses.

Lettie helped with the packing and storing of the furnishings of the caravan. More cups of tea were produced but there was no mention of food. By early afternoon Lettie felt weak from hunger and her weakness made her bold. She enquired about lunch. 'Oh,' said Beryl in a dismissive tone, 'we don't eat until the evening.' So Lettie had to wait. After all, she was family.

Then there are those family members who want to think of themselves as good, but achieve this at the cost of another family member. Andrew's daughter told me what her father had done.

Andrew was born into a wealthy Scottish family. His parents and
their Presbyterian minister told him that his task in life was not to
enjoy his good fortune but to earn it through service to others. He
believed what they said and devoted his life to public service. Duti-
fully he followed his father into the practice of law. He began his
charitable work early so that by the time he married he was already
an important figure in several major charities. The education of his
four children drew him into work with school boards and, since his
fourth child was born with Down's Syndrome, into mental health
charities. His life was one of hard work and devotion to others.

His wife shared his view of life as service to others, but increasingly
she would find herself thinking how pleasant it would be if they
could have time for themselves. If she revealed such thoughts to
him he would seek to humour her and promise some future treat,
but such a treat would not eventuate or, if it did, some demand
would curtail the time he could spend on it.

To comfort herself in her disappointment his wife would then
dream of the day when he would retire. As they got older they did
indeed talk of retirement: they would buy a country cottage, go for
long walks, take proper holidays, perhaps a world cruise. She
dreamed and planned, and he, when tired or frustrated by the lack
of success of his good works, would allow himself to think that he
had paid his dues to God and that his old age would be one of rest
and enjoyment.

Andrew retired from law but many of the charities to which he
had devoted his life refused to let him go, while demands from
other worthy causes poured in. He felt resentful and then guilty,
and worked harder. Six months after retiring he had a stroke which
left him paralysed on his right side. He was immobile and helpless.

He was not an easy patient. His family knew him as a man who
never got angry and who could rationalize away anyone else's need
for anger. Now he was angry, and expressed it in being difficult
and graceless to his family and nurses. When his wife, trying to
commiserate, said, 'It's not fair. You've worked so hard,' he flew
into a rage, using words she'd never heard him use.

Then he lapsed into a deep depression and told all who would
listen that he had not worked hard enough. If anyone tried to talk
about his good works he would sob and say, 'That wasn't enough.'
His doctor prescribed antidepressants, but, as a man who had always

prided himself on his clarity of thought, he could not tolerate the mental woolliness the tablets produced. His wife and doctor conferred and, having agreed that he was at his best, albeit for only an hour or two, after the visit from his physiotherapist, a cheerful, competent Australian girl, the physiotherapy should continue indefinitely. Apart from feeling better in himself he was regaining a few small skills and learning some new ones.

His wife allowed herself a small hope. Then one day she came home from shopping and found that he had dismissed his physiotherapist.

'Why?' she cried. 'How could you do that?'

He said, 'I've been lying here all these months asking myself why I had this stroke. At first I was angry with God because I thought I didn't deserve it. But that was wrong. Now I think I did deserve it. I should have tried harder. Then the other day the physiotherapist said something about how she learned something from me that helped her with another of her patients, and that set me thinking. Perhaps there was still a task for me to do. Last night about midnight – I'd just heard the clock striking – it came to me. It was like God speaking to me through my thoughts. It came to me that this was a lesson I have to learn. I've been responsible for other people through my work. Now that was coming to an end I need to become responsible in other ways. This is how I can look after other people. I've had this stroke for other people. Now these other people – I don't know who they are or how many of them – but they won't have a stroke because I've had it for them.'

His wife, unable to make sense of what he was saying, went for the practical. She asked, 'Why have you sent the physiotherapist away?'

He replied, 'Because she was aiding me in refusing the task God has set me. I have to accept the task. Accept my bed of pain.'

Like Jesus he had sacrificed himself for others. He seemed not to have noticed that he had also sacrificed his wife.

Within families adults have the task of educating the child in all aspects of life. This necessarily involves the adult in correcting the child. Such correction can easily degenerate into continual, carping criticism, especially if the family rule is that those members who hold the power can be unrestrained in their criticism of those over whom they have power. In families where continual criticism is the norm the parents can be unaware that this is what they are doing. A child psychiatrist friend who looked after children diagnosed with attention deficit disorder told me how difficult it can be to get the parents to be aware of what they are doing. Even when the parents manage to grasp the notion that they should praise their child, they do not realize that they are not praising their child if they say, 'What you did was very good. Why can't you do that every time?'

Sometimes the whole family will join together in criticizing one family member who has transgressed the rules. In his very moving autobiography, *Maybe Tomorrow*, which is a paean of praise to his family, Boori Pryor, an Australian folksinger and story-teller, described the immense suffering his family endured, as most Aboriginal families endured, and how he had battled to make his way in the white world. Part of his battle was to be successful without alienating himself from his family. Aboriginal families have rules about how their members should behave and one of these rules was that you do not let success puff up your pride or, in Boori's words, become 'up yourself'.[40]

Not becoming 'up yourself' is a rule not just restricted to Aboriginal families. However, Aboriginal families had good reason to teach their children to be inconspicuous. Any Aboriginal person who became in any way noticeable to the white community was likely to receive brutal treatment from them. Never allowed to be themselves, many Aboriginal people turned to alcohol to deal with the constant threat to their meaning structure. However, now that the social climate in Australia has changed somewhat and many Aboriginal people are seizing the opportunity to succeed on their own terms, they sometimes find that the rule of not being 'up yourself' can create problems, especially with those family members who are envious of their success. In families it is sometimes difficult to distinguish criticism which is aimed at keeping the person criticized safe and criticism which arises out of envy.

In many families criticism comes in the form of 'giving my opinion'. In Lebanon, so a publisher I met there told me, 'any relative older than you feels obliged to give you their opinion'. I heard Tima's uncle speak of giving Tima his opinion as if he were giving her the family jewels, yet the opinion he expressed – on a creative project which Tima was planning and which showed every sign of success – was not a supportive one.

Tima, I observed, dealt with her uncle's opinion in the way many children deal with criticism from their elders. They ignore it. I went with my friend Toby, one of six children, now all grown up, to see Brian Friel's play *Daisy, Daisy, Give Me Your Answer Do*. This play, in part, concerns a married daughter's relationship with her parents. After the play Toby commented on the way that the parents in the play constantly criticize their daughter and give her orders. Toby observed that the daughter reacted in the way that children of such parents always do. He said, 'When the parents ask the children if anything is wrong the children always say, "Everything's fine."'

Some parents never relinquish what they see as their right to be endlessly, cruelly critical of their children. I had a phone call from my friend Paul. He had just celebrated his forty-eighth birthday – if celebrate is the right word. He had been made redundant in the recession of the early 1990s and he had never returned to the level he had previously achieved. Some money would have helped, and, when his father died, he expected that his share of his father's modest wealth would set him up in business. However, he and his wife had just separated, and his mother disapproved – so much so that she manipulated the terms of her husband's will to prevent Paul from getting his share of the inheritance. Paul was very angry and tried to sever every contact he had with his mother. Despite this, she always sent him a birthday card which carried the usual birthday wishes, but with the card she would enclose a letter in which she berated him for his bad behaviour. Despite her eighty years her handwriting remained firm and her sentences clear and to the point. She would not forgive him and she wanted him to know she would not forgive him. She would go to her grave not forgiving him.

When a child grows up in a family where the adults inflict much criticism and little praise the child has to develop defences against that criticism in order to maintain the integrity of his meaning structure. Some children develop a selective functional deafness. They no longer hear the voices of the critical adults. This can be an effective protection, but it means that the child also ignores what might be useful to hear – information about the world and advice about how to make his way in the world. If the child extends his functional deafness to the voices of all those in authority, then he soon transgresses first the rules of his school and then the laws of society. Many of society's misfits and criminals have followed this path.

Other children try to defend themselves against continual criticism by forestalling it. They develop competence in those areas of behaviour most likely to be criticized. In doing so the child takes in the critical parental voice and makes it his, but often *her*, own. The more the child is threatened by the parents' continual criticism, the stricter the standards she sets for herself. If the parents continually criticize the child for being dirty and untidy, she sets herself standards of cleanliness and tidiness even higher than those which her parents demand. If the parents continually criticize the child for not doing well at school, she sets herself the standard of being academically brilliant. If the parents continually criticize the child for making mistakes, she sets herself the standard of being perfect in everything.

To forestall parental criticism in this way the child has to develop an extreme sensitivity to her failure to reach the standard she has set, and to the possibility of such failure. Past errors must be remembered, learnt from, and never repeated.

This way of protecting yourself against criticism by forestalling it is the same pattern of learning experienced by our ancestors when they had to protect themselves against the beasts who would make them prey. Our ancestors had to study the behaviour of the beasts and develop ways of forestalling and outwitting them. When our ancestors made mistakes those who survived had to remember those mistakes and try not to repeat them. Once you have been prey you do not forget.

One of the problems that arises from not forgetting is that we become much more likely to remember our mistakes than to remember our successes. Indeed, we might not remember our successes at all. It often irritates and disappoints me that I have remembered few of the things I got right, whereas I have an exact and detailed memory of most, if not all, of the things I got wrong. This means that I can draw little pleasure from remembering my past. Yet there is much I could enjoy if only I could remember.

Often friends who have known me for a long time speak of happy events of which I have no memory. One friend, Ken, recalled a dinner party which I had arranged some twenty-five years ago. He remembered it with pleasure. At the time I must have felt that it all went well, for I have no recollection of it. Yet I do remember in detail an event involving Ken and his family and an empty petrol can – an event too tedious to relate here, but which left me feeling ashamed of my ineptness and stupidity.

This recollection of those events where we found ourselves prey, first to our hyper-critical parents and then to our hyper-hyper-critical conscience, is analogous to the recollection of savagely trau-matic events which persists in the victims of torture and sexual abuse. There is some evidence that neuronal configurations which are laid down in events which provoke fear are stronger and more impervious to change than those configurations laid down during happy events. There is survival value in not forgetting when you were afraid, but being able to survive does not always mean being able to be happy.

Family – The Tie That Must Bind Us All?

Have you ever had this conversation? You are telling someone about a person who causes you a great deal of pain. You say, 'This person constantly interferes in my life. He expects me to do things for him and I dare not refuse because if I do he gets very angry. He manipu-lates me and gets me to do things I don't want to do. He never praises me or says he cares for me, but he's always criticizing me, and when he envies me, which he often does, he does everything he can to bring me down. What should I do?'

Your listener gives you advice. 'Don't have anything to do with him. Don't invite him to your house and don't go to see him. Don't answer his letters. Don't return his phone calls. When he asks you to do something just say no, and don't respond if he gets angry. He's harming you. You can't have him as a friend.'

You say, 'He's not a friend. He's my brother.'

Immediately your listener says, 'Oh, that's different. You've got to keep in touch. He's family.'

I am familiar with this conversation – as many of us are. The listener who insists that you have to keep in touch with family, no matter how much you suffer, is not pointing to some great, universal, absolute truth that family members have to stay together, but is protecting himself, first, against having to acknowledge tensions and unhappiness in his own family and, second, against the possibility of having to offer support to someone who is not family. If families always look after their own no one has to care for the stranger.

The person who insists that family ties must be honoured no matter what suffering that entails is revealing a deep distrust of people generally. This fear of the stranger hides itself beneath the cloak of sentimentality about the sacredness of the family. Such sentimentality parades itself as a virtue, but sentimentality never is a virtue because it is always the socially presentable face of cruelty. To be cruel we have to see the person to whom we wish to be cruel as an object without that individuality which identifies that person as human. To be sentimental about a person or a group of people we have to do the same. Children are sentimentalized as 'sweet' or 'cute', and not appreciated for the complex beings they are. By sentimentalizing the family we ignore the suffering that goes on in families, we ignore the myriad difficulties even the most loving of families have in getting along together and bringing up children, and we hide our fear of strangers and our unwillingness to care for them.

Those who sentimentalize families are amongst those forces of unreason which bedevil our lives and prevent us from gaining a better understanding of how we could live more happily together. Anyone who publicly questions how families operate is immediately attacked as an enemy who would destroy the fabric of society. Social workers who have to decide whether a child should stay with an extremely inadequate family or be taken into care are criticized for whichever decision they make, and are pilloried if a decision turns out badly. Parents who decide to divorce rather than to continue to inflict their shared unhappiness on their children are berated for failing to maintain the integrity of family life. The high divorce rate reflects just how difficult people find marriage and family life to be.

The criticisms of those who question how families operate are based on the notion that it is actually possible to make decisions which result in everything turning out perfectly. To hold this idea the person has to be totally unaware of what goes on in real life. No decision, no event, ever has only good results or only bad results. The outcome is always a mixture of benefits and deficits. In making a decision we should never ask, 'How can I achieve a perfect outcome?' but 'How can I achieve an outcome where the probability is that the benefits will outweigh the deficits?' A happy family is never perfect, but has simply managed to produce more benefits than deficits for its members.

The degree of realistic thinking needed to assess possible benefits and deficits is not available to those people who, having suffered many disappointments in childhood, maintain the integrity of their meaning structure by depending on fantasy. To survive as children, they might have created fantasies about their family being perfect in order to deny the pain they felt at discovering that it was not. If they carry these fantasies into adulthood and make them an integral part of their meaning structure they find any challenge to their fantasies frightening, and they rush into an unthinking defence. Families are perfect and family ties matter above all else. These are unchallengeable absolute truths.

This way of thinking – the glorification of family with the denigration of friendship – prevents us from examining why, as Naomi said at the beginning of this chapter, being told by a relative to press the play button on the video results in an increase in blood pressure and in the heart rate, and a feeling of intense anger, when such an instruction from a friend might be gratefully received or rejected with a joking, 'Don't be bossy.'

Are we right to believe that families are more to us than friends, or should our aim be to turn our families into a group of friends who have known each other for a long time? Is it possible to do this when our family is part of our meaning structure in ways which a friend can rarely be? After all, our family is, if nothing else, the beginning of our life story.

Of all the stories we construct our life story is the most important. It begins with the stories which we have woven out of our interpretations of what we have been told about our family before we were born. These stories, formed very much under the influence of primitive pride, give to our family history a special significance which an impartial observer at the time would not have seen. Next in our life story are the memories of our interactions with our family when we were children. Such memories may have little relationship to what actually happened.

The Irish playwright Brian Friel has often used his memories of his childhood as an integral part of his work. In one important memory, wrote the critic Fintan O'Toole,

> The boy is about nine years old, and his father is in his early forties. It is summer in the beautiful Donegal town of Glenties, where the boy's mother was brought up. Now, the boy and his father are walking home from a lake with fishing rods across their shoulders. It has been raining all day, so they are soaked to the skin. But, perhaps because the fishing has been good, the boy's father is unusually happy. As they walk along the muddy road into the village, they start to sing.

Fintan O'Toole went on,

> Glenties is at least the imagined setting of much of his work. The childhood holidays there remain so vivid for him that he seems to remember the shape and texture of every tree, every flagstone. It is, perhaps, the nearest he has come to a sense of belonging. The only problem is that he knows that there is no lake beside the road into the village. He cannot have walked along with his father, fishing rods over their shoulders, the two of them singing. The memory, though real, is impossible.

The land around Glenties is a land of lakes, large and small, but there is no lake beside the road into Glenties. Brian Friel and his father fished in Lough Anna, which is high above the town reached by a narrow lane and a climb up a steep hill. Brian Friel's wise comment on this discrepancy was, 'An autobiographical fact can be pure fiction, and no less reliable for that.'[41]

All we ever have is ideas. We can divide these ideas into fact and fantasy – those ideas we have checked against what is going on and those ideas we have not – but, fact or fantasy, if we treat our ideas as being real such ideas have real effects. Brian Friel might never have walked with his father along the road which he remembered, but his fantasy contains a wish, and perhaps a memory of something much less crisp and clear, a moment when he felt a unity and joy with his father. Such a feeling, and many others, spilled over and joined him to the green countryside of Donegal, and imbued him with a sense of belonging.

This sense of belonging to a place is a vital part of the meaning structure of most of us. Even if we have been separated from our family, or have separated ourselves from them, we can feel a powerful tie to the land of our childhood. But, alas, millions of us no longer live where we belong.

Belonging to a Place

In September 1998 Dusan and I were sitting on the couch in his study where, through the windows, we could see the roofs of old Belgrade. Imagine you were shown a photograph of Dusan and me sitting side by side on that couch and, without knowing who we were, you were asked, 'Which of these two people is a Serb?' You would know that Serbs are Slavic people, and so you would unhesitatingly point to me. I have high, broad cheekbones, deep-set blue eyes and blonde (now white) hair. My Slavic ancestors from centuries ago are there in my face. You would also say that Dusan could not possibly be a Serb. It is obvious from his appearance that he is from a Middle Eastern country, a kind of younger, handsomer version of Saddam Hussein, with all of his charisma and none of his wickedness. Dusan himself laughingly admits that there must have been a Turk somewhere among his ancestors. But then genes have nothing to do with what we think.

Dusan showed me a photograph of himself as a schoolboy with his friends on a school outing. In those days, he said, no attention was paid to who was Serb, Muslim or Croat. However, as he told me, 'The teachers always took us to places where some other people had done Serbs harm. This is the place where the Germans shot twenty thousand schoolchildren during the Second World War. The Serbs were always presented as the victims throughout the history we learnt in school. So we couldn't do anything wrong because we were always the righteous victims.'

If you and your family are righteous victims, how could you leave your family? How could you be disloyal? So Dusan, and his wife and two beautiful young daughters, remained in Belgrade through the Bosnian War and the Kosova conflict, even though in his profession Dusan would have been certain of employment in any English-speaking country. He told me, 'Basically I wouldn't like to go from here, because this was where I was born, this is where I learned so many things, this is where I gathered my friendships. Whenever I went outside, whenever I wrote a paper, I wrote it as someone from here. I introduced myself as someone from Belgrade University. Now it may not be the best university in the world, but my father studied at Belgrade University, I studied at Belgrade University, I'm now working at Belgrade University, and I would like my children to get their degrees at Belgrade University. I know in Belgrade where the first university building was two hundred years ago, and I know how many students go there. I know how to find my way around Belgrade – I can pull some strings, I know back doors and life is predictable. Although it's getting less and less predictable because this is not the same city. I feel anxious about this, but still it is less anxious living here in Belgrade than going to London.'

Earlier Dusan had told me the story of his family. It began in 1389, when Prince Lazar suffered a terrible defeat at the hands of the Turks in Kosova. Dusan said that, when he was a child, his grandfather used to tell him stories from the history of Serbia. 'One very important thing was the story of Kosova and how brave Serbian people were to cherish their freedom and not let anyone rule them again after those five bloody centuries under Turkish rule. So they fought. A lot of people died in the first upheaval against the Turks. They fought again against the Turks and a lot of people died. They fought again in 1912 in the Balkan wars. They fought in the First World War, and they wasted a lot of youth and lovely men, and again they fought in the Second World War for all these lovely ideals. But basically what we achieved was not a country of our own but a lot of dead people and a horrible decrease in population, which we didn't know then. So I think we are getting sober only now – after a lot of pain and a lot of realization that we did something wrong to ourselves, since we lost a large percentage of our population.'

The Turks, for all their cruelty, allowed their Serbian subjects to practise their religion, and so it was that the Serbian Orthodox Church kept alive 'the idea of Serbia and its notion that one day the old state would, Christ-like, be resurrected'.[1] Thus it was that in 1689 Patriarch Arsenije Carnojevic encouraged the Serbs living in the Ottoman Empire to rebel and come to the aid of the Austrian army, which had penetrated into Turkish territory. However, on New Year's Day 1690 the Turks crushed the Austrians and the Serbs in battle, and Arsenije led great columns of refugees away from their ancestral homes, mostly in Kosova, the heart of old Serbia.

Dusan's family were part of that expulsion from Kosova. He said, 'My family settled in the town of Panchevo, which is about ten kilometres from Belgrade. It was a long way then, but now it is part of Belgrade really. My family name comes from this Grandma Stoina. Her husband died fighting the Turks, and she came along with two sons, Stoin and Voin. So Stoin's sons were named Stojnov. My great-grandfather was a peasant and he was working on the land. He had no ambitions to become anything else but a plain peasant on the Serbian land. But his son, my grandfather, was something completely else. He wanted to see Europe, so he went to Vienna and studied there, and then started his business in Belgrade. He didn't want to live on his father's land.'

Dusan showed me some photographs of his grandfather and his family and said, 'I can still imagine meeting my grandfather in the street, just as I ran into you in the street today. He used to go to the same restaurant every day where he drank beer with his pals. He and his family moved into this house we're in in 1931. The two shops downstairs in front of the entrance were actually the shops where my grandfather had his picture-framing business. He bought the copyright to sell pictures of the young king, and he made good money out of that. In 1939 he bought a new apartment which was being built. He was due to move into that apartment on 14 April 1941, but on 6 April the Germans attacked Belgrade and bombed that building. So all his effort was destroyed, and we stayed in this apartment, where my father had come to live when he was two or three years old, and this was where my grandfather lived. This very room is the room where I was born, and where I lived when my father was still alive. So I still feel his presence, and can still imagine what this room looked like thirty or forty years ago.'

Dusan showed me a photograph of Belgrade in 1936 and said, 'Even before I was born I was connected to this city. I love these black and white photographs. I prefer them so much to the colour ones. These were happy times. We didn't have much, but we had

better lives. I think I was a happy kid, and being happy had something to do with living here, in this part of the world. If we travelled
we went to the seaside. It's now in Croatia but it was Yugoslavia
then. We loved to go there, but the loveliest part was coming home,
finding everything was as you left it, your toys, your friends.'

He showed me another old photograph. 'This is my mother's
grandfather. I can still go and sit on the very same bench and say,
yes, my great-grandfather used to sit here. This is the entrance to
this building. Somehow it doesn't seem right to move from here.
Who's going to live in this apartment if we leave? Whose pictures
are going to be on these walls?'

Dusan's attachment to his home reveals how our meaning structure can incorporate a place so centrally that to lose the place would
be to put the meaning structure under severe threat. Our sense of
belonging to a place is both an intensely private, individual set of
meanings which we experience more in images and bodily feelings
than in words, and a public, shared set of meanings which relate to
the history and values of the national, racial or religious group with
which we most closely identify.

Richard's attachment to the place of his birth was very strong,
but it was not imbued with the powerful sense of loss and loyalty
which comes from a tragic national history. His knowledge of his
family's history goes back no more than four generations, and it is
a peaceful history. Even though his father had been a professional
soldier who later fought in the Second World War the family was
not caught up in any major national tragedy. Richard chose to move
south, away from his home and family, for reasons of ambition and
career, and his father stayed in Dewsbury in the north. Happy indeed
are the families who have no history.

Richard said, 'I always had the understanding that I would go
away. If you didn't go away you'd never make anything of yourself.
There were very few opportunities within the area I lived in to
progress in any way. It was important to me to travel, but there is
this feeling of home. I had it very strongly a couple of years back,
when I'd been to a conference in Harrogate, and I got the train
from Leeds to Dewsbury. Perhaps it was because I hadn't come in
the car, I'd come up by train, a route I was familiar with but hadn't
travelled on for several years. I got to the station, walked up to
where my father's flat was, and it was like a scene from a film where

you stand for a while, with your case, and feel you've come home. No matter where I went, and where I lived in the world, that would always be home. It would always be Dewsbury, and perhaps that small area of Dewsbury where I was brought up. When I go back, I see places, I see things, and I remember things. Sometimes it can be smells that bring things back. And it brings back a scale as well, because everything seems bigger in your mind, and when you go back it isn't big at all.'

When Richard spoke of how important it was to him that his children knew that they came from a certain part of Dewsbury he showed that he understood, though he would not have used these words, that the place he grew up in was central to his meaning structure. He said that if he did not know his family history and where he belonged 'I just wouldn't understand the way I behave and relate to people. It explains myself to me. It explains my attitudes. Everything about me comes from that background. It's about keeping your feet on the ground. It's about common sense.'

Tima, like Richard, chose to leave her family. Her ambition was to be herself, not a dutiful daughter, wife and mother. She still felt a strong tie to the place where she had spent her childhood, and that tie was all the stronger and more poignant because her home in southern Lebanon was under constant threat from the Israelis.

When Tima was about nine she had asked her father to fill a jar with soil from the family land. 'I still have it,' she said, 'and I've given it to my children now. It *is* the land. It's one and the same, the land and the people, because you're in an open space. There are no buildings to hide the reality: people are not closed up in their small cubicles. They're out in the open. Their doors are open, their homes are open, so the sky and the land are like one and the same. I don't feel that anybody can separate me from my roots. It's not a physical connection. It's a spiritual connection. When I go there it's total bliss for me. It's a very peaceful place. The people are wonderful. They're warm, they're hospitable, they are amazing. It's a pity they don't get a good education. They'd have been a major, positive component of this society, but being so deprived, because they're so far from the capital, they don't get a chance for a good education. I hate the fact that the Israelis are in the south. It doesn't make me feel dispossessed. It makes me feel I want to be there more, and that I must not just sit around and let them take over.'

Whether Tima could visit her home depended on the whim of the Israeli occupiers. Australians, the inhabitants of the Lucky Country, can come and go as they please. Travelling all over the world is part of the Australian way of life. Out of 18 million people 1 million are abroad at any one time. Most are very happy to get back home again.

Irene described herself as 'belonging to the world', but went on to say, 'I'm very patriotic in the sense that I can remember being in Nairobi and walking down the street and looking up and seeing the Australian flag and breaking into tears. I remember the first sight of the Southern Cross when, after eight months, I moved into the southern hemisphere, in Dar es Salaam, and walked on the beach and I said, "There it is! There it is!" I was just so excited to see it. I do feel a citizen of the world in the sense that I feel at home in most places. I don't mind being foreign. But I have a very, very strong love of Australia. My upbringing as a child – standing in the school playground and singing, "There's a land with summer skies," and Dorothy Mackellar's poems, and peppercorn trees, and the laugh of the kookaburra. I love this house. I love coming home. I get homesick – the minute I leave I've already worked out how long it is till I get back. Whereas when I was younger I'd have happily gone off. But it was different then – I was coming back to an unhappy marriage. Whereas here, to me this is serene and peaceful, and all my bits and pieces are here.'

I commented, 'And you're in control of it.'

Irene smiled. 'You've hit the nail on the head there. I think that's what's important to me.'

This sense of being in control, being safe, feeling secure in your identity came out very clearly in the answers my workshop participants gave when I asked them whether they experienced a sense of belonging.

- 'Where I belong is not a geographical place. It is in closeness with others, with my partner, with my dogs, wherever we may be, provided certain very basic comforts are available.'
- 'I belong in England because of its history, language, culture and tradition.'

- 'I belong in England. I wasn't aware of this sense of belonging until I started to go abroad to France and Greece and then visiting relatives in the USA. The USA brought it home to me the importance of our history here. My relatives there took me to visit more family and kept pointing out places connected to their history, like buildings which were no more than seventy years old. I became aware of the feeling of security that a long history gives to me.'

- 'I belong to London. I never cease to tell people that I am a true Cockney born within the sound of Bow Bells.'

- 'I belong where I live now because it is familiar, safe, gives me an identity, and the people there know me.'

- 'I belong in my home village, my marital home and not my family home. I've spent over half my married life in the village, bringing up my children, gathering experiences and friendships. It's the people who are important to me, not the place. If I moved it could be that another place could hold the same feelings. I think I could belong anywhere. Once I've formed relationships and established friends and colleagues, in fact once I've got my bearings, I could belong. It's all about establishing trust.'

- 'I feel I belong with my small children, at home. As long as we're together we're at home. I've travelled and I could live in many places. But where I grew up, the house, the fields, the secret places, I still dream that this is my home, even though it doesn't exist any more. I belong at home, a safe place, a retreat, a rock.'

- 'I belong in Stockholm and the forest. I can go back there and feel at home.'

- 'I belong where I live now, but in my heart I belong to Scotland, the mountains and the glens and the commonality of culture. It is part of my identity – the yearning, longing, belonging. I understand the "dear Green Place".'

- 'I belong anywhere as long as it's by the sea. Living in Wycombe is not good for me. I miss the sea.'

- 'I belong at home, in England. In my early married life we moved every two years and I felt I didn't belong anywhere. I now value being settled. My home is my security, my haven in this world.'

- 'My home is where I belong. It's where my roots are, and the culture and landscapes are familiar and comfortable. It's important to belong, to have a sense of identity.'
- 'I belong in the English countryside where I was brought up. A particular place is not as important as my tie with nature and natural beauty.'
- 'I have nowhere where I feel I belong. I would like to feel that I belong somewhere, especially with my husband and children. Having nowhere makes me feel like no one.'
- 'The more roots you've got in you the more you can move about.'

The statement, 'The more roots you have the more you can move about,' is a simple way of saying that the stronger you feel in yourself (i.e., the stronger your meaning structure) the more the sense of belonging is experienced as a set of meanings which you take with you wherever you go and less as an active attachment which if stretched or severed causes actual pain. The more uncertain you feel in yourself (i.e., the more fragile your meaning structure) the more you need the actual presence of your place to buttress your meaning structure.

Thus the lonely boy J. M. Coetzee described needed to belong to the family farm where, in fact, he was only a visitor. The sense of the boy's loneliness is heightened by the way Coetzee refers to himself as 'he'.

The secret and sacred word which binds him to the farm is *belong*. Out on the veldt by himself he can breathe the word out loud: *I belong on the farm*. What he really believes but does not utter, what he keeps to himself for fear that the spell will end, is a different form of the word: *I belong to the farm*.

He tells no one because the word is misunderstood so easily, turned so easily into its reverse: *The farm belongs to me*. The farm will never belong to him, he will never be more than a visitor: he accepts that. The thought of actually living on Voëlfontein, of calling the great old house his home, of no longer having to ask permission to do what he wants to do, turns him giddy; he thrusts it away. *I belong to the farm*, that is the furthest he is prepared to go, even in his secret heart. But in his secret heart he knows what the farm in its way knows too: that Voëlfontein belongs to no one. The farm is greater than any of them. The farm exists from eternity to eternity. When they are all dead, when even the farmhouse has fallen into ruin like the kraals on the hillside, the farm will still be there.[2]

On the May bank holiday in 1999 Anthony and I were driving from Armagh to Enniskillen through the rich green countryside of Northern Ireland. He was telling me that many of the battles that went on in families, between families and between the two religious groups have to do with land. He said, 'Land is very important. They fight over it and think they can hold on to it. They forget that the land is only lent to them, and it'll be there when they're gone.'

For thousands of years the original inhabitants of Australia must have taken their belonging to the land as being as natural and unremarkable as breathing. It was when the English arrived and began treating them as no-things, the lowest of the low, neither human nor animal, that belonging had to be made conscious and stated over and over in every possible way. Mudrooroo, like many other Aboriginal people, called this belonging 'spirituality' and said, 'This spirituality is preoccupied with the relationship of the earth, nature and people in the sense that the earth is accepted as a member of our family, blood of our blood, bone of our bone, and to show it disrespect or wilfully harm it is tantamount to patricide, matricide or fratricide.'[3]

Pat Dodson, former chair of the National Reconciliation Council, described belonging in terms of meaning.

The land is really the identification of a person's meaning and identification in life. Land and that person is pretty much synonymous. He or she is linked to the stories of that land, to the locations on that land which are part of those stories, to things that the land provides, not just physical sustenance but security and emotional welfare. Land is, I suppose, the warm blanket when you're freezing cold out on the street. It is very much a cloak. With that around you, you can come to your full potential as an Aboriginal person. If you don't have that as your protection, then you're exposed, alienated. You become a non-existent human being, a nobody, and you can't exist as an Aboriginal person. You have to assume some other form of identity.[4]

Sometimes, when we want to strengthen or affirm our sense of identity we simply go and look at where we belong. This is a special kind of looking, where we temporarily relinquish all those meanings that create a defensive shell around us, meanings which have 'I' at their centre – what I am doing, what I am thinking, how I appear to others. When this shell dissolves we can give all our attention to what we are looking at, and what we are looking at becomes intensely real. We become part of that reality. This experience might not last more than a few moments, but it creates a sense of peace like no other.

Of course what is being looked at does not have to be part of where we belong. Trees, flowers, the sea, a candle in preparation for meditation are all amenable to this experience, but where we belong can have a special significance in affirming our existence. The intense feeling of being part of where we belong is the opposite of the feeling of being annihilated.

However, the sense of belonging where you live can be in conflict with what is imposed on you by other people who see you, not as equals, but as second- or third-rate people who know their place and have to keep to it. On my first day in Cape Town in December 1998 I sat in St George's Mall and watched the passing crowd. There was a mixture of nationalities and races, just as there would have been had I sat in one of the outdoor cafés at the Angel, near where I lived in London. Indeed, there was little difference between the crowds at the Mall and at the Angel. They moved with the same kind of assurance and purpose. I wondered if I was being fanciful when I thought that the scene I was witnessing was different from the one I had seen in Cape Town in 1990, when the harsh laws of apartheid were still oppressing black people. Then I felt that the black citizens of Cape Town moved differently, conscious of where they were tolerated and where they were not.

Afterwards I asked my friend Marinella, with whom I was staying, if I had imagined this difference. She said that I had not. She said that she saw this difference in all the black people she encountered. 'They have laws to protect them now,' she said. 'They are sure of their rights.'

In 1993 the journalist Fionnuala O Connor published her account of her interviews with fifty Catholics in Northern Ireland about their sense of identity. She quoted the writer Michael Farrell as saying that, as a teenager in south Derry, he thought of the whole of the Northern nationalist community as 'lacking in self-respect, desperately looking for the South to rescue them'. She commented that this was 'a judgement John Hume and Gerry Adams would second'.[5]

The Troubles in Northern Ireland had gone on for so long that it could be difficult for anyone under forty to 'appreciate how dramatic the change has been in the public profile of Catholics'.[6] In 1964 Patricia and Conn McCluskey started the Campaign for Social Justice, the first group to make a systematic attempt to quantify discrimination against the Catholics in housing and employment. Now in their late seventies, they spoke to Fionnuala about the changes they saw. Conn pointed out how those Catholics who had been educated in the South had more confidence than those who had been educated in the North. He said,

'The ones who went to St Malachy's, in Belfast, they were very inhibited compared to us. They felt inferior. We did too, but less so. Now it's completely changed. Once, recently, I was in Armagh, in the Protestant owned shop: a very up-market draper, austere sort of crowd. In the old days it was nearly like going into church, it was so respectful and restrained. This last time I was in, it was full of young Catholic girls, shouting and laughing and talking like equals.'[7]

Not everyone has that sense of belonging to a particular place. I heard a man on BBC Radio Four say that he had no tie to his childhood home. He added by way of explanation, 'But then I was born in Weybridge.' The explorer Robyn Davidson, on one of her expeditions, joined the Rabari nomads in India. From childhood Robyn had lived in many places. Now she realized that she was, in some ways, less tied to a place than were the Rabaris: 'Even nomads have a place from which they leave. They have a very strong sense of belonging. I've lacked that for most of my life.'[8]

Not everyone finds the land where they live as children a refuge and support that protects them from the unhappiness and uncertainties of childhood. Fay Weldon spent her childhood in New Zealand, but was born in England because her mother, to escape the aftermath of an earthquake in New Zealand, returned to England to give birth to her. When I spoke to Fay about my attachment to the Australian bush and beaches she made it very clear that she did not feel the same way about New Zealand.

She said, 'When I go there I feel very suspicious of it. I look at this beach, which is obviously beautiful, and I don't reckon it. Flying over this country – it looks so small, and it's got little volcanoes and they're so new they haven't mellowed down. They're like porridge – you know when porridge boils you get these little sharp things – I think they're just like porridge boiling. As a child I lived in perpetual fear that the volcanoes were going to erupt, that earthquakes were going to swallow you up – and not without reason. It was the same when we were in Auckland – this is obviously to do with family break-up, and sudden change, which one is well aware of. Even as a child you knew there was a connection between what went on at school or home and what your view of the natural order was. There was a volcano that was meant to be dormant in the middle of Auckland Harbour. I never believed it was dormant. When I went there about five years ago they had discovered that in fact it wasn't dormant. A puff of smoke was oozing from it. I thought, "I told you so!" and got out of there and went to Australia, where the land is more stable.'

Fay might not have felt that she belonged to a land somewhere, but she did know what it means to be uprooted, what it means to become a refugee.

Losing Your Place

I asked Fay if there was anywhere in the world where she felt she belonged. She said, 'The only place where I feel at home is in a room of television writers. It's not a place – it's a room full of people whose backgrounds I understand. Because they're television writers they all drink and smoke too much and are hopeless – and you feel all right. And it's not even that they're very nice to you – they can be terribly bitchy and not pro-you at all, but at the same time you understand where they're coming from. You just feel at home, you share a common history, you know the same kinds of things that they know, and you don't have to explain yourself.'

Groups of disparate people often come together because of the reasons Fay listed. There could be another reason. I asked Fay, 'Has that group got a common enemy?'

Fay replied, 'Their own past. They're all people who are dysfunctional, or they come from slightly dysfunctional families, or they wouldn't be doing what they were doing. You share that in common. I've always known, from the time I was a child, that the friends you had shared the same background. You were friends at school with the refugees. When I was at school in New Zealand my friends were children whose lives had been disrupted. When I went to university, my friends had divorced parents, or peculiar backgrounds. They weren't people from ordinary backgrounds. Then later, being married and in kinds of bohemian circles – artists, painters and the like – all I ever met were victim women. One day I realized that actually there are lots of women who told their husbands to fetch their handbags, and told them to buy new coats and made them dance attendance on them. But they were never the people I knew, and they were never the dinner parties I got asked to. I only met the men who'd been appalling to women and the women who chose to stick around with them.'

Fay might not feel attached to a place but she always remained attached to her mother, her sister and her sister's children. In contrast, I, like many people, lost the place I belonged to when I tried to detach myself from my mother and sister and my ex-husband by putting half a world between us. When my son and I came to England in 1968 we travelled by ship and train because air travel was only in its expensive beginnings. Since then air travel has burgeoned and become less expensive. Over the thirty years I have lived in England I have been able to measure the strength of the Australian dollar by the number of Australians sleeping on my floor. Most have been doing the six-week tour of the UK and the continent, but some have been separating from a faithless spouse, or having a well-earned rest from demanding parents, and some, on sabbatical leave from their university, have been looking for a permanent post overseas, where they can become the person they know themselves to be.

Many of those who fled their family and their place did not return home but became internationalists – people prepared to live in many different countries, depending on where their work and inclinations took them. They joined that huge band of work-driven internationalists. As different kinds of manufacturing and service industries diminished in one area and increased in another, so those with expertise had to follow. In Belfast I met a specialist in textile manufacture whose career, begun in Northern Ireland, had taken him in turn to Australia, Indonesia, South Africa and the USA. 'My daughters like South Africa best,' he said.

Similarly companies with branches and connections around the world expect their employees to pull up their roots and move to suit the company's needs. Some people resist this, and, if forced to move, try to take something of the place they belong to with them. They do not want their children to grow up not knowing the language and customs of the place where they feel their children belong, and so they send their children back home to be educated, or band together with other like-minded parents to provide for the children the same kind of education which they would have received at home. These parents want to make sure that their children hold many of the meanings which the parents hold.

Try as they might, such parents cannot achieve this. Being sent away from your family to Pakistan or Japan to go to school is a very different experience from living in Lahore or Kyoto with your family and going to school, just as it is a different experience from living with your family in Bradford and going to Muslim school or in Milton Keynes and going to a Japanese school. My friend Nez, who has an Egyptian father and a Greek mother, and has lived in England for some years, told me, 'I feel both negatively and positively about "coming from" two cultures – the Arabic and the English culture. As I was growing up I continuously felt this "floating" sensation, never really fitting into either culture or group of peoples. Sometimes I still have those feelings of never being part of either culture. But more so now I feel lucky that my life has been enriched because of the two cultures. I get to see, experience, understand, feel things that I may not have had the chance to do if I were only part of one culture.'

Some parents see the future as one where people will travel a great deal and work in different places, and they want to prepare their children for this future. An executive of an international pharmaceutical firm, whom I met at a conference in England, told me that he travelled widely but mainly divided his time between the USA and the UK. His wife and two small children lived in Florida but sometimes accompanied him on his travels. He said, 'I want my children to think internationally.' At a party I met a woman who seized upon my American companion to get information about houses in his part of California. She explained that every summer she and her husband arranged a house exchange with an American family. She said, 'Every year we go to a different part of the States. We want our children to learn about other people and places, and often you don't get that if you simply go to some holiday hotel.'

In an interview on BBC World Television the journalist Tim Sebastian asked Jost Stollmann, known as the 'Bill Gates of Germany', why, when he left school, he had chosen to study in France and then had gone to the Harvard Business School in the USA. Had he wanted to get away from his country? Jost Stollmann replied that he was not trying to get away; by going away he could see Germany from the outside. 'By doing that I could discover my roots.'[9] This is reminiscent of the saying, 'What does he know of England who only England knows?'

When Sadaaki Numata, the Minister Plenipotentiary at the Japanese embassy in London, was invited to give the graduation speech at Southbank International School he talked about what it meant to be a true cosmopolitan. He explained how the Japanese had changed the value they had placed on 'cosmopolitan'.

Japan has come far in the course of the past 35 years. An American journalist once pointed out that the Japanese word for 'foreign country' *gaikoku* is nothing but *gai* plus *koku*, 'outside' plus 'nation', and that the Japanese term should be thus rendered in English as 'Outnation'. There is some truth in this in the sense that many Japanese used to think of Japan as a unique and cohesive entity, with the rest of the world being 'out' there. I must confess that I felt I was bravely venturing 'out' there when I boarded the ship for America in 1960. In that year fewer than 80,000 Japanese set foot on foreign soil. In 1994 there were nearly 14 million Japanese travelling all over the world. In 1975, around 400,000 Japanese nationals lived abroad, of whom 5,600 were stationed in the United Kingdom. By 1993 the figure had reached 680,000 Japanese overseas, with 56,000 resident in this country. Through such direct exposure, the 'outnation' has been brought much closer home.

Sadaaki Numata quoted Goethe – 'He who knows no foreign language does not truly know his own' – and went on to consider the question of identity.

By 'cosmopolitan', do we mean someone who drifts through the world without any identity to speak of? I think not. A true cosmopolitan is a straddler of cultures with an anchor. Goethe would probably agree that he who does not know his own language cannot know any other. It is such straddlers who can really tear down barriers to mutual knowledge, understanding and affection among the different people of the world.[10]

Travel has changed the pattern of marriage. Until the advent of the bicycle in the late nineteenth century people in the UK usually married someone who lived in their village or within walking distance of the village. The bicycle started a trend which increased and expanded, and nowadays many people marry someone who is not from a village a few miles distant but from a country thousands of miles away. However, even though the modes of travel have multiplied and become easily accessible, what has become increasingly difficult is getting permission to enter those countries whose governments may view unfavourably your national, religious, racial or sexual allegiances. If you are a world traveller your passport, or collection of passports, can become your most precious possession. A passport confirms identity and rights. When the Serbian army was expelling those of Albanian descent from Kosova they took from them not just their money and jewellery but their passports.

There is now what Nigel Harris, in his study of migration, called 'the black economy of nationality'. He wrote, 'Over a few generations, a mobile family might build up a significant portfolio of passports to ease the tiresome rigours of international travel, broaden the potential for work, and avoid irksome legal obligations (such as the commitment to military service) – and assist tax evasion.'

He gave as an example 'a person born in the United States to a couple, respectively from Tanzania and Kenya but originally born in parts of British India which became independent India and Pakistan, who migrates to Canada. Six claims on national status are possible, provided five of the claims are kept secret from the sixth.'[11]

Here national status becomes a moveable feast, selected for prag-
matic reasons, but for the person concerned it must be hard to
decide which of the available nationalities is an essential part of a
sense of identity. Perhaps the only point of certainty that remains
is that, with American nationality, no matter what part of the world
is chosen as home, American taxes must be paid. So much in life
comes down to a matter of money.

Money is a set of ideas which serves two vital purposes.[12] First,
it maintains our physical survival. With money we can buy food,
shelter and clothing. Second, money maintains us as a person. People
who think little of themselves will often work hard to acquire money
so that, in another sense of 'worth', they are worth a great deal.
People who like to think of themselves as not being interested in
money, as caring more about spiritual or humanitarian matters than
about money, are using money as a way of strengthening their sense
of virtue and of identity. We present ourselves to society in terms
of what we earn and own, and society categorizes us in terms of
our financial worth. The rich have more status and power than the
poor.

Money gives us choices. We can see it as our reward for virtue,
and we can feel aggrieved when our much-deserved rewards are
withheld. Money can help us to fulfil our expectations of life, and
comfort us when they are frustrated. The meanings we give to money
are intensely private, yet if we lived alone on a desert island money
would be meaningless, of less use than the sand on the beach. Money
exists only in our relationships with other people. Like our sense
of belonging to a place, the meanings we give to money link the
individuality of our meaning structure to the world around us.

But what happens when our ideas about money are disconfirmed,
when we are no longer worth what we thought we were worth, and
when we can no longer predict our future, as we once did, in terms
of money?

Under the Communist government the suicide rate in Lithuania
was unremarkable, ranging between 25 and 35 suicides per 100,000
of the population. After the collapse of the Soviet Union the rate
of suicide climbed to 46.4 in 1996 and went on climbing, making it
the highest in Europe. In his report on psychiatry in Lithuania the
psychiatrist Rahman Haghighat wrote,

The high rate of suicide can be linked to the disillusionment of the nation, who remain pessimistic and fearful of the future following independence. Under the Soviet regime everyone had a 'job'; those with little skill or ability were also asked to attend a workplace and were given an activity and a regular salary. With the arrival of the market economy, 35% of the population have become unemployed over five years. In the Lithuanian patriarchal society, where men are expected to be the main bread-winners, the loss of status of unemployed men in families causes isolation, loss of self-esteem, depression and alcoholism. The dissolution of the collective farms, the privatisation and redistribution of land in the absence of the previous central government support for equipment, fertilisers and seed, has caused great distress to people who were formerly dependent on a minimal, but guaranteed, standard of living during the Soviet era. It is a huge stress for a nation in a collective economy to be suddenly expected to become self-reliant, in a market economy copied from individualist Western societies.[13]

Suicide is always the statement: 'If I cannot live as me I'll die as me.' Many people in Lithuania found that their meaning structure did not contain the breadth and varieties of meanings necessary to comprehend, much less take advantage of, the changes taking place. Many would have learnt from the Catholic Church's teaching about the Just World to blame themselves for any disaster which befell them. They would be unlikely to struggle against adversity but instead lapse into depression and perhaps take their own lives. Other people, untroubled by a Catholic conscience and able to understand the basic principles of the free market, would seize the opportunity to profit from one very popular commodity: illegal drugs. The Baltic states provided transit points for drugs being smuggled from east to west. However, those people who did not blame themselves for changes in the world order and did not want to be part of the drug trade looked to a third option – migration. If there was no work in Lithuania they would go where there was work. They would become, in the new terminology, economic refugees.

A refugee has been defined as 'someone who has left his or her country or is unable to return to it owing to a well-founded fear of persecution for reasons of race, religion, nationality, membership of a particular social group or political opinion'.[14] This definition does not include those people who are escaping from poverty and who want to make a better life for themselves and their family. They have no rights under refugee law and are dealt with under immigration law which, in many countries, is aimed at preventing those deemed to be economic refugees from claiming asylum.

Those who scorn economic refugees and seek to frustrate their aims fail to recognize how important economic refugees have been in the history of every country. Indeed, for most of human history we were all economic refugees. Hunter-gatherers always move on when food stocks are depleted. However, hunter-gatherers always need to limit the size of their tribe so as not to exhaust available supplies, but, once farming and then industry became the means whereby people sustained their lives, communities and then states usually welcomed migrants, especially if they brought skills and capital. Nigel Harris pointed out that, 'Before the nineteenth century . . . an expanding population was a sign of expanding power, and princes rejoiced at the misfortune of their fellow monarchs in losing their subjects.'[15] Between 1850 and 1900 some 60 million people left Europe for the New World.[16] Migration was essential to sustain growth. As the local population became skilled and moved up the social ladder migrants came to do the work that no one else wanted to do. These migrants then moved upwards and generated wealth. For instance, the Chinese who took their knowledge, skills and industrious habits across Asia acquired capital estimated at $500 billion, which they were able to move into expanding economies like Vietnam.[17]

The great wealth of England was first generated by thousands of migrants who were given the choice of working or dying. These were the slaves taken from Africa. The wealth their owners made from their labours financed the Industrial Revolution, which was then sustained by the influx of economic refugees from Europe and Ireland. The much-cherished British National Health Service would have died at birth if West Indians had decided that life was sweeter, if poorer, in the place which they called home.

From the beginning our ancestors were restless travellers, always moving on until they inhabited most of the fertile land. Yet it was not until the twentieth century that we travelled in such vast numbers, and most did not travel willingly. Most of the twentieth-century travellers were refugees. Some of these travellers were forced from their homes and from their country. Of these, some left when they saw the approaching danger; some waited until the enemy was at their door. Other travellers were able to stay in their own country but lost their homes. By the mid 1990s in Columbia, a country made unstable by the corruption and violence of the illegal drug trade, a million people had been displaced from their homes. The massive Three Gorges Dam, which China started to build in 1994, meant the displacement of some 1.3 million people.[18]

Jean Said Makdisi said of her country, Lebanon, 'We are a land of refugees, a people of refugees, coming from everywhere, going nowhere.'[19] In her glossary of terms to use in crisis she commented upon the word which could be the symbol of the war in Lebanon, *muhajjar* – refugee.

> Actually, the proper translation of 'refugee' is *laji'* with its parallel emphasis on 'refuge or haven'. *Muhajjar* has far more negative connotations, and the nuance is important. While the word *laji'* implies arrival and safety, the word *muhajjar* rests on departure and emigration; and in this particular grammatical form of enforced departure or emigration – the *muhajjar* is one 'one who is made to depart'.[20]

No one is born with a vocation to be a refugee. The word itself came into being in 1685 in reference to the Protestant Huguenots who fled to England from Catholic France. In 1998

> the United Nations High Commissioner for Refugees reckoned that there were 12 million refugees around the world, 3.5 million recently returned refugees and millions more displaced within their own countries. At least 3.2 million Palestinians are still classified as refugees. In Iran alone, some 2 million refugees – from Afghanistan and Iraq – live in border camps. Well over 1 million Afghans have sheltered in Pakistan since 1979.[21]

By April 1999 the United Nations High Commissioner for Refugees had estimated that 1.1 million Kosovan Albanians had been displaced – some 69 per cent of the Kosovan Albanian population.

Forced from their homes, the refugees had nowhere to go. Other people might pity their plight, but other people do not always want to share their country with strangers. It was not just a matter of having to give the refugees homes, money and jobs. Refugees bring ideas and customs which challenge and disturb. Meaning structures have to be protected. Hence countries set limits to the number of refugees they would take.

However, whatever the disaster, someone devises a way of making a profit from it. Smuggling refugees into the European Union proved to be as profitable as smuggling drugs. In 1998 it was estimated that the profit from smuggling people was some $4 billion a year.[22]

Whenever we leave the place where we belong and go somewhere else to live, whether we leave by choice for reasons of ambition or marriage, or in order to better our economic circumstances, or are forced out by those who threaten us, we must, when we arrive at our new abode, make some connection with the new place as quickly as possible. If we fail to do this our meaning structure is continually at risk. As long as our new abode seems to be strange and rejecting of us we lack the certainty and predictability that our meaning structure needs for day-to-day living, while the affirmation of our identity and worth, which we need from those who know us, is very limited or even non-existent. Yet many migrants find themselves in a dangerous limbo. *The Economist* reported that in the UK

> The asylum process takes so long that many migrants put down roots in Britain, marry and have children. Once that happens, it is difficult to repatriate those whose applications are eventually turned down without punishing their families. After taking so long to make up their minds the authorities lose track of many that they reject: refugee organizations estimate that less than a third of asylum seekers whose applications have been denied either leave voluntarily or are deported. In consequence, a twilight world has grown up, inhabited by perhaps 50,000 people with no civil status and no social or political rights.[23]

Neal Ascherson once remarked that we should always watch how refugees are treated because that is how politicians would treat the rest of us if they thought they could get away with it.[24] From my lengthy observations of politicians in different countries it seems to me that few politicians care about the people they represent. Expressed concern for others is often merely a convenient disguise for the desire to make the world be what you want it to be. In politics people with genuine concern for others do not reach high office, or, if they do, the desire to remain in office ensures that such caring vanishes to be replaced by contempt. The game of politics always involves not telling the truth. Democratic systems are adversarial, and politicians on all sides must say what their party tells them to say, even though they may know what they have to say is not the truth. Democracy or dictatorship, claims made by politicians that the political path they propose to follow will be totally beneficial to the people are always lies because no course of action ever has entirely beneficial effects. There are always good effects and bad effects, winners and losers.

Thus all politicians, no matter how great their desire to do good, treat people with contempt. Only the fear of losing office restrains the expression of that contempt. When the fear of losing office is not a factor their contempt knows no bounds.

Although Lebanon by 1998 had returned to a semblance of democracy the country was too riven by different factions for any concerted popular movement to form against those politicians who put their own interests above those of the general population. Looking for profit and glory Prime Minister Rafiq al-Hariri embarked on a grandiose plan to rebuild downtown Beirut, which had been destroyed in the fighting of 1975, but virtually nothing was spent on repairing and replacing roads, the postal service and electricity and water supplies. To travel on the roads of Lebanon, unmarked, potholed, and filled with reckless drivers, was to take one's life in one's hands. The postal service was unreliable to the point of being useless, the phone service so inadequate that practically every Lebanese had a mobile phone. Tima pointed out to me how Lebanese men carried their mobile phones on their hips and, on entering a café, slammed their mobile down on the bar, in much the same way that men used to handle their guns.

Throughout Beirut buildings which had been severely damaged during the war were either inhabited by squatters who risked their lives to do so or were left to decay, with the result that these buildings consisted only of heavy slabs of concrete held in place by rusting cables. In many buildings these slabs of concrete overhung busy pavements. Outside Beirut the concrete frames of unfinished buildings occupied blocks of land which had been carved from farmland.

They had been put up in haste and left unfinished when the money ran out. No attempt was made to prevent anyone from trespassing on these structures. On the road from Baalbek to Beirut I saw a group of young children playing on the fourth floor of one such structure. There was nothing to stop an unwary child from going over the edge of the top floor and plunging to the ground.

Once the mountains and valleys of Lebanon had been green and densely wooded. Greed and war ensured that the famed cedars of Lebanon dwindled to a few meagre groves and all the countryside was denuded of trees. The scrub that was left could not defend the soil against the wind and the rain, and so the ravines of soil erosion burrowed deeply into what were once rolling meadows. Such scrub was prey to fire, either occurring naturally or deliberately set by speculators who wanted to establish quarries which further destroyed the landscape.

Lebanon was indeed the land of refugees. Some had fled from elsewhere and others, though they lived where they had been born, had lost their beautiful country and been given a desert in return.

When I walked around the streets of Belgrade in the late summer of 1998 I felt sorry for the people who lived there. I did not feel sorry for the rich cronies of Slobodan Milošovic who could afford to run up accounts at the expensive clothing stores and grocery shops which sported the advertisements for luxury merchandise from the West; nor was I sorry for the gangsters in their BMWs with darkened windows who, with the threat of a bullet, forced ordinary drivers off the road; but I did feel sorry for those people who had to mend and make do, whose salaries had not kept pace with inflation, and whose savings had been stolen by Milošovic. Most, though not all, of us who live in countries where the politicians have to hide and keep in check the contempt they have for those who elect them, take for granted that we can buy an enormous range of pleasing clothes and delightful food. We can furnish and refurnish our homes, take holidays abroad and entertain ourselves in a huge variety of ways. To show that we are virtuous we might deplore consumerism, but, even though we might have to struggle with some of the pain and anxieties which life can bring, we can comfort ourselves with many pleasures.

Such a way of life was already present in Yugoslavia when Tito died. The country had many resources which could have been developed, but on tourism alone it could have become wealthy. Milošovic held his fellow Serbs in such contempt that he not only denied them a good life but forced them to support his wars, which destroyed their country and their livelihoods.

Whenever we feel contempt for another person we are applying to that person the standards we set for ourselves. If you try to be as truthful as possible you are likely to feel contempt for someone who continually lies. Contempt felt in this way arises in relation to an individual in a specific situation. However, if contempt is directed not at an individual but at a large group of people or, indeed, at the whole human race, then something more profound than the application of a moral judgement is happening. It is primitive pride in action.

The integrity of our meaning structure is always dependent on how we feel about ourselves. If we value ourselves, care about ourselves, judge ourselves in kindly and encouraging ways, then, even though we encounter disasters or people turn against us, we see these events as challenges which we shall master. When we do not value but feel contempt for ourselves, when we do not care for ourselves, when we judge ourselves harshly on impossibly high standards, we see all disasters and rejections as inevitable defeats. In such circumstances it is wise to review how we feel about ourselves and resolve to become our own best friend, but such a course of action is very hard work. It is much easier to leave the job of defending our meaning structure to primitive pride.

An immediate comfort primitive pride can bring is the meaning, 'I might be of little value but other people are much worse than I am.' This meaning allows us to project the contempt we feel for ourselves on to other people.

Such projected contempt provides both comfort and a justification for cruelty inflicted on those seen as contemptible. It is useful both to those who are poor and powerless and to those who seek power. The poor and powerless can feel contempt for people of a different race, or nationality or sexual orientation. Those seeking or gaining power can enhance their standing in their own eyes by denigrating those weaker than themselves. Because he felt contempt for his colleagues Milošovic could be ruthless in his actions to gain and hold on to power. Because he felt contempt for his fellow human beings Milošovic could be ruthless in waging war. But the contempt he expressed was the contempt he felt for himself. What little is known of Milošovic's life suggests that as a young man it would have been difficult for him to accept and value himself. His parents separated when he was young. His estranged father blew his brains out with a shotgun when Milošovic was twenty-one. When he was in his early thirties his mother hanged herself from a light fitting in the family home. How contemptible a son must be if neither parent considers the son's existence sufficient reason for staying alive! Alas, a young man's attempt to hold himself together in the face of great adversity drew other people and events to it which, when combined, led to terrible death and destruction.

Politicians like Milošovic treat their fellow human beings with contempt because they consider them too ignorant and too stupid to understand what is being done to them. They are like children. If adults who are like children can be maltreated, then the same can be done to children themselves.

The sentimentality expressed about children is commensurate with the cruelty inflicted upon them. If adults really cared about children as much as they profess all disputes would be settled in ways which do not involve children. What is needed is for all adults to recognize how easy it is to treat children with the same contempt with which they were treated as children. To do this everyone would have to relinquish the delicious seduction by primitive pride which says to children and younger people, 'I suffered, so you can too.'

Few people are prepared to make this change, and so millions of children have been killed, injured, tortured, maltreated, torn from their homes – and often from their families. In 1997 some 600 refugee children arrived in the UK on their own.[25] They were fleeing terror and persecution. Some had seen family members killed. Many spoke no English and had no family or friends in England. In Africa terrorist forces, such as the Lord's Resistance Army in Uganda, kidnapped children, used them for sexual purposes and forced them, as child soldiers, to kill. In 1999 the United Nations Children's Fund estimated that as many as 15,000 children had been kidnapped in the previous ten years.[26]

The kidnapping of children is not merely a twentieth-century phenomenon. Throughout history children have been seen as objects to be used by adults as they please. Children have been used as sex objects, servants and slaves, and taken from their families and forced to join an alien culture.

As white settlers spread westward across America in the nineteenth century the defeated Indians were forced into reservations, where they were expected to behave in the ways prescribed by the whites. The whites considered themselves to be a civilizing influence, but they did not understand that when we are asked to give up our meaning structures and our world we are being asked to accept our annihilation as a person. Naturally the Indians resisted, so the whites determined to educate the Indian children and turn them into white children.

In 1885 the federal superintendent of Indian schools, referring to his task of making the Indian 'a member of the new social order', envisioned it thus: 'To do this we must recreate him, make him a new personality.' Therefore, remove the children from the demoralizing influence of their families to the boarding school, the more distant the better. They were taken from their grieving parents and kept for years, punished for speaking their own language, and brainwashed of all traces of Indianness. Many died (children died at home, too, this was different); a few entered 'the mainstream of American life'; most returned suspended in vacancy, separate from both cultures.[27]

It apparently did not occur to the whites that they were doing something which the uncivilized Indians had done, something which had aroused such hatred in the whites – kidnapping children.

In their raids on the settlements the Indians if sufficiently angered killed whole families, but in kindlier moods they adopted the children and reared them as their own. Frontier history is full of stories of captured children who were never found or who grew up as Indians changed past recovery. The mother of Quanah Parker, for example, was a child captive who became a Comanche in all but blood; and her subsequent recapture and the failure of her sorrowing white family to reclaim her spirit is an epic of the Southwest.[28]

If a child is taken into another culture early enough in the child's life and if the child is treated as a respected member of that culture then the child will create an identity based on that culture. But, no matter how early a child might be put in another culture, if that child is then not respected by the members of that culture the child is left in a limbo, belonging nowhere.

> In Australia today there may be one hundred thousand people of Aboriginal descent who do not know their families or communities. They are people, or the descendants of people, who were removed from their families by a variety of white people for a variety of reasons. They do not know where they come from; some do not even know that they are of Aboriginal descent.[29]

So begins the book *The Lost Children*, accounts by thirteen Australians of how they were taken from their families and how they had to struggle to find their natural parents.

The first British settlement in Australia was founded at Sydney Cove in 1788. The indigenous people readily showed that they were not inclined to become obedient servants of the crown, and so within a few years institutions run by Anglican missionaries were set up where Aboriginal children were to be taught the virtues of obedience, punctuality, thrift and hard work. The families of these children were allowed to live nearby, but their contact with their children was irregular and sometimes non-existent. 'The missionaries maintained that black children could be brought to the level of white labourers and maids if they were trained properly, and the doubters maintained that it was best to let the Aboriginal population die out of its own accord.'[30]

However, the Aboriginal people failed to die out; in fact their numbers increased after 1850 as the settlers spread into the Outback. Few of these white men who came as settlers brought white women as wives with them. One poem which all Australian schoolchildren learn, *The Women of the West*, contains the line: 'The nearest woman's face may be a hundred miles away.'[31] The white women settlers might not have noticed the faces of the black women, who could be no more than a hundred yards away, but the white men certainly did. So the Aboriginal population grew. Some of these children were born to couples where the white man treated the Aboriginal woman with affection and gave her long-term support, but many were the result of rape or casual usage by white men.

Whatever their background, the children were known as 'half castes', 'quarter castes' and other pejorative terms.

George Orwell once commented on the propensity of governments to set up organizations with names which indicated the opposite of what the organizations actually did. Thus in his novel *Nineteen Eighty-Four* the British government had four main ministries: the Ministry of Peace was concerned with war, the Ministry of Truth was concerned with government control of news, education and the arts, the Ministry of Love, a most fearsome place, dealt with law and order, and the Ministry of Plenty ran an economy where the people lived in poverty. In a similar manner in 1886 the government of Western Australia set up the Aborigines Protection Board. The policy of the Protection Board was made clear in their report of 1909:

> The Board recognise that the only chance these children have is to be taken away from their present environment and properly trained by earnest workers before being apprenticed out, and after having once left the aborigines' reserves they should never be allowed to return to them permanently.[32]

An amendment to the Aborigines Protection Act in 1916 gave the board the right to remove Aboriginal children from their families under any pretext. By 1934 some 1,500 children had been taken from their families, never to return. The children were put in institutions and educated as labourers and servants.

By the 1950s the studies of children separated from their mothers in the Second World War, which showed that this had very deleterious effects on the children, were having some influence on the Australian government's policy on adoption. The Adoption Act determined that Aboriginal babies should be adopted, but only by white parents. Some of these adoptive parents were very loving, but no amount of love could protect the children from the cruel, racist attitudes of most white Australians at that time. However,

> whatever their attitudes, substitute parents had to accept the prevailing view that Aboriginal children were to remain away from their community and culture for as long as possible, preferable forever. Adopting parents were told to destroy any information they may

have learned about their child's origins, so that they might never find out who they really were.[33]

The Adoption Act was framed by people who had decided that when the original identity ceased to exist legally it ceased to exist in actuality. They apparently failed to recognize that what matters most to us is the sense of who we truly are.

Jeannette Sinclair was one of the children taken from their family and adopted by a white family. There is a photograph of her, a pretty eight-year-old, visiting Santa Claus with her brother and sister from the adoptive family. It is the kind of photograph which comfortably-off white parents had taken every Christmas as a means of assuring themselves that childhood is the happiest time of our lives. But Jeannette was not happy. Even though at school she was accepted as a sun-tanned child like the other children, she spent much of her time with the white grandmother, who referred to her as 'that black slut'.

As she got older Jeannette tried to find out about her real family but her adoptive family refused to impart any information, so it was not until she was twenty-seven that she found her mother and discovered that she had brothers and sisters. Later, she said that now,

'I had somewhere where I belonged. That was really great and it was like that hole you walked round with had been totally filled. The first time I went back [to Western Australia to meet my family], that's what it was like although I realize now it can never be really filled in. Ninety per cent of the hole can be filled in but I think you are always missing the ten per cent. That's just my personal opinion. You can never get that ten per cent back because you missed out on the bonding, the fondling and the cuddling. Also you've missed out on building relationships over a period of time: you can't create a relationship out of thin air. And all the trust and everything when it comes to dealing with family, like cousins, takes time.'[34]

But for most of the people who lose their place there is never enough time.

You Can't Go Home Again

The starting point of our life story – the story we construct about ourselves, our past and our future – is the place where we belong. This story, whatever the content, is usually about going away and coming back again. Even when the princess is taken by the prince to his castle to live happily ever after she knows that she always has a home in the hearts of those who supported her through her tribulations. When the poor, weak, scorned boy leaves home to find his fortune it is not enough for him to make his fortune. He has to return home to shame and amaze those who scorned him. Coming home, in one form or another, becomes the end of our story.

Our fictional story, that is. Real life is another matter.

For those who choose to leave their home and go far away, coming back rich and famous can be a dangerous business. Many of those who stayed at home will be envious of you, and those who welcome and praise you may be motivated by greed. Coming back to shame those who once shamed and denigrated you can end in failure because those you wish to shame – like the headmaster who told you you were not capable even of pushing a wheelbarrow – are no longer there. Returning like the prodigal son, a failure, is no better. If you receive help from your family people may think you are getting more than you deserve, and everybody, one way or another, is likely to remind you of your failure.

Being forced to leave where you belong cuts, like death, across your life story. There is first a sense of unreality. This disaster could not possibly have happened. Then there is the mourning for the life you led and story you created which have been lost. Some refugees remain in mourning. They will not look to the future. They will not learn the language and customs of their new home. It is hard to construct a new story when you cannot find an answer to the question, 'Why has this happened to me?' Others say to themselves, 'Life must go on,' and they construct a new story in a new land.

When we leave the place where we belong we remember it as it was when we were there. Our memories are soon out of date. Life in that place moves on, and soon the place where we belong is no longer there. The people there have changed, and we have changed. We can't go home again.

'Everything is sad in exile. Even happiness is sad in exile.' This was an Iraqi refugee trying to explain to television viewers in the UK what it means to be a refugee.[35] No matter how pleasant a new home might be and no matter what opportunities are on offer, what always remains is a longing for the place where you belong. A Bhutanese woman in a refugee camp in Nepal, home to some 90,000 Bhutanese people, told members of the Refugee Council, 'I was tortured by the Bhutanese police when I refused to go and work for them. Then they threw me out of the country. I still take medicine for the torture they inflicted on me. Despite everything, I want to go home. At least let me die in my own house.'[36]

Home is the place where you do not always have to be on your best behaviour. You can put your feet up and expect the people there to do things for you. As a refugee you cannot do that. Refugee children soon learn to be well behaved. Fay Weldon spoke of how, as a refugee child, you learn 'not to rock the boat'. Her mother, so she told me, used to comment on how good Fay was.

My garden in London had on one side a block of council flats and on the other a large hostel for refugee families. The children who lived in the council flats were quite well behaved and well mannered, but whenever they kicked their football into my garden they would call over and ask me to throw it back, and acknowledge my doing so with no more than a cheery wave. If I was not around they would ignore the rule that they should not climb what was a rather dangerous high wall and retrieve their ball. As they saw it, my garden was part of their country and they had a right to go there. The refugee children, when their ball came into the garden, would peer over the wall and, if I was in the garden, say, 'Please, madam, would you give us our ball? Thank you, madam, thank you, madam.' If I was not in the garden they would retire disconsolately and find another game to play. Occasionally one of them would have the courage to come into my garden and retrieve the ball. The wall itself was not a danger, but for them entering another person's territory was. Sometimes through a window I would see them, a little group huddled anxiously beside the wall while one boy, having climbed the wall, ran as fast as he could to pick up the ball and return to the safety of the territory where they were permitted to be. It did not matter that I was kind to them. They knew that kindness can vanish in a world where anything can happen.

Those who choose to leave where they belong for reasons of ambition, work or economic necessity do not have to ask themselves, 'Why in the whole scheme of things has this happened?' But those who are forced to leave by war and terrorism can be haunted for the rest of their lives by the question 'Why?'

There are only three possible answers to this question:

1. It was someone else's fault;
2. It was my fault;
3. It happened by chance.

Marinella chose chance as the reason for her expulsion from her home.

Marinella was born on her Italian parents' farm in Angola. She told me, 'I am an Angolan.' When she married she moved to another farm, where she was still close to her beloved bush. Angola was given independence from Portugal in 1975 but the following year a civil war broke out between the three main political parties: the MPLA, supported by the USSR, UNITA, supported by the USA, and INLA. Marinella said, 'In January 1975 I left my husband and had to fend for myself and my two small children. I tried to cope with the civil war and keep my children safe. Eventually I got a job and settled in Huambo in April 1975. By the end of May we got caught in a major battle in Huambo between the three parties which lasted a week. This put us in great danger. My elder son Marco was lost as the school teachers scattered and left the children behind. A kind parent dropped him off at my hotel and I eventually found him. That event made me decide that I could not expose my children to further trauma and I planned my escape to South Africa, where I had friends. I thought I would return when peace returned, allowing us to continue living in our beloved country.'

After much danger Marinella and her children managed to escape. She drove 800 kilometres through a bush beset by warring troops and reached her parents' farm. Even so, she had not fully realized that it was no longer safe for her and her family in their own country. The Angolan government, to prevent people leaving, forbade emigration. People could leave with only a two-week visa, taking with them Angolan escudos worth no more than 130 rand. Finally Marinella decided that they must go. She planned to drive to Windhoek in Namibia, but the gearbox of her car needed repairing. This proved to be her salvation for, as the rule of law disappeared in Angola, the soldiers on the border were stealing from, raping and killing the refugees. Rather than crossing the border by car, Marinella and her children flew to Windhoek and went on to arrive, penniless, in South Africa.

A friend from Angola met her at the airport and took her to the home of his brother and sister-in-law, who had offered her shelter. Marinella told me, 'For two days I could not speak. For so long I had been busy, working, planning, doing things to make us safe. Now we were safe. There was nothing more I could do. I felt empty. I had nothing to say.' She had sustained so many losses – her marriage, her home, her family farm, her family and her country. For two years she could contact neither her brother, who as a young doctor worked in the hospital at Luanda, nor her parents on the family farm. Her parents and her brother finally escaped from Angola and settled in Portugal.

Marinella had also lost her sense of security. A truth once discovered can never be forgotten. We can never return to our first innocence. Marinella now knew that in life anything can happen. She said, 'Nothing is secure. Everything that you have can be taken away from you.'

Discovering that in life anything can happen for no particular reason, including the loss of that which sustains you economically and as a person, can be very frightening. Life then becomes full of uncertainty. Some people deal with this uncertainty very constructively. They see that, if life is a matter of chance, they can then hope that chance will bring them benefits and that life will get better and not worse. Marinella certainly found this, though her life in South Africa proved to be different from what she had expected when she was a young woman. Many people see in chance disasters the opportunity to learn something that will stand them in good stead in the future, and so they remove from their contemplation of the disaster that sense of waste of time, effort and value which can be so disheartening.

However, many people find that they cannot tolerate the uncertainty involved in answering 'Why' with 'It was chance.' They prefer the Just World answers of 'It was my fault' or 'It was someone else's fault.' Blaming other people for the disasters that befall them – that is, blaming the victim – can save us from the pain of pity, but what do we do when disaster befalls us? Do we blame others and become angry and vengeful, or do we blame ourselves and feel guilty, even depressed? It seems that our physiology prefers the answer, 'It happened by chance.'

Dieter Frey, a Munich psychologist, interviewed accident victims at the University Clinic in Kiel, then followed up their treatment and recovery:

> His 300 subjects were injured at work, driving or playing sports, and suffered everything from broken bones to concussion. Two days after they were admitted, Frey asked them whose fault the accident had been, whether it could have been avoided, and whether the patients believed they could influence their recoveries. Patients who said they had learned something useful from their accidents, but that they could not have avoided them, were out of hospital in just 20 days. They suffered fewer blood clots and heart problems during their stays.
>
> But those who thought they could have prevented the accident, or asked questions such as 'Why me?' remained an average of 40 days. Those who thought they could do nothing to help their recoveries also stayed longer, and stayed off work for an extra two months compared with those who thought that getting well was up to them.[37]

In relatively small disasters where the line of responsibility is clear the answer 'It was my fault' can be dealt with by apology and recompense, and the answer 'It was someone else's fault' allows resort to the law, but in major disasters, where chance, stupidity, incompetence and downright wickedness have combined, laying blame can be so complex as to be, at best, futile and, at worst, destructive. A Yugoslav refugee, now resident in Iceland, said on Radio Four, 'This unfairness is eating me from the inside.'[38]

Even when it is clear that the disaster was someone else's fault or that its effects could have been mitigated by someone who failed to act, what can you do when the people who have harmed or failed you are very powerful?

Diyana told me about what had happened to her in the siege of

Sarajevo. 'I remember – a really painful memory – one morning, early, at the beginning of the siege. A few days before, during the whole week, we had terrible grenades and shellings and lots of people died. We lost electricity as well, so after three days all the things from the fridge and freezer had to be thrown away, so it was the beginning of hunger. I felt the beginnings of hunger, although I had never experienced it before. I was brought up in a happy, wealthy country. Anyway, it was a terrible period for us and nobody could help us. Sarajevo was besieged. Nobody could get in or out. That morning I saw the lights of the cars, the United Nations vehicles – white with a red cross. And I was so happy. It was such a relief. Now they are going to help us, protect us. Now everything is finished and we can get on with our lives. It was a great disappointment after that. At first I was so very happy to see the white vehicles, and after a few months I couldn't look at them without being angry because of course they didn't help us.'

Actually the United Nations could have helped the people of Sarajevo, but Diyana could not let herself go on and on being angry because that anger did nothing but show her how weak and helpless she was. Even if she had gone on to the chamber of the Security Council in New York and told the men there how they had betrayed her and her family she would have achieved nothing. The members and staff of the Security Council would have regarded her as a mad woman. They would have turned away from her and busied themselves with the important business that men always have at hand. Had this happened, it would have been the third time the United Nations had betrayed her.

The second time was when Diyana and her baby Sarah were on a bus with other women and children on a hazardous journey away from Sarajevo and out of Bosnia. They came to a checkpoint manned by the Serbian paramilitaries. Diyana said, 'The soldiers wanted to show off. They wanted to make us afraid – and it was easy, of course, to make women with children – who are already half mad – to make them completely crazy and completely mad – so they were telling us they would throw grenades and kill everybody. There were Serb, Croat and Muslim women with their children, so the soldiers were calling out our names. The Muslim mothers and children, they left them on the bus. The Croat and Serbian women had to get out of the bus. Some of the soldiers were telling us they would kill the Serbs who had betrayed the Great Serbian Cause. There was great confusion – a few drunk soldiers and a few decent soldiers who wanted to check our documents and let us pass, but they had a great problem with the drunk soldiers. I noticed a few very, very young boys and I was afraid of the younger boys because they didn't have any experience and they wanted to show off. They would find it very easy to pull the trigger. And I was very afraid when one of them took my child and I had to go with the soldiers to answer some questions. I was terribly afraid.'

It was at this point that two United Nations armoured cars went by. They did not stop.

'For years,' said Diyana, 'I was always asking myself, "Why did it happen to me?" Because when you've lost what you had back home, you feel as if you've been betrayed, that you've been punished for something you haven't done. So I am asking myself constantly, "Why? Why did it happen to me and what had I done to deserve this?" I had a nice life and that's why I regret it and why I can't make myself at home here. I miss friends, I miss family, I miss the street, I miss the language, I miss the mentality. I miss festivals and songs – everything. It's like a feeling of shame, like some skin disease – everybody can see that you're a refugee. I can't get rid of that – the feeling that everybody can recognize that I am here because I'm forced to be here, I came here because I had to come, and I think everybody can see that I don't belong, that it's not my place, the place I belong to. Like a skin disease, you can't cover that, you can't hide that.'

I said, 'If there hadn't been a war and you came here as a tourist, you wouldn't feel ashamed?'

Diyana replied, 'It is a question of choice. If you have choice you have dignity as well, and you can decide whether to live here or somewhere else. I feel I lost more with that choice than just material things or money. It would be a totally different story if I came to London as a tourist and decided to stay here, to live, to struggle, to survive, but in that case I would have *decided* to do it. And always – I mustn't forget this – I would have had a place to go back to. It wouldn't have to be home but it would have to be somewhere to go back to. Whether it's family or friends, you can go back. But I don't have anywhere to go back to. I don't think about these things because it always makes me feel sad. Not that I feel sorry for myself

– because a lot of people are in the same situation, or a much worse situation. It's just sad when you don't have the possibility to go back, and you have to go on. You're helpless, you can't change things. The only thing I learned when I came here is that there's a lot of tragedy around the world. Maybe I was too ignorant and I didn't think about it the way I think now – about other people, about their suffering. It's something I learnt here.'

'It's certainly sad,' I said, 'but why shame? What are you ashamed of?'

'I can't explain it but that's my feeling. And it is a lack of confidence, of course. When I crossed borders and came to this country I lost all my confidence. I'm struggling to get it back now. The first victory will be to get back my confidence. The other very powerful feeling is the shame – sometimes I feel useless to this country, to these people. And then I get angry, angry with others who made me a refugee, and that's the part I don't want – to poison myself with anger, with hatred. I don't want that. That's why I stop, somewhere around the shame. Of course it's not really a shameful situation, to be a refugee, but when you have to explain your situation to somebody, the first thing it means is that you don't have a home. At the beginning you don't have a job, which is another shame. And you're struggling to get used to a society which is not your society, and maybe society doesn't want you. It's always a question, "Do these people really want me and my family? Do they really feel they should help me? Why should they help me when my people didn't help me?" And there's shame because of that. It's five years now. I think if I want to go on with life and make some improvements and progress, I have to get rid of this feeling. It's the same thing with my husband, but he covers it. He pretends that he's full of self-confidence, pretends we are at home here. But when he and his friends have a cup of coffee, or their first drink, they always speak about back home, about families, about what happened. And always that kind of speaking, and a desperate trying to transport ourselves back home. It's impossible, but at least in stories we try.'

Diyana was trying to make a new life for herself and her family. She was a pharmacist and was studying for her UK qualifications. She said, 'If you want to meet people, to make conversation with them, you have to talk and you have to tell something about yourself. You can't keep saying, "I'm a refugee, I don't have anything."'

Nobody wants to hear that any more. The first time it's all right. Everybody feels sorry for you, feels they understand you, but after that it gets boring for them, and it gets boring for me as well. I'm not just bored but ashamed I haven't changed my situation. And sometimes I feel ashamed because I haven't changed that situation – at least got a good job, so that at the next meeting I can talk about my job and not mention I'm a refugee. I would like to talk about something else but I'm not good at anything else. I can talk about war and about being foreigners, not about much else. I feel sometimes that we from Europe are ignorant, we thought nothing could happen to us after the Second World War. And then it happened in Sarajevo in a terrible way. Now I can better understand other tragedies, but before I was so ignorant about everything. And sometimes I feel I deserve all that's happened to me. I didn't appreciate what I had.'

When we blame ourselves for the disasters that have befallen us we turn against ourselves and can come to hate ourselves. When this happens we immediately feel frightened of other people because if they see how bad we are they will reject and hurt us. So we cut ourselves off from other people by cutting that sense of connection we have with the people we see as friends. We cut ourselves off from our past because all we can see there is evidence of our past wickedness. We cut ourselves off from our future because we believe that all that lies ahead is punishment for our wickedness. We cut ourselves off from the natural world and from society because we consider ourselves too wicked to be part of that. Thus we create the terrible isolation which is the essence of being depressed.[39]

Depression is not just a problem peculiar to refugees. It is a worldwide problem. The 1999 annual report of the World Health Organization showed that depression is the second greatest cause of death in Europe and America after heart disease, and that it is on the rise throughout the world. Depression was clearly linked to radical changes for the worse in people's lives and expectations.[40]

The meanings and their underlying neurological connections which have to do with trying to be good, reward, punishment, shame, guilt and belief in the Just World get laid down so early in a person's life that they can take on the quality of being a fact of life, equivalent to the inevitable passing of time. It is to these early meanings that primitive pride has direct and instantaneous access.

The majority of people have no understanding of how they are their own meaning structure, and how disconcerting, even terrifying, the disconfirmation of parts of the meaning structure can be. Hence within seconds primitive pride can resort to the explanation: 'It was my fault this disaster happened" and thus restore some integrity to the meaning structure. Unfortunately the price of this is depression.

In the face of what has been described as a worldwide epidemic of depressive illness psychiatrists and the pharmaceutical drug industry have responded with, 'Give them more drugs.' Yet, if antibiotic drugs had had the same cure rates as antidepressant drugs they would have been rejected as ineffective within ten years of their discovery.

David J. Nutt, professor of psychopharmacology and head of the Department of Clinical Medicine at Bristol University, and his senior registrar Sam Forshall reported in the *Psychiatric Bulletin* in 1999 that

> Formerly, major depression was regarded as having a relatively good prognosis; however, long-term naturalistic community surveys have indicated that this is not the case as there is a high risk of recurrence and chronicity. Of those who suffered one episode of depression 50–85% will have a second episode, while those who have had two episodes 80–90% will develop a third. With each recurrence a further recurrence becomes more likely and the period in remission tends to become shorter. Recurrent depression is costly, with each episode incurring not only the expense of treatment, but also the loss of productivity and disruption to social relationships, to say nothing of the distress to the sufferer. In addition, surveys consistently indicate that 15% of sufferers of depression go on to commit suicide. With each episode there is a considerable risk of long-term social impairment and chronicity, with estimates varying between 15–30%.

They concluded that 'It becomes very important to develop strategies for the long-term management of depression.'[41] The strategy was to keep the patient taking the drugs. Nutt and Forshall argued that

> The purpose of continuation treatment is to prevent a relapse. It is thought that antidepressant drugs can suppress the symptoms of the

illness without correcting the underlying psychopathological process which continues its natural course. Withdrawal of medication during this time frequently results in the re-emergence of symptoms and relapse . . . It must be remembered that an antidepressant that was ineffective in treating the acute phase is likely to be equally ineffective in the continuation phase. Where no antidepressant can be found, continuation ECT [electroconvulsive therapy, the passing of 100–150 volts through the brain] should be considered.[42]

In the final paragraph of their advice to psychiatrists Nutt and Forshall wrote: 'In trials 20–70% of patients have a recurrence despite prophylactic treatment.'[43]

What the research shows is that the majority of depressed people who are treated in the traditional way with drugs and ECT go on being depressed. In contrast, there is ample research which shows that the talking therapies are effective in helping depressed people. This kind of evidence has been available to psychiatrists for many years, yet most psychiatrists and many general practitioners continue to prescribe drugs to their depressed patients and make no attempt to provide access to counselling or psychotherapy which would allow the patient to explore and perhaps choose to change those meanings which, when disaster struck, led to depression. There are both economic and personal reasons why doctors persist in this error, which has had such devastating effects on many people's lives.

Vast amounts of money are involved. The pharmaceutical drugs industry is second only to the armaments industry in terms of the size of the industrial and marketing undertakings. The pharmaceutical industry is closely linked to the psychiatric profession. Indeed, when the psychiatrist Loren Mosher sent his resignation letter to the American Psychiatric Association after thirty years' membership he wrote, 'The major reason for this action is my belief that I am actually resigning from the American Psychopharmacological Association.'[44]

The psychiatric profession is based on the idea that there are mental illnesses which are the equivalent of physical illnesses with a biochemical and genetic cause. Take that idea away and the whole *raison d'être* for the existence of psychiatry vanishes.

The personal reason for the persistence of the psychiatrists' error lies in the need to maintain the integrity of the meaning structure.

If you have spent your teenage years working hard to get the qualifications to go to medical school; if you then suffer the burdens and humiliations of being a medical student and then a junior doctor; if, in the course of this, you discover that you are never going to be a world-famous brain surgeon and that you do not enjoy the messiness of the various medical specialities; and if you then opt for the orderliness and delicious power over people that psychiatrists enjoy, you do not want to discover that your profession has as much relevance to people's lives as alchemy has to science. Most psychiatrists would no more give up the ideas of mental illnesses and treatment by drugs than Dusan would pack his bags and leave Belgrade.

There are no drugs, legal or illegal, that can solve the problems we have in living our lives and getting along with other people. Our world of interpretations interpreting interpretations is like a world of mirrors with infinite reflections, and no changes in brain chemistry are going to simplify that. Whatever we do is a result of the meanings which we have created, and no meaning, however straightforward it might appear to be, is discrete, a thing in itself. Every meaning comes with many connotations, many reflections.

Take, for instance, the word 'pity'. When I was a little girl my grandmother taught me to say the prayer 'Gentle Jesus', which contains the line 'Pity my simplicity'. I did not know what my simplicity was, but I thought that Jesus pitying it must be a good thing. Now I would argue that our capacity to pity one another is one of the processes that brings us close together. Those of us who grew up in homes untouched by war and civil unrest can only guess at what it must be like to be a refugee, but our capacity for pity enables us to feel benignly about refugees and to offer them help and comfort. However, being pitied can be something a person does not want. Diyana said, 'I don't like pity. It's a kind of humiliation. I don't think people do it deliberately, but it is a humiliation for me when I realize they are sorry for me.'

Alas, what many people feel about refugees, the strangers in their midst, is not pity but hatred. Most people can cope with one or two refugees. They can feel good about themselves because they feel pity. They can feel intrigued by the stranger, whom they see as exotic. But when the number of strangers grows adult pity easily gives way to childhood prejudice.

Australians born before the Second World War were children in a country where a stranger was someone from the city or another Australian state, not someone from a land across the sea. When, after the USA's defeat at Pearl Harbor, American troops arrived in Australia on their way to fight the Japanese, we looked with amazement at them. They spoke just like the actors in the films we watched! We knew that we were part of the great British Empire where the noble white people had shouldered the burden of looking after the incompetent, childlike, devious, untrustworthy people whose skin was a different colour from ours. We acquired uncritically the attitudes of our elders – attitudes which today would be considered very racist. Fifty years on, whenever I returned to Australia I would hear many of my contemporaries, usually in the privacy of their own homes, expressing the racist attitudes of their childhood. They were applying these attitudes to the large number of people from almost every country in the world who were by then Australian citizens. What seemed to disturb my contemporaries in Australia most was seeing these exceedingly foreign strangers occupying those places where the Australians had spent their childhood. When they saw the milk bar that sold the best milk shakes in the world become Patel's twenty-four-hour food store, or the drapery shop that sold them their Sunday best become the Huong video shop, or the cinema that brought magic into their dull lives become a mosque they felt that a vital part of their life story had been stolen and destroyed. They did not understand that these exceedingly foreign strangers had also lost the places of their childhood.

Prejudices linger in the meaning structure of many people even when the historical and economic circumstances which gave rise to them no longer exist. In the nineteenth century many migrants came to England from Ireland. Most were penniless, many starving, and all forced to accept the most menial and poorly paid work. They built the roads and railways which added immensely to England's wealth. The Irish immigrants did not share in this wealth, and neither did the English poor, but, rather than join in common cause with the Irish, the poor of England were pleased to have a group of strangers on whom they could look down. At the same time the rich and powerful in England could feel that the British government's harsh policies against Ireland were justified. The Irish deserved what they got.

A hundred years on, Ireland was a wealthy country and its emi-
grants educated people choosing to work abroad. Yet in the UK
they still suffered from the prejudices of the British. A survey of
Irish members of the public by the Campaign for Racial Equality
in 1997 found that

> although only 20% specifically reported a 'bad atmosphere' at work,
> 79% had been subjected to anti-Irish 'jokes' and remarks. Seventy
> per cent of those surveyed said that they found anti-Irish jokes
> offensive, but only 30% felt able to reject them outright. None of
> the sample had considered taking legal action over any of the abuse
> they had been subjected to. Anti-Irish attitudes were seen to be
> widespread, and the majority of those surveyed could immediately
> identify instances of behaviour which they found insulting, hurtful
> or intimidating.[45]

These anti-Irish attitudes of the British played a significant part
in the division between Protestants and Catholics in Northern Ireland, and the subsequent failure to resolve them. British governments, one after the other, failed to take the problem seriously, and
few British politicians bestirred themselves sufficiently to discover
the differing attitudes of the people in Northern Ireland and to try to
understand the reasons why. Only the news of atrocities in Northern
Ireland and the occasional bomb in England captured the attention
of the British, and then the opinion expressed by many of the British
was, 'We should pull out and let the two sides sort it out among
themselves.' If both sides fought each other to mutual annihilation
the Irish problem would be solved.

The fact that Northern Ireland is just across the Irish Sea, in sight
of western Scotland and an hour's flight from Heathrow failed to
awake many of the British to the realization that they were not
separate from Northern Ireland. A fact is never allowed to get in
the way of a strong prejudice, especially when that prejudice, a
manifestation of primitive pride at work, is concerned with dealing
with the discomfort raised by the failure of the Just World to operate
as it should.

Not everyone who believes in the Just World gets depressed when
they suffer a disaster – only those who choose the 'It was my fault'
interpretation. Many people prefer 'It was someone else's fault.' This

'someone else' can be a large power with what appear to be long tentacles reaching into all likely and unlikely places. In the days of the Cold War Americans were encouraged by their leaders to see the hand of power-hungry Communists everywhere. With the fall of Communism a large part of the human race came to see the imperial power of the USA as a universal threat. The myth of the Protocols of Zion was still flourishing, given new life on the Internet, and so the hand of international Jewry was still being seen as manipulating world events. Meanwhile, in Northern Ireland Ian Paisley knew beyond the shadow of a doubt that the Pope was to blame.

However, an appreciation of a world conspiracy of whatever kind requires some knowledge of geography and history, and can be quite taxing for the brain. Many people prefer something simple and close to hand. What better than 'the council'?

'I've worked hard all my life and I've paid my taxes but what's the council ever done for me? Nothing. But the refugees, they no sooner arrive here than the council gives them a flat and decorates it. Can't do enough for them and nothing for me.'

Thus speaks the voice of racism saying, 'I've been good and I've never got my reward.'

Even though they might publicly deplore racism, when unemployment is a threat to their power governments generally exploit such racist attitudes in order to restrict the number of migrants. All a government minister has to do is murmur the phrase, 'Need to protect jobs.' Newspapers exploit such racist attitudes in order to increase their sales. The *Daily Mail*, under a front-page headline 'brutal crimes of the asylum seekers' reported:

The devastating impact of serious crime by asylum seekers has been uncovered in a *Daily Mail* enquiry. At least 44 major trials in London alone have this year ended in the conviction of asylum seekers and illegal immigrants. Of those cases, 17 were of rape, attempted rape or serious sexual assault, and five were murder or attempted murder. The investigation into this previously unexamined area of the asylum debate comes as Britain faces a crisis with a record 44,000-plus asylum seekers expected this year. It focuses only on the capital's courts and represents a small proportion of such crimes. Literally hundreds of other cases involving asylum seekers and illegal immigrants accused of 'petty' offences such as shoplifting, pickpocketing and mugging have been dealt with by magistrates this year.[46]

In response Duncan Campbell in the *Guardian* took his readers on a short tour of the objects of British racism in the twentieth century. At the turn of the century it was the Russian immigrants who were the threat; by the end of the First World War it was the Chinese opium seller; by 1929 it was the Jews. In 1957 *The Times* was warning white girls about West Indians, and, with the growth of the drug trade, the Columbians and the Nigerians came in for special mention. Duncan Campbell noted that, while some migrants were involved in horrible crimes, 'the vast majority of the immigrants quietly got on with life as waiters, cleaners, nurses, bus drivers and, now, minicab drivers.' He concluded that 'Much has changed, but some things have remained fairly constant. Our murderers and rapists, our paedophiles and fraudsters, our wife-beaters and road-ragers remain, almost universally, of good, solid Anglo-Saxon stock.'[47]

Racist attitudes demonstrate how primitive pride is not concerned with what is actually going on. No account is taken of the benefits brought to a community by an influx of new people. Most immigrants work hard to create a stable life, and thus benefit the economy and the stability of the community. The immigrants bring ideas and customs which add variety to the life of the community. Australians born after the Second World War might have little idea how dull and stodgy Australian cooking was before the New Australians, as they were called, started arriving. The only meals on offer were fish and chips or a plate of meat from a choice of beef, lamb and mutton, grilled, roasted or stewed, and chicken on special occasions, with three overcooked vegetables from a choice of peas, runner beans or chokos, potatoes, baked or mashed, and pumpkin. The only take-aways were fish and chips or a meat pie. I was introduced to sophisticated continental food when I went to Sydney in 1948. Friday night at Florentino's was so exciting. We had spaghetti bolognese, a bottle of Chianti and a cappuccino! It was, however, the start of a revolution. Now the world's cuisine is on offer, not just in thousands of restaurants but in every home, even the homes of those who denigrate all those foreigners who call themselves Australian.

There is another benefit which immigrants bring to a community

– one which challenges those people who hold the erroneous notion that a nation's strength lies in 'the purity of the blood', where only those who share a genetic make-up are allowed to marry one another. 'Pure blood' readily becomes host to those diseases and disabilities which can be inherited by the offspring of such unions. The genetic pool of every community needs to be diverse, and it is immigrants who provide that diversity. Steve Jones, professor of genetics at University College, London, remarked, 'The most important events in the human genetic future have been the invention of the bicycle and the 747.'[48]

The gifts which they have to offer mean very little to the refugees as they struggle to make sense of what has happened to them. Having been driven from their home and arriving in a country where the inhabitants do not want them, refugees experience the fear and helplessness that comes with being prey. The degree to which a refugee experiences anxiety and depression seems to be related not so much to the degree of trauma that person has suffered as to the amount of social support he or she has. Being a refugee along with your family is better than being alone.[49] Left utterly on our own we ask ourselves that most terrible question, 'What will become of me?' and the only answer is the frightened beating of our heart.

Becoming a refugee may mean not just the loss of family but the destruction of the community's family structure. Mudrooroo described how Aboriginal people had

> a network of kinship which was inscribed on the land, on the environment, on the skies. Nowhere was there a singular All-Father; for we had many fathers and mothers and many relations. We were never that solitary figure which was only pictured and made by the master in his image.[50]

Yet this was the structure that Governor Phillip, in founding the British colony, imposed on the native people. Mudrooroo wrote,

> They were ordered by a king, by a governor, by Masters in a pyramid based on class, on the governor, on the free settler, on the soldier and the convict, an ordering quite unlike our own. Against this pyramid we had a tree structure which they did not understand, and so against our families and kinship structures they ordained

what we might call the anti-family, in which everyone was ordered
to do things without any discernible tradition.[51]

The British were anti-family to the Aboriginal people, but they
were also anti-family in what they did to the families of the convicts.
When convict ships left the port of London or Cork the families of
the convicts knew that they were unlikely to see their loved one
again. Those convicts who had been transported for 'the term of
his natural life' might be given a 'ticket of leave', but this did not
allow them to return to Britain. Those who had shorter terms might
not have the money for the fare, and many had already lost touch
with their families back home. Letters took six months to travel
between Britain and Australia, and not all the ships bearing them
completed their voyage. Many of the would-be correspondents could
not read or write. Some wives did manage to join their husband in
the colony, but most convicts, like my great-grandfather James Freel,
had to do the best they could for themselves as a stranger in a
strange land.

My great-grandfather, from what little is known of him, seems
never to have settled down. He married the daughter of a convict,
fathered two daughters and a son, and went to the gold fields, never
to return. His wife, left penniless, gave her daughters away and went
as housekeeper to a man by whom she had another family. This
rejection and shame weighed heavily on her daughters, one of whom
was my grandmother. She married a Scot – my grandfather, who
once told me how, when he was seventeen, his father had ordered
him from his home. It was time for him to earn his own living. He
went, an economic migrant, to Queensland, where he cut sugar
cane, and then to the Hunter Valley, where he became a miner. His
only ties to Scotland were a Scottish brogue and a love of Robert
Burns.

These two rejected children had six children of their own. By
then the story of James Freel had become a family secret. My mother
never spoke of it, but she had accepted the burden of shame. She
became, in effect, a refugee child. She felt that she did not belong.
She never felt safe, except on her own territory, the house and
garden of her own home.

Families do not deal with a major trauma once and for all and
leave it behind them. The effects rumble on, generation after genera-

tion. Aaron Hass, himself a child of two Holocaust survivors, made a study of children like himself, now in their thirties. He wrote, 'The experience of being a child of a survivor is reflected by three words uttered by almost every such person with whom I came into contact: fear, mistrust, cynicism ... The world, for these children of survivors, is clearly a hostile protagonist.'[52]

One of the survivors Hass interviewed said, 'I've always had a need for security – both physical security (having locks and alarms on the doors) and financial security. My dad always said, "Get educated because that's one thing that can't be taken away from you."'[53] (My parents always said the same to me.)

Another interviewee said,

'I have a survivor's mentality. I'll come through situations no matter what. In my work I have to be tough. I am very resilient. I think I inherited a feeling of being a survivor from my parents. I am proud that they managed to live through it, and I'm doubly proud of all the times they used their intelligence or their spirit to save themselves from what looked like certain death. Many times in my life, I've come through a tough situation thinking, "I'm a survivor."'[54]

Suffering does not always make us kind and understanding. One interviewee said, '"For this I survived the Nazis? For this I survived the camps?" This was my parents' frequent anguished refrain – if I talked back to them or if I came home later than I said I would without telephoning to report my delay.'[55]

Martha, a thirty-five-year-old paediatrician said,

'My parents overreacted to everything. For example, if someone stole a five-cent candy from their store, they became totally paranoid and hysterical. Everything was life and death. They were always waiting for the worst to happen. I had no way of understanding that when bad things happened to me, I shouldn't take it personally. If someone was late for an appointment, it didn't occur to me that he could have had a flat tyre or some other good reason. I always felt, "Why is this happening to me?" – just like my parents did.'[56]

It seems that the legacy of the Holocaust did not end with the survivors' children. Some of the survivors' grandchildren are now coming to the attention of therapists. Peter Fonagy, Freud memorial professor of psychoanalysis at University College, London, reviewed some of the psychoanalytic literature on the effects of the Holocaust on the survivors and presented his own case study of one of three third-generation survivors of the Holocaust whom he had treated.

In his general discussion Fonagy spoke of how

> The Holocaust involved a society which appeared to be (and to remain) civilised, turning on a group within it and stripping them of all humanity, dignity and safety. People who could have been expected to treat their compatriots as fellow human beings with intentionality, suddenly began to treat the Jews with hatred and a systematic brutality previously unimaginable even between enemy peoples or between humans and animals. The same people continued to behave in a normal way in other relationships.[57]

'Intentionality' means creating meaning, having thoughts, feelings, desires, needs, acting as an agent. The Germans were treating the Jews not as people but as objects.

In the course of an ordinary upbringing children are occasionally treated as objects by their loving parents. Witness the busy mother in a supermarket car park packing her toddler into his car seat with the same brisk efficiency with which she packed her groceries into the boot of the car. Another time she might have stopped to talk to her child and take his complaints seriously, but now he was just another bundle to be transported safely. In an ordinary upbringing children can cope with occasionally being treated as an object. However, if the parent has herself been seen as an object and treated with hostility and brutality she is likely to have difficulty in treating any of her own children as people in their own right. Children need their parents to accept and mirror their sense of being a person and what that means to the child. This is an essential element in the attachment which links the child to the parent. Without this the parents cannot see and therefore cannot remedy the effects the parents' thoughts and feelings have upon the child. As a child of one such parent I can report that it is very strange and alienating to be aware, as a small child, of what your mother is thinking and feeling, and to know that she is unaware that her thoughts and feelings have any effect on you. To her you are without thoughts and feelings, an object that suddenly and mysteriously produces behaviour which to her is bad or odd.

Fonagy concluded,

Individuals with relatively minor disorganization within their attachment system we expect to withstand trauma more effectively, but it is unlikely that anyone is immune. Once opened, this gap takes perhaps many generations to heal, and through it pass images of horror, including confusions of identity between torturer and victim, guilt and shame, paranoia and helplessness.

Fonagy's client, a fifteen-year-old boy, was quite seriously disturbed. Most third-generation refugees whose families have settled in a new home lead ordinary lives, but certain attitudes which are a result of the refugee experience get handed down from one generation to the next.

When General Pinochet came to power in Chile in 1973 Myriam's husband was jailed and tortured, and her daughter, also Myriam, aged fifteen, was forced into hiding. Later the family managed to escape to England. Looking back at the age of sixty-three, Myriam said, 'Sometimes I feel I was too tough with the children, I didn't demonstrate enough love because the pressure to survive was so strong. I still feel guilty about that, and I know that Myriam repeated the same pattern.'

Her daughter agreed.

'I have had a good life here but for twenty-five years I have had to say to myself you must cope, you must cope, you must cope. I have neglected part of myself, I am emotionally repressed. The insecurity of exile has made me harder with my children. I have constantly been preparing them to be strong, I haven't had time to be affectionate with them. I'm always thinking "You never know what will happen, they must be ready, ready for that knock on the door." I've probably pushed them too hard.'

Myriam's son Sean, aged seventeen, born some eight years after his family was out of danger, said,

'What happened to my mum has become part of everything about me. Without her, I would probably be like the kids at my school; as it is, I feel very different. I haven't decided what I'd like to study after my A-levels but all the things I'm considering are connected with my mum's history: international law, or working in a human rights organization. My mum has always been very harsh with me about homework. She says you only get one shot at an education. I used to want her to leave me alone to watch TV like the other kids, but if we have an argument I'll be sympathetic to her point of view because I know she has experienced some of the most horrible things a human being can experience. From the age of eleven or twelve I felt she gave me too much responsibility. She told me things were up to me. I don't resent her harshness; I see it as part of her history.'

But is this the end of the story? Sean said, 'If I have children of my own I'll be harsh with them, too. That's the only way I know.'[58]

We can hope that Sean went on to encounter no more than the usual difficulties in passing examinations, getting the job he desired, and finding a true love. If so, by the time his children were born he might have been able to reconstrue his concept of 'harsh' and turn it into his way of inspiring in his children a sense of optimism and achievement while being able to demonstrate his love for them in abundance.

Sean, like all migrants, and the children of migrants, also had the task of finding some way of reconciling his tie to the country his family left and his tie to the country which was his home. Every country demands loyalty from its new citizens. When the Conservative politician Norman Tebbit demanded that the 'cricket test' be applied to those UK citizens of Indian or Pakistani descent – when the England cricket team played India or Pakistan, did they cheer the English team? – there was a tremendous row. Tebbit, being British through and through, did not understand that the one great advantage of having several national loyalties is that you can cheer for whoever wins.

What Tebbit was demanding was that all migrants to Britain should abandon their foreign ways and behave like the British. No doubt he was objecting to the way in which most migrants adopt the 'pick and mix' attitude in choosing which attributes to acquire and which to ignore. Some communities of migrants tried to maintain their customs and live in the way their relatives did back home, but even they found themselves choosing elements from the culture that surrounds them. Saris are beautiful and convenient garments, but they often need the addition of a British raincoat or woolly cardigan.

Loyalty, like love and forgiveness, is an emotion, a way of being which we cannot command into existence. What we feel is what we feel, and it is foolish to pretend any different. We can choose to behave in a loyal way, just as we can choose to behave in a loving or a forgiving way, but that sense of attachment, of which loyalty, love and forgiveness are part, grows slowly, often unnoticed.

Jean Said Makdisi called herself 'a wandering person'. She wrote,

When the war began I belonged everywhere and nowhere, one of a breed of human beings so common in modern times, who have moved from place to place, adjusting their papers with their peregrinations. My family came originally from Palestine, but I grew up in Egypt as an outsider. I was educated by Englishmen and Americans, absorbing their culture and values along with those handed down by my Arab ancestors. I was tossed about in the gales the two worlds blew at each other. I married a Lebanese firmly rooted in Arab culture. We lived in America for many years and then we went to Beirut. He was returning home, and I thought that in going with him I could attach myself to his firm roots. But the vine does not share the roots of the oak. It grows its own, and so I have now.

She explained that during the war in Lebanon

From the inside, I watched and recorded. I wrote to master that experience which was consuming me and the world in which I lived. I wrote as a witness to the common experiences of common people, feeling that in the trial of history there should be a record, a vindication of their pain . . . Sharing that pain and writing about it, I came to love the place. Writing about Beirut, I attached myself to it, and made it mine, and myself part of it. Now every inch of that shattered city is mine. I have earned my place in the world.[59]

Others left Lebanon, just as people leave every war-torn country and become wandering people – 'new internationalists', as Linda Grant called them, who buy a passport where they can and work in jobs where taxes are not paid. 'These new internationalists form their own country, an ungovernable one with its own culture, politics and habits of thought, which refuses to tie itself to the allegiances of any nation state, setting its own laws.'[60]

Nabil is one of these new internationalists.

He goes back to Lebanon every summer to see his family. The war is over. As the country cleans up, he could clean up economically if he returned permanently, but in his years abroad he has come to see his homeland through the eyes of the cosmopolitan wanderer: 'It's a beautiful country – sunshine, rivers, beaches. I admire the country. But I went to the south of France and saw exactly what I saw there, and better. Saw in Paris, saw in Spain, saw in England.'[61]

Across the world millions of refugees remained in limbo, in the camps, unable to return or to migrate. Some of these camps became, as the years went by and new generations were born, communities in themselves, where the inhabitants developed customs and loyalties as in any community. Most of these refugees were helpless, in the hands of warring factions and an ineffective United Nations. Some of these refugees could leave the camps, but to do so would mean giving up the grievance which brought them there. For many Palestinians living in the camps is a daily visible reminder to the Israelis and to the world that the Israelis stole their land. To move out of the camps, to settle in Lebanon or another country would mean accepting that their home had gone for ever. They could have thrown away their most treasured possession, the key to the front door of their house, which was in Israeli hands, but to do so, in the eyes of many Palestinians, was to be a traitor.

The idea of being a traitor is not confined to those whose homes have been stolen. For many of those who stayed at home those who leave and never return to stay are traitors.

The Vietnamese had a special name for those who fled the country at the end of the war and did not return – the Viet Kieu. The rest of the world knew them as 'the boat people'. Robert Templer wrote,

The journey they faced to reach countries of asylum were often harrowing. Women and young girls were taken from the boats and sexually abused for days on end by Thai pirates before being dumped alive into the sea; others were wrecked on the sandy atolls of the South China Sea, surviving on rainwater and by eating raw sea birds and fish. Those who reached countries like Malaysia faced hostile governments. In the chaos of escape families were divided and children and parents separated, often forever. Michael, an Australian Vietnamese, saw his young sister dragged off by pirates. She was never seen again.[62]

Despite what they had suffered and the presence of a Communist government in Vietnam, many of the 2 million Vietnamese living overseas wished to return, at least to visit and re-establish links. Once the government signalled that such visits would be allowed some 400,000 a year began to make the journey home.

But, said Robert Templer,

You can never really go home again. The Viet Kieu are a diverse group that defy any easy summation, but once they go back to Vietnam they find themselves compressed into a narrow range of stereotypes. For most Vietnamese, they are a confusing blend of familiar and foreign; on one hand they appear Vietnamese, on the other they are generally richer, better educated and more cosmopolitan. They are envied and scorned for their imagined wealth, held in respect and contempt for their sophistication and familiarity with the West and sometimes regarded as traitors for leaving.[63]

Living up to what relatives and friends in Vietnam expect is not easy.

The image in Vietnam is that all Viet Kieu are enormously successful and wealthy; when they return they are expected to come back laden with gifts, particularly designer clothes and the latest gadgets which cannot yet be found in Vietnam. Viet Kieu stoke these cargo cult images by sending back photographs of themselves with their trophies of success – trips to Disneyland, massive cars and sprawling suburban homes. To return without evidence of success can be a huge loss of face. Jimmy Nguyen, a jeweller in Seattle who spends several months a year in Ho Chi Minh City, rents returning families heavy gold and diamond jewellery. They leave their cars with him as collateral and return the jewellery and a rental fee when they return. 'When they go back to Vietnam they say they own a res- taurant but of course they just work in one; you can't go back and say you are just a waiter in a *pho* restaurant,' he said.[64]

Going home when home no longer feels like home is never easy. When I was in Belgrade in September 1998 Dusan took me to a party where our hostess was the professor of clinical psychology at Belgrade University, a woman in her sixties, very welcoming and effusive, very anxious that her guests should be well provided for. All the guests were psychologists and therapists. The guest of honour, Mirjana, was one of her ex-students, a middle-aged woman who lived in Australia and was visiting her home town of Belgrade.

The professor made a special welcoming speech which we all listened to and applauded. I could not understand her words, but their meaning seemed clear. 'How could you leave us, and, now you're here, how could you go away again?' Afterwards I said to Mirjana, 'Is she making you feel guilty?' Mirjana said, 'Yes, very.'

I was reminded of my recent phone call to my friend Nan in Sydney to tell her that my son was returning to Sydney to work and that he was very happy about this. Nan said, 'He belongs here. You do too. You both do.'

The people who stay do not always understand that those who have left build a life in another place. If you, as the person who has left, do not talk about your new life they never come to understand why you do not return. If you do talk about your new life, you can stir up unhappy emotions. Friends who have stayed may feel rejected when you talk about your new friends. If you have done better than those who have stayed you may create envy, while if you have not done so well your failure may be taken as proof that you should not have left in the first place. It is impossible to give a complete picture of your new home to friends who have never been there, or who have gone there only as tourists and seen it with outsiders' eyes, and so they cannot appreciate, say, how you balance the expense, the danger and the crowds of London or New York against the opportunities those places can give.

The more you put down roots in your new home, the more your

interest and involvement in your old home wanes. If you do not put down roots you feel a stranger in your new home and long for your old. If you do put down roots, when you visit your old home you feel an outsider and, as much as you enjoy your visit, you long to go home.

Thus many of us have become 'the clan of the dispossessed', as Marion Molteno called us in her novel *The Shield of Coolest Air*, 'a clan united by no single language or culture, people, who, having lost their real relatives, pick up new ones in the street.'[65]

'The clan of the dispossessed' is perhaps too sad in its connotations. Perhaps we should use the phrase only when we are feeling sorry for ourselves. When we are feeling confident, or want to make ourselves feel confident, we should use the term chosen by Immanuel Kant and taken up more recently by the modern historian Mary Kaldor and the writer Michael Ignatieff. This word is 'cosmopolitan'. Kant defined cosmopolitan as 'the matrix within which all the original capacities of the human race may develop'.[66] Michael, whose father was born in Russia, his mother in England, and who has worked in Canada, Britain and France, must, he said, have a claim to be a cosmopolitan. 'I wish I spoke more languages than I do, I wish I had lived in more nations than I have, and wish that more people understood that expatriation is not exile: it is merely the belonging of those who choose their home rather than inherit it.'[67]

However, he added a huge proviso.

What has happened in Bosnia must give pause to anyone who believes in the virtues of cosmopolitanism. It is only too apparent that cosmopolitanism is the privilege of those who can take the nation state for granted. Though we have passed into a post-imperial age, we are not in a post-nationalist age, and I cannot see how we will ever do so. The cosmopolitan order of the big cities – London, Los Angeles, New York, Paris – depends critically on the rule-enforcing capacities of the nation state. When order breaks down, as it did during the Los Angeles riots of 1992, it becomes apparent that civilized, cosmopolitan multiethnic cities have as great a propensity for ethnic warfare as any Eastern European country.[68]

This is where the danger lies. Everything is there for us to enjoy – the pleasures and opportunities of cosmopolitan life with the comfort and security of our group and our family – were we to choose to take it. But to do that we would have to solve our greatest problem, the problem of enemies.

6

Strangers and Enemies

On a lovely summer day in June 1999 Anthony and I drove from Omagh in Northern Ireland to Portadown by way of the church at Drumcree. The road, little more than a lane, wound through green fields and overgrown hedgerows. The summer flowers were in full blossom. About half a mile from the church the flags began, the Union Jack and the Orange Order flags, fluttering from every telegraph pole and tall post. In the distance we could see the church and graveyard surrounded by a stone wall on which three men were sitting.

Just before we reached them Anthony parked the car, hid his copy of the *Irish News* and walked a little ahead of me to where the men were sitting. He greeted them in his usual friendly way and explained that I was from Australia and wanted to find out about what was happening at Drumcree.

Two of the men were elderly with weather-beaten faces and toil-hardened hands. The third man, in his thirties, wore a white shirt and business suit trousers and carried a clipboard. He smiled in greeting, listened to the start of our conversation, and then left.

Anyone who knew nothing of Northern Ireland and came across us four talking in the sunshine would very likely have seen two men, their working life over and time hanging heavy on their hands, glad of an opportunity to talk to two visitors. But this was not what was happening.

Anthony was being friendly and polite, asking interested, courteous questions. I did not appreciate until the next day how difficult the situation was for him. He told me, 'I felt almost dishonest because I was talking to two dyed-in-the-wool Loyalists. If they knew I was a Catholic they would certainly not be as nice to me, as polite to me, as if I was someone trying to make sense of what they were doing. They would suspect that I could have a Republican agenda to undermine their views. At best I would have been sent on my way. At worst we could have lost the car.'

'What do you mean "lost the car"?'

'They certainly wouldn't have been sitting there on their own. They would have some contingency plan. Maybe you weren't aware of it, but I was certainly aware that we were not there alone. They were most likely checking us out. They would have gone into the house, made a few phone calls, checked the car number. [The Loyalists and the Ulster Volunteer Force, the illegal paramilitary organization, were believed to obtain intelligence from the Ulster Defence Regiment.[1]] I wouldn't be surprised if the car number wasn't taken today when we were in the Sinn Fein Advice Centre. That's not being neurotic, that's the way security works. People need to know who's there and what goes on.'

Curiously, we were not asked any of the questions usually posed in Northern Ireland to establish the religious persuasion of the person questioned. The two men took our interest as an opportunity to set out the rightness of their position. They explained that they were part of a contingent of Orange Order members who had manned the post continuously since the previous July, when their order was prevented by the Royal Ulster Constabulary and the army from proceeding down Garvaghy Road through the Catholic estate back to Portadown. The men pointed to their outpost headquarters, a large shed at the edge of the graveyard, covered in patriotic inscriptions and flags, and the fields where the army and the Protestant supporters had clashed.

I admired the masses of flags. 'I've never seen so many Union Jacks,' I said, 'not even at the end of the Second World War.'

This seemed to please them. They spoke of Britain and the Empire. Indeed, this spot on the little hillside was to them the heart of the great British Empire, but in fact it was its last outpost. All the other great outposts – Australia, India, New Zealand, Canada, South Africa – paid no more than self-serving lip service to the idea of the Commonwealth, and busied themselves with their own affairs, as did the Scots, the Welsh and the English. Ask the younger generations of English about patriotism and they will talk about the World Cup.

If, in about AD 400, a group of Roman soldiers camped at Drumcree had been left behind when the Roman Empire abandoned Britain and if their descendants were still at Drumcree today, calling themselves centurions and marching in phalanxes, their actions could not be more anachronistic than the actions of these Orange Order men with their flags.

This is one of the tragedies that often besets us. We build up a set of ideas which, at the time we do so, are a reasonable reflection of what is actually going on. We incorporate these ideas into the core of our meaning structure, and they become part of our identity. Then, as time goes on, these central meanings gradually lose touch with what is actually happening. It may be that we have simply not acquainted ourselves with the changes in the world around us, or it may be that both our primitive pride and our moral pride have a vested interest in maintaining these ideas because they hold our meaning structure together and bolster our feeling of self-worth. When the discrepancy between what we thought was the case and what is actually the case is forced upon us, we either have to find the courage to undertake a massive restructuring or we can fight a rearguard action, trying to force the world to be what we want it to be. This is a battle we always lose. Even if we win the war we lose the peace. It is never possible to return to the security of the past.

Sometimes these battles are fought and lost by individuals who refuse to acknowledge that their world has changed. Sometimes there are actual conflicts and wars fought by groups of people who want to make the world what they want it to be. In such wars and conflicts there will be combatants who are simply mercenaries taking part because it is politic to do so and whose interest in the outcome is confined to economic advantage and physical survival, but for others the engagement concerns fighting to survive as the person you know yourself to be. These two elderly men standing there in the summer sunshine were fighting such a war. They dared not contemplate the actuality of events, which showed that the supremacy of the Protestants over the Catholics in Northern Ireland was fast becoming a thing of the past, because this outcome was an immense threat to the integrity of their meaning structure. Their fear of annihilation robbed them of their natural kindness and humanity, with the result that they could view with equanimity the possibility of death and injury to people, even to themselves, if next July led to a return to riots and sectarian killings. They were involved in what was to them a much more serious battle: the battle to survive as a person.

Portadown, and the farms and fields around it, was their home. The customs, practices and beliefs of Protestantism and the Orange Order defined the group they belonged to and the persons they knew themselves to be. The various annual celebrations of Protestantism and the Orange Order were anchor points for them in the formless passage of time. Membership of their group gave them status in their community. They were known and respected by those whom they knew and respected, and such mutual respect was held in terms of one very rigid set of customs, practices and beliefs.

Joel Patton, the founder of a radical movement known as 'the spirit of Drumcree', told the journalist Peter Taylor,

> 'In many ways it's not about 800 Orangemen marching down a road. It's about the survival of a culture, of an identity, of a way of life. It's about our ability to still hold on to parts of the country. The Ulster people have their backs to the wall. They're in retreat. They have been chased from quite a large area of the country and they feel that Portadown, the citadel of Orangism, where Orangism was born 200 years ago, that is the place where they want to take their stand. Drumcree represents that.'[2]

Thus, when this strange woman asked these two men at Drumcree, 'If you had to choose between your march going down Garvaghy Road or peace in Northern Ireland which would you choose?' they could not answer. The question was meaningless. Primitive pride takes no account of the needs of other people except when it is in the interests of primitive pride to do so. For each of the men to contemplate a Northern Ireland where the Unionists shared power and privilege with their enemies was to contemplate his own annihilation as a person. They were not alone in feeling like this. Five months later, when Peter Mandelson, the Northern Ireland Secretary, came to Portadown to explain to an Ulster Unionist meeting the compromises which, he hoped, would lead to Northern Ireland's first successful inclusive government, he was greeted by a large crowd screaming at him, 'Homo, homo, homo!' The crowd then waited two hours in the cold to greet him again on his exit from the meeting. The journalist John Mullin reported, 'There was only a dozen steps to his waiting car, but the hate poured on him as the police struggled to keep the crowd back. He looked terrified.'[3]

Perhaps the men I met at Drumcree were among this crowd. They were not of an age to accept homosexuals, so Peter Mandelson would have been doubly a stranger to them, but one who threatened their own existence. Whenever we fear someone we find it easy to hate that person. These men certainly feared and so hated the Catholic families who lived in the Garvaghy Road estate who, so they told me, 'had the IRA army at their backs.' Both of the men complained to me, 'We've given up ten of our parades. Why should we give up all of them?'

And why should not the residents of the Garvaghy Road estate let this group of men in bowler hats walk down their road if doing so meant so much to them? This part of the parade took only seven minutes. Could not the residents show some tolerance of this quaintness? But to them it was not quaintness but the group with power and privileges demonstrating its strength in order to remind the Catholics who was in charge. To the Catholics this was a double threat – that of physical death and personal annihilation.

In 1997 Robery Hamill, a twenty-five-year-old Catholic, was kicked to death in the town centre of Portadown. The Royal Ulster Constabulary officers in an armoured vehicle in view of the attack did nothing to stop it and apprehend the assailants. Other attacks on Catholics by the Loyalists since the ceasefire included the murder in 1999 of Elizabeth O'Neill, a Protestant married to a Catholic. The Ulster Volunteer Force, which began in Portadown, was believed to have been involved in the murder of Rosemary Nelson, the Lurgan solicitor who represented the Garvaghy Road residents. One such resident, Asling McCann, said, 'It is a nightmare living here. I am thirty-six years old and in my whole life I have never walked through the town centre on my own at night or at the weekend. I have a seventeen-year-old boy who will not go into the town on his own because we know there will be trouble.'[4]

Whenever we think about our enemies, be they the enemies of our national, racial or religious group or our own personal enemies, we are faced with one or both of two threats: the threat to our physical existence and the threat to our existence as a person. The first threat, even though it is potentially lethal, is the easiest to deal with because we do not feel personally threatened. Afterwards reconciliation and forgiveness are not impossible. The second threat, even though there is no physical danger, may make us feel confused and vulnerable, so that we resort at times to some desperate defences. Afterwards reconciliation and forgiveness are extremely difficult, if not impossible.

When covering the war in Bosnia Martin Bell, the renowned BBC journalist, was shot at many times by the Serbs and was eventually quite severely wounded. Yet he did not see the Serbs as his enemy. They were doing their job, as they saw it, and he was doing his. When he returned to England he was persuaded to stand for Parliament as an Independent for the seat of Tatton, held by the disgraced Conservative MP Neil Hamilton. Suddenly he discovered that, for the first time in his life, he had enemies – Neil Hamilton and his wife Christine, a most formidable woman.

Martin told me, 'In journalism generally you have rivals and competitors, both within your organization and in other ones, but you don't have enemies. But clearly, and of course technically, in politics what you have is opponents. There's an old saying that your opponents are in front of you but your enemies are all around you, because they're your rivals. But of course I had two particular enemies through the peculiar nature of the case, because I was threatening their career. Actually they threatened their career. I didn't do it to them, they did it for themselves, and the people of Tatton did for them, but I was the instrument of their removal. Recently Neil Hamilton came to see me about something else and there was no problem, but I don't think Christine could ever bring herself to do that. But I never said anything since I was elected which could be construed as ungallant or discourteous.'

'You didn't return the enmity?' I asked.

'No. I was a bit upset by the campaign, by the ferocity of the legal assault. I had no knowledge of the terrain on which I was operating, which they did. She'd been in politics for more than twenty years and he'd been an MP for fourteen, so they knew the game. Also he was trained in the law, so he knew how to throw lawyers at me. During the campaign I felt angry about that, but I don't like anger, especially in myself, and now it's over I feel really sorry for them – their career is ruined.'

When Martin was standing for Parliament – in effect as the candidate for truth and honesty – the tabloid newspapers did their mighty best to find something dishonourable and disgraceful about his past but they failed. Everyone spoke highly of him, including his two ex-wives, which is a distinction very few men ever earn. Martin played by the rules of fairness and honesty. When he encountered the Hamiltons it was not just their overt enmity which shocked and threatened to destabilize him; it was the fact that they were playing by another set of rules, using the kind of ploys well known to unscrupulous lawyers and politicians. It is not just by humiliating, belittling and treating us as objects that an enemy can threaten the integrity of our meaning structure. An enemy can destabilize us simply by acting to a set of ideas which we cannot comprehend, much less appreciate and predict. This is why we are always so ready to see the stranger as the enemy.

During the 1990s it became fashionable to use concepts from the study of evolution to explain why we behave as we do. For instance, the desire which most young men have for frequent sex with many different partners was explained in terms of the need to father many children and establish genetic dominance, while the helplessness which the depressed person feels was explained as the helplessness of being prey. Such descriptions could rapidly degenerate into simple-minded, unscientific theories about genes determining complex behaviour or about how we are no more than hapless vehicles for action replays of the behaviour of our ancient ancestors. Actually there is a much simpler explanation of why on some occasions we behave in ways similar to the ways we assume our ancient ancestors behaved: we are very slow to learn. For instance, between 1900 and 2000 life expectancy in wealthy countries rose from forty-five to eighty years, yet the ways in which we thought about marriage – an institution founded at a time when death made most unions quite brief – were not modified to allow for this increase in longevity. Even though the law was changed to allow for easier divorce, the expectation that marriage ought to be for life did not. No allowance was made for the fact that a couple who were well suited to one another in their twenties might be very different people in their forties or sixties.

The ideas we hold are of our choosing. Even when other people press their ideas upon us we still choose which ideas to accept and which to reject. Sometimes we choose ideas which are appropriate to the present. Sometimes we choose ideas which have been handed down from generation to generation. Such ideas are often more appropriate to the past than to the present. Many of our ideas about strangers and enemies are ideas from the past.

For most of human history we lived in small groups which anthropologists call bands. Jarel Diamond in his study of the influence of germs, guns and steel on the growth of societies wrote,

> Bands are the tiniest societies, consisting typically of 5 to 80 people, most or all of them relatives by birth or by marriage. In effect, a band is an extended family or several related extended families . . . Probably all human lived in bands until at least 40,000 years ago, and most still did as recently as 11,000 years ago.[5]

In time some bands came together to form tribes of a few hundred people. An adult in a tribe would be likely to know, or at least recognize, every member of the tribe. Living in bands and tribes people could readily identify a stranger. Strangers were not kin and were therefore likely to be killed. It was not until the rise of chiefdoms, groups numbered in thousands, some 7,500 years ago that 'people had to learn, for the first time in history, how to encounter strangers regularly without attempting to kill them'.[6]

It seems that 7,500 years has not been long enough for most people to learn how to separate the ideas of 'stranger' and 'kill'.

The Necessity of Enemies

General Manuel Antonio Noriega, erstwhile dictator of Panama, once remarked, 'Between countries, there is no such thing as friendship. No country is another country's friend. Countries share only interests.'[7] Noriega's life story, which includes a sentence by a US court in 1992 of forty years in jail for racketeering, money-laundering and drug-trafficking, suggests that altruism did not play a large part in his thinking, but his remark does raise the question of whether friendship is possible between groups of people and even between individuals. Are apparent friendships between groups and individuals nothing more than shared interests? When interests change friendships can disappear. Two schoolfriends drift apart when one person goes to university while the other gets a job, or one marries and has children while the other pursues a career. Two groups might come together in defence against a common enemy, only to drift apart, or even into mutual enmity, when peace is secured.

Those of us who value friendship would argue that, while shared interests are important in a friendship, there is something far more important: our need for long-term, secure, trusting, affectionate relationships. Such relationships are essential to the survival of each of us as a person. However, just as a good case can be made for the necessity of friendship in our life, so a good case can be made for the necessity of enemies.

Our organs of perception function in such a way that, for us to be aware of the possible existence of anything, that thing must exist in contrast to something else. This applies both to what we see, hear, touch, taste and smell and to the meanings we create. We cannot see a grey cat in a grey fog. If everybody and everything lived for ever we would have no concept of life because there would be no death. If everybody was universally friendly to one another all the time we would have no concept of friendship because there would be no enmity.

In the contrast friendship–enmity we have a choice. We can focus on friendship or on enmity. The people who focus on friendship would say that they have no or very few enemies. They can see through the propaganda put out by their national, racial or religious group about the group's enemies; if an individual is unpleasant to them, they seek to resolve any differences and, if that fails, they separate themselves from that person. For me one of the joys of getting older and enjoying a modest economic independence is that I feel I do not have to spend one precious minute in the company of someone who wishes to hurt or use me.

Unfortunately the people who focus on friendship are out-numbered by those who focus on – indeed whose lives are consumed by – enmity. What friends they have they take for granted. What interests and excites them is their enemies, be they relatives, colleagues, neighbours or strangers of a different nationality, race or creed. Such enemies meet two important needs: they provide excitement in what otherwise would be a very dull life; and they operate as a distraction from inescapable and unresolvable angers and fears.

We may learn quite early in life to try to meet these needs by creating enemies.

In 1998 one of the children who lived in the council flats on one side of my garden, a blond, blue-eyed boy of ten, was forever kicking a football around the car park that served the block of flats. Whenever he kicked the ball into my garden he would climb up on to the garage roof and call for me or jump into the garden. From the roof he had a clear view into the garden of the hotel on the other side of my house. At that time there were some ten homeless refugee children living in the hotel with their families.

The boy from the council flats was always well dressed and well cared for, but he often had nothing to do and was frustrated because his mother would not let him go across the road to play in the park. One day with two companions he was kicking his football around and repeatedly and deliberately kicking it into my garden. I warned him that if he did that again I would confiscate his ball. He ignored my warning, and so I picked up the ball and carried it into my house. Inadvertently I started a small war.

The boy and his two companions were on the garage roof. He was very angry and had to find someone on whom to vent his anger. Swearing at me was not enough. The homeless refugee children were playing in the hotel garden and taking no notice of the boys on the garage roof. He attracted their attention and began his attack on them. I found his choice of invective very interesting.

He could not attack the homeless children on racist grounds because one of his companions was of West Indian descent and the other was from Ethiopia. So he chose homelessness. 'I live in a nice flat,' he told them. 'Where you are is yuk.' He went on to enlarge on his theme, telling them that his aunt had been in their hotel and seen how dirty and horrible it was. His words were full of venom. The children knew that they were safe behind my stone wall and most of them took themselves off to a distant part of the garden but one lad of about ten stood his ground. He would not have his family insulted. His reasoned arguments were ignored by the three on the flat roof. Frustrated, he went away, but he was too angry to leave it be. He came back and shouted at the trio. I did not see who threw the first stone but soon a rain of stones was travelling both ways across my garden. Fortunately this small war could be brought to an end by one powerful arbiter, the hotel manager.

Alas, there are no powerful arbiters to bring to an end similar disputes between adults. Having witnessed the ferocious violence and hatred expressed by some Serbs, Croats and Muslims, Martin Bell withdrew to what he thought would be a peaceful part of rural England, only to find himself confronted by enmities amongst some of his constituents as great as those he had seen in Yugoslavia, though fortunately the violence was expressed in harassment, not murder. He told me, 'I'd never run into neighbours' groups before I became an MP but they're very, very important. They consume people. Now there are people who don't need enemies, who just want to live in peace and quiet, but when they are denied peace and quiet by a vexatious neighbour it becomes totally obsessive. It ruins their lives. I'm amazed at how common it is.' He went on to tell me about a farmer who held a great many car boot sales, thus annoying his neighbours, and who dealt with any criticism in a very belligerent way.

Martin gave me a copy of one of the monthly reports he routinely gave to his constituents. Like a loving father trying to resolve an argument between fractious children he had written,

> We live in a blessed and peaceful corner of a turbulent world. But even in our part of Cheshire there are certain neighbourhoods which take on the character of war zones. The issues are nearly always about development, and the hostilities are initiated by a very few people who seem to me to need enemies as much as most of us need friends. They provoke and antagonize. They fence their neighbours in, or out, with barbed wire. They build Berlin Walls. They grow giant hedges. They dump rubbish about the perimeter of a victim's garden. They harass. They intimidate. The common decency and tolerance of people – nearly all of the people nearly all of the time – is perhaps too often taken for granted. The occasional defiance and denial of the qualities in our neighbourhood wars have shocked me almost as much as some of my experiences on the darker shores of countries in genuine conflict.[8]

Martin knew that the person at the centre of the conflict was battling his own demons by trying to take out his fear and anger on his neighbours. Even the most skilled therapist finds it extremely difficult to persuade a person bent on acting out his misery to try to understand it, so it was not surprising that Martin was baffled.

To be able to concentrate on friends rather than enemies we need to feel that our meaning structure is not under any major threat. When people disagree with us we see this as their right to have their own opinion. We are not beset by envy because we rank fairness and justice above having everything for ourselves. When people get angry with us we try not to take it personally; we examine the situation realistically in order to accept appropriate responsibility and, when necessary, to make the necessary apology and recompense. It takes considerable self-confidence and wisdom to be able to do all this, and many people simply do not try. It is easier to identify the person or group which we see as a threat and to put our energies into combating that threat. This way we do not have to confront our own essential weakness. Instead, we can assure ourselves that we are better than our enemy.

Threats to the integrity of our meaning structure come from other people. These may be real threats or threats which we have imagined. They may have been real in the past but time and events moved on and we failed to notice. Other people might have told us that we were threatened, and we accepted this without question. We think only of defence and never of conflict-resolution because, as we see it, to offer to negotiate would be to reveal our shameful weakness. Defending ourselves against our enemy can become not just the pattern of our individual lives but the pattern which divides a group or a whole society.

Pat O'Shane is a famous Australian. Like many people from an Aboriginal family she had to battle to get an education and a career. In 1976 she became Australia's first Aboriginal barrister, and in 1981, appointed as the permanent head of the NSW Department of Aboriginal Affairs, she was the first woman to head a government department in Australia. In 1986, as the first Aboriginal magistrate in NSW, she began handing down some controversial judgements which struck great blows for the deprived and dispossessed. I met her in 1997 and she told me about the deep divisions in Australian society. She listed five, and each can be understood in terms of a threat to the meaning structure.

The first was men against women. In the 1980s the government had stressed equal opportunities, but by the 1990s men's antagonism to women was, as Pat said, 'as bad and dangerous as ever'. Such antagonism is common in cultures where boys are brought up largely separated from their mothers and expected to act in a very macho way. Australian boys are not physically separated from their mothers like boys in a traditional Muslim community, but Australian men can set up an invisible wall between mother and son by making constant demands that she not 'bring him up as a sissy'. This forced early separation leaves the boy feeling vulnerable and weak, something he has to hide if he is to be accepted by other males. He remains dependent on his mother, but he resents his dependency and he is angry with his mother for deserting him. One way or another he takes out this anger and resentment on all the women who play a part in his life. Men brought up in this way have little difficulty in becoming soldiers and in starting and maintaining wars and conflicts. They have little interest in resolving conflicts and finding compromises and reconciliation because in their eyes to do so is to act like a woman.

Pat spoke next about how the Australian police were against young people, which reflected 'the fear that adults have of youths who organize themselves into gangs'. This is a particular instance of the way in which the old hate the young, which I wrote about in *Time On Our Side*. There are many adult Australians who hold the view that young people have no right to be unhappy because they are enjoying the best years of their life in the best country in the world. Such views are usually accompanied by statements like, 'You don't realize you've got it made. Now in my day . . .' These resorts to martyrdom are usually an attempt by primitive pride to ward off the recognition of the bleakness and emptiness of their own life for which there will be no recompense or reward. Faced with such lack of understanding, young people can feel very alienated, and with that can come the threat of annihilation against which suicide can be the desperate defence – 'If I can't live as myself I will die as myself.' Australian males between seventeen and twenty-four have one of the highest suicide rates in the world.

Australians claim that theirs is a classless society, and so it is in that Australians do not define their class in terms of their family history. But they do define their class in terms of money. Those who by good luck or hard work have moved upwards can feel what Pat called 'hatred of the poor "dole bludgers"'. This expression of intolerance was increased by the 'radio shock jocks' like John Laws and Alan Jones, who prided themselves on saying publicly what many people said privately. Two years after Pat and I had this discussion it appeared from events that John Laws took the view that, while it was wrong for an unemployed person not to be completely open about his availability for work, it was not wrong for John Laws to be less than frank about his reasons for the opinions he expressed. He felt it was not necessary that he should disclose publicly that he had entered into what he called 'a perfectly reasonable transaction' with the Australian Bankers' Association in which, for a substantial sum of money, he would stop criticizing the banks and instead promote them on his programme.[9] At the same time the former chief executive of the AMP (Australian Mutual Provident Society) revealed that he

> had turned a blind eye to a secret deal between the company and the broadcaster Alan Jones in the early 1990s in which it agreed to a $A7 million debt refinancing scheme for South Sydney Leagues Club, of which Jones was then director of football ... Mr Salmon told the *Herald* that Jones, the [Radio] 2UE personality, had attacked the AMP and himself 'mercilessly' over a sustained period in 1992 and 1993 but then suddenly the attacks seemed to stop. 'I suspect they stopped because somebody – and it certainly wasn't me – was persuaded to provide some support for something he was interested in.'[10]

John Laws and Alan Jones, like other shock jocks, were assisting people to act out their fear and anger instead of helping them to understand it. According to Ian Salmon,

> Jones's attacks on the society and him were so damaging that he was forced to employ security guards at his home. 'We had threats. We had a bullet through the post [and a message] saying this is for you next. That wasn't him [Jones] but [his comments] stirred people's emotions. He should have known better.'[11]

The fear and anger that people with money can feel for people without money comes not just from the concern that they might lose what they have worked hard to acquire. They see their financial rewards for work as part of the functioning of the Just World. If those who did not work were rewarded, did this mean that the Just World had ceased to function?

Then there was the deep division which racism created. Pat spoke of how, centuries ago, when people in northern Europe began living in villages, they had to find ways of getting along with one another. So they invented trolls and other dark little people to be the repositories of their fears. The trolls represent those parts of our meaning structure which, if we subjected them to scrutiny, would challenge the validity of the other parts of our meaning structure. The Aboriginal people, said Pat, were the trolls of white Australians. Boori Pryor, who had spent time performing his dances and stories in schools in order to teach children about Aboriginal culture, found that a great deal of his work involved teaching white children not to be frightened of Aboriginal people.[12] One way in which some adult white people used to deal with their fear of Aboriginal people was to romanticize them – to talk of the Dreamtime and how spiritual they were and in touch with nature. Fortunately, as some Serbs would be the first to tell us, spiritual people do not want or need material things, so there was no point in spending money on education, health services and housing for the Aboriginal people.

Finally, Pat spoke of a division which emerged as the federal government cast its net wider for immigrants. The first shipload of immigrants to arrive soon after the end of the Second World War was made up of people from the Baltic countries, all blond and blue-eyed. White Australians would accept no other. They were very upset when Greeks and Italians started to arrive. I remember when the Maltese were seen as a shade of darkness too far, while the Turks! Another kind of nationalism was created, that of whites whose ancestors arrived in Australia between 1788 and 1940. Such nationalism rehabilitated the skeletons in the cupboards of many families, including mine. A convict ancestor became a reason to boast about one's roots. Such a boast held together many a meaning structure made shaky by the fear of the stranger.

However, this new nationalism did mean that some people confronted the truth about their family history. In many places family history is still something to keep secret. When Professor Henry Louis Gates of Harvard University, himself a descendant of African slaves, visited the Swahili coast in east Africa he found that most of the people there, though they would certainly have been regarded as black in any other part of the world, thought of themselves as Arab or Persian, descendants of the traders from Arabia and Persia. He found that the reason why the Swahili could not accept their slave ancestry, while American blacks could accept theirs, lay in the identity of the enemy, the slave trader. American slaves were bought, sold and used by whites. On the Swahili coast black people were captured, maltreated, sold and used by fellow blacks. The enemy was in the family.[13]

Michael Ignatieff wrote, 'The story of Cain seems to say, at its simplest, that there are no wars more savage than civil wars, no hatreds more intractable than those between closest kin.'[14] Within some families conflicts are fought directly between those who have identified themselves as enemies – sibling against sibling, parent against child, child against parent. However, such conflicts threaten to destroy the family unit, something which can be very threatening to other members of the family and to onlookers for whom the family is their bulwark against the world. Hence many family conflicts get acted out in disguise. Children, even as adults, do battle not with their parents but with people whom they see as being like their parents, and siblings do likewise with people they see as being like their siblings. Often the perception of such likenesses is not consciously recognized and thus becomes the source of great misery for the person concerned. Many a career has been spoiled and many a marriage foundered.

Such sibling conflicts are at their worst when they emerge as ethnic wars. The Serbs, Muslims and Croats of Yugoslavia are such siblings, sharing a common genetic ancestry of Slavic stock mixed with the genes of the many different people who happened to visit this fertile, beautiful land. The differences between Serb, Croat and Muslim have their roots not in genes but in the differing ideas of three different religions – Orthodox, Catholic and Islam – and two cultures – the Austrian-Hungarian empire and the Ottoman empire. As Chuck Sudetic recorded in his history of the Celik family, when Serbs, Croats and Muslims live peacefully together such differences all but disappear. Kupusovici was a tiny village on Mount Zvijezda, a bulwark of earth and limestone that marked the boundary between Bosnia and Serbia. Throughout its long history both Serbs and Muslims lived there. Sudetic wrote,

Many men on the mountain lived for their addiction to plum brandy. They awoke to it each morning and downed it before going to bed at night. Muslim men revelled in the brandy despite the prohibition handed down by the Prophet Muhammad in the Koran, and the Serbs had no such religious prohibition ... Not everyone had a still, and the Celik menfolk in their baggy trousers, black wool cummerbunds, and maroon fezzes would distil the brandy at the Radovanovic place or with the Mitrašinovic men ... Sometimes they would sit up all night arguing and swearing on the pussies of each other's mothers. They would roast potatoes on the fire, trade lies, tell tales, and play practical jokes. One of them might pull out a wooden flute and play a tune that began the *kolo*, the dance they all seemed to know without having learnt it. The Muslim women in their billowing *dimije* and drooping veils would take the arms of their Serb sisters and dance about the yard.[15]

When we are confident in ourselves, when our meaning structure is not under threat, we have no difficulty in accepting that we are similar to other people. We do not have to defend our sense of being an individual by claiming possession of some overvalued, idiosyncratic attribute. But when we feel we are going to be swallowed up and annihilated by events or by the people around us we have to find some aspect of ourselves, however imaginary, to defend our sense of identity. My sister in her seventies would sometimes tell me that someone she knew had seen me, or a picture of me, and had commented to her about my similarity to her. She would add, 'I know you don't like being told this.' Family resemblances were not a problem for me in adult life but in childhood they were. Myra had always been very adept at identifying what would annoy me, though she did not waste time trying to work out why. My angers and irritations were simply evidence of my peculiar nature. Like many unhappy children I fantasized that I did not belong to this family, but a glance in the mirror would prove me wrong. Forced to accept that these were my relatives I tried to assert my individuality at school by being different from the other pupils, but this was not a wise move because I was in an educational system that valued conformity above all else.

This was, however, a better choice than becoming a slavish adherent of some religious, racial or national creed, making myself feel special by belonging to a special group. Even though I might have found comfort and support from the other members of the group, and vented my hatred of myself on the group's enemies, I would have reduced drastically the number and variety of ways in which I could have defined myself; thus I would have become much less of a person. If I define my identity in many different ways – woman, writer, Australian, psychologist, cosmopolitan, mother, friend, swimmer, driver, gardener, *Guardian* reader, lecturer and so on – and list these definitions in differing orders in response to different situations I do not box myself in to a fixed role and a fixed way of behaving. Also, it would be very difficult for me to find one person or one group of people whom I could see as representing the despised opposite of all these definitions and who thus could be an enemy. However, I would still have no control over anyone who wanted to focus on just one of my attributes and see me as their enemy.

Michael Ignatieff, after visiting the Serbian command post in the village of Mirkovci in Croatia during the Serbo-Croat war in 1993, wrote of one of the Serbian soldiers,

> The kind of Serb this man believes himself to have been before the war is not the kind of Serb he became after the war. Before the war, he might have thought of himself as a Yugoslav or café manager or a husband rather than as a Serb. Now as he sits in this farmhouse bunker, there are men two hundred and fifty yards away who would kill him. For them he is only a Serb, not a neighbour, not a friend, not a Yugoslav, not a former teammate at the football club. And because he is only a Serb for his enemies, he has become only a Serb to himself.[16]

When we are afraid our attention and our train of thought become focused on the source of the threat. We abandon many of the complex ideas we acquired in adult life and resort to the simple ideas of our childhood. Faced with danger someone who gave up religious observance the day he left the parental home can find himself praying to God to save him, while someone who prided herself on her scientific world view can find herself thinking, 'If I'd been really good this would never have happened.' The ideas we acquire early in childhood can have an absolute quality that ideas acquired later in life rarely have. Parents who want their children to think in particular ways know this and make sure that their children encounter these ideas early in their life.

I have in front of me two photographs. One must have been taken in about 1937. It is a close-up of a group of people gathered to watch a parade go by. Four adults are looking down very fondly at a four-year-old boy standing in front of the group. The fifth person, presumably the boy's mother, is standing behind him and looking shyly and proudly at the camera. The little boy is dressed in a child's version of a Nazi uniform. In his left hand he holds a German flag and his right arm is raised in a Nazi salute.[17]

We can only wonder if this little boy survived the war and the difficult years that followed. If he did, how did he deal with his past? Did he confront not just the crimes of Nazi Germany but the fact that the people he loved and depended on allowed, indeed encouraged, him to play a small part in supporting those crimes? Or did he deny that it had happened, thus damaging a vital part of his meaning structure, his life story?

The other photograph was in *The Economist* on 11 July 1998, the day before the conflict at Drumcree, when the Orange Order was prevented from walking down the Garvaghy Road. It is a close-up of a baby boy barely eighteen months old. He is sitting in a push chair and wearing a white lacy knit outfit, the kind a loving grandmother would make. Over this outfit he is wearing a large white bib on which is printed the sign of the Red Hand of Ulster and the words BORN TO WALK THE GARVAGHY ROAD. NO SURRENDER. This bib is not just to keep his clothes clean. It is there to brand the child as a Loyalist determined to confront and overcome his enemies.

On 12 July 1998, when the conflict at Drumcree was raging, a Loyalist petrol-bombed the home of the Quinn family in Ballymoney. Three children, Jason, Mark and Richard Quinn, were burnt to death. The child in the push chair would have known nothing about this, yet the bib his mother lovingly tied around his neck made him part of it. As he grew up would he be angry with his parents for imposing their enemy on him, or would he make his parents' enemy his enemy in order to preserve his belief that his parents were always good and always did their best for him?

Young children, of necessity finding complexity difficult, readily absorb a picture of the world where people are clearly divided into one simple contrast, good and bad. Aaron Hass wrote about how the survivors of the Holocaust communicated their angry, suspicious attitude toward all gentiles to their children. For the survivors 'it was not simply the Germans, Poles, Lithuanians, Ukrainians, and other nationalities who participated in the Final Solution. More to the point, it was the goyim.'[18] As a child

> The world, I learned, is divided into two. There are Jews and there are goyim. There are few of us and many of them. Goyim are different from Jews. They are brutish. We are sensitive, humane. They persecute. We study. We must stick to our own, for community and safety. Goyim are to be shunned. They are to be feared. And because Jewish survival is, and has always been, precarious, we must focus our energies on ourselves, our families, and our people. We live in America, but we are Jewish and alien here. It's been like this for generations. We live in their countries and they hate us. And, sometimes, they decide to murder us.[19]

The categories 'good' and 'bad' are absolutely central to our thinking because they are vital to our survival, both physically and as a person. We all see the world in terms of 'good' – that which we approve of, which benefits us and advances our interests, which reassures us and gives us pleasure – and 'bad' – that of which we disapprove, which does not benefit and even harms us, which frightens us and causes us pain. Of course there is an infinite number of ways in which we can define the features of 'good' and 'bad'. If we are wise we do not set ourselves and our fellows impossibly high and rigid standards. My friend Jeannie grew up defining her 'good' as 'I must be perfect and please everybody all the time.' To think otherwise was to be bad. She was dreadfully miserable, but at last she came to understand that she was free to change her definitions. Accordingly, she became fond of her imperfections, and in her dealings with other people she defined 'good' as 'I try to be reasonable.'

In adopting this attitude Jeannie deprived herself of one of the great pleasures that many people enjoy – condemning their enemies. Such people know that their group is infinitely good and their enemies infinitely bad. This way of thinking protects the person from one of the greatest threats to the meaning structure: feeling yourself to be bad. Having an enemy who is immensely wicked is a great comfort because, no matter what you are, your enemy is worse. Enemies are dirty while you are clean. They are cowardly while you are brave. They are stupid while you are clever. They are wildly licentious while you are sexually pure. Writing about the anti-Catholic and anti-Masonic movements in American politics the historian Richard Hofstadter commented,

> Anti-Catholicism has always been the pornography of the Puritan. Whereas anti-Masons had imagined wild drinking bouts and entertained themselves with fantasies about the actual enforcement of grisly Masonic oaths, the anti-Catholics developed an immense lore about libertine priests, the confessional as an opportunity for seduction, licentious convents and monasteries and the like.[20]

The comfort of having an enemy is not just confined to knowing that our enemies are aggressive and utterly selfish while we are peace-loving and saintly in our unselfishness; our stance against the evil of our enemies has a cosmic dimension. Jean Said Makdisi said that in Lebanon 'The warring groups perceive in their battles apocalyptic confrontation, each side seeing the other as the very incarnation of evil and itself as the embodiment of good – each seeking to cast the other out forever.'[21] Meanwhile in 1980 the Moral Majority leader Jerry Falwell assured Americans that they were in no danger from the Soviet Union. 'No matter how militarily superior the Soviet Union is, they could never touch us. God would miraculously protect America.'[22]

Five years later Hezbollah in Lebanon announced its existence to the world in a manifesto which stated:

> No one can begin to imagine the scope of our military strength and capability. No one can even fathom its size. For we do not have a separate military wing which is independent from the parts of our bodies. Everyone of us is a fighting soldier when a call for a *jihad* arises and each one of us carries out his mission in battle on the basis of his legal obligations. For Allah is behind us supporting and protecting us while instilling fear in the hearts of our enemies.[23]

What better protection could there be for a shaky meaning structure than the knowledge that God is on your side! The trouble with

God is that He takes too many sides. In both World Wars each side claimed that they had God's support. As events turned out it became very hard to see in those events the infallible workings of the Just World. Where was God during the Holocaust, or when the bombs rained down on Dresden, or when the mushroom clouds rose over Hiroshima and Nagasaki? Perhaps it is best to claim that God is on your side without looking for evidence that it is so.

Most of us have in childhood the kind of experiences which lead us to believe that we are not good enough as we are. Any person who can assure us merely by their existence that we are acceptable becomes very precious to us. Hence enemies become very precious. Some people keep a stock of enemies and arrange them in a hierarchy so that they have always got someone to feel superior to. Some racists rank their enemies according to the colour of their skin. Hezbollah regarded the West, and particularly the United States, as its staunchest enemy after Israel.[24]

These hierarchies of hate can make a nonsense of the saying, 'My enemy's enemy is my friend.' Polish Jews who escaped the Germans and joined the Polish resistance discovered that the Poles hated the Jews even more than they hated the Germans. Hundreds, if not thousands, of Jews were murdered by their Polish 'allies'.[25]

Having an enemy may be so important that many people will not relinquish this pleasure even though they know full well how terrible it can be to be identified as an enemy and persecuted. Many of the Jews who settled in Israel tried to create a life where enemies were unnecessary, but many did not and instead created the various political and religious factions which caused such misery for Israelis and Arabs alike. Martin Bell told me, 'The Knesset, Israel's Parliament, is the most fractious assembly on earth. They shout at each other and sometimes it gets worse. Sometimes it goes to fisticuffs. If you've got three Israelis together, you've got two political parties and a schism, but held together by the hostility of the Arab world – and I'd have to say the disunity of the Arab world as well – and this has helped them keep their sense of identity as special people.'

Being persecuted by an enemy can be extremely unpleasant, even dangerous, but it can enhance enormously our sense of self-worth and personal power. The temptations of martyrdom are very great. A people brought up on a religion of saints and martyrs, the Republicans in Ireland were offered infinite possibilities of martyrdom by

their enemy, the British, who did not seem to recognize the importance of martyrs for a movement. Peter Taylor in his study of the
Provisional IRA wrote,

> In March 1920 Lloyd George sent the 'Tans' to Ireland to make it
> 'hell for rebels to live in'. This succeeded as they proceeded to
> 'terrorize the terrorists'. On one occasion, a party of 'Tans' captured
> a handful of the enemy at Kerry Pike near Cork, cut off the tongue
> of one, the nose of another, cut out the heart of a third and smashed
> the skull of a fourth. To intimidate the local population who gave
> support to the IRA, they set fire to villages and torched Cork city
> centre in reprisal for an ambush in which seventeen Auxiliaries had
> been killed. But far from denying the IRA their popular base and
> isolating them from the population, the excesses of the 'Tans' only
> increased support for the IRA.

Some months later Terence MacSwiney, the Lord Mayor of Cork,
died in Brixton jail after a hunger strike lasting seventy-three days.
Peter Taylor went on,

> MacSwiney took his place in history not just because of his sacrifice
> but because of his portentous words, 'It is not those who can inflict
> the most,' he warned, 'but those who can suffer the most who will
> conquer.' His words became the epigram of the 1981 hunger strike.
> Lloyd George, like Mrs Thatcher sixty years later, refused to give in.
> On both occasions, the political consequences were momentous.[26]

Martyrdom always claims superior virtue. It needs the contrast
of an enemy and it needs an audience. Martin Bell told me, 'I was
the BBC Washington correspondent for twelve years at the beginning
of the super-power rivalry. The American government seemed to
crave tinpot dictators, whether it was Ayatollah Khomeini, Saddam
Hussein, Noriega, Ortega in Nicaragua – and all these became hate
figures. It was almost as if they needed them. Americans needed
someone to denounce. They needed someone against whom they
could parade their American values. I found it the same with the
Serbs. They believed themselves to be an heroic people and they
needed a dark background against which to shine. They would if
necessary create that darkness themselves.'

It is not enough to be surrounded by the adoring, concerned gaze of the others in your group. Your enemy must see and acknowledge you. To be held in the gaze of your enemy might put you in danger, but such a gaze can be comforting because it assures you that you exist and are important.

Many people, when offered the choice between living comfortably and safely in a society where nobody even acknowledges your existence, much less talks to you, and living in a society where people acknowledge you but only to persecute you, choose the latter. Thus quite a number of elderly people who live on their own and have few friends become convinced that they are the prey of burglars and muggers or of the council, or that some great power is beaming messages at them through their television set. Children who have no friends and whose family is absent or not interested in them, and whose teachers make the mistake of ignoring them when they are well behaved, will deliberately misbehave in order to gain attention, even if it is hostile attention. Being unacknowledged creates the threat of annihilation. The comfort of paranoia is that someone, somewhere is thinking of you.

Unfortunately, the sad truth is that other people think of us only occasionally, if at all. Our favourite topic in our thinking is ourselves and our concerns. Those people who pride themselves on their concern for others are likely to be busy observing themselves being concerned about others rather than giving their full attention to the objects of their concern. One of the vital skills of friendship which people must consciously learn is to pay attention to the other person and to observe and remember the things which are important to that person. The fact that many people are not even aware that they lack this skill is evidence of how little we actually think about one another.

Believing that you and your group are the focus of world attention can be very comforting and supportive but all too often such a belief is based on fantasy, not reality. When I was in Belgrade in 1998 I found that the Serbs I met believed that the attention of the British was focused on the plight of Serbia, the noble victim of its wicked enemies. Not wanting to make it worse for these people whom I pitied and liked so much, I did not tell them that, the Bosnian war notwithstanding, most British people would be hard pressed to find Serbia on the map. When, in the following year, British television screens were filled with pictures of Kosovan refugees, the British people saw people like themselves, looking like them, wearing the same sort of clothes, being persecuted by the Serbs. Then the attention of the British was suddenly focused on the Serbs, but, coming late to the history of Serbia and knowing nothing of what the Serbs had suffered, they did not see Serbia as the noble victim but as the cruel oppressor.

When I was working as a clinical psychologist in the National Health Service I became acquainted with dozens of families whose members had no understanding of one another but who operated simply on their prejudices. In Northern Ireland the Protestant Loyalists who supported union with Britain, the Catholic Nationalists and the British seemed to share the same kind of relationship. When I visited Northern Ireland in May 1999 most people there, both Protestant and Catholic, seemed to believe that the British gave Northern Ireland their full attention. They might be forgiven for thinking that if a country sent its army to patrol their streets it was actually interested in them, but that was not the case with the British. Ed Cairns at the University of Ulster told me that he had always had difficulty in getting his research published in British academic journals because the editors of those journals believed that research done in Northern Ireland could not have any relevance to the rest of Britain. Ed would exchange papers and books with academics from other parts of Britain, but often these packages came to him bearing a green Customs sticker: these academics did not know that Northern Ireland was part of Britain and shared the same postal service.

In June 1999, as the wrangling went on about the implementation of the Good Friday Agreement and the British saw, night after night, on their television screens the Unionist politicians saying 'No', Richard Ingram wrote in his column in the *Observer,*

A handful of Tory MPs and leader writers of right-wing newspapers are about the only people left now who still support the Unionist cause. The general attitude of the people in this country towards Northern Ireland is one of utter weariness allied with the wish that the Irish be left to sort out their own mess. Those of us who have seen billions of our taxes being pumped into Northern Ireland to try to preserve the status quo have little, if any, sympathy for a group of people who, despite their waving of Union Jacks, have always expressed contempt for mainland Britain and its elected leaders.[27]

The Loyalists, while they professed a loyalty to a mythical Britishness, actually despised and distrusted the British government, irrespective of which party was in power. This was an important idea which they shared with Nationalists, who had no difficulty in seeing the British as the enemy. If wishing to govern themselves had been at the top of their list of priorities, and had they been clever, the Loyalists and the Nationalists could have achieved self-government by joining forces to throw the British out. Similarly, as Martin Bell pointed out to me, if the Palestinians were clever they would make their peace with the Israelis in the knowledge that, with no enemy to fight, the Israelis would soon tear their own country apart in factional fighting. However, being clever begins with trying to understand what is actually going on. This means putting aside the fantastical notions created by primitive pride and taking the risk that parts of your meaning structure might be disconfirmed by such understanding. Unfortunately, few leaders in wars and conflicts ever have the courage and wisdom to be clever.

Whenever we try to put aside our fantasies and wishes so that we can see what is actually going on we create a high degree of uncertainty for ourselves. We see that the world does not revolve around us. We see that most people are not regarding us with either friendship or enmity. They are not regarding us at all. They are going about their business, elaborating their own fantasies and tending to their own concerns. To understand why other people behave as they do we need to understand how they see themselves and their world, and the more we try to do this the clearer it becomes that it is not possible to put people into neat, separate categories and thus clarify how we should respond to them. Instead, we can find ourselves liking someone whose political or religious beliefs are anathema to us, or feeling sorry for someone who has committed horrendous crimes, or being tremendously interested in someone whom previously we would have considered utterly boring. In trying to understand the course of events we see that what we thought were simple processes – enemies falling out, say – dissolve into myriad 'variables', as scientists call them: all the factors that play a part in the cause and outcome of a process. The more we look the more we see how very far our fantasies about what was going on are from what is actually happening.

To live with such an understanding requires an ability to tolerate uncertainty. Uncertainty may threaten the stability of our meaning structure because we know that at any minute our meaning structure could be disconfirmed. To avert such a threat many people develop a complete world picture which makes everything explicable and predictable. Absolutely essential to this picture is the enemy.

This way of thinking Richard Hofstadter called 'the paranoid style'.

It is [he wrote] above all a way of seeing the world and expressing oneself. Webster defines paranoia, the clinical entity, as a chronic mental disorder characterized by systematic delusions of persecution and of one's own greatness. In the paranoid style, as I conceive it, the feeling of persecution is central, and it is indeed systematized in grandiose theories of conspiracy. But there is a vital difference between the paranoid spokesman in politics and the clinical para-noiac: although they both tend to be overheated, oversuspicious, overaggressive, grandiose, and apocalyptic in expression, the clinical paranoid sees the hostile and conspiratorial world in which he feels himself to be living as directed specifically *against him*; whereas the spokesman of the paranoid style finds it directed against a nation, a culture, a way of life whose fate affects not him alone but millions of others. Insofar as he does not usually see himself singled out as the individual victim of a personal conspiracy, he is somewhat more rational and much more disinterested. His sense that his political passions are unselfish and patriotic, in fact, goes far to intensify his feeling of righteousness and his moral indignation.[28]

The Internet is always awash with messages from exponents of the paranoid style. Such people have never wanted to keep their knowledge to themselves. They have always seen it as their duty to warn the unwary and, in doing so, show themselves to be both good by caring about others and powerful because they know what is going on.

The exponent of the paranoid style garners information of a particular kind and then organizes it into a comprehensive theory about the world. As Hofstadter described,

The typical procedure of the higher paranoid scholarship is to start with such defensible assumptions and with a careful accumulation of facts, or at least what appear to be facts, and to marshal these facts toward an overwhelming 'proof' of the particular conspiracy that is to be established. It is nothing if not coherent – in fact, the paranoid mentality is far more coherent than the real world, since it leaves no room for mistakes, failures or ambiguities. It is, if not wholly rational, at least intensely rationalistic; it believes that it is up against an enemy who is infallibly rational as he is totally evil, and it seeks to match his imputed total competence with its own, leaving nothing unexplained and comprehending all of reality in one overreaching, consistent theory.[29]

Since it is the theory rather than events which is of prime importance, the paranoid style readily lends itself to the workings of primitive pride.

The enemy, so central to the theory, is no ordinary enemy.

The enemy is clearly delineated: he is a perfect model of malice, a kind of amoral superman: sinister, ubiquitous, powerful, cruel, sensual, luxury-loving. Unlike the rest of us, the enemy is not caught in the toils of the vast mechanism of history, himself a victim of his past, his desires, his limitations. He is a free, active, demonic agent. He wills, indeed he manufactures, the mechanism of history himself, or deflects the normal course of history in an evil way. He makes crises, starts runs on banks, causes depressions, manufactures disasters, and then enjoys and profits from the misery he has produced. The paranoid's interpretation of history is in this sense distinctly personal: decisive events are not taken as part of the stream of history, but as the consequences of someone's will. Very often the enemy is held to possess some special source of power: he controls the press; he directs the public mind through 'managed news'; he has unlimited funds; he has a new secret for influencing the mind (brain washing); he has a special technique for seduction (the Catholic confessional); he is gaining a stranglehold on the educational system.[30]

Such a comprehensive theory with such an enemy at its centre removes all ambiguity and uncertainty from the paranoid person's view of the world. Moreover, it absolves the person of any responsibility for what happens in the world. The enemy is always to blame. Delicious as this denial of responsibility is, even more so is the knowledge that you are in possession of the one and only Absolute Truth.

Knowledge, so it is always said, is power. When we are children we are weak, not just because we are puny, but also because we know very little. Much of what we learn at school does not give us any power, but there are some things which we learn from teachers and other people that lead us to feel that we are getting some purchase on this vague, slippery thing called life. We learn how to do certain things – play the piano, use a computer, ride a bicycle – and we feel that we can act upon the world and get the result we desire. We learn about the world and find that we can make some fairly accurate predictions about, say, what clothes to buy or what film to see. However, all this useful knowledge does not tell us what life is about, how we should live it, and what death entails. We have difficulty enough in coping with day-to-day living. How can we cope with not knowing about the meaning of life and death and how we should live our lives?

What a great relief it is then when someone tells us that they know what life and death are about and how we should live, and that this knowledge is absolutely true and certain. It is so reassuring to know that someone strong and powerful is watching over you and that you do not have to fear death because you will live for ever. A Druze warrior goes into battle fearlessly for he knows that if he dies 'I shall be drinking mother's milk in the morning.' Etaf Aliyan, one of the women active in the Islamic Jihad, was captured by the Israeli police just as she was about to set off on a suicide mission driving a car packed with explosives into Jerusalem. The journalist David Sharrock asked her why she had been prepared to do this. She laughed and said, 'There is a saying of the Prophet Mohammed, blessed be his memory, that through death in the service of others you will come to great good. I would have been singing in my heart at the moment I pressed the trigger, knowing I was going to heaven.'[31]

However, believing in an absolute truth is not without its price. We are constantly presented with evidence that many other people do not share our belief. Dismissing these people as mad or bad does not always work. They may show us by their actions and arguments that other beliefs are possible. This can be an enormous threat to vital parts of our meaning structure, and so we are forced by our fear to do everything we can to shut them up. Such people we see as enemies.

When I was asked to run a workshop for managers from several international companies I expected the participants, who were likely to have a background in science or engineering as well as management, to have a keen appreciation of science and scientific method; some of them, I assumed, would not hold a particular religious belief, and those who did would hold such beliefs as their own private way of making sense of life and would not dream of forcing their opinions on to others.

In our first session I talked about how our physiological make-up means that we can never see reality directly. All that we can ever know are the constructions that we make. One of the participants, a tall man called Luke, quickly identified one of the implications of this. He said, 'Are you saying that there are no absolute truths, only relative ones?'

I replied that there may be absolute truths but we can never be sure. All our meanings are guesses. The other people in the group seemed to have no interest in this issue so I moved on to other matters.

When we broke for coffee I sat at my desk to sort out my worksheets. Luke came and stood over me. His opening words were: 'I am very disturbed by what you said.' He went on to say that he was also very upset that the organizers of the course, of which this workshop was part, had seen fit to invite me; I was quite wrong to say that we could not know absolute truths. He was in possession of the Absolute Truth. He clearly wanted to intimidate me. He talked with such vehemence and was so very angry that I did not try to interrupt him.

Usually when someone with strong religious beliefs raises objections to what I have said I reply that we can hope that our belief is an absolute truth, that we can have faith that our belief is an absolute truth, but to claim that it *is* an absolute truth is to go beyond what the evidence allows us to say. We may be glad when other people share our beliefs; with those who do not we may present arguments to support our beliefs in the hope that these people will see the wisdom of believing what we believe, but to force our beliefs on to other people and to punish and try to silence them is utterly wrong because in doing so we are denying the very nature of our being: we cannot help but have our own way of seeing things. However, with Luke I just waited until he stopped talking and walked away. I felt I was in physical danger.

One rant at me was not enough for Luke. He made some attempts to disrupt the following sessions and he behaved towards me in a discourteous manner. He made a strong complaint about me to the director of the course which, as he showed me with a triumphant look, he believed to be successful. The director, being used to participants making complaints on intellectual or practical grounds, did not grasp the seriousness of the matter. He had what he thought was an interesting theological discussion with Luke. I wondered if he had realized that this was a participant on the course trying to silence one of his lecturers. He later told me that Luke was a 'neo-Calvinist' who believed that 'God is the ultimate objective reality beside which everything is relative'.

Why Luke became so angry in defending a belief held by many more people than neo-Calvinists can be understood in terms of the threat my ideas had posed to his meaning structure, but this was of little comfort to me when I returned to my hotel room later that afternoon and heard on the radio that a nail bomb had exploded in Brick Lane in London. If Luke had been thinking in terms of nail bombs I would have been his target.

Whenever I spend time with someone who adheres absolutely to some absolute belief, even if that person is not threatening me, I begin to feel oppressed and want to escape. When my friend Sandra was telling me about ending her affair with a man who, she discovered, had some paranoid theory about the magical forces which controlled events, she said, 'People with absolute beliefs are like death. They're anti-life.'

Life is about change. People who hold absolute beliefs and want everybody to conform to these beliefs are against change. They do not even allow for the possibility of change. Therefore they have to try to force other people to be what they want them to be. Force always involves some degree of cruelty.

Linda Grant was a journalist who knew a lot of people. When in 1999 NATO began its bombing campaign in defence of the Albanian

Kosovans she looked up her various Serbian connections and through them met many of the Serbs living in London. She wrote,

> Not a single Serb I met spoke of the Albanians in Kosova as if they were anything but an undifferentiated mass, the enemy. Repeatedly, and from some sophisticated people, I heard about 'over-breeding'. The ethnic Albanians and the Serbs may have lived side by side for centuries, but the Albanians are regarded as squatters. The tone many Serbs adopt when they speak of Albanians reminds me of that used by some Israelis towards the Palestinians: that they are backward, alien, that there are too many of them and that they are in the wrong place ... All the men speak repeatedly of the dismemberment of Yugoslavia but only the Serbs continue to call their rump state by that name. They are like those Palestinians known as the Rejectionists, who believe that one day the Israelis will leave or be driven out, and they will get their country back. But they also resemble those Israelis who know – but do not want to admit that they know – what is being committed against the Palestinians in their name.

Would the Serbs ever change and focus on the future, not the past? Linda concluded,

> I grew up from being a child who hated Germans into an adult who had German friends; part of the student generation of the Sixties that had faced the past and moved on from it, sought to construct a new national identity for Germany, built the Green movement, built post-war German pacifism and feminism. I was a child in the land of Rule Britannia, and I'm an adult in a land where there are British who do not obsess over our glorious defeat of the Hun in two world wars, but take their place in the European Community; British who concede that we are no longer a world power but a multi-ethnic state; English people who are allowing the peaceable break-up of their sovereign power. To live in the present or in the future – beyond the bombing: that is the choice the Serbs have to make for themselves.[32]

As Linda showed, people can choose to change. In its history the Catholic Church has not been noted for its tolerance of non-Catholic

points of view, and indeed there are still many Catholics who hold
tenaciously to the belief that they are in exclusive possession of the
one absolute truth; but equally there are many Catholics who have
realized that, if any organization has something of real value to offer
people, then exclusivity and intolerance will hinder rather than help
its work. Like many non-Catholics they know that claiming to be
in possession of the one absolute truth is not so much a sound
philosophical and theological position as a desperate and terrified
whistling in the dark.

A few weeks after my encounter with Luke I went to a family
centre attached to a Catholic girls' school, where I had been invited
to be one of the speakers at the centre's annual general meeting.
The other speaker was the director of family services in the local
council where, as he explained, the previously separate government
departments of health, education and social services had been
meshed together so as to provide a comprehensive service for children. In his talk he described how the tradition had always been
that the child had to fit into the existing services' structure, and no
account was taken of the needs of the individual child. Now the
child was at the centre of the coordinated services, and every service
provider was committed to listening to the child.

It was easy for me to follow on from what the director had said.
I began by describing how, in the traditional ways of organizing
society and the family, children who did not fit into the existing
systems were shown unequivocally that they were bad. My remi-
niscences about this, I could see, rang bells for many people in the
audience. Then I went on to talk about how children and adults
alike cannot help but have their own way of seeing things. I spoke
about our physiological make-up which means that we all have our
own individual interpretations of the world. I was well aware that
there would be a number of people present who, like Luke, would
see the implications this had for relative and absolute truths, but
no one interrupted me, and at the end of my talk I received considerable praise and applause.

Of course my audience might simply have been polite, but my
doubt on this score was dispelled when Sister Mary, who had organized the meeting, said to me, 'I really would like you to talk to our
sixth-form girls. I'm a biologist, and I think it would be very good
if you could talk to the girls about what you've talked about this

evening.' I said, 'Are you sure?' 'Oh yes,' she said and, turning to the Reverend Mother, asked her, 'Don't you agree?' The Reverend Mother did.

During the years that I worked in the National Health Service I spent much of my time listening to people who were severely depressed. What came out time and time again were the fears left over from their religious upbringing: they had been told that, on pain of death or hell, they had to believe in the absolute beliefs of their family's religion. They had been given no choice. Whether their fear was that of Protestant guilt for failing to maintain the absolute standards of the Calvinist conscience or whether it was the fear of failing to please an awesome, demanding, jealous God, it was the fear we feel when we know that we are the prey of something all-powerful and inescapable. This is the kind of fear which cruelty creates.

The cruelty perpetrated by the holders of absolute beliefs ranges from the monstrous to the petty. Human history is the history of wars and conflicts, and almost without exception these have involved clashes between two groups holding different absolute beliefs, or the destruction by one group holding absolute beliefs of those who did not share those beliefs. Of course, the claim for the rightness and virtue of the absolute beliefs held by one warring group was often a cover for the attempt to satisfy the group's envy and greed, but any group or individual claiming great virtue in contrast to wicked enemies is mistaken. No one is ever that good. Whatever our background and beliefs, we all have much the same failings and virtues.

Many of those who hold absolute beliefs would respond with horror to the gross cruelties of murder, rape and torture, but they see nothing inhumane in the petty cruelties which are committed in the name of such beliefs.

To the untrained eye, Northern Ireland, in 1999 and two years into the ceasefire, looked very much like an English county. The army presence which was everywhere during the Troubles was reduced to a few command posts. Police stations were still behind defensive walls, but suburban gardens were tended, streets swept clean, and each town of any size had its inner ringroad enclosing the old market place, now a shopping precinct. Only the shops showed how poor Northern Ireland was in contrast to England. Each mall had shops from the major chain stores, but they were 'down-market' ones which provided for people who had little money. Woolworths was well represented but not the major department stores or the more select supermarkets. Nor were there any expensive little dress shops with the latest fashions. Many of the big firms were still not prepared to invest in a place where the peace had not been secured.

Shopping is for many people an enormous pleasure. My friend Anna Raeburn said she could shop for England, but she is only one of thousands who could make this claim. To be deprived of this pleasure in what could be a wealthy country is cruel. Another enormous pleasure which became extremely popular in England in the 1980s was 'going out for a meal'. Sometimes it was a matter of 'going for a Chinese' or 'going for an Indian', or sometimes it was trying out a new restaurant which someone had recommended.

After our encounter at Drumcree Anthony and I drove to Armagh. First we went to the top of the big hill in the centre of Armagh, past the great grey mass of the Catholic cathedral. Then we drove down to the city centre below the cathedral and parked the car. It was early afternoon and we were hungry.

The sun was shining on the paved open space that had once been the market place. Had this been a country town in almost any other part of Europe there would have been a hustle and bustle of people. There would have been delicatessens and greengrocers selling produce from all over the world, clothes shops, souvenir shops, craft shops, bakeries, restaurants, cafés and bars with chairs and tables spilling out into the square, trees, shrubs, hanging baskets of flowers, benches, ice-cream vendors, musicians, entertainers – altogether a delightful place in which to spend an hour or two. The square in Armagh was bare. The few shops, all of which sold cheap goods, were locked and shuttered. Had this been an English or Australian town Anthony and I would have been hard pressed to decide, out of more than a dozen choices, where and what we wanted to eat. As it was we had to ask a passer-by if there was any café open. Only one, we were told – a little place tucked away behind a wall, where we sat at a rickety table for a toasted sandwich and a cup of tea.

I said to Anthony that I had noticed on our drive that there was not even a Little Chef, one of the chains of drive-in restaurants that are part of the landscape of the English towns and countryside.

'Ah, yes,' said Anthony, 'but if you wanted to open a Little Chef, you'd have to decide whether it was a Catholic Little Chef or a Protestant Little Chef, and what sort of flag you'd have flying over it.'

When we are so busy focusing on our enemy we do not always see how we deprive and harm ourselves. When I lived in Sydney and wanted to go to the beach I could consider a vast range of options from Cronulla in the south of Sydney to Palm Beach in the north. I would decide in terms of the prevailing winds and the likelihood of crowds. The north-west coast of Northern Ireland and County Donegal is magnificent, but the choice for people in Northern Ireland was limited: the Protestants went to the Antrim coast, the Catholics to County Donegal.

The harm we do to ourselves is often caused by the fact that we treat our enemy as an object, not as a person. In so doing, we come to treat ourselves as an object. When we deprive ourselves of a pleasure or comfort we split ourselves in two and become the punisher and the punished – even, if our conscience is implacable, the predator and the prey. Whenever we create these artificial splits in our meaning structure we weaken ourselves, and then in response to this weakness we become even more frightened of our enemy.

Once we become well trained in punishing ourselves we have no difficulty in punishing those people who, in kinder circumstances, we would try to help. When I was in Beirut in 1998 I read an article in the *Daily Star* about the way in which disabled people were commonly treated in Lebanon. One woman, Sylvana Laqis, was quoted as saying, 'People don't believe that we are citizens. They discriminate against us in all aspects. How can I make them believe that we are humans too?'

Warren Singh-Bartlett, the author of the article, wrote,

In Lebanon the disabled are mostly the responsibility of their families. Shut away when they could lead productive lives, the handicapped stagnate. They are victims of shame, superstition and ignorance. The UN believes that up to ten per cent of the population is disabled, many as a result of the war. The Lebanese Sitting Disabled Association estimates a slightly lower figure of seven per cent. Either way, these figures represent a significant swathe of the population, certainly a big enough percentage to make the current situation unacceptable . . . In the past the disabled were believed to be devils, punished by God. Amazingly, attitudes haven't changed that much. The modern approach, propagated by religious organizations, is that the disabled bear the burden of our sins and are therefore to be pitied. It's the punishment metaphor again, but this time the handicapped are the victims.[33]

When I first worked as a psychologist in Australia in the 1960s and then in England in the 1970s disabled people were treated as they are still treated in Lebanon. Justifications from religion were not overtly used because it was taken for granted that handicapped people were not fully human. It is not difficult to punish people when we see them as objects. This is very easy to do when we hold absolute beliefs because, when we do so, we are denying that other people inevitably have their own way of seeing things. Thus we deny other people's humanity, and we have no difficulty in treating them inhumanely.

The untoward death of another person can remind us not only of our own humanity but of the humanity of those with whom we disagree. Such a death always points to our own impending death. This may merely frighten us, or it may remind us of the preciousness of life and show us how trivial our concerns and disagreements are. When we come together to mourn we can be at our most truly human. The bomb which exploded in Omagh in August 1998 was a terrible event, not just because so many were killed and injured but because most people had come to hope that there would be no more such atrocities in Northern Ireland. Not long after, the *Weekly Telegraph*, which advertises itself as 'Britain's Global Newspaper' and is sold all around the world, carried the following story.

David Trimble, Northern Ireland's first minister, faced censure by the Orange Order for breaching its code by attending the Roman Catholic funeral Mass for three children killed in the Omagh bomb. Mr Trimble and Dennis Rogan, the Ulster Unionist chairman – both Orangemen – travelled to the Irish Republic for the service at St Mary's Church in Buncrana, Co Donegal, in memory of Sean McLaughlin and James Barker, both 12, and Oran Doherty, eight. Gerry Adams, the Sinn Fein leader, and Mary McAleese, the Irish president, also attended.

A condition of Orange Order membership is that 'you should

not countenance by your presence or otherwise any act or ceremony of Popish worship.'

It was understood that a formal complaint against Mr Rogan has already been made by members of his Orange lodge in Belfast. Mr Trimble, whose lodge is in Bangor, Co Down, has also been heavily criticised at Orange meetings.[34]

The only time I saw my Auntie Jessie cry was when she came to tell my parents that her youngest son had married a Catholic girl 'behind the altar' – an expression of horror from Protestant paranoid fears about the Catholic Church. I also remember the wedding of another cousin in a Presbyterian church where the Catholic members of the bride's family stood around the churchyard while the service was conducted inside. Fortunately for them, the Pope's injunction against setting foot in a Protestant church did not run as far as the reception.

I wonder how many of the Protestants and Catholics who obeyed such orders asked themselves, 'Why am I doing this?' The holding of absolute beliefs can seriously inhibit our ability to be self-aware.

On a flight from Belfast to London in 1999 I got into a conversation with a man who told me that he had been brought up as a Protestant in Northern Ireland but had spent much of his working life in South Africa. We talked about President Mandela's retirement. This man told me, 'The best man to succeed Mandela would be Buthelezi. He could unite the Zulus, and they are the best of the blacks.' In a continent which has produced many shady characters Buthelezi was one of the shadiest, and he did not share Mandela's passion for compromise. I then asked my companion how he saw the changes in South Africa. He said, 'The person who did the most for South Africa and set it on the right path was P. W. Botha. He did much more than de Klerk, but de Klerk takes the credit.' P. W. Botha believed in the absolute truth of apartheid. As I write this in July 1999 the Truth and Reconciliation Commission announced that P. W. Botha was implicated in the killing of eight young anti-apartheid activists blown up by booby-trapped hand grenades fourteen years ago. P. W. Botha was already likely to be prosecuted for his involvement in the murder by apartheid security forces of Matthew Goniwe, an anti-apartheid activist, and three of his colleagues.[35] You can take the boy out of Northern Ireland but you can't take Northern Ireland out of the boy.

The lack of awareness that comes from the holding of absolute beliefs makes it easy for people to lie to themselves and to dissemble by using a dishonest form of language. A woman interviewed in a television programme about the whites in South Africa said, 'My husband would have a heart attack if my son wanted to marry a black, or even a coloured. We're traditionalists, not racists.'[36]

In the early 1980s, when I was writing *Living with the Bomb: Can We Live Without Enemies?*, I was invited to a theological college to talk to the students about depression. These were the years when it seemed that the horrors of the apartheid regime in South Africa would never come to an end. During the discussion after my talk I mentioned how depression was universal, found in all races and in all recorded history. One of the students, a white cleric from South Africa, queried this. He said that it was well known that the Bantu people never got depressed. Black people, he explained to me, were not affected in that way. I replied that I thought this could not be the case, and I quoted research in transcultural psychiatry to support this. I went on to talk about the work of a friend of mine who in Kenya studied the incidence of depression in black women and the relationship between leprosy and depression. If blacks in Kenya got depressed I could not believe that blacks in South Africa did not. All through this the student regarded me seriously and nodded.

A year later I returned to the college to talk to the students about counselling depressed people. The student from South Africa was in the group and towards the end of the session he asked me the same question – did I not know that the Bantu were impervious to depression, that they were a happy-go-lucky people, unaffected by the kind of things which affect white people in South Africa and cause them to become depressed? I was astounded. This man had spent over a year in a theological college whose teaching emphasized pastoral care and a compassionate awareness of human suffering, yet he still believed that black people did not feel pain in the way that white people did. I said very shortly, 'Well, in the pictures I've seen of them standing beside their bulldozed houses they don't look very happy,' and then went on again to give him the results from transcultural studies which show the universality of depression.

At the end of the session he came up to thank me for an interesting talk and to say goodbye. He was returning to South Africa to take up his ministry. As I drove home I wondered whether I should have taken refuge in facts rather than make him look at the reality of the situation: that he had given his allegiance to and received the blessing from a church whose founder taught that, while suffering is universal, so is God's love. If he acknowledged that black people suffered in the way that white people do, then he could not return to South Africa and accept the way of life there. He would not be able to minister to a white congregation and ignore what was happening to the blacks. He would be forced into dangerous action or anguished impotence and, in either case, isolation.[37]

When I wrote about this man I concluded that his self-deceit was a defence against despair. So it was, but now I would add that it was one of those defences created by primitive pride.

Primitive pride not only defends. It helps us to choose our leaders.

The Leaders We Deserve

Despite the ancient Greeks, the idea of democracy came late to human history. The basic idea of democracy – that we are all equal and free to choose one of our number to act as leader – runs counter to our desire to remain as children looked after by a parent who is all-wise, all-good and all-powerful. With such a parent, so primitive pride would have us believe, we would never encounter threats to our meaning structure; if such a threat ever loomed on the horizon, our powerful parent would deal with it.

We have a choice. We can see our leader as one of us, or we can see our leader as our parent. Leaders have a choice. They can portray themselves as parents with special powers or as one of us, perhaps with some special skills and knowledge, but with no special powers. Leaders as parents may be attacked and overthrown by their subjects when they fail to deliver what their subjects want, but before then they may enjoy enormous power and delicious privileges. Leaders who are one of us have a much less happy time. Many of their subjects will still insist on seeing them as parent-leaders with special powers, and when they fail to deliver what these subjects want they will be attacked and rejected. A leader who is truly one of us has all the pain and none of the pleasure of being a parent-leader. No wonder such leaders are so rare!

It is only very recently in our history that leaders in democracies have portrayed themselves as ordinary people just like those they represent. Franklin Roosevelt shocked and largely delighted Americans when in 1934 he instituted his radio fireside chats as a means of winning voters over to his New Deal programme, thus circumventing a Congress which was likely to obstruct his plans. He would begin his fireside chats with 'My friends,' and when he was campaigning he would add, 'You and I both know,' thus convincing most of his listeners that they shared his insights and opinions. Even so, Roosevelt lived like a prince, wealthy, exclusive, impervious to the demands of marital fidelity. As newsreels and later television show, British political leaders continued to talk down to their constituents, patronizing them in the tones of a sententious parent or schoolteacher. Tony Blair cultivated the tone of 'I'm an ordinary bloke trying to do the best I can for you', which came as a pleasant change from Margaret Thatcher's bullying and John Major's whining complaints about our unsatisfactory behaviour, but those of us who had watched Margaret Thatcher's image progress from the sensible, realistic, busy housewife to the regal figurehead rivalling the Queen waited to see if Blair would be seduced by the pleasures of power.

Lord Acton's observation that power tends to corrupt and absolute power corrupts absolutely is often quoted without any explanation of why this is so. The implication of the statement is simply that people are intrinsically wicked and the more power they have the wickeder they tend to be. Intrinsic wickedness is a catch-all explanation which does not advance our understanding. However, if we look at the use and misuse of power in terms of the efforts we make to maintain the integrity of our meaning structure we can see why some people are seduced by power and others are not.

Power is not a thing which a person can own, but a relationship between that person and other people. If other people see you as being powerful you are powerful; if they do not, you are not. Someone who claims to be powerful, in the absence of anyone supporting that claim, is deemed to be deluded.

Anyone who is seen to be powerful has to decide whether he is actually capable of doing what his supporters believe he can do. This is an act of reality-testing, something we all should be doing for most of the time – that is, seeing whether our meaning structure is as accurate as possible a picture of what is going on. Reality-testing is not a popular pastime because it often throws into doubt important parts of our meaning structure. This seems much more secure when we think of ourselves as intelligent, creative, competent and successful, but reality-testing can show us that we are simply lucky. If we always bear in mind that we actually have little control over what goes on in the world and that things happen by chance we will not believe what our flattering supporters tell us, and thus we will not come to believe that we possess some special quality called power. If, on the other hand, we are unable to accept discrepancies between our meaning structure and what is actually going on but prefer to resort to the services of primitive pride to hold our meaning structure together, we will indeed be corrupted by power. Part of this corruption is the inability to tell the truth either to ourselves or to other people.

Tony Blair always tried to give the appearance of telling the truth, and I think he had the wit to know that many people always take phrases like 'I'll be perfectly frank with you' as the preamble to a lie. However, the test of how truthful a politician is trying to be is to what degree he will publicly admit that there are many problems which do not allow any satisfactory solution. In 1941, when the propaganda machine of Britain and the Empire was assuring the populace that they were fighting a noble war, George Orwell wrote, 'The choice before human beings is not, as a rule, between good and evil but between two evils. You can let the Nazis rule the world; that is evil; or you can overthrow them by war, which is also evil. There is no other choice before you, and which ever you choose you will not come out with clean hands.'[38]

Choosing which of two outcomes is the lesser evil is a great responsibility, and this is a responsibility which few people are willing to undertake. They prefer to place all the blame for the situation on their enemies and let their leader decide what to do. Not all leaders are prepared to accept the responsibility of choosing between two evils. Most prefer to claim that there is a perfect solution – that is, one that benefits them – while blaming their enemies for causing the problem and preventing its solution. Often the perfect solution is one where some outside power comes to save them. This outside power might be God, or the United Nations, or the USA. Alas, all too often God is otherwise engaged, the United Nations is disunited, and the USA will come only if you have oil reserves.

Choosing to see the leader as a parent rather than as an equal has many advantages. It is an effective way of avoiding responsibility. Being responsible is very difficult. You have to make an effort to find out what is actually going on. It often means that you have to recognize that you are on your own. Both these activities can be tremendous threats to your meaning structure. Handing responsibility over to a leader means that you will not be blamed when things go wrong.

The belief in the great parent who can 'kiss it better' is passionately held by many people. Nowadays every therapist has an armoury of ideas and practices which can help people to sort out their distress and go on to live much happier lives, but, whatever each armoury contains, the effectiveness of each depends on the preparedness of the clients to take responsibility for themselves. Many people refuse to do so, and go on living miserable lives, waiting for the good fairy to wave a magic wand, or for the therapist to say the magic word to make their pain vanish and enable them to live happily ever after.

Unscrupulous therapists are likely to present themselves as the good fairy/magic therapist, and never tell clients that the first step towards real change is to take responsibility for themselves. Some of these therapists go on to become very rich, with thousands of gullible followers who get endless enjoyment from talking about the state of their psyche or their soul, and about how special they are because they are in touch with a therapist who has such special powers. These therapists are not very different from many parent-leaders who claim limitless powers and whose followers believe them. In Shiite Islam it is the custom to follow a religious exemplar known as the *faqih* who 'is chosen for his ability to master and fathom the word of God . . . Entrusting religious authority to someone in Shiite Islam entails giving that person the power to determine every religious aspect of life, from details as basic as how to pray, to contemporary moral issues such as test-tube babies.'[39]

Hezbollah's leader Sayyed Hassan Nasrallah described the central role of the *faqih* in Shiite Islam.

We must obey the *Wali al-Faqih*, disagreement with him is not permitted. The guardianship of the *faqih* is like the guardianship of the Prophet Mohammed and of the infallible Imam. Just as the guardianship of the Prophet and the infallible Imam is obligatory, so is the guardianship of the *faqih* ... His wisdom derives from God and the family of the Prophet, and he approaches the divine ... When the *Wali al-Faqih* orders someone to obey and that person disobeys, that is insubordination against the Imam. When the *faqih* orders someone to be obeyed, such obedience is obligatory.[40]

Such obedience might at times seem onerous, but the return on obeying parents is that they protect you. They also let you share in their glory. Parent-leaders are always the embodiment of that version of the history of the group which shows the group in the best light. They are always heroes or heroines in the group's history, just as a child's life story depicts his parents and grandparents as heroes and heroines. When children are unable to depict their parents in this way they feel deprived.

Children always want their parents to tell them how much they love them. Wise parents always do. So do cunning parent-leaders. On the eighth anniversary of the Gulf War Saddam Hussein addressed his people thus:

Peace upon and with you, the people of Iraq, with its men and lofty women, from the comrades of President Saddam Hussein in the leadership and from your brother and son of your people: Saddam Hussein, who is afflicted with love for you – a disease without which no official in the nation can have good health. It is the disease I was accused of having by some Arab officials, who said that Saddam Hussein suffers from the Arab street disease. They thought this was an insult to Saddam Hussein. However, brothers, it is a fact. It gives honour that our disease is love for the sons of our nation in the streets, cities, villages, factories, houses of education and culture, poor alleys and quarters, and rural areas. We hoped this disease would afflict the Arab officials concerned, instead of the disease of loving Zionism and the United States, caving in to them, carrying out their orders and responding to their plans at the expense of the security of the Arabs, their causes and higher interests. God is great, and long live the disease of loving the people and the nation.[41]

No British prime minister, and certainly not the Queen, would address the nation in such a flowery way, but each prime minister, and the Queen and Prince Charles, as well as American presidents and Australian prime ministers, take great pains to be shown enjoying and appreciating what their people enjoy and appreciate. The idea of sharing enjoyment and appreciation with the people carries with it the implication of loving the people, even though the reality of the situation might be very different.

However, no matter how certain people might be of their parent-leader's love, the fact that they see their leader as being powerful means that they know that he is dangerous. Children who love their parents and adults who love their leader might obey with utter willingness and thus have no fear of punishment, but even they fear their parents or their parent-leader because, if he is powerful enough to protect and save them, he is powerful enough to harm them. People who see their therapists as having the power to make them better can also fear that the therapist will use that power to take away, say, their most cherished religious belief.

If we see our leaders as being people like ourselves, without any special access to special powers and absolute truths, then, when we feel frightened of them and what they might do, we can assess our fear realistically. Are we imputing to our leader some magical, imaginary power or does he in fact have the privileges of power – a police force, an army, the legal right to make laws, the temerity to break them – which he can use against us? If we think we are seeing magical powers then we need to take ourselves to task for being so silly. If it is the privileges of real power then we need to work out how best to protect ourselves. However, if we see our leader as our parent we can be in danger of falling into one of the traps such leaders set for their followers.

Parent-leaders always present themselves to their followers as having magical powers and access to absolute truths. Some do this in a very obvious way and some more subtly. The Queen might have her sceptre and orb as symbols of her magical powers and her direct access to God as head of the Church of England, but Margaret Thatcher could convey her access to absolute truth simply by appearing always to know best. Such leaders recognize that, much as their followers want to be protected, they will fear that their leader will use his power against them. To prevent this fear from turning into anger against a leader who might misuse his power, the leader defines the fear as itself a virtue. The fear of the parent-leader, like a child's fear of the parent, makes the person humble, and humble is what a subject and a child should be. When Dusan was trying to explain to me the role of icons in Serbian Orthodox religion he said, 'If you are not afraid of God it is something very bad. If you are not afraid of God you are too proud, too arrogant. You have to be afraid of God, you have to be aware that there is something above your own ego. You have to stand under what He has done.'

People who believe that they are being virtuous when they fear their parent-leader are likely to accept whatever their leader does, especially when they benefit from such actions. They will feel that they are acting virtuously when they attack or profit from an attack on the enemy. A political science professor, Wolfgang Dressen, with great difficulty managed to gain access to the basement of the Cologne tax office, where he found 60,000 files, a complete record of how the region's Jews were robbed during the Holocaust and what happened to the loot. He said, 'German thoroughness means every detail is recorded. And this is just Cologne. Such files are lodged with the local tax authorities all over Germany.'

The *Guardian* reported,

A bailiff's record from the small town of Hennef shows that an auction of 287 items to neighbours of deported Jews yielded 3,492 marks on September 7, 1942. Five pillowslips went to Schumacher for four marks, one bucket to Beielschmidt for one mark, one sewing machine to Schmitz for 30 marks, and so on, exhaustively. 'These files show that literally everyone was involved and knew what was going on,' said Professor Dressen. 'These were free auctions. Nobody forced you to buy a sack of onions or the complete works of Tchaikovsky.' A Cologne city orphanage bought up bedding and children's clothing from a Jewish orphanage which was closed down. City hospitals run by Roman Catholic and Lutheran Churches purchased bedding and furniture that came from Jewish hospitals. The law faculty acquired book collections. The proceeds went to the Nazi state.[42]

Subjects who share the profits of the parent-leader's actions are much less likely to rebel. They are much less likely to speak out against the parent-leader lest they implicate themselves in the guilt. After the Second World War remarkably few Germans admitted that they knew about the concentration camps and Hitler's Final Solution. No wonder these financial records were kept well hidden!

Parent-leaders adopt many of the tactics which less than adequate parents adopt in dealing with their children. They buy their children's silence with gifts and money. Many adult children will not speak ill of their parents lest they be cut out of the will. Some parents fear that their children will band together to oppose them, so to prevent this they exploit sibling rivalry. One woman, Candice, told me how her mother had ensured that Candice and her sister were rivals in everything. This meant that when they were grown women they could not be in the same room without having a spat. When the mother died all that she possessed had to be divided between the two sisters. Both women realized that this could be their biggest fight ever. When Candice put forward a plan, derived from some work she had done on conflict resolution, to decide who should have what in the family home, her sister accepted it. In carrying out the plan they became friendly, and on its successful completion they felt triumphant. It was a victory over their mother, but also a recognition of loss, of all the long years when they could have been friends.

Fostering sibling rivalries has always been the practice of parent-leaders. The principle that underlay the success of the British Empire was 'Divide and rule'. By fostering the rivalries between Muslims and Hindus the British ensured that when they left their territory would not be united but divided into India and Pakistan, that the process of division would be accompanied by a vast amount of murder and suffering, and that the rivalry between India and Pakistan would lead to continuing conflict in Kashmir and, in 1999, to the two governments issuing nuclear threats to each other. The rivalry fostered by Stalin, himself a Georgian, between the Caucasian groups of the Muslim Ingush and Chechens and the Orthodox Ossetians became unrestrained when the USSR collapsed into separate states. When Russia intervened in Chechnya a costly war followed. In 1999 Alexander Lebed, President Yeltsin's former security adviser who negotiated the withdrawal of Russian troops from Chechnya, said that he expected a 'conflagration' to ignite the region.[43]

According to Misha Glenny, a journalist who knew the Balkans well,

> Milosovic's capacity to identify weakness and play two parties off against one another is surely unparalleled in modern history. He is able to deploy this tactic, essentially a policy of divide and rule, in any situation because he is not bound by personal or ideological scruples – he has no final goal (beyond maintaining power in Serbia) and hence no strategy, only tactics. This affords him enormous political flexibility. Milosovic has not been cleansing Kosova because he considers Albanians inferior; he is doing it because he believes it will bring him political rewards of some nature.[44]

The Serbs, so I was told by Serbs, while presenting themselves to the world as a noble nation united against their cruel enemies, invariably fight among themselves. Apparently Milošovic in political life applied to those who opposed him the tactics he learned as a boy in dealing with his family.

Fostering rivalries has more advantages than merely keeping the parent-leader in power. The acting out of rivalries causes crises, and crises, no matter what they are, help to keep the parent-leader in power, for is it not the task of the parent-leader to protect his subjects? In democracies the party in power will, at every crisis, point out that the opposition party, if in power, would be unable to deal with the crisis. 'The whole aim of practical politics,' said H. L. Mencken, 'is to keep the populace alarmed – and hence clamorous to be led to safety – by menacing it with an endless series of hobgoblins, all of them imaginary.'[45] This is very likely to happen in a group where the group's religion teaches that suffering is a virtue and pleasure a vice. Protestantism has always taught that, as Malcolm Fraser when Prime Minister of Australia said, 'We were not put on this earth to enjoy ourselves.' Pope John Paul II wrote,

> What we express with the word suffering seems to be particularly essential to the nature of Man. Sharing the sufferings of Christ is, at the same time, suffering for the Kingdom of God. In the just eyes of God, before this justice, those who share in Christ's sufferings become worthy of his Kingdom. Through their sufferings they, in

a sense, pay back the boundless price of our redemption. Suffering contains, as it were, an appeal to Man's moral greatness and spiritual maturity.[46]

Enemies are necessary because they are a continual source of crises. They bring the group together behind the parent-leader. A crisis will distract the attention of the populace, so that they do not notice the nefarious actions of their parent-leader. A crisis offers the leader and the led the chance to resort to the high moral ground and martyrdom. George Orwell commented, 'Whereas socialism and even capitalism in a more grudging way, have said to people, "I offer you a good time," Hitler has said to them, "I offer you struggle, danger and death," and as a result a whole nation flings its self at his feet.'[47]

A crisis will enable a parent-leader, while claiming to be fighting to defend the rule of law, to break the law. In 1998 the United Nations Human Rights Commission published a report into allegations of abuse of defence lawyers by the Royal Ulster Constabulary officers in Northern Ireland's 'holding centres'. The UN special rapporteur on the independence of judges and lawyers, Param Cumaraswamy, said, 'There is no doubt that there was harassment and intimidation of the lawyers.' Eamonn McMenamin of the firm of solicitors Madden and Finucane said, 'Our clients are regularly told [by RUC officers] their solicitor is a top IRA man, and the officers say, "Your solicitor will end up like Pat Finucane and so will you."'[48]

Pat Finucane was targeted by the Ulster Freedom Fighters because his clients were Republicans and he was believed to be close to Gerry Adams. When he was having supper with his family on Sunday evening, 12 February 1989, UFF gunmen smashed down his door with sledgehammers and shot him fourteen times, leaving him bleeding to death on the kitchen floor with his wife wounded and his children in a state of terror.[49]

To illustrate the point further I could select from a long list of examples of IRA attacks against Loyalists as cruel and inhumane as that of the UFF murder of Pat Finucane. Critics of such violence often condemn it with the phrase 'mindless violence', as if the gunmen are no different from the cartoon figures in computer games like *Doom* who do nothing but kill. Yet the gunmen and their leaders in whatever conflict are thinking and making in their own individual ways interpretations of what is happening, and violence and torture are often the outcomes of such interpretations.

The Meaning of Violence

Violence is a means of communication, a language whose aim is to silence the enemy. Those who are violent are trying to impose their set of meanings on the world and, in doing so, feel that they must silence anyone who through word, deed or mere existence challenges that set of meanings. Violence can seek to silence the enemy through pain or the threat of pain, or it can seek to silence the enemy through exile or through death. A man might seek to silence a woman by raising his hand to her. A group might seek to silence any enemies by expelling them from the territory which the group claims as its own or by killing them.

We assert our individuality and maintain the integrity of our meaning structure through speech. To be silenced by whatever means is a tremendous threat to our meaning structure, and so we have to resist. This is why certain leaders have tried to expel or exterminate the enemy completely. If the leader fails to do this resistance must and will continue. People will fight to the death against enemies who want to impose their ideas and practices on them because they believe, as we all do, that it is better to give up your body than to cease to be the person that you know yourself to be.

Down the centuries when Britain tried to defeat the Irish millions of Irish died and millions went into exile. Yet the British never succeeded in ridding Ireland of the Irish, and, as Kevin Toolis wrote, 'Rebellion and republicanism were in the blood of this defeated people.'[50]

He went on,

All the troops, the barracks, the fortifications, the billions of pounds spent on security, the informers, the intelligence networks of Special Branch, Scotland Yard's Anti-Terrorist Branch, Britain's domestic intelligence service, MI5, and the world's best equipped anti-terrorist defence force, the Royal Ulster Constabulary, failed to destroy the

IRA or mitigate its ambition of forcibly bringing into being a United Ireland. The Republican credo has exhausted the will, the bribes, the threats and the retributions of countless Crown rulers. It has endured the twenty-five years of military occupation by British soldiers, the never-ending procession of its own black-bereted coffins, the cruelties inflicted on its own Volunteers, the hundreds and thousands of lost prison years of its sons and daughters, the stalemates, the setbacks, the grinding poverty. It cannot be bargained with, bought, sold, traded, appeased, cajoled, repressed, diverted, destroyed or rationalized away by economic argument. It is ultimately an ideal, a religion, and its supporters will not stop until they achieve that goal. In a world of broken ideologies Irish Republicanism is the last great political passion in Europe.[51]

The history of Ireland is but one example of what Don Foster, professor of psychology at the University of Cape Town, called 'the dialogue of violence', where each act of violence produces its retribution. The struggle against apartheid was another example. In this dialogue between two enemies one side acts and the other side responds. A response at the same level is often felt to be inadequate. The need to assert one's existence as a person is felt in proportion to the threat that has been made to it, and so the other side responds with greater violence, to which the first side, now threatened, must respond with even more violence. However, as Don Foster pointed out,

Dialogical relations do not have predictable, inevitable outcomes. There are unintended consequences. Dialogical relations are also beset with contradictions. For example, political detention [in the 1980s] was a 'reply' to widespread protests, an attempt to destroy political organizations. It produced, however, unintended consequences: a local 'reply' in the form of further grassroots protests and mobilization (a deepening of political resistance) and a loss for the state of international legitimacy. In this particular instance the state 'replied' again with alternative repressive measures, i.e. restriction orders, in an effort to avoid further loss of legitimacy. However, it could have 'replied' by increasing levels of state violence.[52]

The violence of murder does not always achieve its aim of silencing the vanquished, as long as there are some of the vanquished alive to tell the tale. Telling the tale in story and song has been the means whereby the descendants of the vanquished have maintained their pride in their identity, weaving stories of their ancestors' suffering and courage into their own life stories. As oral histories began to be matched by written and recorded histories more of the vanquished survive in memory to challenge the victors. Moreover, the mass murders which occurred in the Bosnian and other recent wars extended the records of events through the skills of the forensic anthropologists. 'You can murder your enemies, but you cannot hide the bodies or the manner of their death. In those scraps and fragments in the pit reside narratives that can be decoded and can ultimately condemn through blindfolds and bound hands. How bodies fell. How they were murdered.' Clive Snow, a forensic anthropologist working in Bosnia, said, '"Bones are often our last best witness: they never lie, and they never forget."'[53]

Whenever we enter into a dialogue, be it a conversation or a violent exchange, we need to justify our actions. Not to be able to do so weakens our position with respect to the other participants and thus undermines our sense of security. Here primitive pride comes to the rescue, especially when we have not acted with the highest of motives.

Greed and envy are not the highest motives, especially if they have been given an unfair advantage in their expression. When one group takes over the land and possessions of another they have to denigrate the group from whom they have stolen in order to defend themselves against the guilt they would feel if they recognized the injury they have done to other human beings. Thus white Australians have felt impelled to denigrate Aboriginal people. The Protestant Unionists must denigrate the Catholics rather than acknowledge that they themselves are enjoying the fruits of the spoils their ancestors took from the Catholics.

Verbal abuse is a form of violence, but it is a form which invites a more violent response because a reasonable protest against it can be turned into further abuse, thus increasing the feeling of hurt and the need to retaliate. Women who protest about the sexual jokes and innuendoes made by a man are often told by their abuser that they are 'too politically correct' and 'can't take a joke'. If ever I protested to my mother and sister about the hurtful things they said about me they would tell me that I was silly to be so sensitive. Ruth Dudley Edwards gave an interesting example of denying a reasonable complaint about verbal abuse in her book *The Faithful Tribe*, sub-titled *An Intimate Portrait of the Loyal Institutions*.

Two pejorative terms used by Protestants about Catholics in Northern Ireland are 'Fenian' and 'croppy', the latter being closely associated with the Loyalist marching song *Croppies Lie Down*, which celebrates the defeat of the Irish at the Battle of the Boyne. I remember how in the 1960s blacks would try to explain why they found the term 'nigger' offensive, and in the 1970s women would try to explain why they found the term 'ladies' offensive, and how racists and sexist males would respond with bland incomprehension and tell the complainant not to be so silly. I do not know how often Catholics have tried to explain to Protestants why 'croppy' is offensive, but I have met a number of Catholics who are pained by its use against them. Ruth Dudley Edwards gave the bland response to such complaints a further twist. She denied that she had ever heard an Orangeman use the word 'croppy' but only the word 'Fenian' and went on,

> These days, republicans use the word cleverly: when nationalists suffer a negotiating setback or a contentious parade is approved, a republican spokesman will announce that unionists/Orangemen can no longer make croppies lie down, thus pressing a Catholic tribal button. No decent unionist uses the term publicly, but to them, like 'Fenian', it denotes those who wish to destroy the state. Between republican and loyalist riff-raff, however, it is kept in currency. Thus, when some of the dregs of loyalism produced a banner on the Drumcree frontline in July 1998 reading 'croppies lie down', it was a propaganda gift for Sinn Fein.[54]

Here Ruth Dudley Edwards is not only telling the Catholics not to be silly; she is also resorting to a theme which plays a large part in the dialogue of violence, the denial of responsibility. When one side says to the other, 'You've done something wrong,' the side charged can deny responsibility with, 'No, I didn't.' If that fails and the side charged has been clearly seen to have behaved outrageously, the denial can be, 'Unruly elements in our group are responsible.'

Ruth Dudley Edwards would have us believe that the Orangemen leaders who could reprimand David Trimble and impose the discipline of marching on their members could not order the 'dregs of Loyalism' to take down a banner which was offensive to Catholics. But then truth and reason play very little part in the justification of violence.

Those who use violence always want to justify it to themselves and to other people. The nobility of a cause is often claimed as a reason for violence. When the conflict comes to an end the nobility of defending one's people from the enemy can be reworked as an excuse for violence in the peace. The end of the apartheid era brought terrible violence to South Africa. Millions of people could not get work, there was no unemployment benefit, and a generation had grown up educated only in ways of living dangerously. Many young black men used their skills as anti-apartheid activists to attack the police and those with whom they did not agree, to steal, and sometimes rape and murder. Monique Marks, a researcher at the Centre for the Study of Violence and Reconciliation in Johannesburg, talked to a group of young men in Diepkloof in Soweto in order to discover how they justified violence in peacetime.

In 1985 the ANC in exile had called on black youth to 'make the country ungovernable'. Black youth, the victims of much brutality and murder perpetrated by the forces of the apartheid regime, responded enthusiastically. In 1990, because it had entered into negotiations with President de Klerk, the ANC called for an end to the armed struggle. Three years on, with the ANC on the verge of power, when Monique Marks carried out her study, these young men still saw violence as the best strategy for political change. The blame for what one young man, Lumkile, called 'the culture of violence' amongst the black youth lay with the police, who had brutalized young people with their assaults, detentions and murders. Peace was not possible until inequality was eradicated by fighting. Musi said, 'Violence will always be the order of the day because, you see, we Africans always fight to make sure we retain our right and our culture.' Violence had become part of the identity of each of these young men.

Violence was seen as a cleansing force. Musi explained, 'Violence is needed in our country so that we can remove all the bad things that are there. This present regime is like a sickness that must be destroyed violently so that better things can exist and society can be more healthy. So violence is necessary.'

These young men saw themselves as defenders. They saw themselves as energetic, flexible, agile and adaptable, in a position to defend the community against outside dangers. These dangers included not just the actions of the state but also the activities of gangsters and the rival black group Inkatha. They would, they believed, impose the necessary discipline and morality on the community. Immoral people needed assistance from the comrades, as they called themselves, if they were to get back on the right path. If such wrong doers did not learn from the comrades, violence was, as one young man said, 'Another language which people understand'. Sometimes it was necessary to kill the person who did not understand.[55]

All people, no matter how wicked their deeds, like to think of themselves as being good and doing good. Such are the delusions of primitive pride!

Ideology [wrote Don Foster] is not merely a set of ideas [absolute truths] but a process involving widely shared meanings, practices, collective actions and intense emotions which make statements regarding 'what is', 'what is good' and 'what is possible and impossible' ... ideologies provide the means for people to act violently yet, ironically, believe that they are acting in terms of worthy, noble, morally righteous reasons. Thus some Afrikaner nationalists will still claim a 'just war', not against black people, but against communism – a global struggle. In the ideological justification black people were merely the dupes of international communism. Elsewhere, apartheid was ideologically justified through moral arguments of 'separate development': blacks required development and progress, but at their own, slower, pace and their own way since (as the argument went) they were essentially different from the more civilized, developed people of European origins. Leading academics, scientists and theologians provided these moral and purportedly reasonable claims over a sustained period. Of course such claims served to create and silence the various demonized 'others' who wished to challenge such 'rational' arguments.[56]

In carrying out these dreadful acts of violence and justifying them in terms of virtue men are usually practising a skill which many boys are taught – 'the happy knack', as Philip Hodson called it, 'of making themselves feel better by making others feel worse'.[57] The boy justifies his actions in terms of 'he deserved it' and, like the cleric who insisted that blacks never get depressed, 'he isn't really hurt'.

In learning to get satisfaction in this way the boy has to learn to be indifferent to another's pain. To do this he learns to see his enemy not as a person but as an object. This is a curious anomaly in the dialogue of violence. If the enemy is an object then it cannot feel pain, so there would be no point in inflicting pain on it in order to impose your will. In using violence the person sees the enemy as being incapable of feeling hurt while at the same time knowing that the enemy does feel hurt.

Whenever we believe, or try to believe, two opposite things at the one and the same time we harm ourselves because by doing so we create a fundamental flaw in our meaning structure. No matter how much we hate our enemy, how much we despise and denigrate our enemy, no matter how much we ignore all that we have learnt about people generally, that basic form of thought with which we were born, the face, will tell us again and again that our enemy is not an object but a person like ourselves. All our justifications for our cruelty struggle against this ingrained knowledge.

Two Russian men who had been conscripts, raw recruits, in the Soviet army fighting against rebels in Afghanistan in the early 1980s talked on television about their experiences. The first man said, 'I remember how we once rounded up all the women and children, poured kerosene over them and set fire to them.' He looked sad but shrugged. 'Yes, it was cruel, yes, we did it, but those kids were torturing our wounded soldiers with knives.'

The second man said, 'When you kill someone you don't feel calm, you feel indifferent, paranoid, you lose your morality. You become very cold. You become cold blooded. Your soul grows cold because you've been presented with something you don't like doing.'

The first man explained, 'A young soldier might kill just to test his gun, or if he's curious to see what the inside of a human body looks like, or what's inside a smashed head. But there is also the fact that if you don't kill you'll get killed. It is a feeling of being drunk on blood. Often you kill out of boredom or you just feel like doing it. It's like hunting rabbits.'[58]

Some people, when they become depressed and utterly despairing, hating themselves with a hatred which spills out and becomes a hatred of the entire world, turn on their own, much-loved possessions and destroy them. They turn on their loved ones and, if they do not destroy the person, destroy the cherished relationship.

The journalist Neal Ascherson, writing about the savagery of war, said, 'I certainly learned that soldiers who grow savage and prone to atrocity are frightened, weary soldiers, a danger to their own comrades as much as to "the others".'[59] Self-hatred is a terrible force.

In wars and conflicts 'the others' are often women and children. In the dialogue of violence killing children can be part of the plan to exterminate the enemy, but often the violence comes from the man's inner discourse with himself. The weakness and vulnerability of children remind the man of his own weakness and vulnerability, which he has learned to despise. If he acknowledges these feelings and reveals them to his fellows he will be overwhelmed by shame. Better to remove anything that reminds him of his shame. Aaron Hass told the story, 'In the ghetto, there was a little child about four years old. And she was a very happy and friendly child. Even the Nazis liked to talk to her. One day she was walking alone and one of the Nazis asked her if she would like a candy. "Would you close your eyes and open your mouth?" And he shot her in the mouth.'[60] At the war crimes trials in The Hague after the Bosnian war the story was told of the young mother from Srebrenica carrying her baby and being herded along by Serbian soldiers. Desperate, she ran up to a soldier and begged him for food for her baby. With the words, 'Your baby won't be hungry any more,' he cut the baby's throat.[61]

Don Foster noted that 'The most astonishing aspect of ploughing through masses of literature on atrocities of all kinds is to find the sheer neglect of the fact that they are almost exclusively committed by men.'[62] There were some women among the guards in Nazi concentration camps, and some women warders in ordinary jails have been noted for their brutality. Some women are violent to their children, and some violent to their menfolk, and women have never been averse to murder. In recent years there has been an increase in the number of young women serving jail sentences for violent assault. The media reported this in their usual horrified terms of 'I don't know what the youth of today are coming to', but the majority of women, though they would admit to having fantasies of violence when they are very angry, would not contemplate carrying out atrocities, much less actually doing so.

Men commit atrocities against other men, but they also commit atrocities of rape and murder against women. Don Foster saw how 'patriarchy as an ideology serves to legitimate violence against women which in turn serves to sustain relations of domination of men over women.'[63] In a patriarchal society women do suffer at the hands of men, but they suffer in all societies and especially in a war. Many men grow up with an intense hatred of women, and treat this hatred as something not to be combated and eradicated but to be shrugged off – 'that's the way men are'. Research carried out in 1999 by a group of academics for the Zero Tolerance charitable trust, which campaigns against physical and sexual violence against women, found that of the men aged between fourteen and twenty-one questioned, one in two thought that raping a woman was acceptable under certain circumstances, while one in four believed it was justifiable to hit a woman.[64]

Boy babies are not born hating their mother. Indeed, little boys have a passionate love for their mother. For many of them it is the greatest passion they ever feel. However, if they come to feel that their love is not returned, if they cannot cope with the way in which their mother frustrates and disappoints them, they may develop a hatred which they then direct at all women. Little girls can develop a hatred of their father which they then direct at all men, but, while some of these women might murder individual men, and all might disparage and belittle men in general, they do not resort to rape and mass murder.

Rape has always been part of war but it has been little documented. It had not featured as a topic for war artists until Peter Howson went to Bosnia. He had never shied away from depicting the brutalities of life in Glasgow or in the army, but the brutalities of the war in Bosnia changed him. His paintings recorded some of the great horrors of that war, including two paintings about rape. One was of a naked woman struggling in the grip of a man holding her from behind. This was entitled *Serb and Muslim*. The other painting, *Croatian and Muslim,* depicted a scene in a bathroom – a naked woman and two men in combat gear. The family photograph on the wall suggests that this is the woman's own bathroom. One man is pushing the woman's head down the lavatory pan while steadying himself by placing his blood-stained hand on the photograph. The other man is holding the woman's legs apart and raping her from behind. When the commissioning committee viewed the set of paintings done by Peter Howson on his return from Bosnia the men, not the women, on the committee refused to accept the painting of the rape. When I talked to the curator at the museum she told me that the decision had been made on financial grounds. The file of newspaper cuttings about the painting proved to be interesting reading. While some commentators deplored the rejection of *Croatian and Muslim* others said that it could not be a record of an event because, even though Peter Howson had talked to some 150 Muslim women who had been raped, he had not actually witnessed a rape. This is an interesting concept; if all art galleries and museums put it into practice, thus excluding those paintings of scenes which the artist had not actually witnessed, their problem of shortage of space would be solved at a stroke.

The selection committee at the Imperial War Museum had been unanimous in approving another painting by Peter Howson, that of a group of exhausted refugees beside a road, and this was the painting selected. *Croatian and Muslim* was bought by the singer David Bowie.

According to human rights organizations the big difference in the Balkans is that rape has been used as an instrument of policy by Serbian forces and paramilitary groups, and that the victims have been willing to testify to their ordeal. 'Rape is a deliberate weapon of policy in Kosova as it was in Bosnia,' said Regan Ralph of Human Rights Watch, an American monitoring organization.[65]

Rape was official policy for the Hutus when they attacked their Tutsi neighbours in Ruanda in 1994. The mass slaughter of the Tutsi by the Hutus was so vast that the systematic rape of women was overlooked by the world's media. Hundreds of thousands of women were raped and most of them were murdered. Children were raped along with their mothers. It was also official policy to infect the women with Aids; some were allowed to live so that before they died they would infect Tutsi men. Infecting women with Aids was easy because a woman after prolonged rapes would be traumatized and bleeding.

In a BBC television film about these women Clementine told her story. She was seventeen when Hutu men found her hiding in a convent. She said, 'They raped me, one man after another. Everybody took turns. When they'd finished they took acid from a car battery and poured it inside my vagina. Then they broke bottles and pushed the broken glass inside me. They told me we are doing these horrible things to you so that when your brothers win the war they will never find a girl to marry.'

For two months more the killings went on. Clementine lay rotting in hospital. The doctors had fled but the Red Cross brought her food. Hutu patients were rescued but no one would help her. The Red Cross stopped coming and the killers came back. They did not touch her but told her she was going to die anyway. When the genocide was over a doctor found her and arranged an operation which saved her life. The doctors continued to give her free treatment but they knew she could never recover. She had lost her vagina and uterus because the flesh had rotted. She could never have children or even marry because in the operation her genitals had to be closed. She became HIV positive but, because she could not afford the treatment, she was too weak to work to support her mother and two small half-brothers. She said, 'I feel very sad because the rapists are healthy and happy with their families. They have jobs and are working. But me, I don't have a life any more.'[66]

Torturers are men, but what kind of men? Primo Levi wrote,

More and more often, as time recedes, we are asked by the young who our 'torturers' were, of what cloth were they made. The term torturers alludes to our ex-guardians, the SS, and is in my mind inappropriate: it brings to mind twisted individuals, ill-born, sadists, afflicted by an original flaw. Instead, they were average human beings, made of our same cloth, they were average human beings, averagely intelligent, averagely wicked: save for exceptions, they were not monsters, they had our faces, but they had been reared badly. They were, for the greater part, diligent followers and functionaries: some fanatically convinced of Nazi doctrine, many indifferent, or fearful of punishment, or desirous of a good career, or too obedient. All of them had been subject to the terrifying miseducation provided for and imposed by the schools created in accordance with the wishes of Hitler and his collaborators, and then completed by the SS drill.[67]

Primo Levi quoted two remarks from a long interview by Gitta Sereny with Stangl, ex-commandant of Treblinka,

'Considering that you were going to kill them all ... what was the point of the humiliations, the cruelties?' the writer asks Stangl, imprisoned for life in the Düsseldorf gaol, and he replies: To condition those who were to be the material executors of the operations. To make it possible for them to do what they were doing. In other words, before dying the victim must be degraded, so that the murderer would be less burdened by guilt. This is an explanation not devoid of logic but which shouts to heaven: it is the sole usefulness of useless violence.[68]

The useless violence of torture produces pain, and pain silences the tortured. Elaine Scarry in her book *The Body in Pain* wrote, 'Physical pain does not simply resist language but actively destroys it, bringing about an immediate reversion to a state anterior to language, to the sounds and cries a human being makes before language is learned.'[69] Severe pain can silence even those sounds and cries. In 1962 I had part of my right lung removed. The scar from the incision runs from my right shoulder blade around my chest to the bottom of my breast bone. After the operation and in the recovery room my pain was dulled by morphine, but some days later and back on the ward I was told that the two substantial draining tubes which wound their way through my chest would be removed without any kind of pain relief. I was in a hospital where all the patients were expected to be extremely well behaved. What worried me most about the forthcoming procedure was that I would make a noise and shame myself. I need not have worried. The pain from the removal of those tubes, one after the other, left me with mouth agape and utterly silent. It robbed me of all speech, all sounds, all cries. Later, when I read accounts of torture, I wondered how anyone survives such and greater pain which comes not once or twice but day after day, week after week, year after year.

There is another way of silencing the enemy. Patrick Wall, in his study of what he called 'the science of pain', noted that, 'Governments have refined techniques over the centuries for inflicting pain.' However, he went on,

> Individuality can be demolished without pain. In the early 1970s, the British army in Northern Ireland introduced a new high-tech method of interrogation without pain. Arrested men were made to lean at 45 degrees, supported by their handcuffed hands on a wall. A bag was placed over their heads so that they could see nothing. Intensive noise from loudspeakers prevented hearing. If they collapsed they were propped up again. At irregular intervals they were taken out and interrogated but were otherwise left in their unmoving posture of sensory deprivation for days. When these men were examined long after their release, many remained broken zombies, apathetic, tremulous and unable to function.[70]

Our meaning structure requires practically constant contact with the world around it in order to maintain its integrity. Without sensory input against which to test its meanings our meaning structure becomes a vague, shifting collection of fantasies filled with paranoid fears. Torturers and jailers might know nothing about the meaning structure, but they have always known that the violence of degradation and sensory deprivation will destroy a person.

Don Foster noted that in the twentieth century violence became concentrated in the hands of two state structures: military and police. 'It would appear,' he said, 'that no instance of mass atrocity has occurred without a significant degree of militarization.'[71] Militarization usually leads to war, and war is popular with many people because, while a great many people suffer in war, conflict with the enemy can be pleasurable.

The Pleasures of War

Most evenings Camille came to Tima's jazz café, where she talked and laughed with her friends, but on one particular evening she sat huddled and silent beside me at the bar. Even James, our lovely barman, could get few words from her. Although it was a warm evening she was wearing a heavy sweater. She kept pulling the sleeves down over her thin hands and now and then she rocked back and forth in the way small, neglected children do. I put my arm around her, but she neither shrugged me off nor snuggled up to me. James put a drink down before her and, as she sipped it, she talked somewhat disjointedly about how she had been depressed for as long as she could remember. Someone near us mentioned the war and the fighting in Beirut, and Camille said, 'My village is in the occupied territory. I can't go there.'

Her family had been dispossessed and she had come, a refugee, to Beirut. Here she made friends and together they survived the war years, but when the fighting ended those who could left the country while others, though they might still meet at Tima's place, moved on to new jobs, new relationships.

Camille spoke of the war and said, 'It was good then. It was exciting. We were all together.'

I had first heard that said in 1948, when I went to university and met some ex-service men who would often say, 'It was better back in the war.' Some said this when they reminisced about the excitement and the comradeship they had enjoyed, and some when they complained about how the unexpected and ill-defined changes that followed the war left them rudderless and uncertain. In the war their purpose had been clear and the rules for living well defined. Tima said, 'In the war the achievement was to stay alive to the end of each day. If you'd done that you'd achieved something.'

Tima had worked for the Lebanese Red Cross for eight years during the war. She said, 'The first time I went into the emergency room, there was shelling in Beirut and there were bodies piled up in the corridors. I could not grasp it in my head that these people could have been alive, because of the way they looked and the manner in which the bodies had just been thrown around the place. There was no respect for the dead. If you had time, you tried to save the living. But then I got used to it and then it was very easy. I think partly also it's the height of the adrenalin that comes along with this sort of thing that keeps you going. I don't know if "exciting" is the right word, but it's like walking on a rope between two mountain peaks and saying, "This time I'll make it." '

In the war the rules were simple and obvious. Yasmin said, 'During the war you got up, you went to school, you followed a routine. You blocked out what was happening. You did what you had to do.' Amir said, 'In the war the shells could come from the east or the west from the sea. You tried to keep several walls between you and outside, but often you didn't know which walls. But then there were rules. When the war was over there were no rules.'

Jean Said Makdisi told how all she could read during the war was Jane Austen, with her settled, orderly world. 'Structure: that more than anything, I suppose, I craved – an impregnable structure to be cherished in my world where reinforced concrete was collapsing all around me.' She found a new structure in friendships:

> People sat together visiting. Those were the days for friendships. Mere acquaintances became bosom friends. Lips normally sealed in discreet silence whispered secrets that would never have been pried loose in normal times. Old friends became – how shall I put it? – closer than anyone could imagine: they became necessary, vital to each other's existence.[72]

Structure, friendships, excitement – all valuable entities created by participation in wars and conflicts. Ed Cairns told me that, even though people were glad to be at peace, they missed the excitement of the Troubles. Part of his structure was always remembering to listen to the news. Knowing what was happening in this street or that village 'could be a matter of life or death'. He sounded as though he might have missed having the news as an important marker for structuring his day.

The writer Jo-Anne Richards told how, one night in 1996, she and her friend Phetole drove through Diepkloof in Soweto. Phetole said,

> 'This used to be the stronghold of the ANC. The street committees were strong – there was no crime. These days, the crime's creeping in. You know what I miss most now? I miss the sense of purpose.' Phetole, now a civil servant, trained as a guerrilla after 1976. 'I miss the way we believed in a cause, and in our leaders. We had a strong, almost mystical mission. Now our leaders are just politicians. And what is my mission? I have a mortgage and a car payment.'[73]

Having a mission, a common aim, a tight-knit group, united

against an enemy – what greater pleasure can there be! Barbara Ehrenreich pointed out that

> The project of 'socialist constructionism' turned out never to be quite so compelling as the project of war. People who would lay down their lives for their country will not necessarily give up a weekend to participate in a harvest or the construction of a dam. Love of neighbours might stir us, but the threat posed by a common enemy stirs us even more. The sociality of the primordial band is most likely rooted, after all, in the exigencies of defence against animal predators. We may *enjoy* the company of our fellows, but we *thrill* to the prospect of joining them in collective defence against a common enemy.[74]

And then there is the thrill of killing.

Adulphe Delegorgue was both a prolific killer of game and a superb naturalist. In his journeys in KwaZulu-Natal, Gauteng and Northern Province in South Africa between 1838 and 1844 he shot thousands of animals, far more than he needed either for food or for his collection. He kept detailed journals, and there he described 'the feverish excitement' of stalking an elephant – 'that mixture of fear and pleasure which sets the heart thudding against the ribs, that delicious anxiety, seasoned with indescribable anguish, which one experiences in anticipation of a great event such as this, when one's life, housed in its frail shell, is to be thrown into the game of chance against the life of a colossus.'[75]

The hunter, in killing his prey, can be thrilled by his success and even more thrilled by the knowledge that he is alive and his prey dead. In war the prey are fellow human beings. Soldiers are supposed to say that they regretted, indeed were horrified by having to kill. Many do feel like that, but for others killing was just a job that had to be done. Ted Van Kirk, navigator of the *Enola Gay*, which dropped the atomic bomb on Hiroshima, claimed to have 'come off the mission, had a bite and a few beers, and hit the sack, and had not lost a night's sleep over the bomb in 40 years'.[76]

Over the twentieth century, when the casualties in war rose from the thousands in previous centuries into the many millions, when the numbers of dead were so great they could only be estimated, the military sought to present themselves to the public in such a way that the public would forget that soldiers had anything to do with killing. In this the military was quite successful. At the beginning of the Falklands war in 1982 I was invited on a television chat show to discuss the psychological effects of war and to answer callers who phoned with problems about the war. One mother called to say how distressed she was that her son was being sent to the Falklands. 'I was pleased when he joined the army,' she said, 'because it's a good job, but I never thought he would have to fight.'

When the British army moved into Kosova in 1999 as part of the peace-keeping force, that was what the soldiers were seen as by the British – gentle, unaggressive, upright peace-keepers. The guns they carried were no more than a part of their uniform. When a group of soldiers who were being attacked shot dead their attackers the army propaganda machine had to find a way of presenting the story which did not imply that this is what soldiers are employed to do: to kill people. So it came as a surprise to many people that within months of one another two books were published about war and the pleasure soldiers can take in killing. Niall Ferguson's *The Pity of War*[77] and Joanna Bourke's *An Intimate History of Killing* covered different ground but they each agreed that many ordinary men find war an absorbing experience, and that men who are neither psychotic nor sadistic get pleasure from killing people.

William Broyles, a former Marine, said, 'I believe that most men who have been to war would have to admit, if they are honest, that somewhere inside them they loved it too.'[78] Gary McKay as an Australian army officer killed many Vietnamese, but what greatly impressed him was actually seeing his bullets kill a man. 'When another soldier went berserk and massacred many of the enemy, he remembered feeling suffused with joy: "I felt like a god, this power flowing through me . . . I was untouchable." '[79]

James Hebron, a scout sniper in the Marines, thrilled to ' "That sense of power, of looking down the barrel of rifle at someone and saying, 'Wow, I can drill this guy.' Doing it is something else too. You don't necessarily feel bad; you feel proud, especially if it's one on one, he has a chance. It's the throw of the hat. It's the thrill of the hunt." '[80] James Byford McCudden, a fighter pilot in the First World War, said after shooting down a 'Hun', 'I think that this was one of the best stalks that I ever had. I cannot describe the satisfaction which one experiences after bringing a stalk to a successful conclusion.'[81]

There is another thrill– the thrill of getting something right, of winning the approval of those in power over you. The training whereby an ordinary young man is turned into an obedient soldier is brutal and degrading. Neal Ascherson wrote, 'After an infinity of being harangued and insulted and threatened by his commanders, the man with the smoking gun has at last done something "right". He has performed the deed for which he was trained. Somebody, unbelievably, will be pleased with him.'[82]

Lieutenant William Calley, infamous for his part in the My Lai massacre in Vietnam, described the brutal methods by which he had been trained to kill. When he was accused of mass murder he could not understand it.

'I thought, *Could it be I did something wrong?* I knew that war's wrong. Killing's wrong: I realized that. I had gone to a war, though. I had killed, but I knew *So did a million others.* I sat there and I couldn't find the key. I pictured the people of My Lai: the bodies, and they didn't bother me. I had found, I had closed with, I had destroyed the VC: the mission that day. I thought, *It couldn't be wrong or I'd have remorse about it.*'[83]

Many Americans agreed with Calley that he had not done something wrong. When Calley was found guilty and sentenced to hard labour for life for premeditated murder there was a huge outcry. When eventually Calley was released by presidential order into house arrest, the House of Representatives applauded.[84]

Such a response was consonant with the attitude of many Christians during war, despite the fact that the Ten Commandments are clear about killing and that Jesus was utterly unambiguous about the necessity of forgiving one's enemies. Joanna Bourke recorded that

since the thirteenth century, when chaplains joined the British army, religious representatives have always accompanied troops to war, albeit in small numbers . . . Although smaller sects (such as Quakers, Christadelphians, Jehovah's Witnesses, Mennonites, and Plymouth

Brethren) have consistently spoken out against war (and suffered punishment for their views) and many individual clergymen opposed involvement in the Boer War and in Vietnam, during the two world wars clergy from all the major denominations united against a common foe. The First World War was portrayed as a crusade; the Second as a just war. The justifications for armed conflict were recited in almost identical terms in both conflicts: war paved the road to peace; it promoted civilization and nurtured high idealism; virtues such as courage, strength, patience and self-sacrifice could flourish only during a crisis; materialism was to be swept away as entire nations underwent spiritual reawakening. In addition, the church had a duty to see the moral issues which led to the conflict resolved.[85]

This list of justifications shows all the hallmarks of the functioning of primitive pride. It ignores the fact that war leads to war, war degrades people and their environment; courage, strength, patience and self-sacrifice can flourish in peacetime, and no war has ever led to spiritual reawakening. Over my lifetime I have heard many claims from various religious groups that we were on the verge of a spiritual reawakening, but each time we went on as before. When a conflict ended there was much pious talk about forgiveness, but the major churches continued to support state policy. The Church of England was not averse to holding shares in businesses which had an interest in the arms trade.[86] However, the churches' justifications for war did promote that most wonderful pleasure, the glow of feeling morally right.

Islam can offer similar pleasures in wartime. Rima Fakri, a member of Hezbollah's 'Women's Association' said,

> 'I know a woman whose husband was one of Hezbollah's cadre and who had volunteered himself as a martyr. Her husband died in a car crash and this woman was devastated more because he had not achieved martyrdom. You see, martyrdom is the objective of love and the route to victory. It is the topmost status of a lover.'[87]

The topmost status of a lover and the glory of war – what could be finer? Some would disagree. Neither my father, who was a soldier in the First World War, nor my husband, a soldier in the Second

World War, ever put on their medals and marched in an Anzac Day parade. Each of them despised their leaders, who had lied to the troops and wasted so many lives. There were many soldiers who did march on Anzac Day, some out of simple comradeship, especially with those who had died, and some out of a desire to share the glory. This second group, as my father would often point out, demonstrated the inverse relationship between the degree of glorification of war and the degree of closeness to the actual fighting the person experienced.

The glorification of war is one of the fantasies created by primitive pride. When a little band of our ancestors stumbled home after an encounter with a foreign band they might have felt despairing and frightened by their losses, or they might have felt the joy of victory, but, in either case, they would have known that in a short space of time they would have to do it all over again. Telling themselves the truth – that they had lost much and gained little and that victory or defeat was a matter of chance – could defeat them in a way no enemy could, so they conjured up a lie, that they were glorious, their victory or defeat was glorious, and tomorrow they would again cover themselves in glory. This was a lie that had to be told and retold to keep it fixed in place. What better way to do this than to commemorate the lie in stone, to build memorials and cenotaphs, or even cities like Paris, where the vistas along each avenue and all the great buildings are hymns to the glory of war. Along these avenues and past these great buildings come men wearing the flying buttresses of their meaning structures – their uniforms and their medals. Oh, the glory of war!

Who gets the greatest pleasure from war and conflict? Jean Said Makdisi gave the answer.

I ponder, for the ten thousandth time since this damnable war began, on the happiness of the manufacturers and salesmen of arms and ammunition. Every roar, whistle and crash translates itself in my mind to the sound of the cash register, the tinkle of champagne glasses, and the hum of conversation at a very expensive restaurant somewhere. The glisten of shrapnel, the smoke billowing out of someone's ruined home, the rumble of big guns, are all echoed in my imagination as the glitter of jewellery, the smoke of cigars lazily puffed out of appreciative lips, and the rolling of drums for a hip-swinging, carefree dance. The screams of a terrified, burning child become the laughter of those who reap the gains of this havoc.[88]

The gains from this havoc are enormous. The armaments industry is the biggest industry in the world. Second to it is the pharmaceutical industry, which also profits from war and conflict. In 1998 Vanya in Belgrade said to me, 'Everyone in Serbia is on tranquillizers.' In the same year Tima in Beirut told me, 'A couple of months ago there was a small news item in the newspaper saying that in Lebanon last year there were many millions of tranquillizer pills consumed by a population of three and a half million. If I were the editor of a newspaper I would have put this as a banner headline because I don't think this sort of thing should have been overlooked. There's something definitely wrong – there's a lot of stress, people are not being given what they deserve, nobody's asked them, "Tell me what's missing in your life? What can we do to make life better for you?"'

Making life better for people would diminish the profits of the pharmaceutical industry, and stopping wars and conflicts would ruin the armaments industry. Wars make armament manufacturers and their shareholders rich. On 26 March 1999 David Lister of the *Evening Standard* reported,

> British Aerospace became steadily richer today as its equipment, including Harriers and Tornado jets, went to work in the skies above Yugoslavia. BAe, which has suffered since the acquisition of GEC-Marconi earlier this year, soared 15.5p to 425p to become the FT-SE 100's best performer.

During the 1980s many people who had previously put their savings in a building society or a bank were encouraged by the government to invest in shares. Some of these new shareholders chose to invest in individual companies but most bought various financial packages from investment firms, which made the decisions about where the money should be invested. When it became apparent that their money was being invested in the armaments industry, or in industries which injured, or damaged the environment, or used unethical work practices, a considerable number of investors turned to investment firms which claimed to invest only in companies with high ethical standards. However, the morality of ethical investments did not appeal to everyone. When the *Daily Telegraph* asked some financial experts to pick shares that they would include in an unethical portfolio Peter Hargreave of Hargreave Lansdown chose BAe, saying that, 'This is an industry you just cannot go wrong with; it arms both sides and then re-arms the loser.' He went on to say that BAe was part of a so-called 'Rambo portfolio'.[89]

British investors were likely to include more than BAe shares in their Rambo portfolios. By 1999 Britain was selling almost a quarter of the world's arms, and, while part of the trade was of large equipment – planes, tanks, artillery, ships – much was of small arms which made gun-running a profitable business. The organization Saferworld, 'working towards the prevention of armed conflict', issued a report which stated,

British arms brokers can bypass national export controls by buying and shipping weapons from another country (often in Central and Eastern Europe) into war zones. As long as the arms do not touch British soil, the dealers do not need any authorization from the Government. There have been many disturbing examples of British brokers organizing shipments from abroad for which they would have been refused a licence if the weapons had been exported directly from the UK. UK-based company Mil Tech brokered small arms from Albania and Israel to Rwanda in 1994 at the time of the genocide. And in recent times 'arms-to Africa affair', Sandline International organized the shipment of weapons from Bulgaria to war-torn Sierra Leone. These high-profile cases, however, are only the tip of the iceberg. Recent reports have linked British brokers to arms shipments to Angola, Congo-Brazzaville, Democratic Republic of Congo, Eritrea, Sierra Leone, and Sudan.[90]

The end of the Cold War brought a slump in the arms trade, so arms manufacturers turned to 'political control technologies' such as electroshock weapons, surveillance systems, leg irons, thumb cuffs, riot-control vehicles and gas. The market for police technology was reliable and was not dependent on wars and conflicts which waxed and waned. One electroshock weapon, the Talon, so the *New Scientist* reported, was 'capable of emitting up to 250,000 volts. When pushed against an assailant and fired, it produces temporary paralysis. The manufacturer describes the weapon as "affordable self defence that doesn't compromise morals". Prices starts at $39 – two ordinary 9-volt batteries are not included – and it can be bought over the Internet.'[91] The shape of these electroshock weapons lent themselves to being inserted in various human orifices, and so they became a popular weapon for rape and torture.

Political control technologies have a long history in England. The towns of Bristol and Liverpool grew to cities through the wealth from the slave trade. Birmingham grew rich on the manufacture of fetters, chains, padlocks, branding irons and other implements of slavery, and copper wire, iron bars, brass pans and kettles, guns and other such goods to barter for slaves.[92]

Whenever the anti-slavery movement protested at the iniquities of the trade and campaigned for its end someone was sure to say in defence of the trade, 'Jobs depend on it.' The same argument was always used in defence of the arms trade. Workers in armament factories might have earned only modest wages, but their money was as precious to them as were the vast profits made by the manufacturers and the investors. Morality often comes a poor second to money.

Arms can only kill or rust. They add nothing to the value of life. Their very existence is based on the misguided belief that our enemy is not human like ourselves. Whenever Samuel Cummings, who was probably the world's biggest private dealer in small arms, was asked about the morality of his trade, he would say, 'Human folly goes up and down, but it always exists, and its depths have never been plumbed.'[93]

Human folly comes in many forms, but one of our most popular forms of folly is to cling to pleasures and rewards which actually harm us.

Whenever we do something which causes us nothing but pain we try never to do that thing ever again. Whenever we go on doing something which causes us pain there is something in the situation which rewards us. If we want to change we have to identify what in the painful situation rewards us, and ask ourselves whether we are prepared to give that up. Sometimes when we do this we find that we are clinging to something we no longer need. We can give it up and release ourselves from the pain and futility of persisting in something which damages rather than enhances our lives. More often, when we look at the rewards, we see something which we believe is essential to the integrity of our meaning structure. A woman who believes that she is so unacceptable that no one could possibly love her will go on and on being depressed because, as she sees it, if she ceased to be depressed her family who look after her would leave her, and such rejection and isolation would annihilate her. A man who sees his black neighbours as his enemy will cling to his enmity, even though he is frightened by his fantasies of what his neighbours might do to him, because he feels that, if he were friends with his neighbours, he would be a nonentity against their magnificent ebullience and charm, and he could not cope with such a failure.

Having an enemy might not lead to happiness, but we can find that having an enemy is immensely rewarding. Here is a list of the rewards we can get from having enemies – either personal enemies or group enemies. It is not an exhaustive list, nor are all these rewards present in every situation, but the list does show how much we can value having an enemy.

- We can project on to our enemies all those attributes we find unacceptable in ourselves.
- The enemy binds our group together.
- The anger and aggression which would tear our group apart we can turn on our enemy.
- An enemy can be blamed for everything, and we avoid taking any responsibility.
- An enemy provides a simple explanation for why things happen. We do not have to grapple with the complexities and uncertainties of life.
- An enemy can interest and excite us much more than our friends.
- An enemy is a distraction from our own angers, fears and failures.
- We can comfort ourselves with the knowledge that, no matter how bad we might be, we are better than our enemy.
- Having an enemy can seem to be a sign of our strength and our importance in the world.
- An enemy allows us to act out our internal conflicts without having to understand them. We can
  – act out sibling rivalry

- act out hatred of our parents
- act out our fear of growing old and our hatred and envy of the young
- act out our fears that the Just World has treated us unjustly
- act out our fear and hatred of the unacceptable parts of ourselves.

- An enemy allows us to feel special by belonging to a special group.
- We can make sure our children will stay close to us by teaching them about the enemies which threaten us.
- Condemning and criticizing our enemy in public speeches or in gossip can be very pleasurable.
- Our enmity has a cosmic dimension: we are the embodiment of good and our enemy is the embodiment of evil.
- We can enjoy the glory and nobility of martyrdom.
- Having an enemy means that someone, somewhere is thinking of us. We are never forgotten or ignored.
- In seeing our enemy as being uniformly bad we save ourselves the hard work of trying to understand people whose ways of seeing themselves and their world are different from our own.
- In seeing our enemy as uniformly bad we save ourselves from the pain of pity.
- We can profit from our enemy's misfortune and not feel guilty.
- An enemy can provide the excuse to cling to a parent-leader and not take responsibility for ourselves.
- An enemy provides us with the pleasures of war.

These rewards make relinquishing our enemies very difficult. But, if we decided that we could live without our enemies, what would we have to do?

The End of Enmity

Gerry Adams, the Sinn Fein leader, was speaking from vast experience when, during the talks which led to the Good Friday Agreement, he remarked that, compared to creating a peace, 'It's easier to make war.'[1]

So it is. War is destruction, and it is always easier to destroy than to create. It is easier to destroy a relationship than to build up a friendship. To create we have to take account of what is actually going on. We have to be prepared to accept uncertainty and the changes which something new always brings. But when we destroy we can stay within our fantasies. We do not have to ask ourselves whether what we feel is appropriate to what is actually going on. By destroying whatever threatens us we can try to force the world to be what we want it to be.

It is an article of faith among most people in the media that in order for a discussion on television or radio to 'work' there must be disagreement and argument. A discussion where the participants consider the complexities of an issue and compare differing points of view is seen as dull and unwatchable, no matter how amusing or important the matters discussed might be. After recording Trudi, a psychoanalyst, and myself discussing with Professor Anthony Clare the pitfalls of finding a therapist, the producer expressed regret that Trudi and I had not crossed swords. But why should we? We were discussing something which was a serious problem, and we were obliged to tell a little of the tale of the confused, often misguided efforts by representatives of the various kinds of therapies to create a register of qualified therapists. This process, carried out by the members of the UK Council for Psychotherapy, went on for years.

Finally the psychoanalysts fell out completely with all the other kinds of therapists, who ranged from the strictly scientific to the wildly magical. In the end two registers were created, one of all the qualified psychoanalysts and one of all the other therapists. The story of the compiling of these two registers would make a wonderful comic novel, but I should warn anyone considering such a project that the therapists' mafia would soon come to call – with very unpleasant results.

If therapists cannot get along together and find ways of resolving their differences, who can? Traditionally, therapists have not been very interested in seeking reconciliation and compromise with colleagues with whom they disagree. Some therapists are interested in mediation and reconciliation in the specialist areas of divorce and the end of armed political conflicts, but most have always followed the tradition started by Freud of guarding their own patch with the sort of ferocity with which the Israelis guard Jerusalem, and of punishing their heretics with never-ending exile. After all, therapists are only human.

It is only human to want to keep safe the place where we belong, to separate ourselves from those with whom we disagree, and to defend ourselves against attack. It is also human to want to live peacefully with our neighbours and enjoy lasting friendships. Unfortunately, it is difficult to reconcile all these desires. When we feel enmity towards another person or another group it may seem easier to persist in these ways rather than to take steps to resolve that enmity. Such a step could, we fear, be more dangerous than remaining in a state of enmity. The first step renders us vulnerable, and our enemy might see this and attack rather than welcome our peaceful overtures. If our enemy does not attack us but instead welcomes our approach we then have to find new ways of behaving in the presence of our erstwhile enemy, and this uncertainty may make us feel awkward and ill at ease. We have always seen our enemy from afar, a fixed entity, and now we have to deal with the surprising complexities of a real person.

When we find ourselves the object of someone's enmity we may experience two kinds of threat: a threat to our physical safety and a threat to the integrity of our meaning structure. With the first threat a successful defence might be all that we need. We escape, our attackers are driven off, and we can rejoice and relax. With the second threat a successful physical defence is not enough. We need to do something to restore our meaning structure to its former strength, or make it even stronger. In this situation the remedy chosen by primitive pride is often revenge; however, while carrying out our revenge might give us some immediate satisfaction, its consequences give us none. The only safe form of revenge is that enacted solely in our fantasies. Any other form is likely to place us in greater danger.

The Satisfactions and Failures of Revenge

The liveliest of all the workshops I ran were those on the theme of anger, revenge and forgiveness. At the beginning of one of these workshops one woman declared, 'I could take a PhD in revenge.' Her account of how various relatives and friends had offended her and how she had had her revenge by not speaking to them was very amusing and we all laughed. She was pleased with our reaction, but there was no doubt that she meant every word of what she said. This host of friends and relatives to whom she no longer spoke did not seem to have committed any major crimes against her; they simply did not perceive the world in the same way as she did. I thought she was a delightful person, but as the day wore on I found myself becoming increasingly anxious that I might say something which offended her. I was also anxious for her. Anyone who follows a policy of never forgiving an injury will inevitably end up alone and lonely. However, this woman had already foreseen this eventuality and was guarding against it. She now had pet dogs. Dogs will never let you down!

Another woman took up the theme of not forgiving and not speaking. She enacted with a toss of her head and the lift of a shoulder the delight and satisfaction of cutting another person dead. We all laughed at this, but our laughter showed that we understood that such revenge can be employed only when the person feels self-confident and proud. 'How dare that person offend me!' is a statement based on pride. From the other side of the circle another woman spoke. Somewhat nervously she pointed out that not speaking can also come not out of a pride which demands revenge but out of fear. When someone hurt her, she told us, she felt wounded and crept away, not wishing to risk receiving another wound. 'When I meet the person again,' she said, 'I can't engage in any small talk. I don't want even to look at them.'

The pride that turns the defence of silence into a weapon of revenge is itself based on a feeling of personal inadequacy that cannot tolerate a different point of view which, by its very difference, seems to imply a criticism. My mother was profoundly angry and hurt when life and people failed to be what she needed them to be, and she retreated into wounded silence. However, at some time in her youth she had discovered that through this silence she wielded power over friends and family. They wanted to be, as my father would say, 'in her good books', and so they took her silences seriously. No one joked about her silences or ignored them. No one used the word 'sulking'. They all sought to placate her, and eventually she would deign to be placated. Her silences placed the blame for what had happened solely on those who had offended her. Such power without responsibility was too delicious to be relinquished, even though Mother must have been very lonely. She feared strangers, and all her family treated her very warily.

Not speaking as a method of revenge is extremely popular. In a survey psychologists at the University of Toledo in Ohio questioned 2,109 Americans aged between eighteen and eighty about their experience of ostracism. 'Three-quarters of respondents said that they had been ostracized by a loved one, while 68 percent admitted ostracizing a close friend or relative. Men and women were equally likely to be both perpetrators and victims.'[2]

There are two difficulties with using silence as revenge. First, it is effective only when you are in contact with your enemy. There is little point in ostracizing someone who, in the ordinary course of events, you never meet. Hence not speaking is popular in families. The other difficulty is in deciding how you start speaking again to those who have offended you. One of the reasons why such tactics continue for decades in some families is because the person who is not speaking cannot think of what to say to show that he has ended his silence. He may fear what other family members will say when he does. My mother would announce the end of her revenge against her family by making some banal remark about domestic matters, such as, 'Has the kettle boiled?' or 'Have you got anything to go in the wash?' None of us would dare say, 'So you've started speaking again?' because that would have driven her into another angry silence. Instead we would reply with, 'I'll just put it on,' or, 'Do you want me to take the sheets off the bed?', and life would go on as before. It was a bizarre way to live.

Not speaking is not confined to friends and family. In the long days and nights at Stormont in 1998, when the Good Friday Agreement was being negotiated, the Loyalist leaders never spoke to the Republican leaders. It must have been very demanding to maintain such a silence. In all those everyday encounters – walking towards one another down a long corridor, reaching a doorway at the same time, queuing for a meal in the canteen, forced to stand side by side in the gents' lavatory – did David Trimble never say, 'Hi,' or, 'You go first,' or 'Thanks' when he was passed a teaspoon, or agree that the weather was terrible. Apparently not. Gerry Adams, skilled in the ways of the media, made it clear that he operated with friendly good manners. When David Trimble was elected as leader of his party Gerry Adams responded with, 'Well done, David.' No doubt David Trimble's intransigence pleased his supporters, but to onlookers such intransigence simply looked like a back-to-the-wall, desperate defence.

The Good Friday Agreement could not be complete in itself. It needed to be followed by a period of negotiation and compromise which would lead to the setting up of the Northern Ireland Assembly; this in turn would lead to the handing over of considerable powers from the British government to the Assembly. This did not happen. Instead, all sides fell to bickering with accusation and counter-accusation. It looked as if the whole process would end, as all previous attempts to bring peace to Northern Ireland had ended, in utter failure.

In September 1999 the American senator George Mitchell, who had acted as mediator in the discussions leading to the Good Friday Agreement, arrived in Belfast to conduct a review of the agreement. He came for three weeks and stayed for ten, and in the course of those weeks performed a miracle. How he did this we have yet to learn, but during the first few weeks there were hints of what was happening. It seemed that David Trimble was talking to Gerry Adams; indeed, everyone was talking to everyone else, and it was not just, 'Would you pass me the salt, please?' It was a matter of coming to understand one another. The truly extraordinary nature of this understanding was not glimpsed until, at the end of the talks, each party issued a statement.

The Ulster Unionist statement included the words, 'The UUP recognizes and accepts that it is legitimate for nationalists to pursue their political objective of a united Ireland by consent through exclusively peaceful means,' while the Sinn Fein statement said,

> All sections of our people have suffered profoundly in this conflict. That suffering is a matter of deep regret but makes the process of removing conflict all the more imperative. Sinn Fein wishes to work with, not against, the unionists and recognizes this as yet another imperative. We reiterate our total commitment to doing everything in our power to maintain the peace process and to removing the gun forever from the politics of our country.

However, the cause of not speaking was not entirely lost. When the Assembly's cabinet was being set up Ian Paisley's party, the DUP, nominated two members, Peter Robinson as Minister for Regional Development and Nigel Dodds as Minister for Social Development, but both announced that they would not sit down with Sinn Fein. On 2 December the cabinet held its first meeting, but the DUP members held their own exclusive meeting elsewhere. Meanwhile Martin McGuinness, now Minister for Education and seeking to meet the people for whom he was responsible, went to Kilkeel High School, County Down, to meet staff and students. When he arrived 200 Loyalist children walked out of their classes in protest.

No doubt these children were behaving as their parents expected them to behave, but, if they learn from this episode to handle their personal relationships in the same way, their adult lives will be a misery. Whenever someone offends them or fails to agree with their views they will sever relationships with that person, no matter how much that person might mean to them. 'Never darken my door again!' does not promote a happy family life and good relationships with friends and lovers. We all need to learn how to distinguish between disagreeing with a person and actively disliking a person.

When we feel strong in ourselves and straightforwardly dislike someone we organize our lives so that we see as little as possible of that person. When occasions arise where we do have to meet that person we resort to the effective social defence of good manners. It is only when we feel weak in ourselves or that there is a fundamental weakness in our position that we have to resort to not speaking.

At Stormont both before and after the Good Friday Agreement the Republicans were able to speak to the Loyalists, if only in terms of good manners, because they could draw on the strength that came from a clearly defined political philosophy. Basically this philosophy was simple: as one of the leaders of the East Tyrone brigade of the IRA spelled out to Kevin Toolis, 'Our aim is to get the British out of Ireland,'[3] but the thinkers among the Republicans had made the means of fulfilling this aim 'the ballot box, not the gun'.

In developing and maintaining this philosophy the Republicans could draw on the traditions of the Catholic Church, with its emphasis on obedience to an infallible head of the Church. An ex-Volunteer, talking to Kevin Toolis about the Sinn Fein leader Martin McGuinness, said,

> 'Martin was a relatively rare phenomenon in the IRA, he was a thinker at a time when there was a lot of blind faith. "We are right, we might not be able to tell you how we are right but we are." If someone with a bit of education came along they could tie you up in knots. A common response was: "We know we are right and if you don't lay off we'll shoot ye." '[4]

The Loyalists had no coherent aim other than to keep things the same and hang on to what they had. The Protestant tradition presents absolute truths alongside the teaching that individuals are responsible to their own conscience. This always meant that individual Protestants were very prone to take their own beliefs as infallible, absolute truths. When other Protestants did not agree with him the individual was likely to break away from the group and set up his own group. Thus there is only one Catholic Church, yet there are many Protestant churches; in Northern Ireland there were only two Catholic political parties and one paramilitary force linked to one of the parties, but four Protestant parties and three paramilitary forces. The history of the IRA shows that there were disagreements, with small splinter groups – the Irish National Liberation Army (INLA) and later the Continuity IRA – being formed, but all were committed to the idea of a united Ireland. It was the enemy, the IRA, which held the Loyalist groups together. Just as the Israelis needed the Arabs, so the Loyalists needed the IRA. No wonder David Trimble could not afford to say 'Hi' to Gerry Adams!

The Loyalists' lack of a well-defined political philosophy was noted by Dermot Finucane when he was describing to Kevin Toolis what life was like for IRA prisoners in Long Kesh.

'In general I would say that the Republicans know what they were fighting for, Loyalists don't. They came across as street boys, thugs with tattoos, who would attack you when they were drunk. They were not brave men, just uneducated, working class yobs. None of them could articulate why they were in jail. They became more efficient at killing Catholics but that was because of collusion – someone was helping them co-ordinate their attacks.'[5]

Some Loyalists came to realize that they were fighting *against*, rather than fighting *for*. In 1966 Gusty Spence was sentenced to twenty years in Long Kesh for the murder of the young Catholic man Peter Ward. There he became the commander of the Ulster Volunteer Force compound. When in 1974 David Ervine was caught with a gelignite bomb in a stolen car he was sentenced to eleven years. David Ervine told Peter Taylor how, like all other UVF prisoners, when he entered the compound he was interviewed by Gusty Spence, who asked him the question he asked all new inmates: 'Why are you here?' David Ervine was affronted.

'I said, "Possession of explosives," and he says, "No, no, no, no, no. *Why* are you here?" I thought, "Arrogant bastard – for defending my people!" But it was a question which caused me some concern because I didn't know that I'd thought very long about why I was doing what I was doing and why I had subsequently ended up in gaol. I would say that that question was a beginning for me on a road that was about analysis and about trying to understand not only what was happening to me as a person but what's happening to our society, generation after generation. Gusty unlocked the door, pushed it slightly ajar and gave me the offer to walk through it as was my choice. I think that was as good for me as anything that's ever happened to me in my life.'[6]

Peter Taylor commented, 'Spence more than any other person

sowed in the hard soil of Long Kesh the political ideas that were to flourish in the form of the UVF's new political party, the Progressive Unionist Party (PUP).[7] It was Gusty Spence, flanked by Gary McMichael, David Adams and John White of the Ulster Democratic Party and David Ervine, William 'Plum' Smith and Jim MacDonald of the PUP, who announced the Loyalist ceasefire in 1994 and offered 'to the loved ones of all innocent victims over the past twenty-five years abject and true remorse'.[8] By the latter part of 1999 the PUP, along with many members of David Trimble's UUP, had developed a form of unionism which came to be known as 'civic unionism' as distinct from the 'ethnic unionism' of those who rejected the Good Friday Agreement.

The members of the political parties which had developed from the paramilitary forces on both sides – Sinn Fein, the Progressive Unionist Party and the Ulster Democratic Party – had no difficulty in talking to one another. It was the armchair warriors of Ian Paisley's Democratic Unionist Party and David Trimble's Ulster Unionist Party who refused to speak to their enemies and who went on denigrating and attacking them. Here history was repeating itself. Soldiers usually have considerable sympathy for other soldiers who are going through the same experiences, even though they are the enemy.

> On 4 May, 1915, J. H. Early sent a letter to his family in response to a press cutting. He rebuked them with the words, 'You get no "brutal Huns" here.' Then admitted: 'Probably we ought to feel more apoplectic, and it may be due to really outrageous things being over-shadowed by our immediate surroundings and also to a lurking feeling for the poor dogs who must be living the same silly sort of life that we are, behind the sandbags over there.'[9]

During the Second World War studies of the degree to which servicemen hated the enemy showed that 'men without any combat experience hated the enemy more than actual fighters did, and servicemen who had not left the country hated more than those overseas.'[10]

> Furthermore, civilians who had most experience of war (such as people subjected to aerial bombing) were *less* liable to demand

reprisals. Indeed, one major survey showed that the demand for reprisals for the bombing of British cities came most strongly from rural areas such as Cumberland, Westmorland, and the North Riding of Yorkshire where bombs had not been dropped.[11]

I think that there should be an international law which states that the only people to take part in the actual fighting of a war should be those leaders who declared war. The rest of us should simply be spectators. Alas, those who become leaders are usually very adept at manipulating the truth and playing upon their people's passionate attachment to revenge.

Where two enemies think only of revenge conflict cannot end except through mutual exhaustion. An intelligent visitor from outer space might wonder why human beings persist in such a useless and destructive activity as a dialogue of violence. Surely our ancient ancestors in their little bands, so clever at constructing tools, could have worked out that there were better ways of living than engaging in mutual revenge! However, the very uselessness and destruction of revenge shows that it arises not from the application of intelligence and reason to what is actually going on, but from the fantastical notions of primitive pride – notions which are constantly reinforced by society. Parents in the southern states of America teach their sons that it is a matter of honour to always respond to insult with aggression; the Iranian leader Rafsanjani responds to the murder of Iranian diplomats in Afghanistan with, 'I send my condolences to the mourning families and promise them that we will take revenge for the blood of their dear ones.'[12]

When someone attacks us or treats us very badly we often say, 'That was a blow,' even though no physical blow was struck. Inside we are reeling in much the same way as our body reels from an actual blow; we are aware of our meaning structure just as we are aware of our bones. Describing our reaction in terms of changes in adrenalin levels and pulse rate leaves out the most important part of this experience: the feeling that the structure of our being has been shaken.

The blow we receive might shatter, or come close to shattering, some beliefs we have about the world, or another person or people, or our future; whatever the target, it hits the core of our meaning structure – how we feel about ourselves. Our immediate response is to feel that we are less than we thought we were. We feel the shame of being prey.

In this situation some of us cry and turn to other people for comfort; others creep away alone to some private place. Protected by another person's arms or a room with a closed door we shake and feel that we are falling apart; gradually the shaking, both physical and psychological, eases as thoughts come to us which are restorative, defensive, encouraging. Some of these thoughts arise from our observations of what is actually going on while others come from the functioning of primitive pride. A thought based in reality might be: 'It's a shock but it's not as bad as it could be.' Primitive pride readily supplies: 'How dare that person do that to me!'

'How dare that person do that to me!' is partly an expression of immense anger; this is often impervious to the passing of time and events which might be construed as recompense for the insult suffered. I know from my own experience and from what many people have told me that we may go about the business of our lives feeling that we have dealt with all the demons in our past and that we are reconciled to our losses when something happens and a distant memory comes to the fore, and suddenly we are suffused with anger. Primitive pride is timeless, and a threat from long ago is just as dangerous as a threat in the here and now. 'How could that person have done that to me!' is as powerful and as necessary a defence as 'How dare that person do that to me!'

This is how primitive pride restores our self-confidence. 'I am the most important person in the universe and this insignificant fool has dared to insult me,' we tell ourselves. We all, even the most humble and downtrodden, share this belief. It is the expression of the purpose of life, which is to live. It is a wonderful thought, because it ensures that we battle on when common sense tells us that we cannot win, but it is also a dangerous thought if the anger that accompanies it seeks expression through a stupid revenge. It is a better thought than 'It was my fault. I deserve what happened' – which may lead to the prison of depression. The only good that can come out of depression is that you may learn to value yourself and accept the uncertainties of life, but otherwise it is a waste of time and energy; the anger of 'How dare that person do that to me!', on the other hand, can be used constructively.

For us to use this anger constructively we need to recognize how dangerous it can be. If we are wise we dissipate the anger in fantasy. We allow ourselves to dream about what we would have said if only we had thought of it at the time, or about the ghastly fate that might befall our adversary, or about our adversary finally recognizing our true nobility and grovelling at our feet to beg forgiveness. Ridiculous though these stories might be, they are primitive pride at its best, restoring our meaning structure to its original strength without involving us in any more trouble.

However, the matter may be too serious to be resolved by fantasy. We may use our anger to help us to gain redress through the law. This is rarely easy, and we need courage if we are to attempt it. Alison Halford, once assistant chief constable of Merseyside, Britain's top-ranking woman police officer, took her employers to the Equal Opportunities Commission because she had applied for promotion nine times and been rejected. The case was bitterly fought as she found herself attacked and slandered. Nine years on the journalist Simon Hattenstone asked her whether she had ever lost confidence in herself.

> 'No,' she says firmly, 'It was probably one of the most fascinating times of my life.' She *enjoyed* it? 'No.' She relished it? 'Uh, no I wouldn't say that. I was fascinated, I suppose, in that I knew I was fighting for my own survival. They wanted to see me off and they didn't care how they did it.' Is she more respected than when she was in the police force? 'Oh yes. *Yes. YES.* I'm a person. An achiever. It would be very nice to shuffle off my mortal coil having achieved quite a lot.'[13]

Sometimes recourse to the law is not appropriate. The law offers little redress to children who have suffered emotionally at the hands of their parents or siblings. In disputes between national groups international law is applicable only if both parties recognize the jurisdiction of that law. Without the law we have to find some way of dealing with the anger and injury. Some people deal with it by actively forgetting, by saying to themselves, 'Thinking about it will only waste time and hold me back.' Active forgetting diminishes bitterness and allows us to get on with our lives. But there is also repression, where we deny that such a thing happened. Such denial is always damaging because it creates a split which undermines the integrity of the meaning structure, allowing the repressed anger to break through and be directed at inappropriate objects. Thus a parent might beat his child, taking out on the child the anger he feels for the parent who beat him.

Some people choose to remember their injury and deal with it through revenge. Successful acts of revenge are those which give satisfaction and do not allow the enemy to respond. They are very difficult to achieve and require a very close and realistic appraisal of what is actually going on in order to assess the possible consequences of any action. Destroying the enemy completely is never a successful act of revenge. The destruction of Carthage weakened the Roman empire and led to its downfall. Murdering your enemy and escaping detection still leaves you with a lifetime of fearing that you will be found out. Shaming and humiliating your enemy can be successful, provided you end up with the world on your side. Lady Sarah Moon was cheered and applauded when she chopped four inches off the right sleeve of each of her faithless husband's Savile Row suits and gave away the contents of his much-prized wine cellar, but when Margaret Cook revealed marital secrets about her husband Robin when he was Foreign Secretary the general feeling was that she was being unfairly vengeful. The difference between these two acts of revenge was humour.

When our act of revenge is dealt with humour, when we and the onlookers laugh, and even our adversary raises a wry smile, we are showing that we can laugh at ourselves. When we laugh at ourselves we are acknowledging our shortcomings and this is the first step towards reconciliation. In any dispute reconciliation is possible only when both sides are prepared to admit that they share responsibility for what has happened.

Who's Responsible?

At the end of the Second World War, when news of those living in countries occupied by the German forces began to come through, a most remarkable discovery was made. Throughout the war, when the Vichy government in France collaborated with the Germans, we had heard stories of how those few brave French men and women in the Resistance risked their lives to save British airmen and to get

vital information to the Allies. At the end of the war we discovered
that, without exception, every French man and woman was in the
Resistance. How the German forces managed to maintain their control of France for all those years remains a mystery to this day.

A similar mystery emerged at the Truth and Reconciliation Commission in South Africa. It was the Nationalist Party which created
and maintained apartheid, and in each election held during those
years they won the majority of votes, which were white votes. The
blacks did not have a vote. Archbishop Tutu commented, '[The
whites] voted these Nats into power election after election with
increasing majorities. They were enjoying the fruits; now they want
to pretend they didn't support apartheid. Have you ever found
anyone who supported apartheid? No – absolutely nobody supported it, not even the Nats.'[14]

Most of the French who claimed to be in the Resistance and
most of the South Africans who claimed never to have supported
apartheid would be affronted if they were told that they were lying.
They would explain that they would have been active in the Resistance or that they would have been actively opposed to apartheid
but they were always so tremendously busy that they had no time
to do so. What they called 'busy-ness' was a kind of tunnel vision
which focused on certain aspects of their life and ignored other
aspects, especially anything that concerned people outside their
group. They might not have been aware that they were excluding
so much from their view, but outsiders could see this.

In Beirut I met Steve, a musician from New Jersey who was
playing at the new casino. He knew Lebanon and the Lebanese very
well. He told me, 'The Lebanese don't take any notice of anything
new. They're loud, they shout, they don't listen.'

In Belgrade I met a young Englishwoman married to a Serb. They
both worked in the media and had travelled quite widely. She told
me, 'The Serbs are not interested in anything outside Serbia except
what the world thinks of them. My husband travels the world. When
he gets to his hotel he switches on CNN, watches the report on
Serbia, and then switches off.'

For those who could not escape Belgrade focusing solely on everyday matters was a way of surviving. One of the women postgraduate
students at Belgrade University told me, 'I think about leaving, but
I live my life. I study, I don't look outside. I don't know very much

about what goes on. I can't change anything. I'm not in control of my life. I'm helpless.' Foreign newspapers, television and radio were available in Belgrade but stories which had no connection with Serbia seemed to arouse little interest. I thought that the intellectuals would have been interested in what the Truth and Reconciliation Commission were doing in South Africa because this was relevant to any community where there was conflict, but I did not find a single Serb who knew of its existence. When I spoke about it to Dusan he thought I meant Moral Rearmament, a right-wing peace group that was always in the news during the Cold War.

A narrow vision of the world can be very rewarding. Vedo had been a prominent journalist in Sarajevo but, he told me, until he came to London, where he was reunited with his wife Diyana and their daughter Sarah, he did not realize how little he knew of the outside world. In London, though life was difficult in many ways, the outside world did offer him some very promising opportunities. However, it also took away one of the privileges which Yugoslavian men enjoyed, that of treating women as inferior to men, put on earth to cater to men's needs and wishes. The women Vedo met in England, myself included, were quick to put him right.

Focusing narrowly on our own immediate circumstances is a natural response to real threat, but it is also a way of dealing with fear of the outside world, which arises from a feeling of personal inadequacy and a general paranoid style as a way of trying to overcome that inadequacy. Babies are born curious. They are passionate explorers, but any child who learns to feel inadequate, to see the world as dangerous, and who is punished for exploring soon develops the habit of being interested in nothing that is not part of his or her immediate concerns.

When I was a child I very soon became aware that there were two kinds of people: those who were interested in very little and those who were interested in everything. My father was interested in everything. He had had a very limited education, having left school when he was eleven to work delivering groceries with a horse and cart, but his passion for knowing was limitless. Among his friends were men who, like him, had a limited education, who read as widely as they could, books being in short supply, and who entered into endless discussions, usually about politics and economics but about anything which excited their interest.

In contrast my mother focused only on herself, her home and her family. Anything else to her was a waste of time. She and I were constantly at loggerheads over this. She felt that all I needed to know was how to clean, cook and sew, and how to read, write, spell and do arithmetic well enough to get a job in a bank. She was constantly telling me that I was ruining my eyes reading, and she tried to stop me reading the newspapers which my father brought home.

I found it strange that my mother was not interested in all those things which can make a dull life interesting, but I discovered that she was not alone in her view. Such an attitude has nothing to do with formal education. I have met many professional people whose interests were little wider than my mother's. Each would claim that he had wide interests, and this might appear to be the case, but each of these interests was selected because it defended the integrity of his meaning structure and enhanced his view of himself. Anything which did not allow him to take centre stage was of no interest. These people knew nothing of the pleasure that can come from disinterested interest – of knowing about something simply because it is there. Steven Rose, when writing about his years of research, described his reaction when something he had wondered about became, through experiment, abundantly clear. 'I know of no other sensation quite like this sense of joy, at the same time intensely cognitive but deeply emotionally satisfying.'[15]

However, despots, whether they rule the family or the state, do not care for people who are interested in everything because they are dangerous critics. This is why despots prefer to give their people bread and circuses rather than a good education. Tony Blair might have made education the main aim of his government, but what he prescribed was more to do with learning facts and passing state examinations than with making discoveries.

People who are interested in everything are dangerous because they can make comparisons and see things in different contexts. They know that situations are rarely simple contrasts of opposites. They tend to be sceptical rather than trusting, and they can usually see through lies – both their own and those of other people.

The question of responsibility always comes down to a question of truth and lies. When we say, 'I am not responsible,' and we are lying we seek to narrow the context in which our statement can be examined by ourselves or other people. My mother would never accept responsibility for what she did. It was always other people who were responsible. If she had looked outside the confines of her home she could not help but see that other people did not live as we did. If she then asked herself why she might have been forced to come up with an answer that suggested that she shared the responsibility for how we lived. If she saw that she might then have seen that an apology might be necessary. Ordinarily she could manage something along the lines of 'I'm sorry but circumstances forced me to behave as I did', which is not an apology but an excuse. What she could not manage was 'I did that and I am sorry', because she felt that apologizing would put her in a dangerously weak position. By keeping her vision narrow she could feel that she had nothing to apologize for.

My mother's domain was small but she could try to keep her family's vision focused on that terrain, and when she failed to do this she could terrify us into submission. Unlike most political leaders she was not obliged to make, or to appear to make, statements to her family about her conduct. When forced to talk about their responsibility for some heinous crime political leaders often use a ploy well known to practised liars – the bigger the lie the more likely it is to be believed. If amongst your audience there are those who do not believe your lie, the magnitude of your lie will shock them into silence.

Such lies are quite breathtaking. Milošević was interviewed on the Texan radio station KHOU-TV by Ron Hatchett, director of the Lord Byron Foundation for Balkan Studies, who had denounced critics of Milošević as 'neo-imperialists'.[16] He asked Milošević, 'All the American people know is what they see on TV, so how do you explain the fact that many of these refugees are talking about [being] driven out of their homes by the Serbs?' Milošević replied, 'Well, those you saw in TV were told to say that ... they are terrorized by those killers and kidnappers, those rapists, those narco dealers, CNN, you know, I saw with my own eyes at the beginning of the war on CNN, poor Albanian refugees walking through the snow and suffering a lot and you know in Kosova there was spring, no snow ... CNN, Sky, BBC ... they are paid to lie.'[17]

Apparently those of us who have never been dictators simply do not appreciate just how busy dictators are. In his interview with the *Sunday Telegraph* General Pinochet said, 'As General of the Republic

I never accepted torture. I am not just talking about my presidency. Well before, in fact. I never accepted torture. I didn't have time to control what others were doing. To say that is a gross slander.'[18] He repeated this to Christina Lamb of the *New Statesman*, and added, 'There was much to sort out. We had inflation at 500%. We had to recuperate agriculture to provide food for the people and we had to build houses because they were living in shacks and huts. It would be too long to list everything.'[19]

The Chilean National Commission on Truth and Reconciliation reported that 3,197 people disappeared or were killed between 1973 and 1990, when Pinochet was in power.

Apparently President F. W. de Klerk was just as busy. Called to the Truth and Reconciliation Commission he explained, as Antjie Krog reported, that he

> accepts responsibility for some of the repressive measures under-taken by the National Party Government, including the 1985 State of Emergency. De Klerk admits that this may have created circumstances which were conducive to human rights abuses.
>
> 'There is much which was wrong with the NP past and that which was right. It is my responsibility to admit which was wrong.' Yet his submission contains no specifics on any high-profile abuses. He says he cannot provide information on cases he does not know anything about. He cites the case of the Craddock Four. 'If we had known what had happened and who had committed this crime . . . the perpetrators would have been arrested, tried, and, if found guilty, sentenced. No President can know everything which takes place under his management – not even an Archbishop.'
>
> De Klerk says that he sanctioned the use of unconventional strategies but 'they never included the authorization of assassination, murder, torture, rape, assault. I've never been part of any decision taken by Cabinet, the State Security Council or any committee authorizing the instruction of such abuses. I personally never authorized such action.'
>
> De Klerk makes it clear that those who committed abuses had their judgements clouded by overzealousness or negligence. 'It is not my intention to gloss over the many unacceptable things that occurred in the period of National Party rule. They did happen and

I want to reiterate my deepest sympathy for those who suffered from it.'[20]

In making these statements these three men assumed that their listeners would not only accept what they said as the truth but would also overlook the inconsistency inherent in the assumption that a political leader could not possibly know what was going on in his country. Of course it is impossible for a leader to know exactly what every one of his people is doing all the time, but a leader's responsibility for what goes on is different from that of the ordinary citizen. The political leader is responsible for the lawful functioning of the state. Harry Truman, when US President, used to remind himself and everyone else of this with the motto he kept on his desk in the Oval Office: 'The buck stops here.' When a political leader says he did not know what his representatives were doing in carrying out the law he shows that either he is lying or he is incompetent. Incompetence itself requires an apology.

By refusing to accept the responsibility with which they are charged such leaders actively prevent reconciliation. When two sides fall out, be they two individuals or two groups, each has created a particular truth or story. Each side rejects the truth of the other side's story. In developing this each side selects what to include and how to interpret what is included. Reconciliation can be understood as the abandonment of the individual, opposing stories and the construction of a common story.

Michael Ignatieff considered the situation in Yugoslavia in terms of each group's story:

Resistance to historical truth is a function of group identity; nations and peoples weave their sense of themselves into narcissistic narratives that strenuously resist correction. Similarly, regimes depend for their legitimacy on historical myths that are armoured against the truth. The legitimacy of Tito's regime in Yugoslavia depended on the myth that his partisans led a movement of national resistance against the German and Italian occupations. In reality the partisans fought fellow Yugoslavs as much as they fought occupiers and even made deals with the Germans to strengthen their hand against domestic opponents. Since these facts were common knowledge to any

Yugoslav of that generation, the myth of brotherhood and unity required the constant reinforcement of propaganda.

The myth of brotherhood and unity may have been pointing to a future beyond ethnic hatred, but by lying about the past, the regime perpetuated the hatreds it was trying to get Yugoslavs to overcome. By repressing the real history of interethnic carnage between 1941 and 1945 the Titoist regime guaranteed that such carnage would return. Competing versions of historical truth – Serb, Croat, Muslim – that had no peaceful, democratic means of making themselves heard in Tito's Yugoslavia took to the battlefields to make their truths prevail.[21]

Perhaps the great achievement of the Truth and Reconciliation Commission in South Africa will prove to be the construction of just one story. In an interview with the BBC Judge Albie Sachs said of the TRC, 'Volumes of truth actually came out – not the whole truth, that's impossible – but volumes of truth, and it came out not simply from the victims but from the perpetrators themselves, so no one can deny. The denial of the evils of the past is impossible. No one can do that. That's the foundation of reconciliation. There were some extraordinary cases on opposite sides who were trying to kill one another or nearly killed one another and who got together and established a reconciliation, but they were relatively rare. I think that the deep reconciliation is at a more profound national level. We have one story of the past. We don't have a white story and a black story which have nothing to do with each other. We are living on the same map. We're on the same map. That's the great achievement.'[22]

On the evening of 2 December 1999, when each of the pieces of the jigsaw which gave Northern Ireland its own inclusive government seemed to have come together, Jon Snow on Channel Four News interviewed the Nobel Laureate poet Seamus Heaney, who said that in Northern Ireland now, 'All the stories have become one story.'

Reconciliation has to begin with both sides agreeing on what happened. They have to agree on the story. When one side says, 'That didn't happen and I'm not going to discuss it,' or, 'I don't remember and I'm not going to try to find out,' reconciliation cannot take place. It is possible only when both sides say, 'Yes, this happened. This was my part in it. I am responsible for what I did. I am sorry.'

But what do we mean by responsible? That is a tricky question.

We live in a world where we have very little control over what happens and very little choice in what happens to us. There is only one aspect of our lives where we do have complete control and choice, and that is in the meanings we create. It is these meanings which determine what we do. Our responsibility for the occurrence of certain events might be limited but we are always responsible for the meanings we create.

This responsibility we have always been keen to deny. We have blamed our behaviour on the stars, the humours in our body, on God, Providence or Fate, on the machinations of the devil or some malign spirit or alien, or on our instincts, our traits, our personality types, or our genes. Yet, if you listen to what we actually talk about, you will hear something very different. What we think about, talk about incessantly – to the extent that they dominate our media, our politics, our economy and all our relationships – what we try to understand, influence and change are our ideas. What are the laws which set limits to what we do? Very little but ideas. There are physical limitations to what we can do, but most of our behaviour is limited and directed by our ideas. What makes this garment, washing powder, restaurant, car, holiday resort, drink, recipe, school, shampoo, lover, parent, child, friend, political party, economic policy, morality, religion, more desirable than any other? Nothing but ideas. We love ideas because we know that ideas are us. Or, to correct the grammar, we are ideas. We love ourselves and we love ideas, one and the same.

Yet we have this idea that we should deny the importance of ideas. We have this idea that we can create the idea of the influence of the stars, the changes in our body, God, Providence, Fate, the machinations of the devil and other spirits, aliens, instincts, traits, types, genes, and blame these things – yet not things, merely our ideas – for what we do. What a brilliant idea! What better idea can we have, than that we are not responsible for our actions!

This is primitive pride at work, aided and abetted by moral pride, which is always adept at manipulating ideas in order to preserve the incorruptible virtue of the person concerned. Moral pride is a set of ideas which bears some relationship to what is actually going on. It may ensure that the individual can find truth and clarity no matter how uncomfortable such discoveries might be, but all too often it joins forces with primitive pride to dream up wonderful excuses why this virtuous, upright, honest person was not responsible.

We can claim that we are not responsible because whatever happens is determined by God or Allah, or is the outcome of a cosmic battle between good and evil. We can claim that we are not responsible because everything that happens is a result of a worldwide conspiracy. Paranoia is a great way of avoiding personal responsibility.

We can claim that we are not responsible because we were simply obeying orders. In Nazi Germany and apartheid South Africa violence and torture were coordinated and carried out through a bureaucracy which enabled those it employed to claim that they were not responsible because they were doing what they had been told to do by their superiors.

We can claim that we are not responsible because we were victims of our past. Explanations of current behaviour in terms of an unhappy childhood can be turned into excuses for avoiding responsibility. Hillary Clinton thus sought to excuse her husband for his persistent philandering. She said, 'He was so young, barely four, when he was scarred by abuse that he can't take it out and look at it. There was a terrible conflict between his mother and grandmother. A psychologist once told me that for a boy, being in the middle of a conflict between two women is the worst possible situation.'[23]

The leader writer of the Ohio newspaper the *Lima News* saw through this excuse:

> Hillary Clinton's interview has to be the most amazing piece of garbage since this whole thing started. It seems that she is having trouble recognizing that Bill Clinton's philandering is the sole responsibility of Bill Clinton. If he is unable to take responsibility for his own actions – he has yet to do so – then he is unfit for office.[24]

As this leader writer would be the first to point out, Bill Clinton must have known that it was wrong for him to be unfaithful to his wife and to lie to the nation. These ideas were known to Bill Clinton.

He chose not to operate on them, thus he was responsible for what he did.

No matter how many ideas our meaning structure contains it cannot encompass all the ideas that exist at any one time; therefore we cannot be held responsible for actions which run counter to ideas outside the range of all the ideas we have ever encountered. A two-year-old child is unlikely to be able to make a moral distinction between taking a sweet from her mother's cupboard and taking a sweet from a supermarket shelf. An adult, travelling for the first time in a strange country, may not be able to make a moral distinction between making a certain gesture at home and making the same gesture in this foreign place – a gesture which is offensive to the people there.

When ideas lie within the range of someone's meaning structure that person is responsible for whether or not he chooses to use those ideas. At the Nuremberg International Military Tribunal in 1945 Telford Taylor had the task of prosecuting the senior officers of the German army. He dismissed the generals' defence that they were obeying the orders of the head of state. He said, 'There are some universal standards of human behaviour that transcend the duty of obedience to national laws.'[25] The generals could not argue that they had never heard of such standards.

Choosing between a wide array of possibilities takes time. Sometimes we encounter a situation which seems to demand hasty action. Afterwards we may make a plea for diminished responsibility – 'I didn't have time to think' – but we need to prove that time was short and the need for action pressing. Telford Taylor allowed the German officers no such defence: 'The crimes of these men were not committed in rage, nor under the stress of sudden temptation. One does not build a stupendous war machine in a fit of passion, nor an Auschwitz slave factory during a passing spasm of brutality.'[26]

The story with which we are born tells us that actions have consequences. Stories are concerned with the consequences of actions. As children it takes us some time to discover what actual consequences may result, but we certainly know that other people respond to what we do and say, even though we might not be able to predict correctly what other people's responses will be. Nevertheless, many people try to deny their responsibility by blaming the way in which other people have interpreted their actions and words. Many parents locate the cause of their child's behaviour inside the child – it is caused by the child's own wickedness or stupidity, they say, denying that their own actions and words have played any part in determining how the child sees the world. Similarly, many leaders will insist that they bear no responsibility for the actions of their followers. The loudest and most intransigent of the Unionist politicians, the Reverend Ian Paisley, is one such leader.

Ian Paisley founded his own Free Presbyterian Church in 1951. He made many speeches, but these were usually the same speech repeated over and over with a single theme – Roman Catholicism was the enemy and must be fought. Just how he thought it should be fought was open to interpretation. Ian Paisley always denied that he had any connection with Loyalist paramilitaries and that he ever urged his followers to take up arms against the IRA.

In 1980 Margaret Thatcher and the Irish Prime Minister Charles Haughey got together, liked one another (Mrs Thatcher had a passion for rogues, though she had the good sense not to marry one) and, to the fury of Ian Paisley, came to an agreement which, though it did not seem so at the time, laid the foundation for the Good Friday Agreement. Peter Taylor described what then happened.

> Paisley marched into action, condemning the 'historic breakthrough' in Anglo-Irish relations as treachery, betrayal, and every other synonym he could call on. On the night of 6 February 1981, selected members of the press were escorted to a lonely hillside in County Antrim where they found Paisley at the head of 500 men dressed in combat jackets and lined up in military formation. At a command they waved bits of paper in the air, certificates for legally held shotguns.[27]

A shotgun might not be as efficient as an Armalite but it can kill. At the end of 1981 Paisley formed the 'Third Force' (the police and army being the other two) and called for a day of action.

> Loyalist expectations were raised as they saw 6,000 men, with all manner of dress and demeanour, marching through the streets in the pouring rain, carrying cudgels and trying to look like a private army. From the platform outside the town's historic eighteenth

century courthouse, Paisley boomed that he wanted to see 100,000 men on the march in Ulster – the figure Carson had raised for the original UVF. 'We demand that the IRA be exterminated from Ulster,' he roared. 'The aim of the IRA is to destroy the last vestiges of Protestantism in our island home. But there is one army the Republic fears and that every other enemy of Ulster fears and that is the army of armed and resolute Protestants.' With the men of the 'Third Force' drawn up in front of him he threw cautious language to the wind and rain. 'Here are men willing to do the job of exterminating the IRA. Recruit them under the Crown and they will do it. If you refuse, we will have no other decision but to do it ourselves.'[28]

At an Ulster Clubs rally in Larne in 1986 he said, 'If the British Government force us down the road to a united Ireland, we will fight to the death . . . This could come to hand-to-hand fighting on every street in Northern Ireland. We are on the verge of a civil war . . . We are asking people to be ready for the worst, and I will lead them.'[29]

These two speeches were not aberrations but examples of his central theme and style. Peter Taylor asked various members of the Loyalist paramilitary groups how they had interpreted what Ian Paisley said. By 1980

Gusty Spence's son-in-law, Winston Churchill 'Winkie' Rea, had been released from gaol, where he had been since 1973, and was angered to see Paisley marching up and down again. In earlier days 'Winkie' had thought Paisley was Ulster's saviour, but his own experience and his years in gaol had taught him that he was not. 'I used to go to Paisley's rallies,' he told me. 'I listened to what he had to say, "Ulster will fight and Ulster will be right", and I read into that the way he meant. I thought he meant fighting. Now perhaps he did not mean it that way, but I surely put that meaning into it.' I pointed out that Paisley would always emphatically deny that any such interpretation should be put on his words. 'I would accept that,' 'Winkie' replied. 'But at the same time I would ask him to accept what I read into what he was saying and I genuinely believed it.'[30]

Billy Giles said,

'He was the man. I thought that whatever Paisley said was true. Being affected by Paisley was part of being Protestant. We went to his rallies. Tens of thousands followed him, just to hear what he had to say. He was preaching about a situation as if it was the gospel or a biblical text and, because of our upbringing, we were a ready audience. When you're young and caught up in that kind of atmosphere, you can't distinguish one thing from another. On reflection now, I realize he was full of hate.'[31]

When Billy Giles was eighteen he joined the Ulster Volunteer Force. In retaliation for an Irish National Liberation Army murder of a young woman Billy killed his Catholic friend and workmate Michael Fay. He told Peter Taylor,

'The second it happened, I lost part of myself that I'll never get back. You hear the bang, and it's too late. Standing over the body, it hits you. I felt that somebody had reached down inside me and ripped my insides out. You've found somewhere you've never been before and it's not a very nice place. You can't stop it. It's too late. I never felt a whole person again. I lost something that day I never got back. How do you put that back? You can't. You'll never get that back no matter what people say to you or what you say or think. I've done something and been involved in something and I have to live with it.'[32]

Billy was arrested and went to prison. There he did his GCSEs and went on to do an Open University degree in social studies. He wrote a play about his childhood which was later produced in Belfast. His parents were very proud of him. He was released in 1997 and was part of the Progressive Unionist Party negotiating team in the Good Friday Agreement in April 1998. In September 1998 he hanged himself.

Bobby Morton, an Ulster Volunteer Force man sentenced for conspiracy to murder, told Peter Taylor,

'We all have to take responsibility for this [conflict] and not least the politicians. They were only too happy to lead us by the nose at one stage. "Get into them boys!", "Protestant Ulster!", "We will fight and we will die!" Well, they never fought and they never died. It was left to the likes of me to go out and act on their behalf.'[33]

In reply to such comments Ian Paisley said,

'Oh yes, they do blame me. They say I got them put into prison and I've heard them all and I read their magazines. Their slanders are outrageous, and all I can say is that they're not worthy of comment because if they had been worthy of comment, the vast electorate of Northern Ireland wouldn't have voted for me in the way they do.'[34]

Onlookers to events in Northern Ireland found it curious that in all the vox pop interviews the media did in Northern Ireland every person said that they wanted peace, yet many of these people voted not for the politicians who were actively working for peace but for politicians who were obstructing the peace process. This is an example of what psychologists call 'faking good', where we say publicly what we think will make us look virtuous, even though this is not what we actually believe. It is a form of lying which can confound a reconciliation process.

How people interpret what we say raises some difficult questions about responsibility. Other people are free to interpret what we say in any way they like. I have been amazed by the way in which some religious or spiritual people have interpreted what I have written. They have been able to find in my words a confirmation that I have strong religious or spiritual beliefs. This astounds me because I think I have always made clear that, while I feel a passionate connection to what I see in my garden or in the world generally and to other people, I do not feel the need for a belief in some superior being to explain and connect me to the world around me. I can only assume that what I have written in other contexts – perhaps about loving and accepting oneself and taking life as it comes – has meant a great deal to these readers, to the extent that they had to assimilate everything else I said into what they believe, even though this meant attributing to me things which I have not said. I think I write clearly just as Ian Paisley speaks clearly, but I hope that my words are not capable of serious misinterpretation. I often speak in metaphor, but I hope my metaphors are clearly flagged as metaphors. When I speak of primitive pride behaving like a mischievous imp I hope I am not taken to mean that there actually is within each of us a little imp wearing a T-shirt labelled 'PRIMITIVE PRIDE'.

I have not been to any of Ian Paisley's rallies, though I have been watching them on television for many years. When he spoke of 'exterminating the IRA' or 'hand-to-hand fighting on every street in Northern Ireland' and the like it sounded to me as if he was telling his followers to take up arms and kill the enemy. I recall no occasion when he said, 'I am speaking metaphorically.' I recall no occasion when he warned young men not to be so enthused that they took up arms and killed people. Perhaps he did this, but nothing I have seen or read of him suggested that this was so.

We have no control over how our listeners interpret what we say. All we can do is try to make our meaning clear. If we say, 'We must fight the enemy,' we need to make explicit who we are, who the enemy are, and how we should fight them. What we say is our responsibility. If we fail to make ourselves sufficiently clear we need to apologize. If Ian Paisley did not intend that Protestants should take up arms and kill Catholics he should have apologized for not making himself clear.

Ian Paisley insisted that 'I've never asked anybody to do anything that I haven't been prepared to do myself.'[35] When Peter Taylor asked him about Thomas McDowell, who was a member both of Ian Paisley's church and of the Ulster Protestant Volunteers, he gave the Pinochet/de Klerk answer: 'I can't be responsible for everybody who is a member of a church that I pastor, or an organization that I lead.'[36] He insisted, 'I lived my life before God, before my country and, to tell you the truth, I couldn't care less what people say about me, either when I'm living or dead. All I can say is, I'll not be changing. I will go to the grave with the convictions I have.'[37]

Ian Paisley was a man of absolute belief. He preached that every word in the Bible is true. He rejected the Good Friday Agreement and refused to speak to Sinn Fein, but he insisted on his party's right to sit in the Assembly. Again he was claiming power without responsibility.

But the tide of events moved on and left him beached on the sands of his absolute beliefs. On the evening of 2 December 1999

we saw on our television screens pictures of the members of the
Assembly cabinet without ceremony wandering into the cabinet
room and greeting one another like old friends. We saw David
Trimble teasing Martin McGuinness when Martin mistakenly took
the seat reserved for one of the absent DUP members and Martin
grinning at David and saying self-deprecatingly, 'That's the first
mistake.' Then the television crews were ushered out of the cabinet
room. The next pictures we saw were of the news conference called
by Ian Paisley. He sat behind a desk flanked by the other DUP
Assembly members and launched into his usual attack. That day,
he bellowed, was the blackest day in the history of Northern Ireland.
The look in his eyes suggested that it was the blackest day in his
life. All that he had worked for and believed in seemed to be irretriev-
ably lost. Trying to hold our meaning structure together in defiance
of threatened disconfirmation is physically debilitating. Ian Paisley,
once a huge, strong man, now looked old and frail.

Accepting responsibility for what you have done and changing
long-held ideas both require considerable courage. If peace had
come to Northern Ireland it was because enough people were able
to find that courage.

The Sinn Fein leader Martin McGuinness began his political life
when he was eighteen. He believed that violence was necessary to
force the British out of Northern Ireland. He became one of the
leaders of the IRA and devoted his life to the aim of creating a
Republican Ireland. However, as circumstances changed he changed
his views. He told Kevin Toolis,

'Everyone is responsible for this conflict in Ireland. The British
government, the Dublin government, the SDLP, the Unionists, the
IRA, everybody, we are all responsible, and it is only by getting
together and sorting it all out that there will be a resolution. I
haven't got any grand plan or solution but what we are saying is,
let's get together in a room, let everyone express their fears and
their difficulties, and let the people of Ireland discuss what sort of
political structures they want.
   . . . Our position has not changed. We would like to see a unitary
state, we would like to see a thirty-two county Republic, but we
recognize that we are only a small percentage of the total people of
this island. The people of this island might decide on some other

type of structure. I am not going to oppose it. I might oppose it politically but there is no way I would defend anybody's right to use armed force to go against the democratic wish of the people of this land.'[38]

These words proved not to be empty rhetoric.

Ian Paisley and many other Loyalists no doubt would have said that Martin McGuinness was lying. Probably there were times when, frustrated by the slow progress in coming to a political agreement, Martin McGuinness would find his old, hard-line attitudes reasserting themselves, but he had made the first step towards reconciliation. He had said, 'I was responsible. I am sorry.'

Leaders of each side in a conflict used to be able to conduct their negotiations in relative privacy, but with the advent of newspapers and then radio and television much of the negotiating took place with a public audience. Leaders have always been keen to seize and hold the moral high ground, but such a position, like that of martyrdom, requires an audience. No matter how virtuous you might appear to yourself, it will go against you if your audience does not see you as virtuous. The problem for leaders now is which audience to impress. The Unionist audience might have regarded David Trimble and the other Unionist leaders as being courageous and strong in their opposition to Sinn Fein, but their worldwide audience grew increasingly likely to see them as boringly and stupidly intransigent. Perhaps in the intimate talks during the Good Friday review David Trimble came to realize this. Often, as we come to understand another person better, we learn something about ourselves.

Conflicts and negotiations within families and among friends, while they might not draw the attention of the media, do have an audience of family and friends. Often individuals spend years suffering rather than confront the relative or friend who causes them to suffer for fear of being seen as a bad person. I know that there are people who find it shocking that I write about my mother as I do, and they think less of me for that. I have met many women who were attached to a man who caused them much grief. Such a woman might know that her friends and family would cheer if she left him, but she could not do this because in her own eyes she would be a bad person. She might pride herself on being sensitive and caring, and could not bear to think that she had hurt someone, even though that person had hurt her.

In conflicts with family, lovers and friends we have a choice. We can let the conflict drift on with all its attendant miseries or we can utter that challenge, 'We have to talk.' In such a discussion past events are examined with the aim of defining the issues from which the conflict has arisen. As a therapist I would never advise my clients to put such a challenge to the person who had hurt them so much, but some of my clients chose to do so, with very mixed results. Over the years various friends have told me they have done the same, again with the same mixed results. Sometimes the person challenged ran away, either literally or by taking refuge in silence, but when the person did respond there were, generally speaking, three possible outcomes of such a challenge.

The first is where the person challenged responds with, 'Yes, that happened. I accept my responsibility, and I am sorry.' With that response the way is clear for reconciliation and, perhaps, forgiveness. Of course, we have to make sure that the person is prepared to change. There are some people who find apologizing easy because, having done so, they can then go back to doing what they did before. They think that saying sorry makes up for whatever wrongs they have committed.

The second outcome is where the person responds with, 'Well, perhaps something like that happened, but not as you describe it. I'm sorry you were upset, but I was very busy at the time, my health was poor, I had all those responsibilities, you don't know what I had to put up with from your father, you were the youngest, you had things easier than I did . . .' and so on. To an outside observer this might look like an apology but it is not. It is an excuse for avoiding responsibility. 'I'm sorry you were upset' is a statement of pity for someone, but it is the pity we feel for someone whose suffering has nothing to do with us personally. It is not an apology. This and the list of excuses always contain a veiled attack. The person who has issued the challenge is shown to be weak and wicked, while the person challenged seizes the moral high ground. The challenger then has a choice: either to enter into an argument, which will prove fruitless and potentially endless, or to walk away.

The third outcome is where the person challenged says, 'How dare you say that to me! The things that you're talking about never happened. I have never done anything in my life which hurt any-body. There is nothing I should apologize for. You are a bad person and deserve what happened to you.' This response often includes a creative rewriting of history. A mother who sat back while her husband beat their eldest child would in later years ward off criticism from her adult children with, 'I used to say to him, "That child needs love."' Her children knew that she had not done this, but they felt there was nothing they could say.

The first step on the path to reconciliation is to establish what did happen. Responses two and three are refusals to do this. The report of the Truth and Reconciliation Commission in South Africa stated very firmly, 'While truth may not always lead to reconciliation, there can be no genuine, lasting reconciliation without truth.'

In my experience people who produce a genuine first response are rare, but we cannot find them until we ask, 'Can we talk?' This requires courage: we are likely to be talking to someone who gives the second or third response, or alternates between the two.

I wish I had some way of giving those who can only produce the second or third response the courage to accept their own responsibil-ity, but I do not. Their fear of losing the picture they have of themselves and their place in the world, their fear of a conscience punishing them for past misdeeds, may be so strong that it makes it impossible for them to take their relationships with other people into consideration. Usually such people do not love their challenger, and so there is no incentive for them to look after the challenger, particularly if doing so would put them at risk. They might profess a love for the challenger and believe that they are telling the truth, but all they ever feel is a mild, sentimental affection, and then only when the challenger pleases them. They might want the challenger to love them, but not at the expense of allowing that person a victory over them.

One of the saddest, hardest things that we have to do is to accept that those people who in an ideal world would have loved us bounti-fully simply because we existed are limited by their own sense of being unloved and by their jealousy, envy and hate – to the extent that they are unable even to know what generosity and compassion are, much less to exhibit them. It is always hard to accept that a lover who once loved us wildly and passionately has ceased to love us, but even in the pain of heartbreak we can admit that people change and that is the way life is; as time goes by we might even feel glad that that particular love ended. However, to admit that by unlucky chance we have been born into a family where love is in very short supply, that is a sadness we take to the grave. Difficult though it is, the best we can do is not to blame ourselves for being unlovable but to see the situation clearly and do what can be sensibly done to protect ourselves from further hurt.

So, instead of concentrating on trying to change these difficult people, we should treat them like we treat bad weather, something that is there and from which we must protect ourselves. Then we can concentrate on how we respond when someone says to us, 'Can we talk?' Even in the best of circumstances and with the best will in the world reconciliation and forgiveness are not easy.

Becoming Reconciled

Clare in the Community was the heroine of Harry Venning's cartoon strip for the Society section of the *Guardian*. I was very fond of Clare because she encapsulated the experiences of so many people whom I have known. Clare was a social worker, as was her boyfriend Brian and her friend Megan. One day Clare and Megan were having a beer at their pub. Megan said, 'I'm really glad you and Brian are back together.'

'Yeah,' said Clare, 'but we've got a lot of stuff to work through yet, Megan. Which is why we both decided to go to couple counselling. So we can reassess and explore the nature of our relationship in a supportive, non-judgemental environment.'

Megan asked, 'How long do you think you'll go for?'

Clare replied, 'Until the little bastard admits it was his fault.'

Like many people, Clare did not see reconciliation as a mutual process of two people or two groups coming together, recognizing that each had played a part in what had gone wrong, and trying to understand the other's point of view before entering into negotiations. Clare preferred to see herself as totally in the right, Brian as totally in the wrong and duty-bound to make amends to her.

This stance towards any disagreement or falling out, or bitter conflict or war, is very popular because it protects us from the shame and guilt which might arise when we admit responsibility,

and from the anxiety which we may feel when we change our meanings and consequently behave differently; the consequence of this
is that it is more difficult to predict what the outcome will be. In
the short term this defence might appear to keep us safe, but in the
long term it does nothing to ameliorate the situation and indeed
might make it a great deal worse. Whenever we refuse to recognize
the truth of a situation and place all the blame on the other person
we become dangerous to the other person because we are denying
that person's truth, and we are being unjust. These both threaten
the other person's meaning structure. Our adversary must defend
himself against these threats, and so the enmity increases.

Even when we feel with considerable justification that we are not
in the wrong in any way we must consider our own attitudes and
actions if a reconciliation is to be achieved. Reconciliation will
require us to make some changes in our attitudes and actions. If
we are not prepared to do this reconciliation will fail. I was greatly
saddened when, at the end of a discussion with a leading Serbian
journalist who was a strong critic of Milosevic, I asked him what
needed to change if the terrible situation in Serbia was to come to
an end. He answered immediately, 'The policies of America and the
EC.' He did not consider it necessary for the Serbs themselves to
change in any way.

The first step in reconciliation is often the recognition that your
enemy has also had a bad time. One of the amazing things about
becoming a parent is discovering why your parents behaved as they
did, why they got so angry and so tired, why they complained when
you got into bed with them or when they were in the bathroom
and you banged impatiently on the door. My friend Anne, born in
China, was as a young girl fostered by an English couple, who
brought her to England to live. She was very unhappy because the
couple made no attempt to understand her background or her feelings for her new home, but years later Anne, as a mother of three,
could say, 'I see now that I gave my foster parents a terrible time.'

If the Truth and Reconciliation Commission in South Africa
achieved nothing else it made it very difficult for those who did not
suffer under apartheid to say that suffering did not occur. It did
not make it impossible. There are always people who will ignore all
the evidence to the contrary and declare that the world is as they
want it to be. However, faced with the mass of evidence presented

to the commission, many people felt that they had to make some kind of public statement about their feelings. The TRC set up an Internet website which included a Register of Reconciliation, where individuals could make their statement. To me some of these statements were more dramatic than sincere, but others had the succinctness of truth. Deon Stols of Centurion said, 'I am sorry for what I did during the bush war. I am sorry for being a racist during the apartheid years.'[39] Alexa Kirsten of Wellington said, 'I was born in the fifties in the Easter Cape and so grew up being part of the system. I am deeply sorry for any pain caused by my failure to act and stand up for the people of this land who were oppressed. I beg your forgiveness.'[40]

Daniel du Plessis of Vredehoek recognized that as well as making a general apology it was necessary to ask forgiveness of specific individuals.

> On behalf of my family I wish to apologize to our servants for ill-treating them, especially to the family of the woman known to me as 'Liesbet' (Elizabeth) who worked for us many years when we were living in the Free State (OFS). She came from Lesotho and lived in a little hut outside our property. We were living in the mining village of Theunissen. To this day my parents cannot tell me what happened to her when my father was transferred. I know they would also wish to apologize for not treating her properly.[41]

Colin Glen of Johannesburg looked into himself and produced not an excuse but an explanation.

> I deeply regret that I did not take a more proactive stance in fighting the evil of apartheid. I could have done more than I did, and justified my lack of action on the basis that I was 'getting on with my life'. I was influenced by the propaganda of the government of the time, and accepted the censorship imposed on us all without going to the trouble of thinking about the consequences of this. This, despite the evidence of suffering around me. Needless to say, this could not have happened if I myself had not been desensitized and damaged by the harsh Calvinist home in which I was brought up. The lack of wisdom and compassion which was part of me, and the emotional deadness from which I suffered are staggering. I pray that all those

who have been hurt and whose lives have been destroyed by my
lack of action are more aware and compassionate than I was, and
have more wisdom which may enable them to understand the circumstances which led to my lack of action, and, through doing so,
find it in their hearts to forgive me.[42]

Colin Glenn shows how we can be so wrapped up in our own
affairs and so inured to other people's suffering that we fail to take
a critical stance towards what is going on around us. Often we feel
so sure that our suffering is greater than anyone else's that we do
not recognize what is happening to other people. When another
person has inflicted great pain on us and threatened the core of our
being it might not even occur to us that that person also suffered.
Knowing that our enemy is suffering can fill us with the glee of
vengeance, but that is possible only when we are seeing our enemy
as an object and not as a person like ourselves. Knowing that our
enemy is human and knowing that he suffers as human beings suffer
is a necessary step on the path to reconciliation.

This is what Eric Lomax found. As a boy in Scotland Eric Lomax
became passionately interested in railways. In one of those ironies
that abound in life, he found himself as a prisoner of war on the
infamous Burma–Siam Railway. At the beginning of the Second
World War he joined the army as an officer in Signals and was
captured by the Japanese at the fall of Singapore in 1942. As his
autobiography *The Railway Man* reveals, Eric Lomax was one of
those organized, orderly introverts who has to have clear in his mind
just where he is. He constructed a map of Burma and the railway,
and it was his possession of this and his part in the construction of
a radio receiver that led him to fall foul of his captors in Kanchana-
buri – or Kanburi, as it was known to the English prisoners. He
was savagely beaten, tortured by near-drowning, and incessantly
interrogated. The person he hated most was the interpreter. He
wrote,

I hated him more and more. He was the one asking the questions,
driving me on. I was sick of the sight of him, I would have killed
him for his endless insistence, his boring, mechanical curiosity about
things I thought he would never understand. I remembered all the
POW talk about the moment when you are absolutely doomed and

you take one of them with you. It was easier said than done with
two broken arms, but it came to me all the time now and I wanted
to do it. It was the interpreter I would have tried to kill.[43]

The interpreter was a young man called Nagase Takashi. At the
end of the war Eric Lomax still felt a passionate hatred for Nagase.
He wrote, 'In the cold light of day my anger was more often turned
to the Japanese who had beaten, interrogated and tortured me. I
wanted to do violence to them, thinking quite specifically of how I
would like to revenge myself on the goon squad from Kanburi and
the hateful little interpreter.'[44]
Fifty years on his hatred for Nagase had not dimmed:

The more I thought about and thought about it, the more I wished
to do damage to the Kempei men if I could ever find them. Physical
revenge seemed the only adequate recompense for the anger I
carried. I often thought about the young interpreter at Kanburi . . .
he was centre stage in my memories; he was my private obsession.[45]

By chance he was given information about Nagase, who had
become active in charitable causes linked to the Burma–Siam Railway. Eric Lomax was sceptical and rejecting. Then he was sent a
much longer article about Nagase. 'This article described how Nagase
had spent much of his life "making up for the Japanese Army's
treatment of prisoners of war".' It also described 'his ill health, his
recurrent heart disease, and how every time he suffered a cardiac
attack "he has flashbacks of Japanese military police torturing a
POW who was accused of possessing a map of the railway".'[46]
Eric Lomax described how he felt. 'The years of feeling powerless
whenever I thought of him and his colleagues were erased. Even
now, given the information about what he had done since the war,
and my own changing feelings about revenge, the old feelings came
to the surface and I wanted to damage him for his part in ruining
my life.'[47]
Then he was sent a copy of a small book which Nagase had written.
In it was a description of the torture Eric Lomax had suffered. Nagase
wrote,

They poured water into his mouth. I saw his stomach swelling up. Watching the prisoner in great torture, I almost lost my presence of mind. I was desperate to control my shaking body. I feared he would be killed in my presence. I took him by the broken wrist and felt the pulse. I still remember clearly I was relieved to feel an unexpected normal pulse.[48]

By this time Eric Lomax had met Helen Bamber of the Medical Foundation for Care of the Victims of Torture and had been greatly helped by her understanding. He had also, at long last, made a happy marriage. With such support he was able to let his wife Patti write to Nagase, who answered with what Patti called 'an extraordinarily beautiful letter'. When Eric Lomax read the letter,

Anger drained away; in its place came a welling of compassion for both Nagase and me, coupled with a deep sense of sadness and regret. In that moment I lost whatever hard armour I had wrapped around me and began to think the unthinkable: that I could meet Nagase face to face in simple good will. Forgiveness became more than an abstract idea: it was now a real possibility.[49]

Eric Lomax and his wife travelled to Kanburi, where they met Nagase. Out of this meeting was born a firm friendship. He concluded,

Meeting Nagase has turned him from a hated enemy, with whom a friendship would have been unthinkable, into a blood brother. If I'd never been able to put a name to the face of one of the men who harmed me, and never discovered that behind that face there was also a damaged life, the nightmares would have always come from a past without meaning. And I had proved for myself that remembering is not enough, if it simply hardens hate.[50]

Hatred does constrict us, making us less of the person that we might have been. Once the armour of hate had fallen from him Eric Lomax was able to see that Nagase had also suffered. He was a victim of the war just as Eric Lomax was. They both had the courage to say, 'Yes, this happened. I am sorry.'

What are we saying when we say, 'I am sorry'? This was a question argued over by Australians when National Sorry Day was proposed for 26 May 1998. The previous year a Human Rights Commission report revealed to all Australians the plight of those Aboriginal children – an estimated 100,000 – who had been removed from their families. National Sorry Books were made available in many places and people were invited to sign the following statement:

By signing my name in this book, I record my deep regret for the injustices suffered by Indigenous Australians as a result of European settlement and, in particular, I offer my personal apology for the hurt and harm caused by the forced removal of children from their families and for the effect of government policy on human dignity and spirit of Indigenous Australians.

I would also like to record my desire for Reconciliation and for a better future for all our people. I make a commitment to a united Australia which respects this land of ours, values Aboriginal and Torres Strait Islander heritage and provides justice and equity for all.

Many thousands of Australians signed the Sorry Books and some made their own special apology. The New South Wales police commissioner, Peter Ryan, himself an Englishman, apologized to Aboriginal people for the role the police played in separating the stolen generation from their families. He apologized on behalf of the justice system, including the police, the Attorney-General's Department, Corrective Services and Juvenile Justice. He said,

I offer a sincere apology to members of the stolen generations and to all the Aboriginal and Torres Strait Islander people for the prominent role the police played in enforcing past unjust laws. Police over a long time were the public face of the government and as agents of the government police caused unimaginable pain and anguish to Aboriginal and Torres Strait Islander communities and families, particularly mothers and children, by the forcible removal of children.[51]

Many thousands of Australians did not sign the Sorry Books, some because of lack of time or opportunity, some out of fury at being expected to apologize for something for which they thought they had no responsibility. The Minister for Aboriginal Affairs, John

Herron, told the Senate, 'People should not be made to feel guilty for something they had no direct part in. The Labor Party seems to be in the crying game these days – dropping down and crying all over the place. I do not believe that is leadership.'[52] Only someone who fears his own weakness can see apologizing as an act which increases that weakness.

The Prime Minister John Howard said, 'Personally I feel deep sorrow for those of my fellow Australians who suffered injustices under the practices of past generations towards indigenous people.' However, he rejected a formal apology because 'Australians of this generation should not be required to accept blame and guilt for past actions and policies over which they had no control.'[53] In 1999 the Aboriginal Senator Aden Ridgeway wrung from Howard a statement of 'sincere and deep regret for the hurt and trauma suffered by so many indigenous people', but Howard refused to use the word 'sorry'.[54]

Noel Pearson, a very clever Aboriginal lawyer, pointed out the lack of logic in this statement.

As individuals, ordinary Australians cannot be expected to feel guilty about the past. They might be fairly held to account for what happens in their own lifetimes and, perhaps, what they leave for the future. But the Australian community has a collective consciousness, and that includes the past. If that were not so, how could we share and celebrate in the achievements of the past – indeed, feel responsibility for and express pride in aspects of our past – and not feel responsibility for and express shame in relation to other aspects of the past? To say that ordinary Australians do not have any connection with the shameful aspects of our past is at odds with our exhortations that they have strong connections to the prideful bits, like Gallipoli and Kokoda.[55]

To celebrate our virtues we need also to regret our vices. Not to do so is to deny what actually happened. When it is the virtues and vices of our ancestors that are in question we cannot apologize on behalf of people long dead, but we can show that we acknowledge the feelings of their victims, and of the descendants of those victims. Gatjil Djerrkura, the head of the Aboriginal and Torres Strait Islander Commission, said, 'Sorry Day is not about guilt, it is about understanding – for our people, saying sorry is simply a way of recognizing another person's feelings.'[56]

Recognizing another person's feelings requires us to have some understanding of that person's point of view. Sometimes we can be unaware of the extent of our ignorance. When I went to the Omagh branch of WAVE, a befriender organization for the victims of the Troubles, I met Tracy, the coordinator for WAVE in Omagh, and John, a psychologist. They both told me how they had grown up during the Troubles and had known nothing of what life could be like for people who did not live in a country where the people were divided into two antagonistic groups, where an army patrolled the streets and the police themselves were like an army. Tracy told me that when she had gone to England she was amazed to see that the police were not armed. John told me how, when he was sixteen, he went to an international camp in Scotland. There he was surprised almost beyond belief to find that, not just in the camp but on the boat and train and in the streets, people of different religions and national backgrounds were behaving in very ordinary ways.

It is only by talking together, by participating together in some undertaking that we can start to glimpse how the other person sees certain things in ways very different from us. When we do not talk to people we can form all kinds of theories about those people – how they see the world and why they do what they do – but once we start talking to them and taking account of what they say we often see our theories fall apart. This is why psychiatrists wedded to a belief in the reality of mental illnesses spend as short a time as possible in conversation with their patients, and why David Trimble and his fellow Unionists would not talk to Sinn Fein.

To understand another person we need to know what is important to that person and why. Whatever is important to us makes us vulnerable, and so our defence against attack must be strong. Enemies often seek to discover what is important to us so that they can know what best to attack. In the First World War the German Chief of Staff General Erich von Falkenhayn decided that, as Verdun was of supreme importance to the French, it was there that the German army should attack. Verdun, a town on the river Meuse in northern France, was a bastion against a German invasion and a symbol to the French of France's glory. Von Falkenhayn reasoned that, if the German army captured Verdun, France would be finished. He would use his massive artillery to destroy the French. However, because Verdun was so important to France, the French army defended it fiercely. 'They shall not pass' became the renowned cry of the defenders. The siege of Verdun lasted from February to July 1916 and, although the French drove the Germans back, it cost both sides altogether over a million men.

If the French who had vowed 'They shall not pass' had been asked, 'Why is Verdun important to you?' their answers would have reflected how they defined themselves in terms of their French nationality and how they shared in France's glory. We defend fiercely what is important to us because it is a central part of who we know ourselves to be. In negotiations it might be easy to give up things which are not essential parts of our being. Our sticking point is when we are asked to give up something which we see as essential to our being. When interviewed on television about the IRA's refusal to decommission Kevin Toolis said, 'Guns are sacred objects to the IRA. To ask them to give them up is to ask them to give up part of themselves.'[57]

Under the terms of the review by George Mitchell of the Good Friday Agreement, within the space of twenty-four hours the Queen would give her assent to the bill devolving power from the British government to the Northern Ireland Assembly, the Irish government would rewrite part of its constitution, removing those clauses to do with the government's determination to create a united Ireland, the Assembly cabinet would hold its first meeting and the IRA would give General de Chastelain, who was in charge of decommissioning paramilitary weapons, the name of the person who would liaise with the general and begin the process. On 2 December 1999 all these events took place, but the IRA waited until the brink of 9 p.m. to pass their information on to the general. The aim of this timing was to ensure maximum publicity by waiting until all the other events had taken place and then catching the 9 p.m. news bulletins on radio and television. Their actions demonstrated that the IRA leaders well understood that the media, the purveyor of ideas, is mightier than the gun.

The Troubles might be over but many troubles still lay ahead for those who were now responsible for Northern Ireland. Decommissioning might solve the problems of the guns, but how would they solve the problems of the parades so dear to Loyalists' hearts?

All around the world weapons and parades have been the means whereby people – chiefly men – persuaded themselves that they are strong and important. But there are other advantages. In any conflict involving weapons some people on both sides make money. Parades and the like can be seen as a pleasant break from routine, a chance to socialize and gossip. The advantages which we get out of a situation may prevent us from changing. It is easy to give up those things which cause us nothing but pain, but it is difficult to give up anything that yields some kind or advantage or reward. If we want to change we have to identify what advantages and rewards we get out of the situation and ask ourselves whether we are prepared to give them up. For two people or two groups to become reconciled they both need to identify the advantages to each of them in the conflict and ask themselves whether they are prepared to give them up.

What often tips the balance in a reconciliation process is a change in the economic situation. Money relates to the practicalities of life – food, clothing, shelter – and how we see ourselves and our relationships. It is at once objective and subjective, and so our relationship to it is always complex.[58] When a married couple split up it is often money – or the individual's relationship to money – which determines whether they manage to rework their relationship amicably or not. Often the man will use money as a way of breaking his tie to his wife. Where he has always been generous he becomes mean and claims that she is a gold-digger, trying to take from him all that he has. In most divorces the woman ends up poorer, and many women find that this demeans them. In our society being divorced is no longer a matter of shame but being poor is.

An opinion often expressed about the future of Northern Ireland is that economic factors will bring the conflict to an end. The Troubles were very much a working-class war. The middle class on both sides largely stayed out of the conflict while the working-class Protestants and the working-class Catholics fought one another. Both sides were poor and economically had little to lose. If they looked south to Ireland all they saw was a poor country dominated by the Catholic Church.

Then Ireland joined the European Community and life changed. As the benefits from the Community poured in the Church began to lose its grip on the Irish people, especially the younger generation.

By 1999 Ireland had the fastest growing economy in Europe. Many people in Northern Ireland wanted to share in this wealth, but they knew that the industries which created such wealth would not come to Northern Ireland until there was peace. It was significant that, when David Trimble, as First Minister, had the first choice of portfolios, he chose for his close colleague Sir Reg Empey not the finance portfolio, which in other cabinets carries the most weight and power, but the portfolio for enterprise, trade and investment.

As I travelled around Northern Ireland in 1999 I was impressed by the amount of house-building that was going on. I stayed in bed and breakfast places and was amazed at the size and quality of the accommodation. When I visited distant relatives in Narin in County Donegal I asked Anne, who ran a bed and breakfast, what was happening. She told me, 'The business people want a settlement in Northern Ireland. They see what is happening in Dublin and they want a part of it. After the first ceasefire English tourists started to come to Northern Ireland, but there was no accommodation. So people started building extensions to their houses and advertising bed and breakfast. They took out mortgages to build these extensions, and then the ceasefire was broken. That was a terrible blow, so now it is terribly important to them that the settlement succeed.'

However, nothing in Northern Ireland is simple. Conflicts never are. I had seen many new houses, obviously summer homes, in what had been the empty coast of northern County Donegal. Anne told me that these houses were owned by people from Northern Ireland. In Omagh I asked Anthony about all these fine houses. 'Where did they get their money from?' I asked.

Anthony laughed. 'That's what we'd all like to know.' He went on and talked about the black economy. People did things for one another. If you are building yourself a house you get your cousin to do the wiring, another relative to paint it. Money did not change hands, or, if it did, no tax was paid on it. 'We're all rebels,' explained Anthony. 'Some of the goody-goody Protestants used to pay their full tax but now they've stopped.'

I described to Anthony how quickly HM customs and Excise had come after me when, because of illness, I had not sent my VAT return in on time. I said, 'If peace here lasts the bureaucrats will be able to set up their systems and keep tabs on everybody.'

Anthony said, 'That's why a lot of people here don't want peace.'

The same applied in Lebanon and Serbia. In both those countries there were people making money out of the conflict, particularly out of arms and illegal drugs. The success of the Northern Ireland Assembly will be very dependent on how it deals with corruption.

Understanding another person or group does not mean approving of the ideas that person or group holds. When a psychologist tries to understood why a person becomes a rapist or child molester that does not mean that he or she approves of rape or paedophilia, any more than a biologist who tries to understand how cells become cancerous approves of cancer. If we want to prevent cancer we have to understand the process which leads to it. If we want to stop someone from becoming a rapist, a paedophile or an enemy, or to get someone to stop being a rapist, a paedophile or an enemy, we have to understand the process whereby that person reached and stayed in that particular state.

We need to be clear about the ideas we are using to describe the process. Ideas are tools, and some tools are better in certain circumstances than others. A sewing machine is an excellent tool if you want to make a dress but it is of no use if you want to mow the lawn.

If you want to understand a person there is a wide variety of tools/ideas which you can use. You could seek to understand your enemy in terms of evolutionary biology. You could say to him, 'You are exhibiting the behaviour of your distant ancestors in that you are the predator and I am the prey.' Or you could seek to understand your enemy in terms of genes. You could say to him, 'You have the aggression gene.' Or you could seek to understand your enemy in terms of astrology. You could say to him, 'You are a Capricorn under the influence of Mars.' Or you could seek to understand your enemy in terms of the ideas he holds. You could say to him, 'You see me as your enemy because you believe that I wish to harm you.'

In understanding your enemy each of these tools/ideas might seem to provide a satisfactory explanation, but what if your enemy asks you, 'How can I change?' Can you tell him how to root out this distant ancestor lodged in his being, or eradicate an undiscovered gene from his body, or change the date of his birth and develop a shield against the supposed influence of a planet? There is only one tool/idea which can help him change. You can say, 'You can choose to change how you see me.'

To this your enemy can rightfully reply, 'If I do choose to change how I see you then you will have to change how you see me because I shall be behaving differently.'

Reconciliation is not possible unless both sides are prepared to change their ideas.

The word reconciliation implies a return to some peaceful past where current enemies lived happily together as equals. This is rarely the case. There is no such past for the blacks and whites in South Africa, nor for the Protestants and Catholics in Northern Ireland, nor for the Serbs, Croats and Muslims in Yugoslavia, nor for the Lebanese and the Israelis. Nor is there any such past for children who have suffered at the hands of their parents or their siblings. Some erstwhile lovers and friends can look back to a happy past, but they cannot return there because time has moved on and they have changed. Reconciliation is never a going back. It is always a moving on, and part of its process is for both sides to agree on what their future will be.

Having agreed to a mutual changing of ideas, both sides to the conflict have to agree on which ideas need changing and what they should be changed to. Many of the disagreements that take place in the process of reconciliation are over what is acceptable and what is unacceptable behaviour. If we are asked in the abstract how we should behave we can all give a list of virtues, but, when we have to consider this question in terms of actual situations, agreed definitions are hard to reach. One man's terrorist is another man's freedom fighter.

What always bedevils such a discussion are the terms 'virtues', 'vices' and 'values'. I have all the virtues and all the right values and my enemy has all the vices and all the wrong values. Virtues, vices and values are discussed as if they were things inside us and not ideas which determine our behaviour. Perhaps we would do better if we talked about standards of behaviour in relationships with one another. Instead of 'family values' we would have standards of behaviour which defined whether certain behaviour was acceptable or not acceptable. A simple measure would be to determine whether one person was treating another person with the dignity and respect which goes along with seeing the other person as a person, rather than as an object. It is possible to treat someone as a person even if we do not agree with their ideas or approve of their actions. When we treat someone as a person we are treating that person as our equal, human like ourselves. When we treat someone as an object we are acting as a predator and seeing that person as prey. If we want to live in a world where people live peacefully together treating a person as an object must, without exception, be unacceptable.

Viewed in this way it is clear that the corporal punishment of children is unacceptable. In Chapter Four I listed four 'family values', namely:

- demanding a loyalty which ignores the rights and wishes of the individual from whom loyalty is demanded;
- treating those who are not family members as being of no value;
- demanding that individual family members be the kind of person the more powerful members of the family want that person to be;
- criticizing other family members, using them and treating them with discourtesy.

These behaviours are unacceptable.

People who have some degree of power, either in politics, or business, or education, or in the family, are quite likely to claim that they have very high standards. This sounds very virtuous, but often the application of these high standards results in some other less powerful people being treated as objects. Margaret Thatcher was a woman of such high standards. When Brian Keenan, John McCarthy and Terry Waite were taken hostage by the Islamic Jihad in Beirut, Margaret Thatcher produced as an impeccable standard her 'no deals for hostages' policy, and so condemned these three men to five years as prisoners in a most cruel and inhumane system. Margaret Thatcher behaved like the lion who refused to fight the hyenas over a piece of offal. The hostages were to her the offal.

When the United Nations was set up after the Second World War many people felt that at last acceptable standards of behaviour were being defined and agreed on by all the members of the UN. Certainly the standards are there in the UN Charter, but few countries have been prepared either to adhere to them or to chastise and restrain other countries who do not. War might be wrong, but the profits of those who manufacture arms are sacrosanct. Indeed, the richer you are, the more governments will support your nefarious activities. In Africa and south-east Asia millions of people have died or are dying of Aids. The anti-retroviral drugs are expensive, and so South Africa and Thailand set about developing their own versions of Aids drugs at a fraction of the usual price. The American pharmaceutical industry tried to stop them by getting the US government to threaten them with trade sanctions. If this proves to be successful the US government will have killed as many people as it would have done in waging a war on these countries.[59]

Since the establishment of the United Nations many of the conflicts have gone unchecked by the UN on the grounds that one country should not interfere in the internal affairs of another. This excuse was put aside when NATO decided to launch an air war against the Serbs, who were driving the Kosovan Albanians from Kosova. A war tribunal had been set up at The Hague during the Bosnian war to prosecute those who had committed crimes against humanity, and some real progress had been made in establishing and imposing acceptable standards of behaviour. Murder, torture, mutilation, rape, forcible removal of people from their homes and the theft and destruction of their property were defined as crimes against humanity.

> Most significantly [wrote the lawyer Marcel Berlins], there is to be an International Court, to bring under one roof action against those responsible for the most horrible acts of inhumanity, wherever they take place. Yet even that positive move is deeply marred. The country that objects most strongly to the court, and has refused to sign up for it, is the US, which cannot bear the thought of one of its own citizens being accused. It would be ironic indeed if the nation which purported to be the world's moral mentor were to become the wrecker of the most praiseworthy practical step yet taken towards a system of genuinely global justice.[60]

There are times when I can only sympathize with all the people who, when I asked them if they had any enemies, answered, 'America.' I wish that I never ever again have to witness an American president lecturing the world about his virtue, the virtue of his government, and the virtue of 'the American people', but, unless I give up watching television altogether, I doubt that my wish will ever be granted.

The American pharmaceutical industry is wealthy enough to be beyond the dreams of avarice, but the people who run that industry are mean. In American English the adjective 'mean' has two meanings – one to do with being unwilling to part with one's possessions, and the other to do with being aggressive, dangerous, well-defended. To get to the top in large companies people find it necessary to be aggressive, dangerous and well-defended, or, to use what sounds like a nicer word, competitive. In the workshops I ran for management high-flyers I found that, when I tried to demonstrate how the meanings in our meaning structure are all interrelated, the introverts in the workshops were very happy to demonstrate that competition was of supreme importance to them because it gave them a sense of achievement, but the extraverts were forced into fumbling lies as they tried to hide the fact that what mattered most to them was not competition but their relationships with other people. They felt that if this were revealed not only would they be despised by their colleagues but their career would be harmed.

Competition encourages a meanness of spirit. Letting the other side win something, however small, can be seen as a weakness, not a strength. People like to be seen as being generous, but it is often possible to do this without giving anything away. All big companies spend money on sponsoring worthy causes, but this is not out of generosity. Sponsorship is a means of advertising, and the firms select only those causes which enhance their image. The Australian journalist David Marr, writing about race, politics and respectable Australians, said, 'Australians are hugely generous when called upon to make big gestures that cost nothing.'[61]

This is a very different kind of generosity from that described in the report of the Truth and Reconciliation Commission.

> Above all, the Commission tried to listen, really to listen – not passively but actively – to voices that had for so long been stilled. And as it listened to stories of horror, of pathos and of tragic proportion, it became aware of the high cost that has been paid by so many for freedom. Commissioners were almost overwhelmed by the capacity of human beings to damage and destroy each other. Yet they listened, too, to stories of great courage, concluding often

with an astonishing generosity of spirit, from those who had carried for so long the burden of loss and tragedy. It was a deeply humbling experience.

This generosity of spirit shown by many people under apartheid meant that, when the balance of power was changed, they did not take revenge on those who had harmed them. All they asked was that these people join with them in building a new South Africa. Sometimes this generosity of spirit is shown in the way some people will put themselves at risk in order to create a reconciliation process. John Hume, leader of the Social and Democratic Labour Party, ran a great personal and political risk when in 1988, two months after an IRA bomb killed eleven people at Enniskillen, he began discussions with Gerry Adams as part of a process which was, as Gerry Adams noted, much more difficult than making war.

Such generosity of spirit comes from an acceptance of what actually pertains – that is, as much as we like to think of ourselves as being special and other people as being less than us, people are people the world over. Even with our in-built individual perspectives, we are all very much the same. Human needs and desires, angers, hates and fears can be expressed in a multitude of ways, but the basic meanings of these expressions are very much the same for all of us. If we keep ourselves separate from other groups of people we may fail to learn this. The day-to-day separation of Catholics and Protestants in Northern Ireland and the poisonous propaganda put out by the religious and political leaders on both sides meant that both groups saw the other not as ordinary human beings, but as dangerous monsters. By helping the Unionists and the Nationalists talk to one another George Mitchell allowed them to discover that what they had in common was far greater than their differences. In a speech in Dublin while these talks were going on Gerry Adams reminded his Sinn Fein audience that peace-making was hard. He said, 'It means trying to put yourself in the shoes of your opponents. It means resisting the temptation to misrepresent, to hype and to exaggerate.' He went on to pay a tribute to David Trimble. Unionism was 'no longer a monolith'. It had leaders 'who want to set aside the old ways. We need to work with them.' At the same time David Trimble was demonstrating in all his public utterances a generosity towards the Nationalists the like of which had not been seen before.

If we really understand that human needs and desires, angers, hates and fears can be expressed in a multitude of ways, but that the basic meanings of these expressions are very much the same for all of us, it is easy to be generous. We simply extend to other people the indulgence we give to ourselves.

One of the indulgences we like to give to ourselves is to praise ourselves for small achievements. In the negotiations of a reconciliation it is necessary to be generous when the enemy makes some small concession, but mean-spirited people find this hard to do, even when such a gesture would cost them nothing. When, in August 1999, the Irish National Liberation Army called a ceasefire, saying that the war in Northern Ireland was over, Ian Paisley Junior, following closely in his father's footsteps, said that he was 'distinctly underwhelmed' by this news.[62] A cleverer person who understood the importance of generosity in negotiations would have praised the INLA for its decision, while including in his praise a reminder of the 140 and more people the INLA had killed in the twenty-four years of its existence.

Such generosity is not simply a virtue. It is the practice of good science. One thing that psychologists have demonstrated over and over again in both humans and animals is that the most effective way of teaching anybody anything is to reward the right responses and to ignore or not draw attention to the wrong. Whether you are teaching a pigeon to get its food by pecking at a yellow button or an enemy to give up his aggressive ways, this rule applies. With humans the rewards need not be things. Praise from another person is what we value most.

Such praise needs to be given in a sensitive, creative way. Parents who praise their children for everything do nothing but teach their children to take their parents' praise for granted. Some parents and teachers have sought to change the behaviour of the children in their charge by drawing up a schedule of positive reinforcement and then applying it in a routine, mechanical way. Not surprisingly, the children soon see through this, and resent it because they are being treated as if they were stupid animals being passively conditioned to respond in ways which are antagonistic to their way of seeing themselves and their world. The praise that we value is praise from another human being, someone who sees us as another human being struggling with the burdens and difficulties that all people encounter.

The application of good science to conflict-resolution has, since the 1970s, shown some remarkable advances. In the 1950s and 1960s, when jobs were plentiful and the unions strong, conflicts between unions and employers were usually staged in just one way. Union leaders met employers face to face. They argued. Neither side offered any concessions. The union leaders walked out and called a strike. This method of conducting a conflict was futile and destructive. Over the same years divorce became easier, and lawyers, who make their money from an adversarial system, structured divorce as a contest. Only the lawyers profited from this system.

Out of the miseries of these conflicts and the national and sectarian conflicts around the world was born an interest in finding better ways of conducting the negotiations necessary for a reconciliation. The importance of not losing face was recognized; neither party to the negotiations, it was realized, should be confronted with anything that was a serious threat to its meaning structure, because this would produce a defence and prevent the negotiations from moving forward.

Conciliators and mediators have sometimes been very creative in devising strategies for avoiding situations which give rise to such threats and defences. Some of these strategies relate to the physical layout of the place where the negotiations take place. Where the adversaries greatly distrust one another, or fear that their supporters will assume they are consorting with the enemy, they do not sit facing one another until they have reached agreement. Instead they meet in separate rooms, with the negotiators moving between them. Where the adversaries have already met a different strategy can be used. In his review in Northern Ireland George Mitchell decided that meetings between the Republicans and the Unionists should be held in a comfortable sitting room and not across a table in a formal room. He also made it a rule that they should all take their meals together and at such times no issues were to be discussed. There was to be simply polite social chat. He soon found that what he called the participants' 'initial harshness' changed into ordinary conversation. To reduce the pressure on the participants by their supporters he protected them from the media and, at one stage, for better protection, they all moved from Belfast to the comfort and safety of the American embassy in London.

Reconciliation between two groups can take place in a structured way where the structure itself protects the participants and gives a sense of the process along which the participants are moving. Reconciliation between two individuals is much more a matter of chance and danger, unless there is someone else who will act as a negotiator. With two individuals the first to make an overture to reconciliation can put himself in danger, whereas a competent negotiator can sound out the other person without provoking an attack.

A negotiator is essential if one of the individuals has a paranoid view of the other. If you are the object of your enemy's paranoia, every action, even if it is the most conciliating, friendly gesture you could possibly make, will be interpreted by your enemy as some kind of attack. It is impossible on your own to change this situation.

A negotiator is also necessary when the two individuals, no matter how good their intentions, always fight when they are together – a special fight where the couple know their own and the other's part and can run through it with practised ease. A negotiator – a very brave negotiator – can serve to deflect this fight and, perhaps, the two people will find themselves saying something they have not said before many times over. A technique which some counsellors use is to set two rules for the discussion. The first is that the person speaking should not be interrupted or talked over. The second is that when one person stops talking the other person, before responding, must repeat back to the other person the gist of what that person has just said. This means that each person must actually listen to the other.

With some couples locked in enmity it is the fight which keeps them together. One or both of them may fear that if they stop fighting they will go out of one another's life, and that will be intolerable. When one member of a couple wants to move on and the other is frightened of having to build a new life, that person will obstruct all offers of a settlement and deliberately create crises. In these situations a negotiator might be able to point out what is going on.

For reconciliation to work both sides must get to know one another very well and respect, if not approve of, the other person's point of view. Couples who fight will often claim that they know one another very well, but the fact that they fight shows that they do not really understand the other's point of view and certainly do not respect it. In getting to know another person well we find ourselves feeling sympathy for that person, even though that person has been our enemy. We all have our own burdens and suffering. We are all, as Aboriginal people say, 'a poor fella'. However, in getting to know other people we can see their limitations. In theory we are capable of changing and becoming a very different person, but in practice certain parts of our meaning structure will remain unchanged.

In the process of reconciliation we need to have the generosity to allow that our enemy can change in the direction of reconciliation, and we should praise any such change. At the same time, while checking that we are not imposing our own paranoia on our enemy, we need to identify those parts of our enemy's meaning structure which are not going to change. We can find ourselves feeling very sorry for our enemy but also very wary. On my last day in Johannesburg I visited the zoo, and there I saw this old but still magnificent lion. He was lying on a high rocky prominence, surveying the rather dusty acres of the zoo. He had a large stretch of land for his own use, but he did not have the miles and miles of bush that the lions of the Kruger National Park and the Mala Mala enjoy. I had seen such lions, lolling in the long grass and sweet breezes, and going about their own business, doing what they pleased. I felt very sorry for this old lion, but I did not get over the fence, swim the moat and climb up his hill so I could give him a sympathetic hug.

So it can be with our enemies. Sometimes at the end of a reconciliation process we know that we no longer need to fear one another. We can be vulnerable to each other and embrace. Sometimes at the end of a reconciliation process we cannot do this because some of the necessary changes have proved unattainable, but we can arrive at a mutual respect and agree to treat each other with tolerance. Ed Cairns, working at the Centre for the Study of Conflict at Ulster University, said, 'I think that for us to move on, all that we have to do in Northern Ireland is to learn to *tolerate* each other at some level; we don't actually have to learn to *love* each other; we don't have to learn to *forgive* each other. It would be nice if these things came about, but I think that in the first instance we just have to *tolerate* each other, which people are often not prepared to do at the moment.'

Reconciliation and tolerance are one thing. Forgiveness is another.

Is Forgiveness Possible?

One September day in 1998 I was strolling along the Corniche in Beirut, enjoying the sea and the sunshine, when I came upon a small group of people, speaking English and attired in T-shirts and baseball caps. They were accosting passers-by and engaging them in conversation, often very brief conversation, because the person accosted moved away looking very bemused – and not surprisingly. When money is short, when the electricity and water supplies are liable to unpredictable interruptions, when the rainwater pours through the front wall of your flat and the landlord refuses to make any repairs, when the road outside your flat has been dug up and left in a dangerous state, and when daily Israeli jets break the sound barrier over your head, the Crusades do not occupy much of your thoughts. Indeed, you might find it hard to grasp why a group of Western Christians should be apologizing to you for the behaviour of the Crusaders who, between 1095 and 1291, came from Europe to save Jerusalem from the Turks.

In the autumn of 1998 Beirut was on the path of the Reconciliation Walk from Cologne to Jerusalem by a group of Christians, largely Protestant, from the USA, the UK, Germany and Australia. Those doing this walk aimed to meet and apologize to as many local people as possible. They also had plaques to hand out to any dignitaries they might meet. These plaques bore the words,

> Nine hundred years ago, our forefathers carried the name of Jesus Christ in battle across the Middle East. Fuelled by fear, greed and hatred, they betrayed the name of Christ by conducting themselves in a manner contrary to His wishes and character.
>
> We deeply regret the atrocities committed in the name of Christ by our predecessors ... Forgive us for allowing His name to be associated with death.[63]

The Christians on the Reconciliation Walk seemed to have little grasp of history. The Crusaders did do terrible things, but what happened was not just a matter of the Crusaders attacking the Turks. Michael Young, writing in the Beirut *Daily Star*, noted,

The Crusaders spent nearly 200 years under the hot Mediterranean sun. As the Israelis will attest, three generations in this region are usually enough to turn foreigners into locals, at least when it comes to learning the region's less savoury habits. Very quickly, Crusader noblemen established a number of fiefdoms. These often entered into conflict with one another, and, when they did so, they often allied themselves with Arabs.

It is fanciful in the extreme to believe that apologizing in the street will change anything in cultural relations between East and West. All it does show is that a number of decent, if slightly angst-ridden, churchgoers have decided to take up a reverse White Man's burden whereby the past is reinterpreted to underline the immutable cruelty of the West.[64]

The Reconciliation Walkers hoped that Pope John Paul II would join them in shouldering the new White Man's burden. He had already expressed regret for the Inquisition, the recantation of Galileo, the role of Catholics in the Holocaust (though not the role of the then Pope, Pius XII, who failed to condemn what the Nazis were doing), and the burning of any number of heretics. Now it was rumoured that he would apologize for the Crusades.

Apologizing and asking forgiveness for wrongs committed by people long dead has become very fashionable. The *Index of Censorship* listed some sixteen public apologies between 1988 and 1998.[65] Amongst these, the Japanese government apologized for atrocities committed by the country during the Second World War, for forcing captive women into military-run brothels, and for the treatment of prisoners of war. President Clinton issued an official apology to the survivors of a government experiment which infected 399 black men with syphilis without their knowledge. He also apologized for the genocide in Ruanda in 1994, when the international community of nations did not act quickly enough, and he also apologized for the slave trade.

Such practice in apologizing should have stood Bill Clinton in good stead when it seemed that he should apologize for his conduct in his affair with Monica Lewinsky, but apologizing for what you yourself have done can be much harder than apologizing for what others have done. It is much easier to say, 'They shouldn't have done that' than 'I shouldn't have done that.'

All these public apologists show not virtue but ignorance. Only those who have been wronged have the right to forgive. Rabbi Hugo Gryn survived Auschwitz, where he saw his family die. Whenever he was asked whether he had forgiven the Nazis he would say that he was not authorized to offer forgiveness. 'The only ones who could forgive are not here,' he said.

Nevertheless, forgiveness became highly newsworthy. It seemed that everyone wanted to get in on the act. In 1998 the England football team lost its chance of winning the World Cup when one of its players, David Beckham, childishly kicked an opponent in full view of the television cameras. Soon after, the *Guardian* reported that

> The Bible Society is calling for the nation to forgive David Beckham for getting himself sent off during England's World Cup against Argentina. Forty per cent of fans in a TV opinion poll said they couldn't forgive his foul, and this spurred Dr David Spriggs, president of the Bible Society, to ask us all to forgive Beckham his manifold sins. The Archbishop of Canterbury – an Arsenal fan – supports the move.[66]

Many journalists in search of a human interest story would ask individuals who had escaped from a life-threatening disaster or whose loved ones were dead or dying, 'How do you feel?' To this insensitive question they now added, 'Have you forgiven the person who caused this?' and 'Do you want revenge?'

When in December 1997 a Sinn Fein delegation, the first of its kind, went to 10 Downing Street they paused briefly at the door, and Rita Restorick, whose son Stephen was the last British soldier to be killed by the IRA, gave Gerry Adams a Christmas card. It had a dove of peace on the cover and contained a photograph of her two sons. Gerry Adams took the card and the delegation went inside. Immediately the press fell upon Rita. Simon Hoggart reported what happened.

> Some [of the reporters] tried to persuade Mrs Restorick to denounce Adams and the talks. But she was too cool and composed for any of that.
>
> 'Do you want revenge for your son?' they demanded.

'No,' she said.

'Do you think that the people who support murder and who will not condemn it should be invited into the headquarters of British democracy?' they insisted.

'If anything can help to stop the killing, to keep the talks going, to find a compromise, then it's worth it,' she said.

But they didn't give up. Was she aware that Adams had been a senior IRA man? 'If the Berlin Wall can come down, and Nelson Mandela be president of South Africa, surely they can sit down and talk here.'

This woman could handle Jeremy Paxman, John Humphrys and Robin Day simultaneously. She could give courses on how to handle the media, at a thousand pounds a day. Meanwhile we learned once again that there are some people who cope with grief by demanding blood and vengeance, and some who cope by trying to protect others from what they have suffered.[67]

Rita Restorick had had some time to grieve and to arrive at a decision about revenge and forgiveness, but others have not been given such grace by the press. Ed Cairns told me, 'Some people just say, "I am not going to forgive," and that's it. If you go back through the television archives, you'd probably get some wonderful material on Northern Ireland, because people have often been interviewed immediately after the death of a relative, and you get people saying, "Well, I could never forgive them but I don't want anything to happen in retaliation." So presumably there are other people, who didn't appear on television, who said, "Not only do I not forgive them, but I *do* want something to happen."'

Ed Cairns had been given a research grant by a philanthropist interested in science and religion to take part in a large-scale study of forgiveness. 'Forgiveness is a very "in" topic at the moment,' he said. 'For this forgiveness research, they've hired publicists in San Francisco, who've been phoning me up and doing interviews with me. It's their job to get publicity for this forgiveness thing and to raise money. We started off by writing to organizations in Northern Ireland which might have anything to do with forgiveness. One of the interesting things was that when we wrote to these organizations and said we were going to do this, I got at least one phone call and some notes to say, "Of course, you do realize that this is a religious concept, don't you?" What are psychologists doing, thinking about forgiveness? A Catholic priest rang me up from one of these organizations and said, in effect, "What do you guys think you're doing, treading on our turf?"'

The language we use often misleads us. We talk about forgiveness as a thing, but there is no such thing as forgiveness. 'Forgiveness' is a noun for something which does not exist. What does exist is 'forgiving', a verb. 'Forgiving' is an action. It is something we do.

Even when we talk about forgiving, we make it sound far too simple. 'Would you make me a cup of coffee?' we say, and, 'Would you forgive me?' as if forgiving were as simple as making a cup of coffee. In fact, forgiving is one of the most complex things we do.

Forgiving always involves a relationship. Even when it is a question of forgiving ourselves, this is about the relationship involved in the dialogue which goes on inside us most of the time. 'I can never forgive myself,' we say, talking about the person who forgives and the person who is forgiven. Even when we do not disclose to another person that we have forgiven them, our relationship to that person changes. We might feel more warmly towards that person, or we might even cease to think about him altogether. Forgiveness sometimes means that the person forgiven is no longer important to us and so no longer occupies our thoughts. Sometimes we forgive people without even noticing that we have done so.

Sometimes we use the possibility of forgiveness as a bargaining chip. Gusty Spence was released from the Maze prison in 1985, having served eighteen years of his sentence, and in 1994 he was chosen to deliver the ceasefire statement for the combined Loyalist paramilitaries in which he expressed 'abject and true' remorse for the victims of Loyalist violence. Peter Taylor wrote,

I asked him if that included Mrs Mary Ward [mother of Peter Ward, for whose murder Gusty Spence was sentenced]. 'The most important thing to do was to apologize to Peter Ward's mother,' he said, 'and to apologize to all the mothers.' Mary Ward told me that Spence had telephoned her. 'He said he wanted me to forgive him. I said, "Yes, I'll forgive you on one condition, that you bring peace to this country, because I don't want any other mother to go through what I've gone through." My Peter is in my mind every day and night. I said, "I know it's not going to bring Peter back,

but please try and bring peace here."' I asked Mary if she now
forgave Gusty Spence. She said she did.[68]

Mary Ward had had many long years in which to consider the
question of forgiveness. Some people, usually Christians, announce
their forgiveness within a very short space of time.

On 8 November 1987 a group of people gathered at the war
memorial at Enniskillen to commemorate Remembrance Sunday.
Gordon Wilson stood beside his daughter Marie, just twenty-four
and a nurse. An IRA bomb went off, killing eleven people and
injuring sixty-three. Gordon Wilson talked to Marie as she died.

The next day Gordon Wilson said publicly that he had forgiven
Marie's killers. This got tremendous publicity and Gordon Wilson
was widely praised. The Queen commended him. She was very much
in favour of forgiveness, though her own forgiveness did not stretch
as far as her daughters-in-law. At the time I wondered if all this
publicity might leave Gordon Wilson stuck with something he might
later regret saying. I thought of this again when Gordon Wilson
died in 1995.

In Northern Ireland I discovered that I was not alone in thinking
this. In the first phase of Ed Cairns's research focus groups had
been set up, consisting of victim support groups from both sides of
the community, religious groups from both sides of the community,
and victims of the Troubles from both sides of the community –
six groups in all. The victims' groups, Ed told me, 'brought up
Gordon Wilson, and some of them said they thought Gordon Wilson
had a premature death because he wasn't able to handle the forgiveness burden he'd put on himself. Deep down in his heart he hadn't
really forgiven, but he'd been going round saying this so often that
he was sort of stuck with it. And some at the focus group said, "We
know our limitations. We know we can never forgive."'

Ed commented, 'It certainly struck me as strange that they're
saying that basically anybody who says that they have suffered a
loss like that, and they have forgiven the perpetrator, is deceiving
themselves, and the deception will backfire on them, it's something
you can't live with.'

It did not seem strange to me. When we become a victim we lose
somebody or something that is important to us. This loss is a threat
to our meaning structure. However, there are some losses for which

there is appropriate and adequate compensation available. Being
burgled can be a great threat. The thought of a stranger going
through your possessions can be destabilizing, but the arrival of a
new television set paid for by insurance to replace the set that was
stolen can restore stability. But there are other losses for which there
is no compensation, no reward. The loss is a loss for ever. Mary
Ward said, 'My Peter is in my mind day and night.' Gusty Spence
had shown remorse and asked for her forgiveness, but she could
forgive only if he provided the one thing which would be a small
recompense for her Peter's death – peace in Northern Ireland.

Pietermaritzburg in Natal looks like an English country town
under an African sky. On New Year's Eve in 1998 a brother and
sister, James Wilmot, who was twenty, and Kate Wilmot, who was
eighteen, went to a club to celebrate. They planned to walk home
in the early daylight, but they never arrived home. Their naked
bodies were found in the grounds of the high school. They had been
shot in the head.

Three days later their father, the Reverend Lawrie Wilmot, issued
a statement saying that he and his wife had forgiven the perpetrators.
He said, 'As Christians, our sentiments for the perpetrators are
conveyed through the words of Christ, "Father, forgive them, for
they know not what they do." '[69]

At the time I was staying with friends in Pietermaritzburg. The
local paper, the *Star*, carried a large photograph of Kate and James.
It was a snapshot of them standing together beside a small plane.
James had just gained his commercial pilot's licence. Two beautiful
young people, going forward into life. Most parents feel that, as
their children go forward into life, something of the parent goes
with them. We feel that, when we die, something of us continues
in our children. If our children die before us something in us dies.
For most parents, however much we might care about other people,
our children are special, a continual source of wonder and joy. They
are irreplaceable. The loss of them is one for which there can be no
recompense, no reward.

When I encounter parents who say they have forgiven those who
brought about the death of their child, and especially when this
statement is made soon after the death of the child, I can only
wonder whether these parents did not love their child, or whether
these parents did love their child but were afraid of the pain, anger

and despair which acknowledgement of the truth of the loss would bring.

In the public praise of forgiveness it seems that forgiveness is seen as a kind of balm or blessing that falls upon the forgiver and the forgiven, and then they and all around them are at peace. Forgiveness is seen as a virtue – for many a particularly Christian virtue. It is often said that virtue should be its own reward. If we do something virtuous in order to receive a reward or avoid some punishment then we have not acted virtuously but only in our own interests. Jesus was very clear about the necessity of forgiveness, but He did not teach that it was a virtue in itself. You must forgive in order that God will forgive you. When Peter asked Jesus how many times he should forgive, Jesus told him, 'Until seventy times seven,' and went on to tell the parable about the servant who begged his master's forgiveness for not repaying a debt but who would not forgive another servant who owed him money. On learning of this his master withdrew his forgiveness.[70] When Jesus wanted to impress on his disciples the necessity of faith he said,

> Therefore I say unto you, whatsoever ye desire, when ye pray, believe ye shall receive them, and ye shall have them.
> And when ye stand praying, forgive, if ye have ought against any: that your Father also which is in heaven forgive your trespasses.
> But if ye do not forgive, neither will your Father which is in heaven forgive your trespasses.[71]

The bargain with God is stated clearly in the Lord's Prayer, 'Forgive us our trespasses as we forgive those who have trespassed against us.'

Elsewhere in the Bible it is recognized that forgiving can be an effective way of punishing our enemies. In Proverbs we are advised, 'If thine enemy be hungry, give him bread to eat; and if he be thirsty, give him water to drink: for thou shalt heap coals of fire upon his head, and the Lord shall reward thee.'[72] St Paul repeated this advice to the Romans, 'Therefore, if thine enemy hunger, feed him; if he thirst, give him drink: for in doing so thou shalt heap coals of fire on his head.'[73]

For Christians salvation, which is eternal life, means that God has forgiven their sins. If not forgiving puts their salvation at risk, then when they suffer loss they are likely to feel under pressure to forgive those who have injured them. Not that the history of Christianity shows a marked predilection for forgiveness. If it did there would have been no religious wars and Ian Paisley would have been friends with the Pope. Perhaps there is a liking for the idea of forgiveness because the fear of not being forgiven by God can be tempered with the delicious revenge of heaping coals of fire on the enemy's head.

St Paul and the author of Proverbs recognized that when we suffer loss we get angry with the person who has injured us. Anger is a natural response to injury, to being prey. Anger can help us survive physically, puny creatures that we are, and as individuals. When we are angry we can ward off threats to our meaning structure. We need to recognize the importance of anger and to develop many flexible techniques for dealing with our own anger and the anger of other people. Unfortunately, many people learn to see anger as unremittingly wicked. Many people associate anger only with fear. At the Trauma Clinic in Omagh Michael Duffy, the head of the clinic, told me, 'The problem here is that people associate anger with violence. They think that if they get angry they will be violent and no better than the people who injured them.'

Denying that we feel a particular emotion does not make that emotion go away. It is better to accept that it is there, even if we do not act on it. This is what some people very wisely decide to do. Lin and Shaun Russell, and their young daughters Megan and Josie, lived happily in a village safe, they thought, from all harm. One day when Lin and her daughters and their dog were walking along a country lane they were attacked. Lin, Megan and the dog were brutally killed, and Josie, severely injured, was left for dead. After Michael Stone was sentenced for these crimes Shaun Russell issued a statement to the media in which he said,

I honestly can't say I feel emotions like hatred for Michael Stone. I certainly do feel a degree of pity. I have heard about his upbringing. I certainly feel sympathy for his mother and his sister, and what they had to endure.

But I also feel anger. I rang my late wife's parents after the verdict and the sense of desolation and loss in their voices reminded me that they have lost their only daughter, they cannot get her back again.

I have had to endure hearing terrible things said during the trial. It's not very nice hearing your most loved ones referred to as slags and whores. The one thing I can never forgive Michael Stone for is whenever I think of my wife and daughter, the terrible image of them in the mortuary comes back to me first. I hope in time that can recede.[74]

Shaun Russell went on to speak about Josie and her wish for a new dog. 'She'll never get her mother and her sister back but she might get her dog back.'

When we lose someone we love deeply that hurt stays with us for ever. At the end of the fighting in Beirut Jean Said Makdisi said,

Probably the most single dominant feeling now – greater by far than the latent sense of triumph at having survived, greater than sadness and fear, greater even than their closest rival, an immense and overriding fatigue – is the feeling of terrible waste and the anger which accompanies it. One of my dearest friends was shot and killed at a barricade three years ago. I feel her senseless death every day, a fresh raw wound, the pain almost as intense as it was on the first day, when I thought I should burst, and when I knew at last what they meant when they spoke of a broken heart.[75]

We might forgive or at least become indifferent to the people who injured us, but often we find it impossible to forgive them for what they did to someone we love. My friend Lesley told me, 'I can't imagine forgiving anyone for hurting or harming my children. And while I have made great progress in making peripheral the harm my father caused me, I cannot forgive him the life he gave my mother, even though I recognize his own wounds and the fact that she stayed with him.'

We may feel that if we forgive the people who hurt those we love we would be betraying the people we love. Not forgiving shows that we love them; not forgiving shows that we have not accepted what happened. Aaron Hass described how, for the survivors of the Holocaust,

at their very core, what gnaws most obscenely is the *senselessness* of the Holocaust. Survivors cannot be at peace with the Holocaust for this would be treasonous to the memory of their loved ones. They *must* feel outrage and continue to bear witness, to testify to the *innocence* of those who were murdered, and to the guilt of their tormentors.[76]

To talk of choosing to forgive or not forgive shows that we do not understand the process of forgiving. We can choose not to forgive, and this blocks the process of forgiveness. First, we can keep ourselves separate from the person who has injured us. After he returned from the war Eric Lomax refused ever to speak to a Japanese. At the Medical Foundation for the Victims of Torture Eric's doctor Stuart Turner suggested that Eric do this before he went any further with his plans to meet his erstwhile torturer. Rather than have an 'embarrassing meeting with startled Japanese ticket clerks' Eric accepted a friend's invitation to meet a Japanese historian, Nakahara Michiko, who was researching the exploitation of prisoners of war and Asian labourers by the imperial Japanese army on the Burma–Siam railway. Eric found that he was fascinated by this 'considerate and learned woman', and one of the barriers to his meeting with Nagase was removed.[77]

Second, we can constantly rehearse our complaints about our enemy and find again and again evidence of our enemy's wickedness. We can expand our complaints and build a whole paranoid structure where our enemy is not only the sole cause of our unhappiness but the sole cause of all the unhappiness in the world.

It is always much easier to destroy than to create. It is easier to destroy the conditions that foster forgiveness than it is to create those conditions. We can strive to get to know our erstwhile enemy. We can try to turn our thoughts away from rehearsing our complaints about our enemy. However, while we create these conditions, we have to wait and see if forgiveness appears. We cannot call it forth any more than we can call forth any emotion. Emotions are meanings, and they are our own individual, absolute truth. We feel what we feel. We might have misinterpreted the situation and anger or love or forgiveness might not be justified, but feeling angry, or loving or forgiving is what we feel.

We can be in a particular situation, saying to ourselves, 'I am not angry,' when suddenly we find ourselves feeling angry. Even as we said, 'I am not angry,' we saw something in the situation which was a threat to our meaning structure, and we defended ourselves against this threat with anger. In another situation we might want to show the people with us that we are angry, but there is nothing in the situation which threatens us. We can try saying to ourselves, 'Now get angry,' but nothing will happen. To get angry we must either manufacture some threat in the situation or think about another situation which still threatens us and to which we respond with anger.

It is the same with love. We can choose to behave towards another person in a loving way, but we have to see in that person something which we interpret as very special, very appealing, something which does not threaten us but draws us closer to that person. No matter how much that person loves us, no matter how loving we are in our behaviour towards that person, if our meaning structure, with an absolute clarity of vision, does not see those particular qualities in the other person then our meaning structure does not create that interpretation which we call and feel as love.

So it is with forgiveness. We can say that we have forgiven. We can go through all kinds of reconciliation rituals. We can act in all kinds of forgiving ways. We can tell ourselves that we have forgiven, but we cannot choose to summon up the emotion of forgiveness. We might have reached a stage where we see our erstwhile enemy as another fallible, suffering human being, and the past enmity as something understandable and even forgivable, but there has to be something else for forgiveness to be called forth. Our meaning structure has to be able to interpret the situation as one where there can be a letting go of all those meanings that have to do with the fear, hate, anger, hurt, loss, and the past where the enmity occurred. People who feel that they are weak cannot forgive. It takes a strong meaning structure to let go of what was an important part of itself. It is not a cutting off of part of our self but a letting go, like releasing a leaf into a river and letting it be swirled away.

This process of letting go becomes possible only when we recognize that life *is* change. We can go with the flow of change – *wu wei*, as the ancient Taoists called it – or we can fight to remain the same, standing rigid and denying that the world is changing and condemning the changes as wicked. With this stance we become further and further removed from what is actually happening, which is a very dangerous position to be in. The world refuses to conform to our wishes, and we become increasingly frustrated and angry. The people around us might at first admire our intransigence, and some will fear us, but as time goes by they come to see us as ignorant, ill-informed, unaware, ridiculous, unimportant.

If we are to live more wisely we have to recognize that we are part of a world which is constantly changing. We are continually changing, and part of this change is letting go, not just of old enmities but of ideas that are no longer relevant to what is going on.

However, some ideas remain precious to us no matter how much we change. These may be to do with the kind of person we feel we ought to be. It is these ideas which may lead a person to say, 'I can never forgive myself.'

It may be that the memory of what we cannot forgive fills us with a profound sense of shame. Diyana told me about a second incident on the bus journey she and her little daughter Sarah made out of the besieged Sarajevo.

A few days after the checkpoint where the UN soldiers had driven by, ignoring the women whose lives were in danger, they came to a Croatian checkpoint. 'They called me out because I was a Serb entering a Croatian state, and this was the second time Sarah was left on the bus. She was crying terribly because she didn't let me go anywhere without her. And it was a terrible experience, although they didn't do anything to me. I was shaking. It was a few minutes past midnight, and a border in the middle of nowhere. Nobody was around, no buildings, nothing, just the bus. And they took us, a few women, to ask questions in a small shed. One soldier took my documents and asked me where my husband was, and they let us go back. But I was so afraid they would want to kill me – because I was full of stories I heard when we were in that cellar in Sarajevo. The stories filled your mind, and when you go out you don't expect anybody normal. You are expecting only violent people and criminals. *I could have acted better crossing the checkpoints.* When we were in the camp in the Czech Republic I often talked about this with my friend, who was also from Sarajevo and had two small children. We discussed this matter night after night. We couldn't do anything but talk about it, and always I was shaking like a leaf, as if I was about to cross it again, to go through again. That's the worst thing – you can't get rid of that fear. I don't know whether I will ever be able to remember that without shaking, without being afraid, as if it's going to happen again.'

The fear that Diyana described is terrible in itself, but to be in that state of fear and to be exposed to the gaze of others is to be naked in their gaze, a nakedness more exposed and shameful than mere nudity. This is why Diyana could not forgive herself for not showing more courage at the checkpoints. What is more pitiable and contemptible than cowering prey? Geraldine Finucane, who was wounded when Loyalist gunmen burst into her kitchen and shot dead her husband Pat, told Kevin Toolis,

'At the time of the funeral it was very hard for me to get a sense of what was happening because of my injuries. But before I left the house I called the children together and told them not to cry in public. "Outside there will be TV cameras, photographers, hundreds of people. I do not want those who did this see how they have wrecked our lives. I don't want you crying." Other people do cry on camera but I could not do that. It would seem wrong – maybe that is a weakness.'[78]

I am sure that Geraldine Finucane would assure Diyana that in her place she would have been as afraid as Diyana had been, but for a long time afterwards Diyana could not forgive herself for showing such weakness.

Often, when we remember past failures for which we will not forgive ourselves, we feel not shame but guilt. We may feel that it would be wrong not to feel guilty so we refuse to forgive ourselves, and this takes us into the prison of depression where, we feel, we meet the punishment we deserve. Our guilt cannot be forgiven, only expiated. Sometimes we may feel that we ought to have died. Simon Hattenstone told the story of Joseph Glover:

In a terrible irony, Joseph Glover, one of the survivors of the Hillsborough football disaster, has died at the age of 32 after being crushed while unloading a wagon. His brother Ian died at Hillsborough, despite Joseph trying to resuscitate him with the kiss of life. For a long time, he slept on the gravestone of his brother.

Last weekend, the *Guardian* ran an article, 'Those Who Were Left Behind', in which Joseph spoke about his life over the past decade.

Both he and a third brother, John, who had also been at the FA Cup semi-final where 96 fans died, had been told by medical experts that they were so traumatised they would be unlikely to hold down full-time jobs again. He said that until this year he'd never been able to talk about the day or its aftermath. 'I felt so guilty. I felt it was wrong that I survived, especially being with him. Why did I get out?'

It was partly to alleviate their sons' suffering that John Glover Sr helped set up the Hillsborough Justice Campaign to work with the thousands of traumatised survivors as well as the bereaved. The campaign believed that the people of Liverpool had to be more active in their campaign for justice.

Joseph was a lovely, softly-spoken man who was finally learning to come to terms with what he'd seen; he was learning to live again. Last week, he said that there were still many bleak days, but there was a chink of light. His friends say that he had been fired up by the new campaign, driving round town leafleting people, chatting, reminding them why they couldn't forget about Hillsborough.

Joseph died pushing his friend out of the way of a five-tonne marble load and taking the weight himself.[79]

Life presents us with some difficult choices. We can choose to let love come or we can choose not to love. If we love we may suffer loss, and if we see that loss as our fault we may suffer guilt. If we do not love we are lonely.

Writing about life in Beirut after the war there Jean Said Makdisi said,

> Loneliness and emptiness have encroached. When the war began, my mother and two of my sisters lived here. Another sister and my brother used to visit regularly, and I had cousins, uncles, aunts. Today I am alone. Of my husband's large family, only his sister and one or two cousins remain. The others have all gone away. They rarely write or call. Of course, the mail doesn't work well and neither do the telephones, but perhaps the real reason is that they want to forget, to blot Beirut out of their memories.[80]

Forgetting is one way of dealing with the question of forgiveness. We can say to ourselves, 'I will not think about what happened,' and every time we are reminded of the past we firmly turn our thoughts to other things. Sometimes we may say to ourselves, 'Don't think about that,' and sometimes primitive pride blots out the memory. Diyana told me how she wished she had been better prepared for what happened in Bosnia. She said, 'I wasn't prepared at all, and that's why I can't accept it yet. I know everything is lost, that I had. I don't mean materialistic things, I mean people I had been friends with, had connections with. Almost everything is destroyed. But anyway, I prefer to speak about pre-war times. I always want to speak about Yugoslavia, my society, my country, before the war. To say how beautiful it was, or how normal it was. It was a beautiful country, full of nice people. I didn't notice hatred, I didn't notice a wish for destruction. It was nice living there, we had a nice life. Maybe I make it more ideal than it was. But it's my way of protecting those memories. Because what we have now is much worse than what we had before, especially in terms of relationships. That's why I can remember everything from Dubrovnik or Belgrade or Sarajevo. But I can't remember Sarajevo during the war. My husband asked me the names of some people and I couldn't remember because it was during the war. I spent eight months in Sarajevo, eight difficult months, and somehow I succeeded to cover that period, to hide it. From time to time I remember something, but mostly I can't remember names or dates. Even the very ordinary things in my house, somehow I forget them. Because they connect me to the tragedy, and I don't know when I'll be able to think of them again.'

Selective forgetting can be very a useful defence: it protects us against being overwhelmed by feelings of impotent anger and irreparable loss. As time goes by we may become strong enough gradually to look into these closed-off parts of ourselves and accept our helplessness and our losses. However, forgiving and forgetting, though we link them together, may not always be the wisest thing to do. Whenever we forgive or simply choose to act in a forgiving way, we need to decide whether the person we have forgiven will strike at us again. Some moralists like to believe that the person forgiven will from then on be a better person, but that is not always the case. Many people feel it is best to be wary. My friend Irene told me, 'I can forgive most things, I think. Well, certainly anything I've come up against in my life so far, but I never forget. There's always that little thought in my mind, "They did that once, beware of it." It's a warning sign. My husband always said I made marks on the wall. "That's one, that's two." And I do. That's the truth. Very few people would be able to do the same difficult, hurtful thing twice, because I would be aware of it. I don't forget.'

Irene used a significant image when she talked about what can happen in a relationship. She said, 'I was talking once with a good friend and we agreed that relationships are like a window between one person and another. You look in and you start off with a clear image. You see clearly the good and the beautiful in this person, but everything that happens that's negative makes little cracks in the window, and eventually the image becomes distorted until you can't see though the window at all. I think that's what happens in relationships that fall apart, and I think the cracks are what we see – inadequacies, whatever it is about the person. It's not relating, it's not speaking on the same level, the same terms.'

Often when we are not getting on with another person, when every encounter is full of misunderstandings and hurts, when nothing is clearly stated but much is implied, we may feel that we no longer see the person or the situation clearly. If we do isolate an event where we think the other person has attacked and hurt us, and describe it to a third person it will seem so petty and trivial that we demean ourselves by talking about it. We may explain that we feel that this small event is part of a war of attrition carried out by the other person to wound us and bring us down, but in doing so we may be seen as paranoid. If the other person is a relative we may know that these clandestine attacks have their roots in the distant past, but to say so is to invite the charge, 'You should have grown out of that by now.' So we stay silent, and the window never clears.

In 1983, when the threat of nuclear war was at its height, *Punch* carried a cartoon depicting a vicar standing at his church door, bidding farewell to his congregation. A couple are standing in front of him and the man is saying, 'We've been forgiving our enemies like mad, Reverend. What's the story on friends?'[81] Forgiving friends is indeed very difficult. Irene's image of the cracked window encapsulates the confusions, the misperceptions, the inability to find a way to put it right. To clear the window we need to aim at mutual understanding, not forgiveness. If mutual understanding is achieved forgiveness might or might not follow, but, if it is based on mutual understanding, what follows, whether it is mutual forgiveness or simply mutual tolerance, will be appropriate for the relationship as it continues.

Forgiveness between groups is a similarly complex process.

One day in September 1997, when I was in Vietnam, I went in a tiny rowing boat on a large river to see the Perfumed Pagoda. The boat cleared the water by only a few inches and it looked to me as if it was made out of kerosene cans. Such cans loomed large in my childhood. They were made out of tin, stood about two feet high and were a foot or so square. During the war building materials were scarce, so these cans, once their contents had been used, were cut open and used to mend roofs, to turn into guttering, animal feeding troughs, plant pots, kitchen utensils and toys. Cans could be cut in half, flattened and joined with other half-cans to make a large trough or container. I do not remember them being used to make a rowing boat, but it certainly seemed to me that the Vietnamese had mastered the kerosene can technology.

Actually I was travelling in great luxury. There was just my guide, the man who rowed the boat, and myself in the boat. The other boats on the river carried ten or even fifteen people. Fifteen Australians would never fit in one of these boats, but fifteen Vietnamese, all small, thin people, would. No wonder Americans found it so hard to accept that they had lost the war in Vietnam. To be defeated by such tiny people with such minimal technology – oh, the shame of it! No wonder they could not forgive the Vietnamese.

Yet the Vietnamese showed every sign of having forgiven the Americans for what they called the American war. No matter whom I asked – young people who looked to the West for education and ideas, young party members whose future is secured only by the party's supremacy, honoured, privileged old party members or those who gave their youth and health in the struggle – all said the same: 'The American people were not our enemies. It was just a small group of leaders who waged war against us. Americans are not our enemy now.'

In my travels in Communist countries during the Cold War I learned to identify Communist Party members by the fact that they had travelled abroad. My Vietnamese guide spoke excellent English and he had travelled abroad, so, feeling that he would give me an interesting answer, I asked him why it was that the Vietnamese showed no hatred or malice towards America. He described Vietnam as the crossroads of the world; the Vietnamese, he said, had had to adapt to wave after wave of foreign powers criss-crossing their land.

My guide spoke also of the Buddhist monks from India who had crossed Vietnam on their way to China; indeed, on our way up the mountain to the Perfumed Pagoda we visited a Buddhist temple created by one of these monks in a cave some 2,000 years ago. The essence of Buddhism discovered by the Buddha as he sat under the bo tree was that as we are we cannot know reality directly but only through the fictions which we create. Two and a half thousand years later scientists have shown that the Buddha was right. My guide did not say, though I felt it was implied in what he said, that the basic Buddhist philosophy does not lead to those absolute beliefs which are so often the basis of enmity. The Communist regime in Vietnam never banned religion, so the understanding of individual truths continued to exist alongside the absolutes of Communism.

Children in Vietnam were apparently not put through the process of remembering the past as children are in many other countries. I had visited the Museum of War Crimes in Saigon; it was very simple, with little emphasis on the wickedness of their old enemy. When I visited Hoang Tung, an official at the Red Cross International Rehabilitation Unit in Saigon, I asked him if he had ever been to this museum. He said that he had not. He explained that school-children do visit the museum, but that these trips are not seen as part of a programme to keep the war alive in the children's minds. By contrast, in Japan every child is likely to make at least one visit to Hiroshima or Nagasaki. When I was in Hiroshima I saw a great many schoolchildren lining up to sign the visitors' book.

I asked Hoang Tung, who would have been a child during the last part of the war, what effect the war had had on him. He said that he did not think that today the war has any effect on him. 'The war was twenty years ago,' he said.

In Saigon I went on the back of my friend Hai's motorbike to visit a rehabilitation centre some ten kilometres from the city centre. Many people had lost limbs during the war, and prostheses were made and fitted there. The chief technician at the centre told me that he had joined the Vietcong army at fourteen to fight the French. At eighteen he lost a leg in the fighting. Then he went north to work for the army in Hanoi, where he got an education. In 1971 he was sent to East Germany, where he learnt about prostheses and taught the Germans about Vietnam. They were amazed that such a weak, poor country should confront the might of the USA, the most powerful country in the world. He told me that he reminded the East Germans that 'no one can make you a slave if you don't want to be a slave'. He seemed to see no irony in saying this to the East Germans, who were under the rule of the USSR. He seemed less impressed with the Russians, because when he visited Russia he was not treated as well as he had been by the East Germans, who gave and continued to give generously to Vietnam.

For him forgiveness of enemies was not a problem. A small group of people in America – not the American people as a whole – were the enemy. Throughout history the Vietnamese have had to fight different enemies, he said, and when each war was over the enemy was forgotten.

In Hanoi my English friend Gill took me to meet Professor Nguyen Thi Hoai Duc at the Centre for Reproductive and Family Health. She had studied in China and Poland, and travelled widely. This meant that she had to leave her young children with her husband for four years while she worked in Poland. I asked her about the war, and she told me that people try not to remember. When I said, 'You won,' she smiled and shook her head. 'In war no one wins. Everyone loses.'

Gill was doing research into the social services in Hanoi and had come to know the Vietnamese well. Before my visit in 1996 she wrote to me to give me some idea of what I might expect to find. She said,

Every family has a story to tell about living through the American War – and about loss and dislocation and uncertainty. But there are different dimensions. Forgiveness and reconciliation between Vietnamese and Americans? Between Vietnamese and Viet Kieu, the Vietnamese who left before 1975, many of whom are trying to come back? Between the North and South? However you look at it, the Vietnamese seem on the surface to be extraordinarily forgiving, and on an individual level I think that holds true – perhaps it explains the resilience of the Vietnamese, their capacity to move on and not become mired in a resentment of their own history, as seems to have happened in the States. When you see how the MIA [Missing

in Action] teams are still here picking over Vietnam for the bones
of what might remain of less than 100 missing American soldiers –
the difference in psychology is more than stark: micro level accountability and a refusal to let a national wound heal as opposed to a
sense that there is no healing for that depth and magnitude of
national grief, but that by acknowledging what Vietnam gained from
all that it lost it may be possible to move on.

... In any case there are deeply ingrained coping mechanisms
that help provide some continuity of life – such as the way Vietnamese keep the dead alive through ancestral worship – any of the
myriad of religious practices that enshrine the past with the present.
And the political ideology here continues to promote notions of
'community' and of independence through solidarity. President Ho
Chi Minh remains a much loved and politically supported figure –
so there is an effort to retain old cultural values despite the material
rampages of the market economy. It does seem to be a 'healthy
culture' psychologically – trite as that sounds. People live closely
together but keep a sort of internal privacy, not a physical privacy
like the West; they communicate openly (and now also to
foreigners), express emotions in direct and indirect ways, talk endlessly and laugh a lot.

However, it was within the internal privacy of which Gill spoke
that most Vietnamese had to deal with their losses. The Communist
government tried to manage the national feeling about the American
war. According to Robert Templer,

The Communist Party still feels a political imperative to pare the
complexities of the war down to a simple narrative, turning soldiers
into cardboard heroes ... The dead are honoured in cemeteries
with an obelisk bearing the cold inscription: 'Your country acknowledges your sacrifice.' Some of the cemeteries are untended and nearly
derelict; they rarely seem to be a focal point for remembrance.
Officially the war was glorious, not the tragedy it was for the United
States. A sense of the nation as a victim is encouraged in history
and in the constant remembrances in newspapers. Individual grief
is not seen in the same way and so sorrow in Vietnam has often
turned inward. When almost everyone has suffered terribly, it is
hard for anyone to express that suffering.[82]

It was not until 1994, with the title 'Heroic Mother', that the government acknowledged the sacrifices so many mothers had made. Nguyen Thi Lanh was one of these 20,000 mothers. Robert Templer went to visit her, accompanied by the head of the local chapter of the Women's Union. Lanh began her story in language 'that fitted the approved mix of sentimentality and revolutionary rhetoric' but, when she went to talk about herself, 'the cadre's lips soon pursed into a tight bud of disapproval'.

> 'I lost three of my sons and I lived a life that was indescribably horrible,' she said, her eyes flickering up towards an altar where she had placed framed pictures of the dead: four men, all polished and neatly dressed in white shirts, all frozen in handsome youth, the father looking no older than his sons. Two of her sons died in Cu Chi and another at a Viet Cong base in Cambodia. Her husband had died in the French colonial prison on Con Dao Island. She could not bring herself to talk about how it felt to have your children die in war and instead spoke of a life tarred by conflict and the bleak years that followed it. A quiet cough from the Women's Union cadre reminded her to get back to the glories of the revolution and ended this brief glimpse into her private world of loss.[83]

Professor Nguyen Thi Hoai Duc told me that large numbers of older Vietnamese women were depressed. Unable to speak about their losses and their anger, some women turned their anger inward and blamed themselves. Others lived with their silent grief, unable to take advantage of the *doi moi*, or 'renovation', which allowed artists more freedom. '"One of the biggest changes," said a Vietnamese painter, "is now we are actually allowed to be sad."'[84]

Until sadness can be expressed reconciliation and forgiveness cannot be complete.

After a seventeen-year civil war the Lebanese of different religions stopped massacring one another. In 1998 President Hrawi decided that they were ready to marry one another, and introduced a bill to permit marriages regulated by civil rather than religious authorities. There were eighteen recognized different sects in Lebanon, and of course none of the different clergy wanted to give up their power. The end of war had apparently not created any reconciliation.[85]

I asked Tima, 'Is the war over?' She said, 'No. There are many people who don't want it to be over.' I asked, 'Have people forgiven one another?' She said, 'They work together. That's as much forgiveness as there is. There's a lot of anger waiting to come out. Something just has to happen.'

Were there any government attempts to foster forgiveness? There was no kind of Truth and Reconciliation Commission, but had any classes or workshops been set up to help individuals? Camille, who had had experience of such things, told me that the government had set up organizations to help people be aware of the dangers of Aids and suicide and the like, but there was nothing specifically to bring people together.

I asked Tima if the Lebanese talked about forgiveness and ending their differences. She said, 'Some people are very willing; they're not in general against the idea, but do they have a common purpose in order to forgive and go on? No. We have to provide them with a sense of purpose because otherwise only when they live together will they reach this. But as things stand they don't have a common sense of purpose, so we have no civic education, things that can bring communities together, and bring them, not as sects, but as human beings, making their needs equal in the first place.'

To Tima the basic problem was that the Lebanese did not listen to one another. She said, 'There's a general mentality, "I know better. Who are you to tell me?" This attitude is very dominant in people's thinking, and most people who have this kind of thinking don't like to be told anything basically. Even if it's something they know nothing about, people are not willing to be taught or told.'

If people do not listen to one another there can be no reconciliation, no forgiveness.

To listen people have to be prepared to sit down together and talk. In Northern Ireland most of the Catholics and Protestants have never talked to one another. Following our visit to Drumcree Anthony told me that, if the men there had known that he was a Catholic they would not have spoken to him – or to me because I was with him. To them I would have been either a Catholic or a renegade Protestant. I could have tried claiming I was a humanist, but these men would have wanted to know whether I was a Protestant humanist or a Catholic humanist.

I had said to Anthony, 'So what you're telling me is that you couldn't even begin with half a dozen Protestants and Catholics sitting in a circle?'

Anthony replied, 'We're not that far yet. I think that's probably two to five years away at best. But I think it will come. The cracks are showing. On television chat shows you'll see the platform being shared, and that's just being tolerated. Before it was not tolerated. Sinn Fein were even barred from taking part in debates and so were demonized. With the setting up of the Assembly the sight of their elected members talking together might hasten the process of accepting that public platforms can be shared.

Anthony went on, 'If in the course of my work I sometimes have to go into a Protestant house and, if they perceive me as a Catholic, they might be very polite and courteous, but the conversation will not go above a certain level. And they'll find subtle ways of sussing you out. They'll ask leading questions like, "Do you know so-and-so?" "What area of the town do you live in?" And those little giveaway signs and body language will tell them. We'll agree that the Troubles are a terrible thing, but it will be all surface conversation, nothing deep.'

When Ed Cairns drew up his research programme he planned for three kinds of groups – a religious group, a group of people caring for victims, and a victims' group – but there had to be two of each, a Protestant and a Catholic group. The two victims' groups were the hardest to fill. Ed told me, 'My researcher who was organizing the groups found that the religious people and the caring people were quite into forgiveness – but the *victims* – some of them thought that to talk to them about forgiveness was virtually an insult. They said, "How dare you bring up the subject of forgiveness? What right have *you* to ask me to forgive? You don't know what it's been like." Forgiveness was something they didn't even want to think about.'

When we have been badly hurt talking about that hurt and the cause of it can be extremely difficult. I have suffered more physical pain than I would have wished, but I can say that the pain of a protracted childbirth or the removal of part of a lung is as nothing to the pain I felt when I was attacked, betrayed and neglected by those whom I might have expected to care for me. In the scale of human suffering my pain was minuscule, so I can only try to imagine the pain of those who have suffered major losses. Talking about such pain is not easy. I have had many opportunities to talk in safe surroundings about my experiences, and I have been able to use some of my experiences in my work. However, there are some events from the first thirty-eight years of my life about which I have never spoken. The pain is still too great. So I can say that for tolerance, reconciliation and forgiveness to emerge we must talk to one another, but we must also understand and accept one another's silence. Wordless acknowledgement is often the best we can achieve.

To forgive we have to change, but often the people around us do not want us to change because that would mean that they would have to change how they see us. If our community is moving in the direction of forgiveness that will help us to forgive, but if our community is not we might not want to do something of which it disapproves. Moreover, if we go against our community we might find ourselves deprived of what it has to offer. Some communities want to stay as they are. In Northern Ireland there were Protestants who wanted to return to a time when they enjoyed the privileges of power and to stay there; and Catholics who wanted to stay within the absolute security of the Catholic Church. It may be difficult for individuals in such groups to say publicly that they want to move in the direction of forgiveness. During the peace process in Northern Ireland these people, if accosted by a television journalist and asked their opinion, would refuse to speak on camera about their views, while those who did not want to move towards reconciliation were happy to air their prejudices.

The first stage on the path to reconciliation and forgiveness is an acceptance that the loss has occurred, and a mourning of that loss. Yet many people refuse to take this step. They will not move until they can get what they feel is a satisfactory answer to the question, 'Why in the scheme of things has disaster happened?' Since neither God nor man can give them an answer which satisfies them they remain stuck, unable to accept that things happen by chance, and torn between the impotent anger of blaming others and the guilt of blaming themselves. Depression can be understood as a refusal to mourn. This refusal can become a way of life. Some of the depressed people who join self-help groups such as Depressives Associated and the Fellowship of Depressives Anonymous make these groups their community, and there they stay, defining their identity as 'I am a depressive and I shall never forgive myself.' Many of the survivors of the Holocaust who talked to Aaron Hass showed him that they defined themselves as being one of the Survivors. Yet, as Hass said,

> Mourning provides relief. When we mourn we excrete the pain, the sadness, the guilt. And after our body and mind have been expunged, we can re-enter the world afresh, with hope. Survivors, however, have not mourned. They remain locked in their own sphere. Consequently the bitterness continues to sear their soul.[86]

The process of mourning and reconciliation begins with loss, and the acceptance of loss, but for the process to succeed there must be not only acceptance of that loss but acceptance that other things will have to be relinquished. No individual or community gives up privileges willingly. Much of the reluctance of Northern Ireland's Protestants to support the peace process comes not so much from an unwillingness to bring the conflict to an end as from the refusal to give up any of the privileges which they have enjoyed at the expense of the Catholic community. Many of the Unionists were incensed with Chris Patten's report on the Royal Ulster Constabulary. This report recommended not only that the RUC which, since its inception in 1922, had been disproportionately Protestant, should be 'representative of the society it polices', but, even worse, that its name should be changed to the Northern Ireland Police Service and that the Union flag should no longer be flown from police buildings. The old men at Drumcree would have been furious. They might have been pleased that the Queen had honoured the RUC with the presentation of the George Cross, the highest medal for bravery, but that would not help them to change their minds, especially if they suspected that the honour was a bribe.

A successful peace process would also mean that the Catholic community had to give up the privileges of a close relationship with the Church, which provided them with the virtues of martyrdom and a sense of superiority. When I talked to Martin, once a member of the IRA, he said what I had heard other Catholics say, that the Catholic school system in Northern Ireland was far superior to the state system. Martin was reluctant to contemplate any change. Yet self-government would very likely mean a rationalization of the education system which, when student numbers generally were considered, would lead to the closure of some Catholic schools. This was one of the problems which Martin McGuinness as minister for education would have to face.

These are losses in practical terms. There are also losses in terms of ideas. If Lebanon is to become a peaceful community the belief that the family is of supreme importance will have to be discarded and a belief in the importance of a peaceful, multicultural community put in its place. If Serbs are to live peacefully with their neighbours they will have to discard their belief in their superiority over all other people and their image of themselves as virtuous victims no matter what they do. In individuals, many of the products of primitive pride will have to be relinquished – ideas like, 'I am virtuous because I won't forgive myself,' 'I show myself to be strong because I won't forgive,' 'I will not mix with people who are beneath me,' and so on.

And with all this loss, there is the loss of the excitement of conflict and of the advantages which having an enemy can bring.

Perhaps the hardest idea of all to give up is that somehow, some day, we shall be recompensed for our losses. Someone will 'make it better'. Alas, that can never be. That which we have lost can never come again. Other things can come to us, ease our pain and partly fill the gap left by our loss, but what we have lost has gone for ever.

When we have been attacked and suffered loss our first response is to feel angry, and with that anger can come the feeling, 'I will never forgive those who did this to me.' This resolution can change as events unfold. Many of us have suffered such losses and made such a resolution, only to find that as the years go by our enemy has unwittingly acted to benefit us. Our life has turned out to be much better than it would have been had our enemy not been our enemy. We may still feel loss, perhaps the loss of childhood innocence or the idealism of youth, but we may actually feel grateful to our enemy. Forgiveness seems to be irrelevant. Perhaps, as the years go by, we see our erstwhile enemy suffer, and, because we have suffered, we do not rejoice in our enemy's suffering but feel for our enemy, who now knows loss as we know loss. Again, forgiveness seems to be irrelevant. Perhaps our enemy comes to us, not as an enemy but as a fallible human being, and asks our forgiveness, and we give it not because we have already forgiven, but because we have learnt that, while not forgiving might make us feel stronger, it is a strength that is also a prison. If we do not wish to ruin our lives we should decide against choosing not to forgive and instead choose to act as tolerantly and forgivingly as we can possibly manage. To be happy we need to act forgivingly towards those who have injured us, to tolerate those who hold views different from ours, and, in accepting our losses, let them go.

This is why friends are so important. They too have suffered losses for which there is no recompense. No one escapes, though some people's losses are greater than others'. But together we can ease our pain and create the things that show us that, because we and the world are constantly changing, we lose but we also gain.

8

The Art of Friendship

When Brian Keenan returned to Ireland after four and a half years as a hostage in the hands of various militias in Beirut he wrote a book, *An Evil Cradling*, which is not so much an account of his life as a hostage as an account of what it is to be human. He described one incident when he, John McCarthy, Terry Anderson and Tom Sutherland were confined to a cell where he had been beaten by a crazed guard; following this he and his fellow hostages refused to eat in protest at his treatment. He wrote,

> There were many other incidents in this hole in the ground. But each of them was an affirmation of human capacity to overcome despair. I could write at length and try to reveal each of those situations, some hilariously funny, some pathetic, others undignifying and ignoble, but that is not my purpose. For each of these incidents revealed what each and all of us are. We are all made of many parts; no man is singular in the way he lives his life. He only lives it fully in relation to others.[1]

'The essence of humanity is in interactions between people in groups.' This was said by my friend and colleague David Canter who, as a renowned forensic psychologist, spent much of his working life studying people who might be considered to be somewhat lacking in humanity. Yet even these criminals were engaged in interactions with people in groups. They had friends and enemies. Their interpretations of other people's behaviour informed their choices, and the outcome of their actions was largely determined by how other people interpreted their actions. Alone we might commit great crimes or create great art, but what then happens depends on how other people interpret our crime or our art.

The dilemma with which we all have to struggle is how to reconcile our own individual way of seeing things with our need to interact with other people, who all have their own way of seeing things. Just how well we manage this reconciliation is a measure of our humanity.

Solitary though we might be in planning our lives and carrying out our projects, our greatest achievements are those we bring about with other people. Works of art might be produced by individuals working alone, but such work needs the support and appreciation of other people. Most writers will say that in the act of writing they are addressing their readers, a specific group of people which each writer can define. Actors and orators do not simply act or orate, they act or orate *to* a person or people whom they have clearly in mind. Artists are aware of their paintings as they are in their mind and as they might be in the minds of those who will see them. Some artists give their paintings names to direct their viewers' interpretations, but others simply present their work with, 'Make of it what you will.' Some diarists write for a readership of one – themselves – but most write for their future readers in the hope that those readers will interpret their work in the way the diarist desires. What all these people – writers, actors, orators, artists, diarists – want in return is some kind of satisfactory appreciation from others.

Appreciation by others is vital to all of us, but what matters most to us in life? In a number of my workshops I gave the participants a sentence to complete: 'After it's all said and done, what matters most in life is . . .' The answers, of course, were couched in many different ways, but the participants were all agreed that ultimately only four things mattered:

- A sense of having achieved something;
- A sense of having made a contribution to the world;
- Being able to accept yourself and so be at peace with yourself;
- Loving relationships.

Some people listed all four, some two or three, some only one. What was listed most often was loving relationships. What most people feared was dying unloved and alone.

The capacity to enjoy loving relationships is in itself a great achievement. Constructed physiologically as we are, we are always in danger of misunderstanding other people, of threatening their meaning structure and being similarly threatened in return. Attempting such an achievement is something we cannot avoid. No matter how much we might hide ourselves away from other people and try to be self-sufficient in the way we live, one way or another we are still connected to other people. Where I lived in London I had a neighbour, a man, not very old, who was always on his own. He bore the stigmata of having been a long-term psychiatric patient who had been dosed with the major tranquillizers for some considerable time. He always wore the same brown trousers, jacket and sweater, whatever the weather, and, although he and I often passed one another in the street, he never showed any sign of recognizing me. Indeed, he tried to keep his eyes averted from everyone on the busy street. Yet he could not shut everybody out. He had to eat, and so he and I both made our regular visits to the local shops, where he had to enter into some kind of communication with the shopkeepers.

No group of people can live their lives entirely to themselves. Those survivalists who took to the hills to avoid the US government and whatever disaster they foresaw carried with them supplies from the rest of the world. The religious group the Amish might keep themselves separate from modern society, but they still have to sell their produce, and so their economy is intimately intertwined with that of the US, and the US economy is part of the world economy.

Whether we are friends or enemies with our neighbours we cannot cut ourselves off from them. We are part of everything that happens in the world.

In 1795, just seven years after Captain Philip had founded a penal colony at Sydney Cove, Immanuel Kant pointed out that, across the world, a 'right violated anywhere could be felt everywhere'. He spoke of

the inhospitable behaviour of the civilized nations, especially the commercial states of our continent. The injustice which they exhibit on visiting foreign lands and races – this being the equivalent in their eyes to conquest – is such as to fill us with horror. America, the negro countries, the Spice Islands, the Cape etc. were, on being discovered, looked upon as countries which belonged to nobody; for the native inhabitants were reckoned as nothing. In Hindustan, under the pretext of intending to establish merely commercial depots, the Europeans introduced foreign troops; and, as a result, the different states of Hindustan were stirred up to far-spreading wars. Oppression of the natives followed, famine, insurrection, perfidy and all the rest of the litany of evils which can inflict mankind.[2]

By the time Kant was writing about 'Perpetual Peace', where a world federation of democratic states welcomed strangers and foreigners and treated them with respect, colonization had followed trade to most parts of the world. Trade and commerce increased, accompanied by an increasing complexity in the means of communication. More recently, as the connections between people increased in volume, people began to talk about the process of 'globalization': industries were leaving the confines of the nation states and becoming worldwide enterprises. Yet, even though everyone on the planet was part of that process, only some were able to share in the possibilities these processes provided, while others for economic reasons were excluded. Mary Kaldor noted

a growing cultural dissonance between those who participate in transnational networks which communicate through e-mail, faxes, telephone and air travel, and those who are excluded from global processes and are tied to localities even though their lives may be profoundly shaped by those same processes.[3]

These two groups of people do not live separate lives. Those who are excluded from the global processes are the poor. If they live in agricultural areas it is on land owned by the global rich. If they live in the same towns and cities as the global community they do menial work, and, in those economies where the politicians accept the economic dogma that a healthy economy requires a certain level of unemployment, they form that percentage of unemployed deemed to be necessary to create an economy which benefits the rich and the comfortably off. They have to endure as best they can the inequalities of the society into which they were born, or, if they are there as refugees, the burdens of that role. They benefit little from the global processes, but they cannot help but be affected by them.

The poor have no choice but to live in a localized way, involved only in their homes, their work and local affairs. Those who are not poor can choose to live locally, excluding world affairs from their attention. They can pick and choose which of the global methods of communication they will use. They might choose to use the television and the phone but eschew the fax and the e-mail, but, no matter how much they ignore world events and focus on their own local community, they cannot protect themselves from the effects of the global processes. I heard on Radio Four a middle-class woman extolling the virtues of village life and deploring the fact that Barclays Bank had decided to close its branch in her village. This would mean, she said, that people in the village would have to go to the nearest town to do their banking. They would then shop and deal with their mail there, and eventually the village shop and Post Office, deprived of custom, would close. Why was Barclays Bank refusing to give customers what they wanted? She spoke of the bank as it was in the past, when it was a British bank with only British interests. Now, like all the major banks, it was an international corporation, a significant player in the game of world finance.

This is a curious game, and no one in the world can escape from its effects. When I was researching for my book *The Real Meaning of Money* I was puzzled how best to explain to my readers how the system of international finance worked. There were trillions of dollars, pounds, yen and Deutschmarks swirling around the planet every day, yet no one person or organization was in charge of all this activity. There was no one set of rules. Individual countries formulated their own rules, but these were liable to change for political as well as economic reasons. Much of the money circulating was not in payment for goods and services but was money involved in currency dealings by firms trying to offset losses through changes in the values of certain currencies and by dealers who were speculating to make a profit. Much of the money circulating was not money which the person involved actually owned but debt, which is actually no more than a set of ideas used by a lender and a borrower. Finally I decided I could best describe this system of international finance only by a metaphor – that of a game:

It is the sort of game where to be admitted you have to bring your own ball. The players spend their time throwing and catching the balls. It might seem that the aim of the game is for players to acquire as many balls as possible, but it is not. The aim of the game is to keep on playing. The balls must be kept in the air because if the players stop playing or if a large enough number of them decide to take their balls and go home, the whole edifice of the international currency and financial markets will come tumbling down because the balls that are being kept in the air are not just lumps of money but also money's anti-matter, debt.[4]

The state of play in this game affects us all, whether it is in the interest we pay for our mortgage, the value of our money when we go abroad, or the price we pay for a kilo of rice.

In the nation state of the nineteenth century both government and business were organized hierarchically, but the twentieth century saw much of that system wither away. Instead systems organized like networks in industry, finance and government came into being. Power used to be organized vertically, with the owner of the firm or a political leader at the top of a pyramidal chain of command, but now organizations are more like spiders' webs, with people with special technical skills or financial knowledge at the key points in the web. Chief executives are still there in name, but rather than imposing their rule on the organization they are concerned with guiding ideas which have usually been developed by other people through the network. A similar change happened in government as government-owned services and enterprises were sold to private business. Moreover, the economic dogma that for an economy to be healthy it has to grow has been accepted by governments, and so they now involve themselves in promoting business. Where in the nineteenth century governments created political alliances with other states, in the twentieth century they began forming business alliances with other states. This trend is likely to continue in the twenty-first century.

This tangled web of networks traps us all. People with their little patch of power in their part of the networks try to keep their lies, deceits, dishonesty, stupidity and bungling hidden from the rest of us, as people with power have always tried to do; but they, like the rest of us, are caught in the web of communications which covers the world and which no one controls. The instruments of technology – radios, telephones, televisions, computers – are produced in their billions and spread across the planet. Governments cannot control access to this technology and thus access to information. During the Second World War it was impossible for anyone in the free world to communicate with people in countries controlled by Germany and Japan. Anyone who tried to do so would put the recipient's life in jeopardy. During the Kosovan conflict I could not send Dusan a letter but we kept in touch almost daily by e-mail. Dusan could access the worldwide web and read not just the websites of the rival groups involved in the conflict but those of the world newspapers. When I was in Belgrade Dusan was not interested in reading the copy of the *Guardian* I had brought with me because, he said, it was dangerously left wing, but during the conflict he e-mailed me an article by that pillar of left-wing politics in the UK, Tony Benn, writing in the *Guardian*. Dusan wanted to know who was this person criticizing NATO's attack on Serbia.

E-mail is still available only to the globalized few, but television is there for the many now that satellite television covers much of the inhabited world. Television is big business. Tragedy sells, and so television teams follow closely in the wake of any human disaster. Pictures alone are not enough for us. They have to be embedded in a story. We see the middle of the story in the pictures and want to know the beginning and the end of the story. Thus, whether we loll back in our comfortable armchair or watch crouching on the ground with everyone in the village gathered around, we learn about what is happening in the rest of the world. The stories we are being told will have their own particular biases, but the ideas we are acquiring no government can control.

Very often the stories we are told on television reveal to us the interconnectedness of everything that happens in the world. While I was writing this such a story was unfolding in East Timor. As pro-Indonesian militias and sections of the Indonesian army, which had been sent in ostensibly to control the militias, roamed the streets of Dili and other towns, destroying property and killing civilians, the United Nations compound, crowded with refugees, was besieged. The UN foreign workers had been ordered to leave by the UN. On our television screens we saw pictures of Timorese men, women and children, huddled together in the compound. They knew that if the UN left they would be murdered. We could see the fear in their eyes.

We watched these pictures and we knew without having to think about it how we would feel if we were in their place. What we felt for these people and for ourselves is the essence of our humanity. Not to feel for these people as we would feel for ourselves would be a denial of that humanity. We asked, 'Why isn't something being done to stop this tragedy?' We heard the politicians, who are always so ready to lecture us about the importance of morality, shuffle their way through lies and feeble, self-serving excuses. They said that everything that could be done was being done.

What they did not say was that there were problems which arose from the interconnectedness of everything. Indonesia's economy was very shaky. An invasion by UN forces could have brought it down, and that could have started a domino effect, bringing down the similarly shaky economies of other south-east Asian countries, and that would put at grave risk the economies of the West. The international financial ball game could disintegrate.

Even if that economic disaster had not come about something else might have happened to bring down a British government or prevent the election of a Democratic president of the USA. If UN forces had invaded the Indonesian force would have used against them weapons from British, American and Australian industries. Coming home in a body bag would have been bad enough, but what if you had been killed by a US bomb dropped from a British plane steered by an Australian computer system?

We cannot begin to solve the problems created by our tangled web of networks until we are able to discard those ideas about nationality, race, religion, gender, family, friends and enemies which divide our world into watertight, simplistic compartments. We need to develop the complexity of thought that comes from understanding that while other people may belong to a different nationality, race, religion or gender and hold different views from your own, they are not dangerous strangers who must be, at best, avoided, or, at worst, killed. Complexity in our ideas can remove fear and give us a more interesting life, rich with wonderful possibilities. Andrew Marr, writing about the 'Perils of Ethnic Purity', contrasted the people of Unionist Northern Ireland and the people of Dublin:

The Ulster Unionist people [are] huddled inside a simple, singular view of the world that deliberately avoided complexity or intermingling. As a result, today they have no open door to the outside world. It still feels like about 1956 in many parts of the province. And Unionists have suffered the penalties of the besieged – the hot stink of political claustrophobia, desertion by many of their brightest and best, lack of contact with the outside world, paranoia. Their identity is too strong, too single. In 1999, that is a tragic predicament for any people. Ask the Serbs.

Dublin, wrote Marr, used to be 'poor, priest-ridden and reactionary'.

Today, Dublin certainly does have a multiple identity: Irish, European, northern, Catholic, trendy. It is connected and complex, not singular and isolated. It sends soldiers to peacekeeping duties around the world, welcomes passing statesmen, sits at the table at key meetings of the European Union. And, yes, many of its links are still with London. In fact, Irish connections with England are in some ways stronger than they were when Irish MPs sat at Westminster. Ireland is obsessed with English football and English celebrities. The Irish workman has been joined by large numbers of high-earning Irish in the City. And, in return, large numbers of people, who would by any normal standards be English, now insist on their Irish roots.[5]

'Irish, European, northern, Catholic, trendy, connected and complex, not singular and isolated' – this is the kind of complex definition of either an individual or a group which makes it extremely difficult to have an enemy. An Afrikaans farmer in the wilds of Northern Province might fulfil the criteria of an enemy, being non-Irish, non-European, southern, Protestant, non-trendy, singular and isolated, but an Afrikaans farmer and a Dubliner are not likely even to meet, much less meet in conditions which would give rise to enmity. Defining ourselves and our group in complex ways is an efficient means of avoiding all the time-wasting and pain that having enemies can bring.

However, if we are to define ourselves and our group in complex ways we must know and accept that no two people ever see things in exactly the same way. This is not a moral issue; it is a matter of good sense. It is always good sense to find out what *is*. Until we have a fairly clear idea of how we operate and how the world operates we are not in a position to make successful changes to ourselves and to our world. Living within our fantasies, no matter how comforting those fantasies might be, is always dangerous.

If we are to understand that we are physically incapable of seeing reality directly, that all we can ever know are the meanings we create, that the sum total of those meanings is what we experience as 'myself', and that all we can ever know is a woven web of guesses, and to accept that this is so, we need the courage to accept uncertainty. It is really a matter of deciding how happy you want to be. If you can tolerate uncertainty you can then enjoy good fortune when it comes and deal courageously and sensibly with the bad fortune that must also come. If you insist on the certainty of your absolute beliefs both good and bad fortune will make you miserable because you will be unable to create a reasonably accurate picture of what is going on, and your views will diverge markedly from those of other people, especially those whom you choose to see as different and therefore dangerous.

If we can accept the uncertainty inherent in ourselves as meaning-creating creatures, and know ourselves to be, in essence, a meaning structure, then we can save ourselves much pain and misery. We can get rid of the demons in our head, or, better still, avoid collecting them in the first place.

I had a phone call from a man who told me he had read some of my books; he was phoning to find out if I still worked as a therapist. I did not, but we talked for a while on the phone. He told me that he had become depressed when, some eleven years earlier, the work he was doing suddenly came to an end. He believed that if he did not work he was worthless – that kind of worthlessness which meant that he did not have the right to exist. He lived in daily dread of something terrible happening. I asked him where he had got the idea that if he did not work he was worthless. 'From my father,' he said. 'He always worked hard.'

I said what, if he had read my books, he would expect me to say: that our value does not depend solely on the work we do. Work can be useful and pleasant, the money comes in handy, and it is always pleasing to know that we are making a contribution to other people's lives, but there are times when there is work to be done and times when there is not. Locating our value solely in the work we do is as sensible as believing that we are valuable when it is raining and not valuable when it is not. Feeling that we have to earn the right to exist presupposes that we existed in some pre-birth state from which we were so keen to escape that we had to beg God or some man and woman to perform the necessary to bring us into being in this world. I have been told that this is what the philosophy of Rudolph Steiner teaches, and it is certainly implicit in much of the Christian teachings which instruct believers to thank God for their existence, but to believe that we came into the world with a debt which we have to repay is a burden which multiplies the ordinary troubles of this world a millionfold.

This desperately depressed man was intelligent and well educated. Why did he hang on to this belief, a demon which gave him no peace? The intense dread he felt was to him the harbinger of his deserved punishment, annihilation. This was not brought about by the hand of God descending to pluck him from the surface of the world and cast him into outer darkness but by the shattering of his meaning structure, which would come about, he feared, if he acknowledged the anger, disappointment and love he had for the father who had set him such high standards, failed to show him that he loved him simply because he existed, and then died while his son was still a child. He dared not say to himself, 'My father was wrong,' because that would reveal the reality of his irreparable loss and throw into doubt his belief that he had to suffer to be good. The demons of primitive pride might protect us from the terrible realities of our lives that threaten to shatter our meaning structure, but it is a protection bought at too high a price.

When we were little children the threat of the annihilation of our meaning structure was a real danger. We had had so little experience that our meaning structure was easily disconfirmed, and we were completely in the power of adults who could be dangerous. Even so, we discovered that, after being completely overwhelmed by disconfirming events, we could pull ourselves together again. As we got older our meaning structure grew stronger. Events and other people could disconfirm some of the meanings we had created, but there was always enough of our meaning structure unshaken by this disconfirmation to be the continuing 'I'. This 'I' is always there. It might be battered and bruised, terrorized by enemies without and demons within, but it is always there.

This sense of existing which we call 'I' must have evolved when consciousness evolved – or rather, this sense of existing and consciousness are different aspects of the same thing because one cannot exist without the other. In dreamless sleep and in an anaesthetized state there is no sense of 'I'. These are the only states where 'I' disappears. The rest of the time, even when we are telling ourselves that we are about to shatter and disappear, annihilation does not come. 'I' continues to exist. In psychosis the sense of 'I' does not disappear. The person feels exceedingly fragile and is threatened by the smallest of everyday events, but the sense of 'I' continues. There is an 'I' which hears voices and experiences delusions as well as one which feels hungry and needs company. In Alzheimer's disease and the other senile dementias the sense of 'I' remains. As these diseases progress family and friends might feel that they have lost the person they knew, yet the accounts by John Bayley of Iris Murdoch with Alzheimer's[6] and by Linda Grant of her mother with multi-infarct dementia[7] show that, even though these two women changed markedly, Iris and Mrs Grant remained to themselves as 'I'. Mrs Grant would forget details of her life – for example, she forgot that the woman shopping with her was her daughter – but she did not forget the passion of her life, which was shopping. Some people, usually extraverts, will say, 'I don't know who I am,' but there is still an 'I' who does not know who 'I' is.

When we do not understand that we are our meaning structure we cannot understand what is happening to us when we lose confidence in ourselves and feel that we are about to be overwhelmed and annihilated. We resort to all kinds of defences, the most desperate being those behaviours which psychiatrists called mental illnesses.[8] We build these defences out of ideas supplied by primitive pride and so these defences, be they a dependence on obsessional checking and cleaning or a resort to a set of absolute, unquestionable beliefs, put us more and more out of touch with what is actually going on.

When we are locked into a struggle to hold our meaning structure together we behave very selfishly. At best we ignore the people who love us; at worst we harm them. We cannot pay attention to other people because everything we say, think or do is part of the struggle to hold ourselves together. Yet it is a needless struggle. We are fighting to hold together something which cannot fall apart. Part of our meaning structure may shatter, but this is necessary when certain ideas are no longer an accurate interpretation of what is actually going on. However, at the central core the sense of 'I' remains. What is actually going on may be totally unexpected and not at all what we would have wanted. What is actually going on may be utterly horrible, but, if we concentrate exclusively on our mistaken belief that we are about to be annihilated and on our attempts, guided by primitive pride, to ward off that annihilation, we become unable to work out how to deal with this unexpected, difficult situation.

We have a choice. When disaster strikes we can remind ourselves that the shakiness we are feeling is our meaning structure making some necessary changes, that this can take some time, and that it is best to go with the flow of the changes taking place in our meaning structure even though at times that can be difficult. Or we can take up the needless struggle to hold ourselves together. Sometimes it is hard to give up this struggle because, terrible though it can be, it is a very effective way of avoiding the very difficult issues involved in recognizing that our life and the world are not what we thought they were. Many people will hang on to the defence of depression rather than face up to the fact, say, that neither their parents nor their marriage were as they would have wanted.

Often, when listening to someone who has for years been engaged in the struggle to hold himself together, much as I feel immense sympathy for that person, I have the urge to shake him and say, 'Can't you see that you are wasting your life? Can't you see what you are doing to the people close to you?'

However, that would change nothing, except to confirm that person in his belief that he was worthless, and that he should intensify his struggle.

Yet the solution is to struggle less – indeed, not to struggle at all. You do not have to do anything. Just be. You will not shatter and disappear.

We were born just being. We looked around and found the world an interesting place. Then adult voices began instructing us, 'Do this,' 'Be that,' 'Be good,' 'Try harder,' 'Aren't you ashamed?' 'You should feel guilty.' We took what these voices said inside us and lost the ability to *just be*. But it can be found again. The key to this discovery is to understand that it is not wicked to *just be*.

When we are able to just be we no longer have to spend all our time thinking about ourselves, forever asking ourselves, 'Am I good enough?' 'Did I do that right?' 'Did that person notice me?' 'Does that person like me?' Instead we can pay attention to the world around us and to other people. Rather than seeing other people only in terms of ourselves we can look at them as themselves.

If we want to have relationships which are long lasting and loving, which are not rent by pain and insoluble misunderstandings, we must stop listening to all those voices in our head that are forever giving us instructions about what we ought to think and do and be, and have the generosity to let ourselves *just be* what we are.

Just being is not enough in itself to solve the problem of enemies, but it is an essential part of coming to understand our enemies. If we can *just be* we cease to see our enemies only in relationship to us and instead see them whole and as they are. Seeing someone as they are means not just seeing what they do but why they do it. If we understand why people do what they do we can work out what would be necessary to bring that enmity to an end and whether a reconciliation would be possible. We need to ask, 'How does that person see himself and his world?' 'What does he see as a threat to his meaning structure?' 'What is he doing to hold his meaning structure together?'

These are the questions which Brian Keenan, in his own way, asked himself about the men who held him hostage, who beat and terrorized him, yet sometimes showed him kindness. Brian could have spent his long years as a hostage hating these men as his enemy, but instead he chose to try to understand them. He wrote,

> It is always the case when a people feel themselves so totally dispossessed, so unjustly condemned to a condition of absolute poverty that the anguish of it forces them to seek an escape. The need to escape becomes stronger as each community acknowledges its dispossession. Such acknowledgement always carries with it, hidden below the surface, a kind of shame and guilt, an admission of loss of identity, of full humanity, and that shame and guilt grows into anger. When the anger can find no outlet, when there is no recourse within the social structure for redress of grievances, the anger turns inwards and festers. They cannot find value in themselves; they reject and loathe themselves. A man can no longer surrender to such a monstrous condition of life. He seeks power, power that will

restore his dignity and his manhood; that will let him stand with other men and know himself to be their equal. But so filled with anger is he that he must act to reclaim meaning and purpose. With one leap he tries to exorcise his fury.

The man unresolved in himself chooses, as men have done throughout history, to take up arms against his sea of troubles. He carries his Kalashnikov on his arm, his handgun stuck in the waistband of his trousers, a belt of bullets slung around his shoulders. I had seen so many young men in Beirut thus attired, their weapons hanging from them and glistening in the sun. The guns were symbols of potency.[9]

In August 1999 there were young men in East Timor similarly attired and killing men, women and children, looting, burning, destroying homes and businesses. They were not robots or men driven wild by their aggression gene. They were men who held certain ideas. They could kill because they believed that the inhabitants of East Timor were not human like themselves. They believed that killing proved their masculinity. They believed that, as Indonesia owned East Timor, they were acting in their country's interests.

The UN referendum which allowed East Timorese to vote for self-government was a threat to the meaning structure of these men. They had never been part of a democratic state. The idea of sharing democratic power was meaningless to them. They knew only about the taking and holding of power by force because this was the way their country had always been governed. The democracy of the referendum represented to them weakness – weakness they despised. At the same time the referendum was a threat to their power because its success could encourage other minority groups in Indonesia to seek independence. To protect themselves they had to destroy those who threatened them.

At least some of them had an additional reason for their murderous onslaught. They knew that the UN could send in an army to take away all their power and perhaps their lives. Each of them was fighting for his survival both physically and as a person. The *Sydney Morning Herald* reported,

In traditional Javanese culture, a cornered man may revert to the practice of 'sampyuh'. Although his defeat is inevitable, he may

lessen his humiliation by taking down as many of his enemies as
he can before his own death. As the casualties mounted in East
Timor this week, the question is just how far the humiliated Indonesian military is prepared to go with its own 'sampyuh', and how
many innocent civilians will be slaughtered to avenge the vote
against Indonesia.[10]

The Indonesian army expressed much of their *sampyuh* by driving
the East Timorese out of their homes and leaving few buildings
standing, much less habitable.

Sampyuh is a custom not confined to Indonesians. Eric Lomax
remembered 'all that POW talk about the moment when you are
absolutely doomed and you take one of them with you'.[11]

From our perspective we would probably applaud the *sampyah*
of the prisoners of war in the hands of the Japanese and condemn
the *sampyah* of the Indonesian army and militia in East Timor, but
we should note the similarity of the reasons behind it in both groups
of men. *Sampyah* is a means of giving ourselves courage and holding
our meaning structure together. We all want to die feeling good
about ourselves and feeling that other people will remember us
with admiration and affection. The more we understand how other
people see themselves and the world, the more clearly we can see
that, despite our own individual way of seeing things, we are all
very much alike. If we want to live in a peaceful world the first step
we must take is to reach this understanding.

Living in a Peaceful World

A peaceful world seems like an impossibility, but it is something we
could achieve if that was what we all wanted. Unfortunately not
everyone wants to live in a peaceful world, and, even if all of us
did, to achieve a peaceful world we would all have to change, and
that is something we find difficult. Yet we and the world are changing
all the time. The question for us is whether we want to be unthink-
ingly carried along by those changes, constantly surprised that our
life is not what we thought it was or what we wanted it to be, or
whether we want to know what is actually going on so that, at best,

we can steer the course of some of those changes and, at worst, not be caught unaware of what is happening.

However, it is difficult to keep up with everything that is changing. When events in East Timor began to dominate the news a listener wrote a plaintive letter to the Radio Four news programme *PM*. 'Would you please,' the letter went, 'explain about East Timor.' The writer was probably well informed about what was happening in Kosova but East Timor was, until then, a place beyond her ken. The *PM* presenter duly obliged with a short history of East Timor.

Not knowing about something does not protect us from the effects of whatever is going on. One of the advantages of being able to *just be* is that, once you give up spending most of your time struggling to hold your meaning structure together and to think well of yourself, you have much more time to discover what is going on in the world. What goes on in the world might be pleasant or unpleasant, but, when you have no need to put yourself centre stage, whatever is going on is always interesting.

For those of us who would like to do something more than just hope for a peaceful world the study of the causes of enmity and the ways in which enmity can be expressed becomes a necessity. That method of enmity called war has changed quite markedly from the wars conducted by the nation states of Europe in the nineteenth century and the first half of the twentieth century. Mary Kaldor divided wars into 'old' and 'new'. Old wars, she wrote, were 'a specific phenomenon which took shape in Europe somewhere between the fifteenth and eighteenth centuries . . . It was a phenomenon that was intimately bound up with the evolution of the modern state.'[12] By the beginning of the twentieth century nation states were forming alliances with one another to conduct wars. They created massed armies supported by vast supplies of equipment. 'The wars of the first half of the twentieth century were total wars involving vast mobilization of national energies both to fight and to support the fighting through the production of arms and necessities.'[13] However,

the irregular, informal wars of the second half of the twentieth century, starting with the wartime resistance movements and the guerrilla warfare of Mao Tse-tung and his successors represent the harbingers of the new forms of warfare. The actors, techniques and counter-techniques which emerged out of the cracks of modern warfare were to provide the basis for the new ways of socially organizing violence.[14]

This kind of violence Kaldor called 'new wars':

> I use the term 'war' to emphasize the political nature of this new type of violence, even though the new wars involve a blurring of the distinctions between war (usually defined as violence between states or organized political groups for political motives), organized crime (violence undertaken by privately organized groups for private purposes, usually financial gain) and large-scale violations of human rights (violence undertaken by states or politically organized groups against individuals).[15]

These new wars are being fought mainly with weapons of little technical sophistication – small arms and simple mines which kill or maim individuals – yet they are being fought in the context of the ever-developing systems of international communications. According to John Arquilla and David Ronfeldt, writing about the advent of cyberwars,

> Conflicts will increasingly depend on, and revolve around, information and communication – 'cyber' matters – broadly defined to include the related technological, organizational, and ideational structures of a society. Indeed, information-age modes of conflict will be largely about 'knowledge' – about who knows what, when, where and why, and about how secure a society, military, or other actor feels about its knowledge of itself and its adversaries.[16]

Of prime importance in the old wars was the quantity of the armaments and the number of soldiers available. Little was said about the ideas which underlay the decisions about going to war and the deployment of troops. In the discussions that went on in the early 1980s about the threat of nuclear war all the talk was of the size of the bombs and the destruction they could cause; the ideas which led to the building of these bombs and the maintenance of the Cold War were not touched on. Now, in the information age, we can see

clearly what has always mattered in war – the ideas that people hold.
Arquilla and Ronfeldt described what a war in the information
age would be like.

Suppose that war looked like this: Small numbers of your light,
highly mobile forces defeat and compel the surrender of large masses
of heavily armed, dug-in enemy forces, with little loss of life on
either side. Your forces can do this because they are well prepared,
make room for manoeuvre, concentrate their firepower rapidly in
unexpected places, and have superior command, control, and information systems that are decentralized to allow tactical initiatives,
yet provide the central commanders with unparalleled intelligence
and 'topsight' for strategic purposes.

For your forces, warfare is no longer primarily a function of who
puts the most capital, labor and technology on the battlefield, but
of who has the best information about the battlefield. What distinguishes the victors is their grasp of information – not only from
the mundane standpoint of knowing how to find the enemy while
keeping it in the dark, but also in doctrinal and organizational terms.
The analogy is rather like a chess game where you see the entire
board, but your opponent sees only his own pieces – you can win
even if he is allowed to start with additional powerful pieces.[17]

It was an information war which NATO fought in Kosova. Most
of the armchair warriors said that a war could not be won by a
bombing campaign alone. Ground troops needed to be sent in.
NATO proved them wrong because NATO had better access to the
necessary information than the Serbian army.

What does an information war feel like on the ground? The
journalist Rory Carroll met Milos, a Serbian army conscript, on his
way home at the end of the conflict:

Milos, 28, was a private in a mortar platoon of 39 Serb reservists.
Twenty-six died, 13 survived ... At the end of his eight-hour bus
ride to the town of Sjenica in south-west Serbia will be a young
wife, 14-month-old son and a clerical job in the post office. He does
not know how he will cope. 'I'm not the same, I'm not the same,'
he says, tapping his domed forehead. The grey eyes wander when
he talks. Words come slowly. Without realizing it, he twists the

yellow table cloth into a knot. 'We went to exterminate the terrorists wherever we could find them. That was our job. In the beginning it was OK, we pushed them back. It was cold and I wanted a sleeping bag instead of a blanket, but we had enough to eat.'

February turned to March, and talk turned to NATO. At around 9pm on 29 March an officer dropped into his trench and said that warplanes were on their way to bomb them.

Explosions lit up the countryside. No one died, not that night. But the planes came back, every night, then during the day too. 'They knew everything about us. There wasn't anything they didn't know. If we lit a cigarette they could see it. God knows what they were dropping on us, all sorts of bombs. We didn't expect that intensity. We couldn't fight planes with mortars.'

Every day the platoon tried to run, to hide. 'It felt like we went over every inch of Kosova.' Serb civilians stopped bringing them food. Officers were able to warn troops minutes before almost every air attack, but it was of little use. 'We spread out, one of us every hundred metres, but they just picked us off. Bosnia was a spa compared to Kosova. Everywhere there was a smell of bodies. Rotting bodies.'[18]

No matter what kind of war it is, war means death.

In the old wars of the nineteenth century armies fought one another. Civilians were not a target, though they might be caught up in a siege or be victims of soldiers looting and raping. In the new wars civilians are the target, and in destroying civilians something more is being destroyed. The war in Yugoslavia was seen by many outside observers as an old war between three nationalist groups, when in fact it was not. According to Mary Kaldor,

While Serbian and Croatian nationalism were definitely bad nationalism and Muslim nationalism was not quite so bad, such an analysis missed the point that this was a conflict between a new form of ethnic nationalism and civilized values. The nationalists shared an interest in eliminating an internationalist humanitarian outlook both within the former Yugoslavia and globally. Both politically and militarily, their war was not against each other but against the civilian population and against civil society.[19]

An internationalist humanitarian outlook is very threatening to those people who believe that they have access to nationalistic, racial or religious absolute truth, and that they have the right to force the world to be what they want it to be. A humanitarian outlook is one which recognizes that all human beings are people, not objects, and that they all have their own way of seeing things. Throughout our history there have been conflicts between those with absolutist ideas and those with humanistic ideas, and very often the absolutists have won. However, in recent years, during which the new war militias have inflicted mass murder, rape and torture on civilians, politicians in democratic countries have had to take some account of those people who were suffering, even though they were not the people who could keep the politicians in office. The war in Kosova might mark a significant change in how politicians see their duty.

This duty has always been to the people of their own country. Politicians might not have fulfilled this duty very well but they knew where their duty lay. Now it seems that some politicians are recognizing that they have to look further afield; that they owe a duty to the people of the world. To date politicians have had to try to please those in their constituency, who want all refugees returned to whence they came, *and* those who want to help suffering people the world over. Usually politicians have solved this problem by pleasing the group which could return the biggest vote for them, but with the increase in global information available to us all politicians might begin to find that the humanitarians in their constituency outnumber the racists. Apart from the humanitarians, there are many people who do not want a refugee family living next door but at the same time want to help people in need in other parts of the world.

NATO's intervention in Kosova was aimed at protecting the civilian victims of a new war. This action raised many moral issues and questions about appropriate strategies for such an intervention. It was a pity that the tragedy which unfolded in East Timor came so soon after Kosova because there was no time for the governments involved to work out a strategic plan for similar crises and to define a consistent morality applicable at an international level. Morality is indivisible. If it is right for an international force to bomb or invade a country to protect civilians under attack then this course of action must be followed wherever such attacks on civilians occur.

But what do you do when the country perpetuating the atrocities is your ally? By November 1999 Russian forces had invaded Chechnya with the intention of destroying all resistance. Civilians were not spared. Russian aircraft and artillery pounded the Chechen capital Grozny, killing hundreds of people and levelling large tracts of the city. Thousands of Chechens fled. Many were trapped on the border with Ingushetia by Russian troops who refused to let them cross or allow aid agencies and supplies to reach them. At a summit meeting of the Organization for Security and Cooperation leaders of many countries, including President Bill Clinton, pleaded with President Boris Yeltsin to end the conflict. Yeltsin declared, 'You have no right to criticize Russia,' and left the meeting.

During the Bosnian war many people pointed out that the US and European governments would have moved swiftly and effectively to protect the Bosnians had Bosnia been rich in oil. Events in East Timor at first suggested that the likelihood of international protection depends on the colour of the victims' skin. The British and the US government were forced by international protests to support a UN force entering East Timor to establish order there. Truth for politicians is a very malleable commodity. On the morning of 11 September we were being told by the British Foreign Secretary Robin Cook and other politicians that the government could not suspend the sale of arms to Indonesia. Commercial law made this impossible. By the evening of that day it suddenly became possible and sales were suspended. Robin Cook assured the world that he was not embarrassed. Either he lacked the conscience needed in order to feel embarrassment, or he was lying.

The twentieth century was the century of war. At the beginning of the twenty-first century let us allow ourselves some hope. Suppose that in all the wealthy democratic countries there is a generation of political, business and community leaders coming into power who are honestly and firmly committed to creating a peaceful world. They are committed to telling the truth. They know that they do not have the power to bring all conflicts to an end, but they believe that it is possible to set up a cooperative international organization to protect civilians from murder, rape, torture and forced removal by those who are involved in a conflict. Such an organization would have to work out a consistent morality by defining the conditions under which an international force would intervene. They would also have to construct a strategy for such interventions.

Creating a morality and a strategy would be the easy part of their task. The hard part would be changing people's ideas, but unless we do change our ideas another century of war lies ahead of us. Most of the conflicts which are raging at the beginning of the century show no sign of ending, while a significant decrease in the supplies of water to populous parts of the globe is likely to lead to what are now being called 'water wars'. Water is an issue in the Arab–Israeli conflict – who is to control the river Jordan? – while Turkey, Syria and Iraq each claim rights over the Tigris and Euphrates.

What ideas do we need to change?

First, we need to learn to see one another as people, not as things. We must know that, without exception, no one is sub-human, inherently inferior or inherently wicked. We need to recognize that we all have our own way of seeing things, and, even though we might not approve of another person's views, we must tolerate them. Moreover, we should celebrate the difference between us because living in a culturally complex world, rich with a variety of ideas, is more rewarding and interesting than living in a box with a few simple ideas, enclosed and isolated.

Such a change will not follow merely from a public relations campaign and some exhortations to virtue by politicians and religious leaders. In society ideas are slow to change. It took three decades for the horrible sexist language so prevalent up to the 1970s to disappear from public discourse. Privately many men still hold sexist ideas because little in the upbringing of boys has changed, but, because the public expression of sexism is considered unacceptable, women's lives have considerably improved. Much the same has happened with publicly expressed attitudes to homosexuality. Unfortunately, the same has not happened where racism is concerned. British governments have nodded in the direction of racial equality, but no government has dealt effectively with the racism in its police, fire service and military. Racist remarks made publicly can be the subject of a lawsuit, but anyone who is not obviously of white British descent can be subject to discrimination. Australia is certainly a much less racist country than when I was growing up there, but racism directed not just at Aboriginal people but at people from the Middle and Far East, Africa and the Pacific rim still plays a prominent part in defining groups and creating enemies. The racism so prevalent in the USA is clearly seen in the preponderance of black men and women in the country's jails.

Governments have no control over people's private thoughts, but they can influence shared ideas through the laws they pass and through honest advocacy. It was the law that ended bear-baiting, slavery, child labour and the death penalty, and public opinion followed. When the British government banned the use of the cane in schools the predicted insurrections in classrooms across the land failed to materialize, and slowly the idea spread that corporal punishment is not necessary in the education of children. Laws such as these do influence public opinion because governments are consistent in their demand that the law be upheld. It is when politicians say one thing and do another that people see the hypocrisy and refuse to accept the ideas which the politicians promote, no matter how right or beneficial those ideas might be.

Politicians often exhibit massive hypocrisy – particularly when they talk about children. They claim that 'Children are our future', yet their actions ensure that for many children the future is grim. If adults really cared about children no child in the world would live in poverty, lack medical care and education, and suffer the effects of conflict either in a family or in society. The fact that many millions of children are so deprived shows that most adults do not see children as being fellow human beings.

Not being seen as a fellow human being means that these children have the kind of upbringing which makes enemies necessary. If you grow up in poverty, or with a new war raging around you, or in a family where you are abused, beaten or unloved, or with parents and teachers who set you dauntingly high standards where failure is unacceptable, then you need an enemy on whom to project the bad feelings which you can express in no other way. You readily accept the prejudices held by the adults around you concerning the goodness of your group and the wickedness of the group's enemies: these prejudices are a comfort blanket when nothing else is available. Once you have discovered the two great advantages in having an enemy you readily acquire most of the other advantages. It is only a short step from being a child who has been seen by adults as an object of no importance or as a possession to be used by adults, to being a young man with a gun or a woman who despises everyone who is not a member of her group.

If we all came to understand and accept that all human beings are people like ourselves and that we all have our own way of seeing things our society would change completely.

Let us pin our hopes on this rising generation of honest leaders committed to world peace. Their third task would be to define the standards of behaviour against which individual events would be measured. We have accepted universal standards for trade and tele-communications. Perhaps we are close to accepting universal, enforceable standards for human rights. As a UN peace-keeping and peace-enforcing force went into East Timor Kofi Annan, the UN Secretary-General, challenged the UN Security Council to break out of its usual paralysis to respond faster and more effectively when human rights were being brutally ignored. He called for 'a culture of prevention'.

The Geneva Conventions already define the standards for the conduct of war. Information wars and new wars might make it necessary to update these standards. Certainly there needs to be an unequivocal acceptance that mass murder, rape, torture and the enforced removal of groups of people from their homes and work can in no circumstances be tolerated. Simply stating this will not be adequate. There would have to be an efficient means of policing and of bringing to an international court of law those people who broke the law. Any country which refused to be part of this system and insisted on trying its own citizens would be seen as committing a racist act. To say, 'We must try our own,' is to judge the rest of the human race to be inferior.

Our brave new leaders seeking a peaceful world would have to tackle the problem of crime. A peaceful world would depend on a universal respect for the law, but a globalized world has allowed organized crime to flourish. The United Nations 1999 Human Development Report showed that the world's organized criminals have a turnover greater than all but three of the world's economies. The biggest growth area is in illegal drugs. By 1999 this trade supplied some 200 million customers and was worth £250 billions or 8 per cent of world trade. Another growth industry was the trafficking in women and children for sexual purposes. By 1999 this business was worth £5 billion a year.[20]

Crime flourishes because many political, community and business leaders, instead of upholding the law, evade it and profit from their evasions. It is corrupt officials as well as criminals, taking advantage of the slackening of currency controls, who launder the profits from crime to bring it into the legal financial system. According to the International Monetary Fund, by 1999 between $500 billion and $1.5 trillion (or 5 per cent of the gross world product) were being laundered every year.[21] Transparency International, which is a non-governmental organization dedicated to increasing governmental accountability and curbing both international and national corruption, described what corruption does to all of us:

> Corruption is the abuse of public office for private gain. Corruption hurts everyone. It deepens poverty. It distorts social and economic development, it erodes the provision of essential public services and it undermines democracy. Instead of fair competition based on price, quality and innovation, corruption leads to competitive bribery. This harms trade and deters new investment.[22]

Yet in many countries bribery is seen as an essential part of business. Crime and a disrespect for the law are not confined to criminals. People who regard themselves as law-abiding citizens take part in the shadow economy of money which circulates through a country's economy without being included in the legal record of what is earned and what tax is paid. When told by a tradesman that his quote for a job is £200 plus Value Added Tax or £200 in cash we are likely to hand over the cash. When we fill in our tax return we are likely to forget to include some part of our earnings but remember to inflate the size of some of our expenses. The more we earn the more stratagems are available to us to avoid paying tax. On a league table of the shadow economy shown as a percentage of a country's economy Nigeria and Thailand top the table, with a percentage close to 80. The UK and Australia show about 15 per cent while the USA is 10 per cent. *The Economist* explained the USA's low percentage not in terms of the great virtue of Americans but in terms of their relatively low tax burden. Paying a moderate amount of tax, Americans do not feel that they have to withhold from their government what they see as rightly theirs.[23]

Whenever we commit a crime, whether it is omitting a few pounds of income from our tax return or running a crime syndicate involved in illegal drugs, we tell ourselves that there is nothing wrong with what we do. We say to ourselves, 'Everyone does it,' or, 'The government is more crooked than me,' or, 'I help other people with the money I make.' Primitive pride supplies these excuses because if we say to ourselves, 'What I do is not right,' our meaning structure will tremble and threaten to shatter. We and our meaning structure feel secure only when the core of our meaning structure, how we feel about ourselves, is secure. We need to feel that we can live with ourselves, and so, even while we are telling ourselves that we are not good enough, we are also telling ourselves that we are good, or, at least, no worse than the next person.

Solving the problem of crime, like solving any of the major problems that beset us, cannot be done by tackling it only at a social level or only at an individual level. It has to be done at both. Poverty gives rise to much crime, but simply making sure that everyone had an adequate income would not eradicate all crime – though it would reduce it – because many people would still feel that they did not have enough money. Similarly, ensuring that everybody was utterly honest with themselves and with other people would not eradicate crime because, being poor, many people would still need to steal in order to eat.

Crime and poverty, war and conflict will not disappear until we evolve a way of thinking about ourselves in society where we do not divide up society into discrete boxes with impermeable walls, with the box we are in being defined as 'good' and all the other boxes as 'bad'. Instead, we need to think of ourselves as being at the centre of a set of concentric circles whose walls are permeable so that people and ideas can travel freely. We can label these concentric circles in many different ways. One person might see his first circle as 'family', and surrounding that 'friends', and around that 'country', and so on, while another might have her first circle as 'friends', the second 'women', the third 'Irish', and so on. In whatever way the circles are labelled, none is labelled 'good' or 'bad'.

We need our small group around us, knowing us, loving and supporting us, but we should also recognize that we are members of wider and wider communities which, in all, enclose and support us all. We are unlikely to meet all the members of all our communities but we should accept that each has the potential to be a friend.

In his study of the origins of virtue Matt Ridley defined virtue as 'almost exclusively pro-social behaviour, and vice as anti-social behaviour'. He noted that

> Our cultures are not random collections of arbitrary habits. They are canalized expressions of our instincts. That is why the same themes crop up in all cultures – themes such as family, ritual, bargain, love, hierarchy, friendship, jealousy, group loyalty and superstition. That is why, for all their superficial differences of language and custom, foreign cultures are immediately comprehensible at the deeper level of motives, emotions and social habits. Instincts, in a species like the human one, are not immutable genetic programmes; they are predispositions to learn.[24]

Ridley concluded,

> The roots of social order are in our heads, where we possess the instinctive capacities for creating not a perfectly harmonious and virtuous society, but a better one than we have at present. We must build our institutions in such a way that they draw out these instincts. Pre-eminently this means the encouragement of exchange between equals. Just as trade between countries is the best recipe for friendship between them, so exchange between the enfranchised and empowered individuals is the best recipe for co-operation. We must encourage social and material exchange between equals for that is the raw material of trust, and trust is the foundation of virtue.[25]

But how easy is it to establish trust?

Can Your Lover Be Your Friend?

When the daily unfolding of the story of Princess Diana came to an abrupt end with her death the media had to find other topics to be the subject of discussion and so fill their pages of newspapers and magazines. A number of television series where the main characters were a group of friends had become very popular and so friendship was seen as a hot topic. I was soon getting phone calls from journalists who wanted me to explain this or that aspect of friendship. They wanted to know how long friendships lasted, why friends who go on holiday together often fall out, whether people of different generations could be friends, and so on and on.

Questions like what do you do when your best friend is jealous of your baby, or what should you do when your best friend steals your lover, or when your friend bullies you or talks about you behind your back left me wondering whether the journalist was using the terms friend and friendship rather loosely. Surely people who behaved so badly were not friends but just someone we might have the misfortune to know. Simply knowing someone for several years or having to spend a certain amount of time with someone does not constitute a friendship. Over our lifetimes we have relationships with a large number of people but a friendship with only a few because a friendship has some very special qualities. We may share interests with another person but the relationship is not a friendship. We may like another person and yet that person is not a friend. We may share a sexual relationship with another person and even love that person, but the relationship might not be a friendship. Indeed, there is the whole question of whether a lover can be a friend.

The sexual urge itself has nothing to do with friendship. It is entirely selfish. To satisfy the sexual urge a sexual partner does not have to be seen as a human being. The majority of men the world over prefer to see their partner not as a person but as an object. This is one of the reasons why prostitution is so popular.

The majority of men do not see women as full human beings like themselves. This idea is entrenched in many societies. In Dalmatia, I was told by a woman in Belgrade, men refer to a woman as 'it'. In the *Viet Nam News* I read part of a serialized story where the writer Hô Anh Thái described a woman who had been widowed in the war:

A widowed woman is a fragment of the man who died. Some women bear the fate of a fragment, living silently in seclusion, all the while clinging to the dream of finding and putting all those fragments back together again. Others are fragments lying here and there on the road, piercing and cutting the feet of luckier souls as a way of wreaking revenge for their own sad fates.[26]

When I was a child in Australia it was still customary to refer to a widow as the relict of her husband.

Such selfishness and self-absorption is not only related to the sex act. People may see their sexuality as being the essence of their own identity. Brian Keenan spent the first months of his time as a hostage completely alone. Solitary confinement for an indefinite period is the torture which can break the strongest person. In that seclusion little of the outside world is available to confirm our meaning structure. We have to find confirmation for ourselves, and when our own confirmations are disconfirmed by events we are terrified. Of this experience Keenan wrote,

> I am panicking. Panic is a seizure like a fit. It clamps on me iron-hard, and will not let me go. I have been impotent for weeks. I am reduced to this animal thing, to this failure of my genitals to come alive to me. What have they done to me, this final insult and indignity. That most primitive and animal part of me has been ripped from me. Panic becomes rage and rage reinforces the panic and then fear takes them by the neck and hangs them up. I am possessed by fear, by what it means not to be potent any more.[27]

Society's demand that women be virginal brides and chaste wives saved many women from the torment which men suffer when they base their identity on their ability to be sexually active. The sexual freedom now available to women has allowed them to choose the torment of having to prove your worth as a person by repeated sexual acts. Alison Whelan realized that she had done this when she ended what she called 'the most damaging relationship I had ever been in'. She wrote, 'I have been dating since I was eight, having sex since I was seventeen. I am now thirty-two, which amounts to a long time with men in my bed and in my head.' A girlfriend suggested that she go celibate for a while until she worked out what it was she wanted from a relationship.

Considering this question Alison decided that 'My idea of having a boyfriend is someone who loves me no matter what, who won't get angry with me, someone who will not say no to me and is available 24/7. He's my lover, my best friend, my father, my mother and my careers counsellor.' In demanding this paragon Alison made no mention of what she might be able to put into a relationship.

However, she did see that she was wanting the impossible and decided to give celibacy a go. This entailed considerable changes to her social life, but, seven weeks into this strange way of living, she was making discoveries.

> The most frustrating bit is that I'm also learning a lot about myself I simply don't like. I hadn't realized how much I depended upon having a boyfriend as a level of my self-worth. I have lost confidence because I don't have a man around. If my boyfriend was good-looking and successful, then so was I. Take the boyfriend away and I'm a child wobbling around on her first bike without any stabilizers. I feel ugly and seem to be the only single person in the world. It's a struggle going out with my friends because I think, 'What's the point? I can't pull anyone.' [But,] As I inch into week seven feeling mad, I realize this is pure serenity compared to where I was two months ago.[28]

If we rely solely on another person to confirm our worth we lose control of our lives. Another person, no matter how kind, loving and perceptive he might be, is incapable of giving us as much confirmation as we want when we want it. Just as a relationship between a man and a partner he regards as a sexual object cannot be a friendship so a relationship between a woman and a partner who, she believes, alone has the power to sustain her and on whom she must depend cannot be a friendship. These are unequal relationships where one person has the power and the other is weak. A friendship is always a relationship between equals.

Much of our sexual activity and much of our thinking and talking about sex comes not so much from a passion for sex but from a fear of helplessness. The men who kept Brian Keenan and John McCarthy hostages had only two topics of conversation, Allah and sex. Keenan commented, 'Our captors' obsessions with God and sex were not about religion or morality. They were ciphers for their own powerlessness: an impotence they experienced unconsciously at a deep personal level and also in the world of politics.'[29]

Many men feel an impotence at a deeply personal level and also in the world of politics, so sex becomes a kind of whistling in the dark, a denial of their helplessness. One of the reasons why many women in their thirties and forties lose interest in sex and turn to other occupations which they find more satisfying is that, never having been presented with a model of life as 'compete, win or die', they can acknowledge their helplessness; this means that they do not need to use sex as a way of denying it. Having satisfied their curiosity about sex, they turn to other matters.

In a relationship where a man uses sex as a way of feeling powerful and thus maintaining the integrity of his meaning structure the woman will find the integrity of her meaning structure threatened. Such a relationship cannot be a friendship; in a friendship each friend will try to avoid causing distress to the other person. A friend will try to discover what the other person finds most threatening and then refrain from doing it. In a power relationship one person tries to discover what threatens another person the most and then do it in order to have power over that person. Many marriages operate in this way.

I met one such couple when I first came to England. The woman, Pandora, was referred with a diagnosis of anxiety and insomnia to the clinic where I worked. As we talked it became clear that it was anxiety which kept her awake at night, and that this anxiety was concerned with meeting people and with guarding her children's safety. She was a vibrant, immensely likeable woman whose account of her life before her marriage implied that she had been outgoing and sociable, with a sensible approach to the dangers of life. It seemed likely that the change in her could be accounted for by something in her marriage.

However, it was made clear to me by both Pandora and her husband Leslie that the marriage was not to be discussed. He was the strong one and she was the one who needed looking after. She had problems; he did not. If any health care professional challenged this Leslie severed the connection between that professional and Pandora. Under these circumstances Pandora's insomnia was intractable, but the three of us got on well together and we kept in touch over a number of years after I had left the clinic. In that time I came to see what was the pattern of the marriage. It was not about each partner helping the other to maintain the integrity of a meaning structure but about Leslie threatening the integrity of Pandora's meaning structure so that he could maintain the integrity of his.

Leslie felt safest when he felt he had everything under control. He had fallen in love with an exciting woman who did not want to be controlled. He was constantly afraid that another man would steal her from him. He soon discovered that her dominant fear was of being rejected, a fear which she occasionally expressed as a reluctance to meet new people and encounter new places. Leslie realized that by playing on this fear in the teasing and protective ways that many men use with women he could get Pandora to become more and more dependent on him.

Both shared a belief in the importance of the family. Their children became the focus of their interest in what was an increasingly close family. Leslie became the interface between her and the children and the outside world. He presented his need to control those on whom he depended as a desire to look after the family. The children needed to be looked after because they were children. Pandora needed to be looked after because she did not sleep; for her the most ordinary of events could contain the seeds of illness and death for her children and herself. A teatowel which had not been boiled long enough in the wash, or an apple bruised in one tiny place could unleash the worst of her nightmares.

Over time Pandora's fear of people and places increased. Instead of helping her to confront and overcome this fear Leslie responded 'helpfully' by reducing the number of friends they had and the number of social occasions they attended. Occasionally Pandora resented the extent to which he controlled her life, but she had already been seduced by the ease of a life where she made few decisions and took little responsibility.

This pattern of marriage is not uncommon. There are many obsessional introverts who want to enjoy the illusion that they can control part of the universe, and many unself-confident extraverts who want to avoid the hard work of discovering how to survive without being loved by everybody. A marriage between these two can, by mutual weakness, survive through to old age and death, but this is hardly a relationship between equals and therefore not a friendship.

There are other marriages where the couple might be supporting the integrity of the meaning structure until one, in some way, lets the other down. On one occasion Susie Orbach and I were speaking at a conference organized by a marriage guidance agency. Susie discussed several of the couples who had been her clients and talked about how in an unhappy marriage one or both people may have suffered a disappointment. In the discussion which followed one elderly man questioned her use of the word 'disappoint'. For men, he said, a better word would be 'defeat'. Many a man has found himself defeated by his wife. You can be defeated only if you are engaged in a struggle for power, and a woman can be as interested in power in a marriage as a man.

Marriage can be a friendship and the happiest marriages are just that. In a marriage between equals there is interdependence and mutual reliability but there is also an independence which comes from knowing one another so well that trying to control the other person or trying to hang on to the other person becomes irrelevant. Wanting to control or be dependent on a partner can be expressed as a desire to be understood. The argument goes that if you really understood me you would never do anything which would upset me. When John Bayley was asked about his relationship with his wife Iris Murdoch he said, 'I think understanding is one of the most fatal things that can happen in a marriage. It was one of those curious kinds of closeness, where we never bothered each other at all. We just had a sense of being together. We didn't have one of those sinister kinds of closeness. We were more like two animals in a field.'[30]

Sex can prevent a friendship from forming, but it neither makes a friendship nor destroys it. Sex is irrelevant to friendship. When Lyn Barber interviewed Brian Keenan she asked him, if he and McCarthy had such endless, intimate discussions, did they ever discuss the possibility of having sex? Keenan replied,

'No. It never came up even in a jokey way. For some reason it wasn't something you ever thought about or that crossed your mind. I think there was a profounder kind of intimacy – you were wanting to unravel his head. If sex is in some way about validation – and I suppose it is, or should be – you were more interested in whether your own thought processes were valid, or human, and could be understood and believed. And that was much more interesting than sex.'[31]

The Art of Friendship

When we are small children we need to discover that all human beings have thoughts and feelings, and that a relationship consists of an engagement of the thoughts and feelings of two people, one with another. When one person treats another person as an object he or she is denying that the other person has thoughts and feelings. This is a denial of what is actually going on, and it overlooks the fact that the other person is busily interpreting and judging the person who is treating him as an object. If one person does not acknowledge that the other person has thoughts and feelings then no relationship can exist and certainly no friendship.

Even when one person does acknowledge the thoughts and feelings of the other there can still be many barriers to friendship.

The first barrier may be how you feel about yourself. If you do not believe that you are lovable you will not accept that another person might offer you friendship. Indeed, you might not even perceive the offer. Until I was in my thirties I still believed what my mother and sister had said to me and showed me in their behaviour towards me – that I was a thing of no importance, ugly, unlikeable and unlovable. When I look back on those years now I can see instance after instance where I ignored or rejected offers of friendship and love. Because I believed that in every relationship I would be rejected I often got my rejection in first. I am sorry now for all the friendship and love I foolishly lost, and even more sorry for all the people I hurt.

Now in the wisdom of my years I might congratulate myself on never again making the mistake of rejecting friendship, but I discovered I was still prone to a certain error. My friend Heather was a genius at friendship. If she went to a strange town within an hour she would have met twenty people to invite to one of her splendid dinners, or so it seemed to me. When I was planning my trip to South Africa I wrote to John, someone both Heather and I knew, who would be in South Africa at the same time as I was. I thought we could arrange to meet. Time went by and no answer came. I told Heather that I had not heard from John and said, 'I guess he doesn't want to see me.'

'No, no, no,' said Heather with a passion that surprised me. Her voice was always modulated and sweet. 'You must never assume that. Never. He just hasn't got your letter. The mail is terrible. Have you tried ringing him?'

Heather's response shocked me into looking at how I had been thinking. I had assumed I had been rejected, so I certainly would not have contemplated phoning to receive yet another rejection. Heather, on the other hand, never assumed she would be rejected, and so she rarely was.

There are many people who believe that they are not loveable but they do have another necessary precursor to friendship – an interest in other people. At the same time there are many people who are quite well satisfied with themselves but have no interest at all in other people. The focus of their interest is themselves.

As young mothers Joy and I often met at Nielsen Park, a beach on Sydney Harbour which was safe for small children. We frequently talked about the difficulties we had with our mothers. Both these women were utterly self-involved. They were interested only in matters where they were the star players. Joy and I both found our duty visits home boring and frustrating. We devised two games to keep our spirits up. The first was, while apparently listening to our mother talking, to count the number of first personal pronouns she used. For each woman the most overworked words in the English language were I, me, my, mine, myself. In the other game we would think of a topic far removed from our mother's experience and start to talk about it. We then counted the seconds it took her to get the topic under discussion back to herself. Each woman could do that in a flash. Either she started with 'I think' or she ignored what we had said and talked only about her favourite topic. As a psychologist I never patented these procedures as 'Tests Measuring Self-Involvement', but I have certainly used them with many people.

We can also use these tests on ourselves as we listen to ourselves talk. One of the joys of friendship is that we can talk about ourselves. However, this has to be mutual. A relationship where one person talks about herself and the other listens is not a friendship.

Self-involvement is the essence of selfishness, and selfishness makes friendship impossible. We can forgive our friends the occasional selfish act, just as we can like someone who is occasionally selfish, but it is impossible to like someone who is unremittingly selfish.

Sometimes the selfishness involves not being prepared to make the effort even to explore whether a friendship might be possible. Many elderly people will not make this effort and so they remain very lonely. Some years after the death of my father my mother's eldest sister Jessie died, leaving Uncle George to fend for himself, their children now having families of their own to care for. Lonely, he started visiting Mother for a chat and a cup of tea. They had known one another since they were children – more than seventy years. One day Mother said to me, 'I've told George to stop coming. He was taking up too much of my time.'

I recently saw something similar happen between two people who were good friends to me when I lived in Sheffield. Reg had recently been widowed and was digging in his garden when Lettie, who had been widowed some years previously and knew how lonely Reg must have been, passed by and stopped to talk. Reg could have said, 'How about a cup of tea?' and they could have talked, but he was a man who prided himself on never showing weakness. So he said, 'I must get on,' and went on tidying an already immaculate garden.

Perhaps Lettie could have pressed Reg harder or returned another day, but she had uncertainties about herself and about what other people would think. Creating a friendship requires courage. Brian Keenan wrote, 'It needs a commitment to the courage of another person in order to approach them, be honest with them and know that you will not be shunned or rejected by them.'[32]

Lettie might have hung back because, as I mentioned in an earlier story, she knew only too well how horrible it is to be used by other people. In my first thirty-odd years I was used by people who ought to have been caring for me, and I remember my feelings of loneliness and self-disgust when these people presumed upon my kindness and competence. I did not know how to stand up for myself, and I trapped myself, as many women do, by wanting to see myself as being good and wanting others to see me in the same way. From my early childhood I was very competent at anything I put my mind to, but when I was used I could draw no pride from my competence because those who used me never praised or even thanked me. If I had had any sense I would have protested at their selfishness and failed at all the tasks I was given.

Now I do have enough sense to avoid those people who would use me and, when I do accept a task or offer to help someone, I make sure that I am doing so because I want to and not out of a misguided sense of obligation. Nevertheless, I can still be caught out by someone who uses other people.

Some months ago I boarded a train at Edinburgh for the long journey to London. This train had come from Glasgow and was already quite full. I needed a table to work at but a woman in her fifties was sitting at the only table available. When I spoke to her she welcomed me to take the seat opposite her. As I settled myself, putting my work folder and my newspaper ready on the table in front of me, we exchanged pleasantries, as women in such circumstances do, but I assumed that once the steward had poured my tea I would be able to read my paper and then set to work. But this was not to be. The woman went on talking – about how she had been a college lecturer, how she had now retired, how her children were scattered around the world. This could have developed into an interesting conversation had she shown any interest in me. In some of my responses to her I had briefly mentioned something about myself which another person might have found interesting – for instance, that I had been in Edinburgh to give a public lecture – but nothing I said could deflect her monologue. She talked, and I had no role other than to be the necessary appendage, a listener.

Had she been going all the way to London I would have had to find some way of escaping from this role, but as she was travelling only as far as Newcastle I thought that I should have the generosity to listen to her for that time. I knew why she talked like this. No matter that she said, 'I didn't know retirement could be so busy,' she was immensely lonely, with the loneliness of those who need other people in order to feel that they exist, yet, in clinging to other people so desperately, ignoring their interests and using them to assuage their own anguish, only drive them away.

A friendship, as John Bayley said, has to be like two cows grazing in a field. Using other people, treating other people as your own possession cannot create a friendship. Similarly, a relationship based solely on competition cannot be a friendship. Friends may compete in a game fiercely, yet with fun and good humour, but when the competition becomes a matter of pride, of defending your meaning structure because to lose is to be wiped out, friendship is not possible. This kind of competition creates envy – often murderous envy – and the two people involved become predator and prey. Predator and prey can never be friends because they cannot be equal. Many men cannot enjoy a friendship with another man because they believe that the only kind of relationship they can have with another man is a competitive one. Winning is everything. As these men get older they wonder why they are so lonely.

When the responsibility for what happens is apportioned in a relationship where one person is powerful and the other weak, each may blame the other. The weak may blame the strong for being aggressive, and the strong may justify punishing the weak because they are wicked. In a relationship of equals people take responsibility for their own actions. They may explain their behaviour and their feelings, but they do not justify their actions by spurious arguments. The wonderful cartoon social worker Clare in the Community was a past-mistress of the spurious self-justification. Like me she knew that our feelings are our own truth. We might be misguided in our interpretations of what has happened, but when we are angry we are angry, and when we are sad we are sad. However, the word 'feelings' can be slippery.

Clare and her boyfriend Brian were having a beer and arguing. Brian said, 'You can't say that!!'

This infuriated Clare. 'I bloody well can say it, Brian, and let me explain why. Because I have just told you how I feel, Brian. I have claimed my feelings and they are not subject to discussion, debate or negotiation. You cannot argue against them or refute them or contradict them because how I feel is how I feel!'

Brian said, 'And you feel I'm a useless prat.'

'Exactly,' said Clare.[33]

Clare has made what philosophers call a category error. 'Feeling' as an emotion and 'feeling' as a judgement are two different categories, but Clare has put them together as a way of winning her argument. Brian knew that there was something amiss with what she had said, but, being unable to identify the error, he was put in the wrong and felt misunderstood.

Being misunderstood is one of the most common barriers to friendship. Even if we know and accept that another person cannot possibly understand us completely we do expect our friends to be sensitive in their treatment of what is important to us. We can be insensitive to one another in a multitude of ways, but one very common way is to take some aspect of the other person and turn

it into a category which purports to explain the person completely.
A number of people who were refugees told me how hurt they were
when someone took what was simply a fact of their life – that they
had been forced to leave their home – and turned it into a category
which purported to explain them completely and at the same time
denigrated them. A passing comment, 'Maria is a refugee,' could
ignore the fact that Maria was also a wife, a mother, a teacher, a
friend, with a multitude of skills, ideas and attributes. If a person
is seen as being nothing but a refugee then that person has been
denigrated, and such denigration cannot be the basis of a friendship.

Another way in which one person can be boxed into a category
is by being classed as 'someone special'. Being put on a pedestal can
leave the person feeling very lonely. Some people seek such a position
because they believe that being worshipped will prove to be a satisfactory substitute for friendship, but of course it never is. Those
who do not seek this position and who have a realistic estimate of
their ability find being categorized as special false and very alienating.
Friendship is impossible if the other person does not see you and
accept you as the person you know yourself to be.

Most of us have had experiences of being categorized in such a
way that we felt denigrated and alienated. When we were children
our families might have categorized us as 'the useless one', 'the
just-like-his-father one'. At school our teachers might have categorized us as 'the lazy one', and the other children categorized us as 'the
brainy one'. In society we might have found ourselves categorized
as 'the Jew', 'the Fenian', 'the Paki'. Our categorizers became our
predators, and as defensive prey we became very watchful, ready to
detect and attack categorizing whenever it threatened to occur. Such
a stance can be very effective in changing people's attitudes to the
language we use, but it can also lead to misunderstandings. The
person who says, 'Maria is a refugee,' might not be thinking of
Maria as simply a refugee but as a whole, real person.

The only remedy for misunderstandings is to talk. Not that discussions about what I meant and what I thought you meant are
always successful, but if we do not attempt them a friendship will
not develop, or a once successful friendship will fail. Both Brian
Keenan and John McCarthy already knew this when they were first
thrown together in a cell. Five years after their release they again
spent time together on an expedition through the wilds of Chile.

As the train brought them into Santiago at the end of their journey, they both knew that, as John McCarthy wrote,

> It seems like a good moment to clear the air. In other times we voiced our frustrations immediately, realizing that if we did not, they would fester. Our circumstances may have changed, but the need to be open with one another had not.
>
> 'You know, you changing your plans and getting the key to Frank's place really annoyed me at the time.'
>
> 'I noticed. We were bound to get on each other's nerves. I was ready to strangle you and those bloody guidebooks.'
>
> 'Sorry about that.'
>
> 'I'm sorry too.'
>
> Close friends know each other so well that much is communicated indirectly, the fingers on each other's pulse able to pick up every change of beat. But when your own emotional pulse is running erratically it is easy to presume to know what the other is feeling without seeking confirmation. Reactions are read incorrectly and misguide one's response. Such moments of failed communication can create unstated barriers and sometimes a wilful answer like that of a contrary child . . .
>
> Yet the joy of true friendship is that there comes a point when bitchiness is suddenly thrown over; so deep is the relationship that the hurt can be put instantly behind you. A moment of confrontation when problems are aired leads to an affectionate toast, with wine, tea, water or a hug, which puts the world back on to a happier plane where the light is bright and the smiles broad. Happiness is profoundest when it is shared: an expression of love between friends is a wonderful human experience.[34]

Contrast the experience of shared happiness with the sadness that can come from never attempting to 'clear the air'. In my family there was never any attempt to clear the air. Feelings of anger, frustration and contempt were flung about, but we never sat down quietly and talked about what these feelings meant. My mother and I never discussed our relationship. When she died and my sister had to clear the family home she found my school suitcase crammed full of every postcard and letter I had sent to my mother after I came to England. Why my mother had kept them I do not know.

My son and I travelled extensively in the UK and Europe, but Mother had not kept my correspondence in order to keep track of our travels. She always had only the vaguest idea of what I was doing. When she visited me in England she expressed great surprise that I knew my way around Sheffield, a city I had lived in for four years. I wondered if she had preserved these things for the same reason that I keep many things connected with my son – his letters and cards, though not his e-mails, and the pieces of furniture he had made at school. I have the foolish notion that by preserving these things I am in some way keeping him safe. Perhaps my mother kept my letters and postcards, each ending with 'Love, Dorothy', as proof that she was loved. Perhaps she loved me. I do not know, and I find that very sad.

Although I was well aware of the importance of talking to one another I did not attempt this with my mother because I did not have what Brian Keenan called 'a commitment to the courage of another person'. Mother had never had the courage to take responsibility for what had happened. She always excused herself and blamed others. She had never been able to say, 'Yes, this happened and I'm sorry.' As she got older she might have changed. In her last years she became much less censorious, so perhaps she might have managed then what she had never managed in the past. I did not give her the chance to find out.

We need to have the generosity to give the other person the chance to say, 'Yes, that happened. I'm sorry,' and the courage to accept another possible rejection and the sadness for what has been lost. However, when I think of the relatives of some of my clients and friends, who make my mother seem a paragon of sweetness and light, I can see that such courage and generosity might be hard to find.

When we want someone to say to us, 'Yes, it happened. I'm sorry,' we want there to be in that 'sorry' an acceptance of us as we are. Without this acceptance no reconciliation is complete, and no friendship firmly based. When John Le Carré wrote an appreciation of his friend Al Alvarez he described him as a poet, critic, boxer, poker player, kipper fancier and the man credited with discovering Sylvia Plath, and concluded,

I always dress up a little when I call on Al, and give my shoes a polish. I notice he does the same for me. And, when you come to think of it, that's Al. With the profound pessimism that haunts old poets out of hours, and not only poets either, he honours the stranger in you, loves the friend, and resolutely ignores your short-comings. Which, as Al might say, is about as good as it gets.[35]

One of life's great disappointments is when we believe that we have that acceptance from someone who matters to us, and then we find that we have not. A friend, Clarissa, told me how she had always felt close to her sister even though their paths had diverged, her sister marrying and having children while Clarissa pursued a career as a surgeon. When Clarissa drew up her will she wrote to her sister to explain why she had left money not just to her sister's children but to a woman about whom her sister knew nothing. This woman, much younger than Clarissa, had been her first lover some fifteen years before. This relationship mattered a great deal to Clarissa because her lover had managed to do something no one else had ever done: to break through the wall of reserve that Clarissa had built around her, and, in cherishing her, to free her to be herself. The affair ended when her lover moved far away, married and had a family, but she and Clarissa kept in touch. Clarissa in her letter to her sister said, 'She is the nearest thing I will ever have to a daughter.'

Clarissa expected her sister to understand and accept, but she did not. She wrote back to Clarissa, 'I don't understand and it's not right.' Clarissa protested, but her sister was not impressed. Neither woman wanted to break from the other, so eventually their communications were as warm as they had ever been, but, as Clarissa said to me, 'I'll never forget the original rejection.'

Acceptance does not mean that we have to approve of everything our friends do. If our friend does something of which we very much disapprove – say, committing murder or large-scale theft – we might have to bring the friendship to an end because our friend has been revealed to us as someone we did not know. When our disapproval is no more than evidence of a different point of view we should not resort to, 'I love you *but* I wish you didn't . . .', because the second part of the sentence negates the first by showing that we do not accept the other person as he or she is. I wish my friend Lou did not smoke, but my wish comes from the purely selfish consideration that, as I have already lost three close friends to diseases caused by smoking, I do not want to lose any more. However, smoking is an integral part of Lou – it is part of how she thinks of herself, how she negotiates her day-to-day living as well as her whole life – that to reject Lou's smoking would be to reject Lou herself.

It is a matter of accepting that we all have our peculiar habits and idiosyncrasies. If we did not, what would we have to gossip about?

One of the barriers to friendship is that we can be so fixated on another person's peculiarities that we fail to see the person themselves, and so miss recognizing the potential for friendship. Ian Stewart told me how he had made this mistake:

> I have a neighbour who is a practical, self-made man who managed to make a success first of all of being a newsagent, and then a garage owner, and who has lived by the philosophy of 'better safe than sorry'. At first I found him, forgive me, banal, uninteresting, and interested only in what I regarded as the minutiae of life. He would look at a field and would feel compelled to assess the exact number of sheep that were grazing in that field rather than look at the sheep themselves. He was interested in the number of telegraph poles along a road, the number of carriages an engine could pull. He found my impractical, airy-fairy attitude to life irritating and unworthy. Our conversations were guarded, inconclusive and destroyed by a courteous politeness.
>
> However, he had a very good marriage, and during the final days of his wife's life, and afterwards, our friendship grew because we were able to talk about death. From that time onward we have grown in our relationship, and, from an early tentative giggle, he is now able to laugh uproariously at my sense of humour, which includes laughing at myself. The most poignant thing is that he now comes to me and reveals that he has found himself laughing at some of his protective habits. Now I thoroughly enjoy his company and, if he is away for any period, I miss him and feel somewhat apprehensive at his absence. Moreover, I know that, no matter what situation I happen to find myself in, he will be completely reliable and come to my aid without hesitation, as I would him.
>
> Here are two completely disparate characters who are friends. His attitude towards me, of rather benevolent concern for one so out

of touch with the realities of life, is countered on my part with my concern for his inability to enjoy nature for what it is and his need to make nature conform to what he thinks it ought to be. But it is a very healthy amalgam.[36]

What brought Ian and his neighbour together was shared sadness. They had both suffered loss. This is one of the most remarkable things about friendship. Sadness can bring us closer together than happiness can. We can be going through life, dealing with day-to-day affairs, complaining about any small difficulties we encounter, buoyed up by our belief that, while others die, we are immortal, protecting ourselves from any disconfirmation with the sweet lies of personal pride, and then suddenly we are brought to a standstill by tragedy. We are face to face with real life. All our protective armour is stripped away. We see things clearly, and we do not like what we see. We thought that life was fair and just, and we find that it is not. We feel humbled, and understand in a way we had never done before how other people feel when they lose what was dear to them.

What people say in these circumstances often sounds clichéd and trite, but this is so only because they are responding to what always happens in a tragedy. They say, 'Now I know who my friends really are,' as people who they thought were good friends fail to appear and others whom they might have undervalued as friends and acquaintances are at their side. They say, 'Now I know what really matters,' and talk of really appreciating the simple things, of living in the present and making the most of what is ordinary but immensely satisfying, and of valuing love and friendship.

When people share a tragedy they either fall apart or come closer together. Some married couples, faced with the tragic loss of a child, deal with the loss separately and differently – so differently that one cannot accept the other's expression of grief, and so they separate. Other people form a closeness that lasts for life. When in 1999 Walter Pancott, a retired postman, was interviewed on Radio Foyle about his experiences as a prisoner of war in Germany for most of the Second World War he told of the extreme starvation, the filth and the lack of medication which he and his fellow prisoners endured. Many of his comrades died. In the battle which had led to his imprisonment he had been wounded. He felt guilty that the mortar which only wounded him killed his friend. The Red Cross was able to repatriate some wounded prisoners from the camps. Walter said, 'I could have gone home but I wanted to stay with the boys.' He summed up his experiences with: 'I couldn't go through it again but it was the best thing that ever happened to me. At least you realized the value of food.' He had also recognized the value of friends. 'You were glad to get home, but when you were there you wanted to go back. You missed the boys. Derry boys, Belfast boys. All for one and one for all.'[37]

If we want to understand how a mechanism works – say, how a tree draws water from its roots to its topmost branches, or how car tyres adhere to a road surface, or how two people form a friendship – we often see the functioning of the mechanism most clearly in extreme conditions – for the tree in drought and flood, for the car tyres being driven at high speed, and for friendship, in a situation where none of the usual social supports are available.

The writings of John McCarthy and Brian Keenan, who came together in a situation bereft of all social supports, give many clues about how friendships form and why relationships can fail. Extreme conditions required extreme responses which arose from the mutuality of friendship. McCarthy drew a contrast between their relationship in Beirut and on their journey in Chile.

> The profound need we had for mutual support in Beirut is not now so vital. Then we accepted that element of personal surrender: holding oneself in check to give the other room to breathe; affecting greater optimism than one really felt to carry the other through; frankly asking for help – 'I am frightened, don't let me go under.' These things are fainter now. Mutual responsibility, respect and love are still there. But without the spectre of mental and emotional collapse they do not command the old levels of selflessness. We are no longer in survival mode and recognize that relationships demand less when you can stand up and walk out the door.[38]

How was it that this friendship developed between Keenan and McCarthy when such a friendship did not develop between the other hostages? According to Keenan,

In those conditions, discussions turned into debate and debate degenerated into poisonous argument. Men misdirect their anger and aggression on to one another, and mutual support turned into mutual dislike and seething silence. Yet why did John McCarthy and I, who had more reason for mutual antipathy, find a deep, enduring bond of friendship and support that eventually became a prop for others?[39]

Keenan was working class and Irish, McCarthy middle class and English. These backgrounds alone could have been a rich source of antipathy. However, both brought to the prison cell an understanding of the necessity of friendship.

McCarthy came from a family where love and support were never in doubt. He regretted that he did not know his father well because, with his father working in the City and he himself away at boarding school, they spent little time together, but he had a strong relationship with his mother. His parents must have handled the sibling rivalry between him and his older brother Terence extremely well because right from the beginning they were friends. McCarthy wrote, 'I have never forgotten the love Terence showed when he, too, was very young.'[40] When he returned from Beirut his brother was there to help him. He wrote, 'I was delighted that the strong bond we had formed in childhood had stood us in good stead.'[41]

In *An Evil Cradling* Keenan said very little about his family, but in describing his education he showed that his parents were supportive and patient. All his writings show his concern for others and his passionate need to understand his own experiences and the experiences of others, both necessary precursors to friendship.

Keenan and McCarthy each brought to the prison cell contrasting ways of experiencing oneself and of perceiving the world and other people which are typical of the introvert and the extravert.[42] Each of us uses one of these two ways throughout our life, but we each express it in our own individual style. These two different ways are often the grounds for disagreement because the different points of view are so different, but for Keenan and McCarthy what mattered was not the difference but the contrast. Each could supply what the other lacked.

McCarthy was the extravert, the people person. Again and again he writes about the prime importance other people have for him. He described his life before imprisonment almost solely in terms of friends. He wrote that, when he returned home, 'I found that I brought the same intensity that I had established with my fellow hostages to these new friendships. Now, as then, I felt an urgent need to understand people immediately and find a way of working with them';[43] and again:

> I knew that the balance had, perhaps inevitably, shifted in all my friendships. That my friends were so unchanged was a great relief, but I was still uncertain that I could be a true friend as I wanted to be. I didn't think that I'd be able to take on their worries when I was still so unsure of myself and my situation. I was wrong. It took longer than I thought it would, but once I began to see friends more regularly and we had time to talk, I found I enjoyed discussing their hopes and fears with them, just as before.[44]

In trying to get to know his girlfriend Jill Morrell again he experienced the prime fear that all extraverts have – that they will not be liked. When he went on holiday in France with Jill he found that 'I was no longer worried that any break in the conversation meant that I'd done something wrong and was happy to let those moments pass reflecting on the events of the day.'[45]

In Jill he had found a complementary introvert. Her account of her life during the years of McCarthy's imprisonment contains the points of view so typical of an introvert. 'For most of my life,' she wrote, 'I had tended to fit in with people, and try not to upset anybody, but now I found that there was something I cared about more than being liked. If I thought something was right I had to fight my corner.'[46] She needed to have 'an overriding purpose every day'[47] and so the days she spent with McCarthy as he readjusted to freedom were uncomfortable for her. 'The days were difficult to grasp and bend to any particular shape. I couldn't impose any structure on them, or on John, because there was none.'[48] In *Some Other Rainbow* John and Jill said little about how they saw their relationship developing on his return, but there are enough clues in what they say about themselves to show that an extravert and an introvert, no matter how much they care about one another, cannot always get along together.

The two books, *Some Other Rainbow* and *An Evil Cradling*, stand in extravert–introvert contrast. McCarthy's account of his years as a hostage looks outwards to events and people. Keenan's book looks inward in the search to understand how and why. The same contrast is there in the book they wrote together, *Between Extremes*. Here Keenan wrote about an essential part of an introvert's experience: being alone.

> Aloneness is something we carry with us at all times, yet how do we understand it and, more importantly, how do we value it? Most of us hardly know where to begin to unearth this part of ourselves. All our lives we have been told that love, sharing, human community, is the ultimate source of all happiness and well-being. I am convinced that this is not wholly true, and that human happiness is heightened when human beings learn to cope with aloneness; when they learn to navigate without love, companionship or the trappings of religion. Aloneness is not a dreadful place once we understand how to be with ourselves on our own.[49]

Introverts are born knowing how to be alone. Extraverts have to learn this skill, but it is an essential skill because aloneness – the aloneness of our meaning structure – is part of our condition; life often presents us with situations where we must, if we are to preserve our well-being, tolerate being alone. Extraverts who cannot tolerate even the thought of being alone may find themselves tied to someone who causes them pain. They may also become a burden to their friends, who feel that they are being clung to and used.

Extraverts may find the introvert's capacity to be alone quite frightening. At the start of their journey McCarthy wrote of Keenan,

> His face had that closed-down, pensive look I know so well. When we first met that look made me feel excluded, as if I had done something to offend him. But I soon learned that it was his way of concentrating; though his eyes remained open he is looking inward, studying vistas with his mind's eye. He is away in his own place, making sense of something, putting it into a context which he may want to share later.[50]

Introverts may be impatient with or even contemptuous of extraverts, who must be with people and gain their liking no matter what else might be happening, but they may also be amazed by their sheer goodness in their selfless concern for others. I see in several of my extravert friends a degree of goodness to which I, a selfish introvert, could never aspire. Keenan felt the same about McCarthy, particularly when McCarthy nursed him through a near fatal bout of gastroenteritis.

Because McCarthy and Keenan tolerated and appreciated each other's point of view they were able in their prison cell to develop a most efficient system of cooperation. McCarthy wrote,

> As we got to know, love and respect each other, we would each modify our normal reactions to help the other. Sometimes Brian would be furious but would hold down his anger if he sensed that I didn't have the energy for a conflict. For my part I would reject my usual conciliatory tone when I knew Brian was much distressed and needed my support. We learned to use our different styles to make forceful, yet restrained, points to the guards while denying them their usual angry response to criticism.[51]

Because they accepted one another they saw no need, as some of the other hostages did, to win an argument. 'We liked to talk about things,' wrote McCarthy, 'to search each other's memories for information and sometimes have heated discussions. But the idea was never to defeat the other; we didn't want to score points.'[52]

As the years went by Keenan and McCarthy changed.

> At the outset of our friendship it was always Brian who exploded and damn the consequences. Now I was ready to take on the guards and he was calming me, rather than me him. We'd found a balance. We'd grown together not just in terms of affection but in our attitudes, in our views on personal dignity and in a mutual trust that helped us deal with the curious life we shared.[53]

Part of finding that balance was learning about one another. They had plenty of time to tell one another their story until, as Keenan wrote, 'Our life histories were no longer exclusive preserves. For as we told our stories of friends and families we exchanged each other's friends and families until they became our own. People we had never met became vividly real to us.'[54]

Learning the other person's story is a necessary skill of friendship. We need to listen and to remember. A friend knows your story. Not your whole story because only you can know that, but enough of your story to recognize what is painful to you, what is sacred, and what is a joke that can be shared. You might never have sat down with your friend and said, 'This is my story,' but in your conversations your friend picks up the fragments of your story and weaves them into a whole. A friend might not have got the story exactly right – most of us have problems in remembering names – but the effort and intention show that this person is indeed your friend. A friend puts you in his or her own story. A friend remembers what you were like and what you did all those years ago. A friend remembers things about you which you have forgotten, and, while family members who are not your friends might use their memories of you against you, your friend remembers the best and the most charming.

As the story of John McCarthy and Brian Keenan turns into a legend an important part of that legend is their humour, not just their outrageous use of language and the way in which they could turn every obstacle and peril into a cause for mirth, but the way in which they could use humour to bring a person back from the brink where primitive pride closes down, and body and person start to die. Possibly humour has its genesis in primitive pride, with its ability to ignore what is actually going on while, magpie-like, collecting bits and pieces of that reality and weaving them into some self-supporting story. If the story can be mixed with a very reality-based ability, a sense of the ridiculous, then what emerges is a story which is both self-affirming and funny.

Humour is one of our greatest gifts. Life is difficult for each of us, no matter what advantages we might enjoy. Life is always chancy. The unexpected always happens. We can try to reduce the difficulties and guard against the unexpected by claiming to have access to some absolute truth, but absolute truths do not allow for humour. Absolute truths imply some overall consistent pattern in the world. Humour recognizes that there is no such pattern. The randomness of the world and the vagaries of our lives create absurd contrasts,

and the best way to deal with such contrasts is to recognize them
and laugh at them.

Absolutists hate humorists because humorists show that absolutists are wrong. If they can, absolutists kill humorists because they
are such a threat to their meaning structure. The greatly loved
Columbian satirist and journalist Jaime Garzon, who had offended
many powerful people with his criticisms of corruption and abuses
of power, was assassinated in 1999. A student, one of the thousands
of people mourning his death, wrote on a placard, 'How can we
reach peace if we are so stupid as to kill the people who make us
laugh?'[55] For peace and for friendship humour is essential.

Some people believe that life is too serious for laughter. Aaron
Hass in his study of the children of survivors of the Holocaust
wrote,

> As a child of Holocaust survivors, I grew up thinking that laughing
> indicated a certain superficiality. It was not until I reached my
> thirties that I understood the value and necessity of laughter. I also
> had to learn not to begrudge it to others. To my surprise, I found
> this objection to the casualness of life in few of those I interviewed.
> Because laughter was violently wrested from them, they strive to
> recapture it.[56]

We all need to capture and hold on to laughter. Humour reduces
people and events to an appropriate size. Whenever we feel that
our meaning structure is threatened, laughter reduces the threat to
manageable proportions and strengthens our self-confidence even
as we admit our weakness.

Humour brings us closer together in a way that seriousness never
can do. In the dark days of the Second World War, when Britain
stood on the brink of defeat, a radio programme, Tommy Handley's
ITMA, brought a unity across the social divides far stronger than that
inspired by Churchill's speeches. One of the great joys of friendship is
knowing that your friend will share the joke.

Humour and courage go hand in hand because they are both a
matter of taking account of what actually is. To be courageous we
have to leave aside fantasy and wishes and see what is there. We see
that, if I do this, that will follow. If I do that, something else will
follow. We can decide that the first outcome is preferable to the

second. We may be wrong in how we interpret the actual situation or predict the results, but our initial, basic stance is to look reality in the face and see what is actually there.

Seeing what is actually there is a matter of knowing our own truth, what we feel and think, and striving to get as accurate a picture as possible of what is going on around us. Knowing that we are so constructed that we each see our own rainbow, and living with the aloneness of that knowledge, requires courage, but it is only when we accept that each of us has our own way of seeing things that we can find the generosity necessary to live peacefully with one another and to create friendships.

Friendship is not just a matter of shared interests. We may share interests with another person but, if we cannot find the generosity to accept the differences between us as well, then the relationship will not develop into a friendship. On the other hand, we may meet someone with whom we share no interests at all but whose story we listen to intently and absorb. We become curious about this person, who then responds to our attention and becomes interested in us. We each become more and more of a whole person to the other. Out of such a process friendship across the divides of generation, social class, education, nationality, race and religion can grow. Such friendships enrich us because they take us out of our own narrow world and into larger, different worlds. If we can picture ourselves not locked away in our own little box, separate from the boxes that enclose people who are different from us, but at the centre of a set of concentric circles, the whole of which contains everyone, then such friendships allow us to move with ease from one circle to another and to enjoy that freedom.

This way of living is based on acceptance of one another, a mutual acceptance that we are what we are. Out of such acceptance comes trust. Because we know the limitations and priorities of a friend we know the circumstances in which we can trust one another. For instance, I can trust you always to tell me the truth but I cannot always trust you for immediate help because your first priority must be your children. Trust is not a beneficent soup in which we can wallow but it is part of a relationship which needs to be defined, with the definition arising from our knowledge and acceptance of one another.

Friends are indeed precious. We are individuals who are social

animals. We love to gossip. We can be part of a group, part of a
family, or part of a couple, but none of those relationships can
comfort, support and inspire us to the degree that we need and
desire unless within them we all are friends.

NOTES

CHAPTER 1

1 Samuel Butler, *Notebooks* (1912), *International Thesaurus of Quotations*, Penguin, Harmondsworth, 1973, p. 233.
2 *Mamphela Ramphele: A Life*, David Philip, Cape Town and Johannesburg, 1995, p. 38.
3 Robert Fisk, *Pity the Poor Nation*, Oxford University Press, Oxford, 1992, p. 77.
4 Jean Said Makdisi, *Beirut Fragments*, Persea Books, New York, 1990, p. 61.
5 Mark Twain, *Following the Equator* (1897), *Oxford Dictionary of Humorous Quotations*, Oxford University Press, Oxford, 1995, p. 131.
6 Andrew Sullivan, *Love Undetectable*, Chatto & Windus, London, 1998, p. 180.
7 Ibid., p. 231.
8 Ibid., p. 234.
9 *Observer Magazine*, 2 May 1999.
10 *Guardian*, 22 October 1998.
11 *New Scientist*, 3 January 1998, p. 68.
12 Sullivan, op. cit., p. 234.
13 Tim Lott, *White City Blues*, Viking, London, 1999, p. 3.
14 Ibid., p. 8.
15 Sullivan, op. cit., p. 244.
16 Aaron Hass, *The Aftermath*, Cambridge University Press, Cambridge, 1995, p. 182.

CHAPTER 2

1 Richard Gregory, 'Perceptual Hypotheses', *The Psychologist*, Vol. 9, No. 10, October 1996, p. 452.
2 Terence Picton and Donald Stuss, 'Neurobiology of conscious experience', *Current Opinion in Neurobiology*, 4, pp. 256–65, 1994.
3 *New Scientist*, 7 June 1997, pp. 3, 31.
4 *New Scientist*, 26 September 1998, p. 24.
5 *New Scientist*, 12 December 1998, p. 61.
6 *New Scientist*, 21 June 1997, p. 18.
7 Susan Greenfield, Gresham College Lecture Series, *Exploring the Brain*, Lecture 4, 'Growing a Brain', 14 February 1996.
8 Gregory, op. cit.
9 Robin Dunbar, *Gossip, Grooming and the Evolution of Language*, Faber & Faber, London, 1997.
10 Steven Pinker, *The Language Instinct*, Penguin, London, 1995, p. 60.
11 Tom Bowden, *The Silence Calling*, Allen & Unwin, London, 1997; *Antarctica and Back in Sixty Days*, Allen & Unwin, London, 1991.
12 Dorothy Mackellar, 'My Country', in Leonie Kramer (ed.), *Australian Poetry and Short Stories*, Ure Smith Press, Willoughby, NSW, 1991, p. 472.
13 S. Petry and E. Meyer, *The Perception of Illusory Contours*, Springer-Verlag, Munich, 1987.
14 Susan Greenfield, *Journey to the Center of the Mind*, W. H. Freeman and Co., New York, 1995, p. 112.

15 Greenfield, Gresham College Lectures, op. cit.

16 Igor Aleksander, *Impossible Minds*, Imperial College Press, London, 1996, p. 3.

17 Personal communication, 19 January 1999.

18 Quoted by John McCrone, *New Scientist*, 13 December 1997, p. 28.

19 John McCrone, ibid., p. 30.

20 Nick Schoon, *New Scientist*, 25 September 1999, p. 40.

21 Daniel Stern, *The Diary of a Baby*, Basic Books, New York, 1998 p. 43.

22 Daniel Stern, *The Motherhood Constellation*, Basic Books, New York, 1995, p. 100.

23 Ibid., pp. 89–91.

24 Primo Levi, *The Drowned and the Saved*, Abacus, London, 1998, p. 1.

25 Ibid.

26 Ibid., p. 2.

27 Ibid., p. 127.

28 Brandon Hamber, *Do Sleeping Dogs Lie? The Psychological Implications of the Truth and Reconciliation Committee in South Africa*, Seminar No. 5, 1995, Centre for the Study of Truth and Reconciliation, Johannesburg.

29 Levi, op. cit., p. 15.

30 *Der Spiegel*, 28 September 1998; *Guardian*, 24 October 1998, trans. Sandra Smith.

31 *Index*, Vol. 27, No. 3, May/June 1998, Issue 182, p. 11.

32 Steven Mithen, *The Prehistory of the Mind*, Thames and Hudson, London, 1996, p. 135.

33 Otto Fenichel, *The Psychoanalytic Theory of the Neuroses*, Routledge & Kegan Paul, London, 1963, p. 485.

34 Chris Mace, 'Socratic Psychotherapy', *Changes*, Vol. 17, No. 3, 1999, p. 164.

35 *Journal of Personality and Social Psychology*, Vol. 75, 1998, p. 617; *New Scientist*, 4 September 1999, p. 49.

36 Dorothy Rowe, *Breaking the Bonds*, HarperCollins, London, 1989.

37 *Guardian*, 19 June 1999.

38 Hass, *The Aftermath*, p. 93.

39 *Guardian*, 29 July 1998.

40 Stern, *Diary of a Baby*, p. 49.

41 Levi, op. cit., p. 117.

42 BBC Radio Five, 11 May 1998, reported in the *Guardian*, 23 May 1998.

43 Personal communication, 9 June 1998.

44 Hass, *The Aftermath*, pp. 18, 19.

45 Dr D. Premack, 'Words: What they are and do animals have them?', *Cognition*, 37, 1990, pp. 197–212.

46 Dunbar, op. cit.

47 Ibid., p. 1.

48 Ken Richardson, *The Making of Intelligence*, Weidenfeld & Nicolson, London, 1999.

49 *New Scientist*, 4 September 1999, p. 45.

CHAPTER 3

1 Dunbar, op. cit., p. 87.

2 BBC2, 1 April 1998.

3 *Guardian*, 20 January 1999.

4 Ibid.

5 BBC Radio Four, 25 January 1999.

6 Isaac Marks and Randolph Nesse, 'Fear and Fitness: An Evolutionary Analysis of Anxiety Disorders', *Ethology and Sociobiology* 15, 1994, pp. 247–61.

7 Barbara Ehrenreich, *Blood Rites*, Virago, London, 1997, p. 70.

8 This was pointed out to me by my friend John Courtneige.

9 Dorothy Rowe, *The Courage to Live*, HarperCollins, London, 1994.

10 Letter to the *Guardian*, 2 February 1999.

11 Dorothy Rowe, *The Real Meaning of Money*, HarperCollins, London, 1997.

12 Makdisi, op. cit., p. 137.

13 Rowe, *Breaking the Bonds*.

14 Matt Ridley, *The Origins of* Virtue, Viking, London, 1996, p. 191.

15 Rowe, *The Real Meaning of Money*, p. 365.

16 Ramphele, op. cit., p. 106.

17 Ehrenreich, op. cit., p. 94.

18 *Dateline Soweto*, University of California Press, Berkeley and Los Angeles, 1995, p. 44.

19 Quoted by Tim Judah in *The Serbs*, Yale University Press, New Haven and London, 1997, p. 30.

20 Quoted in Ehrenreich, op. cit., p. 201.

21 G. Finchilescu and A. Dawes, *Adolescents' Socio-political Perspective on South African Society: an Investigation into the Effects of Social Change Between 1992 and 1996*, report for the Centre for Science Development, National Research Foundation, South Africa, 1999, 155pp.

22 Richard Nisbett and Dov Cohen, *Culture of Honor*, West View Press, Boulder, Colorado, 1996, p. xv.

23 D. H. Fischer, *Albion's Seed: Four British Folkways in America*, Oxford University Press, New York, p. 690, quoted in Nisbett and Cohen, op. cit., p. 2.

24 Nisbett and Cohen, op. cit, p. 41.

25 Ibid., p. 50.

26 Ibid., p. 52.

27 Con Costello, *Botany Bay: the story of convicts transported from Ireland to Australia 1791–1853*, Mercier Press, Cork, 1987, p. 47.

28 Ibid., p. 48.

29 *The Economist*, 23 March 1996.

30 *The Edinburgh History of the Scots Language*, Edinburgh University Press, 1997, as reported in *The Economist*, 6 December 1997.

31 *Guardian*, 9 December 1996.

32 *The Economist*, 8 May 1993.

33 David Harrison, *The White Tribe of Africa*, Southern Book Publishers, Cape Town, 1987, p. 53.

34 Dorothy Rowe, *Wanting Everything*, HarperCollins, 1992, pp. 78–114.

35 Levi, op. cit., p. 94.

36 Ehrenreich, op. cit., p. 180.

37 Ibid., p. 183.

38 *Children, Culture and Mental Health: Interventions in Conditions of War*, proceedings of the Congress on Children, War and Persecution: Rebuilding Hope, 1–4 December 1996, p. 76.

39 J. M. Coetzee, *Boyhood*, Vintage, London, 1998, p. 9.

40 Ibid., p. 6.

41 Ibid.

42 Ibid., p. 7.

43 Ibid.

44 Ibid., p. 8.

45 Ibid., p. 184.

46 Ramphele, op. cit., p. 182.

47 John Parry, 'Moros and cristianos: racial attitudes in Spain' *International Minds*, Vol. 8, No. 2, 1998, pp. 6–8.

48 Bill Bunbury, *Unfinished Business*, ABC Books, Sydney, 1998, pp. 14, 15.

49 S. Francis, H. Dugmore and Rico, *Madam and Eve's Greatest Hits*, Penguin, Parktown, South Africa, 1998, p. 34.

50 Melissa E. Steyn and Khanya B. Motshabi (eds.), *Cultural Synergy: Weaving Strands of Africa and Europe*, Knowledge Resources, Cape Town, 1996, p. 7.

51 Mudrooroo, *Us Mob*, Harper-Collins, Sydney, 1995, pp 76, 5.

52 Ibid., p. 9.

53 *The Economist*, 25 July 1998, pp. 25–7.

54 Frank Retief, *Tragedy and Triumph: A Christian Response to Trials and Suffering*, Nelson Word Ltd, Milton Keynes, and Struik Christian Books, Cape Town, 1994, pp. 29, 223, 228.

55 *The Economist*, 29 August 1998, p. 38.
56 'Psychotherapy with political activists: reflections on some South African experiences', *Changes*, 1992, Vol. 10, 2, pp. 82–9.
57 Ramphele, op. cit., p. 123.

CHAPTER 4
1 Ian Player, *Zululand*, David Philip Publishers, Cape Town, 1997, pp. 82, 84, 86.
2 Rowe, *The Courage to Live*.
3 Nejla M. Abu-Izzeddin, *The Druzes*, E. J. Brill, New York, 1993, p. 116.
4 *Guardian*, 15 May 1998.
5 Richard Marshall, 'The genetics of schizophrenia: axiom or hypothesis?' in R. Bentall (ed.), *Reconstructing Schizophrenia*, Routledge, London, 1990, p. 42.
6 *Sunday Times*, 2 February 1999.
7 Robert A. LeVine, 'Infant environments in psychoanalysis' in J. W. Stigler, R. A. Shweder and G. Herdt (eds.), *Cultural Psychology: Essays on Comparative Human Development*, Cambridge University Press, Cambridge, 1996, pp. 454–74.
8 Nisbett and Cohen, op. cit., pp. 87, 88.
9 Jean-Paul Sartre, *Words*, Hamish Hamilton, London, 1964.
10 Wally Seccombe, *A Millenium of Family Change*, Verso, London, 1995, pp. 75, 102.
11 *Observer*, 8 December 1996.
12 Letter to the *Guardian*, 7 May 1998.
13 *Guardian*, 6 June 1998.
14 *Guardian*, 9 May 1998.
15 *Observer*, 28 March 1999.
16 Ramphele, op. cit., p. 197.
17 *Independent on Sunday*, 21 December 1997.
18 Pamela Reynolds and Andy Dawes, 'Pain and Blame', Truth and Reconciliation Commission Report, 'Focus on Children and Youth', December 1998.
19 Ibid.
20 *Guardian*, 24 October 1998.
21 EPOCH, *Bulletin*, October 1998.
22 Peter Newell, EPOCH, personal communication, 10 May 1999.
23 Lecture by Murray A. Straus, 'New and More Definitive Evidence about the Benefits of Avoiding Corporal Punishment', 9 June 1998, p. 3.
24 Ibid., p. 4.
25 Murray A. Straus, *Beating the Devil out of Them*, Lexington Books, Jossey-Bass Inc., San Francisco, 1994.
26 Ibid., p. 4.
27 *Guardian*, 4 January 1997.
28 Seccombe, op. cit., p. 2.
29 Ibid., pp. 2, 242.
30 BBC TV, 17 April 1999.
31 Dunbar, op. cit., p. 201.
32 Channel Four News, 19 April 1999.
33 Robert Templer, *Shadows and Wind*, Little, Brown and Company, London, 1998, p. 143.
34 Ibid., pp. 139, 143.
35 *The Economist*, 20 March 1999, p. 46.
36 Hass, *The Aftermath*, p. 39.
37 Hala Jaber, *Hezbollah: Born with a Vengeance*, Fourth Estate, London, 1997, p. 142.
38 Sheldon Kopp, *Mirror, Mask and Shadow*, Macmillan, New York, 1980, p. 83.
39 Templer, op. cit., p. 244.
40 Boori Pryor, *Maybe Tomorrow*, Penguin Books, Ringwood, Australia, 1998, p. 131.
41 *Guardian*, 1 May 1999.

CHAPTER 5
1 Judah, op. cit., p. 46.
2 Cootzee, op. cit., p. 95.
3 Mudrooroo, op. cit., p. 47.
4 Bunbury, op. cit., p. 5.

5 Fionnuala O Connor, *In Search of a State*, The Blackstaff Press, Belfast, 1993, p. 46.

6 Ibid., p. 30.

7 Ibid., p. 31.

8 *Guardian*, 20 August 1996.

9 26 September 1998.

10 Sadaaki Numata, *International Minds*, Vol. 8, No. 2, 1998, pp. 10–11.

11 Nigel Harris, *The New Untouchables*, J B. Tauris & Co., London, 1995, p. 117.

12 Rowe, *The Real Meaning of Money*.

13 Rahman Haghighat, *Psychiatric Bulletin*, 21, 1997, 716–19.

14 UN Convention Relating to the Status of Refugees, Article 1a, 1951.

15 Harris, op. cit., p. 1.

16 *The Economist*, December 1998, p. 21.

17 Templer, op. cit., p. 303.

18 *The Economist*, 19 April 1997.

19 Makdisi, op. cit., p. 251.

20 Ibid., p. 65.

21 *The Economist*, 17 April 1999.

22 *The Economist*, 20 February 1999.

23 *The Economist*, 14 February 1998.

24 Quoted by Francis Wheen, *Guardian*, 21 April 1999.

25 Refugee Council publication, 1998.

26 *Guardian*, 2 April 1999.

27 Angie Debo, *A History of the Indians of the United States*, Pimlico, London, 1995, p. 288.

28 Ibid., p. 288.

29 Coral Edwards and Peter Read (eds.), *The Lost Children*, Doubleday, Sydney, 1997, p. ix.

30 Ibid., p. xi.

31 George Essex Evans in *Australian Poetry and Short Stories*, Vol. I, Ure Smith Press, Sydney, 1991, p. 430.

32 Edwards and Read, op. cit., p. xiv.

33 Ibid., p. xvi.

34 Ibid., p. 192.

35 Channel Four, 13 April 1999.

36 *INexile*, the Refugee Council Magazine, September 1998.

37 *New Scientist*, 5 December 1998.

38 BBC Radio Four, 6 August 1998.

39 Rowe, *Breaking the Bonds*.

40 *Guardian*, 12 May 1999.

41 David J. Nutt and Sam Forshall, *Psychiatric Bulletin*, 1999, No. 23, p. 370.

42 Ibid., p. 371.

43 Ibid., p. 372.

44 *Changes*, Vol. 17, No. 1, 1999, p. 49.

45 *Discrimination and the Irish Community in Britain*, Central Books, London, 1997, p. 3.

46 *Daily Mail*, 30 November 1998.

47 *Guardian*, 2 December 1998.

48 *Guardian*, 25 June 1996.

49 C. Gorst-Unsworth and E. Goldberg, 'Psychological sequelae of torture and organized violence suffered by refugees from Iraq', *British Journal of Psychiatry*, 172, 1998, pp. 90–94.

50 Mudrooroo, op. cit., p. 20.

51 Ibid.

52 Aaron Hass, *In the Shadow of the Holocaust*, Cornell University Press, Ithaca, 1990, p. 36.

53 Ibid., p. 40.

54 Ibid., p. 46.

55 Ibid., p. 51.

56 Ibid., p. 59.

57 Peter Fonagy, Paper presented at the Third Congress of the European Federation for Psychoanalytic Psychotherapy in the Public Sector, 28 March 1998.

58 *Guardian*, 16 June 1999.

59 Makdisi, op. cit., p. 20.

60 *Guardian*, 13 April 1998.

61 Ibid.

62 Templer, op. cit., p. 310.

63 Ibid., p. 310.

64 Ibid., p. 312.

65 Marion Molteno, *The Shield of Coolest Air*, Shola Books, London, 1992, p. 141.

66 Immanuel Kant, 'Idea for a Universal History with a Cosmopolitan Purpose' in *Political*

Writings, trans. H. B. Nisbet, ed. Hans Reiss, Cambridge University Press, Cambridge, 1991, p. 28.
67 Michael Ignatieff, *Blood and Belonging*, Vintage, London, 1994, p. 7.
68 Ibid., p. 9.

CHAPTER 6
1 Toolis, op. cit., p. 68.
2 Peter Taylor, *Loyalists*, Bloomsbury, London, 1999, p. 239.
3 *Guardian*, 25 November 1999.
4 *Guardian*, 1 July 1999.
5 Jarel Diamond, *Germs, Guns and Steel*, Jonathan Cape, London, 1997, p. 267.
6 Ibid., p. 273.
7 *Observer*, 22 June 1997.
8 April 1998.
9 David Lester, *Sydney Morning Herald*, 21 July 1999.
10 David Lester, *Sydney Morning Herald*, 20 July 1999.
11 Ibid.
12 Pryor, op. cit., p. 37.
13 *Into Africa*, BBC2, 10 July 1999.
14 Michael Ignatieff, *The Warrior's Honour*, Chatto & Windus, London, 1998, p. 48.
15 Chuck Sudetic, *Blood and Vengeance*, W. W. Norton & Co., New York, 1998, p. 20.
16 Ignatieff, *Warrior's Honour*, p. 38.
17 *Guardian*, 9 September 1997.
18 Templer, op. cit., p. 107.
19 Ibid., p. 106.
20 Richard Hofstadter, *The Paranoid Style in American Politics*, Harvard University Press, Cambridge, Mass., 1964, p. 20.
21 Makdisi, op. cit., p. 56.
22 Ehrenreich, op. cit., p. 220.
23 Jaber, op. cit., p. 55.
24 Ibid., p. 55.
25 Hass, *The Aftermath*, p. 10.
26 Peter Taylor, *Provos*, Bloomsbury, London, 1998, p. 11.
27 *Observer*, 27 June 1999.

28 Hofstadter, op. cit., p. 4.
29 Ibid., p. 36.
30 Ibid., p. 32.
31 *Guardian*, 5 May 1998.
32 *Guardian*, 8 May 1999.
33 *Daily Star*, 7 September 1998.
34 *Weekly Telegraph*, Issue No. 387, 1998.
35 *Guardian*, 16 July 1999.
36 Channel Four, 13 December 1998.
37 Dorothy Rowe, *Living with the Bomb*, Routledge, London, 1996, p. 10.
38 Quoted by Francis Wheen, *Guardian*, 7 April 1999.
39 Jaber, op. cit., p. 70.
40 Lecture published in Hezbollah's newspaper *Al-Ahed*, quoted in Jaber, op. cit., p. 71.
41 Iraqi TV, Baghdad, in Arabic, 0800GMT, 17 January 1998, picked up and translated by BBC Worldwide Monitoring, quoted in the *Guardian*, 23 January 1998.
42 *Guardian*, 5 November 1998.
43 *Guardian*, 20 March 1999.
44 *Observer*, 18 April 1999.
45 Quoted in *The Economist*, 20 December 1997.
46 Quoted by Patrick Wall in *Pain: The Science of Suffering*, Weidenfeld & Nicolson, London, 1999, p. 65.
47 Quoted by Francis Wheen, *Guardian*, 7 April 1999.
48 *Guardian*, 31 March 1998.
49 Taylor, *Loyalists*, p. 207.
50 Toolis, op. cit., p. 19.
51 Ibid., p. 26.
52 Don Foster, 'Perpetrators of gross violations of human rights', *Journal of Community and Health Sciences*, 4 (2), 1997.
53 Peter Beaumont, *Observer*, 18 October 1998.
54 Ruth Dudley Edwards, *The Faithful Tribe*, HarperCollins, London, 1999, p. 190.

55 Monique Marks, 'Justifications of violence by activist youth in Diepkloof, Soweto', *Temps Moderns*, No. 585, 1995.
56 Foster, op. cit., p. 6.
57 Philip Hodson, *Men: An Investigation into the Emotional Male*, BBC Books, London, 1983, p. 100.
58 *The Cold War*, a Jeremy Isaacs Production for Turner Original Productions, Time Warner Company, 1998.
59 *Observer*, 12 May 1999.
60 Hass, *The Aftermath*, p. xvii.
61 Rule 61, Hearing against Dr Karadzic and General Mladic, 3–5 July 1996.
62 Foster, op. cit., p. 23.
63 Ibid., p. 6.
64 *Guardian*, 25 September 1999.
65 *Guardian*, 4 April 1999.
66 *Condemned to Live*, BBC TV, 1999.
67 Levi, op. cit., p. 169.
68 Gitta Sereny, *In quelle-tenebre*, Adelphi, Milan, 1975, p. 135, quoted by Levi, op. cit., p. 100.
69 Elaine Scarry, *The Body in Pain*, Oxford University Press, Oxford, 1985, p. 4.
70 Wall, op. cit., p. 15.
71 Foster, op. cit., p. 7.
72 Makdisi, op. cit., p. 176.
73 *Guardian*, 12 December 1996.
74 Ehrenreich, op. cit., p. 224.
75 Adulphe Delegorgue, *Travels in Southern Africa*, Vol. I, trans. Fleur Webb, University of Natal Press, Durban, 1990, p. 225.
76 Quoted by Joanne Bourke, *An Intimate History of Killing*, Granta, London, 1999, p. 220.
77 Niall Ferguson, *The Pity of War*, Allen Lane, London, 1998.
78 Bourke, op. cit., p. 13.
79 Ibid., p. 31.
80 Ibid., p. 32.
81 Ibid., p. 56.
82 *Observer*, op. cit.
83 Bourke, op. cit., p. 171.
84 Ibid., p. 194.
85 Ibid., p. 270.
86 Rowe, *The Real Meaning of Money*, p. 346.
87 Jaber, op. cit., p. 91.
88 Makdisi, op. cit., p. 46.
89 *Daily Telegraph*, 16 January 1999.
90 *Update*, No. 23, 1999.
91 *New Scientist*, 5 July 1997, p. 18.
92 Ronald Segal, *Guardian*, 17 December 1997.
93 *The Economist*, 9 May 1998.

CHAPTER 7

1 *Correspondent*, BBC2, 24 October 1998.
2 *New Scientist*, 11 April 1998, p. 18.
3 Toolis, op. cit., p. 77.
4 Ibid., p. 308.
5 Ibid., p. 152.
6 Taylor, *Loyalists*, p. 142.
7 Ibid., p. 141.
8 Ibid., p. 233.
9 Bourke, op. cit., p. 160.
10 Ibid., p. 147.
11 Ibid., p. 161.
12 *Daily Star* (Beirut), 12 September 1998.
13 *Guardian*, 26 April 1999.
14 *Guardian*, 26 November 1997.
15 Steven Rose, *The Making of Memory*, Bantam Books, London, 1995, p. 315.
16 Francis Wheen, *Guardian*, 4 April 1999.
17 *Guardian*, 23 April 1999.
18 *Sunday Telegraph*, 18 July 1999.
19 *Guardian*, 23 July 1999.
20 Antjie Krog, *The Country of My Skull*, Random House, Johannesburg, 1998, p. 104.
21 Ignatieff, *Warrior's Honour*, p. 185.
22 *One Planet*, BBC World Service, 12 December 1998.
23 *Talk*, 2 August 1999.
24 *Lima News*, 3 August 1999, reported in the *Guardian*, 3 August 1999.

25 *The Economist*, 30 May 1998.
26 *Guardian*, 25 May 1998.
27 Taylor, *Loyalists*, p. 174.
28 Ibid., p. 177.
29 Ibid., p. 187.
30 Ibid., p. 175.
31 Ibid., p. 2.
32 Ibid., p. 6.
33 Ibid., p. 96.
34 Ibid., p. 97.
35 Ibid., p. 178.
36 Ibid., p. 63.
37 Ibid., p. 263.
38 Toolis, op. cit., pp. 328, 329.
39 15 December 1997.
40 15 December 1997.
41 16 December 1997.
42 16 December 1997.
43 Eric Lomax, *The Railway Man*, Vintage, London, 1996, p. 136.
44 Ibid., p. 210.
45 Ibid., p. 225.
46 Ibid., p. 239.
47 Ibid., p. 240.
48 Ibid., p. 249.
49 Ibid., p. 255.
50 Ibid., p. 276.
51 Australian Associated Press, 22 May 1998.
52 *Sydney Morning Herald*, 27 May 1998.
53 *Sydney Morning Herald*, 30 May 1998.
54 *Sydney Morning Herald*, 26 August 1999.
55 *Labor Herald*, 1 July 1998.
56 *Sydney Morning Herald*, 27 May 1998.
57 BBC2 *Newsnight*, 13 July 1999.
58 Rowe, *The Real Meaning of Money*.
59 *Guardian*, 11 August 1999.
60 *Guardian*, 3 June 1999.
61 *Sydney Morning Herald*, 1 July 1998.
62 *Guardian*, 8 August 1999.
63 *Guardian*, 28 June 1999.
64 *Daily Star* (Beirut), 12 September 1998.
65 *Index of Censorship*, No. 3, p. 46.

66 *Guardian*, 13 July 1998.
67 *Guardian*, 12 December 1997.
68 Taylor, *Loyalists*, p. 44.
69 *Star*, 4 January 1999.
70 Matthew 18:21–35.
71 Mark 11:24–26.
72 Proverbs 25:21,22.
73 Romans 12:20.
74 *Guardian*, 24 October 1998.
75 Makdisi, op. cit., p. 214.
76 Hass, *The Aftermath*, p. 22.
77 Lomax, op. cit, p. 243.
78 Toolis, op. cit., p. 186.
79 *Guardian*, 15 May 1999.
80 Makdisi, op. cit., p. 215.
81 *Punch*, 16 March 1983.
82 Templer, op. cit., pp. 31, 34.
83 Ibid., p. 34.
84 Ibid., p. 3.
85 *The Economist*, 28 March 1998.
86 Hass, *The Aftermath*, p. 41.

CHAPTER 8

1 Brian Keenan, *An Evil Cradling*, Hutchinson, London, 1992, p. 277.
2 Immanuel Kant, *Perpetual Peace*, trans. M. Campbell Smith, Swan Sonnenschein and Co., London, 1903, p. 139.
3 Mary Kaldor, *New and Old Wars*, Polity Press, Cambridge, 1999, p. 69.
4 Rowe, *The Real Meaning of Money*, p. 278.
5 *Observer*, 4 July 1999.
6 Quoted by Emma Brockes, 'Life After Iris', *Guardian*, 31 August 1999.
7 Linda Grant, *Remind Me Who I Am, Again*, Granta Books, London, 1998.
8 Dorothy Rowe, *Beyond Fear*, HarperCollins, London, 1989.
9 Keenan, op. cit., p. 132.
10 *Sydney Morning Herald*, 9 September 1999.
11 Lomax, op. cit., p. 137.
12 Kaldor, op. cit., p. 13.
13 Ibid., p. 25.

14 Ibid., p. 29.
15 Ibid., p. 2.
16 John Arquilla and David Ronfeldt (eds.), *In Athena's Camp*, National Defense Research Institute, RAND, Santa Monica, 1997, p. 23.
17 Ibid., p. 5.
18 *Observer*, 20 June 1999.
19 Kaldor, op. cit., p. 58.
20 *Guardian*, 4 July 1999.
21 *The Economist*, 28 August 1999.
22 Transparency International, International Secretariat, Otto-Suhr-Allee 97–99, D-10585 Berlin, Germany.
23 *The Economist*, 28 August 1999.
24 Ridley, op. cit., p. 7.
25 Ibid., p. 264.
26 *Viet Nam News*, 2 March 1997.
27 Keenan, op. cit., p. 65.
28 *Guardian*, 29 May 1999.
29 Keenan, op. cit., p. 272.
30 Brockes, op. cit.
31 *Observer*, 22 August 1999.
32 Keenan, op. cit., p. 97.
33 Harry Venning, personal communication.
34 Brian Keenan and John McCarthy, *Between Extremes*, Bantam Press, London, 1999, p. 342.
35 *Observer*, 1 August 1999.
36 Personal communication.
37 12 October 1997.
38 Keenan and McCarthy, *Between Extremes*, p. 341.
39 Keenan, op. cit., p. xii.
40 John McCarthy and Jill Morrell, *Some Other Rainbow*, Corgi Books, London, 1997, p. 84.
41 Ibid., p. 540.
42 Dorothy Rowe, *The Successful Self*, HarperCollins, London, 1989.
43 McCarthy and Morrell, *Some Other Rainbow*, p. 581.
44 Ibid., p. 586.
45 Ibid., p. 574.
46 Ibid., p. 357.
47 Ibid., p. 595.
48 Ibid., p. 588.
49 Keenan and McCarthy, *Between Extremes*, p. 286.
50 Ibid., p. 44.
51 McCarthy and Morrell, *Some Other Rainbow*, p. 109.
52 Ibid., p. 310.
53 Ibid., p. 351.
54 Keenan, op. cit., p. 105.
55 *Observer*, 15 August 1999.
56 Hass, *In the Shadow of the Holocaust*, p. 87.

ACKNOWLEDGEMENTS

The publishers and author are grateful for permission to reproduce copyright material from the following sources:

Books

Aftermath, The, © Aaron Hass

An Evil Cradling, Brian Keenan, Hutchinson

Between Extremes, Brian Keenan and John McCarthy, © John McCarthy and Brian Keenan 1999. Published by Bantam Press, a division of Transworld Publishers. All rights reserved.

Blood and Belonging, Michael Ignatieff, Sheil Land Associates Ltd

Blood and Vengeance: One Family's Story of the War in Bosnia, Chuck Sudetic. Copyright © 1998 by Chuck Sudetic. Reprinted by permission of W. W. Norton & Company Inc.

Blood Rites, Barbara Ehrenreich, Virago Press

Boyhood, J. M. Coetzee, Secker & Warburg

Country of My Skull, Antjie Krog, Random House

Culture of Honor, Richard E. Nesbitt, Dov Cohen, Perseus Books Group

Dateline Soweto: Travels with Black South African Reports, William Finnegan, copyright © 1988 William Finnegan, University of California Press

Diary of a Baby, Daniel N. Stern, copyright © Daniel Stern, M.D.

Drowned and the Saved, The, Primo Levi, Penguin

Grooming, Gossip and the Evolution of Language, Robin Dunbar, Faber & Faber

Hezbollah, Hala Jaber, Fourth Estate

Love Undetectable, Andrew Sullivan © 1999, Jonathan Cape. Reprinted by permission of the author and the Wylie Agency

Memoir by Lieutenant Colonel, M. W. Gonin, held by the Department of Documents at the Imperial War Museum

Motherhood Constellation, The, Daniel N. Stern, copyright © 1995 by Daniel Stern, M.D.

Articles

Television

INDEX

Aboriginal people
  apologizing for treatment of by
    Australians 424–6, 426–7
  and belonging 264
  growth of population 282–3
  kinship network 301–2
  racism and denigration towards by
    whites 164–5, 248
  removal of children from families
    and adopted by whites 283–4
  romanticizing of by white people 327
Aborigines Protection Board 283
absolute beliefs 341–51, 459, 478
  forcing on to other people 341–3
  lack of self-awareness when holding
    349, 350–1
  perpetuation of cruelty by holders of
    346
activity courses 147
Acton, Lord 353
Adams, Gerry 387, 391, 436, 443
African tribes 191–2
Afrikaans 142–3
Afrikaners 142–3, 150–1, 161
age
  and friendship 37–9
aggression
  as survival strategy 218–19
Aids 434
al-Hariri, Rafiq 277
Albanian Kosovans 94, 155, 271, 275,
  343–4, 434
Alec 239–40
Aleksander, Professor Igor 60–1
Alice 6, 16, 24–5, 191, 202, 203
Aliyan, Etaf 341
Alvarez, Al 510–11
Alzheimer's disease 480
Amir 236, 376
Amish 471

Amy 8–9
ANC 366
ancestors, ancient 118, 119, 120–1, 162,
  235–6, 250, 319, 396
Anderson, Terry 238, 469
Andrew 245–7
anger 449–50, 452
Anglo-Zulu War (1879) 179–80
Angola 287
Annan, Kofi 493
Anne 420, 430
Anthony 18, 209, 264, 313–14, 347–8,
  430–1, 463–4
Anzac Day 381
armaments industry 382, 383–4
Arquilla, John and Ronfeldt, David
  486, 487
Ascherson, Neal 276, 369, 379
Asian values 166
asylum seekers 299–300 *see also*
  refugees
Auschwitz 86–7, 96, 443
Australia/Australians 140–1
  and Aboriginal people *see* Aboriginal
    people
  divisions in society 324–7
  and Gallipoli 130
  immigrants 327
  racism in 164, 297, 327, 491–2
  threatening of Sydney suburbs by
    bushfires 77–8
  transportation of convicts to 140,
    302
  white settlers 163, 302
Australian Broadcasting Commission
  116

babies 49, 188–9
  ability to create a story 75–6
  brain of 58

babies – *cont.*
  comparison between Boston and
    Gussii mothers and 189–90
  distinguishing people from objects
    107–8, 162
  effect of experiences on neuronal
    gestalts 59–60
  and the face 70–2, 74, 213
  and meaning structure 89–90
badness
  method of relieving feelings of
    216–17
Bamber, Helen 424
bands 320
Bayley, John 502
Beck, Gad 232
Beckham, David 443
beliefs *see* absolute beliefs
Bell, Martin 318–19, 323–3, 334, 335, 338
Belsen-Belsen camp 87–9
Ben-Gurion, David 105
Bible
  and forgiveness 448
Black Consciousness movement 157–8
Blair, Cherie 208
Blair, Tony 353, 354, 402
'boat people' (Viet Kieu) 308–10, 460
Boer War 151
Bohr, Nils 45
Bosnian war 36, 318, 364, 434, 490
Botha, P.W. 350
Bourke, Joanna
  An Intimate History of Killing 378,
    379–80
brain 44, 62–3, 186–7
  development of neurons 48–9
  and formation of model of the
    world 45–6
  and importance of individual
    personal experience 187
  meanings in our 56–62
  neural net and understanding the
    creation of meaning by 57–8
  operation of like a computer 61–2
  research on functioning of through
    scanning 57
  and vision 47
Britain
  arms sales 383

ban on corporal punishment in
    schools 226, 492
  migrants from Ireland 297
  and Northern Ireland 298, 337–8
British Aerospace 382, 383
British Veterinary Association 24
Broyles, William 378
Buddhism 183, 459
bullying 226
Buthelezi 350
Butler, Samuel 4

Cairns, Ed 39–40, 337, 376, 440, 444,
    446, 464
Calley, Lieutenant William 379
Camille 374–5, 463
Campaign for Social Justice 266
Campbell, Duncan 300
Candice 359
Canter, Professor David 109, 110, 469
Carnojevic, Patriarch Arsenije 258
Carroll, Rory 94, 487
Castle, The (film) 116–17
Catherine 7
Catholic Church
  view of non-Catholics 344–5
characteristics, universal 187–8
Chechnya 359, 490
children 67
  absolute quality of ideas 194–5,
    330–1
  child-rearing practices 189–91, 221–5
  of a close family 240–1
  committing murder 225
  corporal punishment and bullying of
    83–4, 211, 215, 223–5, 226–8, 280,
    433
  criticism of by family 247–8, 249–50
  demand for perfect parents 205–6
  detecting of deceit 200
  and enemies 16–17
  on family being friends 24–6
  fear of being taken over 106
  and friendship 6
  gaining knowledge 341
  given special role by parents 241–4
  influence of by other family
    members 198
  influence of parents on 197, 198

and interpretations 198
kidnapping of 280–1
killing of by parents and threatening
    to 222
killing of in wars 369
learning languages 52
learning to behave as family expects
    213–15
legislation passed to protect against
    assault 226
and life story 78
and meaning structure 65–6, 79–80,
    207, 479
and parents' responsibility 84
protecting against family criticism
    249–50
as refugees 280
and religion 123
and sense of shame 98–9
and sharing 219
and sibling relationships 202–3, 209
teaching of about their enemies by
    parents 219–20
as threat to parent's meaning
    structure 196, 228
and toys 108
treated as objects by parents and
    used for their own ends 222–4,
    280–2, 304–5, 492–3
world divided between good and
    bad as seen by 331–2
Chile 403–4
Chomsky, Noam 52
Christian Education South Africa 226
Christians
    and forgiveness 448–9
Church of England 145, 380
Clare in the Community 419, 507
Clarissa 511
Clinton, Hillary 408
Clinton, President Bill 408–9, 442
Coetzee, J.M. 152–3, 263–4
Cohen, Dov 133, 134, 135, 136, 197, 219
Cold War 299
Columbia 275
communication
    and primates 109
    see also language
communications technology 474–5

Communism 299
competition
    encouragement of meanness of spirit
        435
    and friendship 506–7
concentration camps 80–1, 86–9, 96,
    102
conscience 73, 97
consciousness 43–4, 107, 480
contempt 279–80
convicts
    transportation of to Australia 140,
        302
Cook, Margaret 399
Cook, Robin 490
corporal punishment
    against children 211, 215, 226–8, 433
    banning of in British schools 226, 492
Correspondent 232
corruption 494
'cosmopolitan' 311
courage 520–1
Cresson, Edith 237
Crick, Francis 61
crime, tackling problem of 493–5
Croatian and Muslim (painting) 370–1
Croats 328
Crusaders 441–2
Cumaraswamy, Param 361
Cummings, Samuel 384
cyberwars 486
Cycladian statue 70, 71

Daisy, Daisy, Give Me Your Answer Do
    (play) 249
Dalleo, Graziella 103
Darquier de Pellepoix, Louis 85–6
Davidson, Robyn 266
Dawes, Andy 131, 139, 147, 151, 160,
    170–3
de Klerk, President F.W. 117, 404–5
deceit
    detecting of by children 200
Delegorgue, Adulphe 377
depression 205, 293–5, 351, 397, 481
    and action of primitive pride 90,
        93–4
    and genes 72
    in Kenya 351

depression – *cont.*
  management of 294–5
  as a refusal to mourn 465–6
despots 402
Diamond, Jack 237
Diamond, Jarel 320
Diana, Princess 13–14, 496
disabled
  treatment of in Lebanon 348–9
disasters
  blaming ourselves for 289, 293, 294
  blaming on someone else 298–9
disloyalty
  and families 237–8
divorce 252, 429, 438
Diyana 35–6, 99–100, 289–93, 296,
  453–4, 456
Djerrkura, Gatjil 426–7
Dodson, Pat 264
Donner Party wagon train 235
Dressen, Wolfgang 358
drills 146
drugs 493
Druze 341
  and reincarnation 181–3
Dudley Edwards, Ruth 365, 366
Duffy, Michael 449
Dunbar, Robin 52, 108, 109, 114, 235
Dusan 220–1, 256–7, 401, 475
  attachment to Belgrade 256–7, 258–9
  family background 258
  on icons 137–8, 358
  loyalty to family 233–4
  and nationality 129
Dutch 142

e-mail 475
East Timor 475–6, 483–4, 485, 489,
  490, 493
economic refugees 273–4
economy
  factors for growth of 237
education 144
Ehrenreich, Barbara 118–19, 126, 377
Eichmann, Adolf 105
Eileen 239
Einstein 45
electroshock weapons 383–4
Eli 202

Eliot, Larry 141
Elizabeth 7
empathy 20, 163
Empey, Sir Reg 430
enemies/enmity 194, 217
  comfort and importance of having
    332–4
  condemning of as way of protecting
    oneself from feeling bad 332–3
  contrast between friendship and 4,
    34
  definition 15–16
  easier to persist with then attempt
    reconciliation 388
  enhancement of self worth and
    power by having 334–5
  and family 219–21
  forgiveness of *see* forgiveness
  friends turning into 19–20
  ideas about from the past 320
  link between need for and way
    children are brought up 221
  necessity of 320–52
  needs met by 321–2
  and paranoid style 340–1
  people not sharing absolute belief
    seen as 341–3
  personal experiences of and
    definitions 16–19
  pleasures of war 374–86
  reconciliation with *see* reconciliation
  rewards in having 385–6
  seen to be aggressive 218
  silencing of through violence 362
  as strangers 319
  teaching about of to children by
    parents 219–20
  thinking of as dirty by groups
    217–18
  threats posed by 317–18, 388–9
  treating as objects 348, 349, 368
  understanding of 482–3
  understanding of through just being
    482
  uses of 220
Enniskillen bomb 446
envy 20, 206
Ervine, David 394
Eskimos 52–3

ethnic wars 328
EU commissioners 237
Evans, Justine 170–1, 172, 173
Everett, Hugh 45
extraverts 29–33, 174, 515, 517–18

face, the 69, 70–4, 98, 187, 199, 213, 236, 368
faces
  identifying of those we have seen before 162
Fakri, Rima 380
Falklands war 378
Falwell, Jerry 333
family 177–255
  becoming part of the 184–229
  changes in form of 230–1
  'close-knit' 238–41
  conflicts within 328, 416–17
  definitions 229–30
  discourtesy and criticism of members 244–51
  distinguishing from friends 177
  and enemies 219–21
  family ties matter above all else 251–3
  and friendship 24–7
  handing down of cruelty from one generation to another 215
  influence of members after death 178–80
  and 'internal objects' 204–5
  learning how to fit in with demands of 212–13
  loyalty to 231–8
  and non-divulging of family secrets rule 210–12
  and reincarnation 181–2
  rules about cleanliness 217
  sense of permanence and continuity provided by 180–1
  sentimentalizing of 252
  sibling relationships *see* siblings
  silence used as method of revenge 390–1
  strife caused by members trying to rid themselves of sense of badness 216
  traditional 230
  writing about 210

see also children
family values 229–51, 433
faqih 355–6
Farrell, Michael 265–6
Fay, Michael 412
al-Fayed, Dodi 14
al-Fayed, Mohammed 14
Fenichel, Otto 92
Ferguson, Niall
  The Pity of War 378
Finnegan, William 127
Finucane, Dermot 394
Finucane, Geraldine 454
Finucane, Pat 361, 454
First World War 427–8
Fisk, Robert
  Pity the Poor Nation 14
Fonagay, Peter 304, 305
forgetting
  and dealing with question of forgiveness 455–6
forgiveness/forgiving 389, 441–68
  asking for in relation to wrongs committed in the past 441–2
  as a bargaining chip 445–6
  between groups 458
  by parents after death of children 447–8
  and Christians and the Bible 448–9
  forgetting as way of dealing with 455–6
  and friends 457–8
  impossibility of if loved one is injured or killed 450–1
  involvement of a relationship 445
  need for change 465
  need for mourning of loss 465
  as newsworthy 443
  ourselves 453–5
  and process of letting go 452–3
  research into 444–5
  seen as a virtue 448
  see also reconciliation
Forshall, Sam 294–5
Foster, Don 363, 369, 370, 374
France
  and *Loi Toubon* 141
  Resistance during war 399–400
  and siege of Verdun 427–8

Francis, Stephen 164
Franco 159–60
Fraser, Malcolm 360
free speech and thought 144
Freel, James 302
French, Dr Chris 67–8, 181–2
Freud, S. 184
Frey, Dieter 289
Friel, Brian 249, 253–4
Friends of the Western Buddhist Order (FWBO) 183–4
friendship/friends 320–1
  and acceptance 510–12
  and age 37–9
  art of 503–22
  barriers to 503–8
  being misunderstood as barrier to 507–8
  and 'clearing the air' 509–10
  and competition 506–7
  contrast between enmity and 4, 34
  dangers of 21
  defining 4–5, 6, 7, 8, 9–10
  distinction between acquaintances and 4–5
  division between introverts and extraverts 29–34
  easiness/difficulty in making 34–7
  failure to see the person themselves as barrier to 512–13
  and family 24–7
  finding 3–4
  and forgiveness 457–8
  and homosexuals 21–2, 40
  humour as essential to 520
  importance of underlying meanings being complimentary and not antagonistic 42
  learning the other person's story 519
  and lovers 496–502
  and marriage 27, 501–2
  necessity of 321
  pain of losing 21
  personal experiences and defining of 3–15
  reasons for difficulty in making 41
  rejecting of because you feel unlovable 503–4

  self-involvement and selfishness as barrier to 504–6
  and shared sadness 513–14
  and siblings 208–9
  talent for 27–9
  turning into enemies 19–20
Frontline 116–17
FWBO (Friends of the Western Buddhist Order) 183–4

Garzon, Jaime 520
Gates, Professor Henry Louis 327–8
genes 72, 185–7
Geneva Conventions 493
Gerrard, Nicci 208
Gilbert, Daniel 93
Giles, Billy 412
Gill 460–1
Glen, Colin 421–2
Glenny, Misha 360
globalisation 472–3
Glover, Joseph 454–5
Good Friday Agreement 387, 391–2, 393, 410, 412, 414, 428
gossiping 110
Grant, Linda 209–10, 308, 343–4, 480
Greenfield, Susan 44, 48–9, 58–9, 107, 163
Gregory, Richard 43, 47, 52
groups 111–76
  believing in one's own group as superior 166, 170
  bringing together by shared suffering 139–40
  categories of 116
  changing of 115
  and concept of prey and sacrifice 118–19
  conflict between pride and humility 120
  and conformity 126
  coping when no longer in existence 170–1, 173
  defining of in complex ways 477–8
  defining in terms of those who are excluded 116
  defining yourself and your 116–36
  denial of contact with outsiders 158–60

describing of enemies 217
establishment of hierarchies 112–13
forgiveness between 458
forming alliances and friendships
within 113–14
as friend and enemy 153–76
handing down of ideas to younger
generations 144
and the individual 132–4, 137
and jokes 139
and justice 120–1
and language 141–3
and martyrs 128–9
national 125, 129, 130–1, 144
outsiders and sense of not belonging
174–6
owing allegiance to 137–53
political activist 125–6
provoking shame and guilt as means
of maintaining allegiance 149–51
punishment of members who fail to
meet standards of 151–2, 154
religious 123–6
and scapegoats 126, 126–7, 128, 129
stress of meeting crowd of people
111
treating certain groups of people as
objects 163–4
use of ritual to maintain allegiance
144–7
Gryn, Rabbi Hugo 443
guilt
provoking of to maintain group
allegiance 149–51
Gussii people 189–90, 192, 193–4, 202,
206

Haghighat, Rahman 272–3
Halford, Alison 398
Hamill, Robery 317
Hamilton, Christine 318, 319
Hamilton, Neil 318, 319
Handley, Tommy 520
Hargreave, Peter 383
al-Hariri, Rafiq 277
Harris, Nigel 271, 274
Hass, Aaron 40, 96, 105–6, 303, 331–2,
369, 450–1, 465–6, 520
Hattenstone, Simon 454

Haughey, Charles 410
healing, ritual of 149
Heather 503–4
Hebb, Donald 57, 58
Hebron, James 378
Helena and Ian 41–2, 55–6, 64
Herron, John 425–6
Hezbollah 237–8, 333, 334, 380
Hillsborough tragedy 454–5
Hinduism 119, 181
Hitler, Adolf 146
Ho Chi Minh, President 461
Hoang Tung 459
Hocking, Ann 104–5
Hodson, Philip 368
Hofstadter, Richard 333, 339–40
Holocaust
robbing of Jews during 358
Holocaust survivors
effect on children of third-
generation 303–4, 332
emigration to Israel and treatment
of 105–6
feelings of betrayal felt by 40
not listening to by relatives 81–2
not mourning 465–6
and unforgiveness 450–1
homosexuals 491
and friendship 21–2, 40
honour, culture of 133–6, 197
Honwana, Alcinda 147
Horney, Karen 93
Howson, Peter 370–1
Hrawi, President 462
Human Genome Project 185, 186
human rights 493
humanitarians 489
humanity 469, 470, 476
Hume, John 436
humility 120
humour 139, 519–21
Humphrey, Nicholas 107
Hunter, Kathryn 96–7
Hussein, Saddam 356
Hutus 371–2

icons 137–8
ideas 409, 431
manipulating of by pride 407–8

ideas – *cont.*
  need for change in if we want
    peaceful world 491–2
identity
  and babies 89–90
  defining of one's 88–9
ideology 367
Ignatieff, Michael 311, 328, 330, 405–6
immigrants
  benefits of to a community 300–1
  prejudice and racism against
    299–300
  reconciling ties with country left
    and new home 306–7
Impossible Minds 60
imprinting 202
Index of Censorship 442
India
  and Pakistan 359
Indians 281
individual
  and groups 132–4, 137
Indonesia 476, 483–4
information wars 487–8, 493
Ingram, Richard 337–8
Ingrid 183–4
INLA (Irish National Liberation Army)
  437
instinct 185
intelligence 109–10
interconnectedness 472, 475, 476
'internal objects' 204–5
international finance 473–4
International Monetary Fund (IMF)
  494
internationalists 268–70
  new 308
interpretations 184–5
  and children 198
Intimate History of Killing, An
  (Bourke) 378, 379–80
introverts 29–33, 33–4, 174, 515,
  517–18
IRA 361, 363, 411
  and decommissioning 428
  importance of martyrs to 335
  needing of by Loyalists 393–4
Ireland 297–8 *see also* Northern
  Ireland

Irene 8–9, 18, 20, 31, 32, 261, 456–7
Irish convicts
  transportation of to Australia 140
Irish National Liberation Army (INLA)
  437
Islam 355–6, 380
Israel
  emigration of survivors of Holocaust
    to 105–6
  Jews settling in 334
Israelis
  regarded as enemies by Lebanon 13
Italy
  debate over whether northern
  states should secede from the
  south 124–5

James 10–11
Janna 111, 113–14
Japan 442, 459
  and cosmopolitanism 270–1
jealousy, sibling 206
Jeannie 244–5, 332
Jessica 243
Jesus 448
Jews
  hatred of by Poles 334
  settlement of in Israel 334
  survivors of the Holocaust *see*
    Holocaust survivors
John 427
John Paul II, Pope 360–1, 442
jokes 138–9
Jones, Alan 326
Jones, Steve 301
Jones, Terry 116
Joy 504
Judy 7–8, 18–19, 40, 174–5
Jung 184
just be 481–2, 485
Just World 121, 169, 170, 171–2, 193, 221,
  273, 298
justice 120–2

Kaldor, Mary 472, 485, 488
Kant, Immanuel 311, 471–2
Keenan, Brian 505
  attempt at understanding enemy
    482–3

An Evil Cradling 469, 517
  friendship with McCarthy 33, 502,
    508–9, 514–15, 517, 518
  as hostage 433, 498, 499
Kennedy, President 150
Kenya
  depression in 351
  see also Gussii people
killing
  thrill of in war 377–9
King, Governor 140
Kirsten, Alexa 421
knowledge 341
Kock, Christof 61
Kopp, Sheldon 242
Kosovan Albanians *see* Albanian
  Kosovans
Kosovo 360, 378
Kosovo, Battle of (1389) 130, 257
Kosovo war 487–8, 489
Kruger, President Paul 150–1
Kureishi, Hanif 209
Kureishi, Yasmin 209

language(s) 52–4, 108–9, 110, 141–4
  development of 52
  different meanings for words 110
  and groups 141–3
  learning of by children 52
  as a social activity 108–9
  use of metaphors to convey
    meaning 53–4
Language Instinct, The (Pinker) 52
Laqis, Sylvana 348
Laws, John 325–6
Lazar, Prince 130, 257
Le Carré, John 510–11
leaders 352–62, 396
  and audience 416
  choosing to see as parent 352, 355–7,
    357–61
  lying over responsibility by political
    403–4
  seen as one of us with no special
    powers 352–3, 357
Lebanon 13–15, 122, 162, 308, 400, 431,
  467
  civil war and The Plot 14–15
  and conspiracy theories 14–15

  and families 234, 236
  and forgiveness 463
  giving of criticism in family 248–9
  and Hezbollah 237–8, 333, 334, 380
  Hezbollah and family loyalty 237–8
  lack of reconciliation after the war
    462–3
  lack of reconstruction work in
    Beirut after fighting 277–8
  and refugees 275, 278
  treatment of disabled 348–9
Lebed, Alexander 359
lesbians 24, 231
Lesley 5, 17–18, 30–1, 33, 450
Lettie 245, 505
Levi, Primo 80–1, 82, 85–6, 102, 146,
  372–3
LeVine, Robert A. 189–90, 192, 193–4
Lewinsky, Monica 13, 442
life story 77–8, 80–3, 98, 253
  dangers of not being believed 80–2
  lying about 85–6
Lister, David 382
Lithuania
  suicide rate 272–3
Loi Toubon 141
Lomax, Eric 422–4, 451, 484
lonely hearts adverts 41
Lost Children, The 282
Lott, Tim
  White City Blue 22, 32
Lou 219, 511–12
love 452
lovers
  friends as 496–502
loving relationships 470–1
Loyalists 393–4, 395
loyalty 307
  and families 231–8
Luke 342–3
Luke, Sister 183

McCann, Asling 317
McCarthy, John 33, 433, 469, 508–9,
  514–19
McCluskey, Patricia and Conn 266
McCudden, James Byford 378–9
McDowell, Thomas 414
Mace, Chris 93

McGuinness, Martin 392, 393, 415–16
McKay, Gary 378
McMenamin, Eamonn 361
MacSwiney, Terence 335
Magnus (multi-automata-general-neural-units-structure) 60, 61
Major, John 353
Makdisi, Jean Said 15, 122–3, 125, 275, 307, 333, 376, 381–2, 450, 455
male friendships
    denying of through fear of intimacy 22
Mandela, President 166, 350
Mandelson, Peter 316–17
Marais, Kowie 143
Marcos, Imelda 128
Marcos, President 128
Maria 243
Maric, Johan 138, 154–5, 168
Marinella 265, 287–8
Marks, Isaac 118
Marks, Monique 366
Marr, Andrew 476
Marr, David 435
marriage 319
    changing of pattern of by travel 271
    and friendship 27, 501–2
    mixed in Yugoslavia 99
Martin 19–20
martyrdom 334–5, 380
    and groups 128–9
Mary, Sister 345–6
Maunsell, John 62
Mbeki, Thabo 166
meaning structure 62–9
    aim to maintain its structure as unified whole 64
    and attachment to a place 259, 260
    awareness of fragility of 107
    babies and children 65–6, 79–80, 89–90, 207, 479
    as collection of stories 77
    in danger of falling apart 64–5, 66
    dependence on how we feel about ourselves for integrity of 199, 279, 495
    importance of justice to maintenance of 120

importance in making connection with new place 276
and interpretations 133
intrinsic forms which enable it to function 187–8 *see also* thoughts, forms of
and just being 485
maintaining of through primitive pride 70, 90–2, 94, 117, 128, 152, 188, 196, 279, 293–4, 364, 479
and moral pride 97, 100
and nationality 129, 130
need for confirmation of by other people 78–9
need to compromise 120
and old age 95–6
and reality-testing 353–4
rules of operation 63
as a self-regulating system 92
and sense of 'I' 479–81
struggle to hold together 480–1
threatening of by other people 97–8, 110, 324
threatening of by shame 100, 101, 102
underlying of meanings 63–4
meanings, creation of 43–56, 44, 50–2, 407
and brain 44, 56–62
checking accuracy of 67–8
and contrasts 51–2, 53
difficulty in changing childhood 68–9
and environment 188
individuality of 42–3
influence of past experience on 49–50, 52, 55
and responsibility 407
and story 76–7
Mediterranean cultures 197
Mencken, H.L. 360
Mengele, Josef 87
mental illnesses 480
metaphors 53–4
Michiko, Nakahara 451
migration 273, 274–5
Mike 222
Mil Tech 383
Miles 6, 16–17, 25, 34–5, 191, 202, 203, 205

Millennium of Family Change, A
  (Seccombe) 230
Miller, Andie 157, 160–2
Milner, Lord Alfred 143
Milos 487–8
Milošovic, Slobodan 130, 155, 168, 278,
  279–80, 360, 403
Mirjana 310
Mitchell, George 391, 428, 436, 438
Mithen, Steven 89
Modern Times: Friends 115
Mohamad, Mahathir 166
Molteno, Marion
  The Shield of Coolest Air 311
money 272, 473
Moon, Lady Sarah 399
moral pride 97, 100, 128, 407–8
Morrell, Jill 516
Morton, Bobby 412–13
Mosher, Loren 295
mourning 465–6
Mozambique
  rituals used in 147–9
Mudrooroo 164–5, 264, 301
Mullin, John 317
Münch, Dr Hans 86–7
murder 364
Murdoch, Iris 480, 502
Musi 366–7
Muslims 328
My Lai massacre (Vietnam) 379
Myra 211, 329
Myriam 305–6

Nabil 308
Naomi 177, 253
Nasrallah, Sayyed Hassan 355–6
national groups 125, 129, 130–1, 144
nationality 129–32, 271–2
native, romanticizing of 166
NATO
  and Kosovo 434, 487, 489
necklacing 126–7, 127–8, 129
neighbours 323
Nelson, Rosemary 317
Nesse, Randolph 118
neuronal gestalts 58, 58–9, 60, 72, 195
neurons 57–9, 60, 62
New Scientist 46

Nez 269
Nguyen, Jimmy 309–10
Nguyen Thi Hoai Duc, Professor 460,
  462
Nguyen Thi Lanh 462
Nilsen, Dennis 212
Nisbett, Richard and Cohen, Dov 133,
  134, 135, 136, 197, 219
Noriega, General Manuel Antonio 320
Northern Ireland 313–17, 346–8, 361–2,
  391–5, 406, 412–13, 427, 429, 436
  attacks on Loyalists by Catholics 317
  British view of 298, 337–8
  calling of ceasefire by INLA 437
  Catholics and sense of identity 265–6
  contrast between people of Dublin
    and Unionists 476–7
  decommissioning issue 428
  and Good Friday Agreement 387,
    391–2, 393, 410, 412, 414, 428
  importance of land 264
  and IRA *see* IRA
  Mandelson's visit 316–17
  method of interrogation 374
  need for toleration 39–40
  Omagh bombing 349
  and Orange Order 18, 314, 316, 331,
    349–50, 366
  and Paisley 299, 395, 410–12, 413,
    414, 415
  peace process 438, 465, 466
  Protestant and Catholic relations 20,
    298, 315, 365, 463–4
  refusing to speak to one another 395
  and republicanism 362–3
  Republicans and Loyalists 393
  Republicans and martyrdom 334–5
  view of Britain by Loyalists and
    Nationalists 338
  view that economic factors will
    bring conflict to an end 429–30
Ntombela, Qumbu Magqubu 179–80
Numata, Sadaaki 270–1
Nuremberg International Military
  Tribunal 409
Nutt, David J. and Forshall, Sam 294–5

O Connor, Fionnuala 265–6
object relations 204–5

octopus 46
Omagh bombing (1998) 349
O'Neill, Elizabeth 317
opponents 318
Orange Order 18, 314, 316, 331, 349–50, 366
Orbach, Susie 501–2
Origins of Virtue, The (Ridley) 123–4
Orwell, George 283, 354, 361
O'Shane, Pat 324–5
Others 103–10
O'Toole, Fintan 254
outside world
　　narrow vision of 400–2
outsiders, of a group 174–6

pain 373–4
Paisley, Ian 299, 395, 410–12, 413, 414, 415
Paisley Junior, Ian 437
Pakistan
　　and India 359
Palestinians 308, 338, 344
Pancott, Walter 513–14
Pandora and Leslie 500–1
parades 428–9
paranoid style 339–41
paranormal 67–8, 181–2
parent-leaders 352, 355–7, 357–61
Parry, John 159–60
Patten, Chris 466
Patton, Joel 316
Paul 249
peaceful world, living in a 484–96
Pearson, Noel 426
perceptions 43
　　shaping of by individual experiences 49–50
Petry, S. and Meyer, E. 57
pets 24, 108
pharmaceutical industry 295, 382, 435
Phetole 376
phobias 118
physics/physicists 44
　　quantum and classical 44–5
Picton, Terence and Stuss, Donald 45, 63
Pinker, Steven *The Language Instinct* 52
Pinochet, General 305, 403–4

'pity' 296
Pity the Poor Nation (Fisk) 14
Pity of War, The (Ferguson) 378
place, belonging to a 255, 256–312
　　ability to take set of meanings with you if you are secure in your identity 263–4
　　difficulties in returning home when it no longer feels like home 310–11
　　forced to leave home 287–8 *see also* refugees
　　inability to go back home 285–312
　　lacking of 266–7
　　and land 264
　　losing your place 267–84
　　and meaning structure 259
　　and sense of being in control and secure in one's identity 261–3
　　strengthening our sense of identity and affirming our existence 265
plants 47
Player, Ian 179
Plessis, Daniel du 421
political groups 125–6
politicians 489, 492
　　treatment of people with contempt 276–9, 280
poor 472–3
power 353–4
praise 437
predator, concept of 118, 119–20
prejudices 297, 298
Premack, Dr D. 107–8
prey 126
　　concepts of 118, 119
　　fear of being 129
pride 156
　　conflict with humility within a group 120
　　maintaining of through jokes 139
　　moral 97, 100, 128, 407–8
　　primitive *see* primitive pride
　　turning of shame into 152–3
'pride systems', concept of compensatory 93
primates
　　and communication 109
primitive pride 87–103, 154, 193, 316, 364

closing down of 95–6
and depression 90, 93–4
and form of the face 98
and glorification of war 381
and maintaining of meaning
    structure in face of threat 70,
    90–2, 94, 117, 128, 152, 188, 196,
    279, 293–4, 364, 479
and paranoid style 340
restoration of self-confidence 397
and revenge 389, 396–7
and suicide 96–7
and surviving in dire conditions
    95
Progressive Unionist Party 395
Pryor, Boori 327
    Maybe Tomorrow 248
psychiatrists 295–6
psychoanalysts 388
psychological immune system 93
psychologists 43
psychology 109, 132
psychopaths 73
psychotherapy 149
Punch 457

quantum physics 44–5

racism 165–6
    against immigrants and asylum
        seekers 299–300
    in Australia 164, 297, 327, 491–2
Raeburn, Anna 347
Rafsanjani 396
Ralph, Regan 371
Ramphele, Mamphela 12, 125–6, 157–8,
    173–4, 222
rape
    during war 370–2
rationalization 92, 93
Raven, Charlotte 23
Rea, 'Winkie' 411
Real Meaning of Money, The 473
reality 44, 45
reality-testing 353–4
reconciliation 405, 417, 419–40, 465
    and couples 439–40
    dependence on economic situation
        429–30

difficulty in giving up something
    that we see as essential to our
    being 428–9
disagreements over acceptable and
    unacceptable behaviour 432–3
finding better ways of negotiating
    438–9
first step towards 418
and generosity of spirit 436–7
need for both sides to agree
    406–7
need for both sides to change their
    ideas 420, 432
need for mourning of loss 465
need for understanding of the
    enemy 427, 431–2
and praise 437
recognizing your enemy has also
    had a bad time 420–4
and saying sorry 424–7
taking responsibility for actions
    406–7
    see also forgiveness
Reconciliation Walkers 441–2
refugees 273–6, 285, 286–8, 296, 508
    attitude towards 275–6, 296
    children as 280
    economic 273–4
    effect on third generation 305–6
    experience of anxiety and depression
        in new country 301
    number of 275
    racism and prejudice against 296–7,
        299–300
    remaining in limbo in camps 308
    smuggling of 276
reincarnation 181–3
religion(s) 122–4, 183, 346
    and belief in importance of sacrifice
        119
    defining of groups by who is
        excluded 123–4
    origins in search for justice 121,
        123
    and ritual 149
    and war 379–80
religious groups
Republicans 334–5, 362–3, 393,
    394–5

responsibility 355, 399–419
  and creation of meanings 407
  denial of by blaming the way in
    which other people have
    interpreted your actions 409–14
  denial of in dialogue of violence
    365–6
  denial of 407–8, 417–18
  and keeping one's vision narrow
    402–3
  paranoia as way of avoiding 408
  and question of truth and lies 402–3
  and reconciliation 406–7
  redefining of 118
  refusal to accept by political leaders
    403–5
Restorick, Rita 443–4
Retief, Frank 170
revenge 389–99
  arising from primitive pride 389,
    396–7
  difficulty in achieving successful acts
    of 399
  and humour 399
  recourse to the law 398
  use of silence as 389–93
Richard (cab driver) 191–2
Richard (journalist) 198, 203–4, 231–2,
    239, 259–60
Richards, Jo-Anne 376
Richardson, Ken 110
Ridgeway, Aden 426
Ridley, Matt 496
  The Origins of Virtue 123–4
rituals
  use of in groups to maintain
    allegiance 144–7
  used in Africa to enable children to
    settle back into ordinary life 147–9
Robben Island 11
Romans 164
Roosevelt, Franklin 353
Rose, Steven 402
Rossi, Father 124–5
Royal Ulster Constabulary (RUC) 466
Russell, Josie 449–50
Russell, Shaun 449–50
Russia
  and Chechnya 359, 490

Ruth 127
Ryan, Peter 425

Sachs, Judge Albie 406
sacrifice 118–19
Saferworld 383
St Mark's Church (Belgrade) 137
Salmon, Ian 326
Samir 13–14
sampyuh 483–4
Sandline International 383
Sarajevo, siege of 290
Sartre, Jean-Paul 200
scapegoats 126, 128
Scarry, Elaine 373
Schindler's List 86
Schirra, Bruno 86
scopus umbretta 169
Scott, Betty 212
Sean 305–6
Sebastian, Tim 270
Seccombe, Wally
  A Millennium of Family Change 230
Second World War
  and French Resistance 399–400
  nationality felt during 130
  soldiers' view of enemy 395–6
self-blame 171–2
self-control 212–13
Sellars, Sean 224–5
Serbia 431
Serbs 130, 154–6, 220, 256, 257–8, 335
  conflict with Muslims and Croats
    328
  family loyalty to a saint 233
  and jokes 138–9
  lack of interest in anything outside
    Serbia 400–1
  and Milošovic 279, 360
  and nationality 160
  see themselves as victims 94, 336–7,
    467
  and spirituality 154
  and suffering 167–8
  view of Albanians 344
  war against Croats (1993) 330
Sereny, Gitta 225, 373
sex 22–4, 499–500
  and friendship 502

sex talk 22–3
sexism 491
Shaban, Nabil 122
shadow economy 494
shame 98–102
  turning of into pride 152–3
  use of as means to maintain group
    allegiance 149–51
Sharett, Moshe 105
Shield of Coolest Air, The (Molteno)
  311
Shiite Islam 355–6
shopping, pleasure of 347
Sri Lanka 142
siblings 202–5, 207–10
  arguments about family property
    and inheritance 208
  conflict between 328
  feelings of jealousy towards 206, 207
  friendship between 208–9
  rivalry between 208
silence
  use of in revenge 389–93
Simbo 12–13
Sinclair, Jeanette 284
Singh-Bartlett, Warren 348–9
single parents 231
Sinhalese 142
Sinn Fein 443, 464
Snow, Clive 364
Snow, Jon 116, 129, 209
Snow, Tom 209
Somalia 180
Sonn, Julian 164
sorry, being 424–5
South Africa 160–2, 166–7, 170–4, 265,
  436
  and Afrikaans 142–3
  and Afrikaners 142–3, 150–1, 161
  and Aids drugs 434
  apartheid regime 11–13, 117, 400
  ban on corporal punishment in
    schools 226
  belief by whites that blacks do not
    study behaviour of whites 164
  and Black Consciousness movement
    157–8
  and Botha 350
  and crime 157
  end of apartheid and violence in
    366–7
  essays by schoolchildren on 'My
    Nation and My People' 131–2
  massacre in Cape Town church
    (1993) 169–70
  necklace murders 126–7, 127–8,
    129
  physical violence used against
    children by adults 151–2
  settlement of Dutch at Cape of
    Good Hope 142
  struggle against apartheid 363
  treatment of children 223–4
  tribal languages 143–4
  and Truth and Reconciliation
    Commission *see* Truth and
    Reconciliation Commission
  and Vlakplaas 117
Soviet Union 159, 236
Spain
  Franco's regime 159–60
Spence, Gusty 394–5, 445–6, 447
Spiegel, Der 86
spite 20
Steiner, Rudolph 479
Stephan 160
Stern, Daniel 71–2, 76, 98–9
Steve (Australian theatre director) 138,
  167, 168
Steve (musician) 400
Stewart, Ian 512–13
Stollmann, Jost 270
Stols, Deon 421
Stone, Michael 449–50
story 70, 74–87, 98, 187
  and babies 74–5
  and creation of meaning 76–7
  life 77–8, 80–3, 85, 98, 253
  linking of events 75
  telling of 74–5
'Story of Kieu, The' (poem) 243
strangers
  as enemies 319, 320
Straus, Murray 227–8
Stuss, Donald 45, 63
Successful Self, The 29
Sudetic, Chuck 328–9
sufferers 90–1

suffering 167–70
  and belief in Just World 169
  and Serbs 167–8
  welding together of a group by
    139–40
suicide 170
  in Australia 325
  Lithuania 272–3
  and primitive pride 96–7
Sullivan, Andrew 21, 27, 40
Sutherland, Tom 469
Swahili 327–8
Sydney Morning Herald 130

Takashi, Nagase 423–4
Talon weapon 383–4
Tamils 142
Tan Dun 49
Taylor, Peter 316, 335, 394–5, 410, 411,
    445
Taylor, Telford 409
teachers 225–6
Tebbit, Norman 306–7
television 475
Templer, Robert 236–7, 308–9, 461,
    462
Thatcher, Margaret 353, 410, 433
therapists 355, 387–8
thought, forms of 69–70 *see also* face,
    the; primitive pride; story
Tima 3, 234–5, 241–2, 248–9, 260–1,
    277, 375, 463
Time on Our Side 223, 325
Tito 405, 406
Toby 249
Toolis, Kevin 362, 393, 428
torture 103–4, 372–3
toys 108
Tracy 427
Transparency International 494
travel 268–71
tribal law 120–1
tribes 223, 320
  African 191–2
Trimble, David 391, 394, 395, 415, 416,
    427, 430, 436
Truman, Harry 405
trust 521
Truth and Reconciliation Commission

(South Africa) 117, 129, 139, 400,
    418, 420–1, 435–6
  achievement of 406
  and Botha 350
  recognition of dangers of not being
    believed 82
  research on violations of young
    people 223–4
  setting up of Trauma Clinic in wake
    of 170–1
Turner, Stuart 451
Tutsis 371–2
Tutu, Archbishop 400
Twain, Mark 20
twin studies 185–6

Uganda 280
Ulster Freedom Fighters 361
Ulster Volunteer Force (UVF) 394, 395,
    412
Una 27–8, 208–9
uncertainty, tolerance of 339
unions
  conflict with employers 438
United Nations 433–4
  Human Development Report (1999)
    493
United Nations Children's Fund 280
United Nations High Commissioner
    for Refugees 275
United Nations Human Rights
    Commission 361
United States
  Americans seen as the enemy 19, 434
  functioning of culture of honour in
    southern states 133–5, 135–6
  lack of malice towards by
    Vietnamese 458–60
  necessity for enemies 335
  and pharmaceutical industry 435
  and Somalia 180
universal characteristics 187–8
UVF *see* Ulster Volunteer Force

Van Kirk, Ted 377
Vanya 382
Vedo 401
verbal abuse 364–5
Verdun, siege of (1916) 427–8

Viet Kieu ("boat people") 308–10, 460
Vietnam/Vietnamese 19, 458–62
  acknowledging of sacrifices made by
    mothers in war 462
  and 'boat people' 308–10, 460
  lack of malice towards United States
    by 458–60
  loyalty and corruption 236–7
  My Lai massacre 379
  and prostitution 243
  return of Vietnamese living overseas
    309
violence 362–74
  against women by men 370–2
  committing of by women 369–70
  and denial of responsibility 365–6
  'dialogue' of 363
  justification for 366–7
  and verbal abuse 364–5
virtues 496
vision 46–7, 61
visual modes 47–8
Von Falkenhayn, General Erich 427–8
Voortrekker Monument 12

Waite, Terry 433
Wall, Patrick 373–4
war(s) 374–84, 387, 396
  and armaments industry 382
  Church's justification for 380
  cyber 486
  excitement and comradeship of
    375–6
  glorification of 481
  information 487–8
  killing of children 369
  'new' 485–6, 493
  old 485–6, 488
  people who gain from 381–3

rape in 370–1
and religion 379–80
thrill of killing 377–9
Ward, Mary 445–6, 447
Ward, Peter 394, 445, 447
'water wars' 491
WAVE 427
Weldon, Fay 30, 32, 174, 176, 266–8,
  286
Whelan, Alison 498–9
White City Blue (Lott) 22, 32
Whorf, Benjamin Lee 52
Wiesenthal, Simon 81
Willett Gonin, Lieutenant-Colonel
  Mervin 88–9
Wilmot family 447
Wilson, Gordon 446
Wilson, Timothy 93
women
  committing of violence against by
    men 370–2
  seen as not full human beings by
    men 497–8
Women of the West, The 282
Women's Movement 24
work 478–9
World Health Organization 293

Xenophanes 78

Yasmin 375–6
Yeltsin, President Boris 490
Yo-Yo Ma 49
Young, Michael 441–2
Yugoslavia 99, 129, 168, 278–9, 405–6,
  488

Zero Tolerance charitable trust 370
Zulus 179–80